THE
MEECH LAKE
PRIMER

THE
MEECH LAKE
PRIMER:
Conflicting Views of the
1987 Constitutional Accord

Edited by
MICHAEL D. BEHIELS

With a Foreword by
The Honourable Eugene Forsey

University of Ottawa Press
Ottawa • London • Paris

© University of Ottawa Press, 1989
Printed and bound in Canada
ISBN 0-7766-0291-8 (casebound)
ISBN 0-7766-0230-6 (paperback)

Design: Lesa Moriarity

Canadian Cataloguing in Publication Data

Main entry under title:
The Meech Lake primer

Includes bibliographical references.
ISBN 0-7766-0291-8 (bound)–
ISBN 0-7766-0230-6 (pbk.)

1. Canada. Constitution Act, 1982. 2. Canada.
British North America Act. 3. Canada—Constitutional
law—Amendments. I. Behiels, Michael D. (Michael
Derek), 1946-

JL65 1989.B34 1989   342.71'03   C89-090369-7

61,895

UNIVERSITÉ D'OTTAWA
UNIVERSITY OF OTTAWA

The University of Ottawa Press gratefully acknowledges the financial
assistance of the Faculty of Arts, University of Ottawa.

All the articles in this book are used by permission.

This book is dedicated to all those Canadians who believe in and struggled for the democratization of the process and the substance of our Canadian Constitution

CONTENTS

FOREWORD

Professor Behiels has called his book *The Meech Lake Primer*. He might almost have called it *The Meech Lake Encyclopaedia*, for it provides a comprehensive treatment of this very complex and controversial subject; it gives both sides of the story, by a judicious selection of authors—lawyers, economists, political scientists, historians, statesmen and politicians, representatives of the aborigines and of women. Each facet of the subject has a lucid and scholarly introduction.

The literature on the subject is already voluminous. Some readers may not wholly agree with Professor Behiels' selections. Perhaps many readers will end up saying, with Tennyson's King Arthur, "All my mind is clouded with a doubt." Perhaps the Meech Lake Accord will join the Fulton–Favreau formula of 1964, the Victoria Charter of 1971 and Bill C-60 of 1978 as just one more attempt to remould the Canadian Constitution that didn't come off.

Whether or no, at a crucial moment in our history, Professor Behiels has cast a flood of light upon a subject "of great pith and moment" to every Canadian. We are all his debtors.

EUGENE FORSEY

ACKNOWLEDGEMENTS

No collective anthology of this magnitude can see the light of day without the co-operation and support of a great many people. I owe a debt of gratitude to all of the contributors, especially those organizations and individuals in the voluntary and private sectors who deem our Constitution important enough to devote an inordinate amount of time and effort to express their views on the Accord. I owe a special thanks to professors Tony Hall and José Woehrling for agreeing to write papers specifically for this collection. The collection of the enormous mountain of research material in a relatively short time period was made possible thanks to the help of a very special Canadian, Ann Marie Kelly, as well as my research assistant, Lorna Maclean, neither of whom ever tired of that one more request to find and dutifully xerox another source. I tip my hat to both of them.

In the overall scheme of things, *The Meech Lake Primer* would not have seen the light of day without the full-fledged support and co-operation of the editorial and production staff at the University of Ottawa Press. When, in the deep of winter in 1989, it appeared that the project was grinding to a halt, the entire staff came together in a show of solidarity to ensure that it would survive. I owe a very special thanks to the typist, Deborah Arnold, editor, Janet Shorten, editorial assistants, Jenny Wilson and Marla Sheffer, and production co-ordinator, Pauline Johnston. A great team, indeed! When all is said and done, the team that really made this project possible and helped see it through to fruition is my family, Linda, Marc and Justin. They have all supported my fascination with our Constitution over the past decade and, in particular, my intense involvement with the Meech Lake Accord since it burst onto the national agenda on April 30, 1987. When unforeseen developments threatened to terminate the project, they all, but most especially Linda, rallied around to provide me with the physical, moral and mental support I needed to see the project through to a successful completion.

EDITOR'S NOTE

The idea of a collection of articles on the Meech Lake Constitutional Accord came to me as I watched the hundreds of intervenors presenting their testimony before the Special Joint Committee of the Senate and the House of Commons on the 1987 Constitutional Accord during August of 1987. It was a fascinating and enlightening experience, one that revealed much about the strengths and the weaknesses of the existing process of constitutional renewal. Electricity and tension, intensified by the fact that the vast majority of organizations and individuals had had barely a month to prepare their submissions, filled the Old Railway Committee Room in the centre block of the Parliament Buildings. Canadians from all walks of life and from all parts of the country were eager to participate in the proceedings.

Yet, all too often, the organizations and individuals left the committee room frustrated and angry. They felt that their testimony had fallen on deaf ears. The Meech Lake Accord was being treated by the first ministers and by the two national opposition party leaders as a fait accompli. The "deal," its advocates maintained, could not be amended in any way, shape or form for fear that it would unravel. In sum, Canadian citizens were being denied an effective voice in the renewal of their own Constitution.

This undemocratic approach to constitutional renewal has not stifled the growing debate surrounding the Meech Lake Accord. It is hoped that this collection of articles on all aspects of the Accord and the editor's descriptive and analytical historical introductions will help provide some focus to this debate. If this collection of material serves to awaken more Canadians to the importance of their Constitution and demonstrates how they might participate more formally in its renewal, it will have admirably served its purpose.

M.B.

GENERAL
INTRODUCTION

Canadians are relative newcomers to the exercise of explicit constitutional reform. The British North America Act of 1867 was put together in three short years by the ruling colonial elites and given legislative sanction by the British House of Commons and House of Lords. It stood the test of time and served Canada well for over a century with very few major amendments. For a long time, the vast majority of Canadians, unlike their American neighbours, showed little noticeable interest in their Constitution, as its many clauses pertained primarily to the distribution of powers between the federal and provincial governments. It is only in the past two decades that Canada's political, social and intellectual leaders have had to focus their attention on the question of adapting the Constitution—renamed the Constitution Act, 1867 in 1982—to the myriad of socio-cultural changes that have taken place at all levels of Canadian society since World War II.

Our recent experience with constitutional renewal has been inordinately time-consuming and, more often than not, excruciatingly frustrating. Indeed, it has, on occasion, been downright depressing for anyone directly involved or for those citizens deeply concerned with the all-too-fragile state of national unity. The process has preoccupied and continues to preoccupy the energies and talents of an entire generation of the best and brightest minds in the public, para-public and voluntary sectors. The never-ending discussions and squabbles among politicians, bureaucrats and intellectuals have left the general public battered and bruised, yet only slightly wiser about the nature and import of both the process and substance of the constitutional debate.

The general public has been subjected to innumerable economic and political power plays mixed only occasionally with high principle. Canadians have witnessed too many setbacks and several outright failures, including Quebec's rejection of the highly regarded 1964 Fulton–Favreau amendment formula and the Victoria Charter of 1971. Even when considerable success was achieved, as was the case with the Constitution Act, 1982, there were a great many detractors all too willing to denigrate both the process and the final product. Donald Smiley, a veteran constitution watcher and analyst, declared the Constitution Act, 1982 to be ''a dangerous deed'' because:

> [the] act of changing the elements of the constitution embodying the powers of the provinces was a betrayal of the commitments made to the Quebec electorate in 1980 and created new hazards in the relations between Quebec and the wider Canadian community.[1]

Indeed, this sense of failure and betrayal of Quebec is the primary driving force behind the concerted efforts of the mandarins, ministers and first ministers to resolve what they consider to be the crucial unfinished business of 1980–82—that is, the unfinished business pertaining to their own constitutional prerogatives and interests.

Proponents of and active participants in the creation of the Constitution Act, 1982, while agreeing that it addressed neither the demands of the Québécois neo-nationalists nor those of a reinvigorated, aggressive provincial rights movement, maintained that it went to the heart of a more fundamental dimension of nation building—that is, the role of its citizens. ''The new Constitution,'' wrote Romanow, Whyte and Leeson, ''with its charter of rights, forges a pattern of political participation for citizens to vindicate their interests, and forestall majoritarian tyranny, by enforcing standards of political decency.'' Nevertheless, the achievement was very fragile. The seeds of a more democratic era had been sown in Canadian society and politics. It remained up to individual Canadians from coast to coast to nurture those seeds and to seize ''on this new pattern of political participation and embed it within the culture of Canada,'' before the inertia of the past reasserted itself.[2]

This warning proved to be far more prophetic than its authors might have imagined. Within very short order, the nascent era of a democratized peoples' Constitution with its Charter of Rights and Freedoms was being challenged by a powerful and highly effective reassertion of the traditional agendas of Quebec's role in Confederation and the

seemingly insatiable demands of a reorganized provincial rights movement focused in western Canada. This turn of events was possible
because the amendment formula agreed to in the Constitution Act, 1982
remained the prerogative of the first ministers. As the debate surrounding the Meech Lake Accord would demonstrate, the first ministers were
able to make effective use of their exclusive control over the amending
process to determine both the agenda and the pace of reform. There
were no constitutional or juridical avenues available to individual Canadians or the many voluntary organizations representing a wide variety
of vested interest groups to give them some control over the process
and the substance of the reforms agreed to by the first ministers. The
only avenue open to them was political. If they wished to amend, delete
or add to the provisions of the Meech Lake Accord, they had to convince
one or more of the legislatures, via their premiers, to delay the enabling
legislation with the objective of gaining another federal–provincial conference. Barring co-operation, a province could simply allow the three-
year time period allotted for ratification to elapse. The constitutional
renewal endeavour would have to await a more opportune moment to
resume its course.

The Meech Lake Primer was conceived and produced with several
goals in mind. The first objective is to represent as accurately as possible the views of both the supporters and the critics of the 1987 Constitutional Accord. The material in this wide-ranging collection, addressing
all facets of the Accord, is primarily drawn from the testimony given
before three legislative forums: the Special Joint Committee of the Senate
and the House of Commons on the 1987 Constitutional Accord, which
held its deliberations in August and September 1987; the Senate Committee of the Whole on the Meech Lake Constitutional Accord, which heard
testimony between June 1987 and March 1988; and the Ontario Select
Committee on Constitutional Reform, which held public hearings
between February and May 1988. Other contributors to the Primer found
expression for their respective viewpoints and interpretations in various
learned journals and a spate of Meech Lake conferences whose proceedings were published in monograph form. The Meech Lake Primer provides
the most clearly defined expressions of the conflicting interpretations
pertaining to virtually all of the central aspects of the Accord. There
are many lucid variations on the same themes that add both colour and
insight into the debate, but these, unfortunately, cannot be included
for lack of space in what remains a very hefty yet manageable and
accessible collection.

The second objective of this Primer is to situate the constitutional arguments presented by both the proponents and the critics of the Accord in their appropriate historical, political and social contexts. Very little is known about the historical origins and the evolution of the contemporary constitutional debate outside select academic, judicial and journalistic circles. It is imperative that students and laypersons interested in contemporary constitutional politics be able to place the highly emotion-laden arguments of the protagonists and the antagonists in their proper historical context. Although the past is all-too-readily used and abused, it can, if approached with a keen sense of critical judgement, help the reader distinguish between mere political rhetoric and valid interpretative arguments based on widely accepted and understood facts.

Clearly, it is still too early to attempt to write a detailed historical account of how and why the Meech Lake Accord emerged in the form that it did on April 30, 1987. The process was one that was entirely closed to public scrutiny, as it did not involve, at any stage, a public first ministers' conference. Because there were no other ministers or advisors present during the intense all-night bargaining sessions, it will be up to individual first ministers to reveal in their memoirs the cut and thrust of the deal that eventually emerged in the form of the Accord. Nor is there a plethora of governmental position papers by bureaucrats, as was the norm during the 1970s and early 1980s prior to all the constitutional conferences. Finally, since the ratification process remains to be completed, none of the participants, particularly the three former premiers—Brian Peckford, Howard Pawley and Richard Hatfield—has chosen to speak out publicly about his role in the formulation of the document.

Although it will be many years before historians have access to the position papers and briefing notes of the first ministers, there is sufficient information about the evolution of the constitutional renewal process since the late 1960s that an appropriate and enlightening historical setting can be provided for most of the issues raised in the Accord. It is important to grasp the nature of the public debate involving a wide range of vested interest groups and individuals, as well as the strategic and somewhat chaotic political bargaining that surrounded the Constitution Act, 1982. Only in this way can one fully understand the intensity of the reactions to the Meech Lake Accord. Lengthy descriptive and analytical introductions to each chapter are provided with this goal in mind. The bibliographies associated with each chapter, located at the end of the book, enable readers to gain ready access to a full range of rich primary and secondary material. It is hoped that many will do so.

The public debate that took place after the first ministers signed the Meech Lake Accord in Ottawa on June 30, 1987, has been dominated by several pertinent themes. One theme that transcends all party lines and upon which there is a growing consensus about the need for change is that of process. The Meech Lake Accord, arrived at via the process of executive federalism involving the eleven first ministers, was presented to the Canadian public and the national and provincial legislatures on the basis of a constitutional package that could not, under any circumstances, be amended. Most Canadians—a majority, as polls would demonstrate—were greatly disturbed with an elitist and undemocratic process that turned their political representatives and the legislatures into mere rubber stamps for the late night and early morning decisions of the first ministers. In the words of the Ontario Select Committee on Constitutional Reform, which heard an earful about process from virtually every witness:

> it is very difficult for provincial legislators and the people they represent to perform their proper function of helping the nation achieve an agreeable resolution of constitutional debate when confronted by a virtual *fait accompli* of First Ministers.[3]

At the heart of the problem is the clash between our democratized Constitution, symbolized by the entrenchment of the Charter of Rights and Freedoms in 1982, and the new amendment formula. The amending process remained exclusively in the hands of the first ministers when they flatly rejected former prime minister Pierre Trudeau's amending formula, which included a limited referendum mechanism. This debate over process had its origins in the public struggle that ensued over the Constitution Act, 1982, and it was completely reopened in the heated battle over the Accord. In order to ensure the legitimacy of any and all constitutional reforms, Canadians will have to decide very soon between two courses of action. Do they wish to perpetuate what two political scientists have referred to as "a process of democratic elitism tempered by occasional populist anger,"[4] or do they wish to create a reformed constitutional renewal process within our system of parliamentary democracy that acknowledges to a far greater extent the sovereignty of the people? This debate invariably will involve a thorough discussion of the existing notwithstanding clause, section 33, of our Charter and may indeed lead to its eventual elimination.

There is a second theme that permeates the entire debate and upon which there is definitely no consensus. Should our Constitution encompass a single, unambiguous and lucid vision of a united, yet pluralistic, Canada, or should it express two or more highly divergent and competing visions of the country represented most vividly by the provincial societies and the francophone nationality? This debate was taken up at the highest level by former prime minister Pierre Elliott Trudeau, who asked, "Who speaks for Canada? Is it the provinces or the national government?" Pierre Trudeau's liberal democratic vision of a strong national government greater than the sum of its parts was countered by Prime Minister Mulroney, Senator Lowell Murray and Ontario's Attorney General, Ian Scott, who defended their conception of our Constitution as an ideal mechanism for reconciling competing and potentially divisive visions of the country.

At the very heart of this ideological debate are the two central aspects of the Accord—the distinct society clause and the principle of the equality of the provinces. Should the distinctive nature of Quebec society, however that might be ultimately defined by the Supreme Court, be entrenched in the Constitution as an interpretative clause applicable to the entire Constitution and the Charter except for clauses pertaining to Canada's aboriginal and ethnocultural communities? It was evident at the outset that most critics did not want to address this issue head-on for fear of being denounced as anti-francophone and anti-Quebec. Yet, just two years later, it is now clear that there is widespread public concern about the constitutional and political implications of dealing with the Québécois francophone majority's legitimate concerns for its survival and development in this all-encompassing and open-ended manner. There is also a growing realization that the Accord does not address the promotional and institutional needs of our two linguistic minorities. Should the country be further decentralized by entrenching the concept of the equality of the provinces? Critics have few qualms about denouncing the provincial equality concept as it is expressed in the Meech Lake Accord's limitations on the national government's spending powers, its expansion of the items under the unanimity amending formula and, finally, its granting to the provinces of control over the nomination of senators and Supreme Court justices, as well as the creation of new provinces. Prime Minister Mulroney, Senator Murray and other Accord promoters respond to their critics on this theme by arguing that the Accord represents a more genuine form of federalism, one that corresponds more closely to the highly decentralized nature of Canadian society and the important role played by the provinces in matters of public policy and their implementation. Our Constitution, they contend, should reflect that reality as well as the vision of a strong, interventionist national government.

The third theme that runs through the entire Meech Lake Accord debate pertains to the Charter of Rights and Freedoms. At the heart of this debate is the question of how to reconcile individual and collective rights. Many critics raised the question of whether the protection of individual rights outlined in the Charter should take precedence over collective rights outlined in the Constitution and, in particular, the distinct society clause of the Accord. After considerable soul-searching, all the women's organizations, except those in Quebec, concluded that protection of gender rights *should* be guaranteed primacy at all times and under all circumstances. These organizations proposed two different approaches to achieve this objective. The primacy of gender equality could be guaranteed by making the entire Charter immune from the distinct society interpretative clause. Alternatively, the gender equality clause, section 26, of the Charter could be added to section 16 of the Accord, thereby immunizing only this aspect of individual rights from the distinct society provision.

On the other hand, Canada's ethnocultural and aboriginal organizations express a different concern with, and adopt a different approach to, the Charter of Rights and Freedoms and the Meech Lake Accord. Representatives of both groups have maintained, from the outset of their involvement in the constitutional debate in the late 1970s, that individual rights and collective rights can and should be reconciled in the Charter and the Constitution. They point to the Charter's and the Accord's guarantees for Canada's two dominant cultural and linguistic communities—anglophone and francophone—and their respective linguistic minorities. Their fundamental criticism of the Constitution Act, 1982 and the Meech Lake Accord of 1987 is that neither of these two documents provides the necessary constitutional entrenchment for the collective rights of the aboriginal peoples and the ethnocultural communities. Not to do so is to create a hierarchy of collective rights whereby some communities acquire constitutional status and the political and social powers that flow from that status, whereas other communities are relegated to second-class citizenship and their members face the real threat of gradual integration and perhaps eventual assimilation into the majority communities. Their point is well taken. Once a society makes the decision to provide constitutional protection for one, two or more of its collectivities, it is inevitable that political and social pressures will mount to provide that same protection to other collectivities. The upshot is that more occasions will arise when a member of any one of these communities will find his or her individual rights in conflict with the collective rights of his or her respective community. The judicial system at all levels, but especially the Supreme Court, will need guidance from our legislators on how to handle these conflicts. The Supreme Court's already-heavy agenda will become further overburdened, and its ability to render relatively swift decisions will be impaired.

All of these fundamental issues deserve far more debate and discussion. Their complexity confirms the importance of creating a constitution that is crystal clear in its principles, relatively unambiguous in its specific clauses and accessible and meaningful for the citizens who must live under its authority. The renewal of Canada's more than a century old Constitution is an important and necessary task. All concerned Canadians should prepare themselves as best they can to face that challenge, thereby ensuring a stable and prosperous future for all generations to come. It is the editor's fond hope that this *Meech Lake Primer* will help, in some small measure, to facilitate this task.

Notes

1. Donald Smiley, "A Dangerous Deed: The Constitution Act, 1982," in Keith Banting and Richard Simeon, eds., *And No One Cheered: Federalism, Democracy and the Constitution Act* (Toronto: Methuen, 1983).
2. Roy Romanow, John Whyte and Howard Leeson, *Canada . . . Notwithstanding. The Making of the Constitution 1976–1982* (Toronto: Carswell/Methuen, 1984): xx.
3. Ontario, Select Committee on Constitutional Reform, 1987 Constitutional Accord, *Report on the Constitution Amendment 1987* (Toronto: Queen's Park, 1988): 5.
4. Keith Banting and Richard Simeon, "Federalism, Democracy and the Constitution," in Banting and Simeon, *And No One Cheered*, 18.

CHAPTER ONE

THE GENESIS AND NATURE OF THE ACCORD:

The Proponents Present Their Case

With the signing of the Meech Lake Accord on June 3, 1987, we achieved the most important policy objective in our program for national reconciliation. The Accord met the five objectives sought by the Quebec government, as a condition for endorsing the Canadian Constitution.

(Prime Minister Brian Mulroney, "Notes for an Address to the Association of Francophone Regional Weekly Newspaper Publishers," *Tadoussac*, June 11, 1988)

. . . there can be no doubt that Quebec has come out of the 1987 constitutional negotiations a major winner. The gains are substantial. For the first time in 120 years, the Constitution will recognize Quebec as a distinct society . . . . The Constitution will give Quebec the means to preserve and promote our distinct identity and it will provide a constitutional foundation for the French fact in Quebec.

(Premier Robert Bourassa in the Quebec National Assembly, June 18, 1987, cited in Donald Johnston, ed., *With a Bang, Not a Whimper. Pierre Trudeau Speaks Out* [Toronto: Stoddart, 1988]: 136)

Reprinted with permission — Susan Dewar.

INTRODUCTION

The Meech Lake/Langevin Accord is the second attempt, after the aborted round of negotiations over aboriginal rights, to alter the Canadian Constitution since the inception of the 1982 Constitution Act. The British North America Act of 1867 was both Canadianized and democratized through a made-in-Canada amendment formula and a Charter of Rights and Freedoms that, for the first time, created a constitutional contract between citizens and their government. This new dimension to our Constitution was achieved thanks to a highly organized coalition of lobby groups, including women, cultural communities, linguistic minorities and aboriginal organizations. A majority of the provinces objected loudly and vigorously to this entrenchment of a Charter. Realizing that Canadian public opinion supported a national Charter, nine provinces relented and gave their consent. The Trudeau government had broken the constitutional logjam that had prevailed since 1927.[1]

Most constitution watchers believed that the battle was over. No one predicted that the provinces would recoup their forces and, at their first opportunity, make a concerted and largely successful attempt to attenuate or nullify the impact of the Charter. According to many observers, the Meech Lake Accord addresses exclusively the traditional concern over the relationship between federal and provincial governments. In so doing, it achieves the longstanding objectives of the provinces and the French-speaking nationality in Quebec by constitutionalizing the provincial compact and the two-nations theories of Confederation. If ratified, the Meech Lake Accord will usher in a very different form of federalism from the one that emerged after World War II and eventually found partial expression in the Constitution Act,

1982. Under the Meech Lake Accord's decentralized vision, the "federal" government becomes synonymous with all the first ministers making decisions in annual conferences. The concept of an autonomous "national" government that is greater than the sum of its parts is considered by the proponents of the Meech Lake Accord to be a violation of the true meaning of federalism.[2]

The federalism of national social programs and financial equalization to "have not" provinces that was put into place after the war by both Liberal and Conservative national governments contributed in innumerable ways to the most prosperous period in our history. Paradoxically, this post-war prosperity, albeit highly uneven across the country, also resulted in the emergence of vigorous and ambitious provincial economic and social elites with vested interests in seeing that the political and economic powers of their respective provinces were enhanced.[3]

Led by the nationalist Liberal government of Jean Lesage in Quebec, province building soon became the order of the day. By the late 1960s, the two central provinces had bureaucracies that rivalled Ottawa's. Indeed, the Diefenbaker, Pearson and Trudeau regimes fought a series of rearguard battles against the rising tide of this provincial rights movement but, as events have shown, lost the war. After the block funding agreements in the late 1970s, the provinces demanded, and most often got, increased revenues in the form of federal transfer payments and equalization grants, while shrewdly gaining the lion's share of the political credit attached to the spending of these revenues in virtually any way they saw fit. Provincial empire building was partly subsidized by the federal treasury.

The serious recession of the early 1980s, the difficult but eventual patriation of the Constitution with a Charter of Rights and Freedoms and the enhancement of provincial prerogatives in 1982 led Trudeau and many other Canadians to believe that a new equilibrium had been achieved in Canadian federalism. A negative Supreme Court ruling on a Quebec challenge to the new Constitution Act meant that henceforth the "unanimity" rule could no longer be used by the provinces to hinder the constitutional evolution of the country. No single province, it was agreed, would be able to use a constitutional veto power to extract gains from the national government. Quebec had refused to sign, not because it was deliberately left out of the Constitution, as most Quebec politicians have claimed, but rather because René Lévesque simply could not partake in the process of negotiations because such action would undermine his party's commitment to sovereignty-association.

What the Quebec government of René Lévesque had failed to achieve via the referendum, the Liberal government of Robert Bourassa, elected in 1985, was determined to accomplish through straightforward political power. Bourassa's government simply refused to co-operate in any serious constitutional discussions until Quebec's minimum demands had been granted. A volatile Quebec electorate came to the aid of the Bourassa government's attempt to unravel the 1982 constitutional equilibrium. The national Liberal party's Quebec bastion was severely ruptured in the 1984 national election with the election of a large Tory caucus from that province for the first time since the Diefenbaker landslide of 1958. As a result, all three national parties, thrown on the defensive, were forced to appeal to a highly volatile but crucial Quebec electorate. A crisis-ridden Mulroney government, in order to have any chance at a second term, had to retain most of its Quebec seats. This factor played right into the hands of Robert Bourassa and the nationalist elites who exacted approval of Quebec's constitutional demands in return for their political support.[4]

Bourassa and his nationalist colleagues jumped at signing the Meech Lake Accord because it was such a marvellous deal for the nationalist political and bureaucratic elites of Quebec. Indeed, thanks to Mr. Mulroney and the other premiers, Quebec received considerably more than it asked for. It is Bourassa's stated belief that the Accord will allow Quebec's governing bureaucrats and politicians to legislate in favour of the preservation and promotion of Quebec's majority francophone society without fear that such legislation will be overruled by the courts. Bourassa agreed to the Meech Lake Accord because he believed that the distinct society clause would take precedence over the Charter of Rights and Freedoms. René Lévesque, had he received such an offer from his arch political rival Pierre Trudeau, would have jettisoned the separatist nationalists in a flash and signed immediately! Indeed, René Lévesque's closest constitutional advisor, Claude Morin, as well as his Minister of Finance, Jacques Parizeau, have given their blessing to the Accord because it puts Quebec in a constitutional position to make more gains in the future. An aggressive and shrewd Quebec government could use the Accord, according to Morin and Parizeau, to disrupt the federal system and move Quebec step by step toward independence.

The Meech Lake Accord has been portrayed by its proponents as the ''Quebec Round.'' In fact, a close reading of the document reveals that, although it addresses Quebec's five specific demands, it does so in the context of a whole series of concessions to the provinces. Bourassa's strategy of power politics provided an opportune moment for all the premiers who, in turn, found themselves in a position to exact certain demands from the national government in return for their accept-ance of the Bourassa government's constitutional demands. The premiers demanded and received the constitutional recognition of the equality of the provinces, the right to propose appointees to two impor-tant national institutions, the Supreme Court and the Senate, the right to sign individual immigration agreements with Ottawa and the right to opt out, with full financial compensation, of shared-cost programs created by Ottawa in areas of provincial jurisdiction.

This interpretation of constitutional reform, its process and its sub-stance, has never been accepted by Quebec's nationalists in the bureau-cracy, the government, academia or the press.[5] There is also a vocal segment of the political science community throughout English-speaking Canada that, to put it mildly, was thoroughly disappointed with the outcome of constitutional negotiations in 1981–82. It was soon quite apparent that many provincial governments were not satisfied with the concessions they had wrested from Prime Minister Trudeau.[6] These constitution participants and watchers shared the belief that the Con-stitution Act, 1982 was fatally flawed because the Parti Québécois government led by René Lévesque had not signed the document. Prime Minister Trudeau, they contended, had promised a renewal of the federal system during the 1980 referendum. Their vision of a fundamentally restructured federal system, including a substantially redefined role for Quebec and a devolution of additional responsibilities and powers to the other provinces, had been thwarted. The legitimacy of the Consti-tution Act, 1982 remained tainted while the Quebec government's deci-sion to boycott all constitutional discussions left them frustrated and eager to seek a way out of the impasse.[7]

The opportunity arose more quickly than anyone anticipated once the Conservative party led by Brian Mulroney and the Quebec Liberal party led by Robert Bourassa achieved power in 1984 and 1985, respec-tively. During the 1984 national election, Brian Mulroney had promised Quebec voters that his party, if elected, would pursue a constitutional reconciliation with Quebec. Striking while its political leverage was the strongest it had been in a long time, the Quebec government's Minister of Canadian Intergovernmental Affairs, Gil Rémillard, outlined at the May 1986 Mont-Gabriel Conference on the Canadian Confederation the five conditions that Ottawa and the provinces had to accept in return for Quebec's signature on the 1982 Constitution Act.[8] Rémillard's per-sistent and strenuous lobbying with the premiers paid off when, during their 1986 summer conference, the premiers decided to give priority to

Quebec's five demands. Prime Minister Mulroney, perceiving a "window of opportunity," assigned his newly appointed Minister of State for Federal–Provincial Relations, Lowell Murray, to find the "bottom line" of each of the premiers in a series of bilateral meetings with them over the winter of 1986–87. These discussions showed promise, and Murray recommended that the first ministers meet to see if a deal could be struck. Anyone not privy to the negotiating process that had been going on for over eighteen months was not very confident about the outcome. Much to their surprise, the first ministers signed the Meech Lake Accord on April 30, 1987.

Senator Lowell Murray's testimony before the Special Joint Committee of the Senate and the House of Commons on the 1987 Constitutional Accord vividly illustrates the degree to which he and his government had adopted the arguments of the Quebec nationalist and provincialist critics of the 1982 Constitution Act. First, he views the Accord as a reconciliation with the Quebec government because it recognizes that Quebec constitutes a distinct society. Second, Murray sees the Accord as an affirmation of the partnership between Ottawa and ten provincial governments because it constitutionalizes the equality of the provinces. This view is based on the assumption that Confederation is a compact both of cultures and of provinces. Consequently, all major constitutional amendments must be unanimous in order to be considered morally, politically and legally legitimate.

The Meech Lake Accord, Murray argues, completed the unfinished business of 1982, in that its central provisions accomplished what Trudeau had set out but had failed to achieve because he lacked flexibility and a proper understanding of federalism. The Accord's central provisions, the recognition of Quebec as a distinct society coupled with the linguistic duality of Canada, merely recognized the two most fundamental sociological dimensions of Canada. Murray is fully confident that this dual recognition had been achieved without either affecting the distribution of powers between the federal and provincial governments or threatening to override the Charter of Rights and Freedoms.

The other provisions of the Accord pertaining to spending powers, the amending formula, immigration and appointments to the Supreme Court involved recognizing the distinct society of Quebec in a way that does not create an unacceptable special status for that province. This was achieved by ensuring that these provisions were also made available to all provinces with the entrenchment of the "equality of provinces" principle. In sum, for Murray, the Meech Lake Accord was a very modest but necessary accommodation of Quebec and the other provinces, one that would have virtually no significant impact on the federal system. On the other hand, its ratification would open the way for more comprehensive and radical reforms desired by the western provinces, namely Senate reform, through a system of annual constitutional conferences.[9]

Gil Rémillard came to the position of Minister of Canadian Intergovernmental Affairs steeped in a Québécois nationalist perception of Canadian federalism and the Constitution.[10] He was determined to incorporate the contemporary constitutional aspirations of a dynamic and vibrant, yet beleaguered and fearful, francophone society of Quebec into a fundamentally renewed Canadian constitution. Like all Québécois nationalists, he was outraged at the outcome of the constitutional negotiations of 1980–81 that resulted in the Constitution Act, 1982. Rémillard strongly criticized the Trudeau government for having failed to live up to the true meaning of a renewed federalism promised during the referendum. As a Liberal, Rémillard also blamed the Parti Québécois government of René Lévesque for not having seized the opportunity to achieve the very essence of Quebec's longstanding constitutional demands, the recognition of Quebec as a distinct society. Once this principle was entrenched into the Constitution, it would be much easier to negotiate all of Quebec's other demands by relating them in one form or another to the practical implementation of this principle.[11]

Premier Bourassa followed the directives of his minister to the letter, and Quebec achieved all of its five demands and more in the Meech Lake Accord. Rémillard, in his defence of the Accord before his colleagues in the Quebec division of the Canadian Bar Association, had every reason to be pleased with the results. Declared Rémillard:

> For the first time since the federal compromise of 1867, . . . Quebec had obtained with the 1987 Accord the explicit constitutional recognition of its distinct identity within the Canadian federation, along with new powers and guarantees to ensure its cultural security and the full development of its specificity.

It was Rémillard's belief that by constitutionalizing the cultural and provincial compact theories of Confederation, the Accord established the foundations for the emergence of a true federalism, that is, a genuine confederation.

It is clear from Rémillard's article that it is the existence of a francophone majority nationality in Quebec that constitutes the ''distinctiveness'' of that province. Section 2 of the Accord gives the government of Quebec the right and the responsibility to preserve and promote that majority nationality within the linguistic dualism, not of Quebec, but of Canada. The other provisions of the Accord—effective provincial control over Ottawa's spending powers, expansion of Quebec's control over all stages of immigration with full financial compensation, the constitutionalization of Quebec's right to appoint three of the nine Supreme Court justices, the acquisition of Quebec's "traditional" veto over any reform of federal institutions, the entrenchment of annual first ministers' conferences on the economy and the Constitution and provincial appointment of senators pending Senate reform—all constitute, according to Rémillard, practical and effective means of enhancing the survival and development of Quebec's francophone majority nationality. Premier Bourassa concurred wholeheartedly with this interpretation of the Meech Lake Accord when he stated in Quebec's National Assembly on June 23, 1987:

> Dans les cinq cas, on constate que le Québec a un contrôle plus grand sur son avenir. Il obtient un outil supplémentaire pour se développer. L'addition des cinq conditions et surtout leur effet conjugué donne de l'oxygène, oxygène dont le Québec a besoin.[12]

This certainly was not the viewpoint of the leader of the Parti Québécois, Pierre-Marc Johnson, nor of many other ultra-nationalists, such as Léon Dion, Claude Morin, Jacques-Yvan Morin and Daniel Latouche, all of whom condemned the Accord as another sell-out.[13] Nevertheless, the Liberal government of Robert Bourassa was able, thanks to an effective media blitz, to convince the majority of Quebec's francophone citizens that considerable gains had been achieved in the Accord. Quebec's longstanding concern over the constitutional question could henceforth be laid to rest, and the government would be able to pursue other, more urgent, agenda items, such as free trade and much-needed job creation. It appeared that Rémillard's gamble had paid off in spades. All that remained to be done was to convince the other signatories to the Accord to live up to their end of the bargain and obtain legislative ratification before June 1990.

Notes

1. For overviews of the bitter political struggle for a Charter and patriation, consult Roy Romanow, John Whyte and Howard Leeson, *Canada . . . Notwithstanding: The Making of the Constitution 1976-1982* (Toronto: Carswell/ Methuen, 1984); Stanley M. Beck and Ivan Bernier, eds., *Canada and the New Constitution: The Unfinished Agenda*, Vol. 1 (Montreal: Institute for Research on Public Policy, 1983); Garth Stevenson, *Unfulfilled Union. Canadian Federalism and National Unity* (Third Edition, Toronto: Gage, 1989): 235-266.
2. The first book-length critique of the Accord was Bryan Schwartz, *Fathoming Meech Lake* (Winnipeg: Legal Research Institute, University of Manitoba, 1987).
3. Stevenson, *Unfulfilled Union*, 72-93.
4. David Milne, *Tug of War: Ottawa and the Provinces Under Trudeau and Mulroney* (Toronto: Lorimer, 1986); Jean Chrétien, *Straight from the Heart* (Toronto: Key Porter Books, 1985).
5. For the most recent expressions of the Québécois nationalists' perspective, see Claude Morin, *Lendemains piégés. Du référendum à la nuit des longs couteaux* (Montréal: Boréal Express, 1988); Gilles Lesage, ed., *Le Québec et le Lac Meech. Un Dossier du Devoir* (Montréal: Guérin littérature, 1987).
6. Keith Banting and Richard Simeon, eds., *And No One Cheered: Federalism, Democracy and the Constitution Act* (Toronto: Methuen, 1983).
7. For an articulate representation of this point of view, see Peter M. Leslie, "Submission to the Special Joint Committee of the Senate and the House of Commons on the 1987 Constitutional Accord," in Clive Thomson, ed., *Navigating Meech Lake: The 1987 Constitutional Accord* (Kingston: Institute of Intergovernmental Relations and *Queen's Quarterly*, 1988): 8-11.
8. Gil Rémillard, "Under What Conditions Could Quebec Sign the Constitution Act of 1982?," in Michael D. Behiels, ed., *Quebec Since 1945* (Toronto: Copp Clark Pitman, 1987): 209-220; and his "Speech to the Conference on Rebuilding the Relationship: Quebec and its Confederation Partners," in Peter Leslie, ed., *The State of the Federation 1986* (Kingston: Institute of Intergovernmental Relations, Queen's University, 1987): 97-108.
9. Senator Lowell Murray's interpretation of the constitutional process since 1960 along with its underlying assumptions strongly influenced the outlook and recommendations of the Special Joint Committee of the Senate and the House of Commons on the 1987 Constitutional Accord chaired by Senator Arthur Tremblay and Chris Speyer, MP. See its *Report* (Ottawa: Queen's Printer, 1987).
10. Gil Rémillard, a lawyer and professor of constitutional law, has authored two books: *Le fédéralisme canadien, La loi constitutionnelle de 1867* (Montréal: Québec/Amérique, 1983); *Le fédéralisme canadien, Le rapatriement de la constitution* (Montréal: Québec/Amérique, 1985).

11. Rémillard, ''Under What Conditions Could Quebec Sign the Constitution Act of 1982?,'' 217–218. In 1985, Rémillard believed that it was sufficient to have this principle placed in a preamble to the Constitution, not written in as an interpretative clause. This was also the position of the Quebec Liberal party in its platform literature for the 1985 provincial election. See ''Le Parti Libéral,'' in Lesage, *Le Québec et le Lac Meech*, 53.
12. Robert Bourassa, ''Discours à l'Assemblée nationale,'' in Lesage, *Le Québec et le Lac Meech*, 463.
13. Cf. Lesage, *Le Québec et le Lac Meech*, 83–95, 95–99, 104–109, 118–124, 451–461.

LOWELL MURRAY

THE CONSTITUTIONAL POLITICS OF NATIONAL RECONCILIATION*

1. Introduction

It is an honour to appear before this Joint Committee of the Senate and House of Commons to examine with you the historic 1987 Constitutional Accord.

2. The Accord: An Affirmation of Partnership

Let me begin by considering what this Accord means for Canada. The unanimous agreement of the Prime Minister and the ten Premiers marks significant progress in achieving national reconciliation. It heightens the partnership among governments and provides a sound basis for Canadians to work together toward common ends.

The 1987 Constitutional Accord completes the unfinished business of 1981 and thereby ends Quebec's isolation from the country's constitutional process. No longer is Quebec half in, and half out, of our constitutional family.

I have heard it said that Quebec's signature is not necessary, since the province is legally bound by the *Constitution Act, 1982*. For my part,

* Brief to the Special Joint Committee of the Senate and the House of Commons on the 1987 Constitutional Accord, *Minutes of Proceedings and Evidence*, No. 2, August 4, 1987.

I find it hard to accept the proposition that there is no difference between a Constitution to which Quebec is a proud and willing signatory, and one to which it is not. And I cannot believe that failure to secure Quebec's willing adherence would have had absolutely no effect upon national unity, now or in the future. In my view, Quebec's adherence is more than desirable, it is essential.

Without the Accord and Quebec's participation in our constitutional family, Canada's future would have remained in doubt. The danger posed by Quebec's continued constitutional isolation might have proved very serious indeed. It would not be right to leave to future generations the obligation to resolve this problem, perhaps in more difficult and less tranquil times.

I have also heard it said that the federal government gained nothing in these negotiations, that it gave but did not get. I must reject these contentions totally. Canada is the clear and undisputed winner in the present round of constitutional negotiations. The strengthening of our country, the reconciliation of Quebec, opportunities for economic policy coordination and future constitutional reform are all significant gains as a result of the present round of constitutional negotiations.

The 1987 Constitutional Accord is a limited package of amendments designed to achieve a specific goal. It has been public knowledge since the Edmonton Premiers Conference of August 1986 that governments had agreed to limit the current round to Quebec's conditions and to address issues raised by other governments in subsequent constitutional discussions. Had this agreement not been secured it is unlikely we would have succeeded in our primary goal—the repatriation of Quebec.

In seeking to resolve Quebec's concerns while meeting the shared objectives of all eleven governments, the Accord is a seamless web and an integrated whole. It represents a finely balanced package—the product of negotiation and compromise. As such, it should not be lightly tampered with.

Three objectives will be achieved through the Accord: recognition of Canada's diversity and linguistic duality; respect for the principle of the equality of the provinces; and promotion of cooperation and collaboration among governments. I believe these are essential objectives for our country. They cannot, of course, be fully met by constitutional amendments: they must be anchored in the hearts of Canadians.

But I do believe that these amendments, when they become part of the Constitution, will provide a better reflection of what Canadians want Canada to be: a generous, tolerant and united society, one that

respects diversity and believes that governments should work coopera-
tively within their respective areas of jurisdiction to serve the interests
of the people.

What are the facts? This Accord leaves all individual rights intact.
The Charter of Rights and Freedoms has not been amended, nor is there
anything in this Accord that overrides it. The Accord leaves aboriginal
rights intact, and there is nothing in it that would preclude future reform
to bring justice to Canada's aboriginal peoples. No group has been
pushed to the back of the bus; rather, in repatriating Quebec, we have
made some repairs to the bus before an accident occurred. The policy
of family reunification, established under federal authority, will be unal-
tered. Mobility rights will not be affected in any way. Existing social
programs are not altered by the Accord. And—as I shall be explaining
in detail—the establishment of new national social programs will
continue to be possible.

3. The Quebec Round

Some critics of the Accord assume that First Ministers undertook to negotiate much more than the "Quebec round" on April 30 and June 3. For
this reason, suggestions to improve the Accord and broaden its scope
often are misplaced—well-intentioned though they may be. If any egregious errors in the Amendment are identified, they can—as First
Ministers agree—be addressed immediately, albeit within the context
of the unanimity requirement. There will be ample opportunity to
address other issues and improvements in the second round. But first,
we must end Quebec's isolation, otherwise no second round, no attempt
at further constitutional reform, will have much prospect of success.

The 1987 Accord is not the product of two intensive meetings of
First Ministers. Nor is it the work of a year of intensive discussions
among Ministers and officials.

Unanimity on the Accord would not have been possible at this time
without the benefit of repeated federal–provincial debate on the main
elements of this Constitutional Accord—Canada's linguistic duality,
Quebec's distinct society, the amending formula, the spending power
and provincial participation in Supreme Court and Senate appointments.

These elements of the 1987 Constitutional Accord were built on the
work of decades—the constitutional review of 1968 to 1971, the constitutional exercise of 1975 and 1976, Bill C-60 in 1978, the intensive dis-

cussions of the Constitution from 1978 to 1979 and the negotiations that followed the referendum in 1980, as well as the exercise of 1981.

Following months of impassioned debate leading up to the referendum in the spring of 1980, the people of Quebec finally said "yes" to Canada and to renewed federalism. During the course of the referendum campaign, solemn promises were made by a number of Premiers that Quebec's constitutional concerns would be addressed. The other provinces are ready to say "yes" to Quebec and to further constitutional change in a second round. And now Parliament has the opportunity to say "yes" to Quebec.

In search of the renewed federalism promised to all Canadians in the referendum, the Government of Canada and the governments of nine provinces agreed in November 1981 to a constitutional package. That package included patriation, an amending formula, the Charter of Rights and Freedoms, recognition of aboriginal rights and our multicultural heritage, a commitment to reinforce our regional strengths and the clarification and extension of provincial jurisdiction over natural resources.

This achievement by First Ministers was certainly a substantial and historic one. But it was flawed. The constitutional picture was not complete because of the absence of Quebec from the agreement. For this reason, I and others voted against the resolution on the Constitution in December 1981 when it was tabled before the Senate.

The long years of constitutional debate reached a turning point as a series of events occurred in the period following the proclamation of the *Constitution Act, 1982*. These events included:

(1)   the election of a federal government in 1984 committed to national reconciliation and to working actively to bring Quebec back into the constitutional family;

(2)   the election of a federalist Quebec government in 1985 that had enunciated in its election platform, *Maîtriser l'avenir*, five realistic conditions for ending the constitutional impasse; and

(3)   the subsequent willingness of all Premiers to make the successful resolution of the Quebec issue their constitutional priority.

These events combined to create a window of opportunity that First Ministers seized in the Meech Lake agreement and in the 1987 Constitutional Accord. No one should underestimate this unique conjuncture of forces, and no one should take lightly the consequences that would have resulted from failure.

The role played by this government in creating a window of opportunity can be traced to a key address made by Brian Mulroney at Sept-Îles during the 1984 election campaign. He made bringing Quebec back into the mainstream of our nation's political life a fundamental objective. It was his firmly held view, and one endorsed by the Progressive Conservative Party, that vital elements of the Canadian social fabric would be incomplete until Canadians came to terms with Quebec's place in the Constitution.

In his Sept-Îles address, Mr. Mulroney stated:

> I know that many men and women in Quebec will not be satisfied with mere words. We will have to make commitments and take concrete steps to reach the objective that I have set for myself and that I repeat here: to convince the Quebec National Assembly to give its consent to the new Canadian Constitution . . . . But, knowing the importance and the complexity of federal–provincial issues, I will not undertake a constitutional path with ambiguity and improvisation. To proceed otherwise would risk making things much worse rather than better.

He also signalled his intent to breathe a new spirit into federalism, replacing the bias of confrontation with the bias of agreement and seeking greater coordination and harmony between the two orders of government through an institutionalized First Ministers' Conference. In this environment, the Liberal Party of Quebec set out five conditions for adhering to the Constitution in its position paper, *Maîtriser l'avenir*, which became its platform for the 1985 election. And, after the Liberal Party came to power in that election, Gil Rémillard, Quebec's Minister of Canadian Intergovernmental Affairs, reiterated in an important speech at Mont-Gabriel Quebec's five conditions.

4. The Constitutional Accord/Problem Solving

Let me now turn to the specific elements of the Accord.

Questions have been raised as to why Quebec's distinct society should be recognized in the Constitution.

The *Constitution Act, 1982* is, in large measure, a statement of Canada's fundamental characteristics, including the affirmation of the basic rights and freedoms we all share, the recognition of aboriginal rights and our multicultural heritage, and a commitment to the regional strengths of Canada.

The Charter of Rights and Freedoms dealt basically with individual rights, but a number of collective rights were also affirmed in the Charter and elsewhere in the 1982 Act. Canada is not a melting pot and it is the Canadian experience in marrying collective and individual rights that has played such a critical role in defining our identity. It was the entrenchment of individual rights that allowed us to affirm, in addition, a number of collective rights. But there is some unfinished business left over from 1982.

Nowhere does the Constitution recognize the distinctiveness Quebec brings to Canada, the importance of our linguistic duality, nor the leavening presence of French-speaking minorities outside Quebec and the English-speaking minority within Quebec.

Without acknowledging these central facts, how can the language provisions in the Charter and elsewhere in the Constitution of Canada or Quebec's special system of civil law be explained or understood?

The issue of Canada's linguistic duality and Quebec's distinct society figured prominently in constitutional initiatives prior to and following the Quebec referendum.

Let us not forget that at the First Ministers' Conference in September 1980, Prime Minister Trudeau was willing to recognize "the distinctive character of Quebec society with its French-speaking majority" in a preamble to the Constitution, and a "best efforts" draft to achieve this end was produced. Alas, the Conference ended in failure and, in 1982, other fundamental characteristics of Canada were explicitly recognized in our Constitution, but not our linguistic duality and Quebec's distinct society.

Governments have now agreed to repair that omission and to recognize the existence of English-speaking Canadians and French-speaking Canadians, both present in all parts of the country; that the French-speaking Canadians concentrated within Quebec and the English-speaking Canadians outside Quebec constitute a fundamental characteristic of Canada; and that Quebec represents a distinct society within Canada.

This is a simple fact of our national life, and has been for 120 years of Confederation. The wording of clause 1 of the text expresses this fact and completes some of the unfinished business of 1981.

It also affirms the role of Parliament and all legislatures to preserve the fundamental characteristic of Canada I have just described, as well as the role of the government and legislature of Quebec to preserve and promote its distinct identity.

Let us be clear on two points: nothing in the proposed amendment changes the distribution of powers between the federal and provincial governments. Nor does anything in the proposed amendment override the Canadian Charter of Rights and Freedoms, including women's equality rights. Furthermore, clause 16 of the *Constitution Amendment, 1987* ensures that nothing in this section affects the provisions of the Constitution respecting the aboriginal peoples or the multicultural heritage of Canadians. No existing rights have been made subordinate. Nobody has been pushed to the back of the bus.

Let us now turn to the spending power of Parliament.

As you know, in addition to spending money on programs and activities that fall within its own legislative jurisdiction, Parliament can also spend for purposes to which its legislative authority does not extend, including matters in areas of exclusive provincial jurisdiction.

While the exercise of the spending power of Parliament has provided major benefits for Canadians over the years, spending in areas of exclusive provincial jurisdiction has, in the view of the provinces, on occasion affected their priorities and distorted their budgets.

More recently, provincial governments have claimed that federal decisions on the conditions of existing grants and the levels of funding are compounding the problem.

For this reason, Quebec—and, indeed, other provinces—has sought to establish ground rules governing the exercise of the spending power in areas of exclusive provincial jurisdiction. This question did not spring up suddenly in 1987. The spending power was thoroughly examined by governments in two previous exercises over the past 20 years—in 1968-71 and 1978-79. On both occasions, the federal government was willing to make the exercise of the spending power in areas of provincial jurisdiction subject to a consent mechanism. This would have required the support of at least a majority of the provinces representing at least half the population before a national program could be inaugurated.

In both instances, the federal government agreed to provide compensation to individuals in non-participating provinces with no requirement that the province launch a program or initiative compatible with the national objectives to justify such compensation. And in both instances the federal proposal went well beyond the limited aspect of the spending power contemplated in the current amendments.

The proposal agreed to by First Ministers at Meech Lake and on June 3, in my view, reflects a more appropriate balance between federal and provincial interests than did previous proposals. There will be no provincial consent mechanism, as a number of governments were concerned that this would overly limit Parliament's ability to inaugurate new national programs. Compensation will be conditional on provinces carrying on an initiative or program compatible with the national objectives. And the proposal applies only to new national shared-cost programs.

The terms of the text before you provide for a healthy bargaining process between the two orders of government, one that should favour broad agreement on new national programs with greater regional sensitivity. In this way, it "civilizes" the future use of the spending power, while recognizing that it is legitimate for Parliament to pursue economic and social progress for Canadians.

The seventh clause of the 1987 Amendment will add section 106A to the *Constitution Act, 1867*. The purpose of this provision is not to define or extend the spending power of Parliament. Rather, it is to require that the Government of Canada provide reasonable compensation to the government of a province that chooses not to participate in new shared-cost programs it established on a nation-wide basis in an area of provincial jurisdiction, but only if the province in question carries on a program or initiative compatible with the national objectives.

These proposed changes, I would note, do *not* naïvely assume that governments will invariably agree. But they do encourage agreement by placing a higher premium, for both orders of government, on consultation and collaboration.

Let me be even more explicit. These proposed amendments provide reasonable and feasible means of encouraging collaborative action by governments in a very clearly defined area: that of national shared-cost programs which may be established in the future in areas of exclusive provincial jurisdiction.

Another of Quebec's concerns relates to the amending formula.

The purpose of the amending formula is to ensure constitutional stability by requiring that the fundamental law of the country be more difficult to amend than ordinary statutes, and to provide protection for the constituent units of the federation.

In seeking such protection, *Maîtriser l'avenir* expressed a preference for a veto for Quebec over all major constitutional amendments. However, recognizing that a general veto was unlikely in the aftermath of 1981, *Maîtriser l'avenir* set out a fall-back position: obligatory compensation in all cases of opting out of amendments transferring provincial legislative authority to Parliament (and not just in the case of education and culture, as was required by the 1982 Act); and a veto over changes to national institutions and the creation of new provinces.

While the provinces confirmed their disinclination to alter the general amending formula, First Ministers did agree that a province should receive reasonable compensation in all cases where it opts out of a future constitutional amendment transferring provincial legislative jurisdiction to Parliament.

As I noted, Quebec also wished to ensure its consent would be required for changes to national institutions not already subject to the unanimity rule of section 41 of the *Constitution Act, 1982* and where opting out is not possible.

The provinces felt that a veto for one province alone over section 42 matters would offend the principle of the equality of all the provinces. Rather, they preferred to extend the unanimity rule of section 41 to the matters contained in section 42. This is achieved through the ninth clause of the 1987 Amendment.

Now one rule—unanimity—will apply to all these matters, thus confirming the fundamental equality of the provinces.

But unanimity will be limited to this narrow range of matters. For all other entrenched matters of general application, only the support of the Senate, the House of Commons and the legislative assemblies of two-thirds of the provinces representing 50 per cent of the population will be required.

To critics of this section, I say that the unanimous agreement reached by First Ministers on a complex constitutional agenda on April 30 and June 3 demonstrates two things. First, the federation has reached a new level of maturity. Secondly, unanimity is not a straitjacket. To suggest otherwise is, simply, to quarrel with the facts.

Furthermore, I should note that applying unanimity to this narrow range of matters is much more modest than the Fulton–Favreau formula of 1964 or the March 31, 1976 proposal of Prime Minister Trudeau, both of which would have required unanimous consent for *all* major amendments.

Finally, a word about the Territories. I have not the slightest doubt that unanimous consent will be readily forthcoming when the time is ripe for the Territories to accede to provincial status. There is no reason, in my view, to override the equality of all provinces. The creation of new provinces will alter the numerical operation of the amending formula. Since that formula is subject to the unanimity rule, it does not appear appropriate that its practical operation should be altered without unanimous consent. In the meantime, devolution of powers to the Territories will continue. And the Government will work with the Territorial Governments on constitutional issues.

Quebec also has a fundamental concern with immigration, which is an area of shared legislative jurisdiction with federal paramountcy. Quebec's primary concern is to have an immigration policy which offsets its rapidly declining birthrate, fosters the preservation of a strong French-speaking community in the province and guarantees that Quebec will be able to retain its relative demographic strength within Canada.

Successive federal governments sought to accommodate Quebec's concerns by negotiating the 1971 Lang–Cloutier agreement, the 1975 Andras–Bienvenu agreement and the 1978 Cullen–Couture agreement. The last agreement, on the selection of immigrants abroad, is still in effect and has operated well to everyone's satisfaction. In addition, agreements appropriate to their circumstances have been signed with six other provinces.

While Quebec and other provinces are generally satisfied with the administrative agreements they have concluded with the federal government, Quebec and others seek the capacity to ''entrench'' agreements under the Constitution in order to avoid the possibility of an agreement being overridden unilaterally by the future exercise of federal legislative power.

The third clause of the *Constitution Amendment, 1987* will add sections 95A to 95E to the *Constitution Act, 1867*. Section 95A commits Canada to negotiate an immigration agreement appropriate to its circumstances with any province that so requests. Such an agreement, once concluded, could receive constitutional protection under procedures set out in sections 95B and 95C, and could not be unilaterally changed by either party subsequently. I might remind you that the Accord of June 3, 1987, specifically commits the Government of Canada to negotiate an immigration agreement with Quebec first. Once concluded, this will be subject to Parliamentary debate.

Subsection 95B(2) of the constitutional amendment will ensure the federal government retains control over the national standards and objectives of immigration policy, primarily through its ability to establish classes of immigrants and admission criteria. As well, the federal government maintains responsibility for determining overall levels of immigration, prescribing categories of inadmissible persons, and family reunification.

Let me say that again: there is absolutely no foundation for alarmist suggestions that family reunification will be affected, that the admission of refugees will be affected, or that the existing rights of landed immigrants or citizens—including mobility rights in the Charter of Rights and Freedoms—will be affected by these proposals. This is not a matter of opinion; it is a matter of fact.

Quebec's fifth proposal relates to the Supreme Court of Canada.

The Supreme Court has a significant role in maintaining and interpreting the Constitution and deciding disputes between the two orders of government. It also has a fundamental role to play in applying the Canadian Charter of Rights and Freedoms. The Supreme Court is thus a national institution of fundamental importance, whose existence should clearly be provided for in the Constitution. Similarly, as a vital institution of the federation, the appointment of its members should conform with the spirit of federalism.

Quebec in particular has a special concern about the composition of the Supreme Court. It is the only province governed by a system of civil law, rather than the common law which applies elsewhere in the country. Consequently, since the creation of the Court in 1875, federal law has ensured that a third of the judges represent the civil law tradition.

The Victoria Charter of 1971 included provisions to achieve these ends. Those provisions figured prominently in the 1975–76 discussions. A new "best efforts" draft was produced in 1978–79 and again in 1980. In the course of those discussions, the federal government was always willing to envisage the possibility of provincial participation in nominations to the Court and to protect the proportion of civil code judges from Quebec.

Notwithstanding this long history of discussion and the references in the amending formula to the procedures applicable to amendments to the Constitution respecting the Supreme Court, there is at present only one provision in the Constitution relating to the Supreme Court: section 101 of the *Constitution Act, 1867* merely states that Parliament may provide for "the constitution, maintenance and organization of a general court of appeal for Canada."

The sixth clause of the agreement would add sections 101A to 101E to the *Constitution Act, 1867*. The effect of this would be to entrench the Supreme Court, as well as the requirement that at least three of the nine Justices be appointed from the Quebec Bar. Section 101C provides for a nomination process for appointments to the Supreme Court whereby a nominee acceptable to the federal government would be selected from names proposed by the provinces. However, only Quebec may propose persons for the three appointments representing its system of civil law. In turn, only the other provinces may propose nominees to fill the vacancies representing the common law tradition. This joint appointment procedure will, in my view, conform to the spirit of federalism, as the Supreme Court must decide conflicts between the two orders of government and between governments and individuals.

Why is there provision for a second round of constitutional discussions?

As testimony of their desire that Quebec become once again a full and active participant in Canada's constitutional evolution, the Premiers unanimously agreed at Edmonton in August 1986 that working towards this goal on the basis of Quebec's conditions constituted "their top constitutional priority."

A number of other constitutional issues, such as Senate reform and fisheries roles and responsibilities, are of key interest to some provinces. They agreed to defer discussion on these issues until the Quebec round had been completed. Now that the Quebec round has been completed, a second round of constitutional discussions can be launched to address the interests of other provinces.

To pursue constitutional renewal, a new Part VI of the *Constitution Act, 1982* requires that the Prime Minister convene a First Ministers' Constitutional Conference at least once a year, beginning in 1988. Agenda items will include Senate reform, the fisheries, and such other matters as may be agreed upon.

The term "second round" is used as a matter of convenience to designate the phase of constitutional discussions that will occur after proclamation of the *Constitution Amendment, 1987*. It does not mean that all remaining constitutional issues must be dealt with in one omnibus amendment package. That would be a recipe for failure.

Let me say a word about aboriginal constitutional reform. The Prime Minister has stated that he will not hesitate to convene a further First Ministers' Conference when he is of the view that sufficient movement towards consensus has developed. The Government will be carefully assessing how best to draw lessons from the successful Meech Lake process and apply them to the ongoing work on aboriginal self-government.

Senate reform, which is of special interest to Alberta, will be on the agenda for the next round of constitutional discussions. As a sign of good faith, and until major Senate reform is achieved, the Government has agreed that forthwith it will appoint Senators acceptable to it from names submitted by the provinces. As a result, the second clause of the *Constitution Amendment, 1987* will add a new section 25 to the *Constitution Act, 1867* respecting the procedure for summoning persons to the Senate.

Finally, let me draw your attention to another provision of the *Constitution Amendment, 1987*, which epitomizes our approach to intergovernmental cooperation. The eighth clause of the 1987 Amendment adds a new part XII to the *Constitution Act, 1867*, requiring the Prime Minister to convene annual First Ministers' Conferences on the Economy and such other matters as may be appropriate. This entrenches in our Constitution the substance of the Regina *Memorandum of Agreement* on annual meetings signed by all First Ministers in February 1985, which itself was an outgrowth of the Prime Minister's vision of federalism as stated at Sept-Îles. This will foster better coordination and cooperation among governments in the federation and allow them to better serve the interests of all Canadians.

5. What the Accord Does/Does Not Do

The 1987 Constitutional Accord does not represent a radical departure from Canadian constitutional traditions. Far from it; instead, it is based on a realistic and measured vision of what Canada is and should be. All Canadians can relate to the vision reflected in the Accord.

The Accord reveals a mature and confident Confederation, whose governments are guided by principles of mutual respect and balanced strength. It establishes constitutional ground rules of collaboration and negotiation, rather than rivalry and competition among governments. Fostering better relations between the two orders of government can only benefit the country and its citizens.

An essential part of these ground rules for governments concerns the place of Quebec in Canada. In this regard, the Accord completes unfinished constitutional business and establishes once and for all that the people of Quebec, through their elected provincial government, will participate fully in the nation's constitutional development. Never again will they be bound by a Constitution that does not fully reflect what they are—a distinct society within Canada. It also takes necessary steps to ensure that other wounds are healed and that cooperation is an active principle of intergovernmental relations.

The Accord confirms the principle of the equality of the provinces. The Accord strengthens the legitimacy of national institutions by giving all provinces a role in appointments to key national institutions, and it puts in place intergovernmental mechanisms and ground rules to coordinate economic policies and to pursue constitutional renewal. This is what the Accord has achieved—a creative, dynamic process of change that will place a premium on seeking consensus.

In these ways, the Accord represents a powerful new element in our nation-building and strengthens our unity. And from nation-building comes strength, not weakness. To those who say the federal government has given away too much, I respond that, to the contrary, this Accord now means a more effective federation with a strong federal government at its heart and ten strong, responsible provincial governments. In short, it means a stronger Canada.

Let me be clear about what the Accord does *not* do. Some criticisms of the Accord have tilted at windmills that have nothing to do with what the First Ministers have agreed. Nor do they have anything to do with the key factor that led to success in this exercise: the decision to restrict the scope of discussions to the Quebec round and to complete that unfinished business from 1981 before moving on to other issues.

Nothing in the Accord overrides the Canadian Charter of Rights and Freedoms. The Accord does *not* override the important affirmations of multiculturalism, aboriginal rights, regionalism, or protection of individual rights of the *Constitution Act, 1982*. This Accord enhances the Constitution, without negating what had already been achieved.

The Accord does *not* alter or detract from the preservation and enhancement of our multicultural heritage. The Accord does *not* jeopardize the fundamental equality of male and female persons. The Accord does *not* establish new rights for aboriginal peoples, because the Accord is limited to the Quebec round.

Nevertheless, the Accord brings to an end the impasse in the constitutional reform process. The Government of Canada—and all provincial governments, not just nine of them—may now give active consideration to new avenues of aboriginal constitutional reform.

The Accord does *not* affect existing national shared-cost programs; nor does it alter the federal spending power within areas of federal and mixed jurisdiction; nor does it change many of its uses within provincial jurisdiction. The spending power provision only requires deliberate consultation and negotiation on the use of this power to establish *new* national shared-cost programs within areas of exclusive provincial jurisdiction. Compensation to provinces choosing not to participate in these new programs will be limited to those that carry on programs or initiatives compatible with the national objectives.

As a Canadian, I support an Accord that respects diversity and different circumstances in areas of exclusive provincial jurisdiction while fostering national objectives. As a Canadian, I believe that respect for the nation's diversity should lie at the centre of the Constitution.

6. The Challenge Ahead

There still remains much to be done before the 1987 Constitutional Accord can be proclaimed. The Prime Minister and the Premiers have committed themselves to seek adoption of the constitutional resolution by the Senate, the House of Commons and the legislative assemblies as soon as possible. The challenges before Canadians are all the greater because the requirements of the amending formula call for adoption of identical amendment texts in both official languages by all legislative bodies.

I am encouraged by the adoption of the Accord by the Quebec National Assembly on June 23. This is a tribute to the commitment of Premier Bourassa, his government and, indeed, the National Assembly to the Canadian federation. It is also a clear sign that the aspirations of successive generations of Quebecers have at long last been addressed by the Accord. The action taken by the National Assembly has, of course, formally initiated the amendment process.

In Parliament, this Joint Committee will have a central role in the amendment process. Your public hearings will ensure that the text of the amendment is carefully scrutinized before adoption. If it should come to light that there are egregious errors in the drafting, we would have an opportunity to address them, while bearing in mind that any change would have to meet the test of unanimity.

Your work will also serve as a prelude to a second round of constitutional reform. Hearings will permit Canadians to point out questions and issues that should be addressed in the next round of reform and the priority that should be attached to them. In this way, the Committee can play a role in assessing the next steps in the evolution of our Constitution. This role is all the more important with the entrenchment of annual conferences on constitutional reform.

The words of my friend and mentor—the Honourable Robert Stanfield—on the Meech Lake agreement offer a succinct and eloquent rationale for proceeding to adopt the Constitutional Accord:

> It is not a matter of making concessions to Quebec, it's a matter of the participants of the accord—the federal government and the provinces—reconfirming that English and French speaking people have to live together in mutual respect if this country is going to work.

It was precisely in this spirit of partnership that the Constitutional Accord was reached. And it is in the same spirit that Parliament should now move towards adoption of the *Constitution Amendment, 1987.*

I enjoin you now to heal the wounds of 1981, reunite the Canadian constitutional family and open the way for Canada's future constitutional development.

GIL RÉMILLARD

QUEBEC'S QUEST FOR SURVIVAL AND EQUALITY VIA THE MEECH LAKE ACCORD *

I wish to thank the organizers of this seminar, held under the aegis of the constitutional law and civil liberties section of the Québec division of the Canadian Bar Association, for inviting me to participate in this forum devoted to discussion of the *1987 Constitutional Accord*. Having taken part in the constitutional exercise that resulted in the Accord on June 3, 1987, as the Minister responsible for the matter, I can attest to the exceptional dimension of the Accord from an historical, political and constitutional standpoint, not only for Québec but for the evolution of the Canadian federation as well.

For Québec, the *1987 Constitutional Accord* is a significant achievement among those achievements, often secured after great struggle, that have enabled it throughout its history to guarantee not only its survival, but its ability to express its specificity as a political, social, legal, economic and cultural entity.

For the first time since the federal compromise of 1867, since the milestones that have marked our development as a society—1840, 1791, 1774, 1760—through the 1987 Accord, Québec has won explicit constitutional recognition of its distinct identity within the Canadian federation, along with new powers and guarantees to safeguard its culture and enable its specificity to be fully realized.

The signing of this Accord was the felicitous outcome of a long political process of negotiation and consultation to achieve the primary objective of this constitutional exercise, which was to allow Québec to participate fully as a major, distinct partner in the federation. An act

* In Réal-A. Forest, ed., *L'adhésion du Québec à l'Accord du Lac Meech—Points de vue juridiques et politiques* (Montréal: Les Éditions Thémis, 1988). Translation provided by the author.

of restitution, the Accord is a tangible expression of the determination of Canada's members to remedy Québec's constitutional isolation and thereby complete the patriation initiated in 1981–1982. From this viewpoint, the amendments to the Constitution resulting from the 1987 Accord will, once they are ratified, end Québec's isolation and reestablish the very foundations of a true federalism in which the government partners support, fully and willingly, the Constitution that governs them.

I—Québec Makes its Conditions Known

Québec felt it could voluntarily adhere to the Constitution only if it received satisfactory responses to the basic conditions it was to set forth. In the wake of the referendum in May 1980, the evolution of the federation remained dependent upon the federal government's commitment to renew Canadian federalism through greater recognition of the needs and aspirations of Québec society. Québec refused, in November 1981, to endorse the constitutional agreement signed on April 17, 1982, known as the *Constitution Act, 1982*, because it was not in keeping with the commitment of 1980. Condemned countless times by the Québec government as counter to the particular interests and historic rights of the only society in Canada with a French-speaking majority, the 1981 agreement was incomplete, unfinished and fundamentally unacceptable.

Given a popular mandate on December 2, 1985, the Québec government took the initiative to make known to its Canadian partners, through me, at a seminar in Mont-Gabriel on May 9, 1986, the five conditions to be met for Québec to support the *Constitution Act, 1982*. They were:

(1) the explicit recognition of Québec as a distinct society;
(2) a guarantee of increased powers in immigration matters;
(3) the limitation of federal spending power;
(4) recognition of a right of veto;
(5) Québec's participation in the appointment of judges to the Supreme Court of Canada.

On August 12, 1986, Québec's provincial partners clearly expressed in a joint statement (the *Edmonton Declaration*) their firm intention to make Québec's support their constitutional priority and to enter into discussions for this purpose on the basis of the five conditions Québec had laid down. Subsequently, the 11 federal and provincial first ministers declared, at their annual conference on November 20 and 21, 1986, that they hoped to sign an agreement in the coming months that would enable Québec to become a full-fledged partner once again in the Canadian federation. This new consensus, expressed in the *Vancouver Communiqué*, was to be developed at the initial meeting of first ministers of Canada and the provinces on April 30, 1987, which made tangible the previous declarations of intent. At the close of this meeting, which was decisive in the evolution of a constitutional agreement, Québec and its partners signed at Meech Lake an agreement ratifying the acceptability in principle of the five conditions set forth by Québec. They agreed to mandate legists to translate the agreement into legal terms while respecting its spirit and letter as much as possible. They also agreed to hold a constitutional conference to draft a formal accord.

In the meantime, the Meech Lake agreement was presented for public consultation by the Québec government at hearings held by the Committee on Institutions of the National Assembly from May 12 to 25, 1987.

On the basis of the comments and opinions received by the parliamentary committee, which highlighted the quality and scope of the marked progress made by Québec regarding each of the five conditions set, the Québec Premier agreed with his federal and provincial counterparts to hold a conference in Ottawa on June 2 to give effect to the agreement signed at Meech Lake. By the morning of June 3, Québec and its partners had achieved their objective. They signed a final agreement that meets, from every standpoint, the five constitutional conditions laid down by Québec. The spirit and the letter of the Meech Lake agreement were faithfully reflected in a constitutional document, and the political commitments made on April 30 were rendered in the initial paragraphs of the Accord. By signing the Accord, the 11 heads of the federal and provincial governments agreed to table in their legislative assemblies as soon as possible a resolution authorizing the amending of the Constitution of Canada in accordance with the terms of the *1987 Constitutional Accord*.

The Québec government kept this commitment by tabling the constitutional resolution in the National Assembly, which ratified it on June 23, 1987. Subsequently, the Legislative Assembly of Saskatchewan, the House of Commons and the Legislative Assembly of Alberta also ratified the Accord.* Once the other governments have followed suit, Québec will be able to fully participate once again in discussions with a view to amending the Constitution of Canada.

---

* Translator's note: The legislative assemblies of Prince Edward Island, Nova Scotia, Ontario, British Columbia and Newfoundland have since ratified the Accord.

II—The Specificity of Québec: Cornerstone and Foundation

Considering its particular situation in Canada and on the North American continent, Québec sought, by formulating the five conditions for its support, to obtain the assurance that the Canadian Constitution would allow it to evolve fully within the federation and to have the guarantees and essential means to maintain and develop the characteristics constituting its specificity. Recognition of the distinctness of Québec was therefore a condition for any negotiations likely to result in Québec's adherence to the *Constitution Act, 1982*. The search for satisfactory constitutional responses to the other conditions laid down by Québec was essentially based on the specific identity which defines Québec, notably from the cultural, linguistic, social, economic, legal and political standpoints. Recognition of the distinct character of Québec society therefore became the principle that generated the other conditions, and their common justification.

The new provisions contained in the *Constitution Amendment, 1987*, which gave substance to the gains made in regard to each of the conditions of Québec's support, must therefore be examined according to the principle of Québec's specificity, for it was at the root of all the conditions, marked each stage of the last constitutional exercise and will justify all future uses by Québec of its new powers. In other words, the distinct nature of Québec is the main constitutional foundation on which its future in the Canadian federation rests. The content of the Accord will be briefly discussed from this very special perspective, which explains its general structure.

III—Québec, a Distinct Society[1]

For the first time in its history, Québec has seen its distinct character entrenched in the Canadian Constitution through an explicit provision that will be part of the new section 2 of the *Constitution Act, 1867*, recognizing a pronounced feature of Canadian federalism, which in part justified its establishment in 1867. Its effect will be twofold: it will provide the courts with a mandatory rule of interpretation, stipulating that they must give the Canadian Constitution a meaning and scope in agreement with the fact that Québec forms a distinct society within Canada, and it will give the National Assembly and the Québec government the role of protecting and promoting all the elements that form the distinct character of Québec society. It therefore contains, on the one hand, an inter-pretative rule applicable to all Canadian constitutional laws, including the sharing of jurisdictions and the *Canadian Charter of Rights and Free-doms*, and, on the other, the possibility of using in a dynamic manner the power to effectively maintain and develop that which distinguishes Québec.

The Accord clearly and wisely avoids designating the particular components of Québec's specificity so that there is all the leeway required to ensure its protection and development. Québec's essential characteristics and its cultural security as expressed in many spheres of activity, now and in the future, were not to be restricted. There is no doubt that the French language is a deciding feature of Québec's specificity, which also includes other, equally fundamental components, such as its culture and its political, economic, social and legal institutions.

The new section 2 also recognizes that linguistic duality forms another fundamental component of the Canadian reality that should guide the interpreters of the Constitution. In this regard, it assigns to Parliament and the legislatures of the provinces the role of protecting that which characterizes Canada from a linguistic viewpoint, i.e. the existence of French-speaking Canadians, centred in Québec but also present elsewhere in Canada, and the existence of English-speaking Canadians, concentrated outside Québec but also present in Québec. This is a constitutional basis for the French fact in Québec, because of the very recognition of the concentration of Francophones in its terri-tory. Québec, as a preponderantly French-speaking society, is thereby entrenched as an essential component of the fundamental nature of Canada.

The restrictive provision contained in paragraph (4) of the section was added to fully preserve Québec's power to legislate in linguistic matters and to exercise any right or privilege in this domain. The sec-tion therefore does not add to the constitutional limitations on Québec's linguistic jurisdiction that existed prior to the Accord (s. 133 of the *Con-stitution Act, 1867* and s. 23 of the *Constitution Act, 1982*). Thus, while playing its role in protecting the Canadian linguistic duality by respect-ing English-speaking Canadians in its territory, Québec can confidently pursue the path of strengthening and consolidating the French language and the other features that distinguish it, thus meeting its responsibility to protect and promote its distinctness.

It is quite obvious that, in seeking this constitutional recognition of its distinct character, Québec never meant to escape the application of the *Canadian Charter of Rights and Freedoms* or question the fundamental equality of its citizens. According to the new constitutional provisions, the Canadian Charter will be interpreted, in applicable cases, in accordance with the distinct character of Québec. The courts will therefore have to take into consideration a new interpretative rule and a novel role of protection and promotion, but that will not give Québec a power of derogation similar to that laid down in section 33 of the Canadian Charter. On this point, Quebecers have clearly understood that their rights and freedoms, guaranteed by both the Québec and Canadian charters, will not be jeopardized or diminished.

The new section 2 of the *Constitution Act, 1867* will be interpreted in conjunction with section 16 of the Constitution Amendment. The object of section 16 is to confirm that the existing constitutional principles related to multiculturalism and the aboriginal peoples in sections 25 and 27 of the Canadian Charter, section 35 of the *Constitution Act, 1982* and section 91(24) of the *Constitution Act, 1867* will coexist with the new principles stated in section 2, without any taking precedence over the others. Section 16 reiterates a principle of interpretation of constitutional acts to the effect that the various provisions of the Constitution are to be interpreted in relation to the others. It will be noted that the scope of application of the new section 2 of the *Constitution Act, 1867* differs from that of section 27 of the Charter. The latter applies to the interpretation of the Charter, whereas section 2 applies to all constitutional acts.

In short, section 2 of the *Constitution Act, 1867* will make it possible for Québec to adhere to basic Canadian law with the double assurance that the law will henceforth be interpreted with respect for Québec's distinct character and that Québec lawmakers and governments will be able to fill, with all the necessary latitude, their constitutional role of preserving and promoting the growth of the particular characteristics of Québec society.

IV—Federal Spending Power

Québec's distinct character implies the right of its National Assembly and government to draft, plan and implement the policies and programs most likely to satisfy the special needs of Quebecers. The social, cultural and economic security of this society calls for Québec's full capacity to make the choices it deems appropriate in the areas of its jurisdiction.

Historically, although this capacity has always existed in theory, in practice the presence of the federal government, through its spending power, in sectors of exclusive provincial jurisdiction has limited its scope and application. The consequences of the use by the federal government of its spending power have often been the source of difficulties in Québec, particularly when the object of federal intervention concerned a field in which Québec had exclusive jurisdiction. Each time, Québec found its constitutional leeway to plan and implement programs to solve its specific problems reduced; each time, its capacity to establish criteria for the implementation of major programs could be affected. In a number of cases, it could only decide to preserve its freedom of action at the cost of substantial financial sanctions imposed by the federal government.

Québec's right to say no to federal shared-cost programs, a select tool for the exercise of federal government spending power, and the absence of sanctions or penalties in the event of refusal to participate in or withdrawal from programs therefore became the basic objectives of constitutional negotiations in this area. As Premier Bourassa mentioned, we sought to rein in the federal government's spending power, to prevent it from imposing its priorities on us.

One of the important results of these negotiations is in section 7 of the *Constitution Amendment, 1987*, which introduces section 106A into the *Constitution Act, 1867*. This section will give Québec the option of saying no to new co-financed federal programs in sectors within its jurisdiction, without incurring financial penalties or sanctions. The section gives us the basic leverage to remain what we are. The federal government must now take into consideration the provinces' right to withdraw when it establishes new programs. It will no longer be able to play havoc with the provinces' fields of jurisdiction or act unilaterally, as it has often done in the past.

More particularly, section 106A will introduce the formal, explicit right of the provinces to opt out of such programs. Furthermore, and this is its most beneficial element, it will give the governments that have this new right the capacity to exercise it. It may be claimed that the provincial governments previously had, in theory, the right to refuse to take part in national programs and to sign bilateral or multilateral agreements. However, in practice, the financial cost of the exercise of this power was so high that the occasions were rare when a government was able to refuse federal financing in order to preserve intact its freedom of action in a sector within its exclusive jurisdiction.

By forcing the Canadian government to give reasonable compensation to a province that decides not to participate in a national co-financed program, section 106A gives provincial governments the essential means whereby they can exercise the power to opt out. Financial compensation will be required each time that a national co-financed program is set up in a sector of exclusive provincial jurisdiction when the province that opts out has implemented or will implement a program compatible with the national objectives.

This concept of national objectives is a fundamental element for Québec. It has never sought to eliminate national programs, but to have the opportunity to break with a harmful, paralysing procedure that implied the unilateral establishment by the federal government of national objectives. Section 106A strongly suggests that the federal government will have to agree on national objectives in close collaboration with the provinces. It also puts an end to certain federal practices that consist in imposing on the provinces, in addition to national objectives, compliance with an ever-increasing array of standards, conditions or criteria for the very planning and management of their programs. It introduces a new dynamic into intergovernmental relations, which will help make them more flexible and coherent.

Lastly, section 106A is drafted in such a way that the exercise by Québec of its right to opt out will not result in recognition of federal authority to implement programs in provincial domains. This section simply stipulates the right to opt out; it does not recognize or define federal spending power. To eliminate all doubt in this regard, a second paragraph was added to section 106A, which confirms that the federal government's legislative powers are not amended by the provision. Québec therefore conserves intact its ability to contest in the courts any use of spending power that it feels is unconstitutional.

V—Immigration

Québec has been concerned about immigration matters for a very long time. Every successive Québec government has been aware of the importance and richness of the contribution made by immigrants to Québec society, as well as the difficulties inherent in controlling immigration and integrating new immigrants into the French culture and language.

Also highly sensitive to the decisive role that immigration plays in the demography of its society and its Francophone character, Québec opened negotiations with the federal government more than 20 years ago to obtain more extensive powers in this field. Several administrative agreements have gradually made it possible for Québec to act in this domain. The latest of these was ratified in February 1978 by the Québec Minister of Immigration, Mr. Jacques Couture, and his federal counterpart, Mr. J.S.G. Cullen. It gave Québec powers to select immigrants abroad and certain categories of people who wish to settle temporarily in Québec.

Québec's efforts in immigration matters have been substantial over the last decade. However, given the birth rate in Québec, which has plummeted since the early 1980s, and the major difficulties in integrating immigrants into Québec society, the means available to Québec quickly became insufficient. The selection that Québec could make covered only certain categories of immigrants, and the administrative nature of the Cullen–Couture agreement authorizing it did not prevent the federal government from condemning Québec for its partial powers. Moreover, the establishment of an annual immigrant quota for Québec remained an exclusive federal prerogative. Lastly, the federal government was acting simultaneously with the Québec government in the sensitive sector of immigrant integration, settlement and adjustment.

Given Québec's insufficient power to plan and control its immigration and to establish demographic policies that correspond to its needs and are essential to its cultural security, immigration became a condition that had to be met if Québec was to take its place in the Canadian federation.

The Constitutional Accord of June 3 gives Québec substantial powers in this regard. New provisions will specify the joint legislative jurisdiction attributed under section 95 of the Act of 1867. The new section 95A will make negotiations mandatory with a view to signing an agreement on immigration between the federal government and any province that requests it. The initial paragraphs of the Constitutional Accord of June 3 also stipulate that the Canadian government must sign such an agreement with the Québec government as soon as possible. Lastly, these paragraphs stipulate that the agreement:

(a) will incorporate the principles of the Cullen–Couture agreement;

(b) will grant Québec pre-eminent powers in selecting immigrants ''on the spot'';

(c) will guarantee that Québec will receive a number of immigrants, including refugees, out of the annual total established by the federal government for all of Canada, proportionate to its share of the population of Canada, with a right to exceed that figure by five percent for demographic reasons;

(d) will provide an undertaking by Canada to withdraw services (except citizenship services) for the reception and integration (including linguistic and cultural) of all foreign nationals wishing to settle in Québec where services are to be provided by Québec, with such withdrawal to be accompanied by reasonable compensation.

Section 95B adds that the agreement may have constitutional value. Its content takes precedence over the provisions of sections 91(25) and 95 of the Act of 1867 and cannot be amended without the formal consent of the parties to the agreement. In fact, under the new sections 95D and 95E, amendments to this agreement may only be made under a constitutional amending formula.

The new powers that the Accord of June 3 gives the Québec government will allow the control and planning of immigration that are consistent with our needs. Québec will be able to select most of the immigrants who apply there; its power to select immigrants applying abroad and to accept beforehand most of the aliens who wish to settle temporarily in Québec will be confirmed. The Accord will also guarantee that Québec has the right to select, from among the annual quotas established by the federal government for Canada, its fair share of immigrants, i.e. at least 25 percent of the number that Canada selects, a proportion likely to reach 30 percent in certain cases. Lastly, the new powers include that of exclusive legislation with regard to all programs for the training, settlement and integration of immigrants. This sector, previously handled jointly by Québec and the federal government, is vital, for it determines the quality of the integration of immigrants into Québec society and, ultimately, the maintenance of the balance or relative importance of this distinct society within the Canadian federation. When the federal government withdraws from this sector of intervention, it will have to pay Québec reasonable compensation.

VI—The Supreme Court of Canada[2]

The Supreme Court of Canada intervenes decisively in more than one capacity in the evolution of Canadian federalism and the two main systems of private law found in the country. As the ultimate arbiter of constitutional disputes, its status should be entrenched in the Constitution. Moreover, its composition must reflect the Canadian duality from a judicial standpoint, as it must contribute to the preservation of the specificity of Québec and recognize its unique contribution to the federation. To these ends, Québec sought and obtained constitutional guarantees related to the status of the highest court in the land, its composition and the method of selecting its judges, which will be inserted after section 101 of the *Constitution Act, 1867.*

Since 1982, doubt has persisted about the constitutional status of the Supreme Court, and it has been difficult to know whether or not or to what extent the Court had been enshrined in sections 41(d) and 42(1) of the *Constitution Act, 1982.* Québec wanted to ensure that the existence of the Supreme Court would no longer depend upon the legislative intervention of a single level of government and that its perpetuity would be guaranteed unequivocally by explicit enshrinement in the Constitution.[3]

Québec was very concerned about the composition of the Supreme Court. It wanted to have a guarantee in the Constitution that it would have adequate representation in the Court and a significant role in the process of selecting judges from its territory. The provision of the *Supreme Court Act*[4] that gives Québec at least three of the nine seats on the bench was raised to the level of a constitutional guarantee and included in paragraph 101B(2) of the Act of 1867. Moreover, according to paragraph 101C(3), the appointment of Supreme Court judges from the Bar of Québec must be made from the list of candidates recommended by the Québec government. The other judges will be appointed through a similar process and the appointee must be proposed by the government of one other province, as provided for in paragraph 4 of the same section.

Because of the amendments to sections 41 and 42 of the *Constitution Act, 1982,*[5] any change in the text of these articles of the Constitution regarding the Supreme Court of Canada must be unanimously assented to by Parliament and the legislative assemblies of all the provinces. Québec thereby recovers its historic right to oppose any amendment contrary to its fundamental interests.

VII—Recognition of the Right of Veto[6]

The constitutional amending formula provided for in the *Constitution Act, 1982* was fundamentally unacceptable to Québec. We had to recover certain historic rights that would make it possible for Québec to oppose any constitutional amendment affecting the structure of federalism and running counter to Québec's interests.

This question is inseparable from the other constitutional conditions laid down by Québec. The amending formula is the key to the evolution of the Constitution, and, as such, all the guarantees obtained under the *1987 Constitutional Accord* would have been quite incomplete without the specific protection that Québec sought.

These changes to the 1982 amending formula are of two types. They affect sections 40 and 42 of the *Constitution Act, 1982*. First, the right to opt out with the financial compensation provided for in section 40, which, in its present form, applies only in the event of the transfer of provincial legislative jurisdiction to Parliament in educational and cultural matters, is extended to include *all matters* that may be the object of such a transfer. Québec's capacity to exercise this right to opt out with reasonable compensation is thereby broadened to cover all the areas within its legislative jurisdiction. Québec is given greater protection and can conserve its powers intact without being financially penalized, notably in all the sectors related to its distinct character. The extension of this right to opt out with compensation to all cases of transfer of jurisdiction in favour of the federal government constitutes a guarantee that the Canadian federation will evolve toward the centralization of power only to the extent that the governments and the citizens they represent allow.

The second change made in the amending formula enables Québec to recover its right of veto with regard to federal institutions. By the establishment of the rule of unanimity for any amendment concerning the questions listed in the new section 42, Québec's consent will be required when a major element of the federal structure is affected, be it the representation of the provinces in the House of Commons, Senate reform, reform of the Supreme Court, the inclusion of territories in existing provinces or the creation of new provinces.

The constitutional amending formula is of supreme importance to Québec. We have reestablished our rights and will be better able to safeguard our interests and strengthen respect for our specificity.

VIII—Conferences of First Ministers[7]

The primary, basic objective of the constitutional discussions that preceded the signing of the *1987 Constitutional Accord* was to end Québec's constitutional isolation so that this important partner, henceforth recognized as distinct, could again participate fully in the evolution of the federation and regain its place at constitutional conferences. It was clear to Québec that once this decisive, well-defined step was taken, once a satisfactory response to each of the five conditions required for its support was obtained, it could take an active role in pursuing the constitutional process to renew the Canadian federation.

To ensure that this process continues, an annual conference of first ministers on the Constitution will be mandatory under section 50 of the *Constitution Act, 1982*. Senate reform and the roles and responsibilities in regard to fishing are on the agenda of this conference. Other subjects for discussion yet to be agreed upon will surely be added.

Apart from the annual constitutional conference, the federal and provincial first ministers will participate annually in another forum for intergovernmental cooperation that will deal with the economy and any other appropriate matters. The convening of this conference will be provided for in section 148 of the *Constitution Act, 1867*, which will entrench a practice that has been effectively and fruitfully developed among the partners of the federation over the past few years.

IX—The Senate[8]

Until the reform of the second federal chamber is effected, the provincial governments will contribute to the process of selecting their representatives to the Senate. The Constitutional Accord provides that any vacancy in the Senate must be filled by a person appointed by the federal government but selected beforehand from among the candidates proposed by the government of the province to be represented.

Until the *Constitution Amendment, 1987* comes into force, those appointed to vacant seats in the Senate will be chosen from among people proposed by the government of the province concerned, as provided for under the political agreement contained in the initial paragraphs of the Constitutional Accord.

* * *

The *Constitution Act, 1982* did not meet the needs or profound aspirations of Québec society. In some respects, it ran directly counter to its most legitimate interests. The "reparative" constitutional undertaking was bold and promised to be perilous when the government of which

I am a part took power in 1985. In the months that preceded the address I delivered at Mont-Gabriel in May 1986, all the past constitutional approaches and all the traditional constitutional demands of the Québec government were studied more carefully than ever. The stakes were high: although it was important to restore Québec's place as a major, distinct partner within the Canadian federation, another failure had to be avoided at all costs.

These preliminary studies convinced the Québec government that the common denominator, i.e. the origin of each and every constitutional demand made by Québec, was the recognition of the distinct character of Québec society. Not only can these demands be interpreted solely in the light of this principle, but their justification, their very reason for being, does not exist without it. The recognition of the distinct character of Québec society accordingly became the principle that generated the other conditions laid down by Québec for its support of a new Canadian constitution.

Essential to the reestablishment of Québec's participation in the federation and the moving force behind the other conditions required to do so, the recognition of the distinct character of Québec society was Québec's primary requirement. The Constitutional Accord of June 3 responds adequately by giving us the assurance that this distinct character will influence all Canadian constitutional acts.

From this standpoint, Québec's other conditions, which have been met by the Accord, are new powers essential to the protection and promotion of the distinct character of Québec society.

From the same standpoint, the Accord entrenches a permanent process of constitutional revision. The Accord does not settle all Québec's needs in constitutional matters, but it fulfills the conditions for Québec's participation in the Canadian federal system and in any forum for constitutional discussions. Consequently, once the *Constitution Amendment, 1987* is ratified, and only then, Québec will again be able to contribute fully, with due respect for its specificity, to the renewal of the Canadian federation.

The matters that Québec would like to see broached at the second round of constitutional discussions will obviously be inspired by our traditional demands and, on the heels of the achievements of the 1987 Accord, will be aimed at improving Québec's role in the Canadian federation.

The *1987 Constitutional Accord* will inaugurate a new era of participation by the provinces in the institutions and policies of the federation. It will encourage the cooperation and solidarity essential to Canadian federalism. It is hoped that the attitude of openness that Québec and its partners have shown until now will continue to permeate the discussions to come, in Québec's interest and in that of all its partners in the federation.

Notes

1. See *Constitution Amendment, 1987*, section 1.
2. See *Constitution Amendment, 1987*, sections 5 and 6.
3. See section 6 of the *Constitution Amendment, 1987*, which provides for the insertion of a new paragraph 101A in the Act of 1867.
4. R.S.C. 1970, c. S-19, s. 6.
5. See *Constitution Amendment, 1987*, section 9.
6. *Ibid.*
7. See *Constitution Amendment, 1987*, sections 8 and 13.
8. See paragraph 4 of the *1987 Constitutional Accord* and section 2 of the *Constitution Amendment, 1987* adding section 25 to the *Constitution Act, 1867*.

CHAPTER TWO

CONSTITUTIONALIZING CONFLICTING VISIONS OF CANADA

Those Canadians who fought for a single Canada, bilingual and multicultural, can say goodbye to their dream: We are henceforth to have two Canadas, each defined in terms of its language.

(Pierre Elliott Trudeau, "Say Goodbye to the Dream of One Canada," *The Toronto Star*, May 27, 1987)

First, there is no single vision of Canada; rather there are multiple, often competing, visions which interact with each other in complex ways. The task, therefore, is not to enshrine one to the exclusion of others, but to provide the framework for a continuing dialectic among them . . . .

(Richard Simeon, in K. E. Swinton and C. J. Rogerson, eds., *Competing Constitutional Visions—The Meech Lake Accord* [Toronto: Carswell, 1988]: 295–296)

Reprinted with permission — *The Toronto Star* Syndicate.

INTRODUCTION

The modern process of constitutional renewal began in the mid-1950s with the publication of the multivolume *Tremblay Report* by the Quebec government of Maurice Duplessis. The *Report* reflected the concerns and aspirations of Quebec's traditional clerical-minded nationalists who feared the development of a national social service state controlled from Ottawa. Traditional nationalists demanded that Duplessis curtail Ottawa's intrusion into social and cultural matters, thereby preserving the distinct character and institutions of Quebec's French-Canadian Catholic nationality. Neo-nationalists, while sharing the *Report*'s critique of the new federalism, demanded that a modern, secular and interventionist Quebec state wrest control over all social services from Ottawa. In the hands of a competent Quebec government, these and other services would be used to preserve and promote a modern, yet distinct, Québécois nationality.

Successive Quebec governments, from that of Jean Lesage to that of René Lévesque via those of Daniel Johnson and Robert Bourassa, drew upon two conceptions of Confederation that had emerged in the latter half of the nineteenth century. The first was the belief that Confederation was the product of a compact of the provinces. The second concept contended that Confederation was simultaneously a compact of cultures. Of course, the provincial compact theory quickly found ample support from amongst the various premiers, particularly premiers Olivar Mowat from Ontario and Honoré Mercier from Quebec. In fact, Premier Mercier convened the first interprovincial conference in 1887 seeking to enhance the status of the provinces, acquire greater control over patronage and extract additional subsidies from the national government of John A.

Macdonald. The provinces also gained a degree of political and constitutional recognition through a series of decisions of the Judicial Committee of the Privy Council, which ruled that the provinces were sovereign entities in areas of jurisdiction assigned to them by the British North America Act and circumscribed the authority of the national government's powers under the "peace, order and good government" and "trade and commerce" clauses. The provincial rights movement became an integral dimension of the political culture and increasingly influenced federal–provincial relations. This was especially true by the 1960s, with the emergence of dynamic and aggressive provinces, especially in western Canada, eager to take advantage of Quebec's persistent demands for constitutional renewal in order to achieve some of their own longstanding constitutional objectives.

Initially, the compact of cultures theory was used by leading French-Canadian nationalists, such as Henri Bourassa, to promote an acceptance of a pan-Canadian bilingualism and biculturalism. It was hoped that such a model would provide redress to Catholic and French-speaking minorities spread throughout Canada. Prior to the 1960s, the vast majority of English-speaking Canadians refused to respond positively to this vision. Instead, they preferred to promote a policy of unilingualism, except in Quebec, where a limited form of institutional bilingualism was written into the Constitution as a protection for its English-speaking minority.

Other French-Canadian nationalists, such as Jules-Paul Tardivel and Canon Lionel Groulx, chose to approach the compact of cultures concept quite differently. By combining it with the provincial compact theory and eventually with the concept of self-determination of nationalities, these nationalists made the French-Canadian nationality coterminous with the province of Quebec. Quebec alone was the true homeland of all French Canadians, including expatriates in the rest of Canada and the United States. During the 1950s and 1960s, neo-nationalists, such as Michel Brunet, Marcel Faribault and Daniel Johnson, drew upon this two-nations concept to demand that Confederation be restructured along binational lines. The constitutional restructuring formula adopted by René Lévesque and his Parti Québécois was sovereignty-association, whereas the formula of the Quebec Liberal party after 1966 was "special status" through enhanced powers for Quebec. Nation-state building had become, for contemporary Québécois nationalists, synonymous with province building. Other provinces were willing to support some of Quebec's demands for increased powers as long as the restructuring of the Constitution involved a similar devolution of powers to all the provinces. The principle of the equality of the provinces that underlay the compact of provinces concept could not be eroded by the granting of "special status" (i.e., increased powers) to Quebec.

In the 1960s and 1970s, the successive national governments of Lester B. Pearson and Pierre Elliott Trudeau responded to this conjuncture of provincial compact and two-nations theories by trying to enhance the identification of Canadian citizens with their national government in a variety of ways. Social service programs were expanded, and new ones, like medicare, were added. Regional economic development programs were instituted to address a wide range of social and economic disparities. In 1969, the Trudeau government instituted the Official Languages Act to bring a degree of institutional bilingualism to the bureaucracy and the Crown corporations, thereby opening them up to francophones in an effective manner. Ottawa also made funds available to the linguistic minorities to enable them to acquire badly needed educational and community services. The provinces were offered attractive financial grants to provide second-language education for their linguistic minorities. The provinces were similarly encouraged to begin the process of providing some of their many services in the languages of their respective linguistic minorities.

Coupled with this policy of bilingualism was a policy of multiculturalism that addressed the needs and aspirations of the many growing ethnic communities that had settled in Canada since the turn of the century and whose numbers were reinforced by a heavy influx of new immigrants after World War II. By promoting cultural pluralism, the national government hoped to undermine the binational constitutional restructuring theories of the Québécois nationalists. By encouraging French Canadians to identify more closely with their national government, and participate more fully in it, Ottawa hoped to diminish both the need and the desire of French Canadians to create a separate nation-state for themselves in Quebec.

The Ontario government of David Peterson has been a staunch supporter of the Meech Lake Accord. The statement of his Attorney General, Ian Scott, to the Ontario Select Committee on Constitutional Reform is an excellent summary statement of the belief in a pluralistic, accommodating and all-encompassing Canadian constitution. In taking this approach, Ian Scott is following the lead of a well-defined school of political scientists specializing in federalism and federal societies. This school includes, to name only two of the most outspoken, Richard Simeon and Peter Leslie at Queen's University.[1]

Ian Scott contends that the Constitution should incorporate the provincial compact theory, which at long last gives constitutional recognition to the principle of the equality of the provinces. It should also have room for the cultural compact theory which, by reflecting the sociological reality of the distinct society of Quebec, will give the government and legislature of that province the necessary constitutional clout to preserve and promote that distinct society. The Constitution, according to Scott, should not "freeze into place any single vision of the nature of the country." This is especially true of the vision that envisages the federal government as the national government capable of speaking on behalf and legislating in the interest of Canadian citizens, as individuals and as communities, from coast to coast. As such, the Constitution should, first of all, be able to allow the co-existence of minority language rights, exemplified by federal bilingual policies and programs, alongside the promotion of the collective rights of the majority francophone community in Quebec via the distinct society clause. Secondly, a pluralistic constitution, according to Scott, which places constraints on the federal government's spending powers, will force Ottawa "to see provincial communities as basic points of reference and want national policy to respect and balance regional interests." For Ian Scott, the constitutional renewal process should not be used to create winners and losers by attempting to resolve, once and for all, the constitutional political debate that has occupied the country for over a generation. Instead, that debate should be laid to rest by incorporating in a practical and functional way the various competing visions into the Constitution. The Ontario Select Committee on Constitutional Reform, in its *Report on the Constitution Amendment 1987*, despite ten recommendations for what it considered necessary amendments, adopted the Attorney General's conception of a pluralistic and multivisioned constitution and recommended that the Legislative Assembly of Ontario ratify the Accord.[2]

Pierre Elliott Trudeau, the central architect of the successful constitutional reform process in 1980–82 that culminated in the Constitution Act, 1982, expressed shock, dismay and a sense of betrayal at the nature of the Constitutional Accord reached by Prime Minister Mulroney and the premiers at Meech Lake on April 30, 1987. Hoping to arouse a dormant public and create a groundswell of opposition to the Accord before the first ministers signed a legal version of the draft, Trudeau denounced the Prime Minister for succumbing to the blackmailing techniques of the nationalist-inspired Premier of Quebec, Robert Bourassa, and the greedy premiers from the other provinces who consented to granting Quebec its much-coveted special status in return for control over national institutions through an expansion of provincial veto powers.[3] Trudeau then presented a less polemical yet just as scathing critique of the Meech Lake Accord to the Special Joint Committee of the Senate and the House of Commons on August 27, 1987.[4]

Some seven months later, Trudeau was invited before the Senate Committee of the Whole on the Meech Lake Constitutional Accord, where he spent over six hours outlining in great detail the flaws of the Accord and the danger those flaws presented for the future of the country. His presentation was a veritable intellectual "tour de force." In a straightforward, no-holds-barred fashion, Trudeau demonstrated a thorough knowledge of the constitutional evolution of the country, as well as a keen perception of motivating forces behind the province-building movement and the nationalist movement in Quebec over the past three decades.

Most importantly, Trudeau articulated a passionate yet rationalized vision of a liberal democratic Canada in which the national government, responding to a pan-Canadian general will on social, economic and political issues, emerged as an entity greater than the sum of the provinces. The Meech Lake Accord was fatally flawed and politically dangerous because its dualistic and provincializing vision, if allowed to become entrenched in the Constitution, would in due course displace a truly national vision. Accordingly, it was imperative for Canadians to reject the Accord. Instead, Canadians should strive to create a healthy and viable national government capable of controlling and attenuating these decentralizing and fragmenting forces.

In his statement to the senators, Trudeau systematically demolishes the argument, made by Prime Minister Mulroney and Lowell Murray, his Minister of State for Federal–Provincial Relations, that the Meech Lake Accord was merely building on the Constitution Act, 1982 by remedying the flaws left by Trudeau. First, the fact that Quebec had not signed, Trudeau reminds his detractors, was not his but rather René Lévesque's responsibility. A premier committed to an independent Quebec was not in a position to sign any document. Secondly, the opting-out provision with compensation for culture and education and the notwithstanding clause in the Charter were included as the price Ottawa had to pay to patriate the Constitution after more than half a century of failed attempts.

Trudeau also emphatically rejects the Prime Minister's argument that Trudeau's commitment to constitutional renewal during the 1980 referendum entailed the constitutional recognition of Quebec as a distinct society. Why, he retorts, win the referendum and then grant the Québécois nationalists the constitutional reforms they were asking for? Trudeau goes on to demonstrate that the Mulroney government, by giving in to Quebec's five demands, is not building upon the achievements of the Constitution Act, 1982 by correcting the injustices. Instead, first of all, Mulroney undermined the Charter and promoted dualism rather than bilingualism with the distinct society clause. Secondly, Mulroney legitimized and aggravated the flaw pertaining to the opting-out provision by granting full compensation in all areas. Thirdly, Mulroney totally ignored the existence of the potentially explosive notwithstanding clause in the Charter. Finally, Mulroney made the amending procedure more rigid by extending the provincial veto to national institutions, thereby debilitating the effective exercise of a general national will. The Mulroney government had achieved short-term national reconciliation of the provinces by not requesting a single thing for the national government in return. In both substance and process, the Meech Lake Accord was a throwback to the pre-1982 period when the Constitution was considered to be the prerogative of the prime minister and the premiers, something to be altered by them without consulting in any meaningful fashion the Canadian citizens to whom it really belonged. The premiers had always felt a great deal of reluctance about the Charter, and Mulroney, according to Trudeau, allowed them to reassert in the Meech Lake Accord their control over both it and the constitutional process.

Given Trudeau's interpretation of Canada's constitutional and political evolution since the 1960s, it was inevitable and quite normal that he would speak out loudly and passionately for the defence of the vision of Canada that he shared with millions of Canadians and that he worked so hard to entrench in the Constitution in 1980–82.

Notes

1. Richard Simeon, "Meech Lake and Visions of Canada," in K. E. Swinton and C. J. Rogerson, eds., *Competing Constitutional Visions—The Meech Lake Accord* (Toronto: Carswell, 1988): 295–306; his "Meech Lake and Shifting Conceptions of Canadian Federalism," *Canadian Public Policy/Analyse de Politiques*, XIV (1988): S7–24; Peter M. Leslie, "Submission to the Special Joint Committee of the Senate and the House of Commons on the 1987 Constitutional Accord," in Clive Thomson, ed., *Navigating Meech Lake: The 1987 Constitutional Accord* (Kingston: Institute of Intergovernmental Relations and *Queen's Quarterly*, 1988): 8–28.
2. Ontario, Select Committee on Constitutional Reform, 1987 Constitutional Accord, *Report on the Constitution Amendment 1987* (Toronto: Queen's Park, 1988).

3. Pierre Trudeau, "Say Goodbye to the Dream of One Canada," *The Toronto Star*, May 27, 1987, reprinted in Donald Johnston, ed., *With a Bang, Not a Whimper. Pierre Trudeau Speaks Out* (Toronto: Stoddart, 1988): 8–22.
4. For Trudeau's presentation, see Canada, Special Joint Committee of the Senate and the House of Commons on the 1987 Constitutional Accord, *Minutes of Proceedings and Evidence*, No. 14, August 27, 1987 (Ottawa: Queen's Printer, 1987): 116–158. For a reprint of Trudeau's preliminary remarks, see Johnston, *With a Bang, Not a Whimper*, 23–35.

IAN SCOTT

THE CONSTITUTION AS AN EXPRESSION OF IDEOLOGICAL PLURALISM AND ACCOMMODATION*

Introduction

This Committee has undertaken a historic act of statecraft. In reviewing the Constitutional Accord, it will speak to the whole country of its vision of Canada.

This brief articulates the constitutional vision which underlies the Meech Lake Accord. It situates the Accord within Canada's unique constitutional tradition, and explains how the Accord maintains that tradition and is consistent with the current practice of Canadian federalism. It analyses the concerns which the Committee will seek to address and measures them against that unique Canadian vision of constitutionalism.

The Constitutional Vision of Meech Lake

(A)   Evolution over Revolution

Any attempt to identify the constitutional vision underlying the Meech Lake Accord must be informed by a sense of constitutional history and grounded in an appreciation of the current practice and reality of Canadian federalism. The Accord represents a set of changes which builds upon the Canadian political tradition.

It has been claimed that the document is revolutionary. The Committee will wish to assess the impact of the Accord on the power of the

---

*Brief to the Ontario Select Committee on Constitutional Reform, 1987 Constitutional Accord.

federal government to formulate and implement national policy. Is there a devolution of power to the provinces? Does the Accord confer unspecified but important new powers on the province of Quebec? Does the *Charter of Rights and Freedoms* still apply in the province of Quebec after the Accord?

In addressing these concerns, it is important to begin with the historical context and, in particular, with the effort over the past three decades to update and revise the original Canadian Constitution as defined by the *British North America Act* of 1867.

Until 1982, our Constitution was an act of the British Parliament. Since the mid-1960s, there has been consensus on the need to modernize the Canadian Constitution. It was generally agreed that there had to be some sort of readjustment in the division of powers so as to provide greater scope for provincial autonomy and distinctiveness, particularly the distinctiveness of the province of Quebec. Limits on the federal spending power, a provincial role in the appointment of Supreme Court judges and Senators, and opting out of shared-cost programs were all the subject of detailed constitutional proposals by both the federal and provincial governments in the 1970s. Most of these proposals, including those advanced by the federal government prior to 1981, would have established a far greater role for provincial governments than is provided for in the Meech Lake Accord itself.

By 1981, agreement on wide-ranging constitutional reform had proved impossible. Attention was therefore focused on the need to bring the Constitution to Canada and to give Canadians a *Charter of Rights and Freedoms*.

While these matters were successfully dealt with in the constitutional amendments of 1982, there was at that time little progress on dealing with the agenda of Quebec and of the other provinces in calling for renewal and revision of the federal–provincial division of powers.

The Meech Lake Accord deals successfully with some of what was not achieved in 1982. It deals with the agenda of Quebec. For the first time, Ontario and the rest of the country have an answer to the question: "What does Quebec want?" What is striking about the answer is its limited, focused and modest character. It eschews radical change in favour of incremental adjustments to current constitutional practice.

First, the Meech Lake Accord does not require any changes in the division of powers between the federal government and the provinces. The federal Parliament retains all of its legislative powers. In fact, the distinct society clause, which has been the focus of a great deal of criticism, explicitly provides that it does not limit the powers of Parliament or the provincial legislatures.

Indeed, far from representing a radical innovation, the Meech Lake Accord largely affirms existing practice or formally writes into the Constitution provisions on which there has been widespread agreement. It has long been accepted, for example, that there should be some provincial role in the appointment of Supreme Court judges and Senators. In terms of the amending formula, until 1982 it was widely believed that unanimity was required for any amendment affecting provincial powers. Opting out of shared-cost programs and provincial variations in their delivery have been central features of the exercise of the federal spending power since the 1960s.

Finally, the recognition of the distinctiveness of Quebec has been a cornerstone of both our political practice and our constitutional law since the *Quebec Act* of 1774. One need only look to the special provisions dealing with the province of Quebec in the *British North America Act* of 1867 to grasp the fundamental way in which the distinctiveness of Quebec has shaped our constitutional tradition.

The novelty of Meech Lake and its likely impact on Canadian politics could therefore easily be exaggerated. Predictions of dire consequences would lack a sense of balance and of proportion. They would fail to situate these proposals within the larger history of constitutional reform over the past twenty-five years. The Accord represents a set of changes which have been the subject of widespread debate and examination in this country for two decades. The likely impact of the changes is circumscribed and measurable. In large part, the Accord constitutionalizes existing practices or builds on previous constitutional proposals for which there was widespread support.

(B)   Meech Lake: Compromise over Confrontation

Constitutions differ in a fundamental way from ordinary legislation. Constitutions are not intended to settle, once and for all, the outcomes of political disputes. Rather, constitutions are designed to establish a general framework within which the art of politics can be practised and fostered within a community. This Committee is mindful of the reality that once constitutions are settled, politics continues.

Similarly, constitutions are not intended to freeze into place any single vision of the nature of the country. Instead, constitutions give expression to competing visions as to the nature of the country and establish the conditions for future conflict resolution. Constitutions, to be successful and enduring in a nation such as ours, must be pluralistic. They must be capable of accommodating the differences of geography, custom, language, ethnicity and belief which exist in the political community.

Consider the *British North America Act* of 1867. Some see in the document a vision of Canada as a unitary state. Others argue that the BNA Act was built upon the ideal of Canada as a truly federal state with provincial governments standing on an equal footing with the central government.

The reality is that the BNA Act expressed both of these competing conceptions of the nature of the country. This, indeed, was the genius of the document. Its longevity and success were a function of the fact that it was sufficiently flexible to allow for conflicts over the nature of the country to be worked out over time and according to the circumstances of the day. It did not seek to freeze a particular ideal of the country into the Constitution and impose it, for all time, on those who held to a different vision.

This constitutional vision of pluralism and accommodation is the vision of Meech Lake. The Accord does not purport to settle for future generations the ongoing debates about the nature of the country. Rather than seeking a futile once-and-for-all settlement of fundamental questions, the Accord provides a space within which politics can continue with civility and mutual respect. It sees politics as a continuing exercise in finding compromise and building trust. It rejects polarization and tests of strength.

The Accord's treatment of the language issue exemplifies this attempt to accommodate competing ideals. The language issue in this country over the past three decades has involved conflict between two fundamentally different views of the nature of the country. One view has emphasized linguistic equality and the guarantee of minority language rights across the country. The contrasting view has focused on the distinctiveness of Quebec and the need for the French-speaking majority in that province to protect and express its linguistic and cultural identity.

Meech Lake recognizes the distinctiveness of Quebec society and the role of the Government of Quebec in promoting that distinctiveness. But the Accord also recognizes the presence of the English-language minority in Quebec and the French-language minorities in the other provinces and affirms the constitutional obligation of all governments, including the Government of Quebec, to preserve those minorities. The Accord also gives expression to the fundamental equality of all the provinces by ensuring that the distinct identity of Quebec does not alter the division of powers. Moreover, the signing of the Meech

Lake Accord by the Government of Quebec affirms the legitimacy within that province of the minority language guarantees contained in the *Charter of Rights and Freedoms.*

These provisions exemplify the constitutional vision of Meech Lake. It is an approach which seeks to avoid confrontation and polarization and places a premium on accommodation and mutual respect. It affirms the desirability of each side in a dispute gaining half a loaf as opposed to one side going home empty-handed and hungry.

A second illustration of this spirit of pluralism and compromise is the way in which Meech Lake deals with the struggle between central and provincial interests in this country. As with the language issue, this struggle has revolved around two competing ideals of the nature of the country. On the one hand are those who see Canada as a single national community composed of individual citizens requiring universal, uniform and efficient services. On the other hand are those who tend to see provincial communities as basic points of reference and want national policy to respect and balance regional interests.

Meech Lake refuses to exclude either of these possibilities. Instead, what it seeks are processes through which the ongoing debate between these two contrasting ideals can be carried on. The Accord provides provinces with the right to nominate Supreme Court judges and Senators but, in each case, provides the federal government with the final say in such appointments. The Accord provides for the possibility of immigration agreements between the federal government and individual provinces but reserves the final say on immigration policy to the federal government. The Accord expands the class of amendments requiring unanimous consent, but in no case can either government unilaterally force the hand of the other. A balance of power is established in which agreement and compromise are required before action can be taken. The Accord establishes a framework in which future differences between the federal and provincial governments can be resolved. No specific outcome is dictated by the Constitution. Instead, the outcomes will depend on the political will of the parties and the particular circumstances and pressures of the period in which they arise.

One of the frequent complaints about these proposals is that they do not foreclose the possibility that provincial governments might some day abuse their powers. For example, a separatist Government of Quebec might try to use its role in the appointment of Supreme Court justices to appoint a separatist to the Supreme Court.

It is, of course, true that any government, either federal or provincial, might some day try to ''abuse'' its constitutional powers. There are no words that can be written into the Constitution to preclude conclusively the possibility of such "abuses." The outcomes of such struggles will not turn on the wording of particular provisions in the Constitution. They will, instead, depend on the political will of the respective governments and the support which they can muster for their proposals in the community.

This point can be brought home most vividly by a comparison of the Canadian and American Constitutions. A straightforward reading of the two documents might suggest that Canada ought to be much more centralized than the U.S. The fact that the opposite is in fact the case illustrates the limited role of constitutional wording in predetermining long-term political outcomes.

Meech Lake's attempt to balance and accommodate different visions of the country may prove troubling to those who look to the Constitution for a once-and-for-all and wholly favourable resolution of their particular concern. But the Constitution cannot and should not enshrine a single vision of the country to the exclusion of all others. Meech Lake stands in the tradition of Laurier, Mackenzie King and Pearson in striking a reasonable balance among contradictory ideals. It refuses to identify unity with uniformity.

(C)   Meech Lake and National Reconciliation

The Meech Lake Accord provides a way of purging the Canadian Constitution of what Stefan Dupré, in his testimony before this Committee, termed a "symbolic monstrosity." This symbolic monstrosity is the fact that the *Constitution Act, 1982* was imposed on the province of Quebec without its consent.

During the referendum campaign, the people of Quebec were promised that, in return for a "no" vote, Canadian federalism would be renewed. But the constitutional settlement of 1982 addressed none of Quebec's historic concerns. Equality rights, multiculturalism, aboriginal rights and minority language education were given constitutional recognition. Only Quebec was left out.

Most important of all, for the first time in Canadian history, through the limiting effect of the *Charter*, the powers of a province had been reduced without its consent. Of course, the Constitution of 1982 was legally binding in Quebec. This was precisely the problem. The circumstances surrounding the patriation of the Constitution in 1982 made it a national imperative to secure Quebec's voluntary adherence to the Canadian Constitution.

Meech Lake secures Quebec's adherence on the basis of proposals that are moderate compared to many advanced by a Quebec government in the past 30 years. The Meech Lake Accord represents the very minimum that would be acceptable to any conceivable Quebec government in return for its acceptance of the Constitution.

One basic and quite simple question which confronts this Committee and the people of Ontario is: are we prepared to say "yes" to Quebec? Are we prepared to accept the fact that a francophone space exists within Canada and that it is a permanent and essential feature of our constitutional fabric?

Some may answer that they welcome Quebec's adherence to the Constitution but that they merely want better terms. But in order for this answer to be credible, it must be accompanied by an explanation of what those "better" terms are and whether or not they would adequately accommodate Quebec's concerns. Moreover, it must explain how these better terms are to be arrived at without disturbing the fragile consensus which has already been achieved.

I understand many of the concerns which have been raised before you. Yet the Accord represents a complex, very delicate series of trade-offs among a number of governments after more than 20 years of negotiation. It permits us to take a modest step forward in the job of nation building. I am not persuaded that the changes proposed can be made without disturbing that fragile agreement.

I am well aware of the fact that reservations about the Accord have been expressed in other provinces. What I ask is that this Committee approach its task on the merits and without regard to the fate of the Accord elsewhere. I ask the Committee to consider any faults they might find in the Accord within the context of the overriding objective of national reconciliation and the constitutional morality which underlies it. I remind the Committee that the Accord is not the end of Canadian constitution making. But it is a key middle part, without which, in my view, there is little reason to be optimistic about further progress on the constitutional agenda.

PIERRE ELLIOTT TRUDEAU

WHO SPEAKS FOR CANADA?: DEFINING AND SUSTAINING A NATIONAL VISION *

I would like to say, first of all, that I am extremely happy to appear before the Senate for a variety of reasons. Constitution discussion can sometimes be tedious, but can also be interesting. For my part, I thought rather than get into legal technicalities, which I did, to a certain extent, when I appeared before the joint committee, I would try to put the discussion in historical perspective, show the dynamic forces which are at work in building a country, and try to draw conclusions as to where this particular 1987 Constitutional Accord might lead us.

I am also happy to be in the Senate, because it is the place for sober second thought. As to the House of Commons today, well, it is well known that the three political parties, lest they be accused of offending Quebec, did not want to re-open the accord. Therefore, the second thought, though it might have existed, was not translated into action in the House of Commons.

Incidentally, I think that in itself is a reason to argue that special status or distinct society, or whatever you want to call it, is not really necessary for Quebec. Politically, the importance of Quebec in making or breaking governments is so great that the three political parties did not dare vote the slightest amendment to the accord lest the Government of Quebec, and, perhaps, the people, would not like it. In that sense, then, Quebec *has* a special status in the Constitution by its electoral force. The reluctance of the House of Commons was, I think, also slightly futile,

Debates of the Senate, Vol. 131, No. 132, March 20, 1988. Edited following the version amended by P. E. Trudeau in Donald Johnston, ed., *With a Bang, Not a Whimper. Pierre Trudeau Speaks Out* (Toronto: Stoddart, 1988).

since I have no evidence that in the polls, at any rate, there was a surge of support for those who had initiated the Meech Lake Accord.

Legislators by profession, if I can say that, are supposed to look at the bills or resolutions, the projects that are put before them, with a view to improvement, if they see faults. It is not expected that they should vote them as they are. If legislators see contradictions or inconsistencies, it is their role to move and vote on amendments. It is a laughable proposition to think that a legislator could be told, "Well, pass the bill, imperfect as it is—you will get some other chance in some other bill to correct it." Yet, in a constitutional matter, where the second chance is very unlikely ever to arise because of the rigidity of the amending procedure, this is what the House of Commons has decided to do—pass a resolution with its known imperfections, its known contradictions or known vaguenesses, which will have to be interpreted, and make no effort to correct them. In that regard, I must say that in reading the joint committee report I was surprised to see at page 51 that that committee calmly envisaged that minority rights under the Charter might be diminished, yet made no recommendations for clarifying or changing that. The report says:

> In law, the distinct society clause is *unlikely* to erode in any *significant* way the existing extended constitutional rights of the English-speaking minority within Quebec.

Well, as far as reassurances go, that is not the strongest one I have ever heard—"unlikely to erode in any significant way." It would seem to me that this is a clear case where, at least, every party would have been able to agree or, perhaps, not to agree, but then we would know that the accord was built on a misunderstanding.

Finally, the reason I am happy to be here is that the father of the accord, the Minister for Federal–Provincial Relations in this government, sits in this place. If Senator Murray is not here today, he might be here tomorrow, and, in a sense, it will be another dialogue of the deaf, but I feel he and I have already begun our dialogue. I did publish a letter in *La Presse* and in the English press on May 27, 1987. Senator Murray, on May 30, just three days later, replied to my letter, in *The Globe and Mail*. I had expressed some mild reservations about the accord, and the senator answered in kind with, I must say, a very good letter. I say this without any sarcasm. I have, really, no disagreement on facts that he used in his letter and very few, though perhaps major disagreements, on opinions. So it was a good letter, and I think I will use it as a theme for the rest of the discussion.

In a sense, Senator Murray alleged that the November 5, 1981, agreement was flawed because it had a dark side, or "un côté ténébreux" is what he said in French, arising from three points. First, obviously, Quebec had not signed that agreement. Second, there was an opting out provision in the amendment formula, which I, myself, had denounced as bad, yet, here it was. Third, there was a notwithstanding clause, which I also believed was bad and which remained in the Charter. I want to show in the rest of the presentation how those flaws came about. That means going into the history of the negotiations to a certain extent. I then want to show how those clauses, far from being corrected in the 1987 accord, were made infinitely worse. Finally, towards the conclusion, I would like to suggest what can be done by the Senate, by the provinces and by the people to prevent irreparable damage to Canada's integrity.

Trials and Tribulations of Constitutional Reform

Dealing with the history of this whole matter, I will not say anything about the earlier years, except to remind everyone of what they know. From John A. Macdonald's day on, the history of federal–provincial relations in Canada has been one of frequent disputes and discords between the two levels of government. That is a constant of our history, as it probably is of most federations.

Rather than go into any detail, I will start, as the joint committee did itself, with the Balfour Declaration of 1926, which, you will recall, set Canada on its path to full nationhood.

Essentially, one thing was missing for Canada to achieve that status, and that was the fact that, through no fault of the British government, but because it was a self-imposed obstacle, Canada had not agreed on an amending formula which would permit it to bring back the Constitution and so to have a constitution of its own. Therefore, in 1927, the year after the Balfour Declaration, Mackenzie King convened a federal–provincial conference—Dominion–provincial conference, as they were then called—and asked the provinces to try to seek an agreement on an amending formula.

I will not read the whole story, of course. I will only read from Professor McNaught's *History of Canada*, at page 246:

The decade's surge of provincialism was symbolized by a Dominion–Provincial Conference in 1927 at which the Tory Premier Ferguson of Ontario and Liberal Premier Taschereau of Québec joined in proclaiming the "compact theory" of Confederation—a position which would give near autonomy to the provinces and which saw federal powers as being merely delegated to Ottawa by the provinces.

Naturally the compact theory caused the conference to end in failure. Exactly 60 years and eight prime ministers would pass into history before the provinces were able to find a prime minister of Canada who was prepared to capitulate to that view of Confederation, that is, a compact between the provinces to set up a federal government.

Creating a Sense of National Identity

I intend discussing that today, but before I do I want to say that during those 60 years federal governments were very active in trying to create a national will, a sense of national identity which would lead Canadians to believe that Canada was more than the sum of the wills of the provinces, but that it had a will of its own—"une volonté générale," as Rousseau said, or "un vouloir-vivre collectif" in more conventional terms. There is some national will which is more than the sum total of the provincial wills.

Various prime ministers attempted in various ways to create a body of values to be shared by the Canadian people. Mackenzie King did it by establishing a network of social security which would bind the people together. Mr. St. Laurent, you will recall, did it, first, by amending section 91, or having the British Parliament amend it, so that Canada, at least in things which did not involve the provinces and language and education, could amend its Constitution. Mr. St. Laurent also, of course, stopped the appeal to the Privy Council so that we had a supreme judicial tribunal of our own.

Mr. Diefenbaker brought the Bill of Rights. He was unable to constitutionalize it, because his minister, Mr. Fulton, had not been able to get the provinces to agree to a formula for amending. Therefore, Mr. Diefenbaker's Bill of Rights, which was certainly a nomenclature of values which bound Canadians together in the sense that they all shared certain basic beliefs, was never put into the Constitution, though it remains as an important stepping stone.

Mr. Pearson attempted, with the B and B Commission, to seek ways in which the dissatisfaction of the French-speaking people in Canada—and, to a certain extent, some ethnic groups—could be met in a way which would not divide Canada, which would not create dualism, which, as we shall see later, is what the 1987 accord does. Dualism, by definition, is a division of people. Mr. Pearson was proposing bilingualism, which is a duality of individuals or institutions which tends to unite them rather than separate them. Of course, one of the more recent prime ministers brought in the Charter of Rights and Freedoms, which was entrenched in the Constitution and which was meant to create a body of values and beliefs that not only united all Canadians in feeling that they were one nation but also, in a sense, set them above the governments of the provinces and the federal government itself. So, the people have rights which no legislative body can abridge, therefore establishing the sovereignty of the Canadian people over all our institutions of government.

But all Canadian prime ministers failed in their attempts to assert the national will by patriating the Constitution. The reason is very simple to explain. Every attempt was predicated on the idea that patriation and an amending formula—and, even more, a Charter—could only proceed with unanimous consent, that is, the consent of each and every province. So there was no national will possible beyond that defined by the 11 First Ministers. Of course, that permitted every province to hold the country to ransom by saying, ''Well, I will agree to patriation which is, perhaps, good for the Canadian people. It's the way to express ourselves as a nation. But I will only do it if you give me some rights in exchange.'' I do not like to use the word ''blackmail,'' but certainly there was a process of ''leverage'' being used with the result that Canada could only exist as a full and complete nation by leave, not of its people, but of each and every one of the ten premiers.

Province Building: 1945–1980

I have figures from National Accounts—Income and Expenditures, July 1965, table 37. There was a period in the early 1950s to the middle 1960s where there was an extraordinary amount of growth in the provinces for reasons which everyone knows—new areas of legislation were coming into play, and the provinces saw that it was within their jurisdiction. They were acting to replace the private concept of schools and hospitals.

In a sense, there was a complete reversal of the proportion between federal and provincial spending. From 60/40 federal–provincial, it had gone to 40/60 federal–provincial during those years. The provinces were not only spending a lot and taxing a lot, although some of it was tax given to the provinces by the federal government. The provincial governments grew proudly; they developed expertise; they had competent bureaucracies; and they felt they could manage their own affairs and also manage all of the affairs that, until then, had been managed by the federal government.

This was just a continuation of the tensions which, I recall, had begun in John A. Macdonald's day: a struggle for power, a struggle for money, and generally a struggle for both between both levels of government.

In post-World War II, a whole new operation was put into place. The provinces began acting collectively to force the federal government to transfer powers to them in exchange for their consent to patriation. We start with the Fulton–Favreau formula of 1964. The repatriation process came unstuck, because Premier Lesage and his principal minister, René Lévesque in those days, both backed out of an agreement that they had not only agreed to but had also begun to publicly defend. They were made to understand that they might have a good amending formula, but they had not won more powers for Quebec in the process and, therefore, they backed out.

Two years later Premier Daniel Johnson, whose slogan was ''Equality or Independence!''—equality between the two nations or independence of one from the other—was demanding all the powers needed to safeguard Quebec's identity in preparation for what was to be Premier Robarts' Confederation for Tomorrow Conference, held in Toronto in 1967.

It then came to June 1971, when Premier Bourassa withdrew from the patriation agreement that he had proposed—an amending formula that he had put forward, plus a lot of other powers for the provinces, including some role in the nomination of judges, and so on. He claimed that in exchange for his signature, he should get ''something of substance'' in the social area. In concrete terms, that meant, for instance, that in Family Allowances the federal government would hand the money to the provinces who in turn would pay it out, courtesy of the provincial government, in a way which might vary for socio-economic reasons from province to province. The minister, Marc Lalonde, had worked out an administrative arrangement whereby that might be done without actually transferring power and money, just permitting the province to decide how it should be distributed. That worked well, but it was not a constitutional amendment, and therefore it was not enough. We will hear the same story later on when we come to immigration agreements. It is not enough that the provinces get to manage the federal government's affairs; they want it to be put into the Constitution so that the federal government gives up its power forever rather than just signing an administrative arrangement.

By 1976 Mr. Bourassa had added cultural sovereignty to his demands for Quebec; but by then every other premier had caught on, because every premier realized that his consent was needed to patriate the Constitution. Therefore, he would trade his consent for as much power as he could get in whatever area he thought was important for his province. In other words, each province was in the position to exact its own price for permitting the Canadian people to have a Constitution of their own.

So that I am not talking too abstractly, at this point I will read the provincial demands put together at the interprovincial conference in the summer of 1976, chaired by Premier Lougheed. You will see a familiar number of items in this particular list, which dates back to 1976. It covered the following areas: immigration (dealt with in the accord of 1987); language rights (dealt with in 1982); resource taxation (dealt with in 1982); the federal declaratory power—that is section 92(10)(c) of the Constitution, which would be amended to require provincial consent; annual conference of First Ministers (dealt with in the 1987 accord); creation of new provinces—we get that in the 1987 accord, too; culture, which really was saying provincial paramountcy in culture and all the arts, literature and cultural heritage. That was dealt with also in 1987. Then there was communications. I will read you some speeches later on from Mr. Bourassa and Mr. Rémillard, saying that in culture and communications they feel they have achieved what they want with the "distinct society" clause. The Supreme Court of Canada was included in the 1976 list; the federal spending power—also in the 1976 list; and regional equalization, which we had dealt with in the 1982 accord.

You can say one thing for the provinces: They are bloody consistent! I do not mind saying, as a Quebecer, that Quebec's hand is clearly seen behind all of this. That is the story of 1976.

Let us now go to the summer of 1978. The interprovincial conference was chaired this time by Premier Blakeney, of the NDP. The 1976 conference was chaired by a Conservative; this one was chaired by a Social Democrat, but he had been joined by a Separatist, Premier

Lévesque. As he came to the conference, Lévesque made a declaration. The Quebec declaration said that, while committed to its option of sovereignty association, it could generally go along with the 1976 consensus and most of the other constitutional points raised in Regina. We will come to those. Quebec went on to state that:

> this approach falls within the mandate of the Quebec government to reinforce provincial rights within the present system and also illustrates some of the minimal changes required to make the federal system a serious alternative in the forthcoming Quebec referendum

—forthcoming, but some four years later.

What were these "minimal changes"? Here is the 1978 consensus: "In addition to the 1976 list"—that I have just given to you—"the premiers, in the course of their discussion in Regina, have reached agreement on a number of additional substantive matters on which federal views are invited. First, abolition of the now obsolete federal powers to reserve or disallow provincial legislation."

Well, obsolete, but maybe some people sitting in Ottawa some day will be glad that they are still in the Constitution Act, because disallowance of some provincial acts may some day remain as the only way to avoid the destruction of the federal government.

"Second, a clear limitation on the federal power to implement treaties so that it cannot be used to invade areas of provincial jurisdiction." We are hearing about that nowadays.

"Third, the establishment of an appropriate provincial jurisdiction with respect to fisheries." Well, we have that on the agenda of the next conferences.

"Fourth, confirmation and strengthening of provincial powers with respect to natural resources." That was done in 1982, and, incidentally, for those who say that the provinces got nothing out of 1982—and I will come back to that later—quite a bit of power was transferred from the federal government to the provinces by the November 1981 accord, which became the Constitution Act of 1982.

"Fifth, full and formal consultation with the provinces in appointments to the superior, district and county courts of the provinces." That would be the next step.

"Sixth, appropriate provincial involvement in appointments to the Supreme Court of Canada." This is a modest agenda, as you will see.

"Further, there was a consensus that a number of additional

matters require early consideration: the federal emergency power; the federal residual power dealing with peace, order and good government; the formal access of the provinces to the field of indirect taxation; amending formula and patriation; and the delegation of legislative powers between governments. All premiers expressed grave concern that section 109, concerning provincial ownership of natural resources, had not been carried forward into the proposed new Constitution.''

After this modest beginning in 1976 and 1978, so it went until we reach September 1980.

What happened in September/October of 1980? By that time it had become obvious that the greed of the provinces was a bottomless pit, and that the price to be paid to the provinces for their consent to patriation with some kind of an entrenched Charter—which had been requested as far back as 1971 in Victoria—was nothing less than acceptance by the federal government of the ''compact'' theory, which would transform Canada from a very decentralized, yet balanced federation, into some kind of a loose confederation. That is when our government said, ''Enough. We are going to move unilaterally and we are going to give the people their Constitution and their Charter of Rights. You can like it or lump it, but this is what we intend to do,'' and honourable senators know the rest of the story: The matter went to the courts—and I will come to that in a moment.

Quite frankly, the reason we were determined, and almost desperate, to move without paying this enormous price that the provinces had asked of us in September of 1980 was that we had promised renewal of the Constitution when we were fighting the referendum. At that time we had said we would put our seats at stake that we would bring renewal. I will come to that in a moment.

The Provincial Agenda, 1980

But first, honourable senators, let me just read the somewhat immodest agenda that was put before the federal government in September of 1980 by all of the provinces. Quebec had made a proposal and it became a common stand of the provinces. It was discussed by the provincial ministers on September 11, and then by the premiers at breakfast on September 12; it was then brought over to the Prime Minister of Canada the same day, and here is what the Prime Minister of Canada was told would need to be done to the Constitution if we were to proceed some day with patriation:

> The provinces of Canada unanimously agree in principle to the following changes to be made to the Constitution of Canada. It is understood that these changes are to be considered as a global package and that this agreement is a common effort to come to a significant first step towards a thorough renewal of the Canadian federation.

I do not intend to read all of the details of it, but on the list there is natural resources; communications; Upper Chamber; Supreme Court of Canada; judicature, which repeals section 96 which permits the federal government to appoint judges of superior and provincial courts; family law; fisheries; offshore resources; equalization. Then we come to item 9, ''a Charter of Rights''; but the Charter would have to be brought in with a *non obstante* clause, and with a clause that all existing laws would be deemed valid. In other words, a charter which was grandfathering government rights over the people.

Under item 10, we would get patriation, but with the Alberta amending formula, which, in the event, was the one that we ended up with. Item 11: powers over the economy; item 12: a preamble. The latter is a Quebec proposal, which I might take time to read to you, but you will not like it.

The document that I was handed at that time (and which became known as the Chateau consensus) goes on to say:

> If a satisfactory interprovincial consensus is reached in this way, it must be accompanied, when tabled, by announcement of the following measures:
>
> > As soon as the federal government has given its assent to this consensus, the matter will be returned to the ministers for drafting; Another list of subjects must be established to be covered by the constitutional discussions at the ministerial level in the following months. These subjects are: The horizontal powers of the federal government—spending power; declaratory power; power to act for peace, order and good government—culture; social affairs; urban and regional affairs; regional development; transportation policy; international affairs; the administration of justice . . .

And so on. Therefore, I do not think history will blame us for having said, "Enough; we are not going to trade all of these things just so that the people of Canada can be sovereign in their own land." After all, we had won the 1980 referendum by making a promise of renewal, and it had become obvious that the rule of provincial unanimity, particularly with a Separatist premier heading the government of Quebec, would continue to render impossible the first step towards renewal (i.e. repatriation), as it had, indeed, without interruption since the 1927 conference.

Therefore, in a sense, we were in a Catch 22 situation. The federal government was told that it must renew the Constitution, and that had begun with Premier Robarts' meeting in 1967. Therefore, the federal government of Canada must renew the Constitution, but, on the other hand, they must be prevented from renewing the Constitution until the federal government gave the provinces all the power they were asking for. In other words, for the provinces, the renewing of the Constitution could only mean one thing: transferring more powers to the provinces. The people of Canada could not have their own Constitution until their national government accepted its own dismemberment!

There is an allegation that is frequently made not only by Quebec nationalists but by more serious people such as academics. It was also made by the Prime Minister of Canada; it was made by Senator Murray in an article that he sent to *La Presse* and to *The Globe and Mail* on June 15. Let me read it:

> The solemn promise made to Quebecers during the referendum that federalism would be renewed and the Constitution amended to reflect the *distinct identity* and aspirations of Quebec was unfortunately not kept.

Mr. Mulroney said the same thing on October 21 of last year, which is quoted in *Hansard*. At that time he said that the federal forces—and I know whom he means—had promised that we would renew the confederation, and, in order to prove our good faith as reformers, the allegation is made that we would have had to bring in renewal of a kind that would carry the assent of the very premier, Mr. Lévesque, who was bent on taking his province out of Canada.

If the absurdity of the circular reasoning contained in that proposition is not obvious, let me state it otherwise: I had been writing, speaking and publishing for some 20 years against any form of special status, such as two nations or the two-Canada concept. Of course, I never said that I would renew federalism by giving Mr. Lévesque what he wanted and by giving the provinces what they had asked for in this enormous list of September 1980. I said we would renew the federation, and anyone who had listened to my campaign speeches or the debates on federal/provincial affairs could not possibly assume and, in turn, write in good faith that we had promised to give Quebec some form of "distinct society."

Honourable senators, how could it reasonably be inferred that I was attempting to win the referendum by setting Canada on a course that I had consistently denounced as deleterious to the integrity of Canada; as deleterious as even losing the referendum itself would be? I really take objection not only to Senator Murray but to the Prime Minister and the devil of a lot of academics implying that, somehow, we had made promises to give the Province of Quebec, in a reformed Constitution, what the Separatists and some ultra nationalists were asking. There was no point in winning the referendum if we were going to give to those who had lost it everything they were trying to get by winning it.

Creating the Constitution Act, 1982

We proceeded unilaterally and the resolution we introduced on October 10, 1980, contained none of the flaws which Senator Murray says "tainted" the November 1981 agreement with the provinces. There was no opting out; there was no notwithstanding clause; and, of course, Quebec would have been in on the same basis as every other province. I have here the October 2 proposed resolution for a joint address, but, of course, I will not read it. However, let me point out two things. Sections 1 to 30 set people above governments. The people were getting a Charter with no notwithstanding clause in it. That was the first step in our history to recognize the sovereignty of the people. But, through the amending procedure, it was done even more clearly, because what it says in this resolution is that if we cannot get unanimity on an amending formula—we were hoping it would be the Victoria formula—then we would ask the people to decide what amending formula they wanted. We would give them a choice. Either the people would vote for an amending formula put forward by the provinces—and to make it a serious one there had to be eight provinces to agree on an amending formula, and there was a "gang of eight" which was developing, so it was not a figure taken out of thin air—or an amending formula put for-

ward by the federal government which, in our view, was going to be
the Victoria formula—it says so in the resolution. However, it could have
been changed as a result of negotiations. The people would have had
a clear choice.

This was recognizing the sovereignty of the people over the fundamental act of the Constitution, but, better still, we had a section 42,
which also set up a referendum process in a free-standing way so that
at any time, if there were a deadlock in Canada, the people, as in most
democratic countries, could be called upon to express their views. That
is what we put before the people and the Parliaments in October of 1980.

You will remember what happened. Three provinces asked for a
reference to the Supreme Court, saying that we could not do it unilaterally. A lot of Indians and premiers went and had dinner in London.
There was a House of Lords committee saying that we were very nasty,
but, until the Supreme Court judgment in the middle of spring, we were
doing what seemed, at least to me, what circumstances had forced us
to do after 54 years, that is, from 1927 to 1981.

If Canada could not give itself a constitution of its own, perhaps we
should ask Britain to give it to us. Margaret Thatcher, God bless her—I
do not say that on everything—told me, "If the Canadian Parliament
asks me for something and it has a majority supporting a resolution,
there is nothing much I can do to prevent it." I think the Britons had
in mind—and, I think, wisely—the principle of no independence without
majority rule in Rhodesia, which became Zimbabwe.

However, the courts decided otherwise; they decided that what we
were doing was legal, but, you will recall, they decided it was not conventional by virtue of a convention which was so obscure that they could
not define it. They knew that consent did not have to be all provinces,
but they knew that, somehow, two provinces were not enough. However, they did not know how many in between. That was a vague convention, to say the least. They said our resolution was legal, but it was
not nice. Since I was known to be a person who liked to do things nicely,
I met with the provinces again and we hammered out the November 5,
1981, agreement. It had other flaws. I note that Professor Tony Hall
was before you recently saying that aboriginal rights had been left out
in the bargaining with the provinces. I could add, too, that women's
rights had been left out, not in our draft of September, 1980, but in
the negotiations with the provinces. Two of them wanted Indians and
women excluded, so, in order to get our Constitution and the rest of
the Charter, we took them out.

They, too, were put back in after the signature of November 5, and that is why I return to the Meech Lake and Langevin Block agreement. Everybody but Mr. Lévesque had signed that original accord on November 5, 1981, but, still, we were able to improve it to include women and the aboriginals. Something like that happened between Meech Lake and the Langevin Block. If that could happen, one wonders why other amendments, which were necessary, could not have been brought in.

I think it is important to say here that the November 5, 1981, agreement, which became the Constitution Act, 1982, gave a lot of new powers to the provinces, including Quebec. Apart from the Charter and patriation which the people of Canada were getting, that agreement of 1981 was based essentially on the Alberta amending formula and on various agendas that I read to you which did several things to transfer powers to the provinces.

Remember that the November 1981 accord did not give any power to the federal government. In a sense, it limited the power of all governments, federal and provincial, by a charter, but it actually transferred a lot of power from the federal government to the provincial governments. It did so in the area of natural resources, giving the provinces the power of indirect taxation and the power of external trade. It entrenched equalization payments. These are all things that Quebec had been asking for since 1976 and beyond. I am sure you will remember the list I read to you. It included more power over natural resources, equalization and the right to opt out of certain constitutional amendments, which I had not offered in the Victoria formula, but which the provinces demanded. Well, they got it. They got the right to opt out of certain constitutional amendments, which was something that, until then, they had not had under the British North America Act.

More important still, under section 41, they gained the right of a constitutional veto that no province alone had until then. Every province can stop the federal government and a national consensus from achieving reform in certain defined areas. Until then, under section 91, the federal government could, at least, amend all those things.

There was a vast amount of new power given to the provinces from the list drawn up by the ''gang of eight,'' of which Quebec was one of the more notorious members, so, to those who say that Quebec got nothing I would point out that they did not say, ''Thank you,'' they still got a lot.

Quebec's Five Demands

We come now to Quebec's five demands. They had not got everything in November of 1981. Quebec came up with five demands, and that was called the "Quebec Round." Mind you, on every one of those demands the federal government had offered some concessions in the past, during the 1968–1980 negotiations. Therefore, I completely understand Premier Bourassa saying, "Well, this is our package. We were offered something before. We got a lot in 1981, but we would like some more, since you offered it in the past. Let's get it now." The situation was different from our point of view, because we had offered a lot, bargaining to get a Charter of Rights in the Constitution. But in 1987, Quebec was not offering anything in exchange that I know of, but it was bargaining for more powers in five more areas.

I want to examine them in detail, because frequent allegations have been made that the 1987 process flowed naturally out of the 1968–1980 negotiations. I have the quotes of Mr. Mulroney, Senator Tremblay and practically all of the members of the Joint Committee of the Senate and the House of Commons. I have all of these quotes, which I can get into, but they all say, "Well, after all, the Trudeau government had offered all of these things. What is the big fuss, that they are objecting now to the fact that we are giving them at Meech Lake and in the Langevin Block?"

I want to go into some detail with each one of these five demands to show that the way they were met in 1987 brought Canada in a diametrically opposite direction to the way in which Canada would have gone in each of the other cases. In other words, when, between 1968 and 1980, we were offering certain concessions to the provinces, it was always in a way which was not destructive of the national will, of the reality that there was a Canadian "vouloir-vivre collectif" which would bind everyone, even if everyone and his brother had not said, "Yes, okay." In other words, we were never conceding that unanimity would have to prevail.

The Amendment Formula

I will take the demands in turn. I will start with the veto on constitutional amendments. Well, of course, before Meech Lake there was no veto for Quebec; and the Supreme Court made that quite clear—when the matter was brought before it in 1982—that there never had been a veto for Quebec or for anyone else. There was some kind of convention, that you needed more than a couple of provinces, but none had an absolute veto.

We offered a veto to Quebec in the Victoria Charter. It was a formula—I will not go into details again—which essentially called for the federal government and six provinces. Quebec had a veto, and everyone agreed, except Quebec! But Quebec had proposed it. It was Quebec and five provinces; but the idea of a national will was defined at least in a way which did not permit every province to exercise some form of blackmail.

We offered that formula throughout the 1970s, including in the October 10, 1980, draft. But it was rejected by Premier Bourassa in 1971, and it was rejected by Premier Lévesque and the "gang of eight" in 1980 and 1981. What Quebec was asking for was something that had been offered to them. But they did not want it. Why? Because as soon as they said "yes" to something, then we would have a Constitution and they would not be able to use their leverage to get more.

I take exception to Senator Murray's saying that I proposed unanimous consent on March 31, 1976. Senator Murray, in his testimony on August 4, at page 286 of the proceedings, said:

> I should note that applying unanimity to this narrow range [he is talking about section 41] is much more modest than the March 31, 1976 proposal of Prime Minister Trudeau, which would have required unanimous consent for all major amendments.

I never proposed that. Senator Murray or his people misread the letter that on March 31, 1976, I sent to Premier Lougheed, with a copy to all premiers. I will not read it all. It comprises several pages. Let me sum it up, and I challenge Senator Murray to contradict it tomorrow— if someone wants to work all night to look that up.

What I suggested was three methods of getting patriation with an amending formula. One called for unanimous consent, in which I say, "This approach would introduce a rigidity which does not now exist." Then I suggested two other methods: "The second and preferable alternative would be . . ." and so on. Then I said that "A third and more extensive possibility would be to include . . ." and so on. So there are three possibilities there. I sum it up by saying:

> As you can see [in my letter to Premier Lougheed], there are several possibilities as to the course of action now to take. So far this is clear. So far as the federal government is concerned [my preference] our much preferred course would be to act in unison with all of the provinces. Patriation is such an historic milestone and it would be better if we could get unison. But if unanimity does not appear possible, the federal government will have to decide whether it will recommend to Parliament that a joint address be passed seeking patriation.

What I am saying, in essence, is that we would like unanimity to patriate the Constitution with an amending formula, and we are prepared to wait for unanimity to get it back with an amending formula; but the amending formula itself will not call for unanimity.

So, for Senator Murray to say that Trudeau's proposal would have required unanimous consent for all major amendments is wrong. I was still saying in 1976 that we need to get everyone in in order to get it back from Great Britain. But, once it is back, no unanimity rule; the Victoria rule.

With Meech Lake there is no national will left. Any province can opt out of a constitutional amendment transferring power to the federal government and get full compensation. So a province can opt out in the matter of powers. But then, more importantly, under section 41, any province has a veto; any province can prevent a constitutional amendment wanted by nine other provinces and the federal government on all federal institutions of government—the Senate, the House of Commons, the Supreme Court and the Territories.

When you remember that some of the western provinces are not, shall we say, all that cooperative with the desire of natives to achieve some of the aboriginal and native rights, it is, I think, wrong to have given each province the right to prevent the Government of Canada—and perhaps six or seven other provinces—from exercising the right to agree, for instance, that the Territories should be established into provinces so that in some way the place where the majority of the native people live could achieve some form of self-government, as the provinces themselves had.

So that is why I say that with Meech Lake, on the first Quebec demand, the solution was not like our solution, which respected the idea of a national will binding all; but it was a solution which destroyed the existence of a national will and submitted it to the unanimous consent of every province.

Spending Powers

The second Quebec demand was on limitation of the federal spending power. Before Meech Lake we had made a proposal in June of 1969 which, once again, was predicated on the existence of a national will, and we defined it then as ''an affirmative vote on a majority of senatorial divisions,'' which in effect meant that five to seven provinces plus the federal government could establish a shared-cost program in areas of provincial jurisdiction.

Under that proposal, if a premier did not want to go along, he was not forced to go along, but, rather than have compensation paid into the provincial treasury, as we have in the Langevin formula, the federal government would give the money back to the people (by a form of negative taxation) so that provincial popular sovereignty would be respected in the sense that the people of a province would not be penalized because their premier wanted to thwart the national will.

That is a lot different from what came out of Meech Lake, where there is no effort to seek to establish a national will. On the contrary, there is encouragement given to provinces that want to opt out of national programs by compensation, providing the province carried on ''a program or initiative that is compatible with the national objective.'' Who sets national objectives? Is it Parliament, or is it the 11 First Ministers? That is something that should be clarified before the members vote on this. And what does ''compatible'' mean? Is it something which is not a complete denial of the federal program, or what?

Supreme Court Appointments

The third Quebec demand was a provincial role in appointments to the Supreme Court of Canada. Before Meech Lake, the BNA Act, of course, in section 101, stated that all aspects of the Supreme Court were under the jurisdiction of Parliament.

In the 1971 Victoria Charter, article 27 provided for, as Quebec was asking in its third demand, a provincial role in appointments to the Supreme Court of Canada. That was worked out with Quebec and the other provinces and it had been agreed to. What was the formula? It was that the Attorney General of Canada would always consult with the attorney general of a province from where he proposed to appoint someone to the Supreme Court of Canada. If there was no agreement, the Attorney General of Canada would set up an electoral college, appointed in agreement by both sides, and chaired by someone, if they could not agree, appointed by the Chief Justice of Canada. So there was a proposal for an electoral college to which the federal government would submit three names that had been tested with the province, and that college would choose one.

This was provincial involvement; it might not have been enough, maybe it was too much, but, at any rate, it was provincial involvement of a kind that had been accepted by the ten provinces at Victoria. What we proposed in Bill C-60 in 1978 repeated somewhat the same scheme.

What is in Meech Lake? The federal government gives up its absolute power under section 101 of the BNA Act by having to select judges exclusively from a provincial list. The Meech Lake Accord, in section 101C.(1)—and I am sure you have all read it again and again—states that the government of each province "may" submit names, and the federal government "shall" appoint a person whose name has been submitted. That is what I call remote control of the Supreme Court by the provinces. But it may mortally wound the Supreme Court because of the not unheard of proposition where a province wants to break up Canada and be a spoiler. It says the province "may" submit names, but what if it does not ? Is there some emergency power that will permit us to break the Constitution and fill the vacancies on the Supreme Court anyhow? Or does it mean that, for instance, in the example I have in mind, if Premier Lévesque were operating under this dispensation and we were to end up with only six out of nine Supreme Court judges, all named by the "Anglos," with many judicial cases coming from Quebec —and they would be judged fairly, I am sure—but to the extent that the judgments were not favourable to the Quebec government, you can imagine the kind of mess it would make, apart from the fact it is doubtful whether the court could operate legally if it had, over a long period of time, only six out of nine judges sitting. So there is no provision for breaking that kind of log-jam.

As you know—and I will not go into it, because it is not one of Quebec's five demands—the same applies to the Senate. Some of us in this place—if I can say I am in this place, at least, for this afternoon— were in the House of Commons when one man, Gilles Grégoire, was able to cause a devil of a lot of obstruction by refusing unanimous consent on a lot of things. He really slowed down the work of Parliament. So what would it be if a province sent up twenty-four or six or ten senators? It would be something like when the Irish Home Rulers disrupted the work of the British Parliament.

So I do not think it is a satisfactory way of respecting or establishing the national will. Certainly it is not fair to say that since I had proposed something quite different on the Supreme Court, I should not object to this particular way of appointing judges. That is like saying: You do not mind if something is white. Why object if something is black?

Immigration

The fourth demand of Quebec was a greater provincial role in immigration. Before Meech Lake, section 95 of the BNA Act said that Parliament may make laws in relation to immigration with all and any of the provinces, and provincial laws shall have effect only as far as they are not repugnant to any Act of the Parliament of Canada.

But we recognized that the provinces, though in a subordinate position, had particular demands as to what kind of immigrants they would need for work purposes or language purposes, so we made contractual arrangements. We made them with Quebec, and we made them with other provinces. Otto Lang began in 1971, Robert Andras in 1975, and Bud Cullen in 1978. They were agreements which were renegotiated from time to time to meet different circumstances, but there was no transfer of constitutional power. In fact, because they were contracts they could be changed and renegotiated, but an immigrant who comes to a province is also an immigrant who comes to Canada. You don't cease to come to Canada just because you are going to a province. Most immigrants come to a province because they want to be Canadians. Therefore, our contracts were in respect of the national will of Canadians.

What do we have with Meech Lake? Well, the federal government gives up much of its paramountcy, and it gives it up irreversibly. Once a contract has been signed it will be constitutionalized, so the accord says, and it can only be changed by using the constitutional amending formula, which means that any province can prevent an accord which is favourable to it from being amended in the slightest way.

There are some funny provisions in there, but I will not go into them in detail. There is a guarantee in the Langevin Block agreement that Quebec will be guaranteed a share of immigrants proportionate to its share of the total population of Canada. What happens if people don't want to go to Quebec? Presumably, that means the other provinces cannot take the immigrants they want, because they will be diluting Quebec's share, but, also, Quebec has a right to have 5 per cent more, and similar agreements may be signed with all other provinces. How you can guarantee 5 per cent more to all of the provinces is something I cannot work out.

These are silly things drafted in haste, and the people were told that they could not ever change them no matter how silly they were, because the whole thing might fall apart.

The most offensive clause is the one that says Canada will withdraw services for the reception and integration, including linguistic and cultural, of all foreign nationals wishing to settle in Quebec, with reasonable compensation to be paid to the province for doing Canada's job.

Well, we are all grown-ups. I do not have to make many drawings to get you to understand that if you have government and immigration officials who are determined to make sure that everybody coming into Canada has a conception of Canada as being a pact between provinces, as being a country where only French should be spoken in one province and only English in all of the others, you could have a situation where the national will is thwarted. I keep coming back to the same expression, because I have to answer those who say: "Well, I proposed something on immigration in Cullen–Couture, therefore why am I objecting to this particular proposal in the Constitutional Accord?" It is completely different, because once the provinces have gotten into that area of reception and integration of all foreign nationals, and are being paid to get into that area, they are not going to get out even if the federal government says, "Tut, tut, tut, now, you are not teaching the love of Canada to these people, you are teaching the love of western alienation, or whatever it is."

Once again, I think that if immigrants are going to be taught the theory of provincial sovereignty, it will not make for a strong Canada. We are having trouble enough now trying to build a nation with common values without starting to provincialize immigrants. We can already work on children, since children are under provincial jurisdiction in schools. But are we now to start to work on immigrants so that they have a conception of Canada which corresponds to that which we defined in the Chateau consensus of September 1980? I repeat that an immigrant to a province is an immigrant to Canada, and that Canada has no moral right to give up its jurisdiction in that area.

A "Distinct Society"

Finally, as to the recognition of Quebec as a distinct society, it is a tough one to tackle. But, in essence, what is federalism? It is a form of government where the exercise of sovereignty is divided between two levels of government so that each can legislate, tax and spend in areas of its jurisdiction concerning people within its territory. That is what federalism is. When the Fathers of Confederation discussed the BNA Act in 1867, that is what they had in mind. They gave to the provinces all of the powers outlined under section 92, which were, as jurisprudence tells us, generously interpreted by the Privy Council and by the Law Lords in favour of provincial rights. They gave all of this to the provinces so that they could develop as distinct societies. So what is the big deal?

Of course Quebec is a distinct society with its own language and its civil law, which it has a right to have under section 92.13. Of course it became even more distinct with the "quiet revolution," when Premier Lesage began to use the organs of a modern state to mould that society as a distinct one. And of course it became even more distinct when a Separatist premier was elected and tried to move the people of that province and that society in a completely different direction. It is a distinct society, and nobody is denying that. Nobody would probably even deny that, if you want, we can put it into a preamble somewhere. That might cause some pique with the Newfoundlanders, though, who only came into Canada in the lifetime of most of the people in this room. They could certainly say, "Well, why not us? Newfoundland and Labrador are a distinct society." There might be some dissatisfaction, but, at least, it would be doubtful that any legal confusion would arise. So you have distinct societies, some more distinct than others. I agree, if you like, that I am more distinct than Senator Marchand here—no, no, that's not right, he was distinct before I was.

All right, we are all distinct. But particularly after constitutionalists have been discussing preambles for a long period of time, when you deliberately do not put "distinct society" into a preamble but put it into an interpretative clause, that can mean only one thing—you are giving to the government of that distinct society powers that it did not have before. If you are entrenching the distinctiveness as a special provision, you can only be doing it because you want to give special powers. That is why every time Quebec asked our government for special status or the recognition of its distinct society or sovereignty association, we would resist. It was not a fight for the distinctiveness of the Canadian people— they had that. It could only be a fight for more power for the provincial politicians. Yet Quebec's distinctiveness, I am proud to say, was probably served as well, if not better, through organs of culture like Radio Canada, the CBC, the Film Board and the Arts Council, all creations of the *federal* government, who rewarded quality of production, quality of French and quality of artistry, which was not always found in Quebec institutions.

So why not put distinctiveness in a preamble? If that is what you want, you can encapsulate it there. We had drafted several preambles, one in Bill C-60, which I will not bother reading to you. There was one drafted in June 1980, which I will bother reading to you, but I will not get far, you will see. I see that the first I mentioned was not in Bill C-60— it was in the prologue to Bill C-60. On June 10, 1980, which can be found in the House of Commons *Hansard* at page 1977, I was tabling in the House of Commons an appendix. I suggested an agenda for a meeting of the First Ministers on the Constitution. This reads:

A STATEMENT OF PRINCIPLES FOR A NEW CONSTITUTION

We, the people of Canada, proudly proclaim that we are and shall always be, with the help of God, a free and self-governing people.

Born of a meeting of the English and French presence on North American soil which had long been the home of our native peoples, and enriched by the contribution of millions of people from the four corners of the earth, we have chosen to create a life together which transcends the differences of blood relationships, language and religion, and willingly accept the experience of sharing our wealth and cultures, while respecting our diversity.

We have chosen to live together in one sovereign country, a true federation, conceived as a constitutional monarchy and founded on democratic principles.

Faithful to our history . . .

I think it was pretty hard to beat, but, look, it was panned by the English-speaking columnists, and do you want to know what happened in Quebec? It did not get beyond the fifth word. When we said, "We, the people of Canada," one hullabaloo broke out in Quebec.

So there was one great scandal, because we started the preamble with the words, "We, the people of Canada." The outrage of not only Premier Lévesque but of Quebec intelligentsia and the Quebec media was enormous. Somehow we could not even talk about "the people" of Canada. Of course, it was forbidden to talk about one Canadian "nation," but we found that we could not even mention the people of Canada without offending the Premier of Quebec. Now, I ask you: Do you expect that we could have reached an agreement with the government of that province when we were trying to get a constitution for the Canadian people?

Unfortunately, I go back to Senator Murray, at page 2A:2 of his testimony of August 4. He says:

. . . in September 1980, Prime Minister Trudeau was willing to recognize "the distinctive character of Quebec society with its French-speaking majority" in a preamble to the Constitution, and a "best-efforts" draft to achieve this end was produced.

Prime Minister Mulroney goes a step further, and is even more wrong. He says the same things in his October 21, 1987, speech to the House of Commons, but he leaves out the words "in a preamble." The allegation is made by these two distinguished gentlemen that I had offered to recognize the distinctive character of Quebec's society with its French-speaking majority. Therefore, what was wrong with doing it in an interpretative clause of the Langevin accord?

I will ask historians to go back to the record on this one, because I have a lot of papers here and I will not pretend to sum them up. However, they are available for anyone who would like to follow it up. They are papers which were distributed to the provinces and, therefore, are not secret. They can be found, I am sure, by asking in the House of Commons. I inquired of the officials in Ottawa where Senator Murray had obtained his information. All the evidence they were able to dig up—and I have a letter here from the secretary to the cabinet sending it to me—is a document entitled "Federal–Provincial Conference of First Ministers, being a report of the continuing committee of ministers on the Constitution, to first ministers."

In the preamble, which is not a very good one, there are square brackets between two phrases, which are obviously phrases where no agreement had been reached and they were referred to the First Ministers for a decision. One phrase is "recognizing the distinct French-speaking society centred in, though not confined to, Quebec." The other phrase is "recognizing the distinctive character of Quebec society with its French-speaking majority." In the first case, "recognizing the distinct French-speaking society centred in, though not confined to, Quebec," if it is a sociological act, if it is a historical reality put in a preamble, I might not have objected. I probably would not have if it had brought a Charter of Rights in the Constitution. But I am nowhere on record saying that I accepted that. It is in brackets, so it is something to be decided by the First Ministers.

The other phrase, "recognizing the distinctive character of Quebec with its French-speaking majority," that is the one phrase that I never would have put in a preamble, let alone an interpretative clause. Of course, that is the one that comes up in the Meech Lake Accord.

For greater surety, I got a copy of *The Summary Record of Proceedings* of the First Ministers' conference between September 8 and September 13, 1980. There is an agenda item entitled "The Preamble of Principles." There are three pages dealing with it. It is mainly a quarrel about the people of Canada and whether or not the provinces are freely united. Mr. Lévesque does go on to say that he objects to the preamble because it did not, in his view, "accurately reflect the duality which lay at the base of Confederation.'' Consequently, the Quebec government suggested the following wording:

> Recognizing the distinct character of the people of Quebec which, with its French-speaking majority, constitutes one of the foundations of Canadian duality.

Now, perhaps, we know where the idea of duality came from for the 1987 accord.

As far as the chairman is concerned—that is me—I raised two items of concern, which I have just quoted to you. In the conclusion I do not draw any consensus, because there is no agreement amongst anyone. To draw out of that the authority to say that Trudeau was willing to recognize the distinctive character of Quebec society, with its distinctive French-speaking majority, is really going a bit far.

Conflict of Visions: Duality or Bilingualism

I would like to deal with the difference between the five Quebec demands as met in the 1987 accord and the way they were met before in various attempts, always trying to trade something in exchange for something else, something the federal government did not do, which I will get into if I have time. Over a period of ten years we were trying to negotiate. We would offer one thing. If it would not work, we would try something else. We would take the first one back and put something else on the table, always trying to trade to get a patriation of the Canadian Constitution.

To take all those things as a whole and say, ''You were prepared to give them all when they were completely different. So why are you objecting to the 1987 accord now?'' is really now an operation in duplicity or ignorance. There is a great difference, because what do we have with the Meech Lake Accord?

In paragraph 2(1)(a) there is linguistic duality. In subsection 2(2) there is the role of Parliament and legislatures to preserve the duality. Duality divides groups. We did not use the expression ''French-speaking Canadians'' and ''English-speaking Canadians'' in any of our constitutions. We used the concept of bilingualism. Bilingualism unites people; dualism divides them. Bilingualism means you can speak to the other;

duality means you can live in one language and the rest of Canada will live in another language, and we will all be good friends, which is what Mr. Lévesque always wanted. You speak English, we will speak French, and we will be friends. That is an option. It was a respectable one, one that I fought, but we knew what it meant.

I think we should know what it means also in the Meech Lake Accord. That is subsection 2(2) on linguistic duality and the role of Parliament and the legislatures to preserve that duality. No wonder the French-speaking minorities in the rest of Canada and the English-speaking minorities in Quebec do not like it, and some of them are "humiliated."

Paragraph 2(1)(b) says that Quebec constitutes within Canada a distinct society. Subsection 2(3) mentions the role of the legislature and government to preserve and *promote* that distinct society, including, as I will read to you later, the right to self-determination, which is part of the deal, according to Mr. Bourassa. I am anticipating myself.

What does Meech Lake mean? First, it is amusing to notice that subsection 2(4) says that this section does not derogate from powers, rights or privileges of Parliament or legislatures. Of course, the sections where the federal government is giving up its authority over the Senate, over the courts, and over the spending power do derogate from federal powers. But this particular subsection does not. The provincial politicians are protecting their turf. It happens again in paragraph 101E(2), where there is no derogation from powers of Parliament over the Supreme Court. After all that Parliament has given away in paragraphs 101A to E, it says, in paragraph 101E(2), "except for what we have just given away on the Supreme Court, nothing will derogate from our powers."

Paragraph 106A(2) says that nothing extends the powers of Parliament or the legislatures on the spending power. After it had just *reduced* the power of Parliament, it says, "nothing extends the powers of Parliament or the legislatures." Politicians are very generous with themselves when they are in power, but what is the effect of these clauses on the Canadian people? Well, we do not know. Because "distinct society" was not put in the preamble, but it was put in an operative clause, in an interpretative clause, we do know that it is a clear instruction to the court as to how they should interpret every other part of the Constitution.

Since the business of the court is to interpret laws, we must ask ourselves: How will the courts interpret this particular section? Opinions are divided. You have had experts, as have the House of Commons, saying, "Well, it is an interpretative clause; it does not mean anything," or, "It is an interpretative clause; it can mean a lot." We have different opinions even amongst people around here. I will read Senator Murray again at page 2A:2 of the same date. He states:

> Let us be clear on two points. Nothing in the proposed amendment changes the distribution of powers between the federal and provincial governments. [Nothing changes distribution of powers.] Nor does anything in the proposed amendment override the Canadian Charter of Rights and Freedoms, including women's equality rights.

If I can read English, it means that the proposed amendment of "distinct society" and French and English duality does not change anything. It is there to make Quebec feel good, I suppose, but nothing changes. The joint committee is a little less categorical.

First, you have read what they say on page 51. I am reading from the 1987 Constitutional Accord report of the Special Joint Committee of the Senate and the House of Commons at the top of page 51. It states:

> . . . in law the "distinct society" clause is unlikely to erode in any significant way the existing entrenched constitutional rights . . .

It shows a little less certainty than Senator Murray, but then you get to the "Distribution of powers," on page 45, paragraph 64, and there is even more uncertainty. Quite frankly, I do not like it, because, although it goes in my direction, the joint committee is not taking the responsibility for saying something. It states:

> It might therefore appear difficult to see how the "linguistic duality, distinct society" clauses could affect the division of powers without derogating from the powers, rights or privileges of one level of government in favour of the other.

They are protected by the famous section 2(4). They go on to say:

> Nevertheless, the Joint Committee was advised—

"We are not taking responsibility for this and we are not doing anything about it, but we were advised that:"

The definition of the scope of the legislative power is an ongoing process of allocating subject matters to heads of jurisdiction. Take, for example, the regulation of markets for financial securities. Would such a law be classified as an aspect of the federal "trade and commerce" power, as some say, or of "property and civil rights" within exclusive provincial jurisdiction, as others contend? And what about a new law purporting to regulate the content of radio or television broadcasting?

Yet, there is nothing in the Constitution about broadcasting. The Fathers of Confederation had not read Jules Verne, and there is nothing in there about aviation as well as a lot of other things that they have not thought about. What about a new law on those matters? It goes on to state:

> As new laws are made and challenged before the courts this process of classification of laws into federal or provincial jurisdiction continues. The court docket is limited only by the imagination and productivity of Canada's legislators and lawyers. The ongoing process of the constitutional "classification" of laws by the courts is one of the important areas where the interpretative provisions of the "linguistic duality" and "distinct society" clauses will come into play.

This is not a preamble. These are "interpretative provisions of linguistic duality" and "distinct society" which will come into play. Indeed, if this were not so, then the "linguistic duality" and "distinct society" interpretative provisions would be meaningless—a result that can hardly have been intended by its framers, except, of course, Senator Murray!

Really, the Joint Committee was advised of this and came to no conclusion, but they were honest enough to say it. Other people were even more honest. Read Premier Bourassa. This is from June 18, and is on page 8708, *Proceedings of the National Assembly.*

> . . . the entire Constitution, including the Charter, will be interpreted and applied in the light of this section on the distinct society. The exercise of legislative authority [so, not only the Charter, but also legislative powers] is included, and we will thus be able to consolidate existing positions and make new gains.

Page 9031 also elaborates on that.

Mr. Bourassa's Minister for Federal–Provincial Relations, Senator

Murray's counterpart, was quite clear, also on June 19, at page 8784. He states:

> . . . the distinct society gives us a tool with which to interpret and give real significance to this sharing of legislative authority, because there are grey areas and ambiguities.

In other words, sections 91 and 92 do not say it all. The courts will use the "distinct society" clause to say, "Well, because Quebec is a 'distinct society' it can extend its rights in this or that direction." Mr. Rémillard goes on and gives examples where Quebec's powers can be extended into broadcasting, banking—the very example of the joint committee report about the economic matters—and international relations. On that matter he says:

> The possibility of expressing our views very clearly on the international scene in terms of our specific identity . . . .

I suppose we can say that there is disagreement. At best, this clause is a prescription for discord, but, at worst, it says that Quebec will evolve under a different constitutional rule than the rest of Canada, because only Quebec is a "distinct society." Therefore, when it comes to a matter of interpreting the Constitution for Quebec, there is more than the possibility, there is a probability that the Constitution will be interpreted differently for Quebec than for the rest of Canada. I will come back to that in a moment when I talk about the consequences of this, but I want to draw a conclusion now. Quebec's five demands were all met in ways which weakened the fabric of Canada by denying the existence of a national will over and above the will of the provinces. The 1987 accord brings us back to the "compact" theory of the 1927 conference, that Canada exists as a country not by the will of its people but by the leave of ten provincial governments. To those who say that what we proposed in the 1970s had this consequence, I say that they did not go back to read what we said, or when they went back they made things up.

The Negotiations: The Provinces Emerge Victorious

I come now to the negotiations. I would like to leave time for questions also.

It is important to point out that not one of the five demands was correcting some injustice that had been caused to Quebec in 1982. I am not blaming Quebec—I have always said that it is the job of provincial premiers to try to get more powers. It is the nature of politicians to think that they can do things better than politicians at the other level. However, Quebec was making five demands—not, once again, because it had suffered injustices in the 1981 deal, but because it wanted completely new powers. The proof that Quebec was not badly treated in 1981 is that it was not attempting to correct the things that happened in 1981; the whole operation was one of leverage; of trying to tell Canada that it could have its Constitution if it gave the Province of Quebec more power. That was the sole grievance after 1981 and the Constitution Act, 1982. Quebec had not succeeded in using its leverage to acquire more power. That is where Mr. Lévesque went wrong. He had ganged up with the other seven and had tried to bargain; he was ditched by his partners, and therefore he was not able to bargain for all that he wanted.

However, what he had bargained for within the "gang of eight" was, as I said earlier, largely given to him. So, I repeat, it was not that Quebec was short-changed; it was that Quebec did not get as much power as it was hoped it could have had if it had found in Ottawa a Prime Minister who believed in the "compact" theory.

Therefore, Bourassa was perfectly justified in trying to get more power, because Mr. Mulroney had declared during the 1984 election, and I quote:

> We will have to make commitments to convince the Quebec government to give its consent to the new Canadian Constitution.

It was really up to Mr. Bourassa to trade in that consent for the most power he could get for his province. I always thought he would get some. After all the things we offered in the 1970s, he should be able to get some. I did not think he had much hope for the veto, because he, himself, had thrown it away in 1971, and then Mr. Lévesque threw it away in 1981 and had added that all provinces were equal. Therefore, I thought Mr. Bourassa would fight for it, get, perhaps, four out of the five demands, and grudgingly rejoin the constitutional family.

However, I knew one thing: I knew that the Prime Minister of Canada was in a superb negotiating position. He had campaigned on a program of national reconciliation; he had won with the largest majority in history; he could have convened a federal–provincial conference to end constitutional squabbles, and told all of the premiers that they had better cooperate or else the Canadian people would conclude that the past ten years of bickering were not Trudeau's fault after all, since, even with a nice, new Prime Minister, the premiers were proving to be as quarrelsome as ever. Instead of doing that, he made it clear that he was the one who needed peace at all costs.

Then, I think, everyone must have watched in disbelief, because, even *before* the constitutional talks got under way, he proceeded to throw away all of the trump cards he had: Premier Lougheed wanted the abolition of the National Energy Program; he got it. Mr. Peckford wanted administration of the offshore resources that we had only offered to share with him; he got it. Mr. Johnson wanted to sit in at international summits; he got it, and then it was inherited by Mr. Bourassa. Mr. Peterson wanted to be involved in the free trade negotiations; he got that, too. Even President Reagan got the dismantling of FIRA and the abolition of the National Energy Program even before they were sitting down to discuss acid rain.

Therefore, in such circumstances, the Prime Minister of Canada and his entire cabinet were absolutely no match for Bourassa and his able Minister of Intergovernmental Relations, Mr. Rémillard. Soon after the 1985 election Mr. Bourassa really judged with whom he was negotiating, and he moved in for the kill. When Meech Lake was all over, Mr. Bourassa was able to say—and I quote from the *Toronto Star* of May 4, 1987, under the byline of Robert McKenzie. This quote is en anglais, I am sorry, but it is contained in the *Toronto Star*:

> We didn't expect, after 20 years, to reach an agreement. Then suddenly without warning, there it is—an agreement . . .
>
> We could have waited until next year; we could have waited until after the next federal election. We were under no pressure. I was serene, but when I saw that it was falling to us piece by piece, I said to myself "Bien voilà! There it is."

So much for the federal government's argument, picked up by many of the provinces, that there was and still is a great urgency to the whole matter. Bourassa could have waited until after the next election; why shouldn't we? As for Mr. Mulroney's so-called negotiating skills, I think they should be assessed in the light of Mr. Bourassa's further comment, made at the same press conference, to the effect that he had obtained more in the field of immigration and in the appointment of Supreme Court Justices than he had been seeking. At that point in the press conference Mr. Rémillard chimed in and said that Mr. Bourassa, at the meeting table, successfully argued for even tougher wording, which made the ''distinct society'' clause more powerful than Quebec had originally dared hope. In short, on three of Quebec's five demands—namely, immigration, Supreme Court and the distinct society—Quebec got more than it was asking for. Yet, for good measure, the Prime Minister throws in two items not asked for: the Senate, which we know about, and federal–provincial conferences, of which there were to be two per year, and an agenda which is fixed until the end of time— or, at least, until there is an agreement between Parliament and seven legislatures to change it. However, until the end of time, you will have on the agenda—with no sunset clause—fisheries and the Senate.

It is no small wonder that Premier Pawley could say—and I am quoting now from the Winnipeg *Free Press* under the byline of Francis Russell:

> The Prime Minister did a very good job of mediating. He was fair and sensitive throughout. He did not try to bully or pressure us at all.

No, he did not try to pressure the provinces into accepting more powers; no sir, he would not do that. Premier Pawley goes on:

> Mulroney never once defended the national government's powers, but I felt he was not unhappy that Peterson and I (Pawley) were doing it [that is, defending the national government's powers]. The Prime Minister wanted to find an accommodation. He put pressure both ways. While he never really came out, I felt he was sympathetic to us [that is, Peterson and Pawley]. After all, we were trying to maintain national power.

Very helpful, Mr. Pawley. When the future of this country is decided at a conference of 11 First Ministers, when no one speaks for Canada except a couple of provincial premiers, encouraged by a little wink from the Prime Minister, that is a pretty sombre day.

So Prime Minister Mulroney gave Quebec much more than it had asked for in its Quebec Round. What did the federal government get in exchange? I will have to leave that for my next appearance, because I have a lot to say on that subject.

The federal government certainly did not trade what it was giving to the provinces in exchange for a correction of the flaws with which I was reproached by Senator Murray in the article in *Le Devoir*, namely, the opting-out provision and the notwithstanding clause. Certainly, even in the constitutionalized agenda you would think that the federal government would have put in one or two items, such as native rights, to be discussed at the next conference, or, at least, some power of value to the federal government. Or was it to be another agenda, where Mr. Mulroney would give the provinces their choice of grabs?

I now refer you to Senator Murray's testimony, at page 210:

> I have heard it said that the federal government gained nothing in these negotiations, and that it gave but did not get.
>
> I reject these contentions totally. Canada is the clear and undisputed winner in the current round of constitutional negotiations.

I think it is good to have Quebec in. It would be better if we had it in on better terms. In the short run, it is good; in the long run—I will talk about that in my conclusions.

What did the federal government gain? I will read on. He says, "The strengthening of our country. The reconciliation of Quebec. Opportunities for economic policy coordination and future constitutional reform." You could always have federal–provincial conferences. That is not a great gain in terms of a bargain. You could always call them, so that was not a gain for the federal government. The reconciliation of Quebec? We will see. In terms of the strengthening of our country, I just want to ask the question: How do you make a country stronger by weakening the only government that can talk for all Canadians? That is the story of the 1987 negotiations.

Mr. Mulroney's government of national reconciliation was able to bring temporary peace to federal–provincial relations by negotiating a sweetheart constitutional deal whereby enormous amounts of power were transferred to the provincial governments, and particularly to the premiers—powers over vital institutions of the federal government and power over the people of Canada through a weakening of the Charter.

Viewed in perspective, the negotiations of the previous 20 years had involved much more than the struggle between two levels of government. It had been a struggle to establish the sovereignty of the people over all levels of government, and, by the proclamation of the Constitution Act, 1982, the battle for the people's rights was won. The war was not over, the Charter was not perfect, and we still have no referendum process in the amending formula, but the legal community was seeing to it that the Charter was having a real meaning, and the media was reporting the rights of the people over the rights of government, and people began to discover that they had a community of values, that the bonds of Canadian nationhood existed, and so on.

But that process of constitutionalizing the people of Canada, which had begun in 1982, was stopped in its tracks by the 1987 accord. Eleven heads of government were to meet in secret in the dead of night, transfer unconscionable amounts of power from the national government to the provinces, submit the whole of the Constitution to an interpretative clause which entrenched the primacy of two collectivities, and, finally, decree that no amount of participation by the people of Canada could ever lead to a modification of that accord or of the Constitution itself.

In 1982 the Quebec *government* was not in, because that government had stood for the division of Canada, but the people of Quebec were in. I refer you to a nice article by one of your colleagues, Senator Stollery, in *The Globe and Mail*, dated February 11, 1988, where he makes a tally of those who voted against the 1982 agreement. I do the additions, but the figures are his. Seventy-one Quebec members of Parliament voted for the 1982 Constitution; four of them voted against, and in Quebec's National Assembly, on December 1, 1981, there was a vote as to whether we would or would not condemn Ottawa's and the nine provinces' accord, and 38 courageous Liberals voted against the Péquistes. That is for a total of 109 Quebec elected representatives for the 1982 accord, against a total of 74 against it, four in Ottawa and 70 in Quebec City. That is just tossed out for the benefit of some of those professors who teach that, somehow, Quebec was not in in 1982. It was in legally, and everyone knows that it was in legally and constitutionally. It was not in "morally" or "politically"—I think those are the words of the former President of the Canadian Bar Association, Mr. Yves Fortier. Personally, I do not accept that distinction. Let us count heads of elected representatives and you will see that the Quebecers voted in favour of the 1982 accord.

Under the 1987 accord the Quebec government is in, but the Quebec people stand divided from the rest of Canada as a distinct society. In 1982 there had been a victory of people over power; 1987 was a triumph of power over people.

The Supreme Court and the "Distinct Society" Clause

The Supreme Court, at some point, is going to have to decide, does "distinct society" mean something or does it not? By the time they will have decided it will be too late, either the Quebec nationalists will have been had or the Canadian people will have been had, because if it is decided that "distinct society" and "duality"—linguistic duality—do not mean anything, then the province of Quebec will revert to the position it was in after 1982. It will be bound legally by the accord. But do you think it will be in politically and morally? Do you think Quebec is going to accept that it has been fooled by this phoney drafting, and that it will accept a decision by some five, six or seven judges of the Supreme Court—whatever is a majority—named by Ottawa, "centralizers," "Anglos" for the most part, that "distinct society" has no meaning? Do you think that is a prescription for peace?

If the courts decide that "distinct society" has no meaning, won't we be in exactly the position we were in after 1982, where Quebec was bound legally, as it will be by the 1987 accord, but where some people will argue that it is not bound morally and it is not bound politically?

We have Senator Murray again saying that he could not vote for the 1982 accord because, in conscience, he thought it was not right. I hope that some of you feel that, in conscience, this is not right, either. Senator Murray said, "Without Quebec's participation in our constitutional family, Canada's future would remain in doubt." It will remain in doubt now, believe me, if the Supreme Court goes against it in a deal it thought it made, in a deal that Bourassa and Rémillard spelled out in so many words in the legislative assembly of Quebec. They may say, "He said it meant this and now the courts are saying we were fooled, we were had, we were tricked." Yves Fortier said, "Politically and morally the Constitution Act, 1982 does not apply to Quebec. Those who claim it does are guilty of constitutional heresy." This brings the matter back to the type of reasoning we heard from the Supreme Court in 1981 where it was decided it was legal to go to Westminster, but it was not nice.

But it will not be nice if Quebec has been had in this deal. "Distinct society" would not have any force in law, but it would have tremendous force in the politics of separation, because already Mr. Bourassa, in the quotes I was reading to you, was warned by the then opposition leader, Johnson: "You will have to pay for this . . ." if you don't get from Ottawa what you were supposed to get. I do not think Mr. Parizeau will be any more gentle than Mr. Johnson.

What if, on the other hand, the courts decide that "duality" and "distinct society" do have meaning? I think Canadians would discover, to their surprise, that the accord has empowered one provincial government to subordinate the rights of every individual Canadian living within its borders to the rights of a chosen community, presumably the French-speaking majority. I know what that would do to French-speaking Canadians in other provinces, and I think they know. You cannot go around saying that the Anglos will not have a right to put English even on the French signs in Quebec, but, in the rest of Canada, we are asking you English Canadians to be good, and bilingualism is the way of the future. So we will have what? The possibility of building one Canada will be lost forever. Canada henceforth will be governed by two Constitutions, one to be interpreted for the benefit of Canada and one to be interpreted for the preservation and promotion of Quebec's distinct society—two Constitutions, two Charters, promoting two distinct sets of values, and eventually two Canadas—well, one Canada and something else.

And lest the mistake be made of assuming that the Quebec Round gave Quebec everything that it wanted, we already have Mr. Bourassa in the Legislative Assembly on June 23, reported at page 9031, telling the Leader of the Opposition: "May I remind the Leader of the Opposition there will be a second round?" No. That staunch federalist, Premier Bourassa, had made his position very clear in the Legislative Assembly on June 18, at page 8709. He said:

> . . . the Liberal Party recognizes Quebec's right . . . to freely express [the] desire to maintain or put an end to the federal union with Canada. Basically, it recognizes the right of the people of Quebec to determine their future as they see fit.

He had just got Meech Lake and Langevin—the works. But, "We still have a right to be independent. We have just signed a marriage contract, but clause 1 says I can divorce at any time."

So our government of national reconciliation will have bungled its way into a no-win situation for Canada. There will be a showdown if this thing goes through. I know what is going to happen; but, as I was saying earlier, there are still some blunt tools left in the BNA Act: disallowance, taxation—all modes of taxation, the declarative clause, expropriation for federal purposes, and so on. I would not like to be here to have to use them, but I can tell you one thing: it will be the end of the "*peaceable* kingdom." And it is in vain that hundreds of thousands of French-speaking Canadians will have settled in the rest of

Canada and tried to preserve their identity; it will be in vain that Acadians will have fought for generations against indifference and frequent hostility; and it will be in vain that many generations of Quebec politicians will have fought for the establishment of the French fact in Canada—not in Quebec, in Canada. I refer to Henri Bourassa, the great Bourassa; and *Le Devoir*, in those days fighting for the rights of various French-speaking communities dispersed throughout Canada (e.g., St. Boniface in Manitoba, Rivière de la Paix in Alberta and Maillardville in British Columbia).

That dream will be gone. And even those who thought they could show that "French power" could exist in Ottawa, that it was not such a forbidding place to French Canadians, will find it to have been in vain. It will be in vain also that many thousands, and even hundreds of thousands, of Canadian children will have learned French across the provinces in immersion courses, because they thought that this could be a country working on the basis of two official languages, bilingualism rather than dualism; that they could be united. So, in vain, we would have dreamt the dream of one Canada.

Define Distinct Society and Let the People Decide

So what do we do with the conclusion? Well, the 1987 accord is unlike the parson's egg; it is not only bad in part, it is completely bad. I think it should be put out in the dust bin. And of course the Quebec nationalists will be pretty mad, and there will be some wishy-washy federalists who will be pretty mad, too—those who want to have their cake and eat it too. We should simply remind them of two things: First, that provincial governments have been holding up the process of constitutional reform for 80 years, and, in particular, that Premier Lesage of Quebec backed out of a deal in 1964, Premier Bourassa backed out of a deal in 1971, and Mr. Lévesque was left on the corner by his seven partners in 1981. But no one broke down and wept. Once again, these experts from Queen's or Toronto, or elsewhere, say that "Quebec is in a state of anguish since the 1980 accord because it wasn't in." Not so. Life went on in the province. Sure, the Quebec nationalists will be a bit frustrated if the accord does not go through. That's the real world: "You don't always get what you want. You were offered it before, but you didn't take it. Now we are not offering it to you."

But more important, the second point is that Mr. Bourassa himself said that he could have waited until after the next federal election. Well, my conclusion is that we should do precisely that. In the meantime, what can be done by the people, by the provincial legislatures and by the Senate? Well, the people should demand that every candidate in every federal or provincial election or by-election should state his or her position on the accord. The Meech Lake Accord had not been debated in any Parliament or legislature before being agreed to in April 1987 by the 11 First Ministers. Therefore, the people should ensure that the same mistake is not made again, that it will be debated. And if a majority of federal MPs want to campaign in favour of the accord, and if they win their seats, then the governments of Canada and the provinces can put Meech Lake into the Constitution by using the amending process that exists.

That is what the people can do. They have the right to vote, and they have the right to know what their members of Parliament or the legislatures stand for from here on in. It has been done in New Brunswick already, and it is being done now in Manitoba—and I admire the courage and the independence of mind of a Premier McKenna or a Sharon Carstairs, who have the courage to stand up—not against Quebec, but to ask what the Meech Lake Accord means; and they want to make sure that they stand up for Canada after they have been told what it means.

So in the provincial legislatures, where the accord is not yet passed, members should consider that any amendment to the Constitution of Canada imparts a new orientation to Canada's destiny. So, voting on it should be a matter of conscience and not of partisanship. Members of those legislatures should force the government to ask for a reference to the Supreme Court, as was done by three provinces in 1980–1981.

Before voting on constitutional amendments which will bind Canada for all time, the members have a right to know what will be the effect of the ''distinct society'' clause on women, or on the Charter in general, or on the linguistic minorities. They have a right to know. You don't vote when it is obvious that even the experts don't agree; and when negotiators in Quebec say one thing and senators in the federal government say exactly the opposite. They have the right to know what is the meaning of such phrases as ''programs or initiatives compatible with national objectives.'' They have a right to know if the doctrine of necessity can be invoked if there is a paralysis of the Supreme Court.

So, in provinces where there might be an election of a new premier who had not signed the accord, and in those that have not yet decided, they should make a reference to the Supreme Court. That is in the law;

that is in the practice. And I say, once again, that it is a matter of dignity for a member of the legislature not to vote on something the meaning of which he does not know; and if ever there was a case where the meaning of the Constitution was not clear, it is in the case before us now. So before they vote, let us get a reference. One was obtained in the 1980–1981 period. It took something in the order of three or four months, and then we knew. On this occasion we still have another two years or more before time runs out.

What can the Senate do? Well, it is too late to use tactics, as you did on me in 1978, to threaten obstruction in order to get a reference, which we gave you. I do not think you have the time between now and April 23 to obstruct in any meaningful way. I suggest that the Senate pass amendments that will ensure that the resolution is corrected so that it means, if you believe in it, what Senator Murray says it does mean, that "distinct society" has no effect on the Charter or on the distribution of powers. That is the minimum amendment that you can make, but there are many others that, for a fee, I would be prepared to suggest to you.

Unless you fear that you are offending someone, remember the Langevin accord, paragraph 1 of the operative sector, which states:

> The Prime Minister of Canada will lay or cause to be laid before the Senate and House of Commons, and the first ministers of the provinces will lay or cause to be laid before their legislative assemblies, as soon as possible, a resolution, in the form appended hereto . . .

So they did that. They did not say the Senate could not amend it. They did not say the members of the House of Commons could not amend it. They tried to amend it. The Liberal Party proposed amendments that were not carried, but nothing in the accord says that the Senate cannot amend it.

I would suggest that if you want to know what you are voting on, you should make it clear and say what you think "distinct society" means, and maybe even within this chamber you will find that some Quebecers do not agree with some Ontarians on what it means, I do not know, but the stock and trade of legislatures, from time immemorial, has been to vote on something the meaning of which they assume they know, and then when they realize they do not know they clarify it with an amendment.

Therefore, I conclude that the Senate can and must send an amended resolution back and ask the House of Commons to vote on that.

There is nothing in the Constitution of 1982 that says the Senate has to believe exactly the same thing as the members of the House of Commons. So, if you want clarification, you should amend it and send it back, and the members of the House of Commons can discuss whether the clarification has made it worse; but, at least, the people will have been enlightened as to the real meaning of Meech Lake and the real direction in which the country is going.

I think we should take our chances. Let the people decide once they know what it means. If the members of the House of Commons and senators and legislators of the provinces want to vote against the accord because they do not want it, then the accord should be discarded. The Quebec government might be a bit disappointed, but, then, it set the rules. In 1981 Premier Lévesque agreed that all provinces were equal. That is what they would be: They would get no Meech Lake, but everybody would be equal.

On the other hand, if the people of Canada want this accord, and that is not beyond the realm of possibility, then let that be part of the Constitution. I, for one, will be convinced that the Canada we know and love will be gone forever. But, then, Thucydides wrote that Themistocles' greatness lay in the fact that he realized Athens was not immortal. I think we have to realize that Canada is not immortal; but, if it is going to go, let it go with a bang rather than a whimper.

CHAPTER THREE

DIVINING A DEMOCRATIC PROCESS: The Citizens' Versus the Politicians' Constitution

Three fundamental principles of constitutional change are (1) that the citizens must be consulted directly, either through a constituent assembly or a referendum; (2) that Parliament and the Legislature, as opposed to the executive power, have the right and the responsibility to initiate constitutional reforms as well as approve any amendments proposed by the first ministers; and (3) that any amending procedure lifts constitutional discussions above the level of partisan politics.

(Michael Behiels et al., *The Daily Gleaner*, March 15, 1989)

The procedures being followed for passing the Accord are consistent with established constitutional procedures. They fall within the practice of executive federalism and are consistent with the tradition of a representative parliamentary government.

(Ian Scott, brief to the Ontario Select Committee on Constitutional Reform, 1987 Constitutional Accord, 80)

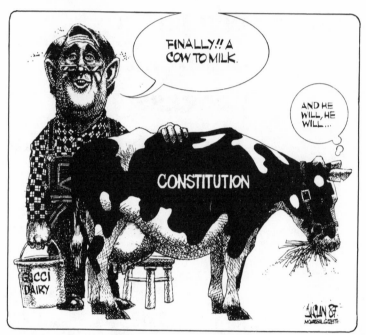

Reprinted with permission — *The Toronto Star* Syndicate.

INTRODUCTION

The issue that generated the most vociferous and passionate critical reaction from the vast majority of organizations and individuals who submitted and/or presented briefs to the Special Joint Committee of the Senate and the House of Commons, to the Senate Committee of the Whole and to the Ontario Select Committee on Constitutional Reform was the *process* adopted by the first ministers. Indeed, many of the representations concluded that the Meech Lake Accord was morally and politically illegitimate because of the secretive, anti-democratic and elitist manner in which it was put together in the middle of the night. "The efforts that the signatories to the accord have displayed to muzzle the Canadian public is [sic] truly indecent," declared Albert Breton in his incisive critique of the process before the senators.[1]

Why this sense of outrage and betrayal over the process rather than the substance of the Accord? To some extent, the fear of being branded as anti-Quebec forced many critics of the Accord to soft-pedal their concerns over the distinct society clause, the very raison d'être of the Accord. The outcry over the *process* was considered important from a strategic point of view. It created a degree of unity and co-operation among the various interest groups and individuals who were concerned with different dimensions of the document under scrutiny. Because of the unanimity of the first ministers and the national opposition parties, there was a general sense of unease and mistrust about the concerted attempt to stifle any meaningful debate. This meant that the dynamic tension between divergent visions of Canadian society and the Constitution was not revealed, as had been the experience leading up to the Constitution Act, 1982.[2] As a result, extraparliamentary opposition emerged, not in the media, which merely gloated over the outcome, but primarily among the leaders of innumerable interest groups speaking on behalf of their respective constituencies.

But these do not constitute the fundamental reason why many Canadians and their associations were so disturbed and perplexed. The real reason resides in the 1982 Constitution Act and its Charter of Rights and Freedoms. The Charter constitutes a popular, democratic dimension to nation building and our national identity. This "constitutional revolution" has resulted in what political scientist Alan C. Cairns has characterized, quite appropriately, as the creation of a citizens' constitution.[3] The Charter's very presence in our Constitution enjoins all Canadian citizens to take an effective interest in protecting that Charter by ensuring that the amending formula, which remained dominated by the first ministers, is not used to undermine or circumscribe the Charter.

The government of Pierre Trudeau used the Charter to galvanize widespread popular support from a whole range of dynamic constituencies, including women, aboriginals, official language minority communities, ethnic groups and civil libertarians. In large measure, this coalition of citizens' groups enabled Trudeau to repatriate the British North America (BNA) Act with an amending formula, albeit one dominated by the provinces. He succeeded where other prime ministers had failed for over fifty years because of their insistence upon the unanimity rule and the provincial demand for additional powers as a quid pro quo. The emergence of this citizens' constitution in 1982 was by and large the product of the socio-economic and cultural changes that had swept over Canadian society following World War II, particularly the arrival of thousands upon thousands of non-francophone and non-anglophone immigrants and the rapid integration of women into the labour force at all levels and in all occupations.

This citizens' constitution was a dramatic departure from the traditional perspective that the Constitution was exclusively a document pertaining to the nature of the division of powers between the federal and provincial governments. From this perspective, the BNA Act was the preserve of the first ministers and constitutional experts in the academic, legal and judicial communities. It rarely struck a resonant chord among the general public. Unfortunately, the achievement of a citizens' constitution in 1982 was only partial and subject to reversal. This was so because of the nature of the compromise at the heart of the 1982 Constitution Act. Ottawa had to settle for a Charter that was hobbled by the notwithstanding clause, while the provincial amending formula of the Gang of Eight repudiated the referendum but allowed full compensation only for opting out in educational and cultural matters. The first ministers, particularly the premiers, as the Meech Lake Accord has amply demonstrated, got the better of the bargain. Their exclusive control over the amending process has allowed them to reinforce executive federalism, to deal a blow to responsible government by denying an effective role to the legislatures and to undermine the very essence of the citizens' constitution gained through the Charter by denying citizens any effective voice in the process.[4]

Viewed in this light, it is fully understandable why the representatives of the various interest groups that had benefitted from the Charter gains in 1982 reacted in such a hostile and outspoken manner when they were effectively excluded from the second indigenous attempt to amend our newly patriated Constitution Act, 1867. Their hard-fought and -won constitutional status was threatened. They had no legal or constitutional mechanism with which to defend either that status or the national vision it represented.

Alan Cairns, in a scathing indictment of the Meech Lake process in all of its facets, raises some of the most incisive and perturbing questions about the future stability of our Constitution. For Cairns, the Meech Lake Accord is a misguided attempt to constitutionalize an outmoded regionalist and dualist perception of the country, held so dearly by the premiers. In taking this approach, the premiers and the Prime Minister are deliberately ignoring the new socio-cultural cleavages of class, ethnicity and race that were incorporated into the Constitution via the Charter and therefore became amenable to compromise and accommodation. It was also through the incorporation of the needs and aspirations of these various social groups and classes into the Constitution that a sense of national community was going to be created. According to Cairns, the only way of reconciling the citizens' and the governments' respective visions of the Constitution is to democratize the amending process to include genuine and effective input from all the legislative assemblies and from Canadians and their myriad organizations. If this is not done, he contends, Canada will face years of constitutional instability with all that portends for our social, economic and political activities.

There is no doubt that the criticism about the elitist and undemocratic nature of the process that produced the Meech Lake Accord rattled the Prime Minister and especially his Minister of State for Federal–Provincial Relations, Senator Lowell Murray. Hoping to blunt some of the criticism and prevent further damage to the integrity of the Accord, Senator Murray offered a defence of the process that mirrored the traditional perception that the Constitution is strictly about federalism and therefore the prerogative of the first ministers. The Meech Lake process, Murray contended, compared favourably with the 1980–81 process that produced the Constitution Act, 1982, and this accounts, in large measure, for its success.[5]

One of the most unabashed supporters of the Accord from the outset was Professor Richard Simeon, Director of the School of Public Administration at Queen's University.[6] Unlike Senator Lowell Murray, Professor Simeon candidly admitted that his confidence was shaken by the "very troubling and powerful" criticisms of the process. He addressed these criticisms directly in his submission to the Ontario Select Committee on Constitutional Reform. "Does the process that we have followed here," Simeon queried, "meet our current standards of domestic legitimacy for constitutional policy-making, or is it so flawed really that the results are unacceptable?" He contends that the process, while far from ideal, was the only available pragmatic, acceptable and workable compromise necessary to acquire Quebec's consent for the Constitution Act, 1982. "Meech Lake," writes Simeon elsewhere, "is a textbook example of 'executive federalism,' or, more generally, of 'elite accommodation' as a style of Canadian decision-making."[7]

Convinced that the process was valid in all respects, Simeon chastises Meech Lake critics for camouflaging their distaste for Quebec's minimum demands behind a smokescreen of concern over process. The procedure adopted by the first ministers was the one set out in the Constitution Act, 1982 and is therefore legitimate. The matters agreed upon were not sprung on an unsuspecting citizenry but had been the subject of discussion in federal–provincial conferences and in national and provincial political party meetings and elections since the 1960s and in particular since the election of the Mulroney and Bourassa governments in 1984 and 1985, respectively. The Accord brings to a successful close, in a very conservative manner, the debates over provincial rights and the role of Quebec in the federal system that have dominated the agenda since the early 1960s. Furthermore, the Accord does not violate the accepted norms of representative, parliamentary democracy because it will have to stand the test of ratification in all eleven legislatures.

Simeon does concede that a process of "elite accommodation," as reflected in the legislatures and among the first ministers, does not allow for the participation of groups and regions that are not represented by these "elites" and therefore raises a valid question of legitimacy.[8] Nevertheless, he concludes that demanding higher standards of democratic decision making at this stage would render an accommodation with Quebec virtually impossible because of the sensitive ethnic cleavages involved. The implementation of a more democratic process, he concludes, should be deferred to future rounds of constitutional reform when the demands of other groups representing a different set of cleavages need to be addressed.

Notes

1. Albert Breton, *Debates of the Senate*, Vol. 131, No. 120, February 10, 1988, 2731.
2. Roger Gibbins, "A Sense of Unease: The Meech Lake Accord and Constitution-making in Canada," in Roger Gibbins et al., eds., *Meech Lake and Canada. Perspectives from the West* (Edmonton: Academic Printing and Publishing, 1988): 121–129; John D. Whyte, "More Than Small Change: The Meaning of Meech Lake for the Canadian Polity," Submission to the Select Committee on the 1987 Constitutional Accord of the Legislative Assembly of New Brunswick, Fredericton, October 20, 1988, mimeo, 3–7.
3. Alan C. Cairns, "Citizens (Outsiders) and Governments (Insiders) in Constitution-making: The Case of Meech Lake," *Canadian Public Policy/ Analyse de Politiques*, XIV (1988): 122.
4. *Ibid.*, 123–124; Michael D. Behiels, "Brief on the Meech Lake Accord," Brief to the Ontario Select Committee on Constitutional Reform, 1987 Constitutional Accord, *Hansard Official Report of Debates*, March 21, 1988, C-727–C-729.
5. Lowell Murray, "The Process of Constitutional Change in Canada: The Lessons of Meech Lake," *Choices* (Montreal: Institute for Research on Public Policy, February 1988).
6. Cf. Canada, Special Joint Committee of the Senate and the House of Commons on the 1987 Constitutional Accord, *Minutes of Proceedings and Evidence*, No. 5, August 11, 1987 (Ottawa: Queen's Printer, 1987): 68–69, for Simeon's presentation.
7. Richard Simeon, "Meech Lake and Shifting Conceptions of Canadian Federalism," *Canadian Public Policy/Analyse de Politiques*, XIV (1988): 22; Ian Scott, Attorney General for Ontario, defended the process of the Meech Lake Accord using many of the same arguments as Professor Simeon. (See Ian Scott, "Brief to the Select Committee of the Legislature on Constitutional Reform," May 4, 1988, 79–84.)
8. Simeon, "Meech Lake and Shifting Conceptions of Canadian Federalism," 22–23; D. V. Smiley, "An Outsider's Observations on Federal–Provincial Relations Among Consenting Adults," in Richard Simeon, ed., *Confrontation or Collaboration: Intergovernmental Relations in Canada Today* (Toronto: Institute of Public Administration, 1979).

ALAN C. CAIRNS

CITIZENS AND THEIR CHARTER: DEMOCRATIZING THE PROCESS OF CONSTITUTIONAL REFORM *

Introduction

The difficulties of the Meech Lake Constitutional Accord begin at the beginning. The very label is inaccurate for the agreement struck at Meech Lake was significantly modified at the Langevin meetings. It is an additional minor irritant that an inappropriate dualism extends to the spelling of Meech Lake which, in the Joint Committee proceedings, is frequently spelled Meach Lake. Regrettably, or perhaps fortunately given my task of writing a short critique of the Accord, there is bigger game in the woods surrounding Meech Lake than such small fry of interest to locational purists and grammarians.

I will not offer an elaborate discussion of the Meech Lake constitutional vision in terms of the substance of the Accord. The Meech Lake process, as well as its substance, expresses a powerful constitutional vision, specifically of the proper role of leaders and citizens in constitutional change which will be discussed below. In order to reduce suspense as to my own position, I hereby express my hope that future first ministers will see themselves as guardians, not owners, of the constitution, and that they will view the Meech Lake procedures as a regrettable aberration, justified if at all only by extraordinary circumstances, but in no way to constitute a model for future constitutional change. To be Meech-Laked twice would surely be considered 'cruel and unusual treatment or punishment,' a provision of the Charter which, unfortunately, is subject to the override.

*In K. E. Swinton and C. J. Rogerson, eds., *Competing Constitutional Visions—The Meech Lake Accord* (Toronto: Carswell, 1988).

The second part of this paper argues that our constitutional theory is in disarray. The federal government Joint Committee hearings, following on the intergovernmental accord, graphically reveal a basic contradiction between those who view the constitution and its modification as an affair of governments, and those who have caught a glimpse of what I call the 'citizens' constitution.' These two perspectives, one of which goes back to Confederation, while the other is a new arrival stimulated by an emerging rights consciousness given constitutional sustenance by the Charter, will not be easily reconciled. Their advocates inhabit divergent moral and political universes. They disagree on the nature of the constitution and, therefore, on the procedures appropriate to changing it.

The relative influence of citizens and governments in constitutional change has varied from the marked impact of civil rights constituencies on the evolution of the Charter in 1980–81[1] to the demobilization of citizens to the status of spectators by the government elites which dominated the fashioning of the 1987 Accord. The competitive coexistence of contradictory views by citizens and governments of the same constitution suggests that Canadians now have a two party system in constitutional matters which is not Tweedledum and Tweedledee.

The two main parts of this paper, respectively labelled 'Some Obstacles to Democracy in English Canada' and 'Whose Constitution Is It?,' are closely related. Disagreement on the answer to the latter lies behind the acrimony over procedures between those who seek to erect and those who seek to erode obstacles to a more participant version of constitutional change. Both parts of this paper suggest that Meech Lake is discordant with powerful strands in contemporary Canadian constitutional culture.

Some Obstacles to Democracy in English Canada

The generational imperialism called constitutional change deserves the closest scrutiny. All long term politics, as Popper reminds us,[2] is institutional. Thus the elaboration of constitutional machinery to mould the behaviour of unborn generations is the supreme act of a free people. Accordingly, as working constitutions are responsive to emerging needs as well as anchored in tradition, the visions which motivate the agents of constitutional change are crucial data for students of the constitution. Such visions are not confined to the substance of proposed changes, but also inhere in the methods employed to achieve them. For example, the referendum instrument employed by the Parti Québécois survives as an honourable part of its constitutional legacy even if its use derailed the drive to sovereignty-association. Equally, the Meech Lake/Langevin constitutional process is inescapably part of the constitutional vision and legacy of those who engineered it. It is a precedent available to inform future acts of constitutional transformation by succeeding generations, and it informs us of the attitudes of our elected servants to their responsibilities as constitutional guardians. Does the process educate and elevate the citizenry? Are citizens encouraged to participate meaningfully in the unfolding of their constitutional fate? Should women, aboriginals, social policy activists, northerners, and those Canadians who are not founding peoples be encouraged to sleep soundly and securely when future first ministers reshuffle in private the constitutional relationships among the governments and peoples of Canada yet one more time?

Regrettably, the answer to these questions is 'No!' At the federal level the nature of the hearings process has hampered public understanding and input in a host of ways identified by group after group which appeared before the Joint Committee—the timing of the hearings in midsummer, the short time given to prepare briefs, the seeming fait accompli which witnesses confronted, and the unworthy suggestions that some of the critics were really anti-Quebec.

The public need for understanding has also been ill-served by the unity of leadership of government and of both national opposition parties behind the Accord. There was no such unanimity over Bill C-60 in 1978, or over the patriation exercise which followed the 1980 referendum. In both cases, the clash of views was highly educational. Further, of course, the disagreements among governments and parties gave public opinion and group concerns an influence discouraged by the more monolithic Meech Lake process.

The muting of the adversarial process in parliament greatly restricts the flow of information and analysis to the public. When it is combined with the executive solidarity of first ministers behind the Accord, major competing visions of Canada are deprived of official spokespersons. It is left to politicians who courageously break party ranks, and pay a price, to a former Prime Minister, to the Senate, and to academics, various interest groups and the media to remind the leaders of eleven governments and of the three national parties that neither their Meech Lake view of Canada nor their elitist secretive processes are unquestioned orthodoxies.

Public understanding and discriminating judgement are hampered by a paucity of information on the jockeying among governments in the Meech Lake/Langevin process. Those who seek to play the role of citizen or informed analyst are reduced to a Canadian version of Kremlinology in which journalistic tidbits are supplemented by selective disclosures of who did what to whom. Is it true that Bourassa was surprised to get more than he had asked for with respect to immigration and the Supreme Court;[3] that Mulroney acted more like a mediator/arbitrator between provincial contestants than the leader/defender of the federal government, but was 'not unhappy' when Pawley or Peterson attempted to speak for national interests;[4] and that the extension of unanimity to the admission of new provinces was, as Spector said, necessary to avoid a breakdown of the deal?[5]

In the Meech Lake process an intergovernmental version of cabinet solidarity applies to the participants in federal–provincial accords which precede formal constitutional amendment, with unfortunate consequences. A 'cabinet-like' solidarity of first ministers from eleven governments is without the redeeming features of its practice within jurisdictions. In the latter, collective solidarity derives from the system of responsible government, and the fact that ministers and their party will share a common fate before a future electorate. The former, however, share no common fate, and do not confront partisan adversaries who can unseat them. Neither electorates nor legislatures can reward or punish a united intergovernmental elite of first ministers. Further, first ministers' solidarity across jurisdictions also inhibits citizen control of governments within jurisdictions. To take the case of British Columbia: little is known of what the B.C. government was seeking in advance of the meetings, of the Premier's behaviour at the meetings, or of the government's subsequent evaluation of the Accord. In the circumstances it is virtually impossible to hold the government accountable for its behaviour. The conflict between executive federalism and eleven systems of responsible government is serious under the most favourable conditions. It is compounded when the private meetings from which agreements emerge are preceded by intensive intergovernmental contact and lobbying to pave the way.

The difficulty in keeping governments accountable for their actions is further aggravated by the smokescreen that Meech Lake was to be the Quebec round, and hence other provinces were to hold back on their constitutional demands. Theoretically, therefore, what the other provinces got, if anything, could not be assessed against any prior understanding of what they sought. This alleged self-control of the other nine provinces was never more than a half-truth for they gained much on the coat-tails of Quebec under the principle of the equality of the provinces. Politically, the image of altruistic provincial governments has the effect of shielding nine premiers from informed criticism, and deflecting attention from the rewards they received for an abstinence they did not practise.

The overall result of the Meech Lake syndrome is a unilateralism of eleven governments which leaves legislators and citizens gasping on the sidelines with an unpalatable choice between an uninformed deferential gratitude for bringing Quebec back into the constitutional family, and an impotent frustration that any flaws they find will be defined away as less than egregious.

The strictures in the preceding paragraphs have a greatly diminished application to the government of Quebec. Both the Parti Québécois and the Quebec Liberal Party developed constitutional proposals, the meeting of which would produce the willing adhesion of the government of Quebec to the constitution. The election victory of the Quebec Liberal Party in December 1985 was followed by the speech of M. Gil Rémillard, Minister for Canadian Intergovernmental Affairs, to a conference in Mont Gabriel in May 1986, at which time he laid down the five requirements of the Quebec government. The Quebec proposals, modified by the process they have gone through and now clothed in legal language, have found their way into the constitution, or will, if the Meech Lake amendments are passed by the legislatures of all 11 governments.

So, from a Quebec perspective the Meech Lake process has been relatively open, the objectives of the government and the constitutional instruments to achieve them were laid out in advance, and the proposed Meech Lake amendments can thus be assessed as adequate or inadequate in the light of known means and ends. The Quebec National Assembly held a reasonably thorough debate on the initial version of the Accord between the Meech Lake and Langevin meetings, and after the Langevin changes the National Assembly debated and passed an appropriate resolution. In such circumstances, the constitutional constituency of journalists, scholars, intellectuals, and engaged citizens in Quebec could have an intelligent debate on Meech Lake. Their counterparts outside of Quebec have not had equivalent possibilities; nor have Québécois in their capacity as Canadian citizens.

The public process of examination and approval by legislatures is fragmented into eleven jurisdictions. As a result, the eleven actors who in secret conclave redefined Canada are never available as a group for collective questioning and challenging. No provincial governments participated in the Joint Committee hearings either as defendant or interlocutor. Joint Committee members were deprived of the opportunity of hearing from Quebec representatives the expansive interpretations of what they hoped would flow from the distinct society clause and the limitations on the spending power. Those who appeared before the Joint Committee and were told that their proposed amendments would unravel an interdependent agreement designed to bring the Quebec government back into the constitutional family could not question the representatives of Quebec or other provinces on this point, for there were none. In general, Quebec participation before the Joint Committee was very limited, which was unfortunate given the shaping effect of Quebec's demands on the outcome.

The women's groups from English Canada, concerned that the distinct society clause might weaken S. 28 equality rights in Quebec, or even the Charter's more general application in Quebec, have lacked an arena in which they can confront the government of Quebec. Citizens and government elites from Yukon and the Northwest Territories, outraged that their aspirations for provincehood have been stifled by the unanimity requirements for the creation of new provinces, are not only denied the opportunity to confront the provincial governments responsible, but are reduced to gossip and speculation as to the identity and objectives of the 'culprits.'[6] It is difficult to disagree with their assessment of the process as dishonourable.

The combination of discussions and decision-making in secret, followed by a fragmented political process in eleven discrete arenas where separate governments seek approval from their legislatures, make it difficult to grasp the total package of constitutional change that is Meech Lake/Langevin. Meech Lake/Langevin is a special Canadian version of divide and rule where the governing elites decide, then divide and explain themselves before separate audiences. In a number of cases, of course, the approval process in provincial legislatures will be perfunctory and formal, with no hearings, and limited debate between government and opposition parties. So far (mid October 1987) in British Columbia a constitutional reform package which will significantly enhance the B.C. government's role in the Canadian federal system is a non-event.

An additional weakness in the process, which has attracted little comment,[7] is the absence of serious justificatory position papers issued by the federal government. This deficiency aggravates the problem of assessing the relationship of the provisions of Meech Lake to any explicit constitutional philosophy. For the long-time constitutional observer, whose files are bulging with federal government documents on the constitution from the late sixties, with the detailed federal position papers which accompanied Bill C-60, with the competing presentations by the 'Yes' and 'No' forces—including the federal government—in the pre-referendum period in Quebec, and with the provincial position papers from Alberta, British Columbia, Saskatchewan and Newfoundland leading up to the 1982 Constitution Act, the pickings from Meech Lake/ Langevin are slim indeed.

We have extensive official rationales for a host of causes that failed—sovereignty-association, fifth region status for B.C., the 1980 proposals for the economic union, and many others. However, for the second most comprehensive package of constitutional change since Confederation we have remarkably little to go on beyond the public knowledge of Quebec's demands. One example may illustrate the point. Under the guise of a transitional measure Canadians have embarked on the most extensive Senate reform in our history. Several observers have described the transformed Senate which will result from the composite provincial–federal government nomination and appointment process as one of the most consequential institutional changes brought about by Meech Lake.[8] Also, with some exceptions the prevailing opinion is that the temporary will become the permanent. This transitional Senate reform, slipped in almost without public explanation, will have a major impact on parliamentary government and probably on federalism.

The inference to be drawn from the proposed nomination/appointment process is that this transitional Senate reform is a response to the intrastate analysis which attributes the weakness of the federal government to its lack of provincial sensitivities. However, as the British Columbia government discovered in its Senate reform proposals of the late seventies to strengthen the region at the centre, the bulk of the Senate's workload concerns matters for which provincial cleavages are of minimal relevance—that the Senate is in fact, however poorly it performs, a reviewing chamber for Canada-wide concerns.[9] How the engineers of transitional Senate reform view its historic primary role in the light of the new nomination/appointment process is unknown.

For some time the Senate has been a useful safety valve in providing governments with cabinet ministers from provinces with minimal representation in the government caucus. Will this be feasible in future Senates composed entirely of appointees from provincial government lists? Occasionally an imbalance in regional representation has been rectified by appointing an intended Minister to the Senate from a province weakly represented in the government caucus. If the availability of this practice is to disappear, as seems inevitable, does that mean that the price of a stronger, more provincially oriented Senate is a less representative cabinet?

To say the least, the almost complete absence of written or spoken explanation of what is intended for this reformed Senate in these and other matters is extraordinary. We have government by oracle rather than government by reason, a circumstance likely to induce either an ineffectual flailing or an exasperated silence from constitutional commentators. The outside analyst/critic is disarmed by the denial of material necessary to an effective dialogue with those elected servants who govern us.

An additional aspect of Senate reform is constitutionally anomalous. The political accord states that 'Until the proposed amendment relating to appointments to the Senate comes into force, any person summoned to fill a vacancy in the Senate shall be chosen from among persons whose names have been submitted by the government of the province to which the vacancy relates and must be acceptable to the Queen's Privy Council for Canada.' This is a repudiation of the role of legislatures in the amendment process which is constitutionally required for Senate reform by clauses 38 (1) and 42 (1) of the 1982 Constitution Act. The combination of executive federalism and party discipline may mean that the presumptuous use of the word 'until' will not be belied by future developments. Nevertheless, legislatures and the citizens they represent have been constitutionally humiliated by the implication that the approval of the legislatures of eleven governments can be assumed. Further, this prejudgement leaves open the possible constitutional embarrassment of a situation in which an anticipatory practice has been implemented and the amendment which it anticipates does not pass. In such circumstances, what is the status of the eleven-government agreement in the political accord? Do we revert to the status quo ante? Or do we just carry on with our anticipations, ignoring their repudiation by one or more governments? Does a future federal government try to apply the Meech Lake/Langevin nomination/appointment process for the Senate in a province whose government has 'scuttled' the package of amendments the process anticipates? This premature anticipation of what is described as a transitional practice may add excitement to undergraduate lectures on the Senate, but it is a novel way to change a constitution.

Whose Constitution Is It?

Both the process and substance of the Meech Lake/Langevin constitutional accord reflect the concerns of governments, with the exception, of course, of Yukon and the Northwest Territories, whose absence from the bargaining table led to the placing of more hurdles in the way of their future advance to provincehood. Governments controlled the process. They met in secret conclaves. They consulted their own interests, albeit in the context of the 'Quebec round.' When they emerged they announced as a pact of honour that they would not break ranks, that in the words of the Prime Minister only egregious errors, as defined by the participants, would justify the reopening of the accord. Consequently, the indirect democratization of the amending process implied by the 1982 Constitution Act requirement of legislative approval was to be rendered as nugatory as possible.

In a narrow, technical sense, this effort may succeed; the constitution may be amended along Meech Lake lines. The reconciliation of the government of Quebec may be achieved. Conceivably the amendments will usher in a period of intergovernmental harmony and cooperative policy-making which will make today's critics and doubters hope that their words were not recorded. While I am happy to be classified as one of the doubters, my doubts are less significant than what the process revealed about the contradictions at the centre of our constitutional life.

Alongside the relative aggrandizement of state power at both levels in recent decades, and the concomitant enhanced capacity of governments to shape their societies, an enlarged conception of citizenship has evolved. This new citizenship changes the relation of the Canadian constitution to Canadian society. Even the most obtuse readers of the briefs presented to the Joint Committee must detect the implicit and explicit assumption of groups and interests defined by gender, by ethnicity, by aboriginal background, by social policy concerns, and by basic conceptions of a national community of rights bearers that the Canadian constitution of the late eighties with its Charter of Rights is a citizens' constitution.

Much of the anger which ran through many of these groups' presentations derived from a sense of outrage at the illegitimacy of governments perceived as playing fast and loose with a constitution which they had forgotten was no longer theirs alone. That anger and frustration were also fed by many witnesses' distrust of what they apprehensively viewed as the provincializing tendency of the package. On the whole, these groups which, at the cost of some ambiguity, may be called Charter Canadians, see themselves as citizens of a national community. They tend to be more sympathetic to the national than to provincial governments, at least in English Canada. They view the national government as a more plausible ally and supporter than the provincial governments whose majoritarianism and sporadic populism they somewhat fear. Without always realizing it they are adherents of Frank Scott's dictum that provincial rights are not the same as minority rights.[10]

Their frustrations with the Meech Lake process are additionally fed by their belief that they should be involved in constitutional change. They have their separate histories of triumphs—memories of when biculturalism was replaced by multiculturalism, when they won S. 28, when their aboriginal rights received constitutional recognition, when Métis were brought under the rubric 'aboriginal peoples' in the constitution, and so on. They also have their memories of defeats, exclusions, and failures—usually the removal of some right or recognition they thought they had won, or were on the verge of winning. Such defeats normally occurred when governments met in secret, and on occasion they were subsequently reversed by vigorous public campaigns. In essence, then, to generalize outrageously, these groups—or at least their elites—look back on a history of hard-won gains which gives them a somewhat precarious niche in the constitutional order. They do not hold their constitutional recognition and their rights as self-confident possessions. They are, accordingly, would-be constitutional actors ever fearful that if their participatory 'rights' are ignored their previous constitutional gains may be eroded. In simple terms, they do not trust governments meeting in secret to represent them.

This new variegated constituency is a product of the constitutional process of recent years, which has politicized and constitutionalized a broad range of interests. The intergovernmental competition for constitutional advantage of the last quarter of a century produced competitive mobilizations of the citizenry as governments sought the justifications appropriate to a democratic political culture. The high-water mark of this tendency was the Quebec referendum which sought popular backing for the pursuit of sovereignty-association. The rhetoric of the federal government from the late sixties onwards stressed that the recognition of citizen rights should be the first item on the constitutional agenda, before the division of powers. In the summer of 1980 Ottawa brilliantly contrasted the rights of the people with the selfish pursuit of governmental advantage, and identified itself with the former through its

'People's package,' and its government opponents with the latter. The same federal government also proposed the use of the referendum device for future constitutional amendments when governments could not agree.

Thus the discourse leading up to the 1982 Constitution Act suggested that governments alone did not always have the authority or legitimacy to implement major constitutional changes. In a halting way a variety of cues intimated that citizens might have a real voice in the drama of constitutional change. Some of them were listening.

The constitutional process induced a variety of interests organized around non-territorial cleavages to see the constitution as a potentially useful instrument for their future advantage. The story has been frequently told of how the alliance between various components of the growing civil rights constituency and the federal government strengthened the Charter and gave credibility to Trudeau's threatened unilateralism. The subsequent success of women's and aboriginal groups in gaining the reinstatement of constitutional protections which had been removed at the behest of several provincial premiers appeared to confirm both the necessity and the utility of political pressure in constitutional politics. Later, aboriginal elites were involved in separate constitutional discussions which focussed on self-government.

Cynthia Williams has discussed the rapid diffusion of a popular language of rights in Canada.[11] Other observers have noted the international sources of rights consciousness,[12] which make Charters of Rights increasingly necessary attributes of statehood in the contemporary era. While the expected divergences in the evaluation of the Canadian Charter are beginning to appear, the fact is that the Charter has taken root. For many groups the Charter is the constitution. The Charter has acquired many defenders, who often focus on particular clauses as the source of their rights and as confirmation of their status in the Canadian community. For the groups involved these Charter recognitions are both status enhancing and a promise of future benefits and protection.

An unanticipated consequence of the Charter and the Constitution Act 1982 is that different parts of the constitution seem, psychologically, to belong to different groups, a phenomenon which gives new meaning to the Innisian aphorism 'Divided we stand!' Women's groups identify with the Charter through Section 28; for traditional third force Canadians S. 27 is their lodestar; for visible minorities sections 15 (1) and 15 (2) are valuable constitutional resources; visible minority women appeal to both S. 28 (for gender equality) and S. 15 (for racial equality);[13] for aboriginals it is a combination of S. 25 of the Charter, S. 24 on the division of powers, and sections 35 and 37 (now obsolete) of the Constitution Act. S. 35, by defining aboriginals to include the 'Indian, Inuit and Métis peoples of Canada,' has expanded the aboriginal community, strengthened its constitutional identity, and exacerbated the cleavages within it. Should the Meech Lake Accord become law, aboriginals and multicultural groups will also look to its clause 16 which asserts that the interpretation clause of the proposed constitutional change—with the words 'distinct society'—does not affect sections of the Charter, the Constitution Act, 1982 and the Constitution Act, 1867 which they identify as theirs.

The conjunction of a growing rights consciousness, the linking to the constitution of groups who previously had little or no constitutional recognition, and the symbolic power of the Charter have modified the Canadian constitutional order in ways that will take decades to work out. This change goes beyond the conventional assertion that the Supreme Court has acquired an enhanced role as a national policymaker. An even more profound change is taking place at the citizen base of the constitutional order. Yesterday's deference to governing elites in constitutional matters has been replaced by a resentment when citizens who think of themselves as constitutional actors are defined as spectators by governments.

In the eyes of many of the group elites, for whom this psychological change is most pronounced, and who see their fate as affected by constitutional change, the constitution is no longer an affair of governments. In addition to the governments' constitution, which tends to focus on federalism, there is a citizens' constitution which the Charter symbolizes. A central task for the constitutional theory and practice of future decades is to find ways in which these two visions, warring in the bosom of the Canadian constitution, can be reconciled. The major site for that reconciliation must be the amendment process where, as Meech Lake exemplifies, their incompatibility is most pronounced.

A constitutional reform agenda which theoretically addressed Quebec concerns, but which in fact became a vehicle for strengthening the provincial role in Canadian federalism, was almost bound to alienate or bypass the concerns of the new citizen constitutional activists. For example, the reform of the process of selecting judges for the Supreme Court by giving nominating responsibilities to provincial governments is a response to the concerns of the seventies—which indeed go back to the 1949 abolition of appeals to the Judicial Committee of the Privy Council—about the impartiality of the Supreme Court as an umpire of federalism. Such a reform, however, does not address the issue of a nomination procedure appropriate to the new jurisprudential concerns which the Court faces in the era of the Charter.[14] Indeed, the proposed reform may make its attainment more difficult because of the operational fragmentation of responsibilities which the proposed nominating/ appointing procedures involve, and the unanimity requirement for their amendment.

The 1982 Constitution Act gave initial constitutional recognition to social categories based on gender and ethnicity, and extended the constitutional recognition of aboriginals beyond the limited 1867 division of powers reference in 91(24) to 'Indians, and Lands reserved for the Indians.' The interpretation clause of the proposed constitutional change which defines linguistic duality as 'a fundamental characteristic of Canada,' describes Quebec as a 'distinct society,' and affirms the 'role of the legislature and government of Quebec to preserve and promote the distinct identity of Quebec' was viewed as a threat by the groups advantaged by the earlier 1982 recognition. The inclusion of S. 16 on the road from Meech Lake to Langevin went only partway to calm the concerns of aboriginals and other ethnic leaders. They pointed out that their groups also constituted fundamental characteristics of Canada, that the interpretation clause with its linguistic duality and distinct society applied to the entire constitution, while the multiculturalism clause of the Charter, S. 27, was an interpretive principle for the Charter only. Women's groups who protested the absence of S. 28 of the Charter (the gender equality section) from S. 16 Meech Lake exemptions were not reassured by the assertions that the potency of S. 28 in the Charter— compared to the weakness of the multiculturalism clause (S. 27)—meant that gender equality rights did not require similar protective treatment.

The complexities of the multiple interpretive criteria which the Meech Lake amended constitution will contain, and what hierarchy if any exists among them, have been discussed by Professor Wayne MacKay of Dalhousie University with a dexterity to which a non-lawyer is happy to defer to.[15] For our purposes, the significant issue is the difference between those cleavages which are linked to governments, and which therefore have powerful sponsors, and the others which are more free floating. Not surprisingly, in a constitutional process dominated by governments the social cleavages invested with special governmental salience received priority attention, hence the distinct society and linguistic duality provisions. It may be, however, that the historic dualist characteristics of Canada singled out by Meech Lake are losing ground to cleavages derived from ethnicity and race.

Finally, of course, a basic assumption of federalism that the territorial particularisms which provincial governments reflect and foster are the primary divisions in Canadian society—an assumption which pervades Meech Lake—is challenged by those who represent the new societal cleavages which the 1982 Constitution Act both reflects and fosters.

Conclusion

Meech Lake underlines a basic contradiction at the very heart of the Canadian constitutional system. The constitutional division of powers from which strong interventionist governments have emerged lends continuing credence to the thesis that federalism in Canada is about governments. That thesis is reinforced by the executive supremacy which party discipline and the theory of responsible government sustain. In the intergovernmental arena of constitutional politics the practice of federal-provincial diplomacy, as Meech Lake almost exaggeratedly confirms, is the very perfection of governmental hegemony when unanimity of governments can be achieved in private.

However, while federalism may still be largely about governments, federalism itself has lost relative status in the constitution as an organizing principle. The constitution is now also about women, aboriginals, multicultural groups, equality, affirmative action, the disabled, a variety of rights, and so on. Since it is not possible to separate clearly the concerns of the governments which dominate federalism from the concerns of these newly constitutionalized social categories, it logically follows that the constitution with its many non-federal concerns can no longer be entrusted exclusively to governments in the process of constitutional change. Government domination of the constitutional process has seriously declined in legitimacy. The intergovernmental bargaining process structures outcomes in terms of one set of cleavages; the public hearings process responds in terms of different cleavages. The latter delegitimates the former.

Those who ran the Meech Lake constitutional show falsely assumed that the Meech Lake agenda could be confined to federalism, and thus could be dominated by governments with little opposition. Meech Lake may succeed and the constitution may be changed accordingly. However, the constitutional contradiction laid bare by the Meech Lake process will not go away. In that sense, both parts of this paper are linked—perhaps even a seamless web as the federal government describes the

Accord—because the dispute about constitutional process derives directly from lack of agreement about whose constitution it is anyway. In the circumstances, it is not surprising that the limited constitutional vision of Meech Lake seems to have a higher degree of support from political scientists who study federalism, and who specialize in territorial particularisms, than it receives from other academic disciplines and from group leaders who respond to an emerging agenda of non-federal cleavages.

Notes

1. Canadian Charter of Rights and Freedoms, being Part I of the Constitution Act, 1982 [enacted by the Canada Act 1982 (U.K.), C. 11, S. 1].
2. K.R. Popper, *The Open Society and Its Enemies*, vol. 1 (London: Rutledge, 1945) at 110.
3. Pierre Elliott Trudeau, *Minutes of Proceedings and Evidence of the Senate and of the House of Commons on the 1987 Constitutional Accord* (No. 14), August 27, 1987, p. 137 (hereafter cited as *Special Joint Committee*).
4. Attributed to Premier Pawley by Frances Russell in the *Winnipeg Free Press*, June 9, 1987, as cited in *Submission of the Honourable Donald J. Johnston to the Special Joint Committee on the 1987 Constitutional Accord*, July 22, 1987, mimeo, p. 7.
5. Norman Spector, *Special Joint Committee* (No. 16), Sept. 1, 1987, p. 13.
6. 'No explanation has ever been given to us by the federal government or anybody else as to why this [veto] power was sought.' Tony Penikett, Government Leader and President of the Executive Council, Government of the Yukon, *Special Joint Committee* (No. 15), August 31, 1987, p. 100.
7. See, however, Ramsay Cook, *Special Joint Committee* (No. 5), August 11, 1987, p. 4709.
8. Thomas J. Courchene, 'Meech Lake and Federalism: Accord or Discord?,' August, 1987, mimeo, p. 33; Eugene Forsey, *Debates of the Senate*, June 26, 1987, p. 1443.
9. Province of British Columbia, *British Columbia's Constitutional Proposals, Paper No. 3, Reform of the Canadian Senate* (Victoria, Queen's Printer, 1978).
10. F.R. Scott, 'The Privy Council and Minority Rights' (1930), *Queen's Quarterly* 37, 668.
11. 'The Changing Nature of Citizen Rights,' in Alan Cairns and Cynthia Williams, eds., *Constitutionalism, Citizenship, and Society in Canada*, Macdonald Commission Studies, vol. 33 (Toronto, University of Toronto Press, 1985) at 99.
12. John Boli, 'Human Rights or State Expansion? Cross-National Definitions of Constitutional Rights, 1870–1970,' in George M. Thomas, *et al.*, *Institutional Structure: Constituting State, Society, and the Individual* (Beverly Hills, Sage Publications, 1987).

13. See the evidence of Ms. Akua Benjamin, *Special Joint Committee* (No. 15), August 31, 1987, pp. 155–56.
14. See the presentation of the Canadian Bar Association, *Special Joint Committee* (No. 8), August 18, 1987, pp. 116–17, and of the Canadian Association of Law Teachers, *Special Joint Committee* (No. 15), August 31, 1987, p. 8.
15. *Special Joint Committee* (No. 3), August 5, 1987, esp. pp. 49–51.

RICHARD SIMEON

POLITICAL PRAGMATISM TAKES PRECEDENCE OVER DEMOCRATIC PROCESS *

What I would like to do in my presentation today is to grapple, and I think that is the right word, with some of the criticisms of the accord which have appeared both here and in other forums and, in particular, to address myself to two crucial sets of questions which go to the heart of the legitimacy of the accord.

First, what is the appropriate process for constitutional decision-making? Does the process that we have followed here meet our current standards of democratic legitimacy for constitutional policy-making, or is it so flawed really that the results are unacceptable? Second, what is an appropriate standard for judging the outcome of such a constitutional process? What are the kinds of tests that we should apply to the results of constitutional decisions?

I think I should say at the outset that the critiques of both the process and the substance of the accord are indeed very troubling and powerful ones. As I have read them, more and more I have found my own confidence in both the process and its outcome pretty severely tested. I really have found myself wrestling with these issues very much in the past few months.

Certainly, I suspect very few of us would say that this is the ideal way to go about changing a constitution. All of us can imagine better ways to do it. All of us can probably see in Meech Lake elements that we wish were not there, and all of us probably feel that, left to ourselves, we could devise a more ideal blueprint for Canadian federalism, but one that would secure a very broad agreement is a different question.

My defence of Meech Lake, therefore, is a more pragmatic one. I do not really ask whether it is the best that we could have done but

---

*Brief to the Ontario Select Committee on Constitutional Reform, 1987 Constitutional Accord.

rather, is it an acceptable, workable compromise or not? The question is not, "Is the process ideal?" but "Does it meet our basic standards, and could we imagine in the real world of politics a much better way we could have done it at this time?"

I also do start all my thinking about Meech Lake with the fundamental premise that it really is essential to find some way that is acceptable to Quebec and to the rest of Canada to secure Quebec's voluntary accession to the Canadian constitutional order. Certainly, I see this as the Quebec round; I see that as the great achievement of the accord and that is the characteristic of the accord which we would really not want to lose, although it has to be done, of course, in ways which are sensitive to our other constitutional values.

The pragmatic question becomes, is there another way in which we could have secured this Quebec accession, and is the way we have done it such an affront to other values that it should be rejected anyway?

My own feeling is that the recognition of Quebec as a distinct society we find in the accord—and that, of course, has been the sine qua non for all Quebec governments in modern times—is the very minimum that we could have expected from any conceivable Quebec government, this one or any other. It is really less than any modern Quebec government has sought, so I think to say no to Meech Lake—at least in its general outline, perhaps not in all its specifics—is to say no to Quebec.

Implicitly or explicitly, I think most of the critics of the accord really are telling us that this goal of achieving Quebec's consent really is not very important, or if it is important, it is certainly not as important as some other constitutional objectives. I know many of the critics have said that they do not wish to upset the agreement with Quebec and that they too wish to see Quebec brought in, but I think relatively few of them have shown how those objectives, meeting their concerns and bringing Quebec in, could be reached.

Let me first look at the question of procedure. As we all know, and I am sure it has been said many times around this table, constitutional decisions are not like ordinary decisions. We somehow expect higher standards of them than we do in other kinds of political decisions.

Until 1982, I think it is important to remind ourselves, we had no agreed formula for amending the Constitution of Canada. Indeed, if one worries about the rigidity here, as one perhaps should, we should realize that for a very, very long time we worked on the assumption that any constitutional change affecting essential features of federalism required the unanimous agreement of all 11 governments. That was the assumption we worked on for years and years and years.

In that sense, what we did in 1982 gave us a bit more flexibility, and we should remember that in the past, constitutional agreement did not require any sort of popular or legislative ratification process, it was only a process of executive authority.

So 1982 did give us a constitutional amending procedure, one which required that most amendments could be made with the consent of Ottawa and seven provinces with 50 per cent of the population; it did provide for opting out of amendments which infringed on existing provincial powers, with the very limited right of compensation, which we have now expanded; and it required the unanimous agreement of all governments for a limited but crucial, and again now expanded, set of amendments, including changes to the amending formula itself.

It is certainly worth noting that the formula of 1982 was indeed criticized for being too rigid and too provincial as to formula, but that is the one we got and, of course, what we got in 1982 did add one more democratic element to the amending process, and that is the requirement of ratification by all the legislatures, so it was no longer a purely executive process.

The way we are dealing with Meech Lake is following that amending process of 1982 precisely. In that sense, I suppose, it meets the first test of legitimacy: is it following established procedures? The answer is that yes, it is. So some of the criticisms of the process have to be directed not at the way this process is going particularly, but at what we did in 1982 and the process that we created then. Insofar as the amending process we agreed to in 1982 was consistent with federalist norms, so is the process we are now following.

Nevertheless, a number of very powerful criticisms have been levelled at how we are doing this. First, of course, is the idea that constitutional change should only be undertaken with the fullest possible public debate of the alternatives and issues. It is illegitimate for a group of decision-makers to spring major change on an unprepared population. Of course, the criticism here is that the 11 first ministers met at Meech Lake and then in Langevin and somehow invented or created a brand-new agreement out of whole cloth which was sort of sprung on us.

There are elements in Meech Lake, such as the provisions with respect to provincial unanimity on the creation of new provinces—although that, I believe, was an element of the Victoria charter—which have indeed received relatively little previous attention. But I think in most respects this notion of somehow this all being new and sprung on us is unfounded.

First of all, the elements in Meech Lake have really been the central elements in Canadian constitutional debates since at least the early 1960s, such things as limits on the federal spending power, provincial role in the appointment of judges and senators, opting out of shared-cost programs. All of them have been extensively debated, have been part of formal constitutional proposals both by the provinces and by federal governments in the past. In many cases, even federal governments have suggested they were willing to accept a considerably greater provincialization in these respects than is found in the accord. In that sense, we have had a long tradition of debating this set of issues.

Second, the fundamental elements of the Meech Lake accord were clearly set out by the current Prime Minister in the 1984 election campaign and, indeed, formed a major part of his appeal for national reconciliation. In that sense, he was not springing it on us.

Third, Quebec itself had publicly stated its conditions for constitutional settlement a year before the Meech Lake accord, and we all had a year to think about that list of five conditions. A few months later, the premiers meeting together had pledged to address that agenda in this round of discussions. So again the issues were not sprung on us.

Fourth, both major federal opposition parties had debated the issues around Meech Lake within their own party forums, admittedly not without some internal division and some soul-searching, as we well know. Both the federal opposition parties had endorsed resolutions well before Meech Lake which were generally consistent with the way in which it went.

While there was indeed a secret process of seeking the optimum conditions for reaching agreement which went on before Meech Lake, and while those two meetings were indeed held behind closed doors, the ideas and alternatives being canvassed were pretty well articulated beforehand. I think the instantaneous commentary we got after the draft agreement was published after the first meeting is a good indication of how well prepared, in fact, we all were. I really do not see this in that sense as a constitutional coup d'état, to use one of the phrases which I have heard said about it.

It is also argued that the legislative debate and ratification of the accord are fundamentally flawed in that they are presented to the legislatures as a fait accompli which has to be voted up or down without change. The reason for this is entirely pragmatic. If one government makes changes, then the issue must inevitably be thrown back into the intergovernmental arena, since all governments, in the end, have to approve the identical text. The question is—and it is a serious question, I think, for the future of how we operate executive federalism—how do we get around that difficulty? I think this is probably the most troubling aspect of the procedure. Of what use is parliamentary and legislative debate that cannot produce change?

I think, though, there are a number of answers. I am not going to articulate them with great conviction, but there are a number of responses to that criticism. First of all, legislatures do have power here. They have the power to say no to the whole agreement, which, as I noted, is not a power they had before. This agreement is going to have to survive 11 legislative votes. That is a high set of hurdles for a constitutional change to meet and a very traditional and important expression of democratic politics in this country.

Second, under the Canadian form of responsible party government that we are all so used to, like it or not, what we are doing here is standard practice. Governments using party discipline are normally able to secure passage of legislation which they put before their legislatures, and governments choose which amendments and changes they are going to accept.

Third, there are ways of putting additional items on the constitutional agenda for future discussion. Indeed, the previous discussion with the Native Council of Canada, I think, raised a series of very interesting possibilities there.

I guess as I look at the procedures we are following here, I would say that the procedures for passing the accord do meet the test of consistency with the established constitutional procedures, are consistent with the norms of a federal system and are consistent with representative, parliamentary democracy as we have developed it in Canada. According to these norms, it has received really a very high degree of consent from all parties in Ottawa, from the government and, we will see, from most of the provinces.

On what grounds could it still be argued that this high degree of consent by accepted, legitimate, political authorities still does not meet our current standards of legitimate consent? I think there are two basic arguments here. The first I have already mentioned, that parliamentary passage should come only after the fullest degree of public discussion and consultation on the issues involved. But as I mentioned, there was extensive prior discussion of these issues before the accord was reached. It seems to me there has been a pretty high level and high degree of public discussion in this and the other legislative forums that have been provided since it was passed. Indeed, it is by no means clear to me that this accord will eventually secure the necessary consent.

The second critique of parliamentary government is one, it seems to me, which legislators like yourselves are going to have to grapple with much more in many aspects of politics in this country, and that is the criticism that, in effect, parliamentary government and executive federalism are in some crucial respects not fully representative. The fact that governments at the first ministers' conference must all be elected and re-elected, that they are responsible to their legislatures and to their electorates and so on is held by this group of critics to be an inadequate means of ensuring that all views and all interests are represented and taken into account.

It is in particular believed that minority groups or groups which are systematically underrepresented in legislatures and cabinets, such as women, will in fact, if they are not present, simply be left out and not taken account of at the table. When we have governments and legislatures whose memberships are not a mirror of the population, and governments and legislatures which have their own interests to protect, this criticism is really saying: "We cannot trust those governments, however democratically elected they are, to represent and speak for the people on constitutional matters. To be represented, one must be present." That is a very fundamental challenge, I think. It is not only on this issue that it is being raised.

In the constitutional discussions, the anger of women's groups, especially because of their perceived and I think accurate perception of being betrayed in the November 1981 conference, adds a huge degree of weight to that criticism which has been articulated especially by women. It gives a lot of weight to the complaint of northerners that their future, if it is not determined, is at least influenced by what was done at the accord and that they were not present at the table.

For these critics, the model of democracy that is being argued is that we need, perhaps in general but certainly in the constitutional process, a much more participatory one than we have been accustomed to in Canada, one in which citizens as a whole should have more say in such decisions, perhaps by a referendum, and in which specific provisions should be made to ensure that important groups are directly present in the decision-making process, as the aboriginal peoples were present at those aboriginal discussions.

The critique is not so much that the Meech Lake process violates our existing standards of democratic decision-making, because I do not think it does. The critique is that it violates our newly emerging standards of democratic decision-making, standards which see our present system as really much too elitist.

I am very sympathetic to many of those sets of concerns and I do think they raise some very deep philosophical issues for how we operate our democracy in such a plural and diverse society as ours. I think in this case that it is a very difficult thing simultaneously to bring about such a delicate, difficult constitutional accommodation as the Meech Lake accord and suddenly to say, "We are going to require that the process meet a new and controversial, little understood set of democratic norms."

It seems to me that executive federalism and representative, parliamentary government may be flawed and are flawed in important respects, but it is hard now to imagine how one would create an alternative process which would command broad assent and which could bring together and make the kind of accommodation which is essential here. It seems to me we should not reject the accord on these grounds, but we should in the future seek to respond in as many ways as we can to some of those new concerns. I think that rather than reject the Meech Lake outcome on this ground, we should turn our attention to the process in the future.

Here in fact one or two elements in the accord are promising. The provision for annual first ministers' conferences on the Constitution opens up much greater possibilities for extensive citizen consultation and discussion prior to the conference itself. The more clearly we know the agenda in advance, the more precise and focused those public discussions and the research and deliberations can be, and the more governments can use legislative committees like this prior to the process rather than after it. I certainly hope that this committee will make a number of recommendations as to how Ontario will gear itself up democratically to carry out these constitutional discussions prior to each of the future rounds. That would be a very important thing for this committee to do.

Those are generally my views on the process. Just to conclude more briefly on the substance, I suppose it is true that one's attitudes about process depend entirely on one's attitude about content and vice versa, so my worries about the process might be a lot greater if I were more worried about the substance of the accord. There are many respects in which the conception of federalism and of Canada embodied in the accord does coincide broadly with my own conception. As I have said, I have long thought it essential to provide some recognition of Quebec as a distinct society. It seems to me that is not only a sociological but also a legal reality in this country.

I strongly endorse the spending power provisions in the document, partly because they set up exactly the right dynamic for federalism, as I understand it. That is to say, it legitimizes federal intervention for major national purposes into areas of provincial jurisdiction for the very first time, or gives it constitutional weight for the very first time, and as well establishes the right balance between national objectives and national concerns in provincial variations. I am actually a great fan of section 106A.

I agree very much with a provincial role in appointment of senators and in particular of Supreme Court judges. It seems to me that those bodies, especially the Supreme Court which is sort of the umpire of federalism, should not be a creature of any one of the two orders of government. This may not be the best way of securing both levels' involvement in Supreme Court appointments, but it is, I think, a reasonable one.

As I said, I do not want to go into a point-by-point evaluation of the accord, although I would be glad to do that later if members wished. I would like to end up with a few general observations.

First of all, I do not believe that the accord is a radical transformation in Canadian federalism or Canadian democracy. I do not see it as a huge change. It does not confer on Quebec significant new powers, and certainly not ones which suggest it is a first step down some slippery slope to independence. I do not think it denudes the federal government of its ability to exercise policy and political leadership in this country. It does not set aside the Charter of Rights.

It seems to me that much of the criticism really is of the perceived kind of tilt, and I admit there is a tilt, towards a more provincialist conception. It is based less on the text of the accord than it is on the larger visions people hold. I think much of the criticism overstates the impact of the accord and much of it fails to recognize that many of the elements in the accord such as opting out, for example, have been long-established parts of our political tradition. In that sense, there is very little that is new here.

Much of the criticism seems to overstate the existing authority of the federal government, as if now the federal government had the right to dictate to provinces what they would do in areas of provincial responsibility. It does not under the existing rules, or a province does not need to participate if the federal government sets up one.

The federal government does not deliver shared-cost programs. Provinces deliver shared-cost programs. We have not had a tradition in which the federal government, even where there are shared-cost programs, sets out highly detailed conditions and restrictions on the way in which the federal government spends the money. Our shared-cost programs have always historically, for good political reasons, given all sorts of room for provincial variation in how those programs will be conducted, quite unlike the American system where its grant and aid programs are just absolutely detailed in setting out every aspect of how a joint activity is done.

Much of the criticism is not so much critique of Meech Lake itself, but really is a criticism of the evolution of Canadian federalism since the 1960s, rather than of this document. Certainly, much of the criticism denies that this is a limited Quebec round and seeks to say, "Let us put a whole lot of new and additional items on the agenda which we think are very important."

As I think about the extent to which Meech Lake reinforces tradition rather than opens up new change, I see Meech Lake more as drawing a line under the past. I see Meech Lake almost as the end of an era rather than a reshaping of our future. That is especially true when you read it in conjunction with the 1982 settlement. By giving us an amending formula, and especially by giving us the charter and constitutional recognition of multiculturalism and other newly emerging dynamic elements of Canadian life, 1982 was a great nationalizing document—I think it was tremendously important in that respect—and it did give new prominence and recognition to aspects of Canadian identity and Canadian values other than our federalism side of our life, and that was tremendously important.

But it had this fatal flaw of excluding Quebec and somehow it did not really respond to that large number of proposals which, as I mentioned, had been debated over many years by provinces in the previous rounds of discussion to provide some redefinition of the federal system. What Meech Lake does is not to set aside 1982 but to pick up on those things which were left out and to reaffirm our federal character. Meech Lake is a solution to a set of problems that had dominated our thinking for a very long time and exorcises some pretty deep wounds, it seems to me.

One response to that is to say that in doing this and reaffirming our federalism, Meech Lake is further institutionalizing and entrenching the primacy of regional and linguistic divisions within our political system, is reaffirming our tendency always to be preoccupied with federal-provincial relations, regional conflicts and so on and so forth. They would also argue that in so reinforcing the federal character of the country, we are perhaps blunting the ability of Canadian political institutions to respond to new identities, new concerns and newly mobilized groups in the future.

Here I think there is a parallel between the procedural criticism, which says we need to reorient our democracy in a more participatory way, and these criticisms which really say we need to reorient our political system from its historic concern with federalism to this new concern with gender, multiculturalism and so on, those nonfederal aspects of our politics. I think that is a very important statement.

I think it can be replied, however, to those views that in fact we would not effectively be able to respond to these new agendas so long as that unfinished agenda hung over our heads. Now with Quebec fully in the fold, with the federal spending power clarified and so on, with that set of issues in a sense out of the way, we are more free to respond to these new dimensions than we might have been before. Many aspects of Meech Lake, as mentioned earlier this afternoon—for example, a provincial role in Supreme Court appointments—point to ways in which a lot of new groups can exploit those varied lacunae that the federal system creates.

I think we will learn, as we have learned in the past, that the responsiveness of our system to new issues and new groups historically is not and has not been achieved in Canada by getting rid of federalism, although many people have argued right since the 1930s that federalism is somehow obsolete and we should get rid of it and that a really modern country is a country with class politics, not with regional politics and so on. But it has had this tremendous staying power, so arguments that we should just set federalism aside are wrong. What we should instead realize is that working in and through the institutions of federalism, exploiting the multiple opportunities for participation and so on that it creates, is where we will find responsiveness to these new concerns.

It is also important in a sense to realize, when we look at the responsiveness of our political system to minorities, that the best guarantee of the justice with which we will treat future minorities is how we have treated minorities in the past. In that sense, it seems to me the meeting of our obligation to Quebec should send a positive signal to other minority groups, rather than a negative one.

Finally, I would just like to conclude with a slightly embarrassed defence of the compromise, ambiguity and contradiction we find in this document. The critics are certainly right to point out that Meech Lake leaves much unresolved, that it is shot through with internal tensions and that some crucial terms are left pretty vague. In a sense, it is unsatisfactory to the constitutional purist whose ideal is precision, clarity, a single vision of the country and so on.

It is true that these contradictions and ambiguities mean that it is very difficult to predict the long-run effects of the Meech Lake accord.

I would say that the Meech Lake accord is open enough that the future of federalism is really going to be determined much more by economic and social changes, by things like whether we have free trade and by the mobilization of citizens' groups than it is by what is said in that document.

We have had historically a lot of constitutional flexibility in this country. Despite the slightly increased rigidity in the amending formula, I do not think we have lost that.

I think that all these ambiguities reflect, not poor draftsmanship or late nights, but rather the realities of constitution making in Canada and of the country itself. We find just as many competing visions embedded in the British North America Act itself. You can haul out of that a centralized vision of the country. You can haul out of that a compact theory of federalism. Ditto in 1982. Look at what we did in 1982. We sent all sorts of contradictory messages. We invented a charter with massive numbers of brand new concepts which had never been nor had any experience in Canadian jurisprudence and so on and so forth.

Meech Lake is just in the pattern of Canadian constitutional documents when we point to its internal tensions. That is for good reason. I do not think there is a single blueprint we can all agree on. As individuals and as a country, we are this complex mixture of interests and identities, Ontarians and Canadians, men and women, defenders of individual rights but also preservers of community. We are centralists on one day and decentralists the next. We have learned that the country really cannot survive if one group's model of politics is imposed on the rest.

It seems to me that we must make modest demands on our Constitution. We must see it as being, at any given time, a somewhat awkward balance which is politically acceptable at that time. We must see it therefore as a continuous matter of unfinished business and not require that each episode of constitution-making, like this one we are just going through, address all the possible issues.

I guess my sense is that Meech Lake is not a definitive reorientation, nor do I see it as foreclosing alternatives in the future. I see it as in a sense reaffirming some very traditional aspects of Canadian politics, but still leaving us free for the political process to work as it should and that should be the real source of political change.

CHAPTER FOUR

DECIPHERING THE DISTINCT SOCIETY CLAUSE

*All the attempts to show that the 'distinct society' means very little
ring hollow upon examination. If it really means so little, what is it
doing there at all? Why was Quebec so insistent upon its inclusion?
Why are Mr. Bourassa and Mr. Rémillard trumpeting so vocifer-
ously about all the wonderful new powers it will give them?*

(Eugene Forsey, submission to the New Brunswick Legislative Committee on the 1987 Constitutional Accord, September 26, 1988, 15)

*The distinct society clause adds one more factor to be taken into
account by the courts in interpreting the meaning of the Charter:
that is, far from overriding or limiting the Charter, as do Sections 33
and 1, the Charter would also have to be interpreted in a manner
consistent with the recognition that Quebec constitutes within
Canada a distinct society.*

(Senator Lowell Murray, *The Ottawa Citizen*, September 10, 1987)

Reprinted with permission — *Le Devoir*.

INTRODUCTION

From the perspective of the Quebec government of Robert Bourassa, the very heart of the Meech Lake Accord resides in the recognition of Quebec as a distinct society. This is not a recent preoccupation of Quebec's political and nationalist elites. With the birth of French-Canadian nationalism in the early decades of the nineteenth century, French Canada's leaders have pursued with determination and vigour the "Dream of Nation" in some form and capacity on the North American continent.[1] This longstanding struggle of the French-Canadian nationality for survival and equality has found ideological expression in a wide variety of concepts. These include republican separatism in the 1830s, binationalism during the Union of the Canadas, provincial autonomy after Confederation and bilingualism and biculturalism at the turn of the century. In recent decades more complex notions such as special status, associate-state status, two nations and sovereignty-association have found currency in the political discourse of Québécois intellectuals and politicians. Invariably, all of these ideologies have influenced relations between the anglophone and francophone communities. Each one of these political strategies for achieving survival and equality of the francophone nationality demands that the English-speaking Canadians share to a greater or lesser degree social, cultural, economic and political power with the francophone communities. Power-sharing arrangements of any kind, especially between confident and dynamic communities, are not achieved without a great deal of tension and, at times, hostility.[2]

The contemporary origins of the concept of recognizing Quebec as a distinct society reside in the response of Quebec's nationalists, old and new, to the emergence of the social service state planned and administered by Ottawa's mandarins and politicians following World War II. A 1956 Quebec Royal Commission of Inquiry on Constitutional Problems, better known as the Tremblay Commission, produced a multivolume report that opposed this development on the grounds that it constituted a serious threat to the survival of the French-Canadian nationality of Quebec. To prevent this from occurring, the commissioners recommended two ways of reforming the Canadian Constitution. The first involved granting the province of Quebec special status: exclusive control over all social security and post-secondary education programs, with the necessary taxing powers to implement its own policies in these areas. The second option entailed creating a genuine confederal system by granting all the provinces greater autonomy and taxing powers in areas of social and economic development. Modern Québécois neo-nationalists preferred the special status approach but for vastly different reasons from the traditional nationalists. Neo-nationalists understood the need for a social service state that had the powers and the conviction to intervene in the economy. With constitutional special status they could create a francophone-dominated Quebec state rather than be at the mercy of the anglophone-controlled Canadian state.[3]

Canadians and their political leaders, in and outside Quebec, have been discussing and debating variants of these two constitutional options ever since. The Royal Commission on Bilingualism and Biculturalism, established by Prime Minister Pearson at the request of André Laurendeau of Le Devoir, perceived Canada as composed of two majority societies or communities, according to the introductory pages to Volume 1 of its Report. The English-speaking pluralistic society was governed through Ottawa and nine other provinces, whereas the more homogeneous francophone society functioned as a fully integrated society only in Quebec, where as a majority it had at its disposal all the necessary socio-economic and political institutions for its continued survival and development. Quebec, as French-Canadian nationalists had long proclaimed, was not a province like the others and deserved to be treated differently by the national government. Furthermore, the dual nature of the Canadian political reality that resided in the distinct nature of Quebec needed to be recognized in a reformed constitution. This dualist and regionalist perspective was adopted and propounded by the Task Force on National Unity, known as the Jean-Luc Pepin and John Robarts Commission, in its 1979 report entitled A Future Together.[4]

While this debate was going on, Jean Lesage's Liberal government (1960–66) committed itself to pursuing special status for Quebec through the mechanism of co-operative federalism, which allowed Quebec to opt out of shared-cost programs and create its own pension scheme. Daniel Johnson's Union National envisaged Quebec's constitutional future in terms of a binational associate-state arrangement between Ottawa and Quebec. René Lévesque's Parti Québécois was born of the desire to achieve political independence for Quebec while maintaining an economic association with what remained of Canada. During the early 1970s, Robert Bourassa's Liberal party committed itself to a policy of cultural sovereignty within the context of a financially profitable federal system. Ottawa's politicians and bureaucrats during the Pearson and Trudeau regimes, while finding it increasingly difficult to keep abreast, let alone understand the full implications, of all these various options, looked for practical and effective ways of responding to the real needs underlying Quebec's growing constitutional aspirations. Their basic objective was to retain intact the existing federal system without succumbing to the growing refrain of demands from Quebec nationalists and other provincialists for radical or fundamental changes that would fracture in an irrevocable manner the Canadian nation-state.[5]

For the neo-nationalists, survival and equality for the francophone nationality of Quebec could be achieved only through the creation of a closer identification between it and the state of Quebec. For some, this Québécois nation-state required complete political independence. For others, a significant restructuring of Quebec's constitutional relations with the central government in the Canadian federalism system would be sufficient. Led by Prime Minister Pierre Trudeau, the national government offered its own model of accommodation. This model entailed greater francophone participation in the Cabinet decision-making process, official institutional bilingualism at all levels in the federal bureaucracy, protection of linguistic minorities through a Charter of Rights and Freedoms and appropriate funding for these minorities through a wide range of socio-economic and cultural development programs. In this model, French-speaking Canadians have language and educational rights that extend from coast to coast, and those rights are supported and protected by their national government.

While the 1982 Constitution Act entrenched this model of linguistic dualism and minority rights, the Meech Lake Accord is an attempt to entrench the Québécois binational, territorial model of dualism through an interpretative clause, paragraph 2(1)(b), recognizing Quebec as a distinct society. This is not just a symbolic preamble, as was originally proposed by all three parties and the Quebec government. Rather, first of all, this paragraph is a powerful constitutional interpretative clause that instructs Supreme Court justices to interpret the entire Charter, except sections 25 and 27, in the light of this sociological reality. Secondly, subsection 2(3) stipulates that "the legislature and the Government of Quebec" have the responsibility to "preserve and promote" this distinct identity of Quebec. Finally, the power of the legislature and government of Quebec pertaining to the "rights or privileges relating to language" is reaffirmed by the non-derogatory subsection 2(4).

If past history is any indication, and it most certainly is, Quebec's majority francophone society will certainly insist that the distinct society clause refers exclusively to their culture and their language rather than to the bilingual and multicultural nature of Quebec society. Indeed, the Conseil de la langue française, while critical of the Meech Lake Accord because the distinct society clause was not defined, recommended strongly to the minister responsible for the application of the Charter of the French Language, Bill 101, that the Quebec government act as if it *is* a distinct society. By implementing wide-ranging legislation based on this premise, Quebec would be defining the term de facto, thereby preventing the Supreme Court from defining it in a way that was detrimental to the interests of Quebec's francophone majority. The overall objective of the distinct society clause, concluded the Conseil, should be to immunize Quebec from "l'uniformisation pancanadienne des valeurs placées dans la constitution de 1982."[6]

This line of reasoning reflected the attitude and arguments of Premier Bourassa and his Minister of Canadian Intergovernmental Affairs, Gil Rémillard, both of whom contended on numerous occasions that Quebec had made juridical and socio-political gains with the Meech Lake Accord.[7] If the Accord is ratified by all parties, the Quebec government, according to Rémillard, will have at its disposal a constitutional mechanism in the distinct society interpretative clause to enhance step by step, in many undefined areas of governmental activity, the powers of Quebec. "Ce que nous avons maintenant avec la reconnaissance du Québec comme société distincte," declared Rémillard, "c'est la possibilité d'utiliser cet élément d'interpretation constitutionnelle, . . . pour démontrer que Radio-Québec est un outil essentiel pour le développement culturel du Québec et . . . pour plaider que les caisses populaires sont vraiment de compétences provinciale, [et] . . . de nous exprimer très clairement sur la scène internationale en fonction de notre spécificité."[8] In short, for Rémillard and Bourassa, Quebec will be able to achieve through the Meech Lake Accord what Ottawa and the other provinces had refused to grant the province since the early 1960s—a considerably expanded and enhanced constitutional special status.

Ramsay Cook, an incisive critic of Quebec's constitutional demands since the early 1960s, expresses strong concern over the fact that the Meech Lake Accord quite deliberately does not define what it means by the concept of Quebec as a distinct society. Consequently, he argues, it is impossible to predict what its constitutional implications are going to be for Ottawa/Quebec relations and for the continued predominance of the Charter of Rights and Freedoms. Once the Supreme Court is called upon to define and apply the clause as an interpretative mechanism for the entire Constitution, including the Charter, the outcome will be divisive and destabilizing. If, on the one hand, the Supreme Court accepts a definition proposed by Quebec nationalists, government leaders and bureaucrats, these nationalists will be pleased with the resulting devolution of further powers to Quebec. Canadians who support the need for a viable national government will be angered and frustrated. On the other hand, if the Supreme Court adopts a definition of the distinct society clause that incorporates Quebec's anglophone and ethnic communities, then Quebec's francophone leaders will be incensed, and the fires of separatism will be stoked. To prevent this from happening, Ramsay Cook calls upon the first ministers to define the term "distinct society" and apply it in a very specific and clearly understood manner. Finally, the *entire* Charter, according to Cook, must be protected from any possible erosion at the hands of the interpretative distinct society clause.

A McGill constitutional professor, Stephen Scott, sympathizes with Quebec's desire to achieve through the Meech Lake Accord a "constitutional commitment to the survival of French Canada, within the Canadian Federation." He objects vigorously to the approach, the concept, the form and the language represented by the distinct society clause adopted by the first ministers in the Accord. For Scott, the distinct society clause would have the same effect as a notwithstanding clause, in that it would enable provincial legislation to violate the Charter even when that legislation was not "demonstrably justified in a free and democratic society." In his view, the Accord's attempt to define the fundamental characteristics of Canada is far too limited, niggardly and humiliating for many Canadians. It does not reflect accurately the socio-economic, religious and ethnic diversity of Canada. In its place, Professor Scott proposes an all-encompassing clause that would acknowledge responsibility to the aboriginal peoples, affirm the socio-economic and political well-being of all Canadian citizens and extol official bilingualism. Furthermore, this preamble, while acknowledging the preponderant role of Quebec in the survival and promotion of its French-speaking

majority, would clearly commit the federal and the provincial governments and legislatures to both the survival and promotion of the French-
and English-language minorities throughout Canada.

José Woehrling, a professor of public law at the Université de
Montréal, has been one of the most prolific defenders of the distinct
society clause. Whereas the defence of most Québécois academics has
been categorical and unqualified, that of José Woehrling is nuanced and
highly sophisticated.[9] He contends that both elements of section 1 of
the Accord—the recognition of the linguistic duality of Canada and the
distinct society of Quebec—will have to be considered simultaneously
by the Supreme Court. He begins his analysis with two important interpretations. First, he contends that the term "distinct society" refers specifically to the francophone society of Quebec rather than to a society
that is bilingual and multicultural. Because linguistic duality is defined
as a fundamental characteristic of Canada while the distinct character
of Quebec is not, Woehrling argues that in the event of a conflict between
the two parts of the clause, the Supreme Court would grant the former
priority over the latter. "La protection et la promotion du fait francophone," he concludes, "ne peuvent remettre en cause la protection de
la minorité anglophone du Québec."[10]

His analysis of the relationship between the Charter and the Accord
brings Woehrling to the conclusion that the Accord will have the effect
of limiting the centralizing and uniformizing potential of the Charter.
The linguistic duality and distinct society interpretative clause of the
Accord will be applied by the courts in defining the terms "reasonable
limits" and "demonstrably justified in a free and democratic society"
in section 1 of the Charter. Conversely, these interpretative sections will
have to meet the social objective and proportionality "tests" administered by the courts in the application of section 1 of the Charter. Used
in this manner, the courts could apply the distinct society clause to justify
a "regionalization" of the Charter in its application to Quebec. This
"regionalization," in Woehrling's view, confirms the decentralizing and
diversifying nature of federalism that is at the heart of the Canadian
Constitution. Woehrling also reminds us that the debate on the distinct
society clause is academic given the existence of section 33, the notwithstanding clause, of the Charter.

On the basis of this interpretation of the Accord, Professor
Woehrling assesses the juridical rather than the political–constitutional
validity of the criticism advanced by various opposition groups. With
regard to the concerns of the francophone minorities, Woehrling believes
that the courts, once the Accord became law, would be forced to give

a much broader interpretation to all of their existing constitutional rights. He does agree with the criticism that the Accord does not allow the francophone minorities to demand new rights from Ottawa and the provinces. This was not the intention of the ''Quebec Round,'' and the failure of the Accord would only weaken the position of the francophone minorities. He then dismisses the concerns of Quebec's anglophone community with the argument that the Supreme Court, following the trend of *all* the cases pertaining to Bill 101, will give priority to the linguistic duality part of the clause over the distinct society part.

Canada's ethnic minorities and aboriginal peoples, according to Woehrling, do not have to be concerned about any juridical fallout, because section 16 of the Accord prevents the application of the distinct society clause to sections 25 and 27 of the Charter and section 35 of the Constitution Act, 1982. Woehrling concedes that the Accord has an important political impact by diminishing the recently acquired ''symbolic'' constitutional status of the ethnic minorities and the aboriginal peoples. It does so by defining the anglophone/francophone duality as ''a fundamental characteristic of Canada,'' while failing to incorporate the longstanding historical presence of cultural pluralism and aboriginality in Canadian society.

Finally, Woehrling addresses the two basic concerns of the women's organizations, namely that the Accord in conjunction with section 1 of the Charter could justify limits on sexual equality rights and, in a more general way, the fear that women's rights will be harmed whenever individual rights are subordinated to collective rights. First, he is willing to concede that if Quebec's distinct society is defined in such a way as to incorporate an unacceptable traditional status for women, then the Accord definitely would undermine the ongoing struggle for sexual equality. Secondly, because the Accord accentuates the recognition of the collective rights of minorities already in the Constitution and the Charter, it will allow the courts to restrict individual rights and hence the equality rights of women as individuals. This problem, while very real, should not be resolved, in Woehrling's view, by reopening the Accord. Instead, he proposes the creation of a parallel accord protecting section 28 of the Charter, to be adopted via the existing amending formula of seven provinces with fifty per cent of the population.

Notes

1. Susan Mann Trofimenkoff, *The Dream of Nation: A Social and Intellectual History of Quebec* (Toronto: Gage, 1983).
2. Michael D. Behiels, "Francophone/Anglophone Relations, 1760–1987," in *The Canadian Encyclopedia* (Second edition, Edmonton: Hurtig Publishers, 1988).
3. Michael D. Behiels, *Prelude to Quebec's Quiet Revolution* (Montreal/Kingston: McGill–Queen's University Press, 1985): 185–291.
4. Canada, Royal Commission on Bilingualism and Biculturalism, *Report*, Book 1. *General Introduction: The Official Languages* (Ottawa: Queen's Printer, 1967); Task Force on National Unity, *A Future Together* (Ottawa: Supply and Services Canada, 1979).
5. Cf. Ramsay Cook, *The Maple Leaf Forever* (Toronto: Macmillan, 1971); Kenneth McRoberts, *Quebec. Social Change and Political Crisis* (Third Edition, Toronto: McClelland and Stewart, 1988).
6. Conseil de la langue française, *Les compétences linguistiques du Québec après l'Accord du lac Meech*, Avis au Ministre responsable de l'application de la Charte de la langue française (Québec, 1988): 72–80, quote 90.
7. "Bourassa est convaincu d'avoir réalisé des gains énormes," *La Presse*, 2 mai 1987; Bernard Descoteaux, "Le français est protégé de façon absolu," *Le Devoir*, 4 juin 1987; Robert Bourassa and Gil Rémillard, *Journal des débats*, Assemblée Nationale du Québec, 12 mai, 18, 19 juin 1987.
8. Gil Rémillard, *Journal des débats*, 19 juin 1987, Vol. 29, No. 128, 874–875.
9. Guy Laforest, "The Meaning and Centrality of Recognition," in Roger Gibbins et al., eds., *Meech Lake and Canada. Perspectives from the West* (Edmonton: Academic Printing and Publishing, 1988): 73–89; André Morel, "La reconnaissance du Québec comme société distincte dans le respect de la Charte," in Réal-A. Forest, ed., *L'adhésion du Québec à l'Accord du Lac Meech—Points de vue juridiques et politiques* (Montréal: Les Éditions Thémis, 1988): 55–63; Nicole Duplé, "L'Accord du Lac Meech: les inquiétudes féministes sont-elles fondées?" in *ibid.*, 65–77.
10. Professor Woehrling provided one of these two legal analyses for the Conseil, and his interpretation no doubt influenced the Conseil's advice to the Minister. Cf. note 6 and Jean-Pierre Proulx, "Deux avis juridiques au Conseil de la langue française," *Le Devoir*, 26 août 1988.

RAMSAY COOK

ALICE IN MEACHLAND *OR*

THE CONCEPT OF QUEBEC AS

"A DISTINCT SOCIETY" *†

> If the recognition of Quebec as a distinct society turns
> out not to mean anything, Quebeckers will realize it and
> begin fighting again.
>
> Claude Morin, *The Globe and Mail*,
> 3 November 1987

No discussion of constitutional matters in Canada should take place
without ready access to a copy of Lewis Carroll's standard reference
work, *Through the Looking Glass and What Alice Found There*. Certainly
that is true of the 1987 Constitutional Accord and especially of Section 2,
which refers to "a fundamental characteristic of Canada" and describes
Quebec as "a distinct society." A moment's thought about those seemingly innocent phrases should remind us of Alice's first discussion with
Humpty Dumpty.

> "Don't stand there chattering to yourself like that," Humpty Dumpty
> said, looking at her for the first time, "but tell me your name and your
> business."
>
> "My name is Alice, but—"
>
> "It's a stupid name enough!" Humpty Dumpty interrupted impa-
> tiently. "What does it mean?"

---

* First published in *Queen's Quarterly* and subsequently in Clive Thomson, ed., *Navigating
Meech Lake: The 1987 Constitutional Accord* (Kingston: Institute of Intergovernmental
Relations, 1988).
†Meachland, like Wonderland, is a purely imaginary place. Meech Lake, on the other
hand, is not a place at all, Erewhon. Meach Lake is, of course, well known to residents
of the Outaouais and careful readers of Quebec maps.

> "*Must* a name mean something?" Alice asked doubtfully.
>
> "Of course it must," Humpty Dumpty said, with a short laugh: "*my* name means the shape I am—and a good handsome shape it is, too. With a name like yours, you might be any shape, almost."

The difficulty with the terms "fundamental characteristic" and "distinct society," as they are used in the 1987 Constitutional Accord, is that they describe something that rather than being "a good handsome shape . . . might be any shape, almost." Like Humpty Dumpty I think that names should have understood meanings. In Section 2 of the Accord they do not.

Historically, at least since the early nineteenth century, francophones in British North America/Canada developed a consciousness of their distinctiveness both individually and collectively. The most obvious badge of that distinctiveness was language while the civil code provided a legal foundation for difference. And, at least until recent decades, Catholicism and the church were linked to that identity. Also, it was long insisted by many nationalists—even when the facts contradicted them—that French-Canadians were naturally an agricultural people (Brunet 133–66; Trudeau 3–91). Finally, and most important, French-Canadian distinctiveness was founded upon an interpretation of the past that made the collectivity unique: the struggle for survival in North America made the "petit peuple" North American, but not Anglo-Saxon, French-speaking, but not French. From that sense of uniqueness grew a sense of mission that assigned French-Canadians the task of continuing that quest for survival and fulfillment as a distinct "race," "people," or "nation" (Cook, *Maple Leaf* 96–122).

Until the 1960s that "people" or "nation" usually included francophones wherever they lived in Canada and even, sometimes, included those who had emigrated to the United States. Moreover, whatever term was used to describe the collectivity—"race," "nation," "people"—it was intended to describe a cultural and sociological entity rather than a political or constitutional one—except perhaps in the case of those who followed Louis-Joseph Papineau (Morissoneau). Of course, within that cultural and sociological definition, those francophones who lived in the St. Lawrence Valley, "the homeland," were central. After 1867, when the province of Quebec was created, that territorial definition was strengthened since it was the one province with a francophone majority. Even so, that distinctiveness was called French-Canadian, more than Québécois. (This confusion of French-Canadian and Québécois often irritated members of the Diaspora, Acadians and Franco-Manitobans, who insisted that their way of being French-Canadian was as valid as that of the Québécois.)

In the period stretching roughly from the Second World War to 1960, as part of the so-called Quiet Revolution, the concept of distinctiveness changed as did the focus of that distinctiveness. Once the obvious facts of industrialization and urbanization were accepted, the "myth" of "ruralism" was rejected. As the outlook and ambitions of francophones grew more secular, the centrality of the church and religion in the definition of distinctiveness was questioned. In some ways French-Canadians seemed to be becoming less "distinctive." Soon it came to be recognized that the dangers and challenges of industrial society made the state a necessary instrument not only of modernization but also as a means of preserving and promoting cultural and sociological distinctiveness (Behiels). And that, in turn, further reinforced the territorial definition of francophone distinctiveness. Without entirely losing sight of the Diaspora, Quebec French-Canadians were becoming Québécois. This term, of course, was not entirely satisfactory since about 20 percent of Québécois were non-francophones and thus not members of what had traditionally been thought of as the "distinct" "people" or "nation." That remains a somewhat confused issue. But what does seem clear is that the contemporary sense of distinctiveness retains from the past an emphasis on language, a sense of a common history (though there is less agreement about its meaning than there once was), and a conviction that Quebec, both geographically and constitutionally, is the focus of that distinctiveness (Cook, *Canada, Quebec* 68–86). But it should also be added that language in the new context means something more than an instrument of a culture in a literary or philosophical sense. In the debate over Bill 101 the issue was clearly power and social mobility, though the matter of culture, purity of language and other traditional preoccupations was not wholly absent. Professor Fernand Dumont summed up the new situation aptly when he observed that "Le langage n'est pas que poésie. Il est aussi le pouvoir" (*Québec et le lac Meech* 137).

The idea that the distinctiveness of Quebec should be recognized constitutionally is far from new. Indeed the very act of creating that province in 1867 was, implicitly, a recognition of distinctiveness. But the British North America Act also included several explicit recognitions of that fact. For example, Section 94 recognized the civil law of Quebec as distinct and, if the intent expressed in that provision had been fulfilled ("uniformity of all and any laws relative to Property and Civil Rights" in all provinces except Quebec), Quebec would have had a "special status" in that area. In addition the special character of Quebec was recognized in Section 133 which not only made French, for the first time, an official language of Canada, but also made Quebec, alone among the original provinces, bilingual. In this, and in some other ways, Quebec has never been a province exactly like the others, for its historic characteristics made some constitutional variations desirable.

It was not until the 1950s, perhaps because some Quebeckers had begun to realize that Quebec's traditional distinctiveness was disappearing under the impact of urban and industrial growth, that arguments began to be devised to justify demands for a wider recognition of Quebec's power to defend its distinctiveness. These arguments were given systematic form in the *Rapport de la Commission royale d'enquête sur les problèmes constitutionnels* (1956), commonly known as the Tremblay Commission. Though that Commission's definition of Quebec's distinctiveness was remarkably traditional—a French-speaking Roman Catholic society, spiritual rather than material in its values and goals—it made a powerful argument for provincial autonomy in areas into which the new federal welfare state was moving, and insisted that Quebec was not a province like the others.

During the 1960s a new political and bureaucratic elite transformed the familiar process of constructing a provincial welfare state into an exercise in nation-building. A new nationalist ideology both legitimized that process and redefined the concept of "distinctiveness" into a Quebec-centred, secular doctrine (Smith ch. 6). Like French-Canadian nationalists in the past, the neo-nationalists of the 1960s were both moderate and persistent. Only a small fringe group demanded outright independence and linguistic uniformity in the manner of nineteenth-century nationalists in Europe and post-1945 nationalists in the colonial world. Instead their demands were for a recognition of the priority of the French language in Quebec, and the recognition of Quebec as a "province pas comme les autres," with, according to the intensity of the theorist's nationalism, a "different status," a "particular status," a "special status," "associate states," or "sovereignty" accompanied by "association." For various reasons—lack of definition, unworkability, federal opposition, lack of popular support, among others—none of these proposed constitutional methods of recognizing Quebec's distinctiveness was realized (Cook, *French Canadian Question* 62–78). But the thrust behind the demand, and the rhetoric supporting it, never totally dissipated even though the "mood" of Quebec altered radically leaving the nationalist movement, at least temporarily, in disarray and even exhaustion (Clift; Bouchard).

Perhaps a rough measure of that new "mood" is the new phrase that has been adopted in the latest attempt to capture Quebec's special character. That, of course, is "distinct society" or, alternatively, "distinct identity," phrases which seem to avoid the implication of "national" or "quasi-national" status. And that, at long last, brings us to the 1987 Constitutional Accord which enshrines these phrases. The point of this introduction has merely been to demonstrate that the idea of French-Canadian/Quebec distinctiveness is not new either historically or in terms of constitutional practice. It is a reality. Therefore to criticize the concept of a "distinct society" as it appears in the Accord is not to reject the fact of that distinctiveness. It is to criticize the Accord for its inadequate reflection of the reality.

Though the term "distinct society" has a familiar ring it assumed a central place in constitutional discussions only after the Quebec Referendum of May 1980 and especially after the proclamation, without Quebec's formal adherence, of the Constitution of 1982. The Quebec provincial Liberal party, in its 1985 programme, set out as one of its conditions for accepting the new constitution "l'inscription, *dans un préambule de la nouvelle constitution*, d'un énoncé reconnaissant explicitement le Québec comme foyer d'une société distincte et pierre d'assise de l'élément francophone de la dualité canadienne" (*Québec et le lac Meech* 53). Other conditions, designed to give meaning to that concept, included a veto on constitutional amendments, limitations on the federal spending power, constitutional recognition of the Cullen–Couture agreement on immigration, and the right of the Quebec government to participate in the nomination of Supreme Court justices from that province.

In his now often cited, but perhaps less frequently read, speech at Mont-Gabriel 9 May 1986, Gil Rémillard, as a minister in the Bourassa government, repeated these conditions, stating that the recognition of Quebec as a "distinct society" should include increased powers in immigration, limitations on the spending power, a veto on constitutional amendments, and the right to "participer au processus de sélection et de nomination de ses juges." This latter condition was especially important, he argued, because the court's rulings touched values "qui font partie essentiellement de la spécificité québécoise comme le droit civil et, sous certains aspects, les droits et libertés fondamentales."

In that speech the Quebec minister made two additional points of importance in light of the subsequent Meech Lake agreement. The first concerned the new Quebec government's view of the Canadian Charter of Rights. After four years of interpretation, he said, the Charter was "un document dont nous pouvons être fiers commes Québécois et Canadiens.'' Consequently the new government would no longer use the *non obstante* clause in relation to articles 2 and 7 to 15. ''Nous voulons que les Québécois soient aussi bien protégés quant à leurs droits fondamenteaux que les autres Canadiens.''

Second, though not listing it as one of his specific conditions, Rémillard expressed a profound concern about the inadequate protection provided for francophone groups *hors* Quebec, especially in the matter of control over schools and the issue of ''sufficient numbers'' required to warrant minority language schools. These matters, he thought, would be part of a new constitutional package (*Québec et le lac Meech* 54–60). These then were the general propositions advanced by the Liberal government of Quebec as a negotiating position in the discussions leading up to the signing of the Meech Lake–Langevin Block Accord.

Before turning to an examination of Clause 2 of that Accord, the one dealing with Quebec as a ''distinct society,'' two observations seem in order. The first is that the description of Quebec as a ''distinct society'' is not part of the preamble, as the Liberal government had demanded, but is rather a substantive interpretive clause covering the constitution and the Charter. Second, all those areas which the Minister outlined at Mont-Gabriel are dealt with separately, meeting Quebec's conditions almost to the letter: a Quebec veto (though now given all provinces) on an extended list of constitutional changes (including Senate reform and the admission of new provinces), guarantees respecting Quebec's role in the appointment of Supreme Court justices (again other provinces receive similar rights), and a limitation on the spending power. Whatever one may think of these provisions they certainly seem congruent with those conditions set out by the Quebec government. To that, however, the Accord adds the interpretive clause, leaving the concept of ''a distinct society'' undefined. Thus the task of giving meaning to that sociological and psychological phrase will be left to the courts. It is not, as is normal, interpreting the application of a defined constitutional term but the definition of the term itself that our elected representatives have turned over to the judiciary. Moreover, it is not just the definition of *any* term that is given the courts. It is the definition of what has always been a primordial aspect of Canadian history and constitutional concern: the relations between French- and English-speaking Canadians and the place of Quebec in the Canadian constitution. What are the problems that are raised by this decision?

Any careful reading of s. 2 of the Accord will demonstrate that it is shot through with contradiction, confusion, and ambiguity. Section 2(a) recognizes ''the existence of French-speaking Canadians, centred in Quebec but also present elsewhere in Canada.'' That, presumably, refers to an ethnic group whose mother tongue is French and whose roots extend back to the beginning of the European part of our history. In addition, s. 2(a) recognizes ''English-speaking Canadians, concentrated outside Quebec but also present in Quebec.'' That, presumably, *does not* refer to an ethnic group but rather to the fact that English is the *lingua franca* of those of many mother tongues other than French. To put this another way, French is both a defining characteristic of an ethnic group and one of Canada's two official languages; English is simply one of the two official languages. These two entities are not, therefore, equivalents though the Accord leaves the unwary with the impression that they are.

Or are they equivalents? Here we come to the question of defining the term ''a distinct society.'' To what does this phrase refer? Is it to ''Quebec'' or to ''the French-speaking Canadians centred in Quebec?'' Those, of course, are not the same. Many francophone Quebeckers, especially among those who have joined the debate over the Accord, believe, or hope, that the term ''a distinct society'' refers to the francophone majority. English-speaking Quebeckers, naturally, fear and reject that conclusion and hope that ''a distinct society'' refers to a bilingual, multi-cultural society. Gil Rémillard, the Quebec Minister of Intergovernmental Affairs, appears to accept the first interpretation; those who speak for Alliance Québec defend the latter.[1]

In the debate in the Quebec National Assembly in June 1987, Premier Robert Bourassa offered what is presumably the official view of his government in this matter. He stated: ''The French language is a fundamental characteristic of our uniqueness, but there are other aspects, such as our culture and our institutions, whether political, economic or judicial.'' These were not defined, he said, because definition ''would confine and hamper the National Assembly in promoting this uniqueness.'' Then, he added—and I italicize:

It must be noted that Quebec's distinct identity will be protected and promoted by the National Assembly and government, and its duality preserved by our legislators. It cannot be stressed too strongly that the entire constitution, including the Charter, will be interpreted and applied in the light of the section proclaiming our distinctiveness as a society. As a result, in the exercise of our legislative jurisdictions we will be able to consolidate what has already been achieved, and gain new ground.

Finally, after a reference to the safeguard clause confirming existing powers over language, he added ''[W]e have for the first time in 120 years of federalism managed to provide constitutional underpinnings for the preservation and promotion of the *French character of Quebec*.''[2]

Here, then, is a crystal clear statement of the view that ''distinct society'' and ''French character'' are interchangeable concepts. But elsewhere only confusion reigns.

Senator Lowell Murray, one of the architects of the Accord, nicely—I refrain from saying intentionally—expressed this confusion when he explained the lack of definition:

> We decided not to define Quebec's distinct society more clearly. If, in the 1930's, anyone had tried to define Quebec's specificity, it might have been said that Quebec was Catholic and French-speaking. I don't think today's politicians would use these kinds of terms to define Quebec's specificity.

Here the reference is exclusively to the francophone majority.

But the learned Senator then continued:

> We all know that we can quickly draw up a list of those characteristics that describe Quebec. There is the obvious fact that Quebec is the only province to have a French-speaking majority and an English-speaking minority. There is also the fact that it uses the civil code and that it evolved under a different Crown for 150 years before the 1763 Royal Proclamation. There are also the cultural and social institutions. As you can see it would be easy to draw up a list, but that list might unduly limit the concept itself (Joint Committee 41).

Now there are two interesting aspects to this part of the statement. The first is that the ''distinct society'' now includes both French- and English-speaking people. Second, and equally revealing, is the fact that Senator Murray's list contains *nothing* that is not already guaranteed in the 1867 version of our constitution: the civil code, control over education presumably being the ''social and cultural institutions'' referred to, and official bilingualism which is what seems to follow from his description of the population's ethnicity. Does that mean that the concept of ''a distinct society'' is merely a description of the *status quo* as established in 1867? That would surely surprise many Quebeckers.

Another witness before the Joint Committee, Yves Fortier, appeared to agree with Senator Murray's second definition, but to go a step further. "Quebec society within Canada is not defined solely by the characteristics of the Francophone majority, and clause 2 states this specifically," Fortier contended. "Quebec's distinctive society is composed of English-speaking Canadians, native people, and people from ethnic groups" (Joint Committee 33). Now I find no reference to "native people" and "ethnic groups" in s. 2. It may be that s. 16, the so-called non-derogatory clause, adds these groups to Quebec's distinctive identity. If so, are the Quebec government and legislature responsible for the preservation and promotion of French, English, aboriginal, and multicultural rights? Again I think that might be an unwelcome surprise to some Quebeckers. "Preservation," maybe. But anyone familiar with the last 20 years of debate over language and culture in Quebec could be forgiven any amount of skepticism about "promotion."

Nor does the Report of the Joint Committee add any light to this obscurity; indeed on this, as on much else, it only obfuscates the matter further. When Zebedee Nungak, of the Inuit Committee on National Issues, himself a Quebecker, expressed the fear that his people might be "out-distincted by a distinct Quebec," the Committee's majority replied that: "The members of the Joint Committee have no doubt that other communities within Canada might also be defined as 'distinct societies' and the fact that they are not referred to in Section 2 does not mean that these other characteristics or other cultural groups have been rejected or given second class status" (Joint Committee 40).

Whether Nungak was satisfied with the Joint Committee's evident reluctance to choose, he may have thought of an Inuit version of Gilbert and Sullivan's insistence that where everybody is "distinct," nobody is "distinct." Or perhaps he was moved to turn to Alice:

"When *I* use a word," Humpty Dumpty said in rather a scornful tone, "it means just what I chose it to mean—neither more nor less."

"The question is," said Alice, "whether you *can* make words mean so many different things."

"The question is," said Humpty Dumpty, "which is to be master—that's all."

As so often, Humpty Dumpty was right. Section 2 is not merely a description of some supposed sociological construct. It is an interpretive clause concerned with the allocation of power. And that is where the issue of who is "master" must be confronted. Let me illustrate.

The "Legislature and Government of Quebec" are given the "role . . . to preserve and promote the distinct identity of Quebec . . . ." It obviously matters very much, in language policy, for example, which of Senator Murray's "distinct societies" is referred to—"French-speaking Canadians centred in Quebec," or a bilingual Quebec? The history of Quebec since 1968 suggests that it cannot be both. Who will be master?

The "Parliament of Canada and the provincial legislatures" have the "role . . . to preserve the fundamental characteristic of Canada . . ." and, apparently, the existing geographical distribution of that characteristic. Does that, for example, mean preservation of a situation in Alberta where it is, evidently, unacceptable to ask a question in French in the provincial legislature? Distinction seems to come in varying fundamental hues. And does preservation include policies devised by the federal government and applicable to the inhabitants of the distinct society of Quebec? When the Canada Council and the SSHRCC make grants to Quebeckers to study the French language in that province, compose Quebec music and poetry, is that merely preserving or is it promoting? The same question might be raised about the CBC/Radio Canada and the NFB/ONF. Under the "distinct society" clause a future Quebec government will be able to challenge federal "promotion" of francophone culture—and perhaps even anglophone or allophone culture—in Quebec on the ground that Quebec, not Ottawa, has the role of "promoting that society's "distinct identity." It is even possible that "reasonable compensation" may be demanded by Quebec when it opts out of federal programmes in this area (*Québec et le lac Meech* 70).[3]

Yet it is surely absurd that, given the proposition that the existence of French- and English-speaking Canadians represents "a fundamental characteristic of Canada," that the federal government and parliament should not have an explicitly recognized "role" to "promote" as well as "preserve" that characteristic. The term "preserve" conjures up the image of an endangered species. Under the new Accord that is surely the potential fate of linguistic minorities unless "governments" as well as "legislatures" are mandated to "promote" as well as "preserve" their languages.

The second area of concern turns on the relationship between the "distinct society" (and "fundamental characteristic") interpretive clause and the Canadian Charter of Rights and Freedoms. Section 16 of the Accord, in exempting s. 25 and 27 of the Charter, s. 35 of the 1982 Constitution Act and clause 24 of s. 19 of the British North America Act from interpretation "in a manner consistent with" clause 2, obviously leaves the rest of the Charter subject to clause 2. That means, at least potentially, that those rights and freedoms, which are the foundation of Canadian citizenship, may vary from one part of Canada to another if, in some way, "preserving" our "fundamental characteristic" or "preserving and promoting" Quebec's distinct identity appears to require it. Attention has frequently, and rightly, been drawn to the impact that this interpretive requirement may have on the "sexual equality" provisions. But that concern should not be allowed to disguise the possibility that "Fundamental Freedoms," "Democratic Rights," "Legal Rights," and "Language and Educational Rights" also fall under this rule of interpretation.

This potential problem is troubling for at least two reasons. First, the Accord's architects, especially Senator Lowell Murray, have on the one hand claimed that rights such as "sexual equality rights" are not subject to this rule of interpretation. ("[I]ls ne cèdent le pas à aucune disposition d'interprétation.") But at the same time Senator Murray has insisted that the Charter cannot be exempt from the interpretive clause because that "viderait virtuellement de tout son sens la disposition ce société distincte" (Murray). Are both arguments possible? Surely not.

Second, if we return to Rémillard's moderate set of conditions we note that he not only indicated the Quebec government's willingness to accept the full application of the Charter, "un document dont nous pouvons être fiers comme Québécois et Canadiens," but he never once suggested that the concept of "distinct society" should be applied to its interpretation, since his party's platform had asked only that the phrase be included in the constitution's preamble. The shift in positions at Meech Lake has never been explained.

To the extent that the interpretive clause (s. 2) could potentially vary the character of Canadian citizenship rights, it is unacceptable. Mr. Justice Lucien Cannon's judgment in the Alberta Press case (1937) remains as convincing now as it was 40 years ago. He stated:

> Every inhabitant of Alberta is a citizen of the Dominion. The province may deal with the property and civil rights of a local and private nature within the province, but the province cannot interfere with his status as a Canadian citizen and his fundamental right to express freely his untrammelled opinion about government policies and discussion of matters of public concern (8 SCR at 123).

It is, of course, easier to identify the problems created by the lack of definition in the "distinct society" clause than it is to arrive at a formula that would both clarify the clause and win the consent necessary for the Accord's approval. The Accord's supporters have concluded that the only acceptable solution is to leave the matter to the courts. That seems nothing less than an abdication of responsibility. Terms like "fundamental characteristic," "distinct society" and "distinct identity" are not legal terms, but rather sociological and psychological. They are, presumably, statements about the shape and values of a community. Those statements require definition by the elected representatives of a democratic society. As Professor Léon Dion has written: "Plutôt que de laisser aux tribunaux le soin de décider à toutes les instances juridiques à partir de cas particuliers, demandons plutôt à nos législateurs d'avoir le courage de définir les objectifs de cette société devant le Québec et le Canada entiers" (Québec et le lac Meech 95). To do less than that almost certainly assures continuing controversy over precisely the issue which the Meech Lake Accord claims to settle, namely, the status of Quebec and of the francophone community within Canada.

But what alternatives exist? One possible approach would be to amend Section 16 to exempt the whole of the Charter from the vague conditions described in Section 2. Having done so, a more specific constitutional provision dealing with Quebec's powers in the language field should be devised increasing the province's control in that sensitive area. Such a clause would fulfill Rémillard's Mont-Gabriel goal: "Nous voulons assurer aux Anglophones du Québec les droits linguistiques auxquels ils ont droits. Ces droits doivent se situer évidemment dans le contexte du caractère francophone de la société québécoise et du ferme désir du gouvernement d'en assurer le plein épanouissement" (Québec et le lac Meech 60).[4]

The adoption of this strategy would remove some of the objections to the Accord that have been heard both in Quebec and elsewhere for it would clarify some of the ambiguity of the "distinct society" clause. And by increasing Quebec's power over language policy it would go a step beyond the original conditions set by the current Quebec government.

In conclusion I would simply reiterate my essential concern. As it stands in the Constitutional Accord of 1987 the "distinct society" clause may mean much or nothing. If it means much, we need to know how much. If it means nothing, we should think again. Otherwise Professor Daniel Latouche may be right that "dans 50 ans, la seule chose qui distinguerait le Québec serait une clause affirmant sa différence" (Québec et le lac Meech 123). Or to return to Alice, we might recall Humpty Dumpty's complaint that he would not recognize Alice at a future meeting since her face was just like everyone else's. He continued,

"Now if you had two eyes on the same side of the nose, for instance, or the mouth at the top—that would be *some* help."

"It wouldn't look nice," Alice objected. But Humpty Dumpty only shut his eyes and said "Wait till you've tried."

Once defined the "distinct society" may not "look nice," but it will be recognizable. And that, in my view, would make the constitution understandable without the aid of a Looking Glass.

Notes

1. The conflicting views are outlined in Dumont, *Le Québec et le lac Meech.*
2. See *Canadian Parliamentary Review*, 10 (1987) for an unofficial translation of this speech.
3. Writing in reference to this matter Professor Robert Décary of the University of Montreal: "Ainsi, la dualité sera-t-il l'affaire des parlements fédéral et provinciaux, tandis que le caractère distinct du Québec sera-t-il l'affaire de seul Québec, s'exprimant par son Assemblée nationale *et par son gouvernement?* . . . le Québec devient le seul maître d'oeuvre de la protection et de la promotion de son caractère distinct. Ensuite, *le gouvernement* du Québec se voit reconnaître un statut constitutionnel relativement à cette protection et à cette promotion, ce qui pourra signifier, notamment, le droit de participer en tant que gouvernement à de nombreuses activités internationales."
4. The position taken by the Lévesque government in 1985, while more restrictive than the Anglophone community in Quebec would find easily acceptable, represents a realistic basis on which to begin serious discussions about allowing Quebec the same power in language matters as is enjoyed by the other provinces. See *Projet 20.*

Works Cited

Behiels, Michael. *Prelude to Quebec's Quiet Revolution.* Montreal: McGill–Queen's University Press, 1985.

Bouchard, Gérard. "Une ambiguité québécoise: les bonnes élites et le méchant peuple," dans *Présentations.* Société royale du Canada 1985–86: 29–43.

Brunet, Michel. *La Présence Anglaise et les Canadiens.* Montréal: Beauchemin, 1958.

Canada. Special Joint Committee of the Senate and the House of Commons on the 1987 Constitutional Accord. *Report.* Ottawa: Queen's Printer, 1987.

Clift, Dominique. *Le déclin du nationalisme au Québec.* Montréal: Libre expression, 1981.

Cook, Ramsay. *Canada and the French Canadian Question.* Toronto: Macmillan, 1966.

————. *Canada, Quebec and the Uses of Nationalism.* Toronto: McClelland and Stewart, 1986.

————. *The Maple Leaf Forever.* Toronto: Macmillan, 1971.

Lesage, Gilles, Ed. *Le Québec et le lac Meech.* Montréal: Guérin littérature, 1987.

Morissonneau, C. ''Mobilité et identité québécoise.'' *Cahiers de Géographie du Québec* 23 (1979): 29–38.

Murray, Lowell. ''Le Canada doit répondre 'oui' au Québec.'' *Le Devoir,* 28 August 1987.

Québec. *Projet d'accord constitutionnel. Propositions du Gouvernement du Québec.* Québec: 1985.

Quebec. *Royal Commission of Inquiry on Constitutional Problems.* Vol. II. Quebec, 1956.

Smith, Anthony. *The Ethnic Revival.* Cambridge: Cambridge University Press, 1981.

Trudeau, Pierre-E. Ed. *La Grève de l'Amiante.* Montréal: Cité libre, 1956.

STEPHEN ALLAN SCOTT

"MEECH LAKE" AND QUEBEC SOCIETY: "DISTINCT" OR DISTINCTIVE?*

I—S'il va sans dire, il va encore mieux en le disant

Many aspects of the *1987 Constitutional Accord* (the "Meech Lake Accord") of June 3, 1987, trouble me profoundly—as they should trouble all who believe in effective government, or in just government, or in both.

I have, however, no difficulty with the principle of including, in the Constitution of Canada, a statement of Quebec's "distinct identity" or "caractère distinct", to use the Accord's terminology. Nor, indeed, am I reluctant to include, in the Constitution, a commitment on the part of the aggregate Canadian Federation—or on the part of its component federal and provincial elements—to "preserve and promote" ("protéger et promouvoir") that identity and character so far as *any* exercise of *governmental authority* can, practically and legitimately, in a free and democratic society, seek or accomplish such a result.

To me, a central aim of our Federation is, indeed, to create a governmental structure which will—within the limits appropriate to a free and democratic society—encourage, and make possible, the survival, in North America, of that distinctive French language and culture primarily, though not exclusively, found in Canada within the Province of Quebec. In short, *"la survivance"*. In a sense this has been—in a moral if not in a juridical sense—an implied term of Confederation. Certainly it lies at the basis of French Canada's support for the 1867 federal union. Article 1024 of the *Civil Code of Lower Canada* expresses a principle

---

*In Réal-A. Forest, ed., *L'adhésion du Québec à l'Accord du Lac Meech—Points de vue juridiques et politiques* (Montréal: Les Éditions Thémis, 1988).

broader than the private law of contract, broader also than the law of Quebec alone:

> The obligation of a contract extends not only to what is expressed in it, but also to all the consequences which, by equity, usage or law, are incident to the contract, according to its nature.

Very broadly stated, what Quebec and its Government appear to seek—and what Meech Lake attempts to give—is a constitutional commitment to the survival of French Canada, within the Canadian Federation. A federal and provincial consensus clearly accepts that the time has come to convert the *implied* term of constitutional *history*, and (within limits) also of *practice*, into an *express* term of constitutional law. The challenge is, first, to *find suitable language* in which to state it, and, second, to *integrate the language chosen into the Constitution in a suitable way*.

Of course, defining the identity of *French Canada*—or of *Quebec*, which is at once more and less than French Canada, and is certainly not the same as French Canada—is no easy thing. Such a definition would be an extraordinary challenge even in the discursive terms of a sociological or historical treatise—let alone in the terse language of a juridical text. How even does one define *the modern Québécois, French-speaking, community*—now including immigrants from many countries, and no longer (almost) exclusively the descendants of seventeenth- and eighteenth-century French settlers on the banks of the St. Lawrence? How does one define *the pluralist Quebec, a geographical and juridical entity*, distinct from any definition of French Canada or of francophone Quebec? Supposing one can achieve such a definition, how can one *integrate it into a balanced constitutional statement*?

The Meech Lake Accord implicitly, and rightly, recognizes that there are limits to what can be accomplished, in a juridical text, in terms of definition of a society. In the end—in the clause proposed for inclusion in the Act of 1867 as its new section 2—, the 1987 Accord declares that Quebec ''constitutes within Canada a distinct society'' (s. 2(1)(b)).

In my view, the proposed provision, taken as a whole, is awkward and inelegant in its language; isolationist in terms and in tone; lacking in the appropriate balance, and context, both in its statement of the nature of our country and in its formulation of constitutional objectives; unsatisfactory for anglophones within Quebec; and even more unfair to francophones outside Quebec. It also, quite unnecessarily, puts itself into the posture of an adversary of the *Canadian Charter of Rights and Freedoms* instead of an ally. In my view, the proposed clause on linguistic duality and the identity of Quebec is, in sum, altogether unsuitable as a statement of the nature of our country, and especially so when framed and proffered as a rule of constitutional interpretation. Indeed, the highly controversial "saving clause" (s. 16 of the proposed *Constitution Amendment*, 1987)—with all its problems for the *Canadian Charter of Rights and Freedoms*—is a direct, though avoidable, and unfortunate, side-effect of the proposed section 2.

In order to get down to particulars, and to substantiate these charges, let me set out the relevant provisions of the 1987 Accord, and then a draft clause of my own, intended as a substitute for the proposed new s. 2 of the 1867 Act. My draft clause, let me emphasize, is simply one possibility, intended to convey my general sense of what should be said, and how it should be said, in order to achieve a fair and balanced juridical statement of the nature of Canada and of Canadian constitutional objectives.

II—The 1987 Accord's Clauses Relating to Linguistic Duality and the Recognition of Quebec as a Distinct Society

Here, first, are the relevant clauses of the 1987 Constitutional Accord:

SCHEDULE, CONSTITUTION AMENDMENT, 1987, Constitution Act, 1867

1. The *Constitution Act, 1867* is amended by adding thereto, immediately after section 1 thereof, the following section:

"2. (1) The Constitution of Canada shall be interpreted in a manner consistent with:

    (a) the recognition that the existence of French-speaking Canadians, centred in Quebec but also present elsewhere in Canada, and English-speaking Canadians, concentrated outside Quebec but also present in Quebec, constitutes a fundamental characteristic of Canada; and

    (b) the recognition that Quebec constitutes within Canada a distinct society.

(2) The role of the Parliament of Canada and the provincial legislatures to preserve the fundamental characteristic of Canada referred

to in paragraph (1)(a) is affirmed.

(3) The role of the legislature and Government of Quebec to preserve and promote the distinct identity of Quebec referred to in paragraph (1)(b) is affirmed.

(4) Nothing in this section derogates from the powers, rights or privileges of Parliament or the Government of Canada, or of the legislatures or governments of the provinces, including any powers, rights or privileges relating to language.''

General

16. Nothing in section 2 of the *Constitution Act, 1867* affects section 25 or 27 of the *Canadian Charter of Rights and Freedoms*, section 35 of the *Constitution Act, 1982* or class 24 of section 91 of the *Constitution Act, 1867*.

III—Draft of a Proposal for a New Section 2 of the Constitution Act, 1867, in Substitution for that Proposed by the 1987 Constitutional Accord

I next offer my own draft:

2. The Canadian federation, acknowledging its special responsibility to its aboriginal peoples, affirms:

(a) its resolve to secure, under the rule of law, the advantages of liberty, equal opportunity, and economic well-being, to all its people, inheritors and bearers of the diverse cultures of many lands;

(b) its resolve to ensure the survival and vigour, throughout Canada, of its two official languages, English and French;

(c) its recognition that Quebec, unique in its French-speaking majority, is a guarantor of the survival and vigour of the French language in Canada; and

(d) its recognition that the French language and distinctive culture are at once a resource and a heritage, and its resolve to ensure their survival and vigour not only within Quebec, their principal historic home, but throughout the federation;

and the Constitution of Canada shall be interpreted accordingly.

IV—A Remarkable Model and Some Comparisons

The Constitution of the United States offers a remarkable model for a constitutional statement of national purposes. It is in the form of a preamble linked to the words of enactment:

> We the People of the United States, in Order to form a more perfect Union, establish Justice, insure domestic Tranquillity, provide for the common Defence, promote the general Welfare, and secure the Blessings of Liberty to ourselves and our Posterity, do ordain and establish this Constitution for the United States of America.

By comparison to this, the Meech Lake clauses are surely a national embarrassment to Canada. I recognize that political compromises necessary in Canada will preclude anything quite so terse and elegant in this country. Still, it is worth noting, and imitating if we can, the *grandeur* of the ideals; the dignity of the language; and the delicacy of the balance in the enumeration of national objectives.

It may be suggested that Meech Lake's proposed new section 2 of the 1867 Act is not intended as a general statement of national objectives, but only to deal with a narrower subject. Yet it is designed to become the first substantive section in our principal constitutional Act, the *Constitution Act, 1867*. It could not be more prominent. And its very preoccupation with one aspect only of our national life is part of the problem, since it thereby excludes all context, balance, and sense of proportion.

It is, surely, a remarkable comment on a constitutional statement of national objectives and character, that it must immediately be subjected to a series of "saving" clauses designed to restrain its operation, and, furthermore, that its appearance immediately prompts large efforts, by many who fear adverse effects, to restrain its operation still further. Thus, the proposed sub-sections 2(1), 2(2) and 2(3) of the 1867 Act cannot (the framers have agreed) be allowed to disturb the federal–provincial distribution of powers; so sub-section 2(4) is added to ensure that there is no derogation from the powers of the Parliament or Government of Canada, or from those of the legislatures or governments of the provinces.

This, of course, only serves to establish that various guarantees of rights and freedoms—notably the *Canadian Charter of Rights and*

Freedoms—are indeed the intended target of the first three sub-sections of proposed section 2. This itself, in turn, produces s. 16 of the 1987 *Constitution Amendment* in response to the latter threat. Section 16 declares that nothing in section 2 affects s. 25 of the *Charter* (the *Charter*'s own "saving" clause for aboriginal rights and freedoms) or s. 27 of the *Charter* (requiring interpretation of the *Charter* "in a manner consistent with the preservation and enhancement of the multicultural heritage of Canadians") or s. 35 of the *Constitution Act, 1982* ("Rights of the Aboriginal Peoples of Canada"), or s. 91(24) of the Act of 1867 (federal legislative jurisdiction over "Indians and Lands reserved for the Indians." (This last, it seems, is thrown in for good measure in conjunction with s. 25 of the *Charter* and s. 35 of the *Constitution Act, 1982.*)

Why these four particular provisions should be "saved" from the impact of the proposed clauses on linguistic duality and Quebec's distinct identity has never been explained. Nor, in my view, *can* it be satisfactorily explained. Indeed, so far as they are intelligible at all, the federal ministerial explanations are entirely specious. Inevitably, every exception from the operation of the clauses on linguistic duality and Quebec's identity simply focuses their operation all the more ruthlessly on the remaining sections of the Canadian *Charter* or other guarantees (such as s. 133 of the Act of 1867 or s. 23 of the *Manitoba Act, 1870*). (Indeed, the special "saving" for s. 91(24) of the 1867 Act detracts from the *general* "saving" of *all* federal powers in proposed sub-section 2(4).) Not surprisingly all segments of society with a concern in keeping intact the operation of the *Canadian Charter* line up to demand the same special protection for their own interest—or, if they are unusually enlightened, to seek the exclusion of the *entire Charter* from the operation of the proposed s. 2 of the 1867 Act on linguistic duality and Quebec's identity. Women's groups; ethnic groups; linguistic minority groups; and others: all wish to keep the *Charter* intact—at any rate for themselves.

The inference is *both clear and inevitable* that if *certain* sections of the *Canadian Charter are* specifically protected from the operation of s. 2, and *others not*, the latter are more vulnerable. This inference is of course underscored, despite denials from Ottawa, by affirmations from Quebec City that the new section 2 *may*, indeed, or even *will*, have a bearing on the availability of the *Canadian Charter*'s guarantees—for example, those guarantees protecting freedom of expression (s. 2(b)), or equality (s. 15)—against restrictive provincial language legislation. (The usual example is, of course, the Quebec language legislation which, under penalty, largely prohibits the use of languages other than French in public signs and posters and commercial advertising.)

As the Meech Lake scheme stands, the proposed ss. 2(1)(b) and 2(3) can be read as declaring, in effect, that Quebec's "distinct society" can justify provincial legislation *prima facie* violating *Canadian Charter* guarantees, *even when the legislation is not "demonstrably justified in a free and democratic society"* (s. 1 of the *Charter*). To me this is unacceptable. The objection of principle, and the risks in fact, are not overcome by my hope, and indeed my expectation, that fairminded judges will attempt to escape such results by one expedient or another. It is not desirable to leave to the courts the task of integrating unsatisfactory provisions into a constitutional scheme. It is wrong to create provisions which must be viewed, in part at least, as problems in damage control.

I would far prefer to design a fair and balanced statement of our national character and our constitutional objectives—a statement which can be integrated into the Constitution *without ANY restraining safeguards*, and which can be allowed *to bring its full interpretive force to bear on the WHOLE Constitution, including* the distribution of jurisdiction and the *Canadian Charter of Rights and Freedoms*. It would be the role of *all* governmental authorities, legislative and executive, to promote these objects, and this could, if desired, be stated; but in my view clauses like the proposed s. 2(2) and 2(3) of the revised 1867 Act would be superfluous. I have not, therefore, included parallel language in my own draft clause.

It is this fairness and balance, and integration into a coherent constitutional scheme, which my own clause attempts to achieve. Its opening words acknowledge our responsibility to the aboriginal peoples. Paragraph (a) summarizes our common social objectives—liberty, equality of opportunity, and economic well-being—all under the rule of law, which is the essence of any just constitutional system. (It would destroy the balance to omit the rule of law here merely because it is also mentioned in the preamble to the *Canadian Charter*.) Canadians are of many and diverse national and cultural origins, and it is right to acknowledge and welcome this fact.

Paragraph (b) of my draft then sets out a commitment to the *survival and vigour of* BOTH official languages, *English* and *French*, THROUGHOUT Canada. This, it seems to me, is balanced and fair to linguistic *majorities and minorities alike*—and particularly to the *French-speaking minorities outside Quebec*. It should be stressed that, under the Meech Lake scheme, French-speaking Canadians, who are declared (by the proposed s. 2(1)(a) of the 1867 Act) to be "centred" in Quebec, are then declared merely to be "present *elsewhere* in Canada" (my emphasis). Not, be it noted, *throughout* the Federation. It follows that no particular provincial legislature—not even the Parliament of Canada—has (under the proposed s. 2(2) of the 1867 Act) any "role" or responsibility "to preserve" a francophone community *in any given province outside Quebec*. For as long as there are *some* French-speaking Canadians, *somewhere* outside Quebec—even in one corner of one province—, that is quite good enough for s. 2(1)(a). Here the English-speaking minority in Quebec fare somewhat better, since they are declared (s. 2(1)(a)) to be "present" *in* Quebec. On the other hand, the only role of Parliament and the provincial legislatures is to *preserve* these "fundamental" characteristics—i.e., the linguistic minorities' presence *in Quebec*, and *somewhere outside Quebec*, respectively—while the "role of the legislature and Government of Quebec" is "to preserve *and promote*" (my emphasis) "the distinct identity of Quebec referred to in paragraph (1)(b)''. This is unbalanced and unfair to both linguistic minorities, English-speaking and French-speaking.

Paragraph (c) of my draft notes Quebec's unique characteristic—its French-speaking majority—and recognizes that Quebec is a guarantor of the survival of the French language in Canada. By contrast, Meech Lake would simply mysteriously declare "that Quebec constitutes within Canada a distinct society''.

Paragraph (d) of my draft adds a special, and explicit, recognition that the French language and distinctive culture are a resource and heritage; and a further recognition that Quebec is their principal historic home; and ends with a commitment to ensure their survival and vigour not only in Quebec but throughout the Federation.

The concluding words of my draft require *the whole Constitution* to be interpreted in the light of these principles. No exclusions are needed, in my view, because my formulation respects, in a balanced way, *all legitimate interests*. Hence the distribution of powers, the *Canadian Charter of Rights and Freedoms*, and everything else in the Constitution, would be governed by my interpretive clause. Though my draft seems to me suitable for enactment in its present form, it could obviously be revised to meet reasoned objections.

A further word on the language of the proposed s. 2, which I described earlier as "awkward" and "inelegant." My point has perhaps been made sufficiently and simply through my comparison with the preamble of the United States Constitution. Let me, however, particularly point to such declarations as that of the existence of groups of people who are centred or concentrated in various places. English-speaking people are centred in one place; French-speaking people concentrated in another. This is grotesque. Can any literate person really welcome such phrases in the opening clause of our principal constitutional instrument—or, for that matter, *anywhere* in our law? Must we descend into barbarism?

V—Quebec Society: "Distinct" or Distinctive

Of all aspects of the 1987 Accord's clauses relating to linguistic duality and Quebec's identity, the declaration (para. 2(1)(b)) "that Quebec constitutes within Canada a distinct society" has attracted most public attention and controversy.

Let me first ask how many urbane and sophisticated French-speaking Quebecers would, in New York or Rome or Paris or London, describe themselves as members of a "distinct society"? Very few, I should think; probably not even Premier Robert Bourassa himself. (At least, whilst keeping a "straight face" and without recourse to explanations.)

Why so? In any normal use of words, Quebec is *not a "distinct society" but a distinctive part of Canadian, North American, and Western society.* Distinct societies are now very rare and usually primitive. Japan before the arrival of Commodore Perry would have offered a good example. Isolated tribes of New Guinea may still offer some instances; perhaps Albania is another. Russia before Stalin's death would have had a good claim to being a "distinct" society; the claim would be more tenuous now though perhaps defensible with a series of qualifications. I think it would be absurd to describe Canada, or any part of Canada, as a "distinct society". We share far too many aspects of our daily lives with the rest of this continent and the western world.

To me, so isolationist a description of Quebec as that in proposed s. 2 (1)(b) is the *last* thing one would wish to see in a constitution, even though the "distinct" society is of course declared to be "within Canada".

What, indeed, is the purpose of such constitutional language? What legal impact will it have? It is clearly not intended to be allowed to affect the distribution of powers (s. 2(4)). But it *may* (it seems) justify measures not otherwise acceptable in "a free and democratic society". (Certainly there are those who argue so.) Yet such results will not easily be accepted by the courts, and would indeed involve breach of international obligations assumed by Canada with Quebec's approval.

The "distinct society" phrase also evokes various past battles of

French-Canadian nationalism. It undoubtedly offers a gesture (though an inarticulate gesture) to that nationalism. Yet the phrase ''within Canada'' seems deliberately designed to defeat any claim to a right of self-determination in the sense of the establishment of a separate state in what is now the territory of Canada. Indeed, in my view *no* segment of the Canadian population is ever entitled to appropriate, in sovereignty, exclusively to *itself*, any part of the national territory. All the territory belongs in sovereignty to all citizens. Provinces are established for the exercise only of constitutionally defined powers, and without any other vocation. When a boundary is established by *any* lawmaking authority for the exercise of defined powers, the population within those boundaries has no inherent right, even if such be their unanimous wish, to the grant of wider powers. The phrase ''within Canada'' would, I submit, reinforce this result, despite the ''distinct society''.

I see nothing in para. 2(1)(b) which, from any perspective, promotes Quebec's short-term or long-term interests. I do on the contrary see an isolationist, even reactionary—and to me undesirable—tone, demeaning to Quebec and to Canada. Why, indeed, does not s. 2(1)(b) read: ''the recognition that Quebec constitutes a distinctive part of Canadian society''?

It occurred to me recently in this connection to look at the history of one of Quebec's internationally distinguished and prize-winning cultural institutions, the Orchestre Symphonique de Montréal. Founded in 1934 with the assistance of the Quebec government, its first musical director was a Montrealer by birth, Wilfrid Pelletier. A Belgian (Désiré Defaux) followed in 1940, and then successively Igor Markevitch (born in Russia), Zubin Mehta (born in India), Franz-Paul Decker (born in Germany), Rafael Frühbeck de Burgos (born in Spain) and Charles Dutoit (born in Switzerland). Its guest conductors, orchestra members, and soloists have come from countless countries. It has toured many countries on this continent, in Europe, and in Asia.

This is not the record of a cultural institution of a ''distinct society''. Rather it is the record of a distinguished institution within a creative, and—as it happens very distinctive—part of Canadian, North American and Western society.

To what advantage, then, are we to include a false, misleading, and pejorative description of Quebec prominently in our Constitution? Is it like de Gaulle's oracular ''Je vous ai compris''? Is it intended to mean all things to all people? Let us at least be clear as to *what it is intended to mean* and *why it is there*. Better still, let us produce something better. Failing this, the case for sheltering *all* guarantees from the operation of s. 2 seems unanswerable.

JOSÉ WOEHRLING

A CRITIQUE OF THE DISTINCT SOCIETY CLAUSE'S CRITICS*

Introduction

On June 3rd, 1987, at Ottawa, the ten provincial Premiers and the Prime Minister of Canada signed a Constitutional Accord by which they agreed to introduce certain amendments to the Constitution of Canada in order to satisfy the conditions fixed by Quebec for its adherence to the *Constitution Act, 1982*.[1] The June 3rd Accord is the result of efforts to finalize and formalize, after several changes had been made, the agreement in principle reached the previous April 30th at Meech Lake.[2] Attached to the Accord is a *Motion for a Resolution to Authorize an Amendment to the Constitution of Canada* which in turn sets out in a schedule the text of the *Constitution Amendment, 1987*. It is here that one finds, divided into seventeen sections, the amendments proposed for the Constitution of Canada.[3]

Featured in s.1 of the *Constitution Amendment, 1987* are certain provisions relating to the recognition of Canada's linguistic duality and the distinct character of Quebec society. For over a year these provisions have attracted lively controversy, some taking the view that the terms used are too ambiguous, others fearing that their inclusion in the Constitution could lead to undesirable results, in particular a weakening of the *Canadian Charter of Rights and Freedoms*.[4] A number of groups fear that their own rights and freedoms are especially threatened. These groups include francophones outside Quebec, anglophones within Quebec, cultural and ethnic minorities, aboriginal peoples and, finally,

---

*Paper written specifically for inclusion in this volume. Translated by Professor Ruth Sullivan.

various women's organizations. I wish to assess in this paper the impact of the Accord's duality and distinct society provisions on the rights of these groups and on the *Charter* in general. This will depend, of course, on how the provisions are interpreted by the courts, a subject over which there is considerable disagreement between supporters and opponents of the Meech Lake Accord. For this reason it will be useful to begin with an examination of the legal meaning and significance of the duality and the distinct identity provisions. I will then consider the general impact of these provisions on the *Charter* and finally I will attempt to assess the eventual effect of these provisions on the rights belonging to each of the groups opposed to the Meech Lake Accord.

The Legal Meaning and Significance of the Duality and Distinct Identity Provisions

Section 1 of the *Constitution Amendment, 1987* provides:

1. The *Constitution Act, 1867* is amended by adding thereto, immediately after section 1 thereof, the following section:
2.(1) The Constitution of Canada shall be interpreted in a manner consistent with
(a) the recognition that the existence of French-speaking Canadians, centred in Quebec but also present elsewhere in Canada, and English-speaking Canadians, concentrated outside Quebec but also present in Quebec, constitutes a fundamental characteristic of Canada; and
(b) the recognition that Quebec constitutes within Canada a distinct society.
(2) The role of the Parliament of Canada and the provincial legislatures to preserve the fundamental characteristics of Canada referred to in paragraph (1)(a) is affirmed.
(3) The role of the legislature and Government of Quebec to preserve and promote the distinct identity of Quebec referred to in paragraph (1)(b) is affirmed.
(4) Nothing in this section derogates from the powers, rights or privileges of Parliament or the Government of Canada, or of the legislatures or governments of the provinces, including any powers, rights or privileges relating to language.

As the text indicates, once the Amendment becomes law the provisions in question will constitute a new s.2 of the *Constitution Act, 1867*.[5] To fully appreciate their meaning and force, one must also take into account s.16 of the *Constitution Amendment, 1987*, which states:

> 16. Nothing in section 2 of the *Constitution Act, 1867* affects section 25 or 27 of the *Canadian Charter of Rights and Freedoms*, section 35 of the *Constitution Act, 1982* or class 24 of section 91 of the *Constitution Act, 1867*.

Together ss.1 and 16 of the *Constitution Amendment, 1987* offer first, official "recognition" of two socio-linguistic realities, namely, Canadian duality and the distinct identity of Quebec; second, a dual mechanism for giving normative force to this recognition; and finally, two "saving clauses" designed conversely to limit the legal effects such recognition might otherwise engender.

Canada's Linguistic Duality

In recognizing the co-existence of anglophones and francophones throughout Canada as well as Quebec's special identity, the Meech Lake Accord simultaneously affirms two duality principles: anglophone/francophone and Quebec/English Canada. The extent to which these two may be ranked or prioritized is a question dealt with below. My purpose at this point is to look more closely at the language used to express the first duality—francophone/anglophone. It will be referred to herein as "Canadian duality"; for the other duality the expression "Quebec's distinct identity" will be used.

The *Constitution Amendment, 1987* asserts that "the existence of French-speaking Canadians, centred in Quebec but also present elsewhere in Canada, and English-speaking Canadians, concentrated outside Quebec but also present in Quebec, constitutes a fundamental characteristic of Canada". The sociological reality addressed by this formulation is the existence of linguistic minority groups, French speakers in English Canada and English speakers in Quebec. From a legal point of view, this recognition of Canadian duality must mean at least that the existence of these minorities is constitutionally acknowledged and protected even though the extent of the protection is not precisely defined.

Quebec's Distinct Identity

The expression "distinct society" appears to have been first used in 1965 by the Royal Commission of Inquiry into Bilingualism and Biculturalism, which used the term in its Preliminary Report to designate the existence in Quebec "[of] the types of organization and the institutions that a rather large population, inspired by a common culture, has created for itself or has received and which it freely manages over quite a vast territory where it lives as a homogeneous group according to common standards and rules of conduct".[6] It thus took almost twenty years from the time the concept of a "distinct society" first entered politico-constitutional discourse for agreement to be reached on its introduction into the Constitution. It remains to be seen what meaning Canadian courts will attach to these words. The *Constitution Amendment, 1987* offers no express definition of Quebec's distinct identity. Moreover, the concept is a controversial one, the question being whether Quebec is properly defined as a *French* society or a *bilingual and multicultural* one.

According to one interpretation, Quebec's distinctive character is derived from the co-existence within its territory of a French-speaking majority, an English-speaking minority and "third-language" groups composed of other cultures and languages. If this is so, the preservation and promotion of Quebec's distinct identity logically should consist in maintaining the bilingualism and multiculturalism of Quebec society. However, in my view, for several reasons, this interpretation of "Quebec's distinct identity" is not a tenable one.

In the first place, the co-existence of a francophone majority and anglophone minority within Quebec is already constitutionally acknowledged in the recognition of duality ("the existence of English-speaking Canadians . . . also present in Quebec"), the precise purpose of which is the protection of minority rights. Logically speaking, then, the recognition of Quebec's distinct identity must refer to something other than the presence in Quebec of an anglophone minority.

There is also the consideration that in a federal system every one of the constituent members is "distinct" in some sense; indeed, it is the distinct character of the member-states, and more particularly their desire to preserve whatever it is that makes them distinct, which explains the choice of a federal form of government in preference to a unitary state. To expressly affirm Quebec's distinct identity—and only Quebec's —therefore suggests that there is a difference in kind between Quebec's distinctiveness and that of the other provinces. This difference consists, in my view, in the fact that *the demographic relationship prevailing in all the other parts of Canada is reversed in Quebec,* which is the home of the only francophone majority in any of Canada's member-states.

Finally, one must give some meaning to the fact that duality is merely *preserved* whereas Quebec's distinct identity is to be *promoted* as well as *preserved.* In Quebec the majoritarian position of francophones, the "French fact", calls for *promotion* and not just *preservation* because of its fragility. However dominant French may be at the provincial level, everywhere else in Canada and the rest of North America it is a minority language. In my view, the June 3rd Accord implicitly recognizes that the francophone majority in Quebec is a "threatened" majority and so must defend its language.

If Quebec's distinct identity derives from the fact that it is the sole province in Canada where the majority language and culture are French, it follows that the preservation and promotion of this identity logically should consist in maintaining and developing the French and franco-phone character of Quebec society, while at the same time, of course, respecting the duality principle.

The Paramountcy of Canada's Linguistic Duality Over Quebec's Distinct Identity

The text of the *Constitution Amendment, 1987* twice affirms that linguistic duality constitutes "a fundamental characteristic of Canada"; as for Quebec's distinct identity, its existence is merely recognized and it is not characterized as "fundamental" in a comparable way. In the event of a conflict between the need to preserve duality and the need to pre-serve and promote Quebec's distinct identity, this clearly established priority would no doubt be noticed by the courts. Even without an express indication of this sort, logically the courts would consider duality to be a matter affecting Canada as a whole, in contrast to Quebec's dis-tinct identity which concerns only one of its constituent parts. In a con-flict which involves concerns of a political nature, national interests would be likely to prevail over specific interests of any one province.

One must therefore conclude that the role of the Quebec legisla-ture in relation to Quebec's distinct identity is subordinate to its role as preserver of duality: the preservation and promotion of the French fact may not jeopardize the preservation of Quebec's English-speaking minority.

The General Impact of the Meech Lake Accord on the *Canadian Charter of Rights and Freedoms*

In this section, after some preliminary remarks on the relationship between the Meech Lake Accord and the *Charter*, I will examine the potential impact of the duality and distinct identity provisions both on the *definition* of *Charter*-guaranteed rights and on their *limitation*. I will then consider the extent to which the Meech Lake Accord may limit the potential power of the *Charter* to bring about greater uniformity in provincial laws.

The Relationship Between the Meech Lake Accord and the *Charter*

One point must be clearly established at the outset: the provisions of the *Constitution Amendment, 1987*, once they become law, will be applicable to the *Charter*. They will form an integral part of the Constitution in the same manner as the *Charter* and, as is well known, each part of a single constitutional or legislative text must be interpreted and applied in relation to the others. Furthermore, s.1 of the Accord expressly declares that "[t]he Constitution of Canada shall be interpreted" in a manner consistent with the recognition of duality and Quebec's distinct identity. The *Charter* is part of the *Constitution Act, 1982* which, as stated in s.52(2) of that Act, forms part of the "Constitution of Canada". Finally, if further argument is required, one could point to s.16 of the Accord which, in providing that the duality and distinct identity provisions do not affect ss.25 or 27 of the *Charter*, presupposes that these provisions do indeed apply to the *Charter*.[7]

My second preliminary point is that the *Charter* will itself be applicable to the Meech Lake Accord, including the provisions dealing with duality and Quebec's distinct identity. These provisions, in other words, do not set aside the *Charter* any more than they supplant it. This follows first of all from the fact, mentioned above, that the *Charter* and the Meech Lake Accord form part of the same constitutional text and will therefore be applied concurrently. Second, because the duality and distinct identity provisions are merely interpretive, they can have effect only in combination with substantive constitutional provisions, including those in the *Charter*.

Notwithstanding this, representatives of certain groups opposed to the Accord, primarily women's groups, have claimed that the duality and distinct identity provisions might not be subject to the *Charter*. Their principal argument is based on what is in my view an erroneous appreciation of the Supreme Court of Canada's reasoning in *Reference re Bill 30*.[8]

The issue for the Court in that case was the validity of a Bill designed to implement a policy of full funding for Roman Catholic separate high schools in Ontario. Those opposed to the policy argued that it violated freedom of conscience and religion as well as the equality rights guaranteed under the *Charter*. This argument was unanimously rejected by the Court, which held that in conferring on the provinces the power to legislate in respect of Catholic denominational schools, s.93 of the *Constitution Act, 1867* necessarily conferred "the jurisdiction to legislate in a *prima facie* selective and distinguishing manner with respect to education whether or not some segments of the community might consider the result to be discriminatory".[9] In other words, in the view of the Court, where a legislature in exercising a power that is expressly conferred on it by the Constitution must unavoidably create differences in treatment, it does not act inconsistently with the *Charter* even though such differences would otherwise be constitutionally impermissible.

Representatives of women's groups opposed to the Accord claim that similar reasoning could be applied to the duality and distinct identity provisions.[10] However, it is clear that the *ratio decidendi* of the judgment is not applicable to these provisions. In the first place, as we shall see below, they confer no legislative (or executive) power. Furthermore, even if they did, they do not unavoidably entail discrimination of the sort prohibited by the *Charter* or indeed any other violation of a guaranteed right or freedom.[11]

Accordingly, insofar as the duality and distinct identity provisions are subject to the *Charter*, any laws adopted to preserve duality and any legislative or executive measures taken to preserve or promote Quebec's distinct identity will have to respect its terms. This means that such measures either must impose no limitation on *Charter*-protected rights and freedoms or must limit them only to the extent permitted by s.1, that is, the limitation must be "reasonable" and capable of being "demonstrably justified in a free and democratic society". As we shall shortly see, it is in the context of this two-stage process, defining rights and freedoms and defining their limitation, that the impact of the Meech Lake Accord provisions is likely to be felt.

The Effect of the Duality and Distinct Identity Provisions on the Definition and Limitation of *Charter*-guaranteed Rights

Once the Meech Lake Accord provisions become law they may be relied on in interpreting any section of the *Charter*, including those that define the content of guaranteed rights and freedoms as well as s.1, which permits their limitation under certain conditions. In other words, the courts may be influenced by the Accord in determining both the *scope* of guaranteed rights and freedoms and the *limitations* they will allow.

With respect to determining the content of rights and freedoms, the provisions of the Constitution most likely to be affected are those that deal with minority language rights, namely s.133 of the *Constitution Act, 1867*,[12] s.23 of the *Manitoba Act, 1870*[13] and ss.16–20 and 23 of the *Charter* itself. As we shall see in more detail when examining the impact of the Meech Lake Accord on the rights of francophones outside Quebec and of Quebec anglophones, the recognition of duality could be used to justify a broader and more liberal interpretation of minority rights than has been offered by the Supreme Court of Canada.

When read with s.1 of the *Charter*, the duality and distinct identity provisions could be invoked to justify restrictions on rights and freedoms judged necessary to preserve duality or to preserve or promote Quebec's distinct identity. This is just what is feared by certain groups opposed to the Accord, particularly women's groups and Quebec anglophones, and it is for this reason they seek an amendment that will clearly establish the supremacy of the *Charter* over the duality and distinct identity provisions. The Quebec Government is firmly opposed to these demands—for good reason in my view. Given the saving clause contained in s.2(4) of the Accord,[14] it is perfectly clear that recognition of Quebec's distinct identity will not affect the division of powers between Quebec and the federal government. If the *Charter* were also sheltered from the application of the distinct identity provisions, they would be totally divested of any real legal force and would operate on a purely symbolic level.

For various reasons, the fears of groups opposed to the Accord appear to be largely overblown. For one thing, the conditions that must be met to justify a restriction on *Charter* rights, as construed by the Supreme Court of Canada, are extremely exacting. A measure that limits a right or a freedom must have a social objective ''of sufficient importance to warrant overriding a constitutionally protected right or freedom", and the means chosen to achieve this objective must satisfy a form of proportionality test.[15]

With respect to the first requirement, the preservation of duality and the preservation and promotion of Quebec's distinct identity will inevitably be considered important objectives after the Meech Lake Accord becomes law. However, there would appear to be little doubt that these two objectives could be deemed of sufficient importance to justify a restriction on *Charter* rights under current law, quite apart from the Meech Lake Accord. In 1982 in *Quebec Association of Protestant School Boards v. A.G. Quebec*, commenting on the goal of preserving and promoting the French language as set out in the preamble to Quebec's *Charter of the French Language*,[16] the Chief Justice of the Quebec Superior Court, Deschênes C.J. (as he then was) spoke to this effect in the following terms:

> The court has not the slightest doubt that this involves a legitimate objective which, to use the words of the Charter, "can be demonstrably justified in a free and democratic society".[17]

The Supreme Court of Canada expressed the same opinion on the legitimacy of Bill 101's objectives in its recent judgment in *Ford v. A.G. Quebec*.[18]

However, the "test" set out in s.1 of the *Charter* has a second branch: the means chosen to attain the legislative purpose must be reasonable, that is, they must meet a form of proportionality test. In the *Oakes* case, the Court acknowledged that "the nature of the proportionality test will vary depending on the circumstances"; however, "in each case courts will be required to balance the interests of society with those of individuals and groups".[19] The Court went on to explain that:

> [there are] three important components of a proportionality test. First, the measures adopted must be carefully designed to achieve the objective in question. They must not be arbitrary, unfair or based on irrational considerations. In short, they must be rationally connected to the objective. Second, the means, even if rationally connected to the objective in this first sense, should impair "as little as possible" the right or freedom in question: *R. v. Big M Drug Mart Ltd.* . . . Third, there must be a proportionality between the *effects* of the measures which are responsible for limiting the *Charter* right or freedom, and the objective which has been identified as of "sufficient importance".[20]

It is certainly possible that the courts will respond to the Meech Lake Accord provisions by relaxing the severity of the proportionality test in future applications of s.1. However, it will still be exceedingly difficult to justify the limitation of a *Charter* right or freedom, whether grounded in the preservation of duality or in the preservation or promotion of Quebec's distinct identity. In any event, the final word on the matter will belong to judges whose duty it will be to apply s.1 of the *Charter* together with the rule of interpretation set out in the Accord. Interpretation provisions of this sort are notoriously unreliable. Given their non-binding status, the courts use them with considerable freedom and do not always attach the same importance to them as the legislator or constitutional framer intended them to have. This makes it extremely difficult to predict how the interpretive rule respecting duality and distinct identity will figure in the decisions of the courts. It is worth noting in this connection that s.27 of the *Charter* (preservation of multicultural heritage), which closely resembles this interpretive rule, has received little attention to date and has resulted in nothing of particular significance.

A second consideration invites a more nuanced assessment of the threat to *Charter* rights represented by the Accord. It is that such rights are more or less vulnerable to restrictions founded on Quebec's distinct identity depending on whether they are collective or individual in character. Fundamental rights, being individual and universal, appear to be inherently less vulnerable: it will be extremely difficult in practice to prove that Quebec's distinct identity requires the limitation of such rights, for by definition they are the same everywhere. This undoubtedly explains why certain feminist groups have been reduced to inventing far-fetched and extreme examples in their efforts to demonstrate that sexual equality rights are threatened by the distinct identity clause.[21] Conversely, collective rights—rights with cultural and linguistic content—*prima facie* are more vulnerable for they are concerned with the very facts that constitute Quebec's distinct identity (language and culture) and they are not inherently universal and fundamental but rather the product of a particular social and cultural situation.[22] However, as we shall see in more detail when examining the Accord's impact on minority rights, the language rights of Quebec anglophones are protected from any limitations that might be imposed in the name of Quebec's distinct identity by the recognition of duality as a "fundamental characteristic of Canada". The rights of cultural and ethnic minorities are guaranteed by s.27 of the *Charter* (preservation of multicultural heritage), which is itself protected by the saving clause in s.16 of the Accord. This section also protects the rights of aboriginal peoples under s.25 of the *Charter* and s.35 of the *Constitution Act, 1982*. As this quick survey suggests, the impact of the distinct identity clause on *Charter*-guaranteed rights, whether individual or collective, must be very modest if not altogether negligible.

This impression is further strengthened when one takes into account s.33 of the *Charter*, which permits Parliament and the provincial legislatures to derogate from most *Charter*-guaranteed rights.[23] In fact, the existence of this provision renders the entire debate concerning the impact of the Accord on the *Charter* somewhat academic, except for the rights that are exempted from the notwithstanding clause. If a Quebec Government wanted to enact a law that restricted one of the rights to which s.33 applies, it would undoubtedly prefer to rely on the notwithstanding clause and answer to the electorate rather than having to come to court and rely on Quebec's distinct identity. With respect to the rights that are exempted from the notwithstanding clause, s.1 of the *Charter* remains the sole method of justifying a restrictive law. It is in this context that the recognition of Quebec's distinct identity could have some effect on the *Charter* when combined with s.1. Having regard to the character of the exempted rights, however, one can safely predict that this effect will be negligible.

Rights that are exempt from the application of s.33 fall into three categories: democratic rights (ss.3–5), mobility rights (s.6) and language rights (ss.16–20 and 23). It is hard to imagine a court accepting the argument that recognition of Quebec's distinct identity somehow justifies a limitation on the right to vote (s.3) or violations of the principle of annual legislative sessions (s.5) or the rule that makes five years the maximum duration of the National Assembly (s.4). As far as I know, even the groups most vigorously opposed to the Accord have never raised these possibilities. The language rights of Quebec anglophones are protected by the recognition of the duality principle which, as noted above, is paramount over the recognition of Quebec's distinct identity. We will return to this point below when we examine the position of Quebec's English-speaking minority. Finally, with respect to mobility rights, one can imagine Quebec some day opposing the entry of ''heterogeneous elements'' into the province because of the threat they represent to its distinct identity and attempting to justify this policy by invoking the relevant provisions of the Accord. However, in my view these provisions would be of no assistance, for in this context too they are neutralized by the recognition of duality as a fundamental characteristic of Canada and by s.27 of the *Charter* (preservation and enhancement of multicultural heritage), which is protected by the saving clause in s.16 of the Accord.

In conclusion, then, it appears that the duality and distinct identity provisions in the Meech Lake Accord will not significantly weaken the protection that is currently accorded rights and freedoms under the *Charter*. On the other hand, as we shall now see, these provisions may limit the potential centralist and uniformist effects of the *Charter*.

Uniformity and Centralization Under the *Charter*

The application of the *Charter* to the provinces is likely to bring about greater uniformity in their laws. The task of giving substance to rights and freedoms raises crucial issues of culture and civilization and involves decisions that effectively define what sort of society we will live in; under the *Charter* this task is performed on a Canada-wide basis, by a judicial hierarchy that is extremely centralized and that uses a uniform ''national'' approach in interpreting constitutional standards.[24]

The issue to be considered here is whether the duality and distinct identity provisions of the Meech Lake Accord will permit courts to reject this uniform approach, where necessary, in order to apply the *Charter* in a manner that takes into account the particular language situation in each province and more particularly shows due respect for Quebec's distinct identity. Most commentators think that they should.[25]

This ''regionalization'' in applying the *Charter* could be effected, in the case of linguistic rights for example, through interpretation of the *content* of particular provisions; however, it is more likely to influence the application of s.1 in the context of efforts to justify particular limitations on rights and freedoms. For example, a limitation that would be considered inconsistent with the *Charter* elsewhere in Canada might be judged acceptable in Quebec if it could be shown to be necessary to preserve or promote the distinct character of Quebec society. Similarly, legislation enacted by an English-speaking province that conferred benefits on its francophone minority but not on other linguistic or cultural groups, although apparently inconsistent with the principle of equality, might be justified in light of the recognition of Canada's linguistic duality.

It has been noted, quite rightly, that even under existing law such ''regionalization'' is amply justified by the *federal principle* on which Canada's Constitution is founded. This principle presupposes and legitimizes the existence at any given time of a degree of diversity in provincial laws, and even in some cases in the application of federal laws to different parts of the country.[26] Thus, the duality and distinct identity provisions of the Meech Lake Accord confirm and in a sense give specific force to the decentralizing and diversifying impact of the federal principle on *Charter* interpretation.

The Effect of the Duality and Distinct Identity Provisions on the Rights of the Various Groups Opposed to the Meech Lake Accord

In this section I will begin with a quick review of the fears and objections expressed by each of the groups opposed to the Meech Lake Accord. I will then attempt to assess how well founded these fears and objections are in light of the conclusions reached above concerning the significance of the duality and distinct identity provisions and their general effect on the *Charter*.

Throughout I will strive as much as possible to stress the legal position of these groups while placing somewhat less emphasis on the questions of prestige that are tied to politico-constitutional symbolism. One must realize that in Canada, since the events surrounding the "repatriation" of the Constitution in 1980–1982, constitutional issues have become stakes in a race for "symbolic positioning" in which groups representing various ethnic and sociological categories all jockey for a privileged place in the constitutional standings. It has thus become possible to speak in metaphorical terms of a "constitutional pecking order".[27] This is due to the fact that the Constitution, and within it the *Charter*, have a dual function: they offer legal protection of rights and freedoms and also confer symbolic recognition on the various groups that comprise Canadian society.

The Meech Lake Accord clearly enhances the symbolic position of the two official language communities and still more that of Quebec's francophone majority. Inevitably the groups that are not mentioned in the Accord believe that their own position, relatively speaking, has been diminished. Their resentment is understandable. Although the positions of francophones outside Quebec and of Quebec anglophones are recognized in the Accord, in the principle of duality which is declared to be a "fundamental characteristic of Canada", this recognition appears to them to be inadequate. Thus, they too are among the groups opposed to the Meech Lake Accord. I shall begin by examining the position of these two groups.

Francophones Outside Quebec

Francophones outside Quebec raise essentially two objections to the Accord: it does not improve the rights they already have under the Constitution, and it does not permit them to claim additional rights in the future.

In the first place, representatives of the francophone minority deplore the changes made in the wording used to express recognition of Canadian duality. These changes, which were introduced between the adoption of the agreement in principle on April 30, 1987, and the adoption of the final Accord on June 3rd, replace the reference to "the existence of French-speaking Canada . . . and English-speaking Canada" with recognition of "French-speaking Canadians . . . and English-speaking Canadians". While the initial wording connotes the existence of two linguistic and cultural *communities*, the second version refers to *individuals* who express themselves in French or in English. In the view of francophones outside Quebec, the first formulation, unlike the second, captures the collective dimension of Canadian linguistic reality. It would therefore have provided a more solid legal and philosophical foundation for the idea of the equality of the French and English languages in Canada, thereby permitting minorities to demand of the courts a broader and more liberal interpretation of the language rights currently guaranteed by the Constitution.[28]

In my view, however, the collective or individual character of rights depends on the interests—collective or individual—that these rights are meant to protect and not on the terminology used to describe them. Language is a collective entity that can be neither used nor preserved except in a group; the purpose of language rights is to permit the preservation and enhancement of the language that is shared by the members of a collectivity. The collective nature of these rights does not disappear simply because they are legally conferred on individuals who individually may claim their benefit. In my view, the recognition of duality as a "fundamental characteristic of Canada", as formulated, has reference to the existence of the French-speaking and English-speaking minorities and logically should compel the courts to interpret the rights they already enjoy under the Constitution in the broadest, most liberal and most far-reaching manner possible. This, after all, is the surest way to secure the existence of these rights and ensure the minorities' survival. However, not all official language minorities derive equal benefit from these rights: while s.23 of the *Charter*, dealing with the language of instruction in education, applies to all provinces, the constitutional provisions concerning official bilingualism (legislative, parliamentary and judicial) apply only to the Provinces of Quebec,[29] Manitoba[30] and New Brunswick[31] as well as the federal level of government.[32]

Certain guarantees relating to the use of French and English in judicial proceedings, included in s.19 of the *Charter* and in various other constitutional provisions, have in recent years been given a very narrow interpretation by the Supreme Court of Canada. In the *MacDonald* and *Bilodeau* cases the Court held that the right of a litigant to choose between French and English as the language he wishes to plead in before the courts does not mean that a summons issued against him must be written in his language of choice or must even be bilingual.[33] The Court was even more stringent in the *Société des Acadiens* case where the majority held that the right to choose the language of pleadings does not include the right to be understood by the court to which the pleadings are addressed.[34] The Court justified this surprising conclusion by emphasizing that the language rights entrenched in the *Charter* are founded on a political compromise and the courts should accordingly be slow to act as an instrument of change in this area.[35]

In my view, if the issues raised in the *MacDonald*, *Bilodeau* and *Société des Acadiens* cases were to come before the Court in the future, after the Meech Lake Accord has become law, logically the Court would be obliged to rule in a manner more favourable to the minorities for whose benefit these rights were introduced. This is what francophones outside Quebec are hoping for. With respect to the other language rights contained in ss.16–20 and s.23 of the *Charter*, the reasoning is similar: the recognition of duality should move the courts to give these provisions the broadest possible interpretation.[36] From this perspective, then, the Meech Lake Accord can be said to offer a modest improvement in the position of language minorities. Of course, the advantage thus acquired will remain theoretical until the courts demonstrate their willingness to regard the recognition of duality as a mandate to give a more liberal interpretation to minority rights.

The second criticism raised by francophones outside Quebec—and undoubtedly the more serious one in their view—is that the Accord will not permit them to seek new rights at the federal or provincial level in the future. This concern appears to be well justified and is the consequence primarily of two amendments to the agreement in principle of April 30, 1987, apparently requested by Quebec. Under the first, the "commitment" of Parliament and the ten provincial legislatures to the preservation of duality is transformed into a mere "role", which imposes no real constraints. Under the second, the duality and distinct identity provisions are supplemented by the saving clause that now appears in s.2(4) of the Accord. It provides that nothing in these provisions "derogates from the powers, rights or privileges of Parliament or the Government of Canada, or of the legislatures or governments of the provinces, including any powers, rights or privileges relating to language". In my view, this clause makes it clear that the recognition of duality and Quebec's distinct identity will not alter the division of powers between the federal government and the provinces, nor will it confer on minorities any rights in addition to those already constitutionally guaranteed prior to the Meech Lake Accord. In practice, any recognition of new rights or freedoms must involve derogating from existing federal or provincial powers, since the rights of citizens against the state always entail corresponding duties and limitations.

The saving clause in s.2(4) was requested by Quebec's negotiators primarily to ensure that the anglophone minority in the province would not be able to rely on the duality principle to get the courts to impose new linguistic obligations on Quebec. The anglophone minority in the province already enjoys a wide range of important language rights, and the fact that it may not rely on the duality principle to ask for more can be easily taken in stride. Its chief concern is to protect the rights it already has from any derogation and, for the most part, as we shall see below, this concern is adequately met in the Accord. The position of French-speaking minorities outside Quebec is quite different. Those who are in a more advantageous position—the minorities in New Brunswick and Ontario—are still far from benefitting from the same favourable conditions as are enjoyed by the English in Quebec. For them, an improvement in status is essential and might have been demanded on the basis of the duality principle if this approach were not precluded by the saving clause which appears to dispense the English provinces (and the federal government, at its level) from having to agree to any additional rights or benefits.

The inability of francophone minorities to rely on the Meech Lake Accord as a basis for demanding *new* rights is underscored by the fact that under the Accord Parliament and the provincial legislatures are given the single role of *preserving* duality, whereas Quebec's legislature and government are charged with the dual role of *promoting* as well as preserving Quebec's distinct identity. This distinction too was asked for by Quebec's negotiators, who regard it as a major gain for Quebec. They take the view that the province's role in promoting its distinct identity will permit the government to obtain new constitutional powers in the area of language. Having regard to the saving clause in s.2(4), this possibility is precluded in my view. What is clear at this point is that the presence of the distinction between *preserving* and *promoting* on the one hand and the existence of the saving clause on the other, both of them introduced at the insistence of Quebec, reduce enormously the advantages that francophone minorities might have derived from the Meech Lake Accord.

The asymmetry in the actual position of francophones outside Quebec and anglophones within would have justified applying different constitutional provisions to these two groups, the position of francophone minorities requiring a *promotion* of their rights while that of Quebec's anglophone minority calling simply for *preservation*. To preserve the fiction of equality, however, the provisions applied are completely symmetrical—which explains the deficiencies in the Accord complained of by the francophone minorities.

It is fair to conclude that the Meech Lake Accord does little to enhance the rights of francophones outside Quebec. Let us bear in mind, however, that the negotiations leading up to the Accord were not designed to satisfy the needs of Canada's minorities but rather to give Quebec the means to protect its majority language. As for the future, the failure of the Accord would clearly confer no advantage on francophone minorities outside Quebec. On the contrary, to the extent such a failure would be apt to weaken Quebec, the chief bastion of the French language in Canada, it could only prove harmful for these groups in the medium and long term.

Finally, one should notice that it is perfectly possible to improve the position of francophone minorities under the Meech Lake Accord without having to renegotiate the agreement. Under s.43(b) of the *Constitution Act, 1982*,[37] language provisions applicable to certain provinces only can be amended by agreement between the federal government and the particular province concerned.[38] Thus, there is nothing to stop a province that so wishes from immediately moving to guarantee its French-speaking minority all the constitutional rights it determines.

Quebec Anglophones

Our analysis of the position of francophones outside Quebec applies equally to Quebec's anglophones. They will draw the same limited advantages from the Meech Lake Accord as the francophone minorities, namely, the possibility of a more liberal interpretation of already existing constitutionally protected language rights. Any attempt to claim new rights will be subject to the same limitations imposed by the saving clause in s.2(4). However, as noted above, these limitations do not have the same concrete significance for Quebec's anglophones as they do for the French-speaking minorities in the other provinces.

Alliance Quebec, the organization claiming to represent Quebec's anglophones, has called for certain amendments to the Meech Lake Accord, the most important of which is the addition of a clause affirming the unqualified supremacy of the *Charter* over the *Constitution Amendment, 1987*. As indicated above, Quebec could never accept such an amendment, for it would eliminate any genuine legal significance from the provisions relating to Quebec's distinct identity. In any event, an amendment of this sort is unnecessary: insofar as the Meech Lake Accord clearly subordinates Quebec's distinct identity to Canada's linguistic duality, the preservation and promotion of the French fact cannot be invoked to reduce the language rights of Quebec's anglophone minority.

To show that recognition of Quebec's distinct identity poses no threat to the language rights conferred on Quebec anglophones by the *Constitution Acts* of 1867 and 1982, a brief survey is needed of the judicial decisions in which these Acts have been relied on to invalidate provisions in the *Charter of the French Language*. I shall argue that this line of cases is in no way called into question by the Meech Lake Accord.

The first constitutional guarantee enjoyed by Quebec's anglophone minority derives from s.133 of the *Constitution Act, 1867*. Section 133, which applies solely to Quebec and the federal government,[39] guarantees bilingualism in Parliament, the provincial legislature and the courts.[40] In 1977, Quebec enacted the *Charter of the French Language*, Chapter III of which, dealing with the language of legislation and judicial proceedings, provided that henceforth Quebec laws would be enacted and published in French only (ss.8–10), and subject to certain exceptions French alone could be used before Quebec courts (ss.11–13). In *A.G. Quebec v. Blaikie*,[41] the Supreme Court of Canada struck down these provisions as being contrary to s.133. Recognition of Quebec's distinct identity will not restore their validity. As noted above, it is only when read in conjunction with s.1 of the *Charter* that the duality and distinct identity provisions have the potential to justify limitations on rights and freedoms. Since s.133 is not part of the *Charter*, it is not subject to s.1 and thus cannot be restricted. It is equally immune from derogation under s.33 of the *Charter*.[42] In fact, the sole way to limit the rights it guarantees is to amend or repeal the section, and this could not be accomplished without going through the procedure for amending the Constitution of Canada.[43]

The second constitutional guarantee enjoyed by Quebec's anglophone minority is included in s.23 of the *Charter* which sets out minority language educational rights.[44] In *A.G. Quebec v. Quebec Protestant School Boards*,[45] the Supreme Court found the "Quebec clause" contained in ss.72 and 73 of the *Charter of the French Language*[46] to be inconsistent with the "Canada clause" contained in s.23(1)(b)[47] and therefore of no force or effect. Is it plausible to suggest that recognition of Quebec's distinct identity will cause the Court to change this ruling in the future and that the limitation imposed by *Bill 101* on the rights guaranteed in s.23 of the *Charter* will be found reasonable and justifiable as a means to preserve and promote this distinct identity? There are two reasons, in my view, for thinking that the answer to this question must be in the negative.

In the first place, the Supreme Court held that s.73 of *Bill 101* does not constitute a *limitation* on the rights guaranteed by s.23, but an attempt to *amend* the section or, still more, to *derogate* from it. For this reason the legislation could not be upheld under s.1 of the *Charter*; s.23 can be amended only by following the procedure for constitutional amendments, and it cannot be derogated from by means of an express declaration under s.33. In other words, s.23 is so specifically worded that it is impossible to limit it without contradicting it, and this is not permitted under s.1 of the *Charter*.

Secondly, even if the "Quebec clause" were to be regarded as limiting rather than contradicting the "Canada clause", recognition of Canadian duality, given its paramountcy over Quebec's distinct identity, would in my view effectively preclude the Court from reversing its judgment. In fact, for obvious reasons, it would give more weight to the judgment. If Canada's linguistic duality is to be preserved, members of the two language groups must be guaranteed a certain mobility across the country, and this includes providing them with the opportunity to have their children educated in their own language in their new place of residence.

In their efforts to defend their special linguistic identity, minorities—including Quebec's anglophone minority—may also rely on certain of the fundamental freedoms, such as freedom of religion, freedom of expression, freedom of the press and other media of communication as well as the right to equality and non-discrimination. While the principal purpose of these rights and freedoms is not to protect the use of language, they nonetheless possess an ancillary linguistic dimension in that the free choice of language constitutes a necessary condition for their exercise. This dimension exists notwithstanding the absence of any express reference.[48] The Supreme Court of Canada has clearly acknowledged that a linguistic dimension implicitly attaches to certain fundamental rights. In the *Société des Acadiens* case,[49] for exam-

ple, the Court held that the right to a fair hearing, which is protected
by the *Charter* and exists at common law as well, includes the right of
the parties, whatever their language, to understand what is going on
in the courtroom and to be understood.[50]

Similarly, in *Ford v. A.G. Quebec*,[51] the Supreme Court held that
the freedom of expression guaranteed in s.2(b) of the *Charter* includes
the right to express oneself in the language of one's choice, at least in
the domain of private relations. The Court went on to declare ss.58 and
69 of the *Charter of the French Language* of no force or effect insofar as
they prohibited the use of a language other than French for public signs
and posters, commercial advertising and firm names. The Court found
that this restraint on freedom of expression was not justified under s.1
of the *Charter* because the prohibition of languages other than French
did not, in its view, constitute either a necessary or proportionate means
to achieve the law's legitimate objective, the preservation of a French
"visage linguistique" in Quebec.

Is it possible that the Court would have felt itself bound to reach
a different result, based on recognition of Quebec's distinct identity,
if the Meech Lake Accord had been in force when their decision was
taken? The answer to this question must clearly be in the negative, in
my view, for the Court would be equally bound to take into account
the principle of Canadian duality and Quebec's role as preserver of this
duality. It would be most surprising if this role were found to be consistent with the outright prohibition of English in public signs and posters,
commercial advertising and firm names. Might the Court be prepared
to accept such a prohibition with respect to other languages, those not
protected by the Canadian duality principle? In my view, it would be
difficult to reconcile the prohibition of other languages with the rule
set out in s.27 of the *Charter* (preservation of multicultural heritage),
especially since s.27 is one of the provisions expressly sheltered from
the effects of s.1 of the Accord by the saving clause in s.16.

Cultural and Ethnic Minorities

In considering the position of ethnic and cultural groups other than the
official language minorities (the "third-language" cultural groups), it
is important to distinguish their fears concerning the *legal* consequences
of the Meech Lake Accord from their grievances concerning its *political*
implications.

The sole provision in the *Charter* specifically devoted to the *cultural*
rights of minorities is s.27, which provides that "this Charter shall be

interpreted in a manner consistent with the preservation and enhancement of the multicultural heritage of Canadians''. Because this is an
interpretive provision, it cannot serve as a direct or immediate source
of additional rights. Its role will eventually be established by the courts
by reading the section together with other *Charter* provisions. Given
the close connection between language and culture, s.27 could have
some bearing on minority *language* rights as well, even though the section
expressly refers to culture alone.

It will also be helpful to recall the text of s.16 of the *Constitution
Amendment, 1987*:

> Nothing in section 2 of the *Constitution Act, 1867* affects section 25 or
> 27 of the *Canadian Charter of Rights and Freedoms*, section 35 of the *Consti-
> tution Act, 1982* or class 24 of section 91 of the *Constitution Act, 1867*.

The sole purpose of this section, it appears, is to ensure that the provisions of the Meech Lake Accord are not interpreted so as to modify in
any way the existing scope of s.27 of the *Charter* or the other constitutional provisions mentioned in the section. This reading is consistent
with the literal meaning of the section and accords with what we know
of its ''legislative history'': it was adopted at the insistence of Ontario's
Premier who hoped to satisfy the demands and calm the fears of the
province's cultural communities, particularly those centered in Toronto.
If s.16 does indeed preserve the existing meaning and scope of s.27 of
the *Charter*, then the Meech Lake Accord in no way threatens whatever
rights might be derived from this provision for the benefit of cultural
and ethnic minorities.

In support of this analysis, I shall briefly examine the impact that
s.27 is likely to have at the present time in the area of language and
culture. Because as yet there is not much case law applying the section,
this examination must be largely speculative.[52] I may begin by noting
that even though s.27, read literally, applies to all cultures, majority as
well as minority, it is relatively clear, particularly in light of its legislative history, that the section was adopted primarily to respond to the
claims of minority cultural groups belonging to neither of Canada's two
principal language communities. Moreover, to the extent the section
is read as protecting the language rights of persons belonging to minorities other than the francophone or anglophone minorities, logically these
rights should relate to their use of their *mother tongue* and not to their
use of the French or English language.

As a rule of interpretation, s.27 is capable of playing both a negative and a positive role. It could be relied on in the first place to *limit* the application of other *Charter* provisions to the extent that these were found to interfere with the adoption of measures necessary to preserve and enhance the cultural (and possibly linguistic) heritage of Canadian minority communities. The equality provisions in s.15(1) of the *Charter* are obvious examples of provisions that s.27 might to some extent counterbalance in this way.[53] The section might, for example, allow a province that has adopted measures favouring a numerically important cultural minority to resist a s.15 attack based on discriminatory treatment. Clearly the entry into force of the Meech Lake Accord would have no effect on the first role this section may play.

In the second place, s.27 could play a positive role if it led the courts to interpret other *Charter* provisions as *implicitly* guaranteeing cultural or language rights in favour of minority communities. Once again s.15(1) offers the greatest promise of fruitful interaction with s.27.

In the area of education, for example, one could certainly argue that the children of a cultural minority who must attend the public schools of the majority do not receive the same benefits as children educated in their own culture and maternal language. Imposing the educational system of the majority on the minority thus creates an inequality in treatment that works to the disadvantage of members of the minority.[54] A similar analysis applies to the linguistic relations between citizens and government bureaucracies: exclusive use of the majority language by government agents has the effect of putting members of the minority in a disadvantaged position.

It is obvious that an interpretation of s.15 together with s.27 cannot be pushed so far as to permit other minorities to claim the full slate of rights conferred on the French and English language minorities by ss.16–20 and 23 of the *Charter*. However, it should be possible for the courts to use ss.15 and 27 to derive certain language rights for the benefit of the "other" minorities that are different and less extensive than those enjoyed by the anglophone and francophone minorities.

Thus, in the area of education these minorities could insist on preparatory language courses in French or in English, where appropriate, designed to better prepare their children to benefit from public education in the majority language; or they could demand the establishment of public schools that would be bilingual and bicultural in the early grades. This reasoning has been accepted by courts in the United States on the basis of equality alone;[55] it is even more persuasive here where appeal may be made to s.15 in combination with s.27. Minorities could equally rely on these provisions to force the provinces to extend financial assistance to minority *private* schools. In each of these examples, if the s.15 argument were accepted by the courts it would impose certain constraints on the provinces in the exercise of their jurisdiction over education, language and culture.

Similar arguments can be advanced in favour of the "official" use of minority languages. The preservation and promotion of a minority culture entail recognizing the value and status of the culture's language within the framework of the operation of government and the civil service.[56]

This positive application of s.27 is obviously much more speculative than the "negative" application described above, given that it is merely an interpretive provision. My point, however, is the following: if the courts are prepared today to treat s.27 as a source of these kinds of linguistic and cultural rights in favour of minority cultural communities, in my view the coming into force of the Meech Lake Accord will not stand in their way. I reach this conclusion, first of all, because of the saving clause in s.16 and, secondly, and more fundamentally, because such recognition of the rights described above in favour of cultural collectivities does not conflict with Canadian duality or the recognition of Quebec's distinct identity—providing always that the preservation and enhancement of multiculturalism do not interfere with the cultural and linguistic integration of Quebec immigrants into the francophone majority.[57]

While the duality and distinct identity provisions in the Meech Lake Accord may not impair the legal rights of cultural and ethnic minorities, they do diminish the relative importance of their "symbolic" constitutional status, a status only recently acquired.

Since 1867 Canada's Constitution has reserved a special place for the two "founding peoples" of the country, anglophones and francophones, whereas the recognition of multiculturalism dates only from 1982. Furthermore, this recognition takes the form of a simple rule of interpretation in contrast to the substantive educational and linguistic rights conferred on the official language minorities by ss.93 and 133 of the *Constitution Act, 1867* and ss.16–20 and 23 of the *Charter*. The adoption of s.27 in 1982 at least gave cultural minorities for the first time the satisfaction of achieving a place in the symbolic constitutional standings, albeit at a rank below that of the official language minorities. Because the Meech Lake Accord recognizes anglophone/francophone duality as "the fundamental characteristic of Canada", while offering no comparable recognition of multiculturalism, Canada's "third-language'' cultural groups are convinced that the status conferred on them under the *Charter* has been reduced. They want the Accord amended so that multiculturalism is also recognized, in the Constitution, as a ''fundamental characteristic of Canada''. This demand obviously conflicts with the claims of the official language minorities and with those of Quebec.[58]

In the final analysis, it appears that the ''third-language'' groups are treating the Meech Lake Accord of 1987 as an opportunity to claim equal status with Canada's ''founding peoples'' and thus are calling into question the ''ethnic hierarchy'' implicit in the *Constitution Act, 1867* and reaffirmed in the 1982 *Charter*. It appears that the ''two founding peoples'' theory and the principle of duality are becoming less and less acceptable to those Canadians who cannot themselves take advantage of them.[59]

Aboriginal Peoples

The position of the aboriginal peoples under the Meech Lake Accord is similar to that of the cultural minorities analyzed above. From a legal point of view, the duality and distinct identity provisions pose no threat whatsoever, for the saving clause in s.16 precludes any derogation from the rights conferred on aboriginal peoples under s.25 of the *Charter* and s.35 of the *Constitution Act, 1982*. On the other hand, there are other provisions in the Accord that indisputably are contrary to the best interests of aboriginal peoples. These have to do with the procedure for amending the Constitution which will require, once the Accord becomes law, the assent of all ten provinces to the admission of the Yukon and Northwest Territories as new provinces instead of just seven as currently required.[60] There is also the failure to include the questions that are still outstanding concerning aboriginal rights in the program of future constitutional discussions provided for in the Accord.

However, the chief grievance of the aboriginal peoples focusses on the constitutional symbolism of the Accord and their concerns in this connection are much more serious than those raised by the cultural minorities. Of the various groups opposed to the Accord, aboriginal peoples constitute the sole group seeking to be recognized itself as a ''distinct society'', for it is the one group that shares Quebec's ''nationalist'' ambitions or at least some of its demands for self-determination.[61] Politically, recognition of aboriginal peoples as a ''distinct society'' would promote acceptance of these demands. It is worth recalling that these demands were renewed only a few weeks prior to the Meech Lake Accord at a constitutional conference which ended in failure.

In contrast to "third-language" cultural groups, the aboriginal peoples can claim an historical legitimacy that is not simply equal but is vastly superior to that of the two "founding peoples". They justly consider themselves to be the true founding peoples of Canada. Yet their existence is not recognized as a "fundamental characteristic" of Canada, not in the Meech Lake Accord, nor elsewhere in the Constitution.

It thus appears that legally the duality and distinct identity provisions do not affect aboriginal rights, not only because of the saving clause in s.16 but equally because there is no competition, even potentially, between the Accord's provisions and these rights.[62] On the other hand, the provisions have an undeniably negative impact on the political position of aboriginal peoples and their place in the symbolic constitutional standings.

Women's Groups

The objections raised by women's groups concerning the symbolic import of the Meech Lake Accord are obviously different from those raised by aboriginal peoples and cultural minorities. Since women do not constitute a cultural or ethnic collectivity, they do not as a group compete with the official language minorities or with Quebec's majoritarian collectivity; nor do they seek recognition of their "distinct identity" or their existence as a "fundamental characteristic of Canada" in the Meech Lake Accord.

The real fears of women's groups over the Meech Lake Accord have to do with the possible impact of the duality and distinct identity provisions on their legal rights, particularly the right to equality. In this connection, two distinct but complementary arguments are made. The first focusses on the restrictions on rights that could result from combining the Accord's provisions with s.1 of the *Charter*; the second concerns a more indirect threat to women's rights originating in the subordination of individual rights to collective rights.

With respect to the first argument, there are those who claim that it is not possible for the provisions in the Meech Lake Accord to be used in conjunction with s.1 of the *Charter* so as to justify limitations on the right to sexual equality. This claim is based on s.28 of the *Charter*, which states that "[n]otwithstanding anything in this Charter, the rights and freedoms referred to in it are guaranteed equally to male and female persons". This provision is said to preclude any recourse to s.1 for the purpose of justifying sexual discrimination.[63] If this interpretation is sound, it should take care of most of the fears expressed by women concerning the effects of the Meech Lake Accord on equality rights. However, if the courts do not accept this interpretation, and so far it appears that they do not, it will be possible to rely on s.1 of the *Charter* in conjunction with the duality and distinct society provisions in attempting to justify violations of sexual equality.

The fundamental question that arises, then, is whether there exists any real possibility of conflict between sexual equality on the one hand and duality and Quebec's distinct identity on the other. There are many who believe that such a possibility is precluded on the grounds that sex has nothing to do with the language and culture implied in the duality and distinct identity provisions.[64] It would appear, however, that the division of social roles between the sexes and the different status enjoyed by men and women form part of the fundamental structures around which cultures are organized and which distinguish one culture from the next. In most if not all existing cultures, there is a division of social roles that works to the disadvantage of women or at least fails to correspond to the contemporary ideal of sexual equality. Given this reality, it is not absurd to claim that the preservation of a traditional culture could be deemed in certain cases to require the perpetuation of existing social roles and thus discrimination against women. If Quebec's distinct society or the existence of duality were thought to be connected to a certain traditional status for women, this might ultimately be legitimated on the basis of the provisions in the Meech Lake Accord.

In my view, there is little basis for anxiety of this sort, especially in Quebec where the consensus in favour of sexual equality appears to be greater than elsewhere in Canada.[65] However, it would be wrong and unjust to dismiss these fears as totally without foundation. They are supported, in fact, by the historic lesson Canadian women have drawn from the case of *Lavell v. A.G. Canada*[66] where the Supreme Court of Canada in the context of debate over s.12(1)(b) of the *Indian Act* appears to concede the very point in question, namely that protection of a threatened minority culture, in this case native culture, could justify the perpetuation of certain sexual inequalities. If one accepts this analysis of the *Lavell* case, it is tempting to apply it by way of analogy to cases involving the protection of linguistic duality or Quebec's distinct society. However, like the argument made regarding the Court's ruling in *Reference re Bill 30*,[67] the analogy suggested here is flawed. In the *Lavell* case, a majority of the Court relied on s.91(24) of the *Constitution Act, 1867* which confers legislative power on Parliament the exercise of which necessarily presupposes distinctions based on race.[68] The duality and distinct identity provisions, we have seen, confer no additional powers or jurisdiction nor do they necessarily imply distinctions founded on race or sex. Conversely, one must bear in mind that s.28 was introduced into the *Charter* at the request of women in order to neutralize the effects of s.27 in particular, precisely because of the events and controversies surrounding the *Lavell* case;[69] and there is an obvious similarity between the provisions relating to multiculturalism on the one hand and the recognition of duality and Quebec's distinct society on the other: in both, the purpose is to protect cultural values which are by nature collective and thus theoretically liable to come into conflict with the sexual equality of individuals.

These considerations concerning the distinction between collective and individual rights bring us to the second argument presented by the representatives of women's groups. This second argument draws attention to the more indirect threat resulting from the fact that the Meech Lake Accord establishes a certain hierarchy of rights and freedoms in which language and cultural rights—rights that are collective in character—rank above individual rights, including equality rights. There is thus reason to fear that in the event of conflict between these two categories of rights, the courts will be inclined to favour the former over the latter.

It is undeniable that the duality and distinct identity provisions in the Meech Lake Accord will increase the importance of the collective rights already enjoyed by minorities under the *Constitution Act, 1867* and the *Charter*. It is also true, in my view, that courts will have to respond to these provisions by giving the collective rights of minorities a broad and liberal interpretation even if in certain cases this means restricting individual equality rights.[70]

Accordingly, it is not impossible for recognition of duality and Quebec's distinct identity to come into conflict with women's equality rights. Indeed, this appears to be demonstrated by several of the hypothetical possibilities put forward by feminist representatives. In developing an internal hiring policy, for example, a provincial government might be forced to choose between an equal access program for its linguistic minority and one in favour of women. If the province decided to prefer the linguistic minority, women could challenge the constitutionality of its decision under ss.15(1) and 28 of the *Charter*. So long as the Accord was not yet law, this challenge might conceivably succeed. Unlike language, sex is one of the grounds of discrimination expressly mentioned in s.15(1), and it is arguable that distinctions based on enumerated grounds call for stricter scrutiny by the courts than those not expressly enumerated.[71] Once the Accord is law, however, the recognition of duality could well tip the balance in favour of the linguistic minority.

There exists, then, a small but real possibility that the Meech Lake Accord provisions relating to duality and Quebec's distinct identity could have a negative effect on the rights of women. Does this justify a new round of negotiations to amend the Accord in order to exclude its application to the *Charter* provisions guaranteeing sexual equality? Considering the difficulties that would have to be overcome in reaching a new compromise, in my view a reopening of the Accord is to be avoided. What the federal government and the provinces could consider, after the Meech Lake Accord comes into force, is amending the *Charter* to provide that nothing in the Meech Lake Accord affects s.28 of the *Charter*. This amendment would require the consent of only seven provinces.

Conclusion

The groups opposed to the Meech Lake Accord object to it first of all on a symbolic level because it does not accord them their rightful place, does not properly ''reflect'' their importance. One must respond to this objection by pointing out that this was not the purpose of the Meech Lake Accord. The idea was not to create an official ''family portrait'' of Canadian society with each group occupying its rightful constitutional place, but rather to resolve the difficulties created by Quebec's non-adherence to the *Constitution Act, 1982*. This problem is of paramount importance, for at stake is the unity of Canada. It thus takes priority over the problems of social justice raised by the opposing groups. On a more concrete level, if a host of new provisions offering equal ''recognition'' to every dissatisfied group were to be added to the Accord, as some have suggested, the import of recognizing Quebec's distinct identity would be diluted to the point where it would lose all real significance.[72]

The groups opposed to the Meech Lake Accord object to it, secondly, from a legal point of view because they fear that it will result in a reduction of the rights secured by them in 1982 under the *Charter*. The first response to this objection is to point out that the real danger to *Charter* rights comes from s.33 which allows derogations from rights and freedoms. Furthermore, as I have tried to show above, the dangers—real or imagined—that may result from the recognition of Quebec's distinct identity are for the most part neutralized, first, by the recognition of Canada's linguistic duality, second, by the *Charter*'s provisions on multiculturalism and, finally, by the two saving clauses included in ss.2(4) and 16 of the Accord.

Apart from this, all groups opposed to the Accord deplore the fact that they were totally excluded from the *process* through which the Meech Lake Accord was adopted. And they recognize that their exclusion from the constitutional amending process is even more likely to occur in the future in that the Accord further institutionalizes first ministers' conferences as the means of introducing important constitutional amendments, such as those relating to the Senate.[73] In other words, the Constitution will continue to be amended at the pleasure of eleven governments and the rights acquired by the various groups in 1982 will be vulnerable to future erosion without their having the means to oppose it. The adoption of the Meech Lake Accord in 1987 demonstrates that however much the *Charter* may "belong" to the people, the procedure for amending the Constitution remains exclusively in the hands of politicians.[74] For this reason, rather than attempting at this point to amend the Meech Lake Accord, which would only ensure its defeat, efforts should go to improving the procedure for constitutional amendment in order to enhance the role of Parliament and the provincial legislatures and, if possible, the role of the Canadian people themselves.[75]

To become law the *Constitution Amendment, 1987* must be ratified before June 23, 1990, by Parliament and each of the ten provincial legislatures.[76] The House of Commons, after adopting it initially, adopted it a second time to override the default of the Senate. At the beginning of 1989 only two provinces have not yet ratified the Accord—New Brunswick and Manitoba—both of which changed governments as a result of elections held after the signing of the Accord on June 3, 1987. The doubts expressed by these provinces focus primarily on the decentralizing aspects of the Accord and on its supposed effects on the rights of certain of the groups whose positions have been explored above. However, it would be surprising if in the final analysis these two provinces, whose political clout in Canada is limited, were to take responsibility for the defeat of the Meech Lake Accord. Such a defeat could only aggravate Quebec's constitutional isolation and would almost surely lead to a resurgence of Quebec nationalism.

Notes

1. The *Constitution Act, 1982*, Schedule B of the *Canada Act 1982* (U.K.), 1982, c. 11. For a chronology of the events leading up to the June 3rd, 1987, Accord, see *The Report of the Special Joint Committee on the 1987 Constitutional Accord* (Joint Chairmen: Arthur Tremblay and Chris Speyer), pp. 1–6.
2. For the text of the agreement in principle reached April 30, 1987, known as the Meech Lake Accord, see *L'adhésion du Québec à l'Accord du Lac Meech—Points de vue juridiques et politiques* (ed. by R.-A. FOREST), Montréal, Les Éditions Thémis, 1988. pp. 221 ff.
3. For the text of the *1987 Constitutional Accord*, the *Motion for a Resolution to Authorize an Amendment to the Constitution of Canada* and the *Constitution Amendment, 1987*, see P. HOGG, *Meech Lake Constitutional Accord Annotated*, Toronto, Carswell, 1988, pp. 62 ff.
4. The *Canadian Charter of Rights and Freedoms* (hereinafter the *Charter*) is Part 1 (ss.1–34) of the *Constitution Act, 1982, supra,* note 1.
5. The *Constitution Act, 1867*, 30 & 31 Vict., U.K., c. 3.
6. *A Preliminary Report of the Royal Commission on Bilingualism and Biculturalism,* Ottawa, Queen's Printer, 1965, p. 111.
7. One should also point out that in a recent appeal, *Reference re Bill 30, An Act to Amend the Education Act (Ont.)*, [1987] 1 S.C.R. 1149, the Supreme Court of Canada declined to view the *Charter* as having a supra-constitutional status such that it could render invalid or prevent the application of other provisions of the Canadian Constitution where these were judged to be inconsistent with the rights and freedoms it guarantees. In the view of the Court, the various provisions of the Constitution do not neutralize or invalidate one another but rather must be read together and interpreted in light of one another.
8. *Ibid.*
9. *Idem,* p. 1206 (per Estey J.). Mr. Justice Estey goes on to compare s.93 to s.91(24) "which authorizes the Parliament of Canada to legislate for the benefit of the Indian population in a preferential, discriminatory, or distinctive fashion *vis-à-vis* others" and he concludes that even if the *Charter* limits the exercise of legislative power conferred by the Constitution, "it cannot be interpreted as rendering unconstitutional distinctions that are expressly permitted by the *Constitution Act, 1867*" (p. 1207).
10. See, for example, L. SMITH, "The Distinct Society Clause in the Meech Lake Accord: Could it Affect Equality Rights for Women?", in *Competing Constitutional Visions—The Meech Lake Accord* (ed. by K.E. SWINTON and C.J. ROGERSON), Toronto, Carswell, 1988, 35, pp. 50–51; K. MAHONEY, "Women's Rights", in *Meech Lake and Canada. Perspectives from the West* (ed. by R. GIBBINS *et al.*), Edmonton, Academic Printing & Publishing, 1988, pp. 159 ff.
11. My opinion on this point is shared by Professors Hogg and Morel: P. HOGG, *Meech Lake Constitutional Accord Annotated*, pp. 15–16; A. MOREL, "La

reconnaissance du Québec comme société distincte dans le respect de la Charte'', in *L'adhésion du Québec à l'Accord du Lac Meech—Points de vue juridiques et politiques*, pp. 60–63.

12. For the text of s.133 of the *Constitution Act, 1867*, see *infra*, note 40.

13. R.S.C. 1985, Appendix II, no. 8. The content of s.23 of the *Manitoba Act, 1870* is similar to that of s.133 of the *Constitution Act, 1867*.

14. On this question, see J. WOEHRLING, ''La modification constitutionnelle de 1987, la reconnaissance du Québec comme société distincte et la dualité linguistique du Canada'', (1988) 29 *Cahiers de Droit* 1, pp. 25–27; J. WOEHRLING, ''La reconnaissance du Québec comme société distincte et la dualité linguistique du Canada: conséquences juridiques et constitutionnelles'', in *The Meech Lake Accord—L'Accord du Lac Meech*, special issue of *Canadian Public Policy/Analyse de Politiques*, September 1988, 43, p. 50.

15. See *R. v. Oakes*, [1986] 1 S.C.R. 103.

16. R.S.Q., c. C-11.

17. [trans.] *Quebec Association of Protestant School Boards v. A.G. Quebec*, (1982) 140 D.L.R. (3d) 33, p. 70. However, in the result, the Chief Justice held that the ''Quebec clause'' contained in s.73 of Bill 101 (which limits access to English public schools to children one of whose parents received their education in English in Quebec and which is therefore inconsistent with s.23 of the *Charter*) is ''disproportionate to the intended aim and that it unnecessarily exceeds reasonable limits'' (p. 89).

18. *Ford v. A.G. Quebec*, [1988] 2 S.C.R. 712, at 777–778.

19. *Supra* note 15, p. 139.

20. *Ibid.*

21. Some have even suggested that Quebec, in an effort to combat a critical decline in the birthrate, might prohibit abortions and restrict women's access to professional training and higher education so as to encourage them to stay home and raise children!

22. On the collective nature of cultural and linguistic rights, see J. WOEHRLING, ''Minority Cultural and Linguistic Rights and Equality Rights in the *Canadian Charter of Rights and Freedoms*'', (1985) 31 *McGill Law Journal* 50, pp. 86 ff.

23. Section 33 of the *Charter* permits the federal Parliament and the provincial legislatures to derogate from most *Charter* provisions, i.e. to render them inapplicable to any law into which the legislature has inserted a simple formula expressing its intention to derogate (the so-called ''notwithstanding clause''). Once such a clause is inserted, the courts can no longer ensure that the law in question complies with the *Charter*; they are limited to a review of the formal prerequisites set out in s.33, namely the presence of a notwithstanding clause that expressly mentions the rights or freedoms to be derogated from. Although the duration of a notwithstanding clause is limited to five years, it can be re-enacted indefinitely. Moreover, there is no limit to the nature or number of laws capable of being thus ''immunized'' against the *Charter*'s application: thus, it would be possible for the

federal Parliament or a provincial legislature to have recourse to s.33 for the entire body of federal or provincial law in force. Only democratic rights (ss.3,4 and 5), mobility rights (s.6) and language rights (ss.16–20 and 23) cannot be made the subject of a notwithstanding clause. The remaining rights and freedoms, including the right to life (s.7) and equality rights (s.15), are all subject to s.33.

24. On this point, see H. BRUN, "The Canadian Charter of Rights and Freedoms as an Instrument of Social Development", in C. BECKTON & W. MACKAY, *The Courts and the Charter* (Vol. 58 in the series of studies commissioned as part of the research program of the Royal Commission on the Economic Union and Development Prospects for Canada), Ottawa, Canadian Government Publishing Centre, 1986, 1, pp. 9 ff.

25. See, for example, T.J. COURCHENE, "Meech Lake and Federalism: Accord or Discord?", in *Competing Constitutional Visions—The Meech Lake Accord*, pp. 128 ff. Other authors contributing to this work adhere to the same idea, in particular Professors Slattery, Swinton, Simeon and MacKay.

26. K. SWINTON, "Competing Visions of Constitutionalism: Of Federalism and Rights", in *Competing Constitutional Visions—The Meech Lake Accord*, pp. 279 ff.

27. E. KALLEN, "The Meech Lake Accord: Entrenching a Pecking Order of Minority Rights", in *The Meech Lake Accord—L'Accord du Lac Meech*, pp. 107 ff.

28. M. BASTARACHE, "La clause relative à la dualité linguistique et la reconnaissance du Québec comme société distincte", in *L'adhésion du Québec à l'Accord du Lac Meech—Points de vue juridiques et politiques*, pp. 33 ff.

29. Section 133 of the *Constitution Act, 1867*. For the text of s.133, see *infra*, note 40.

30. Section 23 of the *Manitoba Act, 1870*.

31. Sections 16(2) and 16(3), 17(2), 18(2), 19(2) and 20(2) of the *Canadian Charter of Rights and Freedoms*.

32. Section 133 of the *Constitution Act, 1867*; ss.16(1) and 16(3), 17(1), 18(1), 19(1) and 20(1) of the *Canadian Charter of Rights and Freedoms*.

33. *MacDonald v. City of Montreal*, [1986] 1 S.C.R. 460; *Bilodeau v. A.G. Manitoba*, [1986] 1 S.C.R. 449. The Court justified its holding in these cases by referring to the express language of s.133 of the *Constitution Act, 1867* and s.23 of the *Manitoba Act, 1870* which appears to confer the freedom to choose between English and French not only on the individuals who plead before the courts but equally on the judges and other court officials. However, I prefer the dissenting opinion of Madame Justice Wilson in the *MacDonald* case (pp. 504 ff.). She argues that the right conferred on a litigant to use his or her own language in judicial proceedings before the courts imposes a correlative duty on the state to respect and accommodate that right. To fulfil this duty, the state must deal with a litigant in the language he understands.

In *A.G. Quebec v. Blaikie*, [1979] 2 S.C.R. 1016, in *obiter*, the Supreme Court expressed the view that under the terms of s.133 judges covered by the section are entitled to render unilingual judgments. Thus, it would not be unconstitutional for a Quebec citizen to have his case decided by a Quebec court in English only. The dissenting opinion of Madame Justice Wilson in the *MacDonald* case appears to me to be equally relevant here.

34. *Société des Acadiens v. Association of Parents*, [1986] 1 S.C.R. 549. Chief Justice Dickson and Madame Justice Wilson wrote dissenting opinions in the case. They held that the right of a litigant to use French or English in any court or in any pleading or process issuing from a court includes the right to be understood by the court addressed.

35. *Idem*, p. 578. However, the majority of the Court took the view that the right to a fair hearing, which is guaranteed by the *Charter* and also exists at common law, includes the right of parties, whatever their language, to understand what is going on in court and to be understood (p. 577).

36. On this question, see J. WOEHRLING, "La modification constitutionnelle de 1987 . . .", pp. 36 ff.

37. "43. An amendment to the Constitution of Canada in relation to any provision that applies to one or more, but not all, provinces, including

    (a) . . .

    (b) any amendment to any provision that relates to the use of the English or the French language within a province,

may be made by proclamation issued by the Governor General under the Great Seal of Canada only where so authorized by resolutions of the Senate and the House of Commons and of the legislative assembly of each province to which the amendment applies."

38. Conversely, under s.41(c) of the *Constitution Act, 1982*, in order to amend a constitutional provision relating to the use of French or English that applies either at the federal level or in all the provinces, it appears that the approval of both federal Houses and *all* provincial legislatures is needed.

39. A provision comparable in substance to s.133 has applied since 1870 in Manitoba: see s.23 of the *Manitoba Act, 1870*. Comparable provisions applicable to the federal government and New Brunswick are also found in ss.17–19 of the *Canadian Charter of Rights and Freedoms*. For detailed analysis of these provisions and of the differences among them, particularly in terms of their formulation, see J.E. MAGNET, "The Charter's Official Languages Provisions: The Implications of Entrenched Bilingualism", (1982) 4 *Supreme Court Law Review* 163, pp. 179 ff.

40. Section 133, for which there currently exists no official French version, provides:

    "Either the English or the French Language may be used by any Person in the Debates of the Houses of the Parliament of Canada and of the Houses of the Legislature of Quebec; and both those Languages shall be used in the respective Records and Journals of those Houses; and either of those Languages may be used by any Person or in any Pleading or Process in or issuing from any Court of Canada established under this Act, and in or from all or any of the Courts of Quebec."

The Acts of the Parliament of Canada and of the Legislature of Quebec shall be printed and published in both those Languages".

41. *A.G. Quebec v. Blaikie*, [1979] 2 S.C.R. 1016.

42. *Supra*, note 23.

43. To amend or repeal the "Quebec branch" of s.133 of the *Constitution Act, 1867*, it would be necessary to use the procedure provided for in s.43(b) of the *Constitution Act, 1982*: see *supra*, note 37.

44. Section 23 of the *Canadian Charter of Rights and Freedoms* provides in particular
    "(1) Citizens of Canada
        (a) whose first language learned and still understood is that of the English or French linguistic minority population of the province in which they reside, or
        (b) who have received their primary school instruction in Canada in English or French and reside in a province where the language in which they received that instruction is the language of the English or French linguistic minority population of the province,
    have the right to have their children receive primary and secondary school instruction in that language in that province.
    (2) . . .
    (3) . . .".

45. [1984] 2 S.C.R. 66.

46. R.S.Q. 1977, c. C-11. The text of s.73 provides as follows:
    "In derogation of section 72, the following children, at the request of their father and mother, may receive their instruction in English:
    (a) a child whose father or mother received his or her elementary instruction in English, in Québec;
    (b . . .
    (c) a child who, in his last year of school in Québec before 26 August 1977, was lawfully receiving his instruction in English, in a public kindergarten class or in an elementary or secondary school;
    (d) the younger brothers and sisters of a child described in paragraph (c).

47. *Supra*, note 44.

48. On this point, see J. WOEHRLING, "La réglementation linguistique de l'affichage public et la liberté d'expression: *P.G. Québec c. Chaussure Brown's Inc.*", (1987) 32 *McGill Law Journal* 878, pp. 880 ff.

49. *Société des Acadiens v. Association of Parents*, [1986] 1 S.C.R. 549.

50. *Idem*, p. 577.

51. *Ford v. A.G. Quebec*, [1988] 2 S.C.R. 712.

52. On s.27 of the *Charter*, see J. WOEHRLING, "Minority Cultural and Linguistic Rights . . ."; J. WOEHRLING, "La Constitution canadienne et la protection des minorités ethniques", (1986) 27 *C. de D.* 171; J. MAGNET, "The Charter's Official Languages Provisions . . .", pp. 173 ff.; M. BASTARACHE, "Le principe d'égalité des langues officielles", in *Les droits linguistiques au Canada*, Cowansville, Les Éditions Y. Blais, 1986,

pp. 539 ff.; R. ANAND, "Ethnic Equality", in *Equality Rights and the Canadian Charter of Rights and Freedoms* (ed. by A.F. BAYEFSKY and M. EBERTS), Toronto, Carswell, 1985, pp. 437 ff.; *Multiculturalism: A Legal Perspective* (Canadian Human Rights Foundation), Toronto, Carswell, 1987; D. BOTTOS, "Multiculturalism: Section 27's Application in Charter Cases Thus Far", (1986) 26 *Alberta Law Review* 621.

53. "15(1) Every individual is equal before and under the law and has the right to the equal protection and equal benefit of the law without discrimination and, in particular, without discrimination based on race, national or ethnic origin, colour, religion, sex, age or mental or physical disability".

54. See V. VAN DYKE, "Equality and Discrimination in Education: A Comparative and International Analysis", (1973) 17 *International Studies Quarterly* 375, p. 384. This does not mean, of course, that the state must grant "official language" status to every language spoken within its territory or provide public education in each of these languages. Various considerations, based on the financial cost of bi- or multi-lingualism or on the necessity of securing a certain level of linguistic homogeneity in society, could warrant limitations on the right to linguistic equality.

55. *Lau v. Nichols*, 414 U.S. 563 (1974).

56. Professor Magnet takes the view that s.27 of the *Charter* can be read as casting an obligation on governments to provide certain services in the language of Canadian cultural communities other than French or English; see MAGNET, "The Charter's Official Languages Provisions . . .", p. 174.

57. Obviously, the preservation and enhancement of the cultures and languages of origin of immigrants do not mean that they are relieved of the obligation to integrate into the society that receives them and to learn the language spoken by that society. Moreover, the integration of minorities into majoritarian culture is necessary if their members are to benefit from genuine equality with the members of the majority. However, "integration" does not mean "assimilation"; minorities must equally be able, insofar as they desire, to preserve and develop their own cultural distinctiveness. On this issue, see F. CAPOTORTI, *Étude des droits des personnes appartenant aux minorités ethniques, religieuses et linguistiques*, New York, United Nations, 1979.

58. On this question, see A. CAIRNS, "Citizens (Outsiders) and Governments (Insiders) in Constitution-Making: The Case of Meech Lake", in *The Meech Lake Accord—L'Accord du Lac Meech, Canadian Public Policy/Analyse de Politiques*, September 1988, 121, p. 136: "For those Canadians who can claim no founding status the stress on priority of arrival as the basis for constitutional ranking is unacceptable, based on a 'rear view mirror vision' . . . and the 'outdated and discredited concept of two founding nations' . . .".

59. It should be noted that many factors currently tend to diminish the concerns associated with the concept of duality; on this evolution, see P. LESLIE, "Canada as a Bicommunal Polity", in C. BECKTON & W. MACKAY, *Recurring Issues in Canadian Federalism* (Vol. 57 in the series of studies commis-

sioned as part of the research program of the Royal Commission on the Economic Union and Development Prospects for Canada), Toronto, University of Toronto Press, 1986, pp. 126 ff.

60. *Constitution Amendment, 1987*, s.9.

61. A. CAIRNS, "Citizens (Outsiders) and Governments (Insiders) . . .", p. 136: "For aboriginal Canadians the designation of others, but not themselves, as a distinct society is an insult and a distortion of history . . . . They claim that their own constitutional recognition as one or more distinct societies is justified by both history and contemporary social and cultural facts".

62. By their very nature the linguistic and cultural rights of aboriginal peoples do not come into conflict with those of the official language minorities nor with those of the francophone majority in Quebec. This is demonstrated in particular by the special status conferred on aboriginal peoples in ss.87, 88, 95, 96 and 97 of the *Charter of the French Language*.

63. See, for example, N. DUPLÉ, "L'Accord du Lac Meech: les inquiétudes féministes sont-elles fondées?", in *L'adhésion du Québec à l'Accord du Lac Meech—Points de vue juridiques et politiques*, p. 68. On the controversy surrounding this issue, see L. SMITH, "The Distinct Society Clause in the Meech Lake Accord . . .", pp. 40 ff.

64. See, for example, N. DUPLÉ, *ibid.*, pp. 72-75.

65. R. JOHNSTON & A. BLAIS, "Meech Lake and Mass Politics: The 'Distinct Society' Clause", in *The Meech Lake Accord—L'Accord du Lac Meech*, p. 32: "On equality, the evidence could not be more clear: Francophone Québécois are markedly more egalitarian than are other Canadians . . . . Francophone Québécois are much more supportive of the efforts to eliminate discrimination against women than are respondents elsewhere". This psychological openness toward equality on the part of Quebec's population, however, is not totally reflected in its institutional and governmental practices; see L. LAMARCHE, "Perspective féministe d'une certaine société distincte: les Québécoises et l'Accord du Lac Meech", in *Competing Constitutional Visions—The Meech Lake Accord*, pp. 23 ff. One should also point out that the organizations representing Quebec women (the *Fédération des femmes du Québec* and the *Conseil du statut de la femme du Québec*) have officially disassociated themselves from the criticisms addressed to the Meech Lake Accord by feminist organizations in English Canada.

66. *A.G. Canada v. Lavell; Isaac v. Bédard*, [1974] S.C.R. 1349.

67. *Reference re Bill 30, An Act to Amend the Education Act (Ont.)*, [1987] 1 S.C.R. 1149.

68. *Supra*, note 9.

69. See K.J. DE JONG, "Sexual Equality: Interpreting Section 28", in *Equality Rights and the Canadian Charter of Rights and Freedoms*, p. 515.

70. I have discussed this point elsewhere; see J. WOEHRLING, "Minority Cultural and Linguistic Rights . . .", pp. 80 ff.

71. On this point, see J. WOEHRLING, "L'article 15(1) de la *Charte canadienne des droits et libertés et la langue*", (1985) 30 *McGill Law Journal* 266, pp. 275 ff.
72. Thus *Alliance Quebec*, the group claiming to represent Quebec anglophones, would like to add to the recognition of Canada's linguistic duality and Quebec's distinct identity a series of provisions equally recognizing the multicultural character of Canadian society and the rights of aboriginal peoples.
73. *Constitution Amendment*, 1987, s.13.
74. A. CAIRNS, "Citizens (Outsiders) and Governments (Insiders) . . .", pp. 125–127.
75. *Idem*, pp. 142–143.
76. To become law, the provisions of the *Constitution Amendment, 1987* relating to the composition of the Supreme Court of Canada and the procedure for amending the Constitution require the agreement of all ten provinces *(Constitution Act, 1982, s.41)*. The provisions relating to duality and Quebec's distinct identity, on the other hand, in my view could be adopted with the agreement of only seven provinces representing at least fifty per cent of the population of all the provinces *(Constitution Act, 1982, s.38)*. For the moment, the various parts of the *Constitution Amendment, 1987* must be adopted as a whole, and thus with the agreement of all the provinces. However, if the opposition of one or more provinces were to prevent adoption of the Accord as a whole, an attempt might be made to sever them and to seek separate adoption of the several parts.

CHAPTER FIVE

THE DILEMMA OF
THE LINGUISTIC
MINORITIES

Most of the English-majority provinces have a poor record in treating their French minorities. Quebec has now caught up with them in this tawdry competition. Pierre Trudeau's program, which the country generally validated, of enhanced minority rights throughout the country, promoted by a federal government of undiminished powers, has vanished. Provincialism and two solitudes triumph.

(Conrad Black, "Constitutional Shambles Replicated by Budget," *Financial Post,* May 17, 1989)

The language sections of the Meech Lake Accord are an honest attempt to address that issue. But, much as we must welcome Quebec's whole-hearted adherence to the Constitution of Canada, the relevant paragraphs of the accord do not, as now formulated, present a completely satisfactory balance between the general commitment to preserve duality and the specific affirmation of Quebec's role to preserve and promote its distinctiveness.

(Commissioner of Official Languages, *Annual Report 1987* [Ottawa: Supply and Services Canada, 1988]: 7)

Reprinted with permission — Alan King, *The Ottawa Citizen*.

INTRODUCTION

Since Confederation, Canada has struggled with the thorny and politically explosive issue of the rights of its religious and linguistic minorities. The British North America (BNA) Act defined those minorities in terms of religion, for educational purposes, to reflect the Protestant community of Quebec, which was predominantly English-speaking, and the Catholic communities outside Quebec, which included French Canadians as well as Irish, Scottish and, eventually, many European nationalities. The linguistic duality of both Quebec and Canada was also recognized in the BNA Act, which made their legislatures and their courts bilingual. The Manitoba Act of 1870 did the same for that province when it was incorporated into Canada. However, these educational and linguistic provisions were abolished by the Manitoba Legislative Assembly in 1890. The Supreme Court restored the bilingual provisions of the Manitoba Act only in the past decade, and the province is struggling to cope with the consequences of this decision. The Northwest Territories were also made officially bilingual in 1885, a provision that was never rescinded when the provinces of Alberta and Saskatchewan were created in 1905. Following a recent Supreme Court decision confirming the bilingual provision in the case of Father André Mercure, both Alberta and Saskatchewan passed legislation severely restricting bilingualism.[1]

Clearly, it has been a long, arduous, uphill struggle for the francophone minorities. The limitations of the BNA Act and the strong and vocal "nativist" sentiments that prevailed in the vast majority of English-speaking provinces well into the twentieth century generated one minority crisis after another—the Acadian schools issue in the 1870s, the Manitoba schools question in the 1890s and the Ontario schools question

during World War I. All these battles humiliated the majority francophone community in Quebec and forced it to come to the defence of
its threatened brethren. In doing so, its leaders, led by Henri Bourassa,
articulated the concept of a bilingual and bicultural Canada that already
existed in the Constitution and needed only the courts and the politicians to enforce it. In the interim, the vast majority of francophones
emigrating from Quebec chose the factories of New England rather than
the farmland of the Canadian West. All these factors made it exceedingly
difficult for Acadians, Franco-Ontarians and French Canadians in the
four western provinces to survive and develop into strong, self-reliant
communities capable of resisting the juggernaught of assimilation.[2]

By the 1950s, the situation of the francophone minorities was
becoming truly desperate. As increasing numbers of francophones left
their predominantly rural communities in search of a wider range of
employment opportunities in the cities of New Brunswick, Ontario and
the western provinces, they found themselves at the mercy of English-
language school systems, government service departments and private-
sector employers. For the better part of a century, the Catholic Church
had provided the francophone minorities with education and social welfare institutions. After World War II, those functions were taken over
by the state, both federal and provincial, thereby placing francophones
at the mercy of anglophone bureaucrats and politicians. As a result, by
1981 the assimilation rates for francophone minorities based on mother-
tongue statistics ranged from a low of 9.75 per cent in New Brunswick
to a high of 72 per cent in British Columbia, with the rates for the other
provinces falling between 30 and 70 per cent.[3]

Only New Brunswick's Acadians, comprising over a third of the
population, were able to entrench in the Charter official status for their
language in the legislature, the courts and the governmental services
of their province. Franco-Ontarians, under Bill 8, have the right to a
limited range of governmental services in their own language, but the
province of Ontario refuses to declare itself officially bilingual. After
decades of linguistic battles, the Constitution Act, 1982 finally
entrenched minority language education rights in section 23 of the
Charter. However, as subsequent events in Alberta and Nova Scotia
have so starkly demonstrated, the implementation of those minority
language education rights has not been without renewed struggles and
increased levels of frustration for the minorities. It took the Alberta
government five years to decide to amend its School Act to comply with
section 23 of the Charter. Even then, it left all the powers of implementation up to the discretion of the Minister of Education and his
bureaucrats.[4]

The Meech Lake Accord, which is a powerful affirmation of the rights of the provinces and symbolizes a highly decentralized form of federalism, has left the linguistic minorities and leaders confused and angry. At the root of this situation is the fact that, in the words of Bryan Schwartz:

> The 1982 Accord strengthened the rights of individual Canadians; the 1987 Accord does not contain a single provision that enhances the court-enforceable rights of anyone. The 'non-derogation' section of the 'Quebec clause' ensures that absolutely nothing in the section can enhance the legal position of an individual in litigation against a government. On the other hand, a major purpose of the 'Quebec clause' is to bolster the position of the Quebec government in court challenges brought by its linguistic minorities.[5]

The recognition of Quebec as a distinct society, coupled with the clause that assigns the legislature and Government of Quebec the role of preserving and promoting this distinct society, serves primarily the interests of the francophone majority. This situation virtually guarantees a collision with the Parliament of Canada, which, under the Accord, has merely the constitutional responsibility to preserve the bilingual nature of Canada, including Quebec. Given the political imperatives of a federal system in which provincial autonomy is sacrosanct, the constitutional responsibilities of the legislature and Government of Quebec as interpreted by the nationalist intelligentsia will take precedence over those of the Parliament of Canada. The same dynamic will occur in all the other provinces, which, henceforth, will have to comply only with the very limited constitutional obligation to preserve the linguistic rights of French-speaking Canadians.

Canada's linguistic minorities, represented by nine provincial francophone associations, as well as the Fédération des francophones hors Québec (FFHQ), Alliance Quebec and the Quebec Association of Protestant School Boards, objected vigorously to the severe constitutional limitation placed upon the Parliament of Canada and the provincial legislatures. In fact, the Accord places no responsibility upon the federal or provincial governments to protect or promote the interests of their linguistic minorities. The francophone minorities generally agreed with the concept of recognizing Quebec as a distinct society and focused their concerns on the lack of a promotion clause. Alliance Quebec expressed strong concern that the distinct society clause would be used to override individual rights and therefore demanded that the entire

Charter remain immune from its interpretative powers. The Quebec Association of Protestant School Boards, noting that the number of English-speaking students in its schools had declined from around 120,000 in 1976 to 66,000 in 1985, wondered why the Prime Minister had not tried to get Premier Bourassa to agree to implement paragraph 23(1)(a) of the Charter, allowing the application of all aspects of the Canada clause to Quebec for English-speaking Canadians.[6]

Professor Michel Bastarache, who has long served as a legal counsel for francophone minorities, has argued that for this reason and others, the Accord does little to strengthen the position of those minorities. The Accord describes Canadian duality in terms of individual rather than community linguistic rights and therefore does not reinforce section 23 of the Charter. Finally, subsection 2(4) of the Accord, which states that the linguistic duality and the distinct society clause cannot ''derogate from the powers, rights or privileges of Parliament or the Government of Canada, or of the legislatures or governments of the provinces, including any powers, rights or privileges related to language,'' works against the minorities. Bastarache contended that:

> despite its role to preserve Franco-Ontarian society and even if the Meech Lake Accord is in effect, the Government of Ontario can repeal Bill 8 respecting French services or Bill 75 granting francophones the right to manage French schools. So there is no guarantee that preservation will even safeguard rights already acquired.[7]

The Mulroney government quietly acknowledged the political clout of the linguistic minorities but refused to address their concerns with the Accord. Senator Lowell Murray defended the linguistic duality clause of the Accord by emphasizing both its symbolic and legal importance for the linguistic minorities. He rejected the demand of representatives of Quebec's anglophone minority that the entire Charter be protected from the distinct society interpretative clause. ''If we were to agree,'' Murray wrote, ''we would risk rendering section 1 of the constitutional amendment virtually meaningless.'' Yet he then went on to argue that ''English-speaking Quebecers are an essential part of'' Quebec's distinct society. The Prime Minister, Murray acknowledged, had attempted to get a clause that would require the provinces and their governments to promote the rights of linguistic minorities, but the premiers objected vigorously. Instead, Murray indicated that his government chose to proceed with promotion of linguistic duality via a revised and strengthened

Official Languages Act, namely, Bill C-72. Increased funds were to be put at the disposal of the provinces and the private sector to encourage them to follow the lead of Ottawa. In short, what could not be accomplished constitutionally, Ottawa would achieve by statute and through its spending powers.[8]

Rather than campaign aggressively for immediate improvements to the Meech Lake Accord, the FFHQ was willing to accept the government's peace offering of a new and improved Official Languages Act. Indeed, when Bill C-72 appeared threatened by opposition in the Tory caucus, the FFHQ's president, Yvon Lafontaine, stated publicly that if Bill C-72 were amended in any fundamental way, the association would advise Premier McKenna of New Brunswick not to ratify the Accord.[9] In a very real sense, the FFHQ had undermined its bargaining position by agreeing at the outset with the Bourassa government's desire to pursue, thanks to the central provision in the Accord, an increasingly unilingual Quebec society. Some FFHQ affiliates felt that the organization should have insisted, from the outset, that Premier Bourassa obtain from a majority of the premiers a commitment to preserving and *promoting* their respective linguistic minorities before giving its consent to the Meech Lake Accord. In fact, the president of the Association canadienne-française de l'Ontario, Jacques Marchand, did reveal before the Ontario Select Committee on Constitutional Reform that Premier Bourassa and Gil Rémillard had promised to protect the rights of francophones outside Quebec. Unfortunately, in the heat of the prolonged all-night discussions, the rights of Canada's linguistic minorities were deemed secondary to those of the majorities.[10]

The FFHQ and its provincial associations, after realizing that their initial political strategy was not going to achieve the desired results for their constituents, decided to withdraw their support for the Meech Lake Accord until the appropriate amendments were made. They want three amendments to the Quebec clause. First, they want the recognition of the collective as well as the individual linguistic rights of francophones. Secondly, the federal and provincial governments and legislatures, they argue, must have the responsibility to promote as well as preserve the duality of Canada. Finally, following the advice of Michel Bastarache, they demand that subsection 2(4) be eliminated from the Accord.[11] Clearly, the francophone associations have come to understand that they cannot advocate an effective and politically viable policy of bilingualism for their constituents while supporting the Quebec government's stated policy of unilingualism.

Georges Arès, speaking on behalf of the Association canadienne-française de l'Alberta, denounces the Accord in a very categorical fashion. He expresses the enormous frustrations and roadblocks faced by Franco-Albertans trying to develop a healthy and vibrant community in a context where, he maintains, it "is obvious that our provincial government is making war on us." The major flaw in the Accord from the vantage point of Franco-Albertans is that it fails to oblige the federal government to promote the linguistic duality of Canada. The Mulroney government's attempt to appease the linguistic minorities with a revised Official Languages Act and increased funds is not a genuine alternative to constitutionally entrenched rights. Arès rejects the Accord's implicit recognition of the political duality of Quebec and Canada. He wants linguistic duality to be defined in terms of minority language communities rather than individual language rights. This, he believes, would strengthen official bilingualism and weaken the concept of language based on territory. He calls upon Prime Minister Mulroney and Premier Bourassa to exercise political and moral leadership by amending the Accord so as to oblige the federal government and Parliament to promote the linguistic minorities.

Alliance Quebec leaders express a sense of betrayal by their provincial government as well as by the Mulroney government in Ottawa. The Accord, they maintain, will destroy the vision and the reality of Canada as a bilingual and multicultural society committed to defending and promoting the rights of individuals and minorities. Alliance Quebec supports the recognition of Quebec as a distinct society providing that all the Charter rights of Quebeckers not be compromised in any manner. To ensure the continued survival of the linguistic minorities, the Alliance recommends that Ottawa and the provinces take on the constitutional responsibility of promoting those communities, alter section 16 to ensure the primacy of the Charter at all times and remove the notwithstanding clause (section 33) from the Charter.

Notes

1. Frances Russell, "Meech Lake Undermines Minority Language Rights," *Winnipeg Free Press*, April 20, 1988; "Language Bill Offers Both 'Oui' and 'Non'," *Regina Leader Post*, April 6, 1988.
2. Arthur Silver, *The French Canadian Idea of Confederation, 1864–1900* (Toronto: University of Toronto Press, 1982).
3. Karen Taylor-Browne, "The Francophone Minority," in Roger Gibbins et al., eds., *Meech Lake and Canada. Perspectives from the West* (Edmonton: Academic Printing and Publishing, 1988): 188–189, Table 2.

4. *Ibid.*, 192–196; E. Apps, "Minority Language Education Rights," *University of Toronto Faculty of Law Review*, 43 (1985); D. Proulx, "La précarité des droits linguistiques scolaires ou les singulières difficultés de mise en oeuvre de l'article 23 de la Charte canadienne des droits et libertés," *Revue Générale de Droit*, 14 (1983); Michel Bastarache, *Les droits linguistiques au Canada* (Cowansville: Les Éditions Y. Blais, 1986).

5. Bryan Schwartz, *Fathoming Meech Lake* (Winnipeg: Legal Research Institute, University of Manitoba, 1987): 214; for a similar viewpoint, see Commission of Official Languages, *Annual Report 1987* (Ottawa: Supply and Services Canada, 1988).

6. Fédération des francophones hors Québec statement to the Special Joint Committee of the Senate and the House of Commons on the 1987 Constitutional Accord, *Minutes of Proceedings and Evidence*, No. 3, August 5, 1987 (Ottawa: Queen's Printer, 1987): 5–23; Société franco-manitobaine statement to the Special Joint Committee of the Senate and the House of Commons on the 1987 Constitutional Accord, *Minutes of Proceedings and Evidence*, No. 11, August 21, 1987, 49–58; Alliance Quebec statement to the Senate Committee of the Whole on the Meech Lake Constitutional Accord, *Debates of the Senate*, December 2, 1987, 2247–2257; Quebec Association of Protestant School Boards statement to the Senate Committee of the Whole on the Meech Lake Constitutional Accord, *Debates of the Senate*, February 3, 1988, 2615–2622.

7. Michel Bastarache statement to the Senate Submissions Group on the Meech Lake Constitutional Accord, *Proceedings*, No. 5, March 18, 1988, 27.

8. Senator Lowell Murray, "The 1987 Constitutional Accord and Linguistic Minorities," *CAUT Bulletin* (March 1988): 7–8.

9. Yvon Lafontaine, *Le Devoir*, 12 février 1988.

10. Association canadienne-française de l'Ontario brief to the Ontario Select Committee on Constitutional Reform, 1987 Constitutional Accord, *Hansard Official Report of Debates*, February 16, 1988, C-177–C-185.

11. Cf. *Le Devoir*, 7 mars 1988; and Pierre Foucher, "*L'Accord du lac Meech* et les francophones hors Québec," in William Pentney and Daniel Proulx, eds., *Canadian Human Rights Yearbook/Annuaire des droits de la personne, 1988* (Ottawa: Les Presses de l'Université d'Ottawa, 1989).

GEORGES ARÈS

THE ACCORD ABANDONS CANADA'S BATTERED AND DEFENCELESS MINORITIES *

Honourable senators, the Association canadienne-française de l'Alberta is pleased to appear before you today to share its comments on the Constitutional Accord of June 3, 1987, better known as the Meech Lake Accord.

The main issue for us is how we can dare to accept the Meech Lake Accord with no changes when it contains serious basic flaws that absolutely must be corrected before the Accord is proclaimed. The signatories to the Accord have all contributed to these flaws, but not a single one is prepared to acknowledge them.

How can we accept such an accord? For ACFA, this defies the imagination and common sense. Canadians from every province and of every political stripe, representatives of numerous associations, have pointed out serious and pertinent flaws in the Accord. We find it inconceivable that politicians could agree to ratify this Accord without correcting these serious flaws.

First, let us note that the Meech Lake Accord does not expressly recognize the rights of the aboriginal peoples on an equal footing with the duality of Canada. For all practical purposes, it enshrines the unequal status of the Yukon and the Northwest Territories. This is a profound injustice to this country's first inhabitants and those of northern Canada, and shows that our present governments lack the political will to consider their aspirations.

There is also a real possibility that the Meech Lake Accord might take precedence over the Canadian Charter of Rights and Freedoms. ACFA fears that the rights recognized in sections 15 and 23 of the Charter may be watered down dramatically because of this precedence.

---

* Brief to the Senate Submissions Group on the Meech Lake Constitutional Accord, *Proceedings*, No. 1, February 29, 1988.

Finally, ACFA is convinced that in the long run, the Accord will lead to the creation of two or three Canadas and will destroy the bilingual Canada that has been built since Confederation. Our politicians and the Meech Lake Accord are heading in the opposite direction from the people of Canada, who increasingly favour bilingualism.

But the most serious flaw in ACFA's view is the lack of any obligation, at least for the federal government, to promote the duality of Canada. Parliament and the provincial legislatures have only an obligation to preserve Canada's fundamental characteristic, whereas Quebec has the responsibility to preserve and promote its distinct society.

Franco-Albertans cannot be satisfied with the response of the federal government that it will be able to use the Official Languages Act to promote Canada's fundamental characteristic. A mere federal act simply does not have the same scope and permanence as the Constitution. Moreover, the whole controversy surrounding Bill C-72 clearly shows the vulnerability of any political will subject to the pressures and narrow views of special interests.

The principle of promotion and the development of official language communities by the federal government must be enshrined in the Constitution. This would counterbalance the lack of promotion by certain provinces, the veiled assimilation policies that some of them implement, and the promotion of Quebec's distinct society. The federal government would thus have the tools needed to prevent the creation of three Canadas: the distinct society of a French-speaking Quebec that may one day become independent; and English-speaking Canada from east to west and in the north, where the preservation of the French fact is ultimately only a long-term strategy of assimilation. Caught between the two, you have the bilingual provinces of New Brunswick and (to some degree) Ontario, whose provincial governments actively promote the duality of Canada. Experience and history show that francophones in western and northern Canada and the Maritimes certainly cannot rely on a similar open-mindedness.

Alberta's current political environment clearly illustrates why ACFA is deeply concerned about the absence of a clause to promote the French fact outside Quebec. Statistics show that without concrete and energetic affirmative action, language minorities assimilate and end up disappearing.

On the one hand, the federal government is not bound by a constitutional obligation to promote them. On the other hand, Franco-Albertans clearly cannot rely on the goodwill of their provincial government to promote its language minority. Think of the Piquette affair and the problems in obtaining the implementation of section 23. Despite two Alberta court decisions, our Minister of Higher Education in Alberta even says that students should learn Japanese rather than French with federal funding. As for court proceedings, Alberta so far refuses to proclaim Part 14.1 of the Criminal Code.

For us Franco-Albertans, who have lost a great deal in many respects since 1885, the mere obligation to protect leaves the door open to assimilation policies by the Alberta government. The English term "preserve" is already interpreted by our government as giving it a licence to maintain the present situation and even to let it deteriorate.

We have fought desperately against assimilation and for our very survival for one hundred years. Even with all of the help that the federal government could give us, Franco-Albertans foresee long years of political and legal battles that will sap their energy and keep them from dedicating themselves to their development as a community. Without active promotion by the federal government, the road becomes not merely difficult but almost impossible.

ACFA feels that paragraph 2(1)(a) overlooks the sociological and philosophical foundations of bilingualism in Canada and considerably restricts the concept of the duality of Canada. A false concept of duality, the political duality of Quebec and Canada, is implicitly recognized in the Accord by the notion of a distinct society in Quebec. The second concept, cultural duality characterized by the existence of two great language communities that presided at the foundation of this country, is affirmed in terms of language only, not language communities.

The text of the June 3, 1987, Accord reduced the recognition of these communities, initially proposed at the meeting at Meech Lake, to recognition of French- or English-speaking individuals. ACFA feels that francophones outside Quebec are the losers in this shift from collective minority rights to individual rights.

We believe that the recognition and endurance of the two great language communities that defined the conditions for the emergence of this country are a basic condition for the existence of the Canadian federation. The notion of the duality of Canada must not only coincide with that of institutional bilingualism but must be rooted in the Canadian reality of the existence of two great cultural and linguistic communities, French and English.

ACFA is happy that Quebec has rejoined the Canadian family and that the rest of Canada has recognized its distinct character. It was necessary for Quebec to be recognized and accepted as a distinct society, but this gain should not have been made at the expense of francophones outside Quebec. In his desire and his haste to obtain an agreement at any cost, Mr. Mulroney yielded to all of Quebec's demands, even relinquishing his historic role in promoting official language minorities.

Mr. Bourassa says that he recognizes a duty toward francophones outside Quebec, but what did he do at Meech Lake? Mr. Bourassa did not demand any constitutional guarantees to protect francophones outside Quebec. Mr. Mulroney betrayed francophones outside Quebec in the constitutional accord, and Mr. Bourassa abandoned us once again.

Yet it would have been easy for Mr. Bourassa to help us in this Accord, because Mr. Mulroney and the other provinces were ready to concede almost anything. So why did Quebec not demand safeguards for francophones outside Quebec? They could have had them for the asking.

ACFA claims that promotion of the duality of Canada by the federal government is not inconsistent with Quebec's distinct society and would not take away any of Quebec's gains. Our existence in years to come largely depends on active promotion by the federal government. The duality of anglophones in Quebec is already being promoted by force of circumstance.

In its own interests, Quebec would be well-advised to work to strengthen francophone communities outside Quebec, first by enshrining the federal government's role in promoting them in the Constitution, and then by its own active promotion of the French fact outside Quebec, including solid, ongoing moral support and tangible and effective financial support. Francophone communities outside Quebec need more than rhetoric and promises. Since Quebec says that it wants to be part of a bilingual Canada, it is high time that it assumed its responsibilities toward francophones outside Quebec and ceased to abandon us whenever it is time to take concrete action as at Meech Lake.

In its political platform entitled *Maîtriser l'avenir*, the Liberal Party of Quebec admits its responsibility to play a leadership role in developing francophone communities outside Quebec and in defending their rights. Is this rhetoric again?

By waging war against Franco-Albertans, the Alberta government is trying to make us "dead ducks," in René Lévesque's famous words. In its own way, the Quebec government is also ensuring that this will happen, that we will be assimilated, by abandoning us at Meech Lake and by failing to assume its responsibilities.

ACFA urges the Senate to do everything in its power to prevent the Meech Lake Accord, as it was signed and now stands, from becoming an integral part of our country's Constitution. Once the Accord is proclaimed, it will be very hard to amend it and to correct the serious flaws that it contains. Once Quebec obtains its distinct society without having to accept the federal government's promotional role, the Quebec government will refuse to make this change once and for all.

Last Thursday's judgment by the Supreme Court of Canada in the Mercure case strikingly shows the need for an enlightened Constitution that expressly recognizes the federal government's role in promoting the duality of Canada. With our past experience, how can we still consider including clauses in the Constitution that not only enshrine historical inequalities once again but also jeopardize the existence outside Quebec of one of our country's two cultural and linguistic communities?

Must we wait another 83 years for the Supreme Court of Canada to confirm the betrayals and abandonments of 1987 as it has just confirmed the betrayals of 1905?

Historically, francophone minorities outside Quebec have always relied on the federal government to protect and promote their interests. In their eagerness to be reelected, federal politicians have not always shown themselves equal to the task. Sir Wilfrid Laurier may be criticized for abandoning Franco-Manitobans in 1897 and francophones in Alberta and Saskatchewan in 1905. But Mulroney, Turner, Broadbent and Bourassa make no better impression. Turner and Broadbent voted in favour of the constitutional accord to buy votes in Quebec, while admitting that it contained serious flaws. After abandoning francophones outside Quebec in the constitutional talks at Meech Lake, Bourassa now seeks to divide and woo them with promises and grants.

What matters to us is to have a constitution that will protect us. If we compare the status of anglophones in Quebec, who have been protected under section 133 of the Constitution since Quebec entered Confederation, we can see the differences between their communities and, say, those of Alberta which did not receive the same protection in Alberta's Constitution in 1905.

Anglophones in Quebec have their own schools. They have their own school commissions, and they have their own universities. What do we have in Alberta? We were used to having these things, such as our own French schools. We do not have them any more; they have been taken away from us since 1905. All of these things are gone.

If we had had the protection of the federal government and our Constitution in 1905, I think that the status of francophones in Alberta today would be quite different and much more comparable to that of anglophones in Quebec.

ACFA believes that it might be more serious to go ahead with the

Accord than to reject it. If the Accord is defeated, our politicians, including Mr. Bourassa, will have the chance to develop a new accord that will truly benefit all Canadians, including francophones outside Quebec, aboriginal peoples, women, the Yukon and the Northwest Territories.

It may not be easy for those who signed the Meech Lake Accord to say that they must start again, but that is what it takes. They must go back to the Accord and make changes to correct the serious flaws that exist.

In closing, we wish to thank the Senate for inviting us to appear and to present our opinion on the Meech Lake Accord.

ALLIANCE QUEBEC

A MINORITY'S PLEA FOR THE SUPREMACY OF THE CHARTER*

Mr. Chairman, I would like to thank you and the members of the committee for giving us the opportunity to speak before the Select Committee on Constitutional Reform. We are pleased to appear before a committee of the Ontario government to discuss what we see as serious and unacceptable shortcomings of the Meech Lake accord. We would like to commend the government of Ontario for holding open hearings on the 1987 constitutional accord, hearings based on the final text of the accord and hearings in the full light of public attention after due time for reflection on the text.

It is with regret and anger that we must say that the governments that are directly representative of our community, that is, the governments in Ottawa and in Quebec City, have abandoned their responsibility to the needs and interests of our community. It is not overly dramatic to suggest that this may be the last public occasion we English-speaking Quebeckers will have to discuss with Canadian legislators why Meech Lake must be changed.

It is not, I believe, wrong for me to hope that here in Toronto, for the first time since the accord was struck, we will be heard openly and reflectively by politicians without the prearranged and partisan conclusions of the debates in Quebec City and Ottawa.

The fact that you have asked Alliance Quebec to your hearings shows clearly that you do not share the view that is rather widely held in Canada today that provincial governments should look only to their own backyards. Your invitation to us shows you understand that the building and amending of the Constitution are more than political deal-making. The Constitution of Canada is not simply a bit of legal paper-

---

*Brief to the Ontario Select Committee on Constitutional Reform, 1987 Constitutional Accord.

work to allow for the smooth running of government in this country. Our Constitution is also the document that defines us as a nation, a document that states what is of most importance to us as Canadians, a document that enshrines a vision of what we are and what we should become.

Today, we would like to discuss with you the vision that lies at the heart of the Meech Lake accord. We will suggest why that vision is inadequate and potentially destructive of the interests of our community and of official language minorities in other provinces, and ultimately destructive of a nobler vision of Canada that inspired us before Meech Lake.

Alliance Quebec represents the English-speaking community of our province. English-speaking Quebec has a long and proud history as an integral and contributing part of Quebec. Since the beginning of the constitutional history of Canada, our community has been recognized as a legitimate and important element of this country with full rights to participate in the life of Quebec and Canada in our own language. Where the state met the individual, in the Legislature and in the courts, our rights to be heard and served in English were made explicit, as were the rights of French-speaking Quebeckers. Section 133 of the British North America Act enshrined the principle of equal footing for what would become Canada's two official languages.

Over the years, our community grew and flourished in the soil of constitutional and political recognition and acceptance. We built schools and hospitals, developed voluntary agencies and public institutions. In recent years our community and its institutions have fared less well, but we still number 800,000 people, more Canadians than at least six of Canada's provinces.

Our community's vision of Canada is clear. It is a vision which we as Alliance Quebec have supported across the country. We believe in a bilingual Canada, a Canada where the English and French languages are equal throughout the country and where all governments work to promote the right of Canadians to live and participate in their official language of choice.

We believe that all Canadians should expect a full complement of basic services in their official language, education, health and social services and government services as well as access to justice in either French or English. We commend the government of Ontario for taking bold steps to provide these sorts of rights and services for its French-speaking minority. The vision of a bilingual Canada seems to lie at the heart of these actions by the government of your province, but we do not believe this vision lies at the heart of the Meech Lake accord.

There are, it seems to us, three views or visions of language in Canada. The simplest and most politically and morally bankrupt of these is that Canada is or should be an English-speaking country. The people who hold this view are in a distinct minority, but they are strong enough at times to stall legislation and intimidate weak politicians. Their narrow, bigoted vision is even intruding into Quebec lately.

The second vision or view is of a bilingual Canada, a vision based on the equality of the two official languages and the provision of a basic complement of individual and minority rights across Canada. This is the vision of which we have spoken and which we hold. This is the vision we believe is found in the 1982 Constitution of Canada, but it is also a vision that proves difficult for governments to realize. In place of this, the best vision of Canada, there has arisen a third view.

This view is one that sees Canada as a nation of duality. Canadians have until recently used linguistic duality and bilingualism interchangeably, but there is in the rhetoric surrounding Meech Lake an emerging definition of duality that is very different from bilingualism. This notion of duality is based not on an inspired vision of the equality of two languages, but rather on the simple, social fact of the existence of two major language groups in Canada. In a pale imitation of bilingualism, this view sometimes works itself up to recognizing the presence of official language minorities within the major language groups, but it does not hold up a difficult yet necessary goal like language equality for governments. It contents itself with a simple description of, and therefore an acceptance of, the status quo. This is the vision of the country that lies at the heart of Meech Lake.

The view that duality and not bilingualism is what characterizes this country also allows governments to shirk responsibility for making language equality a reality. In our own province, it seems to be part of the thinking of a government that allows its language agency to revoke the bilingual status of municipalities and public institutions when the English-speaking population or clientele falls below 50 per cent. Bilingual status in Quebec does not bring with it, as in Ontario, a requirement to provide minority language services. It is rather a dispensation from the prohibition of functioning in the English language. Nevertheless, bilingual status is of critical importance to a number of English-speaking institutions in our province.

The static vision of duality lies behind the Quebec government's rigid reduction of access to English-language schools in Quebec, the ongoing prohibition of the use of one of Canada's official languages on commercial signs, the threat to override fundamental rights if the Supreme Court decides that the sign law violates the Canadian charter, the clamping down on distributors of English-language movies in an attempt to give wider access to dubbed American culture in French. All these actions, we believe, are not inconsistent with the duality view.

Let there be no mistake: There really is a fundamental debate about the nature of our country here in the discussion of the Meech Lake accord. Let there also be no mistake: We have not come to Ontario to seek your direct help on the effects of this vision of Canada's duality in our province. We are ready to fight those battles ourselves. But we are here to say that we believe the Meech Lake accord, which you are charged with investigating and upon which you must give your opinion, compromises the bilingual vision of Canada and weakens our ability to defend our individual rights and our community's interests in Quebec.

The Meech Lake accord has been sold to us by the first ministers as a deal to bring Quebec into the Canadian Constitution. Alliance Quebec has advocated publicly the importance of Quebec becoming a signatory of the Constitution. We have as well supported the idea that Quebec's distinctiveness be recognized within the Constitution, so long as the recognition of that distinctiveness does not compromise the charter rights of Quebeckers.

We have always said that if the supremacy of the charter is recognized, then the Quebec government can take such measures to promote the French language as it sees fit. We were appalled, however, to see how the first ministers dealt with Quebec's demand that our distinctiveness be recognized. Section 2 of the Meech Lake accord outlines two fundamental characteristics of Canada, its duality and the distinctiveness of Quebec's society, and says that the entire Constitution is to be interpreted in the light of these two fundamental characteristics.

But the accord does not include other equally fundamental characteristics of our country, such as the supremacy of fundamental and equality rights in the political life of Canada, the equality of the two official languages, the multicultural nature of our country and the special rights of aboriginal peoples. By not including these other fundamental characteristics, the accord creates a hierarchy of values that the courts of Canada must use to interpret the Constitution. We fear that this hierarchy of values will ultimately work against our interests.

There has been much debate about the implications of section 2 of the accord. Quebec says it gained powers by it. The federal government implies that it does not change anything. Obviously somebody is wrong. If, as Senator Lowell Murray and others have suggested, the duality and distinctiveness clauses of section 2 have little or no impact, then why did the first ministers go to the trouble of protecting the powers, rights and privileges of their governments in subsection 2(4)? Why did they add section 16 which states that section 2 will have no effect on multiculturalism and aboriginal rights as recognized in the 1982 Constitution?

Explicit protection for the rights, powers and privileges of governments, limited protection for multiculturalism and native rights, and no protection for fundamental rights or language equality rights: That is what we see here. As was suggested to you by l'Association canadienne-française de l'Ontario, this looks like a deal for the benefit of governments and not for individuals. This looks like a deal between linguistic majorities. The question has been asked, who spoke for Canada at Meech Lake? We have been asking for eight months, who spoke for the linguistic minorities?

The problems we see arising from the present formulation of sections 2 and 16 have a relatively straightforward solution. Either the supremacy of the charter is guaranteed by strengthening section 16 into a full nonderogation clause of charter rights, or the other fundamental characteristics of this country must be added to section 2 to ensure that the duality and the distinctiveness of Quebec do not stand in isolation as the pre-eminent political values the courts must consider in interpreting the Constitution. Fix section 2 or fix section 16. Without that, this accord does not promote and enshrine the fundamental values that must be at the heart of our Constitution and our country. Without that, this accord should not be approved.

We have already been told in Ottawa and in Quebec that to open the accord would be to destroy it. We have said and we say again, if section 2 and section 16 of the accord do not work to compromise fundamental and minority rights in Canada, if this was not the intention of the first ministers, then make that clear in the accord. Most minority groups in the country have expressed concern about this issue.

If, on the other hand, the duality and distinctiveness clauses do have a potentially negative impact, then we respectfully suggest that you must put the question to yourselves and eventually to the first ministers whether the price of the Meech Lake deal was the supremacy of the charter and the rights of minorities.

These are our main concerns about Meech Lake. There are a number of other concerns noted in our brief, which you have before you. In our view, the accord is seriously flawed in a number of ways. Some of those flaws we can accept. We understand that the quest for perfection cannot be the enemy of progress, but in our estimation, Meech Lake fails to promote a vision of Canada's future based on fundamental principles of individual and linguistic equality. Therefore, the Meech Lake accord is fatally flawed. The basic values of our political life as Canadians are not advanced in this constitutional deal and we say it must be changed or stopped.

Mr. Chairman, you and your committee must write a report on your findings. Are you prepared to write a report which says that the rights of Canadians are unequivocally unaffected by this accord? If you cannot come to that conclusion, are you prepared to say that compromising the rights of Canadians is an acceptable price to pay for securing the accord?

All legislatures in this country are being asked to pass judgement on this accord and all legislatures and legislators will bear direct responsibility for the actions that flow from this accord in Quebec. The best your colleagues in Ottawa could do in their analysis was the following, and I quote from the report of the joint Senate–House of Commons committee published in September 1987:

> In law, the 'distinct society' clause is unlikely to erode in any significant way the existing entrenched constitutional rights of the English-speaking minority within Quebec.

That must rank as one of the most disquieting reassurances in the history of Canada. Somewhere, sometime in this country there must be an honest debate on what Meech Lake means. Alliance Quebec hopes that will happen here in Ontario. As Canada's only English-speaking minority, we face unique challenges in Quebec. We have committed ourselves to meeting those challenges as Quebeckers. We have never turned to other provincial governments to sort out our problems. Therefore, Alliance Quebec has not come to ask that Ontario intervene in the affairs of Quebec. We do, however, ask you to take seriously your responsibility to give national leadership on constitutional and language issues. We therefore call upon you to insist that the following three steps be taken:

1. That the governments of Canada acknowledge their responsibility to promote both official languages.
2. That section 16 be redrafted to ensure the supremacy of the charter, and not just the equality provisions but the whole charter.

3. That you encourage your government to send a clear message to the minorities of this country by stating unequivocally that the government of Ontario will advocate in future constitutional negotiations the removal of the section 33 override clause from the Charter of Rights.

Alliance Quebec's message to you is clear. Help us as Canadians to secure our basic rights and we as English-speaking Quebeckers will make things work for our community in Quebec.

CHAPTER SIX

SPENDING POWERS:

Provincializing

National Programs?

The Meech Lake Accord is deeply flawed, and Canadians should be forewarned of how profoundly it could affect their lives. Meech Lake means, in all probability, that there will be no more 'medicares' in the future—that the bonds of shared, nationwide public services will be weakened.

(A. W. Johnson, brief to the Special Joint Committee of the Senate and the House of Commons on the 1987 Constitutional Accord, August 21, 1987, 1)

The ability of the federal government to foster our sense of national community and to promote nation building will not be diminished . . . . The federal government remains free to propose, renew or modify shared-cost programs without obtaining prior provincial consent or consensus.

(Ian Scott, brief to the Ontario Select Committee on Constitutional Reform, 1987 Constitutional Accord, 40–41)

Reprinted with permission — James F. Todd.

INTRODUCTION

The debate surrounding the proposed amendment to section 106 of the Constitution Act, 1867, which deals with the federal government's spending powers, has been passionate and divisive. This debate did not originate with the Accord. The longstanding battle over the exercise of the federal spending power reflects the power struggle between proponents and practitioners of the politics of a traditional federalism focused on the cleavages of language and province building, on one hand, and advocates of the politics of progressive social reform who are concerned with class, ethnic and religious cleavages, on the other hand. What makes this most recent battle more crucial is the fact that the proponents of the politics of traditional federalism have managed to constitutionalize their vision to the exclusion of the proponents of the politics of progressive social reform. Thus, while generating some of the best analyses of the Meech Lake Accord, the debate demonstrates the degree to which a certain segment of Canada's social, economic and political elites has managed to outmanoeuvre the national social reformers and weaken the existing political culture that underlies the social service state. In the words of Keith Banting, a specialist of the social service state:

> [T]he Meech Lake Accord would reinforce the sensitivity of the Canadian state to the politics of region, language and culture, the historic axis of Canadian politics. The politics of social reform, and the conception of the country and its problems reflected in that agenda, would not gain similar protection.[1]

This situation can be understood only if placed in the context of the historical role that the national government has played in the development of a broad range of universal social service programs, such as medicare, hospital care, old-age security pensions and disability allowances, since World War II. According to a vociferous critic of the Accord and a longstanding social reformer, A. W. Johnson, "one of the distinguishing features of nationhood in Canada—the sharing across the country of certain common public services—has been made possible by the instruments of the Constitution," namely, federal–provincial shared-cost programs or constitutional amendments allowing the federal government to undertake socio-economic programs on its own.[2]

The creation of a political culture conducive to the creation of a social service state was slow to emerge. Governments, particularly those at the provincial level, preferred to spend their tax revenues on private and public projects that contributed directly to capital accumulation. Provincial governments saw little or no political advantage to investing revenues in projects of legitimization, such as health and social welfare programs.

The Depression, followed by World War II, altered this perception, first at the federal government level and then eventually at the provincial level. A vast majority of Canadians from all regions and walks of life chose not to express their renewed sense of national identity through the development of a powerful military–industrial complex, as was the case in the United States. Instead, successive Liberal governments, from that of King to that of Trudeau, through those of St. Laurent and Pearson, shrewdly drew upon this widespread revitalized national consciousness to create and administer, in conjunction with the all too often reluctant provinces, a social service system that strove to enhance the equality of opportunity and condition for all Canadians from coast to coast and from the 49th parallel to the Arctic Ocean. In effect, the national government, after a long search, had found for itself a new national policy to replace John A. Macdonald's old national policy of tariffs, railroads and settlement of the West.[3]

The Constitution Act, 1867 had placed social programs under the jurisdiction of the provinces. The Rowell–Sirois Commissioners had recommended, in their 1940 report, that responsibility for all social programs be transferred to Ottawa. Ottawa pursued this objective during a series of federal–provincial conferences on Reconstruction in 1945–46. The vast majority of the provinces successfully blocked this wholesale attempt to remake the Constitution. Nevertheless, intense public pressure forced the provinces to transfer their constitutional authority over unemployment insurance and old-age pensions to Ottawa. The public's demand for a comprehensive social service system encouraged Ottawa's mandarins and Liberal cabinet ministers to use the national government's spending powers to put into place a wide variety of shared-cost programs to address the social and economic needs of Canadians. As a result, an important dimension of Canadians' sense of national identity, at home and abroad, soon became associated with a myriad of social programs, such as universal old-age pensions, medicare, hospital insurance and unemployment insurance.[4]

During the 1950s, traditional nationalists, the Church and the Duplessis government steadfastly opposed Ottawa's creation of the social service state. At the same time, the emerging neo-nationalists came to understand both the necessity as well as the political and ideological significance of the social service state, in particular its relationship to modern Canadian nationalism and the enhanced role of the national government in the lives of all Canadians. Neo-nationalists responded by demanding that a secular, interventionist Quebec state regain exclusive control over both the funding and the administration of all social service programs, including family allowances, unemployment insurance and pensions. Since the beginning of the Quiet Revolution in 1960, successive Quebec governments have pursued this objective with considerable success. Quebec opted out of most of the shared-cost programs during the decade, with full financial compensation in the form of twenty additional personal income tax points, and gained control over its own fully funded pension scheme, which provides the province with an enormous source of developmental capital. On the other hand, Quebec proved unable to get Ottawa to relinquish control over the hospital insurance and social service programs.[5]

The remaining provinces chose not to follow Quebec's lead in opting out of the shared-cost programs, at least not until Ottawa decided to place severe limitations on the growth of shared-cost program budgets while proceeding with the implementation of the very costly shared-cost program of medicare. Ontario put up a valiant but politically unwinnable battle against medicare, and Quebec began to gain important provincial allies against Ottawa's use of its spending powers to initiate social programs that the provinces considered to be under their own constitutional jurisdiction. This development coincided with the Trudeau Liberal government's decision in the 1970s to move away from shared-cost programs, so as to curtail spending on programs of social legitimization, while increasing spending on programs of capital accumulation during a period of rising unemployment and inflation. This conjuncture of circumstances created a propitious climate for the creation of a new financial arrangement between Ottawa and the provinces for funding the shared-cost programs involving health insurance and post-secondary education. The Established Programs Financing (EPF) entailed block grants to the provinces, based on population size and the Gross National Product, as well as other cash payments and abatements. These unconditional grants allowed the provinces to cut back—in some cases almost one hundred per cent—their share of funds for these programs, thereby effectively undermining the raison d'être for Ottawa's use of its spending powers in the first place.[6]

Once Ottawa realized that the provinces were quickly abusing the flexibility granted to them under the EPF program, the politicians and bureaucrats scrambled to work out a strategy of damage control. Once returned to office, the Trudeau government created the Task Force on Federal–Provincial Fiscal Arrangements (known as the Breau Task Force), which recommended separating the block grants for health and education in order to impose tighter controls over the former. Emmett Hall, in a report for Health and Welfare Canada in 1980, demonstrated just how politically sensitive the field of medicare was for all politicians.[7] Indeed, the Minister of Health and Welfare in the Trudeau government, Monique Bégin, drew upon this identification of Canadian nationalism with social service programs when she introduced a new Canada Health Act to bring an end to the extra-billing that many provinces had allowed to proliferate in the 1970s and early 1980s. All premiers quickly discovered, much to their chagrin, that the Minister had the full backing of a solid majority of Canadians and both opposition parties in the House of Commons. In the end, even the rich and powerful province of Ontario was forced to comply with the new act, enduring a bitter and divisive doctors' strike in the process.[8] Other efforts by Ottawa to re-establish some level of control over the block grants for post-secondary education were unsuccessful, despite a hard-hitting report by A. W. Johnson that received the full backing of the Canadian Association of University Teachers and the Association of Universities and Colleges of Canada.[9]

Given Ottawa's renewed hard line on the major shared-cost programs, the provinces, with Quebec in the lead, decided to curtail, once and for all, Ottawa's spending powers via a constitutional amendment. Quebec feared Ottawa's reimposition of controls, as well as the growing public demand for new national social programs such as day care. By the mid-1980s, Premier Bourassa, assured of support from several other provinces, demanded a constitutional amendment that would allow all provinces to opt out, with full financial compensation, from any new social programs in the area of provincial jurisdiction that were implemented by the national government. After intense discussions, the Prime Minister and the premiers agreed to this request, with the added proviso that the province choosing to opt out had to carry ''on a program or initiative that is compatible with the national objectives.''

This amendment has been hailed by Premier Bourassa because it gives Quebec the flexibility ''it needs to implement measures and programs that, while compatible with national objectives, will more accurately reflect its own needs.''[10] There is a small but vocal group of constitutional experts and social scientists, including Peter Hogg, Richard Simeon, Thomas Courchene, Keith Banting, Andrew Petter and Stefan Dupré, who support the Accord's curtailment of the federal spending power, for various reasons. According to Hogg, the existing Constitution is not entirely clear, and the Meech Lake Accord's amendment to section 106 ''constitutes a clarification of the breadth of the federal spending power.''[11] Richard Simeon concurs, adding that ''the opting-out clause ensures that this power will not be used to subvert the division of powers, and the provinces will be able to vary their programs in accord with local needs.''[12] Thomas Courchene contends that the Accord's section 106A makes the Constitution more federal in nature, thereby more accurately reflecting the sociological reality of Canada as a decentralized confederation of provincial societies. He believes that section 106A will ''encourage the design and implementation of new shared-cost programs.''[13] Andrew Petter, a vigorous critic of the federal spending power on the grounds that it ''compromises both the federal and the democratic character of the Canadian state,'' argues that section 106A does not go far enough.[14]

One of the strongest supporters of the Meech Lake Accord and, in particular, section 106A is political scientist Stefan Dupré, who specializes in federal–provincial fiscal relations. He shares all the points of view expressed above, and he refers to section 106A of the Meech Lake Accord as ''a masterpiece of intergovernmental compromise.'' He believes that it leaves the question of federal grants to institutions under provincial jurisdiction to be decided by future politicians rather than the courts. It obliges the national government to compensate provinces that opt out of future shared-cost programs if they mount compatible programs. At the same time, section 106A legitimizes federally conditioned payments to provinces in areas of exclusive provincial jurisdiction. Professor Dupré notes that section 106A does not in any way curtail national government payments to individuals, the most politically potent vehicle of the federal spending power. He does warn, however, that the ambiguity of the terms in section 106A will prevent federal and provincial politicians from resolving their differences of interpretation in the courts. In short, section 106A will simply reinforce the existing pattern by pressuring federal and provincial politicians into a negotiating process that will result in a politically acceptable consensus on any new shared-cost programs. Finally, section 106A will allow for more provincial variation, especially in the grey areas of the Constitution, while encouraging governments to use "tax expenditures" to achieve their respective social and economic policy objectives.

A very different interpretation of section 106A was advanced by Ginette Rodger, Executive Director of the Canadian Nurses Association (CNA), in her March 2, 1988, presentation to the Senate Committee of the Whole on the Meech Lake Constitutional Accord. Ms. Rodger expressed the CNA's concern with the deliberately vague language of certain terms used in section 106A, such as "compatible" and "national objective." The CNA is concerned that its commitment to the creation of a national program to ensure primary health care services could be thwarted in a couple of ways if section 106A becomes part of the Constitution. Provinces will invariably wish to focus on different aspects of primary health care, thereby undermining any universality. Funds allocated for one national objective, such as primary health care, could conceivably be used for another national objective, such as improved roads. The CNA also contends that opting out threatens universality and accessibility in existing and future health care programs, because all these programs have to reform periodically. The provinces will have ample opportunity to opt out of existing programs during the renewal process, take the funds and create compatible programs. Interested groups and individuals will have to expend large sums of money and time in order to contest, in the courts, the provinces' varying definitions of compatibility. In the interim, universality, accessibility and portability will all be jeopardized. The CNA made two concrete proposals: one, that the term "national standard" replace the term "national objective," and two, that the Senate consider excluding the health care system from section 106A.[15]

One of the harshest critics of the Meech Lake Accord's amendment restricting the national government's spending powers is Deborah Coyne, a constitutional lawyer and policy analyst. She advances three arguments to demonstrate why section 106A of the Accord is fundamentally flawed. Her first argument is that the built-in incentive for the provinces to opt out of any new national social and economic programs, with financial compensation, will invariably weaken Ottawa's role in the creation and maintenance of a shared national community based on greater equality of opportunity and condition. Province building will, in due course, take precedence over nation building as Ottawa's capacity to initiate programs that generate social and political integration is curtailed by the Constitution.

Ms. Coyne's second argument pertains to the ambiguity of the terms of section 106A: "national objective," "program or initiative" and "compatible with." This ambiguity will erode the powers of our legislatures and legislators because the inevitable disputes involving social policy formulation, rather than strictly principle, will be resolved by Supreme Court justices. The current flexibility has enabled the national government to respond to rapidly changing social and technological circumstances despite the highly rigid division of powers in the Constitution Act, 1867. Deborah Coyne's third, more general, argument is to the effect that the restriction on Ottawa's spending powers, when taken in conjunction with the other measures of the Meech Lake Accord pertaining to provincial appointments to the Senate and the Supreme Court and the annual first ministers' conferences, entails an excessive devolution of powers to the provinces.

The central argument of both individuals and associations critical of section 106A of the Accord addresses the very nature or kind of government structure under which Canadians desire to live. According to these critics, an already highly decentralized federal system of government will evolve, in due course, into an even more decentralized confederal system with the de facto residual powers being exercised by the provinces rather than by the national government. What particularly motivates their concern with constitutional reform and the Meech Lake Accord is the belief that if Canada is to survive as a dynamic nation-state in an increasingly interdependent and competitive world, it must have a national government with a sense of purpose and the constitutional capacity to achieve whatever collective objectives Canadians aspire to.

Notes

1.   Keith G. Banting, "Federalism, Social Reform and the Spending Power," *Canadian Public Policy/Analyse de Politiques*, XIV (1988): S91; his "Political Meaning and Social Reform," in K. E. Swinton and C. J. Rogerson, eds., *Competing Constitutional Visions—The Meech Lake Accord* (Toronto: Carswell, 1988): 163–173.

2. A. W. Johnson, "The Meech Lake Accord and the Bonds of Nationhood," in Swinton and Rogerson, *Competing Constitutional Visions*, 147. See also his statements to the Special Joint Committee of the Senate and the House of Commons on the 1987 Constitutional Accord, *Minutes of Proceedings and Evidence*, No. 11, August 1987 (Ottawa: Queen's Printer, 1987): 33–49, to the Ontario Select Committee on Constitutional Reform, 1987 Constitutional Accord, *Hansard Official Report of Debates*, March 9, 1988, and to the Senate Committee of the Whole on the Meech Lake Constitutional Accord, *Debates of the Senate*, Vol. 131, No. 126, March 16, 1988, 2850–2857.

3. Garth Stevenson, *Unfulfilled Union. Canadian Federalism and National Unity* (Third Edition, Toronto: Gage, 1989): 151–158.

4. J. L. Granatstein et al., *Twentieth Century Canada* (Second Edition, Toronto: McGraw-Hill, 1986): 313, 339–344, 379; J. L. Granatstein, *Canada 1957–1967. The Years of Uncertainty and Innovation* (Toronto: McClelland and Stewart, 1986): 169–197.

5. Michael D. Behiels, *Prelude to Quebec's Quiet Revolution. Liberalism versus Neo-nationalism 1945–1960* (Montreal/Kingston: McGill–Queen's University Press, 1985): 187–194; Roger Marier, "Les objectifs sociaux du Québec," *Canadian Public Administration*, 12, No. 2 (1969): 181–197.

6. Stevenson, *Unfulfilled Union*, 162–169.

7. Health and Welfare Canada, *Canada's National-Provincial Health Program for the 1980s: A Commitment for Renewal* (Ottawa: 1980).

8. Stevenson, *Unfulfilled Union*, 171–174.

9. A. W. Johnson, *Giving Point and Purpose to the Federal Financing of Post-secondary Education and Research in Canada* (Ottawa: Queen's Printer, 1985).

10. Québec, *Débats de l'Assemblée nationale*, 18 juin 1987.

11. Peter Hogg, "Analysis of the New Spending Provision (Section 106A)," in Swinton and Rogerson, *Competing Constitutional Visions*, 157. In fact it is precisely because Québécois nationalists believe that section 106A constitutionalizes Ottawa's spending powers in areas of provincial jurisdiction that they condemn the Meech Lake Accord. See Andrée Lajoie, "The Federal Spending Power and Meech Lake," in *ibid.*, 175–185.

12. Richard Simeon, statement to the Special Joint Committee of the Senate and the House of Commons on the 1987 Constitutional Accord, *Minutes of Proceedings and Evidence*, No. 5, August 11, 1987, 72. See also Banting, "Political Meaning and Social Reform," 162–165.

13. Thomas J. Courchene, "Meech Lake and Socio-economic Policy," *Canadian Public Policy/Analyse de Politiques*, XIV (1988): S66.

14. Andrew Petter, "Meech Ado About Nothing? Federalism, Democracy and the Spending Power," in Swinton and Rogerson, *Competing Constitutional Visions*, 187–201. Advancing the opposite argument is Malcolm Brown, "An Economic Perspective," in Roger Gibbins et al., eds., *Meech Lake and Canada. Perspectives from the West* (Edmonton: Academic Printing and Publishing, 1988): 131–136.

15. Ginette Rodger's statement to the Senate Committee of the Whole on the Meech Lake Constitutional Accord, *Debates of the Senate*, Vol. 131, March 2, 1988, 2807–2816. For a similar critique see the Canadian Council on Social Development's statement to the Special Joint Committee of the Senate and the House of Commons on the 1987 Constitutional Accord, *Minutes of Proceedings and Evidence*, No. 12, August 25, 1987, 36–53.

DEBORAH COYNE

THE MEECH LAKE ACCORD AND THE SPENDING POWER PROPOSALS: FUNDAMENTALLY FLAWED *

Introduction and Overview

Among the more controversial provisions of the Constitutional Accord recently concluded by the First Ministers are those involving a limitation of the federal spending power. Under the Meech Lake Accord, the federal government is required to provide reasonable compensation to any province that decides to opt out of new national shared-cost programs in areas of exclusive provincial jurisdiction, if the province carries on a program or initiative compatible with the national objectives.[1]

The federal government argues that the purpose of the provision is not to define or extend the spending power of Parliament, but simply to limit it in certain specific circumstances to accommodate some of Quebec's longstanding objections to the unrestricted exercise of the power. To support its position, it points to subsection 2 of proposed section 106A of the Constitution Act, 1867 that states that ''nothing in this section extends the legislative powers of the Parliament of Canada or of the legislatures of the provinces.'' Indeed, according to the federal government, the spending power is in fact strengthened since it is now explicitly mentioned in the Constitution. Ironically, this view is also shared by many critics who are opposed to any acknowledgment of the right of the federal government to spend in areas of provincial jurisdiction under any circumstances, however circumscribed.[2]

In my view, the constitutional limitations on the federal spending power are fundamentally flawed for three critical reasons. First and foremost, the federal government has failed to appreciate the broader, intan-

---

* *CAUT Bulletin* (January 1988).

gible importance of national social and economic programs in contributing to our sense, however fragile, of shared national community. Such programs reflect our commitment to helping out the weaker regions and to reducing inequalities of income and wealth among individual Canadians. In short, the proposed spending power limitations are at odds with our commitment to promoting greater social justice and a fairer, more compassionate society.

The Meech Lake Accord proposals will severely constrain the federal government's ability to initiate new programs and impose critical national standards in a variety of areas that may require national action in the future. Examples include child care, a comprehensive disability insurance scheme, a national science and technology strategy, a national commitment to improve the quality and accessibility of post-secondary education, the integration of our social assistance and employment policies, new services to cope with our aging population, and environmental protection. Instead, we will end up with a patchwork quilt of national social and economic programs—a checkerboard Canada guided by cash register politics—something that will increasingly attenuate our sense of national community.

A second fundamental flaw in the proposed constitutional limitations on the spending power relates to their ambiguity and the effective shift of important political powers to an ill-equipped judiciary. The spending power of both the federal and provincial governments already has a secure, albeit unwritten, constitutional basis, and the absence of an explicit reference in the Constitution has enhanced its utility as a means of injecting needed flexibility into the all too rigid federal–provincial division of powers that has existed in more or less the same form since 1867. The spending power has permitted the federal government to respond sensitively to emerging issues of national importance, notably, medicare, post-secondary education, and social assistance policies. And in response to provincial criticism, administrative options have been built into programs that have allowed Quebec, for example, to opt out of the Canada Assistance Plan (CAP) with fiscal compensation, and to vary the nature of family allowances, without impairing the necessary federal leadership role. For the future, it is critical to maintain a similar degree of flexibility.

Yet the Meech Lake Accord will inevitably detract from this flexibility and severely impair the future evolution of the spending power as an instrument for change. More importantly, its constitutional entrenchment transfers critical powers to ill-equipped judges to decide a whole range of essentially political/policy questions such as what constitute "national objectives," or when a "program or initiative" is "compatible with" such initiatives so that a provincial government is entitled to reasonable compensation.

If some explicit constitutional limitation is judged to be necessary, then as was suggested in the 1969 federal discussion paper on "Federal–Provincial Grants and the Spending Power of Parliament," the final solution of the constitutional position must logically be considered only within the framework of a more comprehensive settlement of the division of powers and responsibilities between the two levels of government. To do otherwise amounts to a serious abdication of federal leadership in constitutional negotiations. As Donald Smiley has succinctly noted, "Embodying the restriction on the spending power in an inflexible manner in the constitution may well amount to a resolution of recent political difficulties at the cost of hobbling future policy makers in meeting the [economic, political and social] problems which will undoubtedly confront them."[3]

A final reason why the spending power proposals are fundamentally flawed is that they set in motion undesirable political dynamics that will seriously damage our coherence as a nation and our ability to pull together to meet the national and international challenges that lie ahead. In this connection, the spending power proposals must be assessed in the overall context of the Accord, which involves a substantial devolution of power to the provinces and significant shift of political dynamism on matters of national importance away from the federal Parliament, as well as the undermining of the Charter of Rights and Freedoms. The most relevant provisions of the Accord include the distinct society clause, the constitutional entrenchment of at least two annual first ministers' conferences, the extensive veto powers over constitutional change given to the provinces, and the effective transfer to the provinces of the power to appoint members of the Supreme Court of Canada and the Senate—two critical national institutions.

The political dynamics generated by the spending power proposals will compound and accelerate this shift of power to the provinces. Perhaps most importantly the provisions make it far too easy for provinces to opt out of a shared-cost program with compensation. This not only raises the spectre of significant variations among provinces with respect to, for example, child care arrangements, but also puts in question the willingness of the federal government to even attempt to implement any such initiative at all. More specifically, why would the federal government proceed to initiate and develop a new program and incur the heat of raising the necessary tax revenue, only to transfer the money anonymously to the provincial government, which will reap the political credit for the delivery of the program or initiative?

The relationship between the spending power provisions and the Charter of Rights and Freedoms must also be assessed. For in addition to gravely weakening the federal government, the Accord undermines the Charter and our commitment as a people to respect and promote basic rights and freedoms. This is most evident in the distinct society clause, which will permit the Quebec government to override the Charter. But more generally, the application of the Charter to most provisions of the Accord is seriously and unacceptably in doubt as a result of the specific reference to certain Charter rights in only a couple of the Accord provisions.

Constitutional reform is not simply a matter of First Ministers and the trading of executive, legislative and judicial powers with little consideration for the rights of individuals who will inevitably be affected by the changes. The proposals to impose constitutional limitations on the spending power are no exception, and it is important to ensure that our Charter rights, particularly the broad guarantees of equality, can still be asserted against both levels of government in the exercise of their spending power. Thus, at the very least, a new section should be inserted in the Accord that explicitly states that nothing in the Accord affects any of our basic rights and freedoms in the Charter.

But this is only a second-best solution. The Meech Lake Accord and the spending power provisions are fundamentally flawed. It is necessary to go back to the constitutional bargaining table to seek a better accord that will more effectively accommodate Quebec's special concerns with respect to linguistic and cultural security, but that will also ensure that Canada continues to function coherently as one nation. And this time all Canadians must be allowed and encouraged to participate in creating any new arrangements that will so fundamentally influence our evolution as a nation for years to come. In this way, we can all examine in a constructive manner the significant challenges to the Canadian society and economy that lie ahead and the respective federal and provincial roles in meeting those challenges. Nothing less than the future of Canada as a progressive, dynamic nation is at stake.

I   The Spending Power and Our Sense of National Community

The value of national social and economic programs, including those in areas of exclusive provincial jurisdiction, in contributing to our sense of national community has been underestimated to date. It was certainly not sufficiently appreciated by the federal government in negotiating the Meech Lake Accord.

To begin with, the quantitative and qualitative importance of the federal spending power to individual Canadians can be gauged by examining the annual inventory of federal–provincial programs published by the Federal–Provincial Relations Office. The highlights for the fiscal year 1985–86 have been summarized by Frank Carter in a recent article entitled ''How to Tame the Spending Power.''[4]

In 1985–86, federal cash transfers to the provinces amounted to $20.2 billion, and the value of federal tax transfers equalled $6.9 billion. The total $27 billion accounted for 19.4% of the federal spending estimates for that year.[5]

With respect to total provincial revenues for 1985–86, major federal transfers for equalization, welfare assistance and post-secondary education are estimated to represent over 40% of provincial revenues in the Atlantic provinces, over 30% in Quebec and Manitoba, 20% to 25% in British Columbia, Saskatchewan and Ontario, 13% in Alberta, and 70% in Yukon and the Northwest Territories. Finally, with reference to specific joint programs, the federal government transferred over $5 billion with no strings attached to the have-not provinces under the equalization program, $3.5 billion for welfare assistance under the Canada Assistance Plan, $4.5 billion for provincial medicare and hospitalization, $1 billion for extended health care, $2 billion for post-secondary education, and $7 billion in tax point transfers under the Established Programs Financing arrangements for health care and post-secondary education.

The need for such massive transfers is of course closely related to the gap between the expenditure responsibilities of the provinces and their revenue raising capacities—something that varies significantly among provinces. As Maslove and Rubashewsky note in the 1986 edition of *How Ottawa Spends*, ''some provinces can provide a package of public services at lower tax rates than others, either because the fiscal capacities of the provinces differ or because the per capita costs of providing services differ due to factors such as population density. Thus, if as a matter of equity, all Canadians should receive these services at similar costs, the financial involvement of the federal government is required."[6]

To some extent, this fiscal gap is addressed explicitly through unconditional transfers to provincial governments under the equalization program. The commitment to such equalization was given constitutional status in section 36 of the Constitution Act, 1982. Subsection (1) provides that "Parliament and the legislatures, together with the government of Canada, and the provincial governments, are committed to (a) promoting equal opportunities for the well-being of Canadians; (b) furthering economic development to reduce disparity in opportunities, and (c) providing essential public services of reasonable quality to all Canadians." Subsection (2) then goes on to set out expressly the commitment of Parliament and the government of Canada "to the principle of making equalization payments to ensure that provincial governments have sufficient revenues to provide reasonably comparable levels of public services at reasonably comparable levels of taxation."

Some observers, notably conservative economists whose overriding fixation with reducing the federal deficit leads them to advocate the elimination of virtually all federal spending on shared-cost programs, argue on efficiency grounds that all federal fiscal transfers to the provinces should now be funnelled through the equalization program on an unconditional basis.[7] The current Intergovernmental Affairs Minister in Quebec, Gil Rémillard, goes even further. He argues that this is now constitutionally required under section 36 and that Ottawa's spending authority for public services can be exercised only through the unconditional equalization system and not through conditional grants whereby Ottawa attempts to impose national standards.[8]

In sharp contrast, other constitutional experts believe that section 36 will not be given any real meaning by judges and will therefore have little impact on federal–provincial fiscal arrangements. According to Andrée Lajoie, for example, section 36 is a declamatory clause expressing a vague statement with no real application. "At best it serves an ideological purpose."[9]

Still others argue that the current equalization program that equalizes provincial fiscal capacities only to a Representative Five Province Standard itself violates section 36, which now requires the payments to conform to a Representative National Average Standard in order to discharge the obligation to ensure "reasonably comparable public services."[10] Alternatively, compliance with section 36 may require a complete shift in the basis of the program to the equalization of real income per capita rather than the equalization of tax rates among provinces.

Finally, section 36 may also require conditions to be attached to the equalization grants so as to link the payments, for example, to the elimination of interprovincial barriers to trade or to adjustments in the provincial minimum wage.[11]

The impact of section 36 of the Constitution Act, 1982 on the federal spending power and federal–provincial fiscal relations, in general, is clearly controversial and will be discussed further in Part II of this paper. It is sufficient to emphasize here that the advocates of eliminating or severely restricting the federal government's ability to attach conditions to transfers to the provinces are prominent among those who fail to appreciate or prefer to ignore the importance of the spending power in building our sense of national community.

The rationale for using the federal spending power to enable Parliament to contribute towards programs in fields of provincial jurisdiction and establish minimum national standards is perhaps most clearly expressed in the 1969 federal government Discussion Paper. The argument was made that the justification ''is to be found in the very nature of the modern federal state—in the economic and technological interdependence, in the interdependence of the policies of its several governments, and in the sense of community which moves its residents to contribute to the well-being of residents in other parts of the federation.''[12]

In terms that presage those of the debate almost twenty years later, the Discussion Paper went on to provide examples of the interdependence that dictated federal action: "The effectiveness of pollution control, for example, affects the people in neighbouring provinces; provincial educational systems contribute or fail to advance the economic growth of Canada as a whole; and the equality of opportunity across the country, or the lack of it, affects the well-being of Canadians generally. . . . Moreover, the mobility of Canadians—increasing year by year—itself creates a kind of interdependence: a person in almost any part of Canada, accustomed to the expectation that his children will sooner or later move to other parts of the country, develops an interest in the public services in other provinces as well as public services in his own province—hospital and medical care being the most obvious examples.''[13] More generally, since a province will inevitably wish to avoid incurring costs that will provide benefits to other provinces or other residents, a federal role is essential to ensure an optimal level of spending.[14]

In retrospect, it is now very clear that the major shared-cost programs, particularly in the area of social policy, have been extremely important to the process of social integration in Canada. As Keith Banting has recently pointed out, universal social programs represent one of the very few spheres of shared experience for Canadians, an important aspect of our lives which is common, irrespective of region or language. As the national debate over the Canada Health Act demonstrated, for example, our national health care program has a natural constituency right across this country in a way that the National Energy Program never could.[15]

The federal government is the only government in our federal system that brings the national perspective to bear on such critical issues as: "What in terms of living standards, and particularly in terms of public services, does it mean to be a Canadian citizen?"[16] Equally, it is clear that if there is a national interest in the provision of certain public services, the federal government has a critical role to play in establishing national minimum standards and some measure of uniformity across provinces.

In this connection, it is interesting to note that Claude Forget, a former Minister of Social Affairs in Quebec, argues that the federal spending power has been and continues to be the most important method for harmonizing social policies in Canada.[17] Although he also argues for a form of constitutional restriction, he emphasizes that the federal power to initiate shared-cost programs and to impose national standards must not be impaired. Instead, the federal government should restrict the spending power to the pursuit of (1) national standards determining the program in question, and the expenditures that may legitimately be made in connection with it; and (2) national standards determining who is entitled to benefits or payments from a given program, and under what conditions.

In emphasizing the need to maximize flexibility in the exercise of the federal spending power in areas of exclusive provincial jurisdiction, one must acknowledge of course that certain national social programs, notably medicare, have been "born in the provinces" and that the provinces have frequently acted as catalysts for reform.[18] But it does *not* follow that "it is usually far more difficult to mobilize the national electorate in favour of a new social initiative than it is a provincial electorate" or that "national politics is [necessarily] preoccupied with mediating among competing regional, cultural and linguistic interests and that it is within the less diverse provincial units that economic and social issues occupy central stage."[19]

The very nature of a federal system such as ours encourages valuable experiment and innovation in a wide range of areas by *both* levels of government. Often, the initiative for progressive change will occur at the provincial level; but we must then ensure that the federal government has the ability, as it did in respect of medicare, to devise a national program with national standards to ensure that all Canadians can benefit from such progressive initiatives. Furthermore, as recent experience demonstrates all too clearly, the provinces do *not* exhibit a general tendency towards social progress, especially under conditions of fiscal restraint.

The implementation of a comprehensive national disability insurance scheme based on social insurance principles and involving the elimination of lawsuits as a means of compensation is an example of a future national initiative involving the exercise of the federal spending power and the imposition of national standards relating to public administration, comprehensiveness, accessibility, portability and universality, similar to medicare. Yet the federal government would be building on progressive initiatives in a number of provinces, notably, Quebec's public system of no-fault, no-tort automobile insurance that is now integrated with the workers' compensation system, and major social reforms under way in Ontario.[20]

In my view, the Meech Lake Accord limitations on the exercise of the federal spending power in areas of exclusive provincial jurisdiction will gravely undermine the federal government's ability to establish national programs with minimum national standards. Not only will the courts be involved in deciding essentially political questions and thereby hamstringing our elected representatives, but the ease with which provinces can opt out will mean that we will end up with, for example, significant regional variations in a future child care program or a future environmental protection initiative. This, in turn, will result in unacceptable distinctions among Canadian citizens depending on one's province of residence and will increasingly attenuate our sense of national community.

II Excessive Ambiguity and an Inappropriate Role for the Judiciary

The second fundamental flaw in the proposed constitutional limitations on the spending power relates to their ambiguity and the unacceptable shift of important political powers to an ill-equipped judiciary. In order to better understand this criticism, it is necessary to outline the existing constitutional basis for the spending power and the nature of the concerns expressed by the provinces, especially Quebec, in the constitutional reform discussions over recent years. It will then be possible to assess whether any explicit constitutional limitation is in fact desirable and, if so, in what form.

The "spending power" has been defined in a number of ways for constitutional purposes. Perhaps the most useful is the definition set out by the late Elmer Driedger in 1981: "Spending power means the power of Parliament to make payments to people or institutions or governments for a purpose, the subject matter of which is not necessarily one in relation to which it may exclusively make laws."[21]

Although this definition may appear at first glance to be somewhat convoluted, such a formulation is necessary because, as Driedger points out, the legislative power in the Constitution Act of 1867 is conferred by reference to *classes of subject*. The key sections—sections 91 and 92—do not list *purposes*. Thus both levels of government may carry on many activities of a business or commercial character or may spend money on something, the subject matter of which falls within the exclusive legislative powers of the other level of government. When the federal government, for example, gives money to a university, this is not making laws in respect of education. Or when British Columbia owns and operates a ferry service between the mainland and Vancouver Island, this does not involve making laws in respect of navigation and shipping—an area of exclusive federal responsibility.

The specific constitutional source for the spending power is the subject of some debate. According to the late Frank Scott, spending is a valid exercise of the Crown prerogative power and the only constitutional requirement for Crown gifts is that they must have the approval of Parliament or of the legislature.[22] Making a gift is not the same as making a law. Generosity is not unconstitutional and the federal government may attach conditions to any gift and establish criteria that must be met by the recipient.

Other commentators, such as Donald Smiley, Joseph Magnet and Gerald LaForest, prefer to ground the spending power on a combination of the federal legislative authority in respect of public debt and property (s.91(1A)) and taxation (s.91(3)), and the power in s.102 to spend the Consolidated Revenue Fund.[23] This approach draws support from the following comments of Lord Atkin in the leading case, *Reference re Employment and Social Insurance Act*, in 1937: "That the Dominion may impose taxation for the purpose of creating a fund for special purposes, and may apply that fund for making contributions in the public interest to individuals, corporations or public authorities, could not as a general proposition be denied."[24]

Lord Atkin, however, then went on to establish certain parameters to this ability to spend and to attach conditions to the receipt of the funds. After examining the proposed federal legislation to establish a national program of employment and social insurance he found it unconstitutional in that it was clearly legislation in relation to a subject matter within provincial jurisdiction—property and civil rights. Ultimately a constitutional amendment was required which explicitly transferred legislative responsibility for unemployment insurance to the federal government.[25]

The *Employment and Social Insurance Act* case established the basis for the rather imprecise limitations on the federal spending power that have evolved over the years. In general, the legal interpretation has ensured that the federal government has reasonably broad powers to make payments to persons, institutions and governments and to attach conditions thereto, provided that the program or initiative cannot be characterized as legislation or regulation directly in respect of a subject matter of provincial legislative power.[26]

Certainly the federal government has not hesitated to exercise this power with respect to a wide range of both unconditional and conditional transfers. The most prominent examples of payments to individuals are family allowances and old age security.[27] The three major shared-cost programs involve medicare, transfers for post-secondary education, and the Canada Assistance Plan.

The provincial criticism of the exercise of the federal spending power has generally focussed on conditional grants and subsidies to governments which, it is argued, constrain provincial freedom to determine their expenditure priorities and the range and quality of service. Thus unconditional transfers for equalization purposes or for post-secondary education have not been a real source of controversy, at least not since the Established Programs Financing arrangements of 1977, which no longer tied federal transfers to the health care and post-secondary education costs of the provincial government, but only to the growth in the economy (GNP) and provincial populations.[28]

Transfers under the Canada Assistance Plan are also not particularly controversial since they involve very minor conditions, notably the commitment by the province not to refuse welfare assistance to those in need on the basis of the recipient's province of origin and to establish a procedure for appealing administrative welfare decisions. Moreover, under the CAP, special administrative arrangements were concluded that have allowed Quebec to opt out completely and receive equivalent tax-point concessions in lieu of cash transfers, following Quebec's insistence that its social services not be subject to national standards.

The provinces have been voicing increasing concerns, however, over the rigid CAP requirement for needs-testing as the means of determining a person's eligibility for social assistance. This is preventing an urgent reorientation of social assistance towards the provision of a wider range of social services on a universal basis regardless of need, and the provision of income supplements to encourage people to seek and maintain meaningful work. Perhaps ironically for the provinces, as a review of CAP opens up, pressure is already mounting from social policy groups for even wider reforms that involve the implementation of firm national standards for both income support and social services, similar to proposals made during the social security review in the 1970s.

The most recent and well-publicized federal–provincial dispute over the use of the federal spending power to impose national standards arose in respect of the Canada Health Act. Transfers for medical care and hospital insurance have always been highly conditional: the provinces are required to ensure that their plans conform to firm national standards in respect of accessibility, universality, transferability, comprehensiveness and public administration of programs. These conditions were confirmed in the new fiscal framework established in 1977 by the Established Programs Financing Act.

In 1983–84, the federal government reacted to widespread concerns that extra-billing practices and hospital user fees were seriously eroding the universality and accessibility of provincial medicare programs. The Canada Health Act was subsequently enacted, which imposed severe financial penalties on any province that did not take steps to ban extra-billing and user fees.

Despite much strong provincial criticism, all provinces have now complied with the legislation and none has chosen to challenge it in the courts. Legal challenges have been brought, however, by the Canadian Medical Association and, more recently, by the Ontario Medical Association in respect of Ontario's Health Care Accountability Act.[29] In addition to arguments based on the infringement of certain Charter rights of doctors[30] and a broad attack on the constitutionality of any national standards imposed by the Canada Health Act, the medical associations argue that to the extent that the application of national standards has been extended to matters that have nothing to do with accessibility but that relate to the management of the health insurance programs, the federal government has acted unconstitutionally. More specifically, paragraph 12(2)(b) of the Canada Health Act provides for the right to arbitration when there are disputes between the provincial governments and provincial medical associations. As Claude Forget notes, this provision would have the effect of making the rates for medical fees established under arbitration or conciliation a national standard that has nothing to do with accessibility.[31] If the courts ultimately decide that such a provision is valid, this may amount to a major extension of the federal spending authority. Clearly, regardless of the outcome, the case will serve to clarify further the parameters of the federal spending power.

The legal challenge to the Canada Health Act remains at a preliminary stage and one can expect to see further arguments raised. One of these will be that the punitive financial sanctions imposed on the provinces infringe section 36 of the Constitution Act, 1982, in that they prevent a provincial government from discharging its constitutional obligation to provide reasonably comparable public services at reasonably comparable levels of taxation. Such an argument would certainly mesh well with the view of provincialists such as Gil Rémillard, noted earlier, that section 36 now precludes the federal government from imposing national standards altogether and will ultimately require the federal government to make all transfers for public services pursuant to the unconditional equalization program.[32]

In my view, however, this interpretation of section 36 is wrong and indeed denies the relevance of our federal structure and the importance of retaining the ability of the federal government to harmonize provincial social and other policies to national standards. One can equally and more persuasively argue that national standards and conditions are essential to a proper discharge of the constitutional commitment to promote equal opportunities for the well-being of Canadians; to further economic development to reduce disparity in opportunities; and to provide essential public services of reasonable quality to all Canadians (section 36(1)). Moreover, a recent court decision involving a taxpayer's challenge to federal spending to fund provincial programs on health, welfare and post-secondary education held that section 36 in fact authorized the federal government to undertake such spending.[33]

The trend in public opinion in Canada today is towards a greater federal role in setting national standards not only with respect to health care, social policies and education, but also in a wide range of other areas of public policy such as environmental protection. For example, just as there was widespread national support for the Canada Health Act, pressure is rapidly increasing for the reimposition of conditions on transfers for post-secondary education. In particular, the 1985 Johnson Report entitled ''Giving Greater Purpose to the Federal Financing of Post-secondary Education and Research in Canada''[34] highlighted how, in the absence of any conditions or incentives, the provinces have allowed their grants to universities and colleges to fall off significantly, while federal transfers to the provincial governments have steadily grown with increases in GNP and population in accordance with the current Established Programs Financing arrangements.

Given the national interest in high-quality, post-secondary education, it is important as a minimum first step for the federal government to require the provinces to escalate their support for universities and colleges at the GNP rate, as suggested in the Johnson Report. Future conditions might also involve ensuring the portability of all credentials, whether technical, educational or professional, greater access to provincial institutions by out-of-province residents, an enhanced role for the federal Secretary of State in the Council of Ministers on Education, the allocation of more funds to basic and applied research, more cooperative education programs, and changes in the traditional tuition system. In this connection, it is interesting to note that the Canadian Association of University Teachers recently called for new federal legislation modelled on the Canada Health Act—a Post-Secondary Education Financing Act, which would require provinces to meet specific objectives with respect to funding levels, accessibility, academic freedom, financial assistance to students and the removal of barriers to disadvantaged groups.

Pressure for an enhanced federal role in establishing national standards will also emerge as governments begin finally to undertake a fundamental review of social assistance and employment policies and seriously consider the possibility of integrating the tax and transfer systems. At the very least this will likely result in more national standards attached to transfers for social assistance under the Canada Assistance Plan, especially in respect of income support levels and the range and quality of social services. In addition, already a variety of specific provincial welfare practices have come under attack, notably, the so-called ''man in the house rule'' and the recovery of inadvertent overpayments in such a way as to push the recipient below the poverty level.[35] The federal government may well consider it desirable in the near future to ensure the elimination of these practices in all provinces. At the same time, however, existing CAP requirements such as for needs-testing (discussed earlier) may be dropped or substantially changed.

Certainly there is no lack of possible future federal–provincial friction in respect of existing and future shared-cost programs. The critical question is whether the potential friction is such as to require a constitutional limitation on the federal spending power, and if so, how?

In my view, there is no need for an explicit constitutional limitation at this time. As discussed above, the spending power already has a secure constitutional base and has been, and will continue to be, sufficiently circumscribed through legal interpretation. In addition, Quebec's particular concerns have been accommodated over the years such as through the opting-out provisions under the Canada Assistance Plan or the arrangement to allow for provincial variation of family allowances in 1974. Such administrative options can continue to evolve to meet future contingencies.

The exercise of the federal spending power is fundamentally a question of politics and public policy, and sufficient flexibility is critical. As Driedger succinctly concluded, conditional grants may create political problems, but not constitutional or legal ones. Disputes should therefore be settled by intergovernmental agreement and, for example, ratified by statute.[36]

In any event, to entrench limitations on the power as proposed in the Meech Lake Accord is unacceptable for a number of reasons. First, it will result in a transfer to the judicial branch of critical power to determine government policy and alter spending priorities. As one observer notes: "Not even the staunchest advocate of judicial activism can successfully argue that [Supreme Court Justices] Brian Dickson or Bertha Wilson are the best qualified persons to determine whether the education policies of Bill Vander Zalm or the health policies of Robert Bourassa are 'compatible with the national objectives.' "[37]

Moreover, as the recent landmark decision in *The Minister of Finance of Canada* v. *Robert James Finlay* indicates,[38] the Supreme Court of Canada is prepared to expand significantly its rules of standing to permit private individuals with a sufficiently direct and personal interest to bring legal challenges in respect of government spending pursuant to federal–provincial shared-cost arrangements. More specifically, the court has allowed Finlay to sue the federal Minister of Finance for a declaration that the federal payments to Manitoba under the Canada Assistance Plan are illegal and for an injunction to stop them as long as the province fails to comply with the conditions set out in the arrangements. When this development is combined with the new constitutional role for the courts in respect of national shared-cost programs set out in the Meech Lake Accord, we can undoubtedly expect a spate of lengthy, expensive and more often than not counter-productive legal challenges by a wide range of individuals and public authorities.

The noted constitutional and legal philosopher, Ronald Dworkin, has suggested that a distinction should be drawn between matters of principle and matters of policy in determining the appropriate parameters for the role of the judicial branch.[39] Judges are suited by their training and their role to decide questions of principle and have a duty to protect the rights of individuals and minorities against the encroachment of others and restrain the pursuit of the majority interest in politics. Elected governments and legislatures, on the other hand, have the competence, authority and duty to make policy and, in the constitutional context, to enact measures that will make the community as a whole better off. Although it is of course difficult in practice to distinguish between principle and policy, the spending power limitations in the Meech Lake Accord clearly shift the resolution of important matters of policy to the judiciary. This will seriously impair the ability of our elected representatives to act in the national interest.

Beyond this overriding concern over the unacceptable abdication of power to the judiciary, specific criticisms of the Meech Lake Accord provisions focus on their unacceptable ambiguity, the ease with which provinces can opt out of national programs, and the inability of the federal government to establish firm minimum national standards.

John Whyte, the Dean of Queen's University Law School, has set out no less than six areas where serious questions of interpretation will arise, all of which will "create immense disincentives to the federal government to embark on social welfare or other programs."[40] These questions can be summarized as follows:

(1)   What is a national shared-cost program? Does it require a particular type of financing formula such as matching grants?
(2)   What is meant by spending in an area of "exclusive provincial jurisdiction"? Does there only have to be a provincial aspect to the expenditure program? If so, the spending power provisions will be given a very wide application.
(3)   What is a "program or initiative"?
(4)   What is "reasonable compensation"?
(5)   What is a "compatible" program or initiative, and who will determine the compatibility?
(6)   What counts as "national objectives"? Is it not likely that they will apply only to the broader ends or aims of the program in question, and therefore preclude the imposition of national standards or the means to those ends? Does the federal government have the exclusive right to determine the national objectives?

Constitutional expert Eugene Forsey argues that the reference to a ''program established by the Government of Canada'' will mean that the national objectives could be set by a pronouncement of the Government in a White Paper, a speech by the Prime Minister or Minister most directly concerned; and the courts might rule on the basis of this that a provincial program or ''initiative'' was eligible for compensation. ''Parliament would, again, be subordinated to the courts, and provinces might be able to raid the federal treasury for support of mere tokenism.''[41] In addition, it is clear that ''national objectives'' mean much less than ''national standards'' since, in contrast to the spending power provisions, the immigration provisions in proposed section 95B(2) of the Constitution Act, 1867 *do* explicitly mention ''national standards and objectives.''

The Canadian Council on Social Development (CCSD), along with many others, notes that ''national objectives'' can be interpreted as the lowest common denominator of provincial compliance, and if ''compatible with'' is interpreted as ''not in opposition to,'' we are in danger of losing both the federal role in, and the national character of, social policy. In addition, it is clear that there are inexorable pressures on provinces to use their limited fiscal resources in ways that may not be in the best interests of the Canadian population as a whole. Notable examples include ''the use of extra-billing and user fees to limit access to health care, or the current trend for provinces to reduce social assistance payments to levels well below even the provincially determined level of need for certain groups of people.''[42] More generally, the CCSD concludes that the excessive ambiguity of the provisions will impede the urgently required *national* efforts to develop a new approach to income security, social services and employment opportunities.

Al Johnson, a former Deputy Minister of Health and Welfare and a veteran of federal–provincial negotiations over a wide range of shared-cost programs such as medicare and post-secondary education, argues that medicare would not have been possible under the Meech Lake Accord rules.[43] Both Alberta and Ontario were vigorous opponents of the federal plan for ideological reasons. They preferred to leave the operation of health insurance schemes to the private insurance companies and disagreed with the principles of universality and comprehensive coverage. Under the Meech Lake Accord, John Robarts could have opted out of the program and given Ontario's share of the money to the private insurance companies, or used it to build new highways. The federal government retains no effective bargaining lever to entice recalcitrant provinces into the scheme. Medicare would have been doomed.

Jack London, another constitutional expert and a member of the federal Task Force on Child Care, argues that the Meech Lake Accord gravely diminishes the federal incentive, both political and bureaucratic, to initiate or engage in a significant national day care program because the appeal of a national, homogeneous impact would be gone.[44] In particular, the opting-out provisions will effectively preclude a strong unilateral federal initiative in committing substantial expenditure to day care and, in any event, the provinces would get all the political credit. Since it is not clear that the provinces would be required to adhere to national standards with respect to, for example, unlicensed suppliers and non-profit day care centres, we will likely end up with an inadequate patchwork system in a balkanized Canada.

Even a supporter of the Meech Lake Accord, constitutional lawyer Andrew Petter, acknowledges certain unacceptable ambiguities in the provisions.[45] It is not clear, for example, whether ''national objectives'' will be limited to ''subject matter'' objectives such that child care funds must be spent on ''child care.'' It is also not clear whether tax deductions and tax credits fall within the definition of ''national shared-cost programs.''

Finally, many observers have noted the ambiguity with respect to the application of the provisions to ''programs established . . . after the coming into force of this section.'' It is not clear whether future extensions or amendments to medicare, for example, will qualify as post-Accord programs and therefore be subject to the opting-out provisions. If this interpretation is accepted, existing national programs could be seriously eroded.

All the foregoing concerns apply to a wide range of future initiatives that may be desirable, especially in new areas where the division of legislative authority is not clear. For this reason, it is preferable, in my view, to retain maximum flexibility in the exercise of the federal spending power and to avoid explicit constitutional limitations. But, if such limitation is nevertheless considered essential, it must be determined only after a full and free public debate and in the context of a review of the current division of powers to account explicitly for the new areas of concern.

In this connection, the 1969 federal proposal is instructive.[46] It consisted of four prongs. First, there would be an explicit constitutional provision conferring on Parliament the power to make *unconditional* grants to the provinces. This power would be unrestricted, beyond perhaps some general commitment to the elimination of regional disparities. Second, no decision would be made with respect to the power to make payments to "persons or institutions" in matters of provincial jurisdiction, until consideration had been given to the distribution of legislative powers. Third, there would be no constitutional restriction of Parliament's ability to make grant-in-aid programs involving only some of the provinces, and therefore no compensation would be available for non-participating provinces.

Finally, conditional grant-in-aid programs involving all of the provinces *would* be subject to constitutional restriction. The federal government would not proceed with a program unless a "national consensus" existed, such consensus to require the agreement of three of the four senatorial districts and at least two western provinces and two Atlantic provinces. The federal government would then compensate the *citizens* of a non-participating province by a sum equal to the average per capita payment to participating provinces multiplied by the province's population.

I would still agree with Donald Smiley who criticized this proposed compensatory mechanism on the grounds that it is tantamount to rewarding individuals by Parliament "as the by-product of the frustration of national purposes by the government which represents them."[47] Nevertheless, in stark contrast to the Meech Lake Accord, at least the proposals do not make it too easy to opt out. Moreover, the 1969 proposals preserve the incentive for the federal government to initiate new programs by allowing the federal government to retain the political credit for any tax revenues raised and stipulating that the fiscal compensation goes to the citizens of the non-participating province, not the provincial governments. In addition, although still unsatisfactory, the 1969 proposals ensure that at least five provinces would participate in a uniform national program and thereby decrease the chances of a patchwork quilt result. In contrast, under the Meech Lake Accord, any number of provinces can opt out.

A more innovative proposal to limit the financial spending power has been put forward recently by Frank Carter, a former Deputy Secretary of the Cabinet for federal–provincial relations and subsequently, from 1977 to 1984, a special advisor on the Constitution.[48] Carter suggests that the Constitution provide that monies otherwise payable to a province that opts out of a shared-cost program would be kept in a fund until after the holding of the first provincial election following the elapse of a three-year period. If, after the election, the province still refused to participate, the accumulated funds (and the monies payable thereafter) would be paid by the federal government to the people, but in a way that would facilitate its retrieval by the provincial government through its own taxes. According to Carter, this arrangement would recognize the ultimate sovereignty of a province in fields of its own jurisdiction. At the most, it would impose delay and an electoral test on a province wishing to stay on its own. At the least, it would provide an incentive for both sides to seek solutions.

The Carter proposals certainly merit consideration in future constitutional reform discussions. They have the particular value of emphasizing the need to consult and meaningfully involve the people of Canada in any new initiative and might contribute to more open, responsive government at both levels.

III The Dangers of a Balkanized Canada

A final fundamental flaw in the proposed constitutional limitation on the federal spending power relates to the unacceptable political dynamics that are generated, particularly when viewed in the context of the overall Meech Lake Accord and other relevant provisions in the existing Constitution. More specifically, the spending power provisions, however limited in scope, are simply part of an overall agreement that incorporates a serious and, in my view, debilitating shift of power and dynamism from the federal Parliament to the provinces. Canada is already one of the most decentralized federations in the world; the Meech Lake Accord will potentially make us ungovernable. And when this is combined with the undermining of our Charter, it will certainly impair progress towards greater social justice and a fairer, more compassionate society.

In examining the overall context of the Meech Lake Accord, four sets of provisions must be singled out: the new amendment procedures, the constitutional entrenchment of the First Ministers' Conferences, the provincial role in appointments to both the Senate and the Supreme Court of Canada, and the distinct society clause, particularly its effect in undermining the Charter.

With respect to the amendment procedures, the Accord proposes to extend the rigid requirement for the unanimous consent of all provinces to cover changes to critical national institutions—the Senate and the Supreme Court of Canada—as well as for the establishment of new provinces. In addition, it loosens and expands the general amending procedure to permit opting out with fiscal compensation by any province that dissents from any amendment affecting the division of powers.

The extension of the unanimity rule means that the chances for any meaningful change to our federal institutions, notably Senate reform so that the Senate can more effectively protect and represent the interests of the weaker regions, are now extremely remote. But even more importantly, giving the provinces such extensive veto powers increases their bargaining leverage in virtually any area of federal–provincial negotiations. This ability to use the threat of the veto to extract concessions on unrelated matters opens the door to political blackmail and paralysis, and risks effectively immobilizing national efforts to achieve greater social and economic justice.

The loosening of the general amendment procedure means that it is now far too easy for a province to opt out of future adjustments to the division of powers that may be required to meet the critical challenges that lie ahead, notably in the areas of environmental protection, telecommunications, science and technology, education and the integration of our employment and social assistance policies. More generally, as Garth Stevenson notes, "the opting-out procedure suggests that a province's adherence to Canada is only conditional and that the province is free to accept or reject national decisions depending on whether it finds them convenient."[49]

Constitutional amendments have occasionally been required in the past to permit the implementation of national programs, notably, unemployment insurance (s.91(2A)) and pensions and supplementary benefits (s.94A).[50] One must ask oneself what would have happened to the nature of our national unemployment insurance scheme if Quebec or any other province had been able to opt out with full fiscal compensation. At the very least, our ability to meet the national challenge of devastating levels of unemployment would have been severely compromised. Yet the Meech Lake Accord would now allow such an unacceptable situation to arise in respect of any future constitutional amendments pursuant to the general amending formula.[51]

The constitutional entrenchment of annual First Ministers' Conferences both on the economy and other matters, and on the Constitution, is a second element of the Meech Lake Accord that will compound the debilitating shift of power away from Parliament to the provinces. In effect, we are creating an unaccountable third level of government that may eventually reduce the federal Parliament and provincial legislatures to mere ratification chambers in respect of decisions taken by the First Ministers. The federal cabinet and the Prime Minister will no longer speak for Canada. Instead, eleven First Ministers will collectively speak for Canada, and our position in international and domestic issues will inevitably be fragmented and reduced to the lowest common denominator of rival provincial interests. Again, in combination with the spending power limitations, it will become increasingly difficult for the federal government to carry out its critical leadership role in pursuit of the national interest and to strengthen the national community.

Third, the Meech Lake Accord effectively hands over the power of appointment to the Supreme Court of Canada and the Senate—two key national institutions—to the provincial governments. This represents a very serious abdication of federal responsibility with respect to both the judicial and legislative branches of our national government and an unacceptable alteration of our federal system.

The character of the Supreme Court will gradually be transformed since it is inevitable that the provincial nominees will be ideologically inspired. The impact on the nature of the Court's decisions in respect of our basic rights and freedoms guaranteed in the Charter and on issues of federal–provincial division of powers will be potentially very far-reaching.[52]

Similarly, the Senate will be transformed into a body that simply reflects the untidy sum of rival provincial government interests. Moreover, there is nothing to ensure that the Senate will not stalemate or frustrate the activities of our national legislators in the House of Commons. Furthermore, really meaningful Senate reform is precluded by the virtually unattainable requirement of the unanimous consent of all provinces for any future amendments regarding the Senate.

Finally, a general underlying danger of the Meech Lake Accord is its effect in undermining our commitment to respect and promote basic rights and freedoms guaranteed in the Charter. The concern over the status of the Charter vis-à-vis the Accord arises as a direct result of the distinct society clause which, in the view of many constitutional experts, gives the Quebec government the power to override the Charter.[53] The addition of Article 16 in the early hours of the morning on June 3rd which singles out the rights of aboriginal peoples and our commitment to multiculturalism in the Charter for special recognition simply confirms this view. In addition, the recent Supreme Court decision in the Separate School Funding case indicates, among other things, that political compromises in the Constitution will take precedence over Charter rights in certain circumstances.[54] To resolve this unacceptable situation, at the very least a new section should be inserted in the Accord that explicitly states that nothing in the Accord affects any of our basic rights and freedoms guaranteed in the Charter.

A clear statement of the supremacy of the Charter is as important to the spending power provisions as to all the other provisions in the Accord. More specifically, given the very real potential for significant variations among provinces in respect of national programs, if such programs can be implemented at all, it is clear that our rights to equality and mobility will be adversely affected. As the Canadian Advisory Council on the Status of Women succinctly points out, national shared-cost programs are fundamentally about equality and our commitment to equal opportunity.[55] It is therefore critical that the Charter, particularly the equality and mobility guarantees, applies to the spending power provisions.

But ensuring that the Charter takes precedence over the Accord is only a second-best solution. In my view, the Meech Lake Accord and the spending power provisions are fundamentally flawed. It is my hope that our First Ministers will recognize the need to go back to the constitutional bargaining table and seek a better accord that will more effectively accommodate Quebec's special concerns with respect to linguistic and cultural security, but that will also ensure that Canada continues to function coherently as one nation. An open and extensive public debate will provide a constructive opportunity for all Canadians to examine the significant challenges to the Canadian society and economy that lie ahead and the respective federal and provincial roles in meeting those challenges. It will allow all Canadians to discuss alternatives to the Meech Lake Accord that really *will* result in a stronger, more responsive national government, rather than lead to national disintegration. Nothing less than the future of Canada as a progressive dynamic nation is at stake.

Notes

1. Clause 7 of Constitutional Accord, 1987; proposed s.106A, Constitution Act, 1867.
2. The most notable of these critics are the nationalists in Quebec.
3. Donald Smiley and Ronald Burns, "Canadian Federalism and the Spending Power: Is Constitutional Restriction Necessary?" (1969) 17 Can.Tax J. 467, at p. 479.
4. Frank Carter, "How to Tame the Spending Power" (October 1986) Policy Options pp. 3–7.
5. In fiscal year 1986/87, $28.6 billion in cash and tax points were transferred from the federal government to provinces and municipalities for programs with joint or intergovernmental administration. This represented almost one-quarter of the federal budget.
6. A. Maslove and B. Rubashewsky, "Cooperation and Confrontation: The Challenges of Fiscal Federalism" in *How Ottawa Spends 1986* (1986) pp. 95–118, at p. 97.
7. See, for example, William Watson, "Section 36 Federalism" (June 1987) Policy Options and William Watson, "Simpler Equalization" (October 1986) Policy Options.

8. Gil Rémillard, "Ottawa Cannot Impose its National Standards" *Le Devoir*, June 1, 1984.
9. Andrée Lajoie, "Education—The New Offensive By Spending Authorities" *Le Devoir*, March 6 and 7, 1984.
10. See, for example, Peter Cumming, "Federal–Provincial Fiscal Arrangements and the Search for Fiscal Equity Through Reformulation of the Equalization Program" in Ontario Economic Council, *Ottawa and the Provinces*, Vol. 1 (1985) pp. 96–124.
11. See, for example, Yves Rabeau, "Bien-être social—ou bien-être provincial: vers une refonte du programme de péréquation" (1986) Cdn. Public Administration pp. 237–258.
12. Government of Canada, *Federal–Provincial Grants and the Spending Power of Parliament* (1969) pp. 20–22.
13. *Ibid.*
14. In economists' terms, this is the so-called externality rationale.
15. Keith Banting, "Universality and the Development of the Welfare State" John Deutsch Institute, Queen's University (1985) pp. 7–14.
16. Malcolm Taylor, *Health Insurance and Canadian Public Policy* (1978) p. 181.
17. Claude Forget, "The Harmonization of Social Policy" in Mark Krasnick (Research Coordinator), *Fiscal Federalism* (1986) (Macdonald Commission Studies Vol. 65) p. 97. Forget prefers to use the idea of "harmonization" to analyze public affairs in Canada, rather than the traditional ideas of centralization and decentralization.
18. Andrew Petter, "Meech Won't Stall Social Reform in the Provinces" *The Globe and Mail*, June 30, 1987.
19. *Ibid.*
20. See generally D. Coyne, "Compensation Without Litigation" (April 1986) Policy Options, for details of the various related initiatives under way or under study.
21. Elmer Driedger, "The Spending Power" (1981) 7 Queen's Law Journal 124, at p. 125.
22. Frank Scott, "The Constitutional Background of the Tax Agreements (1955) 2 McGill Law Journal 1.
23. See, for example, Smiley and Burns *supra.* note 2; Joseph Magnet, "The Constitutional Distribution of Taxation Powers In Canada" (1978) 10 Ottawa L. Rev. 473, 476; Gerald LaForest, *The Allocation of Taxing Power under the Canadian Constitution* (Canadian Tax Foundation, 1967); see also Ken Hansson, "The Constitutionality of Conditional Grant Legislation" (1967) 2 Man. L.J. 191, 194.
24. *Reference Re. Employment and Social Insurance Act* (1936) 3 D.L.R. 644 (J.C.P.C.).
25. Section 91 (2A) of the Constitution Act, 1867 was enacted in 1940.
26. The most recent case to follow the *Reference Re. Employment and Social Insurance Act* and to uphold the constitutionality of the major shared-cost programs involving medicare, post-secondary education and social assistance

is *Winterhaven Stables Ltd. v. A.G. (Canada)*, (1986) 29 D.L.R. (4d) 394 (Alta. Q.B.). The decision is currently under appeal. See also *Central Mortgage and Housing v. Coop College Residence Inc.* (1975) 13 O.R. (2d) 39 (Ont.C.A.).

27. Family allowances were upheld as a valid exercise of the federal spending power in *Angers v. M.N.R.* [1957] Ex. C.R. 83. Old age security payments initially were made pursuant to explicit federal authority in section 94A of the Constitution Act, 1867. However, the contribution element has now been completely phased out, and OAS payments are funded entirely from federal revenues.

28. Note, however, that following the federal Finance Minister's announcement in 1985 that the rate of increase in equalization payments would be reduced to achieve savings of $2 billion by 1990, the Quebec finance minister has threatened legal action to challenge the proposed cutback. The other have-not provinces are equally upset.

29. See Amended Statement of Claim, Supreme Court of Ontario File #1217/85. *The Canadian Medical Association, Dr. James MacPhee and Ruby Evelyn Kelly v. AS (Canada) and AG (Ontario)*.

30. Sections 7 and 15 of the Charter.

31. Forget, supra note 17, p. 112.

32. See discussion supra at notes 8 and 9.

33. *Winterhaven Stables Ltd. v. A.G. (Canada)*, supra note 26.

34. The Johnson Report was submitted to the Secretary of State in February 1985.

35. Ontario has recently taken legislative steps to eliminate the ''man in the house'' rule. The recovery of overpayments practice is currently under attack in Manitoba: see *The Minister of Finance v. Robert James Finlay* discussed infra, note 37.

36. Elmer Driedger, supra note 21.

37. Mark Crawford, ''Supreme Court Opened Door to a Constitutional Deal'' *The Gazette*, May 27, 1987.

38. *The Minister of Finance of Canada v. Robert James Finlay* (1986) 33 D.L.R. (4d) 321 (S.C.C.).

39. See Ronald Dworkin, *Law's Empire* (1986).

40. John Whyte, Memorandum for the CCSD Concerning the Meaning and Potential Impact of Section 7 of the 1987 Constitutional Accord, August 13, 1987 (mimeographed).

41. Eugene Forsey, Submission to the Special Joint Committee on the 1987 Constitutional Accord, July 1987 (mimeographed).

42. Letter to the Prime Minister, May 22, 1987. See also CCSD Brief to the Special Joint Committee on the 1987 Constitutional Accord, August 25, 1987 (mimeographed), and the similar range of concerns raised by the Canadian Advisory Council on the Status of Women in its brief to the Special Joint Committee, August 20, 1987 (mimeographed).

43. Al Johnson, Submission to the Special Joint Committee on the 1987 Constitutional Accord, August 1987 (mimeographed). See also Leonard Shifrin,

"Ottawa's Boasting of Day Care Is Nonsense" *The Toronto Star*, July 13, 1987.

44. Jack London, "How Meech Lake Would Balkanize Canada" *The Toronto Star*, May 20, 1987.

45. Andrew Petter, supra note 18.

46. See federal government Discussion Paper, supra note 12. Note that the federal government again suggested the possibility of negotiating spending power limitations during the constitutional negotiations in 1978, but subject to the caveat that "restrictions on the federal spending power should not deprive us of effective means to achieve such national goals as equal treatment of Canadians, regardless of their residence and alleviation of disparities among provinces and regions." See "An Agenda for Change": notes for comments by the Prime Minister at the Constitutional Conference, Tuesday, October 31, 1978.

47. Smiley and Burns, supra note 3.

48. See Carter, supra note 4.

49. Garth Stevenson, "Constitutional Amendment: A Democratic Perspective" 1984 Socialist Studies p. 269.

50. Note that in the 1969–71 constitutional reform debates leading to the abortive Victoria Charter, Quebec focused on a key amendment to section 94A that would have given the provinces effective overriding authority in matters of social policy and over all programs relating to income distribution and social security such as family allowances, youth allowances, manpower training allowances and unemployment insurance. As the federal government noted in its 1969 Discussion Paper, the Quebec approach reflected a particular view of the Constitution and "the case for programme integration." More specifically, Parliament ought not to have the power to spend except where it has the power to regulate. Instead a single authority—the provincial government—should be able to integrate programs in the fields of income redistribution and social security and adapt every program to the specific demographic, income and regional structure of the province, without taking into account the situation in the rest of the country. See federal government Discussion Paper supra note 12, pp. 18–20.

51. It should be noted that the current general amending formula does allow a dissenting province to opt out of amendments relating to "education or other cultural matters," with fiscal compensation. These were viewed as areas of particular concern to Quebec.

52. See, for example, the concerns expressed by the Canadian Bar Association in its submission to the Special Joint Committee on the 1987 Constitutional Accord, August 1987 (mimeographed).

53. See, for example, the submission of Professor Raymond Hébert to the Special Joint Committee on the 1987 Constitutional Accord, August 1987 (mimeographed).

54. See, for example, the following comments of Madame Justice Wilson in *Reference Re Bill 30, An Act To Amend The Education Act* (June 1987) at p. 48:

''It was never intended . . . that the Charter could be used to invalidate other provisions of the constitution, particularly a provision such as s.93 which represented a fundamental part of the Confederation compromise.''

55. Canadian Advisory Council on the Status of Women, Brief to the Special Joint Committee on the 1987 Constitutional Accord, August 20, 1987 (mimeographed).

STEFAN DUPRÉ

SECTION 106A AND FEDERAL–PROVINCIAL FISCAL RELATIONS*

Section 106A responds to a Quebec demand for limitations on the federal spending power that is as old as the agony of constitutional reform this country has suffered since the mid-1960s. In this brief paper I shall examine s.106A in the light of the following perspectives: (1) the art of federal–provincial compromise; (2) its potential for judicializing federal–provincial fiscal relations; and (3) its long-term impact on the conduct of these relations by our eleven first ministers and their ministers of finance.

Two preliminary observations are in order. First, if anyone did cheer the Constitution Act of 1982,[1] I was not among them. As far as I am concerned, Keith Banting and Richard Simeon could not have chosen a more appropriate title for the collection of essays they edited on the subject.[2] To me, a Constitution deemed in part illegitimate by the bipartisan resolution of the Quebec National Assembly has been a symbolic monstrosity. In that s.106A, along with the rest of the Meech Lake/Langevin Accord, may yet receive the approbation of Canada's eleven parliamentary assemblies and thereby purge the constitutional landscape of this monstrosity, its passage into constitutional law will receive my standing applause.

If my first observation brands me as a biased constitutional observer, my second may brand me as an incompetent constitutional forecaster. Given that so many of the means of remedying the symbolic monstrosity of 1982 found our eleven governments shackled by the unanimity chains of s.41, I was confidently predicting, as recently as March of 1987, that the youngest freshman in my class would reach the

---

* In K. E. Swinton and C. J. Rogerson, eds., *Competing Constitutional Visions—The Meech Lake Accord* (Toronto: Carswell, 1988).

age of mandatory retirement from judicial office by the time we got our constitutional house in order. As I delightedly stand on the brink of being proved wrong on this score, I gladly live with whatever skepticism this invites concerning the validity of my forecast of the impact of s.106A on fiscal federalism.

Section 106A and the Art of Federal–Provincial Compromise

Stripped to its bare essentials, and therefore of the textual uncertainties I shall examine in the next part of this paper, s.106A(1) creates a constitutional obligation whereby the federal government must compensate a province that chooses to opt-out of a future national shared-cost program in an area of exclusive provincial jurisdiction. To trigger this obligation, the opting-out province must undertake a measure that is compatible with the program's objectives. Section 106A(2) adds that the federal–provincial division of jurisdiction, as we have come to know it, is not thereby affected.

Viewed as an exercise in the art of federal–provincial compromise, s.106A is a masterpiece. The federal spending power has been derived from s.91(3) ''The Raising of Money by any Mode or System of Taxation'' and s.91(1A) ''The Public Debt and Property'' of the existing division of jurisdiction.[3] These two sections have come to mean that the federal government, having applied its tax powers under s.91(3) to the raising of monies paid into the Consolidated Revenue Fund that is the Public Property of s.91(1A), can dispose of those monies in any manner it chooses, even though the object served comes under provincial jurisdiction. Such monies can be disbursed in the form of federal transfers, conditional or unconditional, to individuals, institutions or provincial governments.

David M. Cameron and I have characterized the federal spending power as the ''single most dynamic element of Canadian federalism.'' In our words:[4]

The manner in which the spending power has been applied in different ways at different times has been a source of centralization and decentralization, of symmetry and asymmetry, of unity and disunity in Canadian federalism—all of these without ever altering so much as a comma in the text of the (Constitution Act of 1867). In the process the spending power has made nonsense of the allegedly ''water-tight'' compartments into which the [Constitution] Act divides federal and provincial jurisdiction. "Water-tight" compartments are not "money-tight."

In the annals of federal–provincial fiscal relations, the spending power has spawned federal payments to individuals (e.g. family allowances, adult training allowances), to institutions (universities, municipalities) and to provinces (from categorical conditional grants through the unconditional equalization payments now enshrined in s.36 of the Constitution Act, 1982 to the umbrella shared-cost grants of the Canada Assistance Plan). It has also come to be hedged by various limitations. Some of these limitations have been the outcome of explicit compromise, e.g. provincial configuration of family allowances; provincial (Quebec) opting-out of various shared-cost programs in the 1960s. Other limitations have been bred by the sheer political force of provincial opposition. I have long been fond of making the point that interposition, the eminently American state practice historically invoked in that country against the enforcement of Court decisions, was successfully invoked in Canada by Premier Duplessis against the federal spending power—in this instance, federal payments to universities. Indeed, it can be observed that:

the legacy of the university grants episode has severely circumscribed the application of the federal spending power to universities, municipalities, and other institutions under provincial jurisdiction. For practical purposes the scope of the federal spending power has increasingly been limited to the making of payments to individuals and to provincial governments.[5]

The point, as Cameron and I summed it up, is that "Politics can effectively inhibit what the Constitution permits."[6]

It is from the perspective of this well-known history that I view s.106A as a stunning expression of the art of compromise. It is silent on the matter of federal payments to institutions which are under provincial jurisdiction. As such, it implicitly recognizes the effectiveness of the political limitations on such payments, while leaving their future configuration to coming generations of politicians and citizens. It is silent on the matter of federal payments to individuals: the Victoria Charter's flirtation with a constitutional limitation on adult training allowances was not rekindled. Accordingly, the most visible and politically potent manifestations of the federal spending power are uncurbed. And as for what s.106A addresses, it creates a federal obligation towards an opting-out province, rather than a limitation on the application of the spending power to federal–provincial shared-cost programs. One searches s.106A in vain for any of the limitations with which past products of the constitutional reform industry sought to hedge the initiation of shared-cost programs by Ottawa. I refer to the generic idea of requiring the registration of consensus by a substantial majority of provinces, either through their premiers or through a provincially instructed upper house before a shared-cost program can be launched. Section 106A leaves this idea to gather dust on the same library shelves as stock the federal White Paper of 1969, the Quebec Beige Paper of 1980 and the intervening products of the constitutional reform industry. Finally, s.106A features a *quid* for the *quo* of the constitutional obligation it imposes on the federal government vis-à-vis an opting-out province. Its explicit reference to shared-cost programs with national objectives in areas of exclusive provincial jurisdiction shifts the legitimation of these manifestations of the federal spending power from judicial *obiter dicta* to the black letters of constitutional text.

In summary, I discern in s.106A what is indeed a masterpiece of compromise. It bypasses federal payments to institutions that are effectively confined by the political process. It equally bypasses federal payments to individuals and therefore brooks no limitations on future federal recourse to this politically potent spending instrument. What is left are shared-cost programs, and here a federal constitutional obligation vis-à-vis an opting-out province is exchanged for the explicit legitimation of federally conditioned payments to provinces in areas of exclusive provincial jurisdiction. That Quebec's longstanding demand for limitations on the federal spending power can be met to its satisfaction through this minimalist approach can only be called a triumph in the art of ''getting to yes.''[7]

Section 106A and the Judicialization of Federal–Provincial Fiscal Relations

It is one thing to describe the content of s.106A in the everyday language I have used so far. It is quite another to reflect upon its formal wording. The text of s.106A is awash with uncertainties and ambiguities that can only be definitively resolved by the Supreme Court of Canada. To be sure, there will have to be recourse to the courts before s.106A produces a judicialization of federal–provincial fiscal relations. Before addressing the likelihood of this eventuality, textual analysis is in order. In my mind, untutored in the law but schooled in the fiscal relations that the text of s.106A addresses, the following questions arise.

(1) What is a ''shared-cost program''? The answer may be that it is any provincially administered program financed in part by a province, in part by the federal government. The vocabulary of federal–provincial fiscal relations, as developed by the ministers and officials who conduct these relations, has suggested a narrower definition: a shared-cost program involves a predetermined federal share (percentage) of program costs whose level is annually set by provincial spending decisions. Thus we were told at the time established program financing was initiated in 1977 that shared-cost programs in the fields of post-secondary education, hospital and medical insurance would be replaced by block funding. Henceforth, provinces would no longer dictate federal spending by determining the rate of increase in the federal obligation to share a set proportion of the costs incurred. Subsequently, through the Canada Health Act,[8] block funding was reconditionalized through federal recourse to fiscal penalties against provinces that violate a federally prescribed code of conduct.[9] Does block funding geared to a code of conduct constitute a shared-cost program?

(2) What is a *national* shared-cost program? Presumably what is invited is a distinction between what in the practitioner's lexicon is a bilateral federal–provincial program tailor-made to the needs of a particular province and a multilateral federal–provincial program offered on like terms to all (most? several?) provinces. Is there a point at which a series of bilateral federal–provincial shared-cost initiatives such as those spawned pursuant to the alphabet soup of DREE, DRIE and ERDA could be taken as constituting a national shared-cost program in an area of exclusive provincial jurisdiction (which DREE, DRIE and ERDA do not likely occupy)?

(3) What is an area of exclusive provincial jurisdiction? Before taking refuge in the comforting words of s.106A(2), we should remind ourselves of Claude Morin's observation that the federal–provincial relations carried out under ss.91 and 92 are littered with claims and counter-claims that seek to distinguish or confound urban affairs and municipal institutions, training or research and education, the economy or employment and anything.[10]

(4) What is the ''program or initiative that is compatible with the national objectives'' that an opting-out province is supposed to carry on? Is an ''initiative'' less than a program and, if so, does the national shared-cost program constitute a shopping list for provincial initiatives

any one of which, if implemented, would offer grounds for federal compensation? The umbrella nature of a shared-cost program like the Canada Assistance Plan is a strong reminder that this question is pertinent. As for what constitutes "compatibility" with the "national objectives" (the objectives in the federal legislation or the federal spending estimates or such portion of these objectives as might be deemed "national"), questions abound. And then there is the matter of what, if anything, distinguishes objectives from conditions or criteria or codes of conduct.

(5) What is the "reasonable" compensation to which an opting-out province may be entitled? Perhaps this compensation is to be "reasonable" in relation to the share of costs that the federal government pays in other provinces. Perhaps this compensation is to be "reasonable" in relation to the fiscal effort which the opted-out province, given its fiscal capacity and need, must exert in order to mount its compatible program or initiative. Who knows?

Who knows indeed? I have raised these illustrative questions to establish that s.106A is a showcase of uncertainty. I will now argue that this very characteristic leads me to discount its potential for judicializing federal–provincial fiscal relations.

Why have federal–provincial fiscal relations been virtually exempt from governmental recourse to the courts in the past? It is well to remember that these relations have been conducted over more than half of a century by governments of widely different political persuasions. The co-operative phases of these relations have been generously interspersed with the most conflictual episodes in the annals of Canadian federalism. If governments avoided head-to-head litigation over the spending power even when their relations were at their most acrimonious, this must be because they perceived that the disadvantages of court-dictated resolutions outweighed the advantages.

Again and again, negotiated solutions have enabled governments to avoid definitive court rulings that could be as damaging from a federal perspective as from a provincial one. That the Supreme Court might deem a particular set of conditions as disguised federal legislation in a field of provincial competence has posed a risk which federal governments have been loath to run. That it might, on the other hand, legitimize detailed conditions or the federal financing of universities has posed an equally unpalatable risk from a provincial perspective. Meantime, federal and provincial finance ministers, with their joint concerns for the revenue and debt positions of government and their capacity to achieve financial tradeoffs quantified in tax points or cash, have had their own stake in avoiding judicial fetters.

And could Quebec, or for that matter any other province, have ever hoped to achieve compensated opting-out via a judicial route? No constitutional doctrine that I can think of would have permitted a court to fashion compensated opting-out. This practice, which has encompassed payments to institutions as well as shared-cost programs, could only have been invented by federal–provincial negotiation. The multiple uncertainties and limitations which in the past have made governments loath to resort to litigated solutions are in the main untouched by s.106A. What is new is the added legitimacy of federal conditions and the enhanced certainty of federal compensation to an opted-out province when this becomes a constitutional obligation.

I consider that the added legitimacy which s.106A accords to federal conditions actually *reduces* the possibility that federal–provincial fiscal relations might become judicialized because it is a deterrent to *private* litigation, not only over future programs, but past programs as well. It seems to me that a constitutional challenge such as the one envisaged to the Canada Health Act by the Ontario Medical Association in the heat of the extra-billing issue is a far more risky undertaking with s.106A than without it.

As for head-to-head litigation between governments, potential judicialization of fiscal relations must be posited on the hypothesis that the equilibrated balance of terror which has deterred recourse to the courts in the past has been disturbed. But why should governments seek to test whether day care, let us say, is "early childhood education," and therefore an area of exclusive provincial jurisdiction subject to compensated opting-out, or is instead "labour market adjustment," and therefore beyond the reach of s.106A as an area of concurrent jurisdiction? I can discern the possibility of judicialization if I posit that a national (multilateral) shared-cost program which governments mutually agree deals with an exclusively provincial matter has been pursued to the point where it has been authorized by Parliament, and the federal finance minister has been unable to negotiate a level of compensation that is acceptable to his counterpart from an opting-out province. It is only in the face of such a conjuncture of events that I consider judicialization a reasonable possibility, and even here, the prospect of a court-imposed settlement that attempted to juggle tax points, equalization and cash is likely a strong deterrent to intergovernmental litigation.

In sum, the prospect that s.106A may have the net effect of judicializing federal–provincial fiscal relations appears trivial.

Section 106A and the Conduct of Federal–Provincial Fiscal Relations

In this setting, I find it reasonable to anticipate that s.106A will have minimal consequences for the conduct of federal–provincial fiscal relations. If anything, it will simply reinforce a pattern of conduct that is in line with trends whose outline has emerged with growing clarity in recent years. I refer to (1) the tendency for federal–provincial initiatives to encompass matters that occupy the gray areas of the division of jurisdiction; (2) the growing prominence of bilateral federal–provincial shared-cost arrangements tailor-made to the particular economic and social circumstances of individual provinces; and (3) enhanced recourse to tax expenditures as a means of pursuing national and provincial objectives.

The modern Canadian welfare state was erected in large part through the application of the federal spending power to shared-cost programs, including the very specific categorical conditional grants that waxed and waned between 1945 and 1965. Once in place, the welfare state does not require reconstruction from scratch. The new avenues of government intervention have shifted from the educational, health and social matters most likely to impinge upon objects of exclusive provincial jurisdiction to matters in which the elements of economic and social policy are intertwined. These lie precisely in the gray areas of the division of jurisdiction where education shades into research, municipal affairs into development and housing, and social infrastructure into economic adjustment. In all of these areas there is ample room for federal–provincial acrimony and indeed for what Alan Cairns calls "competing unilateralism."[11] But one would be hard pressed to conjure an initiative that would constitute a federal intervention in a matter of exclusive provincial jurisdiction and hence trigger s.106A. A federal initiative that so intervened would have had to be transparently designed with this end in mind. If so, s.106A might come into play, but the resulting asymmetry that arose from compensated opting-out will have been intended by politicians rather than being an outcome to which they have been fated by the Constitution.

Where there is good reason for intentional asymmetry in federal–provincial fiscal relations, bilateral undertakings of the DREE–DRIE–ERDA variety are the logical instrument for marrying federal and provincial objectives, not national shared-cost programs encompassed by s.106A. Involving as they do a mixture of economic and social objectives and constitutionally underpinned as they are by s.36 of the Constitution Act, 1982, bilateral arrangements permit just about any kind of government intervention in which national objectives are sensitive to provincial peculiarities. I suggest that such sensitivity is precisely what is suited to the age that lies beyond the welfare state, that of economic and social adjustment in a global environment.

Finally, it is important to bear in mind that tax expenditures have been displacing spending programs as enormously potent instruments for the achievement of economic and social objectives by federal and provincial governments. Where desired, these instruments, particularly in the form of income tax credits, can be designed to produce their intended effects whether or not a federal–provincial tax collection agreement is in place. In any event, they are untouched by s.106A.

In sum, I consider that s.106A will have minimal consequences for the conduct of federal–provincial fiscal relations precisely because it does not encompass the realm where the action lies. These relations will remain the preserve of our eleven first ministers and ministers of finance. Like the country that produces them, they will be conflictual as well as consensual, competitive as well as co-operative, asymmetrical as well as symmetrical. And they will remain insulated from the dead hand of any particular generation of constitution writers and from the opinions of a judiciary with no particular claim to fiscal expertise or sensitivity.

Notes

1. Constitution Act, 1982 [enacted by the Canada Act 1982 (U.K.), c.11, s.1].
2. K. Banting and R. Simeon, eds., *And No One Cheered: Federalism, Democracy and the Constitution Act* (Toronto: Methuen, 1983).
3. Constitution Act, 1867 (U.K.), c.3. See the Appendix to *Competing Constitutional Visions—The Meech Lake Accord* for relevant sections and the text of the 1987 Constitutional Accord.
4. D. M. Cameron and J. S. Dupré, "The Financial Framework of Income Distribution and Social Services" in S. Beck and I. Bernier, eds., *Canada and the New Constitution: The Unfinished Agenda*, Vol. I (Montreal: Institute for Research on Public Policy, 1983) at 340.
5. *Ibid.* at 341.
6. *Ibid.* at 341.
7. R. Fisher and W. Ury, *Getting to Yes* (Boston: Houghton Mifflin, 1981).

8. S.C. 1983–84, c.6.

9. J. S. Dupré, ''Reflections on the Workability of Executive Federalism'' in R. Simeon, ed., *Intergovernmental Relations*, Macdonald Commission Studies, Vol. 63 (Toronto: University of Toronto Press, 1985) at 19.

10. C. Morin, *Quebec versus Ottawa* (Toronto: University of Toronto Press, 1976) at Chapter 5 and *passim*.

11. A. Cairns, ''The Embedded State: State–Society Relations in Canada'' in K. Banting, ed., *State and Society: Canada in Comparative Perspective*, Macdonald Commission Studies, Vol. 31 (Toronto: University of Toronto Press, 1986) at 82.

CHAPTER SEVEN

WOMEN'S RIGHTS:

Does Meech Lake

Undermine the Gains

of 1982?

We do not believe that the entrenchment of this clause (linguistic duality/distinct society) will in any realistic way erode the present constitutional protections of individual rights, including gender equality rights.

(Special Joint Committee of the Senate and the House of Commons on the 1987 Constitutional Accord, *Report* [Ottawa: Queen's Printer, 1987]: 56)

As far as women are concerned, the wording in Meech Lake is muddy and unclear, and all our hard-won gains under the Charter are threatened. The tragedy is that this time, for selfish political reasons, Meech Lake is being rammed through unchanged, no matter what the public says . . . . Isn't there anyone up there in Ottawa who cares to speak up for Canada?

(Doris Anderson, *The Toronto Star*, April 9, 1988)

Reprinted with permission — Alan King, *The Ottawa Citizen*.

INTRODUCTION

The various elements of the women's movement were all catapulted into the constitutional renewal process in early February 1979 when the only consensus that emerged from a First Ministers' Constitutional Conference was the decision to transfer jurisdiction over marriage and divorce to the provinces. This decision had been taken without any consultation with the Canadian Advisory Council on the Status of Women (CACSW)—a federal body—or the National Action Committee on the Status of Women (NAC)—a voluntary organization—both of which were founded in 1972. Women's organizations in Manitoba successfully lobbied their premier to oppose this constitutional change, and the matter was deferred. Prior to this unannounced action, women's groups had not been overly concerned with constitutional law.[1]

In her preface to a collection of studies devoted to women and constitutional issues, Doris Anderson, the president of CACSW, was prompted to declare in the fall of 1980:

> Women constitute 52 percent of the population. It is *our* constitution, *our* lives that will be affected. It is, therefore, important that any new constitution reflects the realities and needs of our lives as workers, homemakers, mothers, wives and citizens. It is up to the women of Canada to make sure that the constitution gives all of us equality and good government for the next 100 years. Let the debate begin.[2]

The women's movement was going to be drawn away momentarily from its necessary preoccupation with the crucial socio-economic objectives expressed, partially, in the insightful and far-reaching recommendations of the 1970 *Report* of the Royal Commission on the Status of Women.[3]

After more than a decade of failed attempts at constitutional renewal, the Liberal government of Pierre Elliott Trudeau, on October 6, 1980, proposed to patriate unilaterally the British North America Act with an amending formula and a Charter of Rights and Freedoms. It became apparent that the women's movement could ignore only at its peril the opportunity to entrench gender equality in the reformed Constitution. The women's movement had been conspicuous by its absence from the process at both the bureaucratic and political levels. In response to the rhetorical question, "What business is this of ours?," Mary Eberts replied that women stood to be affected by virtually every change that could be made to the Constitution, beginning with the Charter of Rights and Freedoms through changes in federal institutions, family law and spending power provisions. It is up to women, Eberts concluded:

> to make sure that we are included in the constitutional review process, and that the perspectives and goals of women are taken seriously. We have a special, historical relationship to the constitution, as we had to fight so hard for so long to be included in even its minimal provisions. Let us not stop now.[4]

This new struggle would prove to be far more difficult than anyone in the movement or the media could have imagined. In fact, the intensity and bitterness of the struggle reminded contemporary women of the far longer and more numerous battles for basic legal rights—such as the rights to vote, to hold public office and for women to be legally recognized as persons in their own right—fought by the first generation of feminists.[5] Yet the contemporary women's movement proved to be far more effective in many ways, because it was better organized and therefore able to galvanize the support of the general public via the electronic media. The resilience and determination of the modern feminist movement were demonstrated by the fact that when CACSW, under pressure by the Liberal government, cancelled its planned constitutional conference slated for February 1981, an Ad Hoc Women's Committee on the Constitution was formed promptly to fill the political vacuum.

The Ad Hoc Committee organized, in very short order, the Ad Hoc Conference on Women and the Constitution to lobby, along with NAC, CACSW and the National Association of Women and the Law (NAWL), for amendments to the Charter of Rights and Freedoms, in particular for a general-purpose clause on gender equality. These organizations won the battle for a general-purpose clause, section 28 of the Charter, only to see it threatened by the notwithstanding clause—section 33—that the provinces insisted upon as the price of their approval. After a second major lobbying effort, section 28 was given immunity from section 33. Consequently, once the dust had settled, the women's movement had gained some of the legal rights its proponents deemed necessary for the continued advancement of the cause of all Canadian women.[6]

These gains came in section 15 of the Charter, which outlines the nature and scope of equality rights with provision for affirmative action, and in section 28, a general-purpose clause immune from the notwithstanding clause (section 33), which guarantees the application of the Charter of Rights and Freedoms equally to males and females. While these new legal rights were considerably less than had been expected, there was also a valid concern among some informed women about how the courts were going to interpret the relationship between sections 1, 15 and 28 of the Charter.[7] Others, like Katherine de Jong, concluded a lengthy study of section 28 of the Charter on a more positive note:

> Canadians want the *Charter of Rights* to be used to promote sexual equality. Section 28 makes this absolutely clear. The principle of sexual equality is now a legal standard of the highest priority.[8]

It is therefore not surprising that all five national women's organizations—NAC, CACSW, NAWL, Women's Legal and Education Action Fund (LEAF) and the Ad Hoc Women's Committee on the Constitution—immediately expressed their very strong concerns to the Special Joint Committee of the Senate and the House of Commons on the 1987 Constitutional Accord that the Meech Lake Accord threatened to jeopardize their hard-fought and hard-won gender rights, section 28 of the Charter.[9] In fact, two issues came to dominate, in short order, the focus of attention of these women's organizations. The first involved the question of process and resurrected painful memories of the 1980–82 experience. The second involved the question of substance. Once again, Canadian women were placed in the awkward and uncomfortable position of having to choose between the protection of gender rights and the national aspirations of francophone women from Quebec whose organizations defended the distinct society clause of the Meech Lake Accord.

As in 1980–82, the women's movement came to realize that it had very little effective political power when it came to influencing both the agenda and the outcome of constitutional reform. Women were not an integral part of the mainstream institutional network of bureaucrats and politicians who control the "executive federalism" of first ministers. This reaffirmation of the political impotency of the women's movement was both humiliating and depressing once the women's organizations realized that it was virtually impossible for them to catalyse an effective extraparliamentary pressure movement, as they had in 1980–81. "The political skirmish was decisive," writes Susan Riley about the Meech Lake process. She continues:

> [W]omen lost. The organized women's movement lost. On Parliament Hill, its representatives ran into indifference more chilling than hostility. Women asked for a serious hearing and they got "trust me, sweetheart." When they persisted, they were accused of being hostile to Quebec's desire to become a "distinct society," of being anti-French. Their motives were questioned, their legal arguments ignored and their political clout called into question.[10]

Operating in a context that lacked the crisis overtones of the 1980–81 constitutional reform talks, the women's organizations proved incapable of convincing the first ministers or the national and provincial legislatures and their constitutional committees to make important and necessary amendments that would protect section 28 of the Charter from the linguistic duality/distinct society clause of the Meech Lake Accord. The women's movement had lost enormous ground in Ottawa with the political watershed that brought the Mulroney Conservative government to power in 1984. This was fully understood by representatives of the national organizations only when they appeared before the Special Joint Committee of the Senate and the House of Commons on the 1987 Constitutional Accord. During the hearings, they were stonewalled by a common front of Conservative, Liberal and New Democratic members who gave priority to the achievement of a political deal with the government of Quebec over legal concerns about the Charter. Distorting what had transpired during the hearings, the Committee stated in its *Report* that:

> the great weight of constitutional opinion put before the Joint Committee, however, leads to the conclusion that the fears that entrenchment

of the "linguistic duality/distinct society" interpretative clause will cause such an erosion are not justified.[11]

The *Report* cavalierly dismissed the women's organizations' strong contention, backed by sound legal advice, that the Accord placed the gender equality rights clause of the Charter at risk. Beverley Baines has demonstrated in a brilliant and devastating critique of Chapter VI of the Committee's *Report* that the Committee simply did not understand what the women's organizations were saying. It demonstrated this clearly in its misleading, inconsistent, distorted and illogical account of the women's submissions and testimony. Contrary to what the *Report* states, the women's organizations (a) all supported the linguistic duality/ distinct society clause; (b) did not recommend special status for gender rights; and (c) did not demand a "guarantee" of "automatic para-mountcy" for their Charter-based equality rights. In large measure, the *Report* simply ignored the bulk of the testimony of the women's organizations while acknowledging the testimony from a dozen male intervenors and two Quebec women's organizations that supported the Committee's position. In sum, the *Report* was a put-up job and lacked any credibility.[12]

To some extent, the women's organizations allowed themselves to be neutralized by the first ministers, Parliament, the legislatures and the various constitutional committees. As was the case in 1980–82, they were torn between competing loyalties. At that time, the desire to entrench equality and gender rights in a Canadianized constitution over-rode the fundamental objections of nationalist-oriented Québécois women's organizations that were opposed to a centralizing and unifor-mizing Charter. Considerable dissension and tension had ensued.[13]

In 1987, the national women's organizations made a valiant attempt to avoid the problems encountered during the initial struggle over the Charter. They refused to be put in a position of having to decide priorities, thereby threatening the fragile but important unity they had fostered since 1982. Furthermore, with the aggressive Mulroney Conservative government, there was a new agenda of reconciliation with the provinces, in particular with the Liberal government of the province of Quebec. If national women's organizations wished to get a favourable hearing on their new agenda items, such as day care, it was important not to alienate the incumbent administration. After considerable deliberation and some dissension, these national organizations consciously refused to make a choice between defending women's Charter-based rights and the defence of the collective rights of Quebec's francophone majority via the entrenchment of the distinct society clause in the Constitution. All supported the entrenchment of the distinct society clause in the Constitution while at the same time demanding that section 28 of the Charter be protected from the interpretative power of such a clause. When critics pointed out that such an approach would transfer the distinct society clause into a symbolic preamble without legal weight, dissension was once again rampant within the women's national and provincial organizations. In an attempt to reconcile the various factions, the Canadian Research Institute for the Advancement of Women commissioned a report that provided a "cultural pluralist" explanation for the divergent but "not incompatible" positions of Québécois and Canadian feminists.[14]

The Fédération des femmes du Québec (FFQ), supported by the Quebec Council on the Status of Women,[15] strongly defended the Meech Lake Accord for recognizing Quebec as a distinct society. The FFQ expressed its concern directly to the Prime Minister that the distinct society and spending powers clauses were not better defined[16] but opposed any formal reopening of the Accord for fear that such action would bring about its demise. The FFQ categorically denounced the claim that the distinct society clause threatened the rights of Quebec women either directly or indirectly. Yet the FFQ contradicted itself when it argued "that the concept of a distinct society is a neutral concept within the context of women's rights" while claiming that the progress Quebec women have made in integrating into the political culture "is linked to the concept of a distinct society." Québécois nationalism is portrayed as a positive force when it provides benefits, while the FFQ considers that ongoing vigilance can prevent fallout from any of its potentially negative dimensions. Nevertheless, in order to ensure harmony in the women's movement, the FFQ was willing to support NAC's recommendation that section 28 of the Charter be made immune from the distinct society clause by placing it in section 16 of the Accord.[17]

While the Quebec women's organizations pleaded for the acceptance of the two-societies or two-nations concept, which allowed them the full autonomy deemed necessary to pursue their aspirations via the Quebec state, other Canadian feminists began to ask tough legal questions about the potential impact of the distinct society clause on equality rights for women. Lynn Smith analyses the three central ways—creating a constitutionally stated justification for limiting equality rights, immunizing legislation from the Charter by defining it as a fundamental compromise of Confederation and interpreting the Meech Lake Accord as a symbolic statement that places a lower priority on gender rights than on collective rights of nationalities—in which gender equality rights could be affected by the distinct society clause. She concludes that "there is reasonable cause for concern that the proposed new s. 2 will directly or indirectly tend to restrict the scope of Charter equality rights, both inside and outside Quebec."[18] Beverley Baines, in her brilliant and persuasive testimony before the Ontario Select Committee on Constitutional Reform, comes to the same conclusion. She refutes effectively the predominantly male claim that the Accord does not override the Charter while demonstrating the women's organizations' claim that the Charter may indeed not apply to the Accord as written. To overcome the serious risks that this situation creates for women's equality rights, she recommends that the entire Charter be inserted as an interpretative clause into section 2 of the Accord.[19]

In her incisive submission to the Ontario Select Committee on Constitutional Reform, Mary Eberts, who provided legal counsel to the Ad Hoc Committee of Women on the Constitution and who holds a watching brief on all matters pertaining to women and the Constitution, provides an overview of all aspects of the Accord that create problems for women. Reiterating the critique of all five national women's organizations, she analyses the undemocratic nature of the existing constitutional amending process involving the first ministers. This process virtually excludes input from Canadian women despite their historical association with the Constitution. The use and abuse of nationalism by the Prime Minister and the Special Joint Committee to castigate Canadian women as anti-Quebec while portraying Quebec women's organizations as the only voices that count have added, in her estimation, even more "sequelae of cynicism and distrust" about the process. Because the Accord constitutionalizes "executive federalism" by calling for annual meetings on the Constitution, the situation for Canadian women will be aggravated rather than improved. In order to ensure meaningful ongoing consultations with citizens' groups and special constituencies, it is important that the government provide them with the necessary operating funds so that they are immune from unsavory political pressure tactics. She also rejects the Special Joint Committee's recommendation that a permanent joint committee be established to monitor the impact of the linguistic duality/distinct society clause on the Charter and recommend changes if necessary. Such intervention would not be benign and would force women into an expensive mode of eternal vigilance.

On the substance of the distinct society clause, Ms. Eberts explains why it is both valid and realistic that women be concerned about the clause's threat to equality guarantees. In outlining the process of argument that a plaintiff must go through in order to convince a court that a particular piece of legislation violates the equality guarantees, she demonstrates how and in what degree the distinct society interpretative clause will come to bear upon the courts' deliberations on sections 15 and 1 of the Charter, and how section 16 of the Accord immunizes aboriginal and multicultural groups from the distinct society provision. Her example pertaining to language training for recently arrived immigrants is very telling and not very easily dismissed. Given the nature of Canadian jurisprudence, Supreme Court decisions involving cases from Quebec dealing with conflicts between gender equality and the distinct society clause will affect decisions in cases from other parts of Canada. Does this mean that, in time, Canada will be able to characterize itself as a distinct society?

Notes

1. Katherine J. de Jong, "Sexual Equality: Interpreting Section 28," in Anne F. Bayefsky and Mary Eberts, eds., *Equality Rights and the Canadian Charter of Rights and Freedoms* (Toronto: Carswell, 1985): 494–499.

2. Doris Anderson, "Preface," in Audrey Doerr and Micheline Carrier, eds., *Women and the Constitution in Canada* (Ottawa: Canadian Advisory Council on the Status of Women, 1981): v.

3. Canada, Royal Commission on the Status of Women, *Report* (Ottawa, 1970).

4. Mary Eberts, "Women and Constitutional Renewal," in Doerr and Carrier, *Women and the Constitution in Canada*, 3–27, quote 25; a very convincing argument for entrenching an effective equality rights provision for women in any new Charter was made by Beverley Baines, "Women, Human Rights and the Constitution," in *ibid.*, 31–63.

5. Mary Eberts, "Sex-based Discrimination and the Charter," in Bayefsky and Eberts, *Equality Rights and the Canadian Charter of Rights and Freedoms*, 184–185.

6. See Chaviva Hošek, "Women and the Constitutional Process," in Keith Banting and Richard Simeon, eds., *And No One Cheered: Federalism, Democracy and the Constitution Act* (Toronto: Methuen, 1983): 285–291; Penny Kome, *The Taking of Twenty-Eight: Women Challenge the Constitution* (Toronto: The Women's Press, 1983): 39–81; and de Jong, "Sexual Equality: Interpreting Section 28," 500–512.

7. In 1985, Mary Eberts provided a lengthy analysis of how the courts might conceivably devise a Canadian approach to interpreting and applying the equality guarantees pertaining to sex-based discrimination. She analyses the range and kind of arguments the courts have resorted to in determining

and then justifying sex-based discrimination in Canadian legislation. Eberts argues that "including section 28 as part of the reasoning process avoids the essential artificiality of first applying section 1 and then resorting to section 28, and it accords to section 28 some of the status of a statement of principle which its proponents sought for it." See Eberts, "Sex-based Discrimination and the Charter," 199–229, quote 216.

8. De Jong, "Sexual Equality: Interpreting Section 28," 512–528, quote 528.

9. See various issues of Canada, Special Joint Committee of the Senate and the House of Commons on the 1987 Constitutional Accord, *Minutes of Proceedings and Evidence* (Ottawa: Queen's Printer, 1987): Canadian Advisory Council on the Status of Women (CACSW), No. 10, August 20, 1987, 82–106; National Action Committee on the Status of Women (NAC), No. 13, August 26, 1987, 21–42; National Association of Women and the Law (NAWL), No. 2, August 4, 1987, 79–97; Women's Legal and Education Action Fund (LEAF), No. 3, August 5, 1987, 110–137; Ad Hoc Committee of Women on the Constitution, No. 15, August 31, 1987, 127–156.

10. Susan Riley, "The Meech Boys. Are Women Up the Lake Without a Paddle?," *This Magazine* (December 1987/January 1988): 31. For similar concerns about the process, see Nadine McDonnell, "The Meech Lake Accord: Saying Yes to Quebec and No to Women?," *Priorities*, XV, No. 4 (Winter 1987): 10.

11. Canada, Special Joint Committee of the Senate and the House of Commons on the 1987 Constitutional Accord, *Report*, Chapter VI, The 1987 Accord and Charter Rights (Ottawa: Queen's Printer, 1987): 55–68. Senator Lowell Murray readily adopted the rationalizations of the Committee in his "Could the Meech Lake Accord Override Sexual Equality Rights?," *CAUT Bulletin* (February 1988): 8–9.

12. Beverley Baines, "Gender and the Meech Lake Committee," in Clive Thomson, ed., *Navigating Meech Lake: The 1987 Constitutional Accord* (Kingston: Institute of Intergovernmental Relations and *Queen's Quarterly*, 1988): 43–52.

13. Hošek, "Women and the Constitutional Process," 289–290; Kome, *The Taking of Twenty-Eight*, illustrates the fact that the Quebec women's organizations, as opposed to individual women, were conspicuous by their absence from the struggle for section 28.

14. Barbara Roberts, *Smooth Sailing or Storm Warning? Canadian and Quebec Women's Groups on the Meech Lake Accord* (Ottawa: Canadian Research Institute for the Advancement of Women, n.d.): 1–24. See also Ginette Busque, "La petite histoire politique du Lac Meech," *FFQ petite presse*, septembre 1987, 2–3.

15. See the Quebec Council on the Status of Women's testimony before the Special Joint Committee of the Senate and the House of Commons on the 1987 Constitutional Accord, *Minutes of Proceedings and Evidence*, No. 15, August 31, 1987, 79–91.

16. Supporting the position of the Bourassa government, the Quebec Council disagreed on this point, stating: "It is true that the concept of a distinct

society encompasses a great deal, but we believe that an attempt to define it could restrict its scope." See *ibid.*, 82.

17. The Quebec Council would not support the NAC's amendment because it contended that "section 28 of the Canadian Charter contains specific wording that gives constitutional paramountcy to the equality between men and women." See *ibid.*

18. Lynn Smith, "The Distinct Society Clause in the Meech Lake Accord: Could It Affect Equality Rights for Women?," in K. E. Swinton and C. J. Rogerson, eds., *Competing Constitutional Visions—The Meech Lake Accord* (Toronto: Carswell, 1988): 35–54, quote 53; Lucie Lamarche argues that section 16 of the Accord was sheer political expediency and the government does not consider it politically necessary or profitable to reopen the Accord to guarantee women their legal equality. See "Perspective féministe d'une certaine société distincte: Les Québécoises et l'Accord du Lac Meech," *ibid.*, 21–33.

19. Beverley Baines, testimony before the Ontario Select Committee on Constitutional Reform, 1987 Constitutional Accord, *Hansard Official Report of Debates*, February 3, 1988, C-47–C-61; Baines' legal advice to the Canadian Advisory Council on the Status of Women led that organization to make a similar recommendation to the Joint Committee. See the CACSW's brief to and testimony before the Special Joint Committee of the Senate and the House of Commons on the 1987 Constitutional Accord, *Minutes of Proceedings and Evidence*, No. 10, August 20, 1987, 84–86, and the Senate of Canada, *Proceedings of the Senate Submissions Group on the Meech Lake Accord*, No. 5, March 18, 1988, 33–42.

FÉDÉRATION DES FEMMES DU QUÉBEC

ARE WOMEN'S RIGHTS THREATENED BY THE DISTINCT SOCIETY CLAUSE?*

The Quebec government has already ratified the constitutional agreement arrived at by the 11 premiers. We fully realize that an eventual re-opening of the Accord might bring about its demise.

Quebec's condition, that its specificity be written into our most basic act, was met; we consider this to be a minimum, and we feel it should not be debated once again.

Last May, in a letter sent to Mr. Mulroney and to Mr. Bourassa, the federation expressed its concerns with regard to the definition of the concept of a distinct society and to the government's spending power. In our presentation today, we would also like to study the concept of a distinct society within the context of equal rights. Several feminist groups have said that the recognition of a distinct society would imperil women's rights: such is not our opinion.

In our brief, the concept of a distinct society will therefore be discussed from two standpoints: equal rights and the definition of the concept itself as well as of cost-shared programs.

I would first like to discuss Quebec as a distinct society and equal rights. This is more than likely the subject about which you are most anxious to hear our point of view.

Several feminist groups, as well as the Canadian Advisory Council on the Status of Women, have said that the concept of a distinct society might pose a threat to women's rights. According to the studies conducted by these groups, it is possible that the other provinces might also claim that they have a distinct character because of the different references made in the Accord to the equality of the provinces. In its presentation to your committee, the group LEAF discussed distinct societies.

* Brief to the Special Joint Committee of the Senate and the House of Commons on the 1987 Constitutional Accord, *Minutes of Proceedings and Evidence*, No. 13, August 26, 1987.

This, I believe, explains in part the concerns expressed by groups outside of the Province of Quebec with regard to the application of the concept of a distinct society. These groups are usually much more distrustful of provincial authorities than we are.

However, if only the Province of Quebec is recognized as a distinct society, we strongly hope that our sisters will not see threats where we feel they do not exist. In answer to the question: Does the concept of a distinct society threaten Quebec's women? the Fédération des femmes du Québec answers: No.

This is why. The purpose of the Accord is to bring Quebec into the Constitution, and the protection of the French language, of our culture, our educational system, our network of social services, our volunteer associations, and so on, does not create a situation particularly apt to jeopardize women's rights.

According to our understanding of section 16 of the Accord, section 25 of the Canadian Charter of Rights and Freedoms, concerning native people, and section 27, concerning multiculturalism, were expressly mentioned in section 16 because the new section 2 of the Constitution Act of 1867 could be interpreted to mean that the recognition of Canada's fundamental characteristics and of Quebec's distinctiveness could undermine the rights provided for in those sections. But since the revised section 2 of the 1867 Act does not refer to matters that can, given their very nature, affect women's rights, we thought it quite plausible that only sections 25 and 27 of the Charter be mentioned.

I should say that the Fédération des femmes du Québec does not consider itself expert on constitutional matters. We did, however, consult a great number of people concerning our interpretation of section 16. Several of these people, whose credibility could not be questioned by this committee, agreed with our interpretation of the section.

Therefore, according to our analysis, the Meech Lake agreement does not pose an explicit nor even a potential threat to Quebec women's rights. We are not trying to say that women's rights in the Province of Quebec will never be threatened. What we are trying to say is that the history of women's rights clearly illustrates that it is not necessary to bring the concept of a distinct society into play for our rights to be compromised or threatened, and that the concept of a distinct society is a neutral concept within the context of women's rights.

Nor do we want the concept of a distinct society or Canada's fundamental characteristics to be used to set back women's rights. In the Province of Quebec, the respect of women's rights is more and more becoming part of the political culture. As a matter of fact, the progress we have made with regard to the status of women is linked to the concept of a distinct society.

I will come back to our specific conclusions on this point a little later on. I would like to bring up a subject that other women's groups have not brought to the attention of this committee: the definition of the concept of a distinct society. In our letter we sent to Messrs. Mulroney and Bourassa, last May, before the signing of the Constitutional Accord, we deplored the fact that the concept of a distinct society had not been defined. I repeat that we are fully aware that the Province of Quebec has already ratified the Accord. We do not think it will be possible to make any changes whatsoever to this clause that seems to be at the very heart of the Meech Lake agreement.

However, in an attempt to perhaps simply influence the way in which this concept might later be interpreted, we want to reaffirm before this committee that, despite the importance that the language question has for us, the concept of a distinct society also involves other fundamental aspects. Although we realize that the definition Mr. Claude Ryan used in his beige paper on the Canadian federation is neither perfect nor all-encompassing, we would still like to use it here. His definition goes beyond language and culture and includes fundamental aspects that, we believe, are proof of our vitality.

According to Mr. Ryan's definition, our distinctiveness as a society includes our laws, our legal system, our municipal and provincial institutions, our volunteer organizations, our media, our arts, our literature, our educational system, our network of social and health care services, our religious institutions, our savings and loans institutions, as well as our language and our culture.

Therefore, the concept of a distinct society is relatively complex. Even on a strictly linguistic level, we are not convinced that all the aspects or the effects of this concept have been analysed. We therefore feel it is essential that even the linguistic question be included in its entirety. What we are saying here is that the fact that we belong to Quebec's francophone majority should not cause us harm at the federal level. Generally speaking, because we belong to this majority, we are unable to develop a national strength in the Canadian sense of the term, and, by the same token, are excluded from those benefits given to national groups as well as those given to linguistic minorities.

We would very much like to discuss this question in order to find out how the federal government will view this concept. It does not have to promote the concept of a distinct society, this is Quebec's responsibility. The federal government will have to recognize the existence of a distinct society. Will the fact that Quebec is a distinct society be taken into account in certain federal policies or programs?

The Fédération des femmes du Québec could use the financing of women's groups as an example. Without ever referring to the concept of a distinct society, last spring, we explained the problems we had in trying to obtain financial support similar to that offered other groups that enjoy a national status. These problems were due to the fact that the federation does not meet the women's programs' territorial criteria.

As far as the concept of a distinct society is concerned, we would like to state that our basic position would not coincide with the request that the Accord be amended in order to protect us. Although it is true that we do not recommend that the Accord be amended, the Fédération des femmes du Québec would not object to an amendment whose purpose would be to include section 28 of the Canadian Charter of Rights and Freedoms in section 16 of the Constitutional Accord, as was suggested by the National Action Committee on the Status of Women.

As a matter of fact, the intention of the signing parties to respect equal rights was expressed under circumstances to which the courts will probably never be able to refer. When Mr. Lowell Murray appeared before this committee, he explained that the Accord would not threaten equal rights. We hope that his testimony will be able to be used by the courts. We would, however, have preferred that the parties to the Accord appear before this committee and explain that they had no intention whatsoever of threatening equal rights. In its decision handed down on June 25 of this year concerning Ontario's Bill 30, the Supreme Court referred to the documents used by the Court of Appeal to interpret section 29.

The following is an excerpt from the judgement:

> In arriving at this interpretation of section 29, the majority relied heavily on the intention of the drafters of the charter, as it appears in the minutes of proceedings and evidence heard by the Special Joint Committee and the House of Commons on the Constitution, 1980–1981.

If some very clear, categorical statements are made here, they will have some weight in the future.

Strictly from the point of view of legal drafting or from a theoretical point of view, clause 16 of the Accord may indeed look rather clumsy. Our analysis has shown that the addition of section 28 of the Charter to sections 25 and 27 can be justified as follows: Sections 25 and 27 are both interpretation sections. Section 28 of the Charter is also an interpretation provision. We can perhaps discuss this question later, because I see that some of the committee members do not agree with our opinion. For the reasons we have given, the explicit reference to section 28 in clause 16 of the Accord would be allowable.

However, we in the Fédération des femmes du Québec feel that the inclusion of a reference to section 28 of the Charter would be done, not because it is necessary to protect rights that are apparently threatened, as is the case for sections 25 and 27 of the Charter, but to provide a logical confirmation of the nature of clause 16 of the Accord, which seems to have been the First Ministers' intention in any case. In our opinion, the amendment is necessary in the interests of consistency, rather than to reassure certain groups.

The inclusion of a reference to section 28 of the Charter in section 16 of the Accord would not affect the substance of new clause 2 of the Constitution Act, 1867 and would not upset, in our opinion, the order of interpretation established in that clause. We would certainly not support any amendment that could jeopardize the very essence of the Accord.

We would like to conclude by saying that had clause 16 not been inserted, we would not even have felt it necessary to make these comments.

We will now discuss the spending power. Clause 7 of the Accord, which amends section 106 of the 1867 Constitution Act, leads us to make some comments and to ask some questions.

Constitutional recognition of the federal government's spending power in fields of exclusive provincial jurisdiction confirms what could be described as the existing situation.

In our comments to Mr. Mulroney and Mr. Bourassa last May, we made the point that the complex problems arising out of the spending powers occur in both the political and legal spheres.

We acknowledge that the spending power has been used in the past in extremely judicious ways as regards the interests of women. For example, the federal government required that health care be provided free of charge before it would provide funding for the provincial medicare program. Quebec was originally opposed to this requirement. There was also the example of the battle against extra billing that was waged by Ms Monique Bégin.

However, the spending power can also be used to work against our objectives in some areas. One example is child care.

A federal Parliamentary committee recently suggested that the main way of helping parents should be to give them money directly rather than invest in infrastructures to increase the number of day care spaces.

Women's groups interested in the issue have always asked that priority be given to non-profit organizations in the creation of child care spaces. This is a policy put forward by the Quebec government.

Even though the amounts invested by the Quebec government have never been adequate, its approach to day care is in keeping with our demands. If the federal government were to give money to parents directly, the results would be catastrophic, because the development of the whole network of child care services would be jeopardized. For this reason, we think it is essential that the extent of federal involvement in areas of exclusive provincial jurisdiction be specified, and that the meaning of certain terms be better defined.

We also have many questions about national objectives. For example, in the case of child care again, would the objectives be to assist parents with children, to offer the necessary child care services to all the children of Canada, or to assist parents with children by providing funding for a national child care network? Who will be defining the national objectives—the federal government alone or the federal government in co-operation with the provinces? At what point will an objective no longer be national? For example, if half of the provinces decide not to participate in a federal program, will it still be a national program? Is the reference to general or to specific objectives? Is there a distinction made between the characteristics, standards and objectives of a program? Another of our many questions is how will national objectives be defined in the case of a program that could have an impact on the distinct society concept? We think that, out of respect for provincial jurisdictions, these questions must be clarified, as must the terms "initiative" and "compatible". "Compatible" does not necessarily mean that an initiative must be of the same type, or that its objectives be similar. In an extreme case, the "compatible" could even mean "that does not run counter to".

In conclusion, therefore, we repeat that we are pleased to see that Quebec is recognized as a distinct society within Canada. However, we deplore the fact that the extent of this recognition is not spelled out more clearly. We think the language and culture are fundamental components, but they are not the only components of our distinct society.

As to the relationship between the implementation of the Accord and equality rights, we have been unable to conclude that the Accord poses any particular danger. We want our rights to be respected, and we do not think that the struggles we have engaged in to date will lose their meaning once the Accord is ratified.

Finally, we hope that future consultations on the Constitution will give us an opportunity to intervene in time to influence the direction of government policy. We also hope we will be given reasonable notice.

We have found it extremely stressful to have to prepare our presentation in such a rush on an issue as fundamental as the Meech Lake Accord. Thank you for your kind attention.

MARY EBERTS

THE CONSTITUTION, THE CHARTER AND THE DISTINCT SOCIETY CLAUSE: WHY ARE WOMEN BEING IGNORED?*

This Committee will be hearing from women's groups who are concerned about the Accord's failure to acknowledge the significance of the Charter's sex equality guarantees. You may hear, too, from those who assure you that there is "nothing to worry about"; indeed, women's groups have received this "reassurance" from several sources, sometimes delivered with an attempt at kindness, sometimes delivered with contempt.

Yet women continue to be concerned, and my remarks today are intended to offer you some insight into why. Accordingly, I speak on two main themes, firstly the process of constitutional renewal as it affects women, and secondly the provisions of the Accord itself.

Women and Constitutional Renewal

Although almost no accounts of it appear in "mainstream" constitutional scholarship or official government texts, women's involvement in constitution making has a long and significant history. Like the aboriginal peoples and like men and women in Quebec, the ordinary women of Canada have for some decades seen a strong link between the country's constitutional arrangements and their own destinies. This year marks the sixtieth anniversary of women's active pursuit of a voice in constitution making, and the tenth anniversary of contemporary women's preoccupation with constitutional renewal.

* Brief to the Ontario Select Committee on Constitutional Reform, 1987 Constitutional Accord.

It was in 1928 that the Supreme Court of Canada heard the Reference case on the meaning of the word "Persons" in the then *British North America Act, 1867*, a Reference case precipitated by women because they could not sit in the Senate, and their right to hold judicial office was challenged, simply because of their sex. The Supreme Court of Canada ruled that women were not "Persons,"[1] and it was only when an appeal was taken to the Privy Council that the ruling was overturned.[2]

Fifty years later, in 1978, in the dying moments of a meeting of First Ministers, Prime Minister Trudeau conceded to the provinces jurisdiction over marriage and divorce. The provinces had not pressed for this concession, and it was greeted with alarm by women's groups who recognized that it would make custody and support orders even more difficult to enforce in a federal system, and could threaten the existence of an effective uniform law on divorce. Only after months of lobbying by women was the initiative stalled.[3]

In these first two episodes of modern-day constitutional history, women learned how essential it is to bring vigilance and persistence to bear on the constitutional renewal process. That lesson would be relearned over and over in the next ten years.

The period of constitutional renewal from 1978 to 1988[4] has had, for women, several salient characteristics:

1. Constitutional decisions of great significance to women are made by men without notice to women, without consultation, and in the absence of any essential awareness of women's interests.

2. If there is to be any hope of reversing constitutional decisions made in this way, women must be prepared to act on very short notice and with a massive show of strength and solidarity. Circumstances dictate that they do so as volunteers, with but slender resources at their disposal, because women control none of the established, official processes of constitution-making.

3. When action is taken in an attempt to reverse an initial decision that ignores their interests, women find that male decision-makers, in the short interval since its making, have developed an enormous attachment to the new-minted status quo, and a desire to maintain it almost for its own sake.

4. Resistance to women's concerns about constitutional initiatives ranges from the patronizing "Trust us" to ridicule, misrepre-

sentation of women's position, and silencing. Women are also threatened that if they do not accept the deal as configured, the alternative will be worse.

5. Although women are told to speak with one voice, or run the risk of not being listened to, decision-makers also tell some women that, because of their regional, political or other characteristics, they have no right at all to be heard in the debate.

6. If any gains are made by women, these should be regarded as fragile, liable to be reversed without notice or consultation at the next meeting of male constitution-makers.

7. Gains for women, and equality guarantees in general, are particularly liable to be sacrificed in the interests of provincial powers.

This pattern of women's involvement in constitution-making was first evident in the making of the present *Charter of Rights*. The version of the *Charter* first tabled in 1980[5] had been developed without any process of consultation with women; moreover, almost no women were involved in the political and civil service teams doing constitutional renewal in the years leading up to 1980. Because of the earlier activism about jurisdiction over marriage and divorce, and because of the outstanding leadership of women like Doris Anderson, women were able to make a strong showing at the Special Joint Committee hearings on the Constitution in 1980,[6] and the federal government did introduce some changes to the proposed equality guarantees in response to women's representations.[7]

The changes were not, however, fully responsive, and when women pointed this out, the realities of male constitution-making were quickly apparent. The federal Minister responsible for the Status of Women first told women "Trust us."[8] When that didn't work, certain women faced an election, to choose between their loyalty to the Minister and his government on the one hand, and the women's constitutional process on the other. The resulting cancellation of the CACSW conference on the Constitution, resignation of Doris Anderson, and spontaneous generation of the February 14, 1981, Ad Hoc Conference of Canadian Women on the Constitution are well-known history.[9] What is not so well known is that during that period, women known as "big L" Liberals were effectively silenced: called to loyalty (and silence) in the councils of the Party, or regarded with suspicion in the women's lobby because of their Party loyalty, real or imputed.[10] This was women's first experience of the rule of thumb that women must have certain "credentials'' (or not have certain others) in order to speak out on constitutional issues. The proponents of the Meech Lake Accord used this technique with cynical deliberation during this past summer's debate on the Accord at the federal level.

The Ad Hoc lobby was successful in having section 28 inserted into the *Charter*, as a statement of principle about the equality of women and men. However, as Chaviva Hošek has pointed out in her analysis of women and the *Charter* lobby, this represented only one small part of the women's agenda.[11] And small though that victory may have been, it and the earlier improvements to section 15 were dealt a sudden and serious blow in November of 1981, when all the First Ministers except for Quebec's agreed to the ''November Accord'' adding the override provision, section 33, to the *Charter*.

The record is unclear whether the First Ministers actually agreed in their all-night session in November 1981 to include both section 15 and section 28 under the override; whatever may have been their intent, by the time the first drafts of the Accord were made public, both sections were subject to the override. Thereafter, the politicians stayed very loyal to the work of the drafters, and a national lobby was required to lift section 28 out from under section 33. Efforts to have section 15 similarly excluded were unsuccessful.

In this lobby two notes that would recur in 1987 with respect to the Meech Lake Accord were sounded: governments told women of the dire consequences to women if women were successful (i.e., affirmative action for women would be stopped by section 28 and legislatures without an override would be powerless to stop that), and women were directly pitted against the provinces, who wanted the override as a hedge against the diminution of their powers represented by the *Charter*'s fundamental guarantees.[12] A third theme also surfaced: women were told that the override could be a benevolent instrument to relieve against wrong-headed decisions of the Supreme Court of Canada, which couldn't really be trusted to give a generous meaning to the *Charter*.[13] Six years later, politicians were to reverse themselves dramatically, exhorting women to ''trust'' that the Supreme Court would protect equality rights from the impact of the Meech Lake Accord's ''distinct society'' clause.

The process of formulating and approving the Meech Lake Accord has, to date, exhibited the same regrettable characteristics as the earlier *Charter* process. In my view, however, the disease is somewhat more virulent this time around, with considerably more sequelae of cynicism and distrust.

For some two years, prior to the drafting of the Meech Lake Accord, the five Quebec conditions for adhesion to the *Constitution Act, 1982* had been clear.[14] Discussion had proceeded, publicly and privately, on those conditions. Yet at no time before its signature was a draft of the Accord, containing clauses 2 and 16 (the sources of so much concern for women), made public for discussion and comment. So, effectively, women were excluded from the run-up to the Meech Lake meetings, because what turned out to be a problem for women was never on the table. This fact alone makes the Special Joint Committee's apology for the process followed in the "Quebec Round" of talks somewhat unconvincing.

The meetings of First Ministers which produced the Accord were not at all representative of women; none of the Premiers and almost none of their senior advisors were women, and no effort was made to have at the meetings any expert with a particular expertise or perspective on women. All this is, of course, distressingly familiar, as is the fact that once the agreement was signed, loyalty to it became the order of the day. In order to enforce that loyalty, and rebuff the criticism of women who discerned problems with the Accord, various stratagems were resorted to. All of them, once again, echo the measures employed in 1980 and 1981.

High on the list of deterrents to real debate is the threat that any change to the Accord will make it unravel or fall apart. Women who seek such change are thus portrayed as the potential wreckers of Confederation. The portrayal is not a subtle one: Prime Minister Mulroney publicly endorsed Lysiane Gagnon's charge that Anglo-Canadian women were a "Trojan Horse" for the foes of Quebec's enhanced participation in Confederation.[15]

Strongly linked with this portrayal of women critical of Meech Lake is the assertion by the federal government and the Special Joint Committee that Quebec women are the only women whose voices count on the issue of whether the distinct society provisions of the Accord will have a negative impact on women.[16] The message sent by Ottawa is: Quebec women may speak, all others hold your tongues, because the Accord is not your business. This, of course, is merely a repetition of the 1981 dictum that "big L" Liberal women should not, or could not, comment on the constitutional scene. But it is potentially much more divisive.

The federal strategy threatens the coalitions between women inside and outside Quebec that have been operating for years, in national women's organizations, other national citizens' groups, and informally.

And just as "big L" Liberal women were put to the choice in 1981 between supporting their party and their government, or supporting Doris Anderson and the women's lobby, women inside and outside Quebec face the choice of whether they are "for Quebec" or "for women." And the reason they face that choice is because the federal government and its closest allies among the provinces have said that no woman can be both—they have, by their manipulation of the issue, told all Canadian women, wherever they live, that they must be either for Quebec or for women. If they are for Quebec, they will drop their complaints about Meech Lake; if they are for women, they will persist with the complaints and run the risk of wrecking Confederation. To tell women across Canada, who have worked together for years to improve the status of women, that they must make these choices is insulting and totally unrealistic. Any idea that a sensible middle position can be reached is never allowed on the agenda.

The absurdity of the false dichotomy engineered by the federal government becomes clear when we consider what else they are telling women. First, there is the "trust us" approach: we really didn't mean to eclipse women's rights and we're sure we didn't.[17] This is heard publicly and in private meetings, but when the government is asked to "make assurance doubly sure" by inserting clarifying language into the Accord, it either lapses into its false dichotomy (don't ask us to make our assurance concrete, to do so will wreck this fragile bargain), or its other "trust" line surfaces. This time, women are told "trust them," meaning the Supreme Court of Canada. The Joint Committee Report exemplifies this approach, suggesting that the Supreme Court can be relied upon to smooth out the problems with the Accord.[18] Such a position pays no heed to the Court itself, which has said in important *Charter* decisions that it gives little weight in interpreting the *Charter* to what politicians say it means.[19]

If the "trust us, trust them" approach to reassuring women does not work, then less kindly means are tried. Government authorities controlling the "discourse" on Meech Lake keep changing the questions women must answer before their concerns will be taken seriously. Women are told that the government's experts advise that there are no problems with the Accord, yet those expert opinions are never revealed or subjected to public debate. When women respond with expert evidence about the dangers of the Accord for equality rights, these experts are either ignored altogether or flatly contradicted, without reasons.

Yet, at times the pretense that there is a legal debate among experts is maintained, and women are told that they will be listened to if it can be shown that there is a problem. However, the standard of proof for such a showing is readily manipulated. The Accord itself says that section 16 is there to ensure that the distinct society clause does not "affect" multiculturalism and aboriginal rights provisions of the *Charter* and *Constitution Act, 1867*. When women show that their equality rights could also be "affected" by the Accord, and ask for the same reassurance, women learn that, now, to be affected is not enough: women must prove beyond a reasonable doubt that their rights will be overridden.[20] When all else fails, the legal positions put forward by women's advocates are misrepresented, as is the case in the Special Joint Committee Report. Thus publicly mischaracterized, on the record, the women's arguments are then rebutted.[21]

Sometimes, however, when women make legal arguments, the answer is that the decisions on the Meech Lake Accord are political ones.[22] Attempts to address political issues in political terms bring rejoinders that we are dealing here with statecraft, with national survival, transcending the merely political, and only the eleven First Ministers really know the essentials of statecraft.

Many commentators will doubtless say in these Ontario hearings, as they have said elsewhere, that the process leading to the signature of the Meech Lake Accord was seriously flawed and should not be followed in the future. Their contention is that executive federalism carried to an extreme is no real way to amend a Constitution, because it offers no opportunity for real consultation on issues of lasting importance. Even the Special Joint Committee recommended changes in the process for the future,[23] although it found no fault with the Quebec Round. I agree with such criticisms of the process, and further suggest that its failings have a particularly serious impact on women and others in the equality-seeking sector. I have outlined above women's perspective on the crucial steps in constitutional renewal over the past ten years. With the Meech Lake Accord, and possible implementation of the recommendations about *Charter* oversight made by the Joint Committee in 1987, the problems will be exacerbated, not relieved.

The Accord establishes regular yearly meetings of the First Ministers as a constitutional fact of life in Canada. Thus, there is institutionalized the real possibility that women could have to respond, yearly, to whatever may be the current version of the November Accord or the Meech Lake Accord. And such a response will have to come after the fact of an agreement, when positions are entrenched, and the threat of "unravelling" can always be made. There are at the present time no satisfactory mechanisms to ensure that there can be adequate public consultation prior to the signing of a deal at a First Ministers' meeting. Substantial reforms to the largely in-house, intergovernmental bureaucratic process would be needed to allow for prior public consultation. The alternative to prior consultation, of course, is consultation after any agreement has been concluded but before implementation. But, for such consultation to be any more than a rubber stamp from the government side or exercise in cynicism for the citizen,[24] governments must commit, in an enduring way, to listen to what is said and allow it to make a difference. There can be no more of the manipulation by false crisis that has been the hallmark of the Meech Lake ''process.''

Whether the commitment is to prior or to subsequent consultation, there is a further pre-condition to any effective process. The watchdogs of executive federalism, located in citizens' groups and special constituencies, are essentially volunteers. If they are in groups at all, the funding of these groups is modest and already committed. Without sustained funding, these individuals and groups simply will not be in a position to comment effectively and make a real contribution to public debate, particularly on a year-in, year-out basis. Moreover, when citizens must respond quickly to a lightning stroke of constitution-making, as was expected in the federal Meech Lake Accord hearings, they do not have the time and resources to do the national consensus building in their own organizations that is itself so critical to maintaining the root-hairs of Confederation.

The strains placed on the non-governmental sector by annual First Ministers' meetings and constitutional conferences do not end there. We have already seen in some of our communities an example of the potentially divisive brokering that can go on with an annual constitutional conference as its focus. Messages are being made that if certain groups will mute their concerns about the Meech Lake Accord, *their* particular topics will appear on the next First Ministers' agenda. This reduces constitution-making to the level of an employer playing one union in its shop off against another; it is hardly worthy of a process that is supposed to produce a fundamental document that guides us all across the generations.

Yet we face not only the annual First Ministers' conferences, but also the prospect of Parliamentary oversight of the *Charter*, if the Special Joint Committee's recommendation is accepted. Their report recommends the establishment of a standing Joint Committee of the Senate and the House of Commons on Constitutional Reform. This Committee would be given the task of reviewing the operation of the *Charter*, and if any difficulties arise in the interpretation of the *Charter* and the linguistic duality/distinct society clause, they could be flagged and ''dealt with'' at that time.[25] Presumably, given the other recommendations on this Committee, dealing with the *Charter* problem could involve making a recommendation to the conference of First Ministers that an appropriate constitutional amendment be considered.

However, it should be remembered that a process conceived with this benign purpose will not be confined to benign uses. The override, section 33, was seen by some of its proponents as a protection against anti-libertarian or anti-*Charter* rulings of the Supreme Court. Yet its use in its first few years of life included protecting anti-trade union measures, and shutting the *Charter* out of the province of Quebec.

So, too, with the *Charter* oversight function of this proposed Committee. In the past several months, the Supreme Court of Canada has made three important women's rights rulings,[26] the most recent of which occurred in the Morgentaler case released last Thursday, January 28. Rulings like this, as well as those demonstrating problems with the linguistic duality/distinct society clause, could become subject to Parliamentary review and thereby be placed on the conveyor belt to reversal by the First Ministers. The cost in resources and time of monitoring this process, as well as the other aspects of the run-up to the First Ministers' conferences, as well as going to court to secure these victories in the first place, will be an impossible tax on the women of Canada. Attempts in the United States to roll back women's constitutional victories show us that this is not an empty fear, as does our own constitutional history—in which we see sections 15 and 28 confined by section 33 so soon after their passage, and *Charter* rights in general made subject to the linguistic duality/distinct society clause in the Meech Lake Accord only six years after the *Charter* is entrenched.

The Accord and Equality Rights

The Meech Lake Accord proposes to add a new section 2 of the *Constitution Act, 1867.* It would provide:

> 2.(1) The Constitution of Canada shall be interpreted in a manner consistent with
>> (a) the recognition that the existence of French-speaking Canadians, centred in Quebec but also present elsewhere in Canada, and English-speaking Canadians, concentrated outside Quebec but also present

in Quebec, constitutes a fundamental characteristic of Canada; and
(b) the recognition that Quebec constitutes within Canada a distinct
society.

(2) The role of the Parliament of Canada and the provincial legislatures
to preserve the fundamental characteristic of Canada referred to in paragraph (1)(a) is affirmed.

(3) The role of the legislature and Government of Quebec to preserve
and promote the distinct identity of Quebec referred to in paragraph (1)(b) is affirmed.

(4) Nothing in this section derogates from the powers, rights or privileges of Parliament or the Government of Canada, or of the legislatures
or governments of the provinces, including any powers, rights or privileges relating to language.

This linguistic duality/distinct society clause has been the focus of
much of the concern of women's groups about the impact of the Accord
on equality rights. My focus, too, is on this clause and its companion,
clause 16, although that is not to say that I find the rest of the Accord
problem free.

To understand at least some of that concern, it is useful to return
to the sixth point about women and constitution-making, set out above:
gains made by women should be regarded as fragile, liable to be reversed
without notice or consultation. The "gains" being reversed by the Meech
Lake Accord are the equality guarantees in the *Charter*, in effect for only
two to five years when the Meech Lake Accord was signed. So new are
the equality guarantees that the first case to explore the meaning of section 15, in force since 1985, was not argued in the Supreme Court of
Canada until October, 1987.

Why women see the linguistic duality/distinct society clause as a
threat to the equality guarantees can best be explained in light of the
process of argument that one must go through in order to establish in
Court that a particular statute violates the equality guarantees. There
is still some uncertainty about the exact nature of that process, because
provincial Courts of Appeal have issued conflicting decisions and there
is as yet no authoritative pronouncement from the Supreme Court of
Canada, but some of the basic outlines are nonetheless clear.

The applicant must first show that the law in question violates a
particular *Charter* guarantee. In the case of the section 15 equality guarantees, such a showing would involve, at least, establishing that the party
complaining is treated differently under the law than others who are
"similarly situated" to that party, and that the distinction has some

negative impact on the party. Under the test established by the British Columbia Court of Appeal, the person must also show that the distinction and the result are "unreasonable and unfair," although the Ontario Court of Appeal does not impose such an added requirement.

Once a violation of section 15 is established, the party wanting to uphold the law must show that it is, in the words of section 1, a "reasonable limit" and "demonstrably justifiable in a free and democratic society." In the course of considering this question, the Court will examine several factors: what is the purpose of the law, is the purpose of such importance that it justifies overriding the right that has been violated, and what is the relationship between the purpose of the law and the means chosen to carry it into effect? This last question prompts a Court to consider whether there is a rational (well thought out) connection between the purpose and the law, and to examine whether the effects of the law on the individual are proportionate. A law passed for a constitutionally acceptable purpose may still be unconstitutional if its effects on the individual are so severe that it would not be appropriate to ask him or her to endure them in order to further that particular legislative purpose.

The inquiry under section 1 is a very thorough one. A Court will often be guided in its deliberations by looking at sections of the *Charter* and Constitution other than the one directly at issue. As Mr. Justice Dickson (as he then was) says in *R. v. Big M Drug Mart*, [1985] 1 S.C.R. 344,

> . . . the purpose of the right or freedom in question is to be sought by reference to the character and the larger objects of the *Charter* itself, to the language chosen to articulate the specific right or freedom, to the historical origins of the concepts enshrined, and where applicable, to the meaning and purpose of the other specific rights and freedoms with which it is associated within the text of the *Charter*.

The linguistic duality/distinct society clause could have an impact in an equality rights argument at either of the two stages outlined above, that is, during the consideration of whether section 15 has been violated at all, or during the analysis under section 1 as to whether the violation of equality rights is justified.

The Accord could affect section 15 analysis in one of two ways. The first is suggested by the decision in *Re Bill 30 (Ontario Separate School Funding Reference*, [1987] 1 S.C.R. 1148). There, it was held that because section 93 of the *Constitution Act, 1867* authorizes legislation with respect to denominational schools, a law extending government funding to Roman Catholic schools (but not to other denominations) could not be attacked under section 15 of the *Charter* as a denial of equality on the basis of religion. As Professor Hogg summarizes the decision: ''The *Charter* does not render unconstitutional a distinction that is expressly permitted by another part of the Constitution.''

Professor Hogg does not see the new section 2 as expressly permitting a distinction, in a way that would immunize it from review under section 15. Women's groups point out that it is too early to tell how the Supreme Court of Canada will interpret section 2. If the governments speak in good faith when they say they don't mean to harm women's equality rights, why not clarify that position now in a non-controversial amendment?

Even if section 2 does not specifically authorize discrimination in a way that would put it beyond the reach of section 15, it could still have an impact on section 15 analysis. Consider the test applied in the British Columbia Court of Appeal: is it unreasonable or unfair to deny someone equality? A person arguing that a law passed to further linguistic duality or the distinct society violates her equality rights might well face an argument that says: Yes, of course it does, but not ''unfairly'' or ''unreasonably'' given the importance of these objectives. Thus her equality claim might expire at the section 15 stage, and she would never reach the section 1 analysis.

Even if the linguistic duality/distinct society clause does not affect the case at its section 15 stage, it is sure to do so at the section 1 analysis. The existence of the linguistic duality/distinct society clause is one of the factors that a court will consider when determining whether a violation of section 15 is reasonable and justifiable.[27] Its impact may be shortly described by saying that henceforth section 1 will be read as follows:

> The *Canadian Charter of Rights and Freedoms* guarantees the rights and freedoms set out in it subject only to such reasonable limits prescribed by law as can be demonstrably justified in a free and democratic society (committed to linguistic duality and the promotion of Quebec's distinct society).

The Joint Committee took the position in its report that this type of impact was not worth becoming alarmed about. It's just ''constitutional business as usual,'' they wrote, arguing that any provision of the *Charter* or Constitution would have this impact on any other. Section 15 was already subject to qualification by the other provisions of the Constitution, and no new curb on equality rights was being effected.

Such a justification ignores the simple mathematical fact that a right qualified by a certain number of factors becomes more qualified when more factors are added to the pool of qualifiers. Progressive addition of more qualifications on equality rights will dilute them, even if it does not change the basic analysis applied to *Charter* questions. It also ignores the issue of weight. It is quite likely that a court will give substantial weight to the language of the proposed section 2 even if it is styled a principle of interpretation. Courts have given considerable weight to the principle enunciated in section 27, dealing with multiculturalism, even though it is ''just'' an interpretive clause. Moreover, the sense of occasion and significance imparted to Meech Lake by governments themselves may enhance its weight in court; in the *Bill 30* case, for example, the Court attached great significance to the fact that section 93 was part of a fundamental constitutional compromise. Thus this new factor added to the pool of potential qualifiers of equality rights is a serious one.

Another telling fact remains. The government's argument that section 2 adds no new threat to existing rights breaks down in the face of section 16 of the Accord. That clause explicitly provides that nothing in section 2 ''affects'' aboriginal and multicultural provisions of the *Charter* and *Constitution Act*. Obviously, it was contemplated by the Meech Lake framers that section 2 would have some effect beyond constitutional business as usual or they would not have included this clause. There has never been a satisfactory explanation for protecting aboriginal and multicultural provisions from the reach of section 2, but not protecting equality rights. Consider this consummate illogic from the Special Joint Committee:

> Many of the constitutional experts that appeared before us testified that section 16 is unnecessary. Certainly it generates more heat than light. Adding section 28 of the Charter to it would accomplish little because section 28 only guarantees equal application to men and women of rights and freedoms referred to elsewhere in the Charter. But reaching into section 15 of the Charter to add gender equality rights to the 'protected list' while leaving all other Charter rights 'unprotected' would be even more arbitrary. What about religious discrimination? Freedom of expression? Religious freedom? Racial discrimination?[28]

Implicit in the use of the term "even more arbitrary" is the acknowledgement that section 16 as it now stands is, indeed, arbitrary.

The potential for mischief inherent in section 2 can be illustrated by an example. I offer one with some diffidence, because of the treatment accorded examples in the summer 1987 round of Meech Lake Accord hearings and discussions. Women were told that without examples of what could go wrong, their arguments were unconvincing. If examples were offered, they were described as racist, unrealistic or anti-Quebec, if they contemplated any legislation by Quebec that put the distinct society ahead of women's interests. If they suggested that any other government could put linguistic duality ahead of women's interests, the examples were styled as speculative or absurd, because the prospect of any government doing anything unconstitutional was remote. Responses like these ignore Canadian history: governments in this country have all, from time to time, done things which courts have found to be unconstitutional. They also ignore the essential nature of an example: it is, by definition, speculative, because the events in it have not happened. Criticizing women's examples for being examples is the height of constitutional double-speak.

The present example is, in fact, drawn from an existing government program, and an existing *Charter* challenge being organized by Canadian women. CEIC has a program of subsidized language training for recently arrived immigrants, giving tuition subsidies and living allowances to qualified persons so that they can learn one of the official languages. Women are effectively precluded from receiving living allowances in a large number of cases by several rules of the program. One of these disqualifiers is that no "sponsored" immigrant can receive subsidized training; the majority of sponsored immigrants are women. Another rule restricts the training to "labour destined" immigrants; only one person per couple may qualify, and these are most often judged to be the male in the family. Thirdly, subsidy is not available if language training is not needed for entry to the labour market. The prevalence of low-income job ghettoes for immigrant women (in, e.g., the garment industry, cleaning and light manufacturing), where women work with others speaking their language, means that women lose out under this rubric as well.

Assume that an agreement is concluded between Quebec and Canada, pursuant to subsection 2(a) of the 1987 Constitutional Accord, for Quebec to take over provision of services "for the reception and integration (including linguistic and cultural) of all foreign nationals wishing to settle in Quebec." Assume, too, that Quebec were to leave all, or even some, of these elements of the present language training policy in place.

A number of groups dedicated to immigrant and visible minority women are already organizing to challenge the federal language training program as a denial of women's equality rights. In defending it, the federal government could rely on the linguistic duality but not the distinct society clause. Quebec, on the other hand, could invoke the stronger distinct society rubric to justify its program. Would there be two separate court rulings on essentially similar programs? If the Quebec program were upheld by the Supreme Court of Canada, because of the distinct society aspect of its defense, would such a ruling influence the court also to uphold the federal program?

This hypothetical example highlights an important issue that is almost always ignored in the discussion of the Meech Lake Accord. The Supreme Court of Canada is the final court of appeal for all of Canada, including Quebec. Cases from Quebec dealing with conflicts between sex equality and the distinct society will, once decided by our highest court, be in our jurisprudence for citation in other sex equality cases, arising in other parts of Canada. It is thus not at all true to say that the relation between sex equality and the distinct society is a domestic matter, for Quebec only. As long as the Supreme Court is the highest Court in Canada, its jurisprudence affects us all. And we have seen in the Court's recent pronouncement that its judgments make philosophical and value statements; they don't simply reach conclusions. It will not help the women of Canada to have a clearly articulated statement that the interests of women must be subordinate to those of their national or linguistic group, because in a pluralistic society with many national and linguistic groupings, and strong constitutional and Accord protection for multicultural values, such a statement will not be confined to Quebec.

I will close on a historical note. In 1974, the Supreme Court of Canada faced the question of whether a woman's equality interest should prevail over the interests of the group of which she was a member: in *Attorney-General of Canada v. Lavell, Isaac et al. v. Bedard*, [1974] S.C.R. 1349, Indian women challenged the statutory removal from them of their Indian status when they married non-Indian males. The majority of the Court ruled against the equality argument, saying that constitutional jurisdiction over Indians gave the federal government the right to impose requirements for having or keeping Indian status that discriminate against women. That the Bedard and Lavell case is about the conflict between sex equality rights and one type of "distinct society" is clear from Justice Laskin's description of the argument in the case:

It was urged, in reliance in part on history, that the discrimination . . . is based upon a reasonable classification of Indians as a race, that the Indian Act reflects this classification, and that the paramount purpose of the Act to preserve and protect the members of the race is promoted by the statutory preference for Indian men.[29]

It is widely recognized by jurists and constitutional scholars that the language of section 15 of the *Charter* was designed to prevent a repetition of the unfortunate reasoning of the Bedard and Lavell case. Now, two years after section 15 came into force, women are wondering whether the wheel has come full circle.

Notes

1. [1928] S.C.R. 276. The Order-in-Council setting up the Reference case was dated October 19, 1927.
2. In *Edwards v. A.G. Canada*, [1930] A.C. 124.
3. See the accounts in M. Eberts, ''Women and Constitutional Renewal,'' in A. Doerr and M. Carrier, eds., *Women and the Constitution in Canada* (Ottawa, Canadian Advisory Council on the Status of Women, 1981), 3, at 5, 15–20, and C. Hošek, ''Women and Constitutional Process,'' in K. Banting and R. Simeon, eds., *And No One Cheered: Federalism, Democracy and the Constitution Act* (Toronto, Methuen, 1983), 280, at 284.
4. For accounts of the period, see Eberts, and Hošek, *supra*, note 3, as well as Penny Kome, *The Taking of Twenty-Eight: Women Challenge the Constitution* (The Women's Press, 1983) and Katherine J. de Jong, ''Sexual Equality: Interpreting Section 28,'' in A. Bayefsky and M. Eberts, eds., *Equality Rights and the Canadian Charter of Rights and Freedoms* (Toronto, Carswell, 1983), 493, at 494–512.
5. For the text of the draft *Charter* submitted to Parliament, consult the useful chart at p.23 ff. in Robin Elliot; ''Interpreting the Charter—Use of the Earlier Versions as an Aid,'' (1982) *U.B.C. Law Rev.* Charter Ed.
6. For the text of the brief submitted by Doris Anderson's Canadian Advisory Council on the Status of Women, see ''Women, Human Rights & the Constitution: Submission to the Special Joint Committee on the Constitution,'' November 18, 1980, reproduced in 2 C.H.R.R. C/35 ff.
7. See Minister of Justice and Attorney-General of Canada, ''Government Response to Representations for Change to the Proposed Resolution,'' January 12, 1981. At p.7, the Minister comments, ''I want specifically to compliment the Advisory Council on the Status of Women for a particularly fine brief as well as for an impressive presentation before you. The work of the Council has greatly influenced the government as have the presentations of the many witnesses who have spoken on this subject on behalf of women's groups, the handicapped, and others.''

8. For accounts of the dinner at which this speech was made, and the energizing effect it had on opposition to the draft *Charter*, see Marilou McPhedran, "Section 28—Was it Worth the Fight?" in Charter of Rights Educational Fund, *The Study Day Papers* (January 13, 1983), 4.1, at 4.2 and Kome, *op. cit.*, *supra*, note 4, 34.

9. See Kome, and Hošek, *op. cit.*, *supra*, notes 3 and 4. For the text of Resolutions passed at the Ad Hoc Conference, see Bayefsky and Eberts, *op. cit.*, *supra*, note 4, Appendix VII, 634 ff.

10. This phenomenon is alluded to in Hošek, *op. cit.*, *supra*, note 3, at 289. The primary basis of this comment, however, is the author's own experience and observation as a known "big L" Liberal at that time.

11. See Hošek, *op. cit.*, *supra*, note 3, at 295–296.

12. Though these comments stem from the author's personal recollection of this period, they are also described in Kome, and Hošek, *supra*, notes 3 and 4.

13. The author recalls several conversations in which this point was made to her by A. Alan Borovoy, General Counsel of the Canadian Civil Liberties Association, who was a supporter of section 33.

14. Originally set out in June 1985 in a Quebec Liberal Party manifesto entitled *Maîtriser l'avenir*, and reaffirmed and clarified by the Minister of Intergovernmental Relations at a symposium in Mont-Gabriel in May, 1986, these conditions were:
    1) Recognition of Quebec as a distinct society;
    2) A greater provincial role in immigration;
    3) A provincial role in appointments to the Supreme Court of Canada;
    4) Limitations on the federal spending power;
    5) A veto for Quebec on constitutional amendments.
    At their meeting in Edmonton in August 1986, the provincial premiers agreed that their first priority was to begin negotiations on these five conditions.

15. Ann Rauhala, "Comment on goals irks women's groups," *The Globe and Mail*, August 20, 1987, A9.

16. For example, *The Report of the Special Joint Committee of the Senate and the House of Commons on the 1987 Constitutional Accord* states, at para.32, p.144:
    > On the other hand, two of the major women's groups in Quebec, including La Fédération des Femmes du Québec, told the Committee that they do not share the fears expressed by the national women's groups. The Joint Committee places great weight on the testimony of these Quebec women. They should know better than anyone what the distinct society is all about. They live in it. They constitute about half its population. They have obviously given careful thought to possible conflict between Charter "equality rights" and the collective interests of the "distinct society" and they have concluded that there is in fact no real potential for conflict.

17. In a letter dated July 31, 1987, sent to Beth Atcheson of the Women's Legal Education and Action Fund, Prime Minister Mulroney stated:

Recognition of Canada's linguistic duality and Quebec's distinct society is not premised upon the gender of Canadians or Quebecers. Therefore, this recognition could not be used to discriminate on the basis of sex. The linguistic and cultural values encompassed by section 2 of the *Constitution Amendment, 1987* apply to all individuals.

Moreover, section 28 of the Charter makes it clear that, notwithstanding anything in the Charter, all of these rights are guaranteed equally to men and women. I am of the view that this section, combined with the substantive guarantee of equality in section 15, offers a very strong protection to women which should not be affected in any way by the recognition of Canada's linguistic duality and of Quebec's distinctiveness.

To the same effect, concerning the strength of section 28, are remarks of the Hon. Lowell Murray, Minister of Federal–Provincial Relations, in "Le Canada doit répondre « oui » au Québec," *Le Devoir*, August 28, 1987.

18. See, for example, these statements in paras.64 and 65 of the Report, *op. cit., supra*, note 16, at 68:

> 64. The real issue, it seems to us, is whether the courts should be trusted with the responsibility of striking the proper balance between Charter rights and "reasonable limits." And if the courts are to have their hands tied with respect to certain Charter rights, but not others, where should the line be drawn?
>
> 65. The Joint Committee believes that the issue of the reasonable limits, if any, on gender equality rights and other Charter rights should be left to the courts to decide.

Along its route to this conclusion, the Committee took quite a different view of section 28 from that earlier espoused by the Prime Minister: "Section 28 simply guarantees that Charter rights are to be guaranteed equally to men and women. It does not define the content of those Charter rights. If, therefore, an interpretative provision were able to cut down or even overrule a substantive Charter right, then it would be only the diminished or non-existent Charter right that men and women were entitled equally to share." Para.59, p.67.

19. See, for example, *Reference re Section 94(2) of the Motor Vehicle Act*, [1985] 2 S.C.R. 486.

20. The provisions of section 16 of the Accord provide that "Nothing in section 2 of the Constitution Act, 1867 [the "distinct society" clause added by section 1 of the Accord] *affects* section 25 or 27 of the *Canadian Charter of Rights and Freedoms*, section 35 of the *Constitution Act, 1982* or class 24 of section 91 of the *Constitution Act, 1867* (emphasis supplied)." Many women's groups argued that the Charter's equality rights were just as liable to be "affected" by the distinct society clause as were the sections mentioned in section 16. However, note that in describing these arguments, the Special Joint Committee used language like this extract from para.5, p.56:

> We do not believe that entrenchment of this [distinct society] clause will *in any realistic way erode* the present constitutional protections

of individual rights including gender equality rights. (emphasis supplied)

The Committee phrases the question before it in this way, at para.40, p.63:

. . . we must first determine whether the "linguistic duality/distinct society" rule of interpretation will have a *negative* effect on these [gender equality] rights. (emphasis supplied)

And, in para.46, p.64, it seems that the Joint Committee is looking for proof that the linguistic duality/distinct society rule of interpretation "would have an impact on section 15 itself to permit inequality or discrimination."

21. The nub of the Special Joint Committee's mis-statement of women's position is found at paras.26 and 27, p.143:

26. Major national women's groups, including the National Association of Women and the Law, Women's Legal Education and Action Fund, and the Ad Hoc Committee of Women on the Constitution, took the position that unless they could be given a guarantee that under no circumstances "could" the linguistic duality/distinct society rules of interpretation have any effect on gender equality rights, then the 1987 Accord should be amended to establish the absolute paramountcy of those rights.

27. Their fear was that using these new rules of interpretation, a court might refuse to invalidate a law despite the fact that it involved gender-based discrimination on the grounds that the law furthered the cause of Canada's linguistic duality or Quebec's distinct society. They wanted, in other words, an affirmation that gender equality rights were absolute, and they did not want to give to the Courts the power or the responsibility of weighing this right against the competing demands of social, historical or cultural facts which the courts might conclude justified some measure of limitation of the right.

22. See, for example, the probably unintentionally candid statement of the Special Joint Committee at para.3, p.55:

We acknowledge that what began as a legal argument grew into an important matter of public policy and perception.

23. Report, chapter 14, "The Process of Constitutional Change," p.129 ff.

24. See the explicit acknowledgement at para.13, p.132 of the Special Joint Committee Report that " . . . practical politics being what they are, it is clear that flexibility *after* First Ministers have made a decision will always be limited . . ." (emphasis in original).

25. Report, para.35, p.145.

26. These cases are *Action Travail des Femmes v. C.N.R.*, [1987] 1 S.C.R. 1114, *Robichaud and C.H.R.C. v. Treasury Board*, [1987] 2 S.C.R. 84, and *R. v. Morgentaler*, [1988] 1 S.C.R. 30.

27. Even the experts whose opinions were respected by the Joint Committee agreed that this is so, as explicitly acknowledged by the Committee in para.48, p.65 of the Report.

28. Report, para.33, p.144.

29. [1974] S.C.R. 1349, at 1386.

CHAPTER EIGHT

ETHNOCULTURAL MINORITIES: The Struggle for Constitutional Equality

We cannot support a Constitution that ignores the multicultural reality of Canada, one whose underlying rationale is the outdated and discredited concept of two founding nations. A country that gives greater rights to its citizens based on their belonging to ethnic groups that came to Canada sooner is not our vision of what Canada is or should be. We are all immigrants or descendants of immigrants. We must be all treated equally and fairly.

(Thor Broda, Ukrainian Canadian Committee, brief to the Special Joint Committee of the Senate and the House of Commons on the 1987 Constitutional Accord, *Minutes of Proceedings and Evidence*, No. 7, August 13, 1987 [Ottawa: Queen's Printer, 1987]: 100)

For these reasons we believe that the immigration provisions of the 1987 Accord represent a reasonable and workable solution to Quebec's demand for greater control in immigration matters as a condition of giving its willing assent to the Constitution.

(Special Joint Committee of the Senate and the House of Commons on the 1987 Constitutional Accord, *Report* [Ottawa: Queen's Printer, 1987]: 106)

Reprinted with permission — *The Toronto Star* Syndicate.

INTRODUCTION

The ethnocultural movement's struggle for equality in Canadian society and for recognition of such in our Constitution is quite recent compared with that of the women's movement. Perhaps this is why its success in 1980–81 was marginal. This partial success in 1980–81 also helps explain why the ethnocultural movement's leaders fought so hard between the Meech Lake and Langevin meetings to protect what was considered to be merely a foothold in the door of our Charter. Only in this way could the ethnocultural movement keep alive its deeply cherished aspiration for the entrenchment of collective equality rights within the Constitution at some future conference of first ministers, to supplement the individual rights of ethnic Canadians protected by subsection 15(1) of the Charter. In its quest for collective equality rights, the ethnocultural movement has encountered the deeply rooted belief that there is a given hierarchy of collective rights that must be protected and, indeed, entrenched in the Constitution. Gaining public support for the concept of the equality of individual rights would prove to be far easier than gaining support for the concept of the equality of collective rights.

Until the 1960s, bicultural and bilingual dualism remained the dominant conceptual approach for historians, social scientists, journalists, politicians and bureaucrats trying to come to grips with the conflicts and tensions that often characterized the relationship between Canada's two founding European communities—francophone and anglophone.[1] Large-scale non-anglophone and non-francophone immigration during the administration of Prime Minister Wilfrid Laurier (1886–1911), most of it to the Canadian Prairies, was met with an Anglo-conformity policy that advocated assimilation of these immigrants to a unicultural, British-Canadian, Protestant and English-speaking way of life. Ethnic groups, such as the American Blacks, East Indians, Chinese and Jews, who were deemed not amenable to assimilation, were excluded by a very restrictive immigration policy. Immigrants from all parts of Europe who were admitted into Canada were subjected to enormous economic, social and institutional pressures to assimilate into the Anglo-Canadian way of life. By the late 1920s, once a second wave of European immigrants had settled in Canada's urban centres, some Canadian opinion makers started to think in terms of the "melting-pot" concept, that is, eventual assimilation of all immigrants and Anglo-Canadians into a new Canadian type. Some began to refer to an emerging Canadian mosaic.[2]

The response of Quebec's francophone majority to this process of mass migration was twofold. First, its political, intellectual and religious leaders objected vigorously and loudly to the national government's policy of mass migration on the grounds that it was motivated by a desire to dilute the francophone proportion of the Canadian population. Second, French-Canadian Catholic school authorities streamed all non-Catholic immigrant children, including Jewish children, into the Protestant schools while attempting to integrate and eventually assimilate European Catholic children into the francophone culture by enrolling them in the Catholic school system of Montreal.[3]

World War II was a watershed in the socio-cultural development of contemporary Canada, in more than one respect. Some immigration restrictions were lifted, and this allowed a momentary flood of European refugees and immigrants into the country. Yet a true liberalization would have to wait for the new 1967 Immigration Act. The two million non-French and non-British immigrants, mostly European, who settled in Canada between 1945 and 1961 reinforced, demographically and politically, the strength of many longstanding ethnocultural communities. Between 1901 and 1981, the ethnic composition of the Canadian population changed significantly. In 1901, Canadians of British origin comprised 57% of the population and the French Canadians 30.7%, while Canadians of all other ethnic origins made up only 12.3%. By 1981, the proportion of Canadians of British origin had fallen to 40.2% and that of French Canadians to 26.7%, whereas all other ethnic groups comprised 26.8% of the total population. There were 6.3% of Canadians who were classified as being of mixed British and French origins.[4] By the mid-1950s, the Anglo-conformity model was in disrepute, and in its place emerged the concept of the "vertical mosaic."[5] With the arrival of John George Diefenbaker as prime minister in 1957, there emerged a new political awareness on behalf of Canada's ethnocultural communities, particularly in the three Prairie provinces, whose voters contributed heavily to the Diefenbaker landslide in 1958. Political commentators and members of the ethnic communities began to speak of the emergence of a "Third Force" in Canadian politics and society.

It was becoming increasingly apparent to many observers that cultural pluralism was the emerging, if still only reluctantly accepted, social pattern of Canadian society. This was especially true in all of Canada's major metropolitan centres where the vast majority of post-war immigrants had settled, found work, got married and were raising their families. The rise of neo-nationalism and separatism in Quebec during the 1960s provided the ethnocultural movement with an opportunity to gain input into an important dispute over public policy pertaining to francophone–anglophone relations. In 1962, the Pearson government established the Royal Commission on Bilingualism and Biculturalism (the B & B Commission) with the mandate to:

> inquire into and report upon the existing state of bilingualism and biculturalism in Canada and to recommend what steps should be taken to develop the Canadian confederation on a basis of an equal partnership between the two founding races taking into account the contribution made by other ethnic groups to the cultural enrichment of Canada and the measures that should be taken to safeguard that contribution.[6]

Sensitized to the growing political clout of this "Third Force" through numerous briefs and public testimony, the B & B Commissioners decided to devote an entire volume of their *Report* to the contribution of these other cultural groups to Canadian society. The general thrust of the *Report*'s sixteen recommendations encompassed "the implementation of an official government policy of multiculturalism and multilingualism designed as a model of integration for immigrant ethnic collectivities."[7]

Responding to the rise of neo-nationalist and separatist movements in Quebec, the Trudeau government provided enhanced statutory support for the bilingual conception of the role of the national government and national institutions in its Official Languages Act of 1969. Canada's numerous and rapidly expanding ethnocultural communities, led by a new generation of better-educated and more militant leaders, felt they had been outmanoeuvred. They fought strenuously for the implementation of the recommendations of Book IV of the *B & B Report*. In 1971, the Trudeau government, eager to avoid giving any official recognition to the two-nations theory that might be extracted from the concept of biculturalism, and determined not to accept the principle that language and culture are indivisible, responded to the entreaties of the ethnic community leaders by proposing a policy of multiculturalism within a bilingual framework.

The federal multiculturalism policy had four objectives: (a) financial support for all cultural groups showing both the need and desire to maintain and promote their continued development; (b) assistance to members of ethnic groups to overcome cultural barriers to integration; (c) fostering of national unity through the promotion of intercultural contacts and exchanges; and (d) support for all immigrants desiring to acquire one or both of Canada's official languages. The first objective met with some criticism from liberal and social democrats on the grounds that the fostering of "ethnic separation, enclavement and retention of traditional values" would impede the development of either a strong national consciousness or class consciousness. Conversely, many of the ethnocultural organizations and their members objected strongly to the fourth objective because it provided no protection for or recognition of non-official minority languages. For these groups, "language and culture are indivisible; therefore multiculturalism is meaningless without multilingualism." Throughout the 1970s, increasing emphasis was placed by these leaders on the acquisition of collective minority rights in the areas of education, language and religion.[8]

To carry out its new policy, the Trudeau government appointed, in 1972, a minister of state responsible for multiculturalism through a Multiculturalism Directorate within the Department of Secretary of State. The minister sought and received advice from the ethnocultural communities via the Canadian Consultative Council on Multiculturalism set up in 1973 (restructured and renamed the Canadian Multicultural Council in 1983). The Multiculturalism Directorate funded a wide variety of programs to help break down cultural barriers and promote intercultural and interracial understanding and eventual integration of individual immigrants. The Directorate also channelled funds to voluntary ethnocultural organizations to help them with collective consciousness raising and the creation of cultural enrichment programs that included "heritage" or minority languages.[9]

Throughout the 1970s, representatives of the ethnocultural movement lobbied to have multiculturalism recognized as one of the fundamental characteristics of Canada on a par with bilingualism in the reformed and patriated Constitution. The Liberal government of Prime Minister Trudeau supported and encouraged this aspiration. Yet, when the government tabled a *Resolution for a Joint Address to the Queen to Patriate the Constitution* in the House on October 6, 1980, the Charter made no mention of multiculturalism. Before the Special Joint Committee of Parliament on the Constitution, established in late October, 1980, representatives from various ethnocultural organizations argued for the entrenchment of multiculturalism in the Constitution, not merely in the preamble, as well as the recognition of non-official minority languages.

The Canadian Ethnocultural Council (CEC), formed in 1980, co-ordinated the lobby efforts of many of these national ethnocultural organizations for a reinforced Charter. In response to this lobby, the Minister of Justice, Jean Chrétien, proposed that an interpretative clause, section 27, be added to the Charter stating: ''This Charter shall be interpreted in a manner consistent with the preservation and enhancement of the multicultural heritage of Canadians.'' This proposal was accepted by the Special Joint Committee and included as one of the sixty-seven substantive amendments in its *Final Report* to the House. In fact, section 27 was dropped during the meeting of first ministers and was reintroduced to the Charter only when the Trudeau government tabled a new *Resolution* on November 20, 1981.[10]

Following the ratification of the 1982 Constitution Act, a controversial debate ensued over the nature and import of the interpretative section 27 and its relationship to the rest of the Charter. Some, such as Clare Beckton, contend that:

> Section 27 is an important statement of principle which must be read with section 15 to ensure that the guarantee of equality is interpreted in a manner that is consistent with the preservation of multicultural values.

He goes on to argue that under subsection 15(2), affirmative action programs can be established to preserve and enhance the multicultural heritage of Canada.[11] Still others, such as Evelyn Kallen, demonstrate persuasively that the equality rights provisions of our Charter do not provide any protection for the collective cultural rights of Canada's ethnic communities. In Kallen's view, section 27 is a ''motherhood'' clause because:

> the provisions of the Charter favouring *majority* ethnic rights over minority rights serve to perpetuate the *vertical* mosaic. Thus the multicultural dream of an *egalitarian* mosaic remains a dream deferred.[12]

Only the inclusion in the Charter of collective language and religious rights for the ethnocultural minorities would bring true equality.

Given the nature of this debate and the perceived limitations of the Constitution Act, 1982, it is not surprising that the CEC, like many other national organizations, found itself on the horns of a dilemma when faced with the Meech Lake *fait accompli*. It was caught between its mandate of promoting the constitutional goals of its affiliated organizations and its fear of losing support for important prospective multicultural legislation by politically alienating the Mulroney government.[13] Following considerable deliberation, the CEC decided to support the Meech Lake Accord because it recognized the need to obtain the formal approval of the Quebec government for the 1982 Constitution Act, which included the Charter of Rights and Freedoms. In its brief to the Special Joint Committee, the CEC then proceeded to make seventeen recommendations, some of which, had they been endorsed by the Committee, would have completely undermined the interpretative powers of the distinct society clause, as well as many other provisions of the Accord. A number of the CEC's affiliates also presented moving testimony before members of the Special Joint Committee. The Chinese Canadian National Council, the German-Canadian Congress, the National Association of Canadians of Origins in India, the National Association of Japanese Canadians and the Ukrainian Canadian Committee indicated their wholehearted support for the CEC's recommendations and in some cases went much further in their criticisms of the Accord. The National Congress of Italian Canadians also submitted a brief to the Special Joint Committee but was not heard. Instead, it found an outlet before the Ontario Select Committee on Constitutional Reform some months later.[14]

Underlying the CEC's critique of the Accord were two fundamental principles: the first pertained to the process of constitutional renewal, while the second addressed the inherent inequality of the Accord, the Charter and the Constitution Act, 1867. The CEC was deeply disturbed with the undemocratic process of constitutional renewal and reiterated that "Constitutions cannot be imposed *upon the people*, but should be built with the consensus *of the people*." The CEC requested a six-month extension of the Committee's hearings, which, it maintained, should be the rule for all subsequent constitutional amendments. It denounced the Accord's entrenchment of the first ministers' and ministers' powers, namely, executive federalism, to sanction federal–provincial agreements on immigration without Parliament's approval. It also objected to the extension of the unanimity formula to national institutions and the creation of new provinces. The CEC argued that a more flexible formula would be more conducive to change while failing to acknowledge that its general approval for the Accord was a tacit consent for the reintroduction of unanimity in the constitutional process.

On the question of substance, the CEC made a powerful plea for the immediate constitutional recognition of equality for all Canadians, a matter that could not be left to a second or subsequent round of discussions. It argued that any statement of the fundamental characteristic of Canada had to include a recognition of multiculturalism on par with the recognition of linguistic duality, because the two, in reality, were interwoven. Both of Canada's linguistic communities in the 1980s were multicultural, and this important sociological reality could not be overlooked if effective equality for Canada's ethnocultural communities were ever going to be achieved. The German-Canadian Congress, in a very forceful presentation on this issue, declared that "failure to include a statement of the multicultural nature of Canadian society could lead to an emasculation of section 27 of the Charter and indeed of multiculturalism in Canada."[15] In fact, the Ukrainian Canadian Committee declared that it felt betrayed by the Quebec government and the francophone minorities outside Quebec. In 1980–81, it had supported official bilingualism and entrenchment of minority language rights with the promise that in the next round Canada's ethnocultural groups would receive reciprocal support from the francophone community for official recognition of multiculturalism. "We cannot support a Constitution," declared the Committee's spokesperson, "that ignores the multicultural reality of Canada, one whose underlying rationale is the outdated and discredited concept of two founding nations." The Committee was willing to entertain a similar deal in the Accord: a multiculturalism clause in exchange for the linguistic duality/distinct society clause.[16]

The CEC had lobbied vigorously between the Meech Lake Accord of April 30 and the final version that emerged from the Langevin Block in Ottawa on June 3, 1987, and managed to obtain a partial victory. The Accord's section 16 immunizes section 27 of the Charter from the linguistic duality/distinct society clause. This partial victory did not satisfy the CEC, because section 27 on the preservation and enhancement of the multicultural heritage of Canada applies only to the Charter and not to the Constitution Act, 1867. This, in effect, creates a hierarchy of rights, because the entire Constitution, once the Accord is ratified, will have to be interpreted in a manner that recognizes bilingualism and the distinct society of Quebec. This hierarchy, in the words of the CEC, "relegates multiculturalism to the 'back of the bus'." True equality can be ensured only if the Charter is given explicit priority over the Accord.[17]

The CEC also envisaged several other ways in which equality could be pursued. In an attempt to enhance linkages with other ethnic and non-ethnic minorities, the CEC recommended that the aboriginal peoples be further consulted on ways of guaranteeing their rights, and that Parliament and the provincial legislatures be given the responsibility to *promote* as well as preserve linguistic duality. It was also important that Canada's multicultural diversity be reflected in the composition of both the Senate and the Supreme Court by ensuring that the principle of merit rather than patronage prevail in the appointments to these institutions.

Going to the very heart of the Accord, the CEC recommended strongly that the term "distinct society" be clearly defined.[18] Its chief concern was the manner in which the undefined concept of distinct society in tandem with the decentralizing immigration provisions of the Accord could be used to balkanize Canada's national immigration policy and practices. The CEC feared that the concept of distinct society could "be abused at any future point to keep out immigrants from certain countries." It rightly pointed out the contradiction between the federal government's commitment to defining Canadian citizenship as a nation founded on the principles of equality, diversity and community and its decision to allow the transfer of immigration services "for the reception and integration (including linguistic and cultural) of all foreign nationals wishing to settle in Quebec" (the Accord). This process could conceivably allow the government of Quebec to reject the federal Multiculturalism Policy and pursue a vigorous policy of assimilation of its ethnocultural citizens. In light of this eventuality, the CEC recommended that the Accord include a statement of the government of Quebec's role in the preservation and promotion of multiculturalism in that province.[19]

Given Evelyn Kallen's analysis of the serious shortcomings of the Constitution Act, 1982, it is not surprising that her critique of the Meech Lake Accord is, without doubt, the most severe by anyone concerned with achieving collective rights for Canada's ethnocultural communities. In her view, the Accord further entrenches "the special and dominant status of Canada's two founding peoples—English/Protestant and French/Catholic 'charter groups'," set out in the Constitution Acts of 1867 and 1982. In so doing, the Accord relegates the ethnic and non-ethnic minorities to second and third positions in the pecking order of minority rights. In the Constitution Acts of 1867 and 1982, the "charter groups" are afforded positive and specified protections through defined rights, whereas ethnic and non-ethnic minorities are extended only negative, unspecified and generally undefined rights. The Meech Lake Accord, in her estimation, "serves to further augment constitutionally established status inequalities between and among ethnic and non-ethnic minorities in Canada." She concludes her analysis on a pessimistic note, stating that the Accord "may be interpreted as a retrogressive amendment which harks back to the constitutional priorities behind Canada, vintage 1867." If this is indeed the new reality, the ethnocultural communities have an arduous and prolonged struggle ahead of them if they wish to achieve true collective equality.

Notes

1. Michael D. Behiels, "Francophone/Anglophone Relations, 1760–1987," in *The Canadian Encyclopedia*, Vol. II (Second edition, Edmonton: Hurtig Publishers, 1988); Ramsay Cook, *Canada and the French-Canadian Question* (Toronto: Macmillan, 1966).
2. Howard Palmer, "Reluctant Hosts: Anglo-Canadian Views of Multiculturalism in the Twentieth Century," in R. Douglas Francis and Donald B. Smith, eds., *Readings in Canadian History. Post-Confederation* (Second Edition, Toronto: Holt, Rinehart and Winston, 1986): 185–199; Jean Burnet, "The Social and Historical Context of Ethnic Relations," in R. C. Gardner and R. Kalin, eds., *A Canadian Social Psychology of Ethnic Relations* (Agincourt: Methuen, 1981): 17–35.
3. Michael D. Behiels, "Neo-Canadians and Schools in Montreal, 1900–1970," *Journal of Cultural Geography*, 8, No. 2 (Spring/Summer 1988): 5–16.
4. Warren E. Kalbach, "Growth and Distribution of Canada's Ethnic Populations, 1871–1981," in Leo Driedger, ed., *Ethnic Canada. Identities and Inequalities* (Toronto: Copp Clark Pitman, 1987): 100, Table 8.
5. Cf. John Porter, *The Vertical Mosaic* (Toronto: University of Toronto Press, 1955). Consult Evelyn Kallen, *Ethnicity and Human Rights in Canada* (Toronto: Gage, 1982) for a solid if somewhat dated general treatment of several aspects of ethnicity as they relate to the question of human individual and collective rights.
6. Canada, Royal Commission on Bilingualism and Biculturalism, *The Cultural Contribution of Other Ethnic Groups*, Book IV (Ottawa: Supply and Services Canada, 1969): 3.
7. Evelyn Kallen, "Multiculturalism: Ideology, Policy and Reality," *Journal of Canadian Studies*, 17, No. 1 (Spring 1982): 53; Jean Burnet, "Multiculturalism in Canada," in Driedger, *Ethnic Canada*, 67–68. Two of the ten B & B Commissioners were J. B. Rudnyckyj and Paul Wyczynski, Slavic post-World War II immigrants to Canada.
8. Kallen, "Multiculturalism: Ideology, Policy and Reality," 53–58, quotes 54 and 57; T. C. Christopher, "The 1982 Canadian Charter of Rights and

Freedoms and Multiculturalism," *Canadian Review of Studies in Nationalism*, XIV, No. 2 (1987): 334–335.

9. Michael R. Hudson, "Multiculturalism, Government Policy and Constitutional Enshrinement—A Comparative Study," in Canadian Human Rights Foundation, ed., *Multiculturalism and the Charter: A Legal Perspective* (Toronto: Carswell, 1987): 64–72; Burnet, "Multiculturalism in Canada," 69.

10. Hudson, "Multiculturalism, Government Policy and Constitutional Enshrinement," 72–79; Christopher, "The 1982 Canadian Charter of Rights and Freedoms and Multiculturalism," 336–337.

11. Clare F. Beckton, "Section 27 and Section 15 of the Charter," in Canadian Human Rights Foundation, *Multiculturalism and the Charter*, 1–13. Similar views are expressed in G. L. Gall, "Multiculturalism and the Fundamental Freedoms: Section 27 and Section 2," in *ibid.*, 29–58; Raj Anand, "Ethnic Equality," in Anne F. Bayefsky and Mary Eberts, eds., *Equality Rights and the Canadian Charter of Rights and Freedoms* (Toronto: Carswell, 1985): 81–129; and Christopher, "The 1982 Canadian Charter of Rights and Freedoms and Multiculturalism," 337–341.

12. Evelyn Kallen, "Multiculturalism, Minorities, and Motherhood: A Social Scientific Critique of Section 27," in Canadian Human Rights Foundation, *Multiculturalism and the Charter*, 123–137, quote 127–128. Dale Gibson is also very sceptical of the legal protection provided by section 27, in his "Protection of Minority Rights Under the Canadian Charter of Rights and Freedoms: Can Politicians and Judges Sing Harmony?," in Neil Nevitte and Allan Kornberg, eds., *Minorities and the Canadian State* (Oakville: Mosaic Press, 1985): 31–51.

13. Preliminary discussions of Bill C-93, an Act for the preservation and enhancement of multiculturalism in Canada, were already under way, and the Bill was introduced into the House for first reading on December 1, 1987, just a few months after the signing of the Meech Lake Accord. The government hoped that this development would help to weaken the growing opposition to the Accord within Canada's ethnocultural communities.

14. For the testimony of these groups, consult, respectively, Canada, Special Joint Committee of the Senate and the House of Commons on the 1987 Constitutional Accord, *Minutes of Proceedings and Evidence*, No. 7, August 13, 1987 (Ottawa: Queen's Printer, 1987): 61–70; 70–80; 80–88; 88–97; and 97–111. For the testimony of the National Congress of Italian Canadians, consult Ontario Select Committee on Constitutional Reform, 1987 Constitutional Accord, *Hansard Official Report of Debates*, February 17, 1988.

15. See the German-Canadian Congress's testimony, *Minutes of Proceedings and Evidence*, No. 7, August 13, 1987, 72–73.

16. Ukrainian Canadian Committee, *ibid.*, 97–111, quote 100.

17. The Chinese Canadian National Council emphasized that section 16 of the Accord should be deleted and replaced with: "The Charter of Rights and Freedoms is applicable to the entire 1987 Constitution." *Ibid.*, 64.

18. The National Association of Canadians of Origins in India contended that the expression "distinct society" conferred special status on the French in Quebec, thereby aggravating the impact of Bill 101: "Some of the legislation has created enormous difficulties for the non-French in Quebec. In some cases their lifestyles have totally deteriorated and economic opportunities have diminished, and some have become displaced persons in their own country." *Ibid.*, 81.

19. For an incisive and severe critique of the immigration provisions of the Accord, consult Orest M. Krulak, "Constitutional Reform and Immigration," in Roger Gibbins et al., eds., *Meech Lake and Canada. Perspectives from the West* (Edmonton: Academic Printing and Publishing, 1988): 210–211. He concludes: "In sum, the Meech Lake Accord, in its immigration section, has far-reaching implications for national unity in Canada as well as for Canada's future economic prosperity. Canada is and has become culturally diverse over the years. The Accord can profoundly effect [sic] that diversity and that has overtones for the unity of this society." *Ibid.*, 210.

CANADIAN ETHNOCULTURAL COUNCIL

A DREAM DEFERRED: COLLECTIVE EQUALITY FOR CANADA'S ETHNOCULTURAL COMMUNITIES*

A constitution states the basic principles and laws of a nation which determine the powers and duties of the state and guarantee certain rights to its people. As well, the constitution symbolizes the substance of a nation reflecting its ideals and vision to its own people and to the rest of the world.

The Canadian Ethnocultural Council (CEC) endorses the need for the 1987 Constitutional Accord, especially as it relates to Quebec's involvement. While the citizens of Quebec were protected by the terms of the 1982 Constitution Act, the lack of their voluntary signature was a most unfortunate absence in that otherwise important historical development. We therefore repeat our congratulations to the Prime Minister and all the Premiers for their efforts in reaching an Accord. The spirit of co-operation was rare and praiseworthy.

Bringing one sector of Canadian society into the Constitution must, however, not take place at the expense of another. The mutual accommodation among Canadians is generous enough that equality for one must equally ensure equality for all. We are, as a people, co-operative enough that we do not have to gain rights at each others' expense. Ethnic minorities have gained rights over the years through various developments, and it would be unthinkable that such rights would be gained at the expense of others, namely the aboriginal peoples or those of British or French origin.

The CEC has some grave concerns regarding the potential effects of the Accord on ethnic minorities, multiculturalism and immigration policies. We, therefore, urge improvements to the Accord to ensure that these areas are not adversely affected. Just as Parliamentary hearings

---

* Brief to the Special Joint Committee of the Senate and the House of Commons on the 1987 Constitutional Accord, *Minutes of Proceedings and Evidence*, No. 7, August 13, 1987.

in 1980–81 immeasurably improved the 1982 agreement, we are confident that the hearing of the "Special Joint Committee on the 1987 Constitutional Accord" can improve the new Accord. This brief is meant to assist in the betterment of the Accord so that all Canadians can be proud of it. Constitutions cannot be imposed upon the people, but should be built with the consensus of the people.

It is important that the concerns we raise be addressed at this time and not be delayed to a second round. We feel that equality should be guaranteed, and there is no reason to delay equality to a later date. We urge the First Ministers to meet again and make improvements to this Accord before it is entrenched.

We should also note that we are concerned that hearings on this important matter are being held in a speedy manner during summer months which is not conducive to thoughtful consideration by all Canadians. We therefore urge you to seek an extension of your mandate by at least one month.

This brief makes two types of recommendations: the first is for improvements to the Accord, and the second is for recommended courses of action for first ministers or governments in the years ahead.

Multiculturalism: Section 1

The "linguistic duality" clause (section 1 of the new Accord, officially known as section 2(1)(a) of the Constitution Act, 1867) gives prominence to the linguistic duality of Canadians. Any recognition of the diversity of Canadian society is good for multiculturalism and in that the recognition of linguistic duality is positive. It is obvious that cultures cross linguistic duality, that each linguistic community is composed of several cultural groups and that cultural groups straddle the two linguistic communities. Hence, each linguistic community is multicultural in itself.

The following excerpts from "Multiculturalism: Building the Canadian Mosaic", the recent report of the Standing Committee on Multiculturalism, observe the increasing cultural diversity of English-speaking and French-speaking Canadians:

Multiculturalism and Bilingualism as Complementary Policies
Part of the consciousness of human rights is the acceptance of diversity. This is demonstrated in that the confluence of multiculturalism and bilingualism is becoming more and more evident.

In 1969 the *Royal Commission on Bilingualism and Biculturalism* sadly observed that:

Since economic, social and linguistic factors all play a part, the Francophone community, being economically weaker than the Anglophone, cannot easily attract immigrants. This is evident in Montreal and elsewhere in Canada. Because of this imbalance between the two societies, most members of non-British, non-French groups gravitate almost instinctively to the Anglophone side. (Vol. IV, pp. 5–6)

Sixteen years later, in 1985, the *Macdonald Commission* noted a significant change:

English Canada is now multicultural, defined by language rather than by shared British past. The metropolitan centres of Anglophone Canada are home to a diverse population of many cultural backgrounds and various countries of origin. French Canada, too, is now multicultural. Because of the Quebec government's recent language policies, it is no longer possible automatically to equate French speakers with the descendants of the approximately 65,000 ''habitants'' who remained after the retreat of the French Empire from North America more than two centuries ago. In little more than two decades, the concept of French-speaking Québécois has expanded to encompass a multicultural population, including immigrants from Haiti and refugees from Vietnam. In relative terms, therefore, the growing tendency is to define French-speaking Quebec by language rather than by common past. (Vol. 1, p. 8)

Perhaps the best testimony to the complementary nature of bilingualism and multiculturalism is illustrated in four recommendations in the Annual Report 1985 of the Commissioner of Official Languages. He not only endorses multiculturalism but is fully supportive of the teaching of Heritage Languages. The Commissioner recommends that the Federal Government:

1. develop an inter-cultural relations program to encourage ethnic groups to strengthen their ties with official-language minorities (Anglophones in Quebec and Francophones outside Quebec);

2. establish an information program on the complementarity of bilingualism and multiculturalism for ethnic community leaders and organizations and official-language minorities;

3. encourage the teaching of languages other than the official languages (Heritage Languages) at all levels;

4. encourage the teaching of an official language to immigrants to help them integrate into their communities. (Comments in parentheses are added.) (p. 25)

The linguistic duality clause recognizes the bilingual nature of our society, it ignores Canada's multicultural reality. Following the first draft of the Accord of April 30, the CEC and others pointed out the absence of the recognition of multiculturalism. In response, the first ministers added a new section (#16) to the Accord of June 3 which states that nothing in the Accord would affect the Multiculturalism Clause (section 27) of the Charter of Rights and Freedoms. Thus, as it stands, the entire Constitution will be interpreted in a manner recognizing bilingualism, but only the Charter which is a part of the Constitution will be interpreted in a manner recognizing multiculturalism. This clearly gives multiculturalism a lower status in Canada than bilingualism. It relegates multiculturalism to the "back of the bus".

Recently the Supreme Court of Canada made a distinction between the Charter and the rest of the Constitution which makes the matter of multiculturalism in the Accord so much more important.

In its decision in the matter of full funding for Roman Catholic Separate High Schools rendered on June 25, 1987, the Supreme Court ruled that certain sections of the Constitution are "immune from charter review". While we do not wish to discuss the particular case, as it is considerably complex in itself, this ruling highlights that the protections within the Charter are good for the Charter itself but may not apply to matters raised in other parts of the Constitution. Section 16 of the Accord states that nothing in the Accord "affects section 27" of the Charter. What it does confirm is that the status of section 27 will remain in effect for the Charter only. Section 16 does not extend its recognition of multiculturalism to the whole Constitution.

In the event of a conflict between this Accord and the Charter, the bottom line will always be that the Accord takes precedence.

It is the belief of the CEC that the multicultural diversity of Canadians is as equal a fundamental characteristic as our linguistic duality. Both must apply equally in law and both must be recognized throughout the Constitution of Canada. Indeed, the very fact that these two characteristics are dealt with differently begs explanation. If they were given different status, one is left to ask why. No one has provided the reason.

Further, our Constitution is also of tremendous symbolic importance. It describes who we are. If the Constitution does not treat multiculturalism and ethnic minorities in a decent manner—why should anyone else?

The rights of linguistic minorities must also be fully ensured and in this regard it should be the role of Parliament and the provincial legislatures not only to preserve our linguistic duality but to promote it as well.

The CEC has found it repugnant that Alberta MLA Léo Piquette was recently asked to apologize for speaking French in the Alberta legislature. On July 3, 1987, we wrote to Premier Don Getty asking him to intervene and ensure a sensitive and fair settlement to the controversy.

Aboriginal organizations have unanimously voiced disapproval of a lack of aboriginal protections in the Accord. The CEC has been on record since 1981 as supporting the desire of the aboriginal peoples for self-government. They should be consulted for redrafting sections to guarantee their rights.

> **Recommendation 1**: The CEC recommends that section 1 of the Accord (section 2 of the *Constitution Act, 1867*) be improved as follows:
> • by adding the following section:
> 1.2(1)(c) The recognition that the multicultural heritage of Canadians also constitutes a fundamental characteristic of Canada.
> • by making additions as italicized:
> 1.2(2) The role of the Parliament of Canada and the provincial legislatures to preserve *and promote* the fundamental characteristics of Canada referred to in paragraphs (1)(a) *and (1)(c)* is affirmed.

> **Recommendation 2**: The CEC notes its support for the expressed desire for aboriginal self-government and recommends that representatives of aboriginal peoples be consulted with a view to redrafting sections of the Accord to guarantee their rights, instead of the present wording of section 16.

A further problem that arises is that by ensuring the sanctity of two clauses of the Charter, in section 16 of the Accord, namely sections 25 and 27, the other sections do not have the same protection and could be overridden. Of special concern to us is section 15 which disallows discrimination based on "race, national or ethnic origin, colour (or) religion".

We are also concerned that this could adversely affect gender equality as guaranteed in sections 15 and 28.

> **Recommendation 3**: The CEC recommends that section 16 of the Accord be rewritten as follows:
> 16. Nothing in this Accord affects the Canadian Charter of Rights and Freedoms.

"Distinct Society": Section 1

In recognizing that Quebec constitutes within Canada a distinct society, a justifiable effort is made to preserve and promote the French language and culture in an otherwise English-speaking North America. As ethnic minorities, we understand and share the desire to have the wealth of one's cultural heritage recognized, preserved and promoted.

The Accord, however, has not defined the nature of this "distinct society". While those of us observing or participating in the constitutional debate today have some understanding of what is intended, it is unrealistic that courts ten or twenty years from now will remember the intent of this section. Further, it is not even currently understood in a similar manner by all concerned.

In the view of the CEC, which does draw its membership from every province of Canada, the distinctiveness of Quebec is based on the following factors. The province of Quebec observes the Civil (Napoleonic) Code, and it is the principal domain of the French language and culture in Canada.

Having said that, it should be clear in the Constitution that Quebec and the people of Quebec, like every other province of Canada, are culturally diverse. Just as Ontario is not uni-cultural and British, Quebec is not uni-cultural and French. Quebec has, on one scale, a minority Anglophone population. On another scale, Quebec has a sizeable population, at least 10%, who are of neither British nor French origin but who linguistically are Francophones or Anglophones. The cultural definition of Quebec is indeed multicultural with a distinct French character. Defining the distinctiveness will ensure that it is universally understood and, as such, preserved and promoted. Leaving the term "distinct society" ambiguous can defeat the very purpose that was intended. It is also possible for some future government of Quebec to declare that it was distinct and that somehow Quebec was not multicultural.

It is now important for the Accord to recognize that Quebec in itself is multicultural and that the Government of Quebec has a responsibility in promoting this aspect of diversity.

Recommendation 4: The CEC recommends that the Accord define the term "distinct society", and clarify that the Government of Quebec has a responsibility to preserve and promote the multicultural heritage of the province.

The Senate: Section 2

The presence of senators from minority ethnic communities has traditionally been significantly lower than the presence of Canadians from those communities. At present, some 15% of senators are from minority groups compared to 33% in the Canadian population.

In August 1983, in our brief to the "Special Joint Committee on Senate Reform", our Council called for approximately one-third of the seats in the Upper Chamber to come from ethnic minorities. In the context of the Accord, the responsibility of appointments is now to be shared by the Prime Minister and the Premiers; consequently, we urge that both levels of government make every effort to ensure that the Senate better reflect the cultural and racial diversity of Canada.

> **Recommendation 5**: The CEC urges the Prime Minister and Premiers to ensure that the presence of ethnic minorities in the Senate be increased to better reflect the diversity of Canadian society.

Immigration: Section 3

This Accord can allow for the powers of Parliament regarding immigration policy to be overridden by federal–provincial agreements. In section 3 of the Accord, section 95 B. (1) of the Constitution Act, 1867, an agreement between federal and provincial ministers will have the force of law, and take place "notwithstanding class 25 of section 91 or section 95" which is the clause in the Constitution that gives Parliament the exclusive legislative authority in matters regarding "Naturalization and Aliens". Section 95 gives Parliament primacy in matters relating to immigration. The word "notwithstanding" leaves the traditional and constitutional division of powers up in the air and subject to change by agreement between the federal government and any single provincial government. We could end up with a checker-board of immigration policies across the country.

> **Recommendation 6**: The CEC recommends that section 95 B. (1) of section 3 of the Accord be improved by removing the words "notwithstanding class 25 of section 91 or section 95".

Through section 95 C. (2) (a) in section 3 of the Accord, an amendment to a federal–provincial agreement can be made by the normal channels of approval by the Senate and the House of Commons, or "in any such manner as is set out in the agreement". Such other manner could well mean a confidential exchange of letters between a federal and a provincial minister. This means that such a secret agreement can replace, in totality, the parliamentary and, hence, the public process. This section of the Accord could well circumvent Parliament.

Recommendation 7: The CEC recommends that section 95 C.(1)(b) of section 3 of the Accord be removed, to ensure that federal–provincial agreements on immigration will be approved by Parliament.

Supreme Court of Canada: Section 6

As Canada becomes increasingly multiculturally diverse (one-third of Canadians are from minority ethnic groups and this proportion is growing), there is a need for the Supreme Court to be fully sensitive to this diversity. Just as one-third of the bench is from the civil bar, i.e. from Quebec, and there is an accepted need to increase the presence of women, we have long advocated that a tradition, written or unwritten, be established to ensure some minority presence. With the death of Chief Justice Bora Laskin in 1984, there have been no replacements from minority communities.

As sections 15 and 27 (Equality Rights and Multiculturalism) of the Charter become increasingly relevant, minority interests become more the issues of serious consideration of the Supreme Court. Such consideration will be enhanced by minority presence on the bench. At the same time, the continuing message and symbolism to the entire justice system will be evident. We are pleased that when the CEC met with Prime Minister Brian Mulroney on June 18, he stressed that he agreed that minority presence was necessary and would give this matter top priority when the next appointment arose.

Recommendation 8: The CEC urges the Prime Minister and Premiers to ensure that the presence of ethnic minorities on the Supreme Court be increased to better reflect the diversity of Canadian society.

The process for provincial nominations in the Accord, namely section 101C of section 6 of the Accord, can unnecessarily politicize the appointment process. Further, the process does not provide a mechanism to overcome an impasse if the federal government does not accept the provincial nominations. Without such a mechanism, it is conceivable that certain vacancies can remain unfilled for extended periods of time, leaving the court short of its full complement for such periods. The ambiguities in this Accord make it so much more important that there not be such disruptions in the Court and that there be a national perspective rather than a provincial bias of those appointed.

Recommendation 9: The CEC cautions the Special Joint Committee to ensure that quality of appointment, rather than political affiliation, becomes the prime objective of the Supreme Court appointment process.

Shared-cost Programs: Section 7

The sections on shared-cost programs could allow for some provincial programs to become sub-standard. We recognize the need for national programs to be regionally sensitive, but one of the reasons for having a national government is to ensure national standards on certain issues.

The section deservedly received much debate among the First Ministers on June 2 and 3, as some wanted to ensure better protection for the role of the federal government. While this second meeting did improve the section to some extent, the term "national objectives" would be better replaced by "national standards" which is more definitive.

Recommendation 10: That in Section 106A. (1) of section 7 of the Accord, the words "national objectives" be replaced by "national standards".

Conferences on the Economy and Other Matters: Section 8

The section that calls for annual federal–provincial conferences on the economy "and such other matters as may be appropriate" can prove to be a positive federal–provincial means of co-operation. It is our hope that these meetings deal with various matters of importance to Canadians and that within three years the subject of multiculturalism and its various related economic, social and cultural aspects be addressed with a view to having an upgraded and co-ordinated set of policies in these areas, across Canada. Such a discussion would supplement annual meetings of the "Council of Federal–Provincial–Territorial Ministers Responsible for Multiculturalism" recently recommended by the Standing Committee on Multiculturalism and cover issues such as justice, education, immigrant integration, race relations, cultural heritage, heritage languages and health and social services.

> Recommendation 11: The CEC urges the First Ministers to address the subject of multiculturalism and its various related economic, social and cultural policies at a federal–provincial conference of First Ministers within three years.

Amendment by Unanimous Consent: Section 9

While we are pleased to see unanimous consent over the 1987 Constitutional Accord, there is little guarantee that there will be unanimous consent for future amendments. Indeed, on matters of minority rights, which sometimes are not the most fashionable issues, a single province can withhold approval for all of Canada. While the principle of unanimity is an extremely important one, its reality may be more elusive. Indeed, several have noted that the probability of real Senate reform or creation of a new province through this process will be made impossible, as big provinces will not want to give up seats. Further, we are concerned that there is no role for the Territories in the new process.

> Recommendation 12: The CEC recommends that the section be improved with a view to providing greater flexibility in the amendment process than is suggested in the Accord and ensure a role for the Territorial governments.

Constitutional Conferences: Section 13

As with the annual meeting of First Ministers on the economy, the annual meeting concerning the Constitution can prove to be positive.

However, the process must be open and public. All accords, now and in the future, must be open to public scrutiny, debate and understanding. As we have noted earlier, constitutions cannot be imposed on the people from on high. If the citizens are to respect and uphold the Constitution of our land, they must feel comfortable with it. They must understand it and must not be afraid of it. Interest groups and individuals must be able to have input into the process of constitutional amendment and development. As in the past, open discussion improves the Constitution and has a greater chance of ensuring that it reflects the wishes of the people.

> **Recommendation 13**: The CEC recommends that all future constitutional amendments agreed to by First Ministers be subject to a debate period of at least six months before final approval, during which time a committee of Parliament will conduct open hearings across Canada to obtain input from the people in every region and province of Canada, and that aboriginal rights be addressed in the near future.

Non-obstantive Clause in the Charter

Since the Canadian Charter of Rights and Freedoms was entrenched in 1982, the CEC and numerous others have been concerned about section 33, the "non-obstantive clause". The sections that can be overridden are far too important and it should be clear that they need apply at all times. It would be appropriate for the Accord to delete section 33 of the Charter to ensure the permanent status of sections 7 to 15.

> **Recommendation 14**: The CEC recommends that the Accord include a section that would repeal the non-obstantive clause of the Canadian Charter of Rights and Freedoms—section 33.

Immigration to Quebec: Preamble to Accord (Commitment 2 (b))

The Accord allows Quebec its share of immigrants—plus five percent. Traditionally, Quebec has been more in favour of increasing immigration levels than other provinces, recognizing the socio-economic advantages of a growing population and also responding to its own demographic needs. Quebec's pro-immigration stands provide the Accord with a positive approach and sets an example for all First Ministers.

In obtaining this level of immigration, it is important that equal treatment be provided to people from all parts of the world and that the Government of Quebec engage in recruitment efforts as much from European countries as from other countries. While we understand the preference for French-speaking people, it is important that linguistic requirements do not result in a return to the quota system. The Government of Quebec, therefore, should be open to potential immigrants who are learning French and are demonstrating a willingness to do so. It is important that the concept of "distinct society" not be abused at any future point to keep out immigrants from certain countries.

> **Recommendation 15**: The CEC recommends that the Accord specifically indicate that the Government of Quebec will ensure a flexible system of immigrant determination that is non-discriminatory based on country of origin or linguistic origin, in the spirit of section 15 of the Charter.

Immigrant Integration: Preamble to Accord (Commitment to 2(c))

The Accord gives Quebec the right to opt out of immigrant integration programs and other provinces can follow if they wish. The wording of the clause, however, is ambiguous. It says that the federal government will withdraw immigrant integration services "for the reception and integration (including linguistic and cultural) of all foreign nationals wishing to settle in Quebec" (parentheses as in Accord).

First, it is important to remember that immigrants migrate to Canada the nation, they do not immigrate to a particular province. In fact, it would seem that this section runs contrary to the federal government's recent efforts to make Canadian citizenship more meaningful. While the section does say that citizenship sources will remain federal, it should be clear that there is more to Canadian citizenship than the processing of certain documents. For an immigrant, attaining citizenship is, and should be, the formation of emotional ties to Canada and the development of a consciousness of the nation and a patriotic frame of mind. If immigrant integration services are provided by the province, the focus will likely be on the province concerned rather than the country.

We are particularly pleased with the government's proposed preface to a new Citizenship Act which recognizes Canada's diversity:

> Diversity is the essence of Canada, harmony its strength, tolerance its overriding quality. In their cultural and linguistic origins, in their hopes and beliefs, in their talents and ambitions, the Canadian people are as varied as the landscape they inhabit, and the climate they experience. However, as citizens, they share a common purpose: to continue the development of a great nation, where freedom is founded on the principles of equality, diversity, and community.
>
> Under the Constitution, Canada is bound to respect the heritage and values of the many diverse cultural groups that enrich the Canadian personality. Under established practice and this Proclamation, Canadians everywhere have a personal obligation to contribute to the well-being of their neighbours, and the development of the country as a whole. It is the interaction and fulfillment of individual rights and obligations that build and maintain a nation.
>
> ("Proud to Be Canadian: A Discussion Paper", p. 19)

Second, as other provinces can also sign similar agreements it is possible to end up with immigrants being taught citizenship matters from provincial perspectives, rather than a national perspective. In the event of a provincial government dedicated to the province's separation or sovereignty from Canada, the integration services could even have an anti-Canadian focus.

Third, the mention of "cultural" services is too ambiguous. If Canada is indeed multicultural, what cultural services are entailed? What does opting out of reception and integration services entail? It is our conclusion that it could be used by a province to opt out of the federal Multiculturalism Policy in its main aspects. Provinces could opt out of its immigrant integration and cultural heritage services. This could result in some provinces recognizing the multicultural reality of Canada and committing services to it, while other provinces reject it.

Coupled with the "distinct society" clause, it is fully possible that some future government of Quebec, especially a separatist one, would be able to opt out of the federal Multiculturalism Policy and declare that Quebec, in its distinctiveness, was uni-cultural—French—and, hence, assimilationist. The diverse cultures of Quebecers would be ignored, not recognized or supported, and newcomers to Quebec would be forced to assimilate into the French-Quebec culture. It is important that immigrants have some choice in integration on matters such as language of education for their children. An assimilationist scenario is possible under this Accord—albeit, we hope, less probable.

> **Recommendation 16**: The CEC recommends that the Special Joint Committee change this section with a view to ensuring that it is Canada, rather than any province, that takes primacy in the process of immigrant integration and the development of citizenship for new Canadians.

> **Recommendation 17**: The CEC recommends that the section add the words ''notwithstanding the federal Multiculturalism Policy and its intent as it applies to all of Canada''.

EVELYN KALLEN

THE MEECH LAKE ACCORD: ENTRENCHING A PECKING ORDER OF MINORITY RIGHTS*

Introduction

For the many scholars and concerned citizens who followed the arguments presented during the constitutional debates of 1980–82, the
current controversy surrounding the provisions of the Meech Lake
Accord arouses a sense of déjà vu. Throughout both 1980s constitutional
debates, amendments designed to further entrench the special and dominant status of Canada's two founding peoples—English/Protestant and
French/Catholic "charter groups"—have assumed top priority. Accordingly, the collective (linguistic, religious and broader cultural) rights of
this country's majority ethnic groups have consistently taken precedence
over the corresponding rights of Canada's ethnic minorities.[1] In parallel
vein, throughout both debates, the minority rights of subordinate, non-
ethnic populations in Canada have been accorded lower priority than
the rights of ethnic collectivities.

From a human rights perspective, this paper will argue that constitutional amendments specified in provisions of the Accord do not serve
to promote national unity and group equality across the country. Rather,
in keeping with earlier (1982) constitutional amendments, especially the
Charter of Rights and Freedoms, the provisions of the Accord serve to
augment and to ossify long-institutionalized status inequalities among
Canada's ethnic and non-ethnic minorities. The paper's analysis of the
provisions for minority rights in the Charter and in the Accord will reveal
that the Accord endorses a hierarchy of minority rights which entrenches

* *Canadian Public Policy/Analyse de politiques*, Supplement to XIV (1988): S107–120.

ethnic status disparities between the three broad categories of founding/ charter, immigrant/multicultural and aboriginal minorities and which reconfirms existing status inequalities between ethnic/non-ethnic and among different non-ethnic minorities in Canada. Further, insofar as the Accord fails to address the Charter-endorsed human rights of non-ethnic minorities (women, aged, disabled, homosexual, etc.), the paper will demonstrate that constitutional protections afforded non-ethnic minorities under the Charter could be seriously diminished.

The Human Rights Approach

Individual and collective human rights derive from the fundamental nature of humankind as a species. Individual human rights represent the biological oneness of humankind. Collective human rights represent the cultural differences between distinctive ethnic groups within the human species. Together, individual and collective human rights represent the twin global principles of human unity and cultural diversity. As specified in the International Bill of Human Rights (IBHR) and associated covenants, protections for individual and collective human rights essentially represent universal, *moral guidelines*, the global standards to which the laws of ratifying states should conform. What this means is that human rights principles are *prior to law*: laws themselves may violate or endorse human rights principles.

Individual human rights are rooted in the premise that all human beings are full and equal persons. All human beings, as such, have a fundamental right to life and to freedom, equality and dignity in all life pursuits. Freedom to decide, equality/equivalence of opportunity and dignity of person can be conceptualized as "natural rights" which accrue to every human being simply by virtue of belonging to the human species. Insofar as human rights are natural rights, they do not have to be earned; they can be claimed equally by all human beings notwithstanding differences among individuals with regard to abilities, skills, resources or other personal attributes, and notwithstanding differential group membership and loyalties. Individual human rights can be said to be inalienable human rights, but in their exercise, they are not absolute. For each person's individual human rights are conditional upon the corresponding rights of others. Human rights thus entail social responsibilities: each human being must not violate, indeed, must respect the parallel human rights of others.

In their incorporation of these fundamental principles, the bulk of the provisions of the IBHR and of the parallel codes adopted by various national and sub-national governments throughout the globe address a common, threefold theme: the right of every human being to participate in the shaping of decisions affecting his/her own life and the life of his/her society; equitable access to economic opportunities and resources, and recognition of the equal worth and dignity of all persons. In sociological parlance, we may say that every human being *qua human being* has the inalienable right to equal/equivalent access to political, economic and social power within the society.

The basic principle behind *collective human rights* is the right of ethnic collectivities *as such* to freely manifest their cultural distinctiveness and thus to express legitimately their group differences. The distinctive elements of ethnocultures may be expressed in language, religion, politico-economic design, territorial links or any combination of these and/or other defining group attributes. Regardless of the specific cultural attributes emphasized at any given time, insofar as its ethnoculture is in itself consistent with human rights principles, every ethnic group has the collective right to develop, express and transmit through time its distinctive design for living (Kallen, 1982:14–17).

The principle of collective human rights relates in its most pristine form to the culturally homogeneous, autonomous ethnic group whose unique ethnoculture is transmitted and perpetuated within the traditional, socio-geographic boundaries of its people's ancestral homeland. Today, as a consequence of world wars, international migration and myriad, disjunctive global forces, traditionally holistic ethnic communities have experienced geographical dislocation, membership fragmentation, cultural diversification and, not infrequently, the acquisition of minority status. Further, with the development of modern, multi-ethnic societies, status differences between minorities have become institutionalized within established systems of ethnic stratification.

These global developments have rendered problematic the *interpretation* of the international human rights principle of collective rights. The author has previously addressed the scholarly debate surrounding current, legal interpretation of the concept of collective rights under the provisions of the IBHR (Kallen, *op.cit.*). In this connection, the one facet of ethnicity which differentiates among collective claims is that of territoriality. Internationally, a "people" whose territorial/ethnocultural boundaries potentially or actually coincide with the geo-political boundaries of a state unit can be conceptualized as a "nation". As applied to ethnic groups within the boundaries of a given state unit, this interpretation is more problematic. Nevertheless, there is growing support among legal scholars not only for the view that all ethnic communities can claim collective cultural rights but also for the argument that all ethnic communities which can demonstrate a continuing, integral association between the people, its ancestral territory and its distinctive ethnoculture within the boundaries of a given state unit can claim collective national rights (nationhood claims).

In light of the foregoing discussion of international human rights principles, we will now address the kinds of human rights claims which can be put forward by Canadian minorities today.

The Canadian Context

Collective Rights Claims

In its application to the current Canadian context, the foregoing human rights framework suggests a threefold division among Canadian ethnic groups, on the basis of the differential nature of their collective claims, into the broad categories of founding (English/French), immigrant (multicultural) and aboriginal (Indian, Inuit and Métis) peoples. While ethnic groups within all three categories are able to put forward collective cultural claims, not all ethnic groups can legitimately make nationhood claims. Insofar as immigrant/multicultural ethnic groups cannot provide evidence for ancestral/territorial links to a particular geographical area within Canada, they cannot, justifiably, make nationhood claims. Alternatively, the collective, nationhood claims put forward by founding/ charter and some aboriginal peoples derive their legitimacy from a demonstrable link between ethnicity and territoriality. The constitutionally recognized and historically grounded link between French-Quebeckers and Quebec, their ancestral homeland, underscores Franco-Québécois' claims to nationhood. Aboriginal peoples' nationhood claims rest on the demonstrable link between particular aboriginal peoples, their traditional aboriginal territories and their living, *land-based* ethnocultures.

Individual and Categorical Rights Claims

Under statutory human rights legislation at the provincial and federal levels, and under the constitutional provisions of the Charter, all Canadians, as individual persons, can put forward claims for redress against perceived violations of their individual human rights. Additionally, s.15(2) of the Charter permits members of disadvantaged minorities to put forward claims, individually or collectively, for redress against the adverse impact of systemic discrimination upon the minority as a whole. In order to distinguish between these kinds of claims and individual or collective human rights claims, the latter claims will be conceptualized as categorical rights claims.

In light of the foregoing discussion, we may posit the following typology of minority rights claims in Canada:

1) *Individual Rights Claims* can be put forward by individual members of ethnic or non-ethnic minorities who perceive that they have been personally subject to acts of individual or institutional discrimination (e.g., Black, Sikh, female or gay applicants denied jobs on the grounds of race, ethnicity/religion, sex and sexual orientation, respectively, can make complaints for redress [job opportunities]).

2) *Categorical Rights Claims* can be put forward, individually or collectively, by members of ethnic or non-ethnic minorities who perceive that the minority as a whole has been disadvantaged through the collective, adverse impact of systemic discrimination (e.g., aboriginal or disabled persons/minorities lacking job qualifications as a consequence of categorical denial of adequate educational opportunities can make claims for redress [special education and training programs]).

3) *Collective Rights Claims* can be put forward by minority ethnic collectivities whose members perceive that the minority as a whole has been subject to cultural discrimination (e.g., aboriginal, multicultural or subcultural minorities whose distinctive cultural practices/lifestyles have been denigrated, suppressed or destroyed can make claims for recognition and protection of their unique designs for living).

4) *Nationhood Claims* can be put forward by minority ethnic collectivities with demonstrable links to an ancestral-territorial base or ''homeland'' within Canada whose members perceive that the minority as a whole has been subject to national discrimination, i.e., denial of their collective right to self-determination as internal nations within their own territorial bounds (e.g., Inuit of Nunavut and Franco-Québécois can make nationhood claims).

Caveat

The human rights framework presented in the foregoing pages will inform the analysis to follow. A caveat may be in order here: Prior to our analysis, each case for particular claims will be articulated from the viewpoint of the minority claimant, for it is the human rights claims of Canada's minorities which are at issue in the discussion.

In the following pages, we will examine constitutional provisions for minority rights in Canada. Our analysis will reveal that, contrary to international guidelines, an entrenched hierarchy of minority rights can be discerned.

Minority Rights and the Canadian Constitution: Equality or Differential Treatment?

Insofar as constitutional provisions are in accordance with fundamental human rights principles, they should afford equal/equivalent protections not only for the individual rights of all persons but also for the collective rights of all ethnic groups within the state. Yet, Canada, from Confederation, has been constitutionally predicated on the inegalitarian notion of special group status. Under the Confederation pact and the subsequent *Constitution Act of 1867*, Canada's "founding peoples"— English/Protestant and French/Catholic ethnic groups—acquired a special and superordinate status as the majority or dominant ethnic collectivities, each with a claim for nationhood within clearly delineated, territorial boundaries (Upper Canada/Ontario; Lower Canada/Quebec). Moreover, under the terms of s.93 and s.133 of the 1867 Constitution, the collective, religious/educational and language rights of the two "charter groups" were protected even outside of their respective territorial jurisdictions, in localities where their members constituted *numerical* minorities.

By way of contrast, under the terms of s.94(24) of the 1867 Constitution, aboriginal nations, lumped together under the racist rubric of "Indians", became Canada's first ethnic minorities. The provisions of s.94(24) gave the Parliament of Canada constitutional jurisdiction to enact laws concerning Indians and lands reserved for Indians. Under ensuing legislation, notably the various *Indian Acts*, once proud and independent aboriginal nations, living and governing themselves within the territorial bounds of their indigenous homelands, acquired a special and inferior status as virtual wards of the state.

Later immigrant ethnic groups, without constitutional provisions for special status—superior or inferior—came to acquire a minority status in Canada which, for all but the favoured few from the "Golden Triangle" (British Isles/NW Europe/United States) was below the superordinate rank of the two founders but above the marginal position of the aboriginal minorities. With the advent of Canada's (1971) multicultural policy, the collective claims of these "multicultural" minorities for equal status and equivalent cultural rights were increasingly voiced (Kallen, 1982b).

By the 1960s, increasing Anglo(Euro)-Canadian domination, not only outside but also within Quebec, evoked the self-perception of Franco-Quebeckers as the *minority* charter group. Dissatisfaction with their subordinate status within their own provincial domain gave rise to Franco-Québécois nationhood claims. The special status of Quebec as a nation/state was to be realized within Canada, or without.

The long-term outcome of these constitutionally rooted developments has been the creation and institutionalization of the Canadian "Vertical Mosaic" (Porter, 1965), the established ethnic hierarchy dominated by Anglo(Euro)-Canadians and internally stratified into three differentially ranked minority categories (Franco-Québécois, multicultural and aboriginal). For purposes of the present paper, the significance of these constitutionally based status differences is that they afford differential bases for collective claims: claims based on special (founding or aboriginal) status and claims based on equal (multicultural) status. Moreover, a direct consequence of this tripartite division between founding, aboriginal and multicultural minorities and the differential nature of their collective claims is that the three sets of minority rights claims are in competition, if not in direct conflict with each other.

The crucial question, at this point, is: To what extent have each of the three sets of claims been recognized during the two 1980s constitutional debates and to what degree have the collective rights of minority claimants been specified and protected through ensuing (1982 and 1987) amendments?

The analysis to follow may serve to shed light not only on the ethnic priorities underscoring the amending process but also on the concomitant version of Canadian "unity in diversity"—on both ethnic and non-ethnic grounds—entrenched through constitutional amendments.

Phase One: The Charter of Rights and Freedoms (1980–82)

Throughout the 1980–82 constitutional debate legal scholars who voiced support for constitutional entrenchment of a Charter of Rights and Freedoms argued that an entrenched Charter would override existing legislation and would thus render all discriminatory laws throughout the country inoperative (Kallen, 1982a: ch. 9). Moreover, it was argued, an entrenched Charter would serve to eliminate existing disparities in the provisions of federal and provincial human rights legislation as it would provide the standard to which all legislation should conform (ibid.).

It follows from this line of argument that a constitutionally entrenched Charter should provide all Canadian minorities with an equal/equivalent basis for making claims for redress against perceived human rights violations. But, is this in fact the case? Is the Charter truly an egalitarian human rights instrument or is it informed by established ethnic and non-ethnic group priorities which serve to render some categories of Canadians *more equal* than others?

In order to answer this question at least three variables relating to the nature of the provisions of the Charter must first be taken into account.[2]

1) *Negative vs Positive Protections*

Negative protections guarantee only non-interference by the state in the exercise of human rights by individuals or groups. Positive protections, on the other hand, obligate the state to take appropriate measures, including the provision of resources out of public funds, in order to guarantee the full exercise of rights.

2) *Specified vs Unspecified Protections*

Unspecified protections apply generally; they do not specify particular target populations. Specified protections, on the other hand, apply specifically to particular, enumerated target populations.

3) *Undefined vs Defined Rights*

Undefined rights are not spelled out with regard to meaning and content. Accordingly, the nature of the state obligations and of the protections to be afforded are neither clarified nor elaborated. Defined rights, on the other hand, are spelled out with regard to meaning and content, and the protections to be afforded by the state are delineated.

When the foregoing variables are taken into account in assessing the provisions of the Charter, it becomes evident that the Charter is not a truly egalitarian human rights instrument. Rather, together with related (1982) constitutional provisions, it can be seen to perpetuate and to further legitimate long-institutionalized status inequalities between and among different ethnic and non-ethnic populations in Canada.

Ethnic Inequalities

The special and superordinate status of Canada's two founding peoples is reconfirmed and bolstered through Charter provisions protecting their collective rights. Under Charter ss.16–21 and s.23, *positive, specified* protections are afforded for *clearly defined* English and French language and educational rights. Under Charter s.29, the constitutionally entrenched, *positive, specified* protections for the *clearly defined* religious denominational education rights of Protestant and Catholic religious collectivities throughout Canada are reconfirmed.

Conversely, there are no parallel protections for the collective linguistic and religious rights of multicultural or aboriginal minorities. Charter s.27 mentions the "multicultural heritage" of Canadians, but the vagueness of this provision leaves its interpretation entirely in the hands of the courts. Certainly, s.27 affords no *positive* protections for minority rights as this provision neither *specifies* nor *defines* the nature of the rights alluded to. Similarly, Charter s.22 provides only a vague, *negative* protection for non-official language minorities by allowing, but neither *specifying* nor *defining*, their linguistic rights.

Constitutional amendments (s.35 and Charter s.25) represent a positive move to improve the constitutionally entrenched, special and inferior status of Canada's aboriginal peoples by recognizing their collective, aboriginal rights. Yet, these provisions afford only *negative* protections for the aboriginal and treaty rights of Indian, Inuit and Métis minorities.The nature and content of collective, aboriginal rights are not elaborated, and, after four constitutional conferences convened for the singular purpose of defining aboriginal rights, these remain *undefined*.

The unwavering priority given the collective rights of Canada's founding peoples over the parallel rights of multicultural and aboriginal minorities was evident throughout the amending process. There was never any significant opposition to amendments reconfirming and expanding the collective linguistic and religious rights of the two charter majorities. Minority rights, however, proved to be far more expendable. Support waxed and waned as amendments protecting particular minority rights became easy pawns in the long, drawn-out political chess game between Ottawa and the provinces.

In the original (1980) version of the Charter, there was no mention of the notion of "multicultural heritage". Accordingly, there was no provision even alluding to the collective, cultural rights of ethnic minorities. In response to extensive lobbying by representatives of a large number of ethnic minorities, towards the end of the negotiations s.27 was added. In the view of many scholars, however, this provision represented only a tokenism—a "sop to the ethnics"/a "motherhood" statement (Kallen, 1987).

Similarly, the original amendment (then, s.24) which addressed aboriginal peoples' rights was a negatively phrased provision which allowed that the existing rights and freedoms that pertained to the "native peoples of Canada" would not be denied. Later, in response to sustained lobbying by representatives of aboriginal minority groups, another amendment (then, s.34) was added which specified the populations to be included under the rubric of "aboriginal peoples of Canada" as Indian, Inuit and Métis and which recognized and affirmed their aboriginal and treaty rights. Yet, this hard-won amendment proved to be highly vulnerable to the ongoing moves of the intergovernmental political chess game, and it was deleted by then Prime Minister Trudeau in the concluding stages of federal/provincial negotiations in order to win majority provincial support for patriation of the Canadian Constitution. Ardent lobbying by aboriginal groups and their supporters led to the later re-instatement of the amendment, in diluted form, as s.35 of the *Constitution Act* (1982). In the new s.35, the qualifying adjective, "existing", was added before "aboriginal and treaty rights", a change which some scholars contended was designed to ensure that the *as yet undefined* collective rights of aboriginal peoples would not be expanded in the future (Kallen, 1982a).

Like aboriginal people's rights, women's rights proved to be negotiable pawns in the constitutional chess game and s.28, guaranteeing the equality of men and women, was added to the Charter's provisions, then deleted, and finally re-instated (at the same time as s.35) in the final stage of the negotiations.

In the foregoing discussion, we have argued that inegalitarian (1982) constitutional provisions for collective rights can be seen to perpetuate and to reinforce Canada's established ethnic hierarchy. In the discussion to follow, we will argue that a parallel situation obtains with regard to the individual and categorical rights of non-ethnic minorities. Moreover, when we compare the Charter's protections for the human rights of ethnic vs non-ethnic minorities, we find that the latter clearly are the more "fragile freedoms" (Berger, 1981).

Non-ethnic Inequalities

Under "Equality Rights", s.15(1) and s.15(2) of the Charter provide the key constitutional underpinnings for individual and categorical rights claims based upon the notion of "equal status". While there is general agreement among scholars that the non-discriminatory grounds of s.15 are "open", i.e., that claims can be put forward by minorities not enumerated in its provisions, enumerated minorities are afforded *specified* protection for their human rights, while non-enumerated minorities have only *unspecified* protection. Enumerated minorities, specified on the grounds of race, national or ethnic origin, colour, religion, sex, age, or mental or physical disability, thereby have a firmer basis for claims than non-specified minorities. Even among the different enumerated minorities, a covert status hierarchy can be found. Ethnic (aboriginal and multicultural) minorities and women have specified human rights protections under other Charter provisions (s.25, s.27 and s.28, respectively), whereas other enumerated minorities do not. In light of the fact that the provisions of s.15 of the Charter are subject to the possibility of provincial government override under s.33, while s.25, s.27 and s.28 are not vulnerable in this respect, it becomes apparent that aboriginal and multicultural minorities and women enjoy greater Charter protections than do other minorities enumerated under s.15.

The foregoing analysis suggests that the provisions of s.15 of the Charter can be seen to underscore a status hierarchy in which enumerated minorities with other constitutional protections (namely, aboriginal and multicultural minorities and women) rank highest; other enumerated minorities (namely, those specified on the basis of race, age or physical or mental disability) rank second; and non-enumerated minorities (namely, unspecified populations whose minority status is based upon sexual orientation, political belief, criminal record or other grounds) rank lowest. Given this interpretation, it would not be surprising if some version of the American approach to equality rights, involving three levels of judicial scrutiny—strict, intermediate and minimal—were to be adopted by Canadian courts in their assessment of the claims made by non-enumerated minorities, enumerated minorities without other constitutional protections, and enumerated minorities with other protections, respectively (see Tarnopolsky, 1982:ch.1). Should this happen, the discriminatory implications of the inegalitarian nature of the Charter's differential protections for Canada's minorities could be profound, for it would follow that the lower the status of the minority the greater would be the burden of proof upon the victim of discrimination (*ibid.*).

Phase Two: The Meech Lake Accord (1987)

At the beginning of this paper the author expressed a sense of déjà vu with regard to the ethnic and non-ethnic group priorities which appeared to inform the constitutional amending process behind the Accord. In light of our analysis of the 1980–82 amending process and of the provisions of the Charter, we will now attempt to provide evidence for our initial impression and for our main thesis, namely, that the 1987 Accord serves to further augment constitutionally established status inequalities between and among ethnic and non-ethnic minorities in Canada.

The precedence accorded Canada's two founding majorities over all of the country's minorities became evident in the earliest stage of the debate when the First Ministers agreed, in April of 1987, to recognize Quebec as a "distinct society", ostensibly for the purpose of bringing Quebec into the Constitution, i.e., to remedy the fact that the patriated 1982 Constitution came into effect without the approval of then Quebec Premier René Lévesque and his provincial government.[3] The move provoked immediate concern among aboriginal and multicultural minorities, and their representatives urged the First Ministers to ensure that a "distinct society" amendment would not erode or diminish their constitutionally recognized, collective rights. In response, Prime Minister Mulroney and the Premiers added a clause to this effect. Women's groups and other minority organizations followed suit, seeking similar protections in an amended Accord.[4] In this connection, minority spokespersons pointed out that, to date, legal precedent has supported the view that the corpus of the Constitution, and, presumably, the Accord, supersedes the Charter.[5]

On June 3, 1987, the Prime Minister and all ten Premiers agreed to place the Accord, the *Constitution Amendment, 1987*, before Parliament and the provincial legislatures for adoption (Government of Canada, August, 1987:1). In the months to follow, Canada's various minorities, notwithstanding their disparate, particular constitutional concerns, were virtually unanimous in their expressed opposition to the provisions of the Accord, especially with regard to s.2(1)a and s.2(1)b, recognizing the existence of French-speaking Canadians and English-speaking Canadians as a "fundamental characteristic" of Canada and recognizing that Quebec constitutes a "distinct society" within Canada.

French-speaking Ontarians and English-speaking Quebeckers expressed concern that the Accord's provisions would override or weaken constitutional guarantees for their collective and individual rights under the Charter. Spokespersons for Franco-Ontarians expressed the fear that the "distinct society" provision would relegate the role of Ontario (and, similarly, the other provinces) to French language preservation without the necessary, distinctive cultural context currently provided in French language schools where history and other subjects are taught from a Franco-Ontarian perspective. Notwithstanding s.2(4) of the Accord, Franco-Ontarians fear that their distinctive cultural heritage within Canada will be lost. Representatives have expressed dissatisfaction with the limitations of the negative protections afforded under s.2(4) and they have pressed for positive guarantees for their collective rights.[6]

Anglo-Quebeckers have voiced similar concerns regarding the erosion of their constitutionally recognized rights under the Charter by the provisions of the Accord. Alliance Quebec, a group representing Anglo-Quebeckers, has called on Ottawa to amend the Accord so as to make it clear that nothing in the "distinct society" clause could override constitutional guarantees for their rights under the Charter.[7]

Representatives of multicultural minorities have been even more vehement than spokespersons for "official language" minorities in declaring their opposition to the provisions of s.2(1) of the Accord. Some have argued that this section of the Accord sanctions the ensconced, superordinate, ethnic status of the French and English majorities, thereby relegating non-English and non-French minorities to the status of second class citizens within Canada. The Canadian Ethnocultural Council, a coalition of more than 30 national, ethnic organizations, has contended that s.2(1) of the Accord clearly gives priority to English/French bilingualism over multiculturalism.[8] Multicultural spokespersons have asserted with one voice that the Constitution should be amended so as to include a reference to multiculturalism in its opening clause.[9]

Equally adamant in their rejection of the provisions of s.2(1) of the Accord, representatives of aboriginal organizations have contended that the recognition of Quebec as a "distinct society" without parallel recognition of aboriginal nations as "distinct societies" seriously undermines constitutional protection for aboriginal peoples' rights. In this connection, a representative of the Inuit Committee on National Issues asked the Joint Committee for some commitment in the Accord which would obligate Ottawa to address the still outstanding issue of aboriginal self-government.[10] Aboriginal leaders also have expressed concern that the provisions of s.41 of the Accord requiring amendment by unanimous consent of the provinces will make it more difficult for the Northwest Territories and the Yukon Territory—jurisdictions representing substantial numbers of aboriginal Canadians—to gain provincial status. Echoing this view strongly, the Justice Minister of the NWT charged that the Accord treats the two northern territories as "colonies of Canada" and further reinforces their subordinate status by enhancing the powers of the provinces at their expense.[11]

Needless to say, these ardently voiced concerns imply aboriginal minorities' underlying renunciation of the long-institutionalized, paternalistic mode of relations between Canadian governments and aboriginal peoples.

Among Canada's non-ethnic minorities, women's groups have been most resolute in articulating their strong opposition to the provisions of the Accord which they view as favouring the collective rights of ethnic groups (majorities and minorities) over the individual and categorical rights of women and other non-ethnic minorities. Women's representatives have objected to s.16 of the Accord on the grounds that this clause singles out multicultural and aboriginal groups as minorities whose constitutionally recognized rights are not affected by the Accord amendments, implying (by omission) that the rights of other minorities not mentioned would thereby have less recognition and protection.[12] Similar objections have been raised against s.2(1) of the Accord. Women's lobby groups have voiced concern that this section of the Accord could weaken women's equality rights by directing the courts to give priority to policies designed to promote French/English bilingualism.[13]

Accordingly, women's organizations have pressed for an amendment to the Accord giving specified protections for women's rights so as to ensure that the courts would give more weight to Charter provisions guaranteeing sexual equality (s.15 and s.28) than to s.1 of the Accord.[14]

Some women's representatives have expressed fears about the potential, sexist consequences within the province of Quebec if the "distinct society" provision supersedes Charter provisions against sex discrimination. They have voiced concern that Quebec's "distinct society" status could empower the provincial government to enact legislation that would infringe on women's rights in Quebec. They suggest, for example, that women's access to skill training outside the home could be restricted in order to promote larger families.[15] Similarly, they suggest that Quebec could replace affirmative action programs aimed at increasing the proportion of women employed in the civil service with programs that would be "language-oriented".

While these views are strongly supported by women's groups outside the province of Quebec, within that province the "distinct society" provision has been strongly endorsed by the Fédération des femmes du Québec.[16] Spokespersons for the Quebec Council on the Status of Women have also expressed the view that the "distinct society" clause will not affect women's equality rights under the Charter.[17]

Briefs to the Joint Commission from a number of national organizations representing other non-ethnic minorities have echoed the concern expressed by many women's groups that the Accord undermines equality rights. There appears to be strong support for the recommendation that a provision be added to the Accord to ensure that the Constitution of Canada shall be interpreted in a manner consistent with the Charter.[18] Women's concerns regarding the discriminatory implications of s.16 of the Accord have also been raised by other minorities. A brief from the Canadian Association for Community Living, representing the rights of Canada's disabled minorities, contended that the Accord served to legitimate an apparent hierarchy of minority groups by affording different and unequal protections for different groups.[19] A March of Dimes spokesperson voiced fears that the hard-won rights of mentally and physically disabled Canadians—the last minority category to be enumerated under s.15 of the Charter—would be at risk under the provisions of the Accord.[20]

Organizations representing non-ethnic minorities also have expressed concern about the potential undermining of national, cost-shared programs by the provisions of s.106A(1) of the Accord which allows provinces to opt out of these programs and yet receive funding for a program or initiative that is compatible with the national objectives. The vague wording of this provision, it has been argued, could lead to a scenario where provinces accept federal funding but provide no alternative program by shifting the onus to the private sector through the provision of certain initiatives.[21] A specific concern raised by the March of Dimes was that this provision would impede the efforts of the federal government to introduce a comprehensive disability insurance program much needed by Canada's disabled minorities. In similar vein, women's organizations have objected to the provisions of s.106A(1) of the Accord, arguing that these provisions could impact negatively on efforts to establish national child care programs.[22]

At the end of August, 1987, an ad hoc coalition of community organizations representing ethnic and racial minorities, women, disabled minorities, unions and human rights groups sent an open letter to Canada's Premiers calling on them to delay ratification of the Accord in order to allow for public analysis and debate.[23] The coalition argued that once again, in 1987 as in 1981, the Canadian Constitution was being amended with virtually no direct participation or input from Canada's minorities. The letter pointed out that the Joint Committee on the Constitutional Amendment had allowed less than two months for briefs from the public and argued that this highly restrictive time frame had prevented many minority organizations from properly informing and consulting with their membership.

What this implies is that particular minority concerns have been unequally voiced and represented in the constitutional debate over the provisions of the Accord. Moreover, insofar as minority organizations have focussed their reaction to the Accord on its potential threat to the minority rights of their own constituencies, what becomes apparent is that the most vulnerable and least powerful minorities are those least likely to have had their concerns articulated. Some women's groups, for example, have recommended only that recognition of women's equality rights be added to the provisions of the Accord. But would such an amendment be adequate to ensure the recognition and protection of the rights of disabled women? And what about the rights of aboriginal women, Black women, Black lesbians and other members of multiple minorities?

The Meech Lake Accord: Entrenching a Pecking Order of Minority Rights[24]

When we analyze the provisions of the Accord, using the same three variables employed in our earlier analysis of the Charter (negative vs positive protections; specified vs unspecified protections; and defined vs undefined rights), our thesis that the Accord serves to perpetuate and ossify constitutionally entrenched ethnic and non-ethnic group inequalities can be seen to have strong support.

As in earlier constitutional provisions, top priority is accorded the collective rights of Canada's two founding majorities whose superordinate status is reconfirmed through the *positive, specified* protections of s.2(1). The subordinate ethnic status of Canada's non-English and non-French minorities is reinforced by the weaker, *negative, unspecified* protections afforded their *undefined* collective rights under s.16 of the Accord.

Even less support is afforded under the Accord for the rights of non-ethnic minorities whose minority rights are not only *unspecified* and *undefined*, but, indeed, are nowhere mentioned.

Probably the most telling comment on the Accord-endorsed minority "pecking order" is that Canada's most vulnerable minorities—those disadvantaged by multiple minority status and those most clearly in need of *positive, specified* human rights protections—are those whose human rights are most seriously violated through omission.

Legal and Policy Implications of the Pecking Order

What are the implications of this apparent hierarchy of constitutionally entrenched minority rights for claims put forward by representatives of the variously ranked minorities? Insofar as claims are made under constitutional provisions, a great deal will depend on the legal inter-pretation of the wording of these provisions by the judiciary. According-ly, minorities whose rights are protected only by *negative, unspecified and undefined* provisions will have the weakest claims on the state.

With regard to public policy, a number of other factors also are germane: These include public support or lack of support for minority claims, lobbying/voting power of minority constituencies, perceived threat to majority hegemony posed by minority claims and financial expenditure involved in the settlement of minority claims.

Taking these factors into account we propose the following scenario with regard to minority rights claims:

1) Individual rights claims brought before federal and provincial human rights commissions will continue to be the easiest kind of claims to settle. Minorities enumerated in the non-discriminatory grounds of human rights codes in their jurisdiction will have stronger protections than non-enumerated minorities, whether or not enumerated minorities also are specified under s.15 of the Charter. In the case of non-enumerated minorities, specified under the Charter's provisions, minority rights claims may take the form of Charter challenges to existing Codes.

2) Categorical rights claims allowed under s.15(2) of the Charter will prove more difficult to settle, particularly in the absence of mandatory affirmative action policies. Insofar as mandatory programs would be sup-ported largely out of public funds, it is unlikely that widespread public support will be forthcoming from Canadian taxpayers. Should the consti-tutional provisions of the Accord be enacted, however, public policy in support of bilingualism would be strengthened and affirmative action in this sphere would likely take precedence over other minority claims.

Where statutory legislation allowing for programs of affirmative action is in place, minority claims will continue to be brought forward, but satisfactory settlement of claims will depend in large part on avail-ability of funding and on willingness of employers, educators and other majority powers to make appropriate adaptations to existing practices and facilities. For example, the claims of disabled (sight, hearing and mobility-impaired) minorities for equivalent accessibility to public services already have solid public support, but the costs involved in making the appropriate adaptations to existing facilities and/or to building new, disabled-adapted facilities are enormous. In the case of women, claims for equal pay for work of equal value also are gaining public support (in some jurisdictions, in the form of special legislation), but, again, the costs involved in the implementation of affirmative action prohibit swift settlement of such claims.

3) The strength and viability of collective rights claims brought forward under the Charter's provisions will depend on the relative status of the minority claimant in the constitutional pecking order, and the concomitant degree to which public policies reinforce claims. Should the constitutional provisions of the Accord be enacted, the superordinate status of claims put forward by charter/founding claimants will be strongly reinforced. In any case, minority (linguistic) rights claims made by Francophones outside Quebec and Anglophones within Quebec are far more likely to succeed than are parallel claims made by non-official language minorities. A similar argument holds in the case of minority claims for public funding for religious denominational schools. Minority (religious) rights claims made by Catholics outside Quebec and Protestants in Quebec are far more likely to succeed than are parallel claims made by non-Protestant and non-Catholic minorities (Moslems, Jews, Buddhists and others).

4) Nationhood claims are the least likely of all the types of minority rights claims to be settled to the satisfaction of the minority claimants. In the case of the Franco-Québécois claim, the Accord probably will serve its ostensible purpose, namely to diffuse and contain the dream of nationhood. In the case of aboriginal claims, the Accord presents yet another obstacle to be overcome in endless negotiations with governments. In general, the constitutional underpinnings of nationhood claims are vague and open to opposing interpretation, the financial costs are prohibitive, the threat to majority hegemony looms large, and it is doubtful that such claims would ever be endorsed through public policy. At the present time, the (originally proposed) nationhood claims of the Franco-Québécois, the Dene Nation and the Inuit of Nunavut represent a "dream deferred".

Concluding Comments

The main thrust of this paper's analysis has been to demonstrate that the Meech Lake Accord perpetuates and ossifies the Charter-endorsed hierarchy of ethnic and non-ethnic minorities in Canada. However, this observation should not be taken to mean that the Accord simply reinforces the 1982 constitutional status quo. Rather, the analysis presented in this paper has attempted to show that the provisions of the Accord can be seen to weaken the constitutionally recognized rights of Canada's minorities. This position is strongly supported by a number of current, legal scholars (Mackay, 1987; Smith, 1987; Swinton, 1987). Therefore, in closing, we suggest that the Accord may be interpreted as a retrogressive amendment which harks back to the constitutional priorities behind Canada, vintage 1867.

Notes

1. The minority concept is employed in this paper in the accepted sociological sense rather than in a numerical (or political) sense. *Minorities* are social categories whose members occupy a subordinate political, economic and/or social status in the society *relative to* the dominant status of corresponding, majority categories. The concept focuses on power disparities among social categories, not on differential population numbers.
2. The author's typology draws upon legal and broader, socio-political interpretations of Charter provisions put forward by a number of different authors. Particularly relevant sources include: Tarnopolsky and Beaudoin (1982); Eberts (1985); Flanagan (1985); Gibson (1985); Morton (1985); Beckton (1987); and Magnet (1987).
3. *The Toronto Star*, 21.08.87.
4. *Ibid.*
5. *Ibid.*:22.08.87.
6. *Ibid.*:07.07.87.
7. *Ibid.*:19.08.87.
8. *Ibid.*:07.07.87.
9. *Ibid.*:11.07.87.
10. *Ibid.*:17.08.87.
11. *Ibid.*:19.08.87.
12. *Ibid.*:22.08.87.
13. *Ibid.*:27.08.87.
14. *Ibid.*:21.08.87; 27.08.87.
15. *Ibid.*:17.08.87.
16. Courchene, in *Canadian Public Policy/Analyse de Politiques*, XVI, note 2. It should be noted, however, that other voices have been raised. Atcheson (1987) has pointed out that some women in Quebec disagree.
17. *Ibid.*:01.09.87.
18. *Canadian Human Rights Advocate (CHRA)*, Vol.111:8, Sept. 1987.
19. *Ibid.*

20. *The Toronto Star*, 20.09.87.
21. *CHRA, op. cit.*
22. *The Toronto Star*, 20.09.87.
23. *CHRA, op. cit.*
24. *Ibid.* The author has borrowed the term "pecking order" from the head-line of this issue of the *CHRA*: "Constitutional Amendment Opens Door to Pecking Order on Human Rights".

References

Atcheson, Beth (1987) Commentator on The Meech Lake Accord, Panel Discussion, Osgoode Hall Law School, York University, North York, November 23, 1987.

Beckton, Clare F. (1987) "Section 27 and Section 15 of the Charter" in Canadian Human Rights Foundation (CHRF): *Multiculturalism and the Charter* (Toronto: Carswell).

Berger, Thomas R. (1981) *Fragile Freedoms: Human Rights and Dissent in Canada* (Toronto: Clarke, Irwin and Co.).

Canada Act, 1982.

Canadian Charter of Rights and Freedoms, Canada Act:1982.

Canadian Human Rights Advocate, Vol. 111:8, Sept. 1987.

Canadian Human Rights Foundation CHRF (1987) *Multiculturalism and the Charter: A Legal Perspective* (Toronto: Carswell).

Constitution Act, 1867.

Constitution Amendment, 1987 (The Meech Lake Accord).

Eberts, Mary (1985) "The Use of Litigation Under the Canadian Charter of Rights and Freedoms as a Strategy for Achieving Change" in Neil Nevitte and Allan Kornberg, *Minorities and the Canadian State* (Oakville: Mosaic Press).

Flanagan, Thomas (1985) "The Manufacture of Minorities" in Nevitte and Kornberg, *op. cit.*

Gibson, Dale (1985) "Protection of Minority Rights Under the Canadian Charter of Rights and Freedoms: Can Politicians and Judges Sing Harmony?" *in* Nevitte and Kornberg, *op. cit.*

International Bill of Human Rights (United Nations: 1978).

Kallen, Evelyn (1982a) *Ethnicity and Human Rights in Canada* (Agincourt: Gage).
——— (1982b) "Multiculturalism: Ideology, Policy and Reality", *Journal of Canadian Studies,* 17:1:51–63.
——— (1987) "Multiculturalism, Minorities and Motherhood: A Social Scientific Critique of Section 27" in CHRF, *op. cit.*

MacKay, Wayne A. (1987) "Linguistic Duality in Canada and Distinct Society in Quebec", Paper presented for the Conference on the Meech Lake Accord, University of Toronto, October 30.

Magnet, Joseph E. (1987) "Interpreting Multiculturalism" in CHRF, *op. cit.*

Morton, F.L. (1985) "Group Rights Versus Individual Rights in the Charter: The Special Cases of Natives and Québécois" in Nevitte and Kornberg, *op. cit.*

Smith, Lynn (1987) "The Effect of the 'Distinct Society' Clause on Charter Equality Rights for Women in Canada", University of Toronto, October 30, *op. cit.*

Swinton, Katherine (1987) "Competing Visions of Constitutionalism: Of Federalism and Rights", University of Toronto, October 30, *op. cit.*

Tarnopolsky, W.S. (1982) "The Equality Rights" in Tarnopolsky and Beaudoin, *op. cit.*

Tarnopolsky, W.S. and Beaudoin, G.A. (eds.) (1982) *The Canadian Charter of Rights and Freedoms: Commentary* (Toronto: Carswell).

CHAPTER NINE

PROVINCIALIZING NATIONAL INSTITUTIONS: The Amending Formula, the Senate and the Supreme Court

If some of the proposed Meech Lake changes to the Constitution turn out badly, they will be virtually impossible to retract. Amendments dealing with federal institutions will require unanimity, and realistically they can be achieved only when the federal government can and does give things away.

(Robert Jackson, "Meech Lake Agreement Will Fracture Canadian Federalism," *The Ottawa Citizen*, June 11, 1987)

As a result of the Meech Lake amendments, it will become impossible to impose a Senate reform proposal on Alberta that was unacceptable to the Alberta Legislative Assembly—as it was possible, in 1981, to impose limits on the Legislative jurisdiction of Quebec's National Assembly without its consent.

(Senator Lowell Murray, "Keynote Speech to the National Conference on Senate Reform," Faculty of Law, University of Alberta, May 5, 1988, 15–16)

Reprinted with permission — Roy Peterson, *Vancouver Sun*.

INTRODUCTION

The debate over constitutional reforms pertaining to such national institutions as the Senate and the Supreme Court has been the preoccupation primarily of politicians and political scientists. Their concern is with the traditional cleavages in Canadian society between Ottawa and the provinces and between Canada's two linguistic communities. Federal politicians want to improve the legitimacy of national institutions. Provincial politicians want to ensure that any reform of the Senate and the Supreme Court would enhance rather than curtail provincial autonomy. French-Canadian nationalists have been concerned with the alleged centralist bias of the Supreme Court of Canada since its creation in 1875. Their concern was heightened in 1949 when the Supreme Court became the final court of appeal in all matters. They particularly feared the Supreme Court's potentially biased involvement in cases pertaining to the constitutional distribution of powers between Quebec and Ottawa.

The concern of Québécois neo-nationalists with the nature and modus operandi of the Supreme Court became a major preoccupation when the Charter of Rights and Freedoms was entrenched in the Constitution Act, 1982. The neo-nationalists interpreted the Charter primarily as a clever strategic political ploy by the Trudeau government to destroy the central elements of Bill 101, the Quebec Charter of the French Language. They were determined that Quebec, along with the other provinces, should gain control over all appointments to a fully entrenched Supreme Court so as to ensure that the Supreme Court would not interpret the Charter in a manner adverse to Quebec's interests. One Charter scholar, Michael Mandel, has declared that the Charter has precipitated the legalization of politics. Given the provincialization of Supreme Court appointments via the Meech Lake Accord, it is now quite conceivable that Canadians will experience the wholesale politicization of the Supreme Court. If so, the demarcation lines between the legislature, the executive and the judiciary will certainly be further blurred.[1]

Proposals for the reform of the Supreme Court have been an essential part of virtually every contemporary effort at constitutional renewal, beginning with the discussions leading up to the Victoria Charter in 1971.[2] In the late 1970s, reform of the Supreme Court was an integral part of the various proposals for constitutional renewal, including (a) the 1978 Trudeau government's Constitutional Amendment Bill, Bill C-60; (b) *Towards a New Canada*, the 1978 *Report* of the Canadian Bar Association (CBA) Committee on the Constitution; and (c) the 1979 *Report* of the Task Force on Canadian Unity (Pepin–Roberts Commission), entitled *A Future Together*. The CBA wanted explicit constitutional recognition of the principle of juridical independence, while some provinces and intellectuals demanded changes to section 96 of the Constitution Act, 1867, which gives Ottawa the power to appoint the judges of the higher provincial courts.[3]

While these were important issues, most of the attention was focused on the Supreme Court of Canada, its jurisdiction, size, regional representation, appointment process and need to be constitutionalized. The federal political elite perceived reform of the Supreme Court as a way of giving it greater authority and legitimacy as a national institution. Provincial political elites and commentators, on the other hand, strove to make the Supreme Court more sensitive to Canada's provincial and cultural diversities through control over the appointment process. The Trudeau government, the CBA and the Pepin–Roberts Commission all agreed on the need for and importance of the entrenchment of the Supreme Court in the Constitution, as well as the retention of its jurisdiction as a central and final appellate court. The CBA wanted the number of judges on the Supreme Court to remain at nine and questioned the convention of regional quotas for provinces other than Quebec. Both Bill C-60 and the Pepin–Roberts Commission favoured increasing the number of judges on the Supreme Court to eleven, but each proposed different quotas for the provinces.

Finally, all three groups—the Trudeau government, the CBA and the Pepin–Roberts Commission—called for an end to the unilateral appointment of Supreme Court judges by the federal government. Both the CBA and the Pepin–Roberts Commission wanted the federal government to retain the power to appoint the Supreme Court judges once they were vetted and approved by a Judiciary Committee of a reformed Senate working in camera or in public. The Trudeau government's proposal was a revised but rather convoluted version of the amendments in the Victoria Charter. Ottawa would nominate candidates and then seek the approval of the appropriate attorney general. If approval were denied, a "nominating council" would arbitrate the dispute by selecting either the federal or the provincial nominee. A reformed Senate, renamed the House of Federation, would then confirm or reject all candidates for Supreme Court judgeships.[4]

Very few politicians or constitutional experts were pleased with the reform suggestions, especially the appointment proposals. W. R. Lederman, professor of law at Queen's University, was highly critical of all three proposals for the selection of judges: ''As a system, such ratification provides only for the avoidance of downright poor nominations; it does not provide for positively seeking out the best available nominees in the first place.'' He proposed that any appointment process begin with a system of nominating commissions for all judicial appointments, including the Supreme Court.[5] Given the lack of a consensus on the appointment question, there were no direct changes made to the judicial system in the Constitution Act, 1982. Instead, fundamental aspects of the Supreme Court were indirectly constitutionalized by subjecting them to either of two new amending formulas. Any changes to the composition of the Supreme Court would henceforth require, under section 41(d), the unanimous consent of Parliament and the ten provincial legislatures. Other basic changes were subsumed under sections 38(1) and 42(1)(d) and required only consent of Parliament and seven of the provincial legislatures comprising fifty per cent of the population of Canada.[6]

A debate ensued about the constitutional and political implications of these new amending procedures. Professor Lederman, supported by other colleagues, maintained that the changes ''in effect 'constitutionalized' the Supreme Court itself.'' Confusion reigned as a result, because sections 41(d) and 42(1)(d) ''are clearly inconsistent with the first part of section 101 of 1867 which deals with 'a General Court of Appeal for Canada'.'' Lederman went on to propose a three-tiered classification system of the Supreme Court Act to help the federal government out of its dilemma.[7] On the other hand, Peter W. Hogg, a professor at Osgoode Hall Law School, argued that section 101 of the Constitution Act, 1867 remained in full force and that sections 41(d) and 42(1)(d) of the Constitution Act, 1982 were inoperative.[8] This confusion was unhealthy, and it was clear that something would have to be done at the earliest possible date. Peter Russell argued that the uncertainties "would be best overcome by making explicit provisions for the Supreme Court in the formal constitution." These provisions should restrict themselves to defining "the Court's basic function, the composition of its bench and the method of appointing judges, as these are the matters of greatest concern to the country's political élites."[9]

Following the Constitution Act, 1982, most of the attention was focused on the procedures for appointments to the judiciary. This concern was sparked by a plethora of judicial appointments made during the final months of the Trudeau government, through late 1983 and early 1984. Both the Canadian Association of Law Teachers (CALT) and the CBA were upset by these events and, in 1984, set up special committees that were mandated to analyse the existing methods of judicial appointments in Canada and to recommend reforms. In 1985, both committees produced reports that were endorsed formally by their respective associations. In the words of Jacob S. Ziegel, the CALT committee's co-chairperson:

> The single and most pervasive criticism made by the committee was that the federal system was too politicized and too often was calculated to lead to appointments being made for the wrong reasons.[10]

The CALT fully endorsed its committee's recommendation calling for the establishment of ten provincial judicial nominating councils and two federal judicial nominating councils—one for the Federal Court and a second for the Supreme Court. The *Report* of the CBA Committee on the Appointment of Judges in Canada, better known as the *McKelvey Report* after its chairperson, contended that political considerations were too prevalent in the selection and appointment of judges in Canada and proposed a system of advisory councils for federal judicial appointments. Both organizations had arrived at the conclusion that neither the CBA's National Committee on the Judiciary—which had screened names for the federal government since its inception in 1967—nor the existence since 1974 of a special advisor on judicial appointments in the Ministry of Justice's office was "sufficient to cure the defects in the existing system." Both organizations lobbied the federal Minister of Justice, the Hon. Ray Hnatyshyn, throughout 1986 and early 1987 but received only a very lukewarm, non-committal response.[11]

Like most Canadians, neither the CBA nor the CALT was aware of what the national government had in store for the Supreme Court in its constitutional reform discussions with Quebec and the other provinces. They were both surprised and dismayed at the result of these negotiations. The Meech Lake Accord proposes to fully constitutionalize the Supreme Court by adding sections 101(A) to (E) to the existing section 101 of the Constitution Act, 1867. These new sections 101(A) to (E) stipulate that the Supreme Court, composed of a chief justice and eight other judges, would remain as the general court of appeal for Canada. At least three of these judges have to come from the province of Quebec. In the event of a vacancy, the provinces would submit lists of names of qualified people to the Minister of Justice for consideration for appointment to the Supreme Court. Finally, sections 41 and 42 pertaining to the amendment formulas of the Constitution Act, 1982 were rolled into a new section 41, which requires unanimous approval of the provinces, the House of Commons and the Senate for alterations to the Supreme Court.

There was widespread approval for the long-overdue entrenchment of the Supreme Court in the Constitution, especially since the symbolic gain involved entailed no operational problems. However, Supreme Court watchers such as Peter Russell would have liked to have seen the Meech Lake Accord "acknowledge the judiciary explicit as a third and separate power established by the Constitution."[12] Francophones were generally pleased because the reforms went much farther than the Bourassa government had requested. An elated Robert Décary said that he could not have asked for more and that he knew of no other constitution that entrenched so much. Guy Tremblay was similarly delighted that the confusion of 1982 had finally been resolved and that Quebec, as a distinct society, stood to gain considerably from provincial input into the selection process. Anglophones, on the other hand, while pleased with the constitutionalization of the Supreme Court, felt that the appointment procedures were flawed because they gave the premier of Quebec exclusive control over one-third of the Supreme Court with no deadlock-breaking mechanism.[13]

Gérald Beaudoin, a well-respected professor of constitutional law and a member of the 1977–79 Pepin–Robarts Commission, is one of the staunchest and most unabashed defenders of the Meech Lake Accord. He has been a very strong and longstanding proponent of the cultural and provincial compact theories of Canadian federalism. He maintains that it is high time that both theories be entrenched in the Constitution. The first objective is achieved via the Accord's linguistic duality/distinct society clause, which he supports without reservation. The second objective is accomplished through the provincial veto over changes to national institutions and through section 106A, which curtails the national government's spending powers in areas of provincial jurisdiction. Beaudoin is also a strong advocate of an entrenched Charter of Rights and Freedoms and maintains that the courts can be relied upon to discover and chart the delicate balance between individual and collective rights, a balance so essential to a bilingual, multicultural and federal society.[14]

Professor Beaudoin's strong advocacy position on the Meech Lake Accord has its origins in what he perceives to be the fundamental flaw of the Constitution Act, 1982. The 1982 amending formula did not "adequately protect Quebec's position within the central institutions." All the fundamental dimensions of the Supreme Court had not been constitutionalized. Under the current situation, many aspects of the Supreme Court can be changed unilaterally by Ottawa without the formal consent of one of Canada's two founding peoples, as represented by the province of Quebec. The Meech Lake Accord gives Quebec a veto over important alterations to the Supreme Court while entrenching the civil law component by guaranteeing at least three of the nine judges come from Quebec.

Professor Beaudoin is particularly delighted with the Supreme Court appointment process, which he describes as "provincial lists and double vetoes." Provincial participation in the selection of judges, he contends, "respects the fundamentals of federalism and, in the case of Quebec, reflects the distinctive character of that province's legal system." In the case of Quebec, Beaudoin is confident that political negotiations will settle any deadlock that might ensue between the Canadian prime minister and the premier of Quebec.

On the question of the Senate, Professor Beaudoin expresses considerable scepticism about the viability of an appointed Senate in a North American federal system. Provincial interests are, in his view, better protected by the premiers through "a distinctly Canadian institution, known as 'executive federalism'." Professor Beaudoin favours interstate federalism over intrastate federalism, and this accounts for his support for the Meech Lake Accord's interim measure pertaining to Senate reform. Indeed, he strongly doubts the temporary nature of the Meech Lake Accord provision allowing the provinces to nominate senators. Any and all proposals for an elected Senate, he contends, will encounter strong opposition both from the members of the House of Commons, who want to protect their powers and prerogatives, and from the premiers, who want to maintain their ability to speak on behalf of their citizens and defend the integrity of provincial autonomy.[15]

The CALT and the CBA felt humiliated by the fact that they had been outmanoeuvred by the provinces in the Meech Lake fait accompli.

Both organizations sent letters of protest to the Prime Minister complaining that their respective recommendations for judicial nominating councils and advisory councils had been completely ignored by the first ministers. "In our view," wrote the CALT's representatives, "giving the provincial governments an *exclusive* nominating power will merely add another level of political partisanship to the existing tier."[16] In its submission, the CALT reiterated its belief that the defects in the existing system of appointments could not be cured by palliatives. It restated the essential criteria for the selection of members of the judiciary and argued that a system of judicial nominating councils could fulfill these criteria without impinging upon the provincial and federal governments' prerogatives to make the final appointment. If this compromise position were not acceptable to first ministers, the CALT stated, then its members were not prepared to accept the appointment procedure outlined in the Accord.[17]

The issue of greater provincial input into, and in some cases control over, national policy issues has been on the constitutional agenda for a very long time. Senate reform has been discussed since shortly after Confederation in 1867. At the first interprovincial conference in 1887, the premiers expressed their concern that Ottawa's control over the Senate threatened provincial autonomy. They wanted half the senators to be appointed by the provinces and all senators to be given limited terms.[18] While the appointed Senate was created to defend the interests of the regions in Ottawa and to temper the democratic excesses of the elected House of Commons, its members became increasingly beholden to the Conservative and Liberal prime ministers and their respective parties that had appointed them to office. In reality, the Senate had become a house of patronage. More often than not, senators were ill-prepared to break party ranks in defence of regional interests when the two collided.[19]

Until the 1980s, the existence of the unanimity convention surrounding constitutional change coupled with the real *politique* of a Senate veto over any constitutional changes proposed by the first ministers and the legislatures rendered all discussions academic and ultimately futile. The Constitution Act, 1982 removed the Senate's veto power over constitutional reform and breathed life into the Senate reform movement that had been gaining momentum in western Canada during the 1970s. The emergence of an increasingly interventionist and centralist national government after World War II had revived the flagging debate over the Senate. The provinces' incapacity to restrain or modify policy initiatives of the House of Commons on matters such as medicare, the national energy program and, more recently, regional economic incentive programs by resorting to the Senate brought increasing calls for Senate reform. The four western provincial governments, pointing to what they believed to be a historically imbedded pattern of political alienation during several decades of Liberal rule in Ottawa, were very dissatisfied with the lack of institutional reform in the Constitution Act, 1982. "While western provincial governments," argues Roger Gibbins, "successfully protected their own status and jurisdictional interests, they failed to advance the *national interest* of their constituents."[20]

In the aftermath of 1982, increasing pressure was brought to bear upon western premiers, from many quarters. Well-funded lobby groups, such as the Canada West Foundation and the Canadian Committee for a Triple E Senate, as well as a plethora of regional political movements and many prominent businessmen, such as Israel Asper, and constitutional experts, such as Howard McConnell, encouraged the premiers to adopt the alternative constitutional vision expressed in the formula of the "Triple E" (Elected, Equal, Efficient) Senate. All of these groups and individuals perceive the "Triple E" Senate as the only means of offsetting the political dominance of the two central provinces' representatives in the House of Commons.[21]

As a result of this mounting political pressure, no western Canadian politician who valued his seat, in either a provincial legislature or the House of Commons, could publicly support maintaining the status quo of the Senate. It was not surprising, then, that the western premiers, led by Premier Getty of Alberta, demanded that the question of Senate reform be placed on the agenda of the annual constitutional conference until the matter could be resolved to their satisfaction. In the interim, the Meech Lake Accord adds section 25(1) and (2) to the Constitution Act, 1867, which allows the provinces to submit a list of candidates for the Senate from which the prime minister then makes the appointment if one of the candidates is deemed suitable for the Upper House. This compromise solution was strongly defended by the four western premiers, especially Premier Getty and his constitutional advisor, Peter Meekison. Before the Special Joint Committee of the Senate and the House of Commons on the 1987 Constitutional Accord, Professor Meekison defended the Accord as a good deal for western Canada, because it extended the idea of provincial equality by giving every province a veto over Senate reform. He discounted the argument that the interim arrangement for provincial appointment of senators will become permanent because of the unanimity formula. Senate reform will remain part of the bartering process with Ottawa and the provinces, which will support it in return for something else. Speaking more bluntly before a western Canadian audience of sceptics, Meekison stated that "the pressure for reform will increase because the requirements of an annual conference will eventually force governments to find an acceptable compromise solution." As part of that compromise, "the principle of equality, while laudable, will in all probability be modified."[22]

Proponents of a "Triple E" Senate were incensed at the Meech Lake Accord's amendments pertaining to Senate reform. Spokespersons for the Canada West Foundation stated that the Accord's Senate reform proposals are "the political equivalent of the AIDS virus: an ailment whose symptoms are initially innocuous but build progressively to a debilitating, uncurable and inevitably fatal condition."[23] The Canadian Committee for a Triple E Senate objected vigorously to the Accord's "Triple P" (Premiers Perpetuating Patronage) Senate and asked instead for the suspension of all Senate appointments until wholesale reform was achieved.[24] The general attitude of the western Canadian critics was expressed very lucidly and forcefully by Israel Asper before the Special Joint Committee:

> There must be linkage between the passage of Meech Lake, which I refer to as the Quebec amendment, and the adoption of what I call the western amendment, namely the economic bill of rights and a triple-E Senate. Linkage is essential, because without it, I assure you, there will never be an equitable western amendment.[25]

David Elton, the longtime president of the Canada West Foundation and "Triple E" advocate, delineates very nicely the Catch-22 situation created by the Meech Lake Accord for Senate reformers. It was very difficult to achieve reform before the Meech Lake Accord. Yet the Accord itself has aggravated the difficulty by imposing unanimity, "an Achilles' heel which will thwart further reform." This crisis is the direct result of an undemocratic constitutional amending process dominated by first ministers. Elton is very sceptical that the premiers will (a) readily abandon the "Triple P" option handed to them in the Accord; (b) make all their Senate appointments solely on merit; or (c) refrain from making nominees. In his view, the only way Senate reform is going to be achieved is by creating "the necessary political incentive to induce First Ministers to reform the Senate." This can be accomplished in two ways. Under the existing Accord, premiers can make provisions for elected provincial nominees, and this would eventually force the prime minister's hand. The Accord could be amended to suspend all further Senate appointments until Senate reform was a reality. This "legal timebomb" would eventually force the first ministers to act. Clearly, with or without Meech Lake, the Senate issue is here to stay until the reformers' aspirations are met in a satisfactory manner.

Notes

1. Cf. Michael Mandel, *The Charter of Rights and the Legalization of Politics in Canada* (Toronto: Wall & Thompson, 1989).
2. One early proponent of fundamental reform was Peter Russell, "The Jurisdiction of the Supreme Court of Canada: Present Policies and a Programme for Reform," *Osgoode Hall Law Journal*, 6, No. 1 (October 1968): 1–38.
3. Canadian Bar Association, Committee on the Constitution, *Towards a New Canada*, Chap. 9 (Ottawa: Canadian Bar Association, 1978); Jérome Choquette, *Justice Today* (Québec: Gouvernement du Québec, Ministère de la Justice, 1976).
4. W. R. Lederman, "Current Proposals for Reform of the Supreme Court of Canada," *Canadian Bar Review*, 57 (1979): 687–701. Reprinted in his *Continuing Canadian Constitutional Dilemmas* (Toronto: Butterworths, 1981).
5. Lederman, "Current Proposals for Reform of the Supreme Court of Canada," 698–700. James C. Macpherson makes a strong case for any and all reform proposals exposing the Supreme Court appointment process to public scrutiny now that the Charter of Rights and Freedoms is constitutionalized. Cf. "The Potential Implications of Constitutional Reform for the Supreme Court of Canada," in Stanley M. Beck and Ivan Bernier, eds., *Canada and the New Constitution: The Unfinished Agenda*, Vol. 1 (Montreal: Institute for Research on Public Policy, 1983).
6. Cf. Peter W. Hogg, *Canada Act 1982 Annotated* (Toronto: Carswell, 1982).
7. W. R. Lederman, "Constitutional Procedure and the Reform of the Supreme Court of Canada," *Les Cahiers de Droit*, 26, No. 1 (mars 1985): 195–200; Joseph Magnet, *Constitutional Law of Canada* (Toronto: Carswell, 1983): 39; Ronald Cheffinns, "The Constitution Act, 1982 and the Amending Formula: Political and Legal Implications," in Edward P. Belobaba and Eric Gertner, eds., *The New Constitution and the Charter of Rights* (Toronto: Butterworths, 1983): 53.
8. Hogg, *Canada Act 1982 Annotated*, 92–94; Barry Strayer, *The Canadian Constitution and the Courts* (Second Edition, Toronto: Butterworths, 1983): 32–33.
9. Peter H. Russell, "Constitutional Reform of the Judicial Branch: Symbolic vs. Operational Considerations," *Canadian Journal of Political Science/Revue canadienne de science politique*, XVII, No. 2 (June/juin 1984): 232.
10. Jacob S. Ziegel, "Federal Judicial Appointments in Canada: The Time is Ripe for Change," *University of Toronto Law Journal*, 37, No. 1 (1987): 2.

11. *Ibid.*, 3–24, quote 11.
12. Cf. Eugene Forsey's testimony before, and brief presented to, the Special Joint Committee of the Senate and the House of Commons on the 1987 Constitutional Accord, *Minutes of Proceedings and Evidence*, No. 2, August 4, 1987 (Ottawa: Queen's Printer, 1987): 97–123, 2A:71–2A:98; and Peter Russell, "Meech Lake and the Supreme Court," in K. E. Swinton and C. J. Rogerson, eds., *Competing Constitutional Visions—The Meech Lake Accord* (Toronto: Carswell, 1988): 99.
13. Robert Décary, "L'Accord du Lac Meech et la Cour suprême du Canada," in Réal-A. Forest, ed., *L'adhésion du Québec à l'Accord du Lac Meech—Points de vue juridiques et politiques* (Montréal: Les Éditions Thémis, 1988): 89–96; Guy Tremblay, "La réforme des institutions et de la formule d'amendement dans l'Accord du Lac Meech," in *ibid.*, 79–87; Stephen A. Scott, "The Supreme Court of Canada and the 1987 Constitutional Accord," in *ibid.*, 131–148; Peter McCormick, "Toward a Provincial Role in Judicial Appointments," in Roger Gibbins et al., eds., *Meech Lake and Canada. Perspectives from the West* (Edmonton: Academic Printing and Publishing, 1988): 45–50.
14. For a full elaboration of Gérald-A. Beaudoin's views, see his testimony before, and brief presented to, the Special Joint Committee, *Minutes of Proceedings and Evidence*, No. 2, August 4, 1987, 63–79, 2A:13–2A:41.
15. Both Guy Tremblay and Jacques-Yvan Morin maintain that genuine Senate reform has been stalled indefinitely by the Accord's interim measure and the required unanimity. Quebec will never agree to the "Triple E" Senate according to Morin. Tremblay, "La réforme des institutions et de la formule d'amendement dans l'Accord du Lac Meech," 87–89; Morin, "Les blocages concertés de l'Accord constitutionnel de 1987," in Forest, *L'adhésion du Québec à l'Accord du Lac Meech*, 128–130.
16. For copies of the letters, consult their briefs submitted to the Special Joint Committee. For their respective testimonies, see Canada, Special Joint Committee of the Senate and the House of Commons on the 1987 Constitutional Accord, *Minutes of Proceedings and Evidence*: CALT, No. 15, August 31, 1987, 6–22; CBA, No. 8, August 18, 1987, 111–139. It is clear from the questioning of the CALT delegates by the committee members that the committee members considered the proposed judicial nominating councils to be overly dominated by the legal profession and not representative enough of the general public's interest.
17. Peter Russell's excellent analysis of the Accord's Supreme Court proposals brought him to agree with the CBA's and CALT's compromise solution in hopes of achieving ideological pluralism on the Supreme Court and making the process more accountable. He doubted that the current practitioners of "executive federalism" and elite accommodation would be willing to accept such a compromise. Russell, "Meech Lake and the Supreme Court," 110–112.
18. J. Peter Meekison, "Meech Lake and the Future of Senate Reform," in Swinton and Rogerson, *Competing Constitutional Visions*, 113.

19. Cf. the forthcoming Randal White, *The Voice of Region: On the Long Journey to Senate Reform in Canada* (Toronto: Dundurn Press, 1989).

20. Roger Gibbins, "Constitutional Politics and the West," in Keith Banting and Richard Simeon, eds., *And No One Cheered: Federalism, Democracy and the Constitution Act* (Toronto: Methuen, 1983): 119–132.

21. A very sound and rational argument for the "Triple E" Senate is made by Professor Howard McConnell, "The Case for a 'Triple E' Senate," *Queen's Quarterly*, 95, No. 3 (Autumn 1988): 683–698.

22. Cf. J. Peter Meekison's testimony before the Special Joint Committee, *Minutes of Proceedings and Evidence*, No. 10, August 21, 1987, 40–58; and his "Meech Lake and the Future of Senate Reform," 118.

23. Canada West Foundation, Constitutional Reform Committee's testimony before the Special Joint Committee, *Minutes of Proceedings and Evidence*, No. 4, August 6, 1987, 22–40, quote 22.

24. Canadian Committee for a Triple E Senate before the Special Joint Committee, *Minutes of Proceedings and Evidence*, No. 15, August 31, 1987, 41–59.

25. Israel Asper before the Special Joint Committee, *Minutes of Proceedings and Evidence*, No. 8, August 18, 1987, 6–25, quote 7. See also Howard Palmer, "The Flaws of the Meech Lake Accord: An Alberta Perspective," in Gibbins et al., *Meech Lake and Canada*, 37–44.

GÉRALD BEAUDOIN

CONSTITUTIONALIZING QUEBEC'S PROTECTION AT THE SUPREME COURT AND IN THE SENATE*

Introduction

On June 3, at dawn, after nineteen and a half hours of tough negotiations, the "Eleven" reached agreement on the legal version of the Meech Lake agreement of April 30, 1987. This document had been drafted by public servants between April 30 and June 2.

The difference between the Meech Lake and Ottawa agreements exceeds the difference between an agreement of principle and a legal document. Several saving clauses were added, including two on the two most controversial items—the distinct society and the federal spending power—a third on Parliament's authority over the Supreme Court and a special saving clause on native rights and multiculturalism. Other important amendments were also made.

The following is a legal analysis of the Meech Lake and Ottawa Accords.

I. The Amending Formula

The amending formula currently enshrined in the *Constitution Act, 1982* does not adequately protect Quebec's position within the central institutions. In fact, at the Supreme Court level, there is no guarantee that the Court's civil law component (one-third of members) is truly protected. With regard to the Senate, some jurists have claimed that Quebec effectively has a veto by virtue of the combined force of Section 23 of the *Constitution Act, 1867* and Section 43 of the *Constitution Act, 1982*.

---

* Excerpts from brief to the Special Joint Committee of the Senate and the House of Commons on the 1987 Constitutional Accord, *Minutes of Proceedings and Evidence*, No. 2, August 4, 1987.

However, doubt persists. The fusion of Sections 41 and 42 of the *Constitution Act, 1982* proposed by the Meech Lake and Ottawa Accords effectively means that changes in the composition of the Senate and the Supreme Court require unanimity, which now gives Quebec adequate protection within these two important central institutions.

Granted, the amending formula becomes more complicated. However, we must not exaggerate. Although the "Eleven" must be unanimous with regard to central institutions and a number of other matters, the basic formula of seven provinces comprising 50% of the population remains constant.

The formula proposed at Meech Lake still seems realistic. After all, that the rule of unanimity be extended to topics as fundamental as proportional provincial representation in the Commons, the annexation of territories to existing provinces and the establishment of new provinces does not make the amending formula a straight-jacket. Among the new areas that require unanimity are several closely related to items in 1982.

Almost every amending formula put forward since 1927 has included a few items that required the unanimity of all governments.

Mackenzie King (1927 and 1935), Louis St. Laurent (1949), Diefenbaker (1960), Pearson (1964 and 1968) and Trudeau (1971, 1979, 1980 and 1981) wanted to avoid the unanimity rule as much as possible; but they accepted it for certain hand-picked items.

II. The Supreme Court

No one opposes entrenching the Supreme Court in the Constitution, on the contrary. This Court decides between the two levels of government in cases of conflict, and interprets the constitutional *Charter of Rights*. Entrenchment has been discussed since at least 1949, at the time when our Supreme Court became truly supreme. Established in 1875, the Supreme Court exists by virtue of a simple federal statute. As with other federally created institutions, it was appropriate to enshrine its existence in the Constitution.

No one opposes entrenching the civil law component of the Supreme Court. In a federation with two legal systems and one supreme court of appeal, this goes without saying. This is the first time that the civil law component of the Court has been *unequivocally* enshrined in the Constitution. The wording of Section 41 was not clear enough on this point. Quebec is guaranteed at least three of the nine judges. Thus, Section 6 of the *Supreme Court Act*, as amended in 1949 when the Court grew from seven to nine justices, is being enshrined.

The impartiality of judges and the mechanism for removing them from the bench are enshrined in the Constitution. We can only be delighted.

A formula to entrench the provinces' participation in the appointment of judges, something that goes without saying in a federation, has been sought for decades. Established practice in this regard dates back to 1875 and does not respect the fundamentals of federalism; the current process is unilateral. I know of no constitutional expert who has not drawn attention to this shortcoming of the Canadian federation.

Particularly since 1968, formulas for appointing judges in a manner more in keeping with the spirit of federalism have been examined carefully.

Several formulas have been put forward: 1) mandatory consultation with the provinces; 2) ratification by a second house or by provinces of the choice of persons designated by the federal executive; 3) alternating provincial and federal lists; and 4) provincial lists and double vetoes. The Meech Lake Accord favours this latter formula.

In the United States, the President appoints judges but, under the Constitution, his choice must be ratified by the Senate. The Senate has a veto and has used it approximately twenty times. The system works.

Incidentally, it would be difficult to predict how, once appointed to a supreme court, a judge will behave. When he appointed Governor Earl Warren to the Supreme Court, President Eisenhower thought he would follow a conservative path (strict constructionism). The reverse proved true.

In a federation such as ours, where the constitutionality of laws is monitored closely, Supreme Court decisions have a strong influence on federalism, another reason to observe the principles of federalism.

The Meech Lake agreement provides that the federal executive appoint judges on the basis of lists prepared by the provinces and, in the case of Quebec, on the basis of the list for Quebec. This is a formula of concurrent vetoes.

Contrary to the Victoria formula of 1971, no provision has been made in the event of a deadlock. Under the Victoria formula, which provided for provincial participation, an arbitrator would resolve deadlocks, meaning that, in practice, the final decision could rest with someone not elected to office.

I do not believe that the resolution of deadlocks through political negotiations between two elected, democratic governments is, in itself, a mistake. This solution seems as good as, if not better than, arbitration. No one knows what the future holds. It would seem that practices and even agreements will be established to enable both parties concerned to reach a *modus vivendi*.

Under the terms of the Meech Lake Accord, the Prime Minister of Canada has broad powers in this area. In common law provinces, he may, in the event of a deadlock, appoint a judge from a province other than that which tradition or rotation dictates. The provinces have everything to gain by nominating a suitable candidate when, according to tradition and practice, it is their turn to do so. In the case of Quebec, which is entitled to three judges, the situation is slightly different. The two First Ministers must reach agreement. Negotiations will in practice settle any deadlock.

The President of the Canadian Bar suggested the 1986 *McKelvey* formula endorsed by the Canadian Bar. It provides for the establishment of an advisory committee in each province or territory, consisting of a representative of the Department of Justice of Canada, the Attorney General of the province concerned, the Chief Justice, a representative of the Canadian Bar and the provincial Bar and two public representatives selected by committee members. This Committee makes its recommendations to the Government of Canada.

There is nothing unusual in the federal government having the final word on the appointment of judges to the Supreme Court. However, the provinces should at least be entitled to be consulted. In fact, they should participate more actively in the appointment process.

In every respect, the Meech Lake formula is preferable to the current formula which entrenches total unilateralism.

Lastly, it should be pointed out that, except for the existence of the Supreme Court, its civil law component, the removal of judges from the bench and the appointment of judges, the Parliament of Canada retains the powers already provided under Section 101 of the *Constitution Act, 1867*, through a clause of the Ottawa Accord of June 3, 1987— excellent! The Federal Parliament will continue to update its organic act of 1875 concerning the Supreme Court.

It is all well and fine to say that judges are being given too much power. If they are, it did not begin with the Meech Lake Accord.

As early as 1867, tribunals were entrusted with the definition of such vague expressions as "peace, order and good government", "property and civil rights" and many more.

In the *Constitution Act, 1982*, broad expressions such as "other cultural matters" or "multicultural heritage" were used. The same holds true of political compromises.

Court interpretations are an inevitable part of constitutional law. The draftsman is often obliged to use relatively broad and general terms or expressions. Constitutions cannot be altered every year. Our courts are experienced with this system.

Where the constitutional draftsman lacks precision or courage, the Supreme Court establishes justice and points the way.

Through the Supreme Court, the French language was re-introduced to Manitoba in 1979 and 1984, after having been *illegally* abandoned by the Legislature for approximately one century. Through the Supreme Court, equality before the law was recognized in the *Roncarelli* case. Through the Supreme Court, freedom of the press was recognized in 1938 as implicitly protected by our Constitution.

Lastly, in conclusion, because the Supreme Court is defined in Section 41 in terms of its existence, composition and the method of appointing judges to and removing them from the bench, it is to be expected that the number of judges will remain at nine, including three from Quebec, and that that court will continue to act as a general court of appeal. In my opinion, the number of judges should remain at nine and, when required (sickness, absence), *ad hoc* judges selected among retired judges of the Supreme Court, superior courts or appeal courts should be used. Furthermore, to ease the judges' burden and to unify criminal law, an intermediate criminal court with appeal with leave to the Supreme Court should be established.

III. The Senate

In every federation, the second house represents the federated states or provinces, landers or cantons. Members of this house are elected, appointed or delegated.

Between 1864 and 1867, the Fathers of Confederation spent long hours debating about the Upper House. They wanted it to be a place for sober second thought.

They dismissed the idea of a directly or indirectly elected Senate such as that of the United States. It was probably a mistake to attempt to transpose the idea of an Upper House, designed for a united country and developed over the course of a long political evolution unique to the United Kingdom, to a federation and one on North American soil.

The Canadian Senate has probably been the subject of more reform projects than any other institution. No radical reforms such as those which occurred in the United States in 1913 and the United Kingdom in 1911 and 1949 have come to pass in Canada.

The Canadian Senate, which has the same powers as the House of Commons with three exceptions (non-confidence vote, money bill, constitutional amendments), does not dare use its full power precisely because it is not an elected body. Of course, it does render good and loyal service to the country, but it does not play the same role as the

American Senate. This vacuum was partially filled by the provincial premiers. Over the years, we have acquired a distinctly Canadian institution, known as "executive federalism", "the government of the eleven", an institution now embedded in our traditions and considered of major importance.

Between 1977 and 1982, we flirted with the idea of a Senate modelled on the German Bundesrat. This was the topic of several reports. Since 1982, fashion has favoured an elected Senate, but no one would be so bold as to say when or whether it will come into existence. In 1978, the Prime Minister of Canada recommended that the provinces appoint half of the members of the Senate for the duration of the term of office. While awaiting Senate reform, the Meech Lake Accord provides for two concurrent vetoes. The Prime Minister selects senators from lists developed by the provinces. (These senators will remain in office until age 75.) The Prime Minister may request another list; when necessary, he may allow himself to wait; the quorum in the Senate is low; the Prime Minister may take his time. Moreover, this system purports to be temporary! However, where institutions are involved, what is temporary may be lasting. Perhaps one day our Senate will be elected. Alberta has put forward the Triple E formula: Elected, Equal, Effective. Reform will not occur easily. The House of Commons may not be anxious to place a rival at its side. The country may not want a possible "mirror" of the House of Commons. An elected Senate will only be acceptable if it adequately performs its role. The provincial premiers would like to speak on their behalf. Such is the situation with or without the Meech Lake agreements! The NDP suggests abolishing the Senate.

One question concerning the Senate remains. What will be the political affiliation of senators? Without doubt, practices and traditions will be created. The party spirit is less strong in the Senate than in the House of Commons, but it exists nonetheless. Occasionally, it may be very strong, as in the debate over free trade. Sometimes a Prime Minister appoints a member of a party other than his own to the Senate, or appoints someone who will sit as an independent.

If the Senate is not to become an elected body within a given time frame, we must consider the reform proposed by the bill introduced by Minister Crosbie, based on the House of Lords reforms of 1911 and 1949. A non-elected house could be given limited authority in legislative matters, as has been the case for the House of Lords since 1911, and for the Senate since 1982 for constitutional amendments.

If ever the Senate were to become an elected body, the non-confidence vote and dissolution issues would have to be settled, as well as the conditions and duration of the term of office. This debate would form part of phase II.

CANADIAN ASSOCIATION OF LAW TEACHERS

DEMOCRATIZING OUR LEGAL SYSTEM: THE CASE FOR JUDICIAL NOMINATING COUNCILS*

1. Our Committee was appointed in 1984 pursuant to a resolution adopted at the annual meeting of the Canadian Association of Law Teachers (CALT) on May 29, 1984, to study the existing systems of judicial appointments in Canada and to make recommendations for changes. The resolution was inspired by widespread concern about abuses in judicial appointments and other public appointments made in the dying days of the Trudeau administration. (Our Association's concern about Canada's system of judicial appointments was not new; the problems had already been discussed at earlier annual meetings in 1967 and 1968.)

2. The members of our Committee are drawn from a wide spectrum of law schools across Canada and are currently as follows: Professor Jacob S. Ziegel (University of Toronto, co-chairperson); Professor Gerald Gall (University of Alberta, Edmonton, co-chairperson); Professor William Angus (Osgoode Hall Law School, Toronto); Professor Joost Blom (University of British Columbia); Professor John E. Brierley (McGill University); Professor Ian Bushnell (University of Windsor); Professor William Charles (Dalhousie University); Professor Patrice Garant (Université Laval); Professor William Lederman (Queen's University); Professor Douglas Schmeiser (University of Saskatchewan and Law Reform Commission of Saskatchewan); and Professor Carl Barr (Brock University, observer).

3. Our Committee submitted its report and recommendations to the annual meeting of the CALT held in Montreal May 29–June 1, 1985. Our recommendations were strikingly similar to the recommendations in the report of the Special Committee on Judicial Appointments of the Canadian Bar Association (CBA) released in August 1985 although there

---

* Brief to the Special Joint Committee of the Senate and the House of Commons on the 1987 Constitutional Accord, August 13, 1987.

were no formal contacts between the two committees and each worked independently of the other. The report and recommendations of our Committee were adopted by an overwhelming majority of the members present at the plenary session of the Association held on June 1, 1985. Attached hereto are a copy of the recommendations (exhibit 1) and of the CALT resolution adopting the recommendations (exhibit 2). We are also supplying the Joint Committee separately with two copies of a volume entitled *Judicial Selection in Canada: Discussion Papers and Reports* (February 1987) prepared by our Committee and distributed earlier this year among government ministers and other officials and among Canadian law libraries.

4.   Our Committee was of the view that defects in the existing system of federally appointed judges and, to a lesser extent, in the system of provincially appointed judges were fundamental and systemic and could not be cured by such palliatives as a Canadian Bar Association type screening committee or the appointment of a special assistant on judicial appointments to the federal Minister of Justice. In the Committee's view, what was needed was an entirely new approach and one that would satisfy the following requirements:

> First, the method of selection of desirable candidates must be as objective as possible. This means that it must focus exclusively on their merits as individuals, as professionals, and on their qualities as prospective judges for the particular posts for which they are being considered. Second, the method of selection must be free from political partisanship and ties of friendship and familial connections. Third, the members of the selection committee must be broadly representative of the major constituencies that are concerned with the quality of the Canadian judiciary: the legal profession, incumbent judges, the federal Minister of Justice and the provincial attorneys-general, and the public at large. Finally, the selection process must be accessible and fair in the sense that every lawyer who wishes to be considered for judicial appointment will be entitled to put his name forward or to have others do it.

5.   Our Committee felt that in the Canadian context a system of Judicial Nominating Councils (JNCs) could meet these requirements without denying provincial and federal governments their constitutional authority to make the actual appointments. In selecting the Judicial Nominating Council as the most appropriate vehicle for the nomination of candidates to judicial office the Committee was influenced by the British Columbia

and Quebec experience with similar bodies established in those provinces for the appointment of provincial court judges and by the experience of the 31 or so states that have adopted a Missouri type plan in the United States.

6.   Our Committee recommended the establishment of three differently composed Judicial Nominating Councils: (a) one for each province for the appointment of superior and appellate court judges to sit in that province; (b) a Judicial Nominating Council for the appointment of judges to the Federal Court of Canada (trial and appellate division) and to other federal courts and judicial tribunals; and (c) a Judicial Nominating Council for appointments to the Supreme Court of Canada. The composition of each Judicial Nominating Council would depend on its function. However, except in the case of appointments to the Supreme Court of Canada and the Federal Court of Canada, each Judicial Nominating Council would include a representative of the federal Minister of Justice and the provincial attorney-general, representatives of the provincial Bar, the Chief Justice of the Court in which a vacancy is to be filled, and one or more members of the public. In the case of the Judicial Nominating Council for appointments to the Supreme Court of Canada, the Committee recommended the following composition:

- the Chief Justice of Canada
- a nominee of the Canadian Judicial Council
- a nominee of the attorney-general(s) of the province or provinces from which the candidate is likely to be selected
- 2 members of the Bar to be selected on the same basis as the bar member of the Federal Judicial Nominating Council
- a member of the public to be nominated by the other members of the Council

7.   Our Committee deeply regrets that both our recommendations and the almost identical CBA recommendations appear to have been ignored in those provisions of the Meech Lake Accord dealing with appointments to the Supreme Court of Canada. Our Committee does not oppose the introduction of a provincial role in the nomination of Supreme Court of Canada judges—on the contrary, provincial participation is entirely in accord with our May 1985 recommendations. What we do criticize is the entrenchment of a nominating and appointing procedure that ignores the public interest in a broadly based, constituency oriented nominating procedure and that instead vests nominating and appointing powers exclusively in the federal and provincial governments. Our

Committee expressed these sentiments in a letter to Prime Minister Mulroney (exhibit 3) dated June 11, 1987. They were reiterated in a unanimous resolution adopted at this year's annual meeting of the Association in Hamilton on June 3, 1987, and communicated to Prime Minister Mulroney and the provincial premiers on June 11, 1987 (exhibit 4).

8.   In our view, the Meech Lake Accord provisions are deficient in the following respects:

(a) They fail to reflect the new and predominant role of the Supreme Court of Canada since the enactment of the Canadian Charter of Rights and Freedoms in 1982. The Court is an independent arm of government under the Canadian constitution and will be made formally so if the Meech Lake Accord is implemented. As guardian of the Charter and of the Canadian constitution at large the Court arbitrates conflicts between the individual and the state represented by the federal and provincial governments. It is ironic therefore that the Meech Lake Accord makes no provision for public input or accountability in the appointment of future judges to the Supreme Court of Canada but treats such appointments as the exclusive concern of the federal and provincial governments;

(b) Future appointments to the Supreme Court may become more politicized rather than less, but politicized for the wrong reasons. They will be politicized if a provincial government sees its nominating power as a vehicle for satisfying non-judicial goals and as a means for extracting other concessions from the federal government, or if the federal government rejects the provincial list of nominees because of political differences between it and the provincial government. These fears are not illusory; well documented instances show how the judicial system can suffer when the provincial and federal governments are at odds with each other over the form and substance of judicial appointments.

(c) The Meech Lake Accord sets a bad example with respect to appointments to other courts at the federal and provincial levels. Implicitly it rejects the need to reform the existing appointments procedure and implies that it is basically sound. Prime Minister Mulroney was himself a strong critic of the patronage system of appointments practiced by his predecessor. It is disturbing therefore to find that he appears to have forgotten his earlier reservations. It is equally ominous that the federal government still has not publicly responded to the CALT and CBA recommendations on judicial appointments though each of these recommendations was adopted two or more years ago.

9. Despite our criticisms of these features of the Meech Lake Accord, in our view it is not too late to correct the deficiencies. It could probably be done without formally amending the Accord. What it would require is acceptance by the federal and provincial governments of the concept of Judicial Nominating Councils for all federally appointed judges, and by the federal government proceeding to establish the appropriate councils with provincial concurrence and participation.

10. If a Judicial Nominating Council were to be established for appointment to the Supreme Court of Canada along the lines recommended by us, it would include at least one representative of the provincial government from whose jurisdiction the appointment is to be made as well as representatives of that province's Bar. Although provincial participation *per se* would not exclude the province's right under the Accord to make independent nominations, we would hope that the provinces would agree in advance to endorse the nominations put forward by the Judicial Nominating Council. They would have a strong inducement to do so because the federal government would also have to commit itself not to depart from the list of nominees prepared by the Council without very good reasons, and also because the establishment of provincial Judicial Nominating Councils would for the first time give the provinces a formal role in the nomination of judges for appointments to the provincial superior and appellate courts.

11. If this compromise solution is not acceptable to the federal and provincial governments, then we would regretfully have to conclude that the current provisions in the Accord on appointments to the Supreme Court fall significantly short of what the Canadian people are entitled to expect and should not be entrenched in the Canadian constitution. There is evidence of widespread public dissatisfaction with appointments to high public office based on narrow partisan considerations. The need for integrity and objectivity is greatest in the making of judicial appointments because of the tenured position of judges and the remarkable powers they now exercise under the Canadian Charter. We expect our judges to behave with complete integrity once they are appointed. It is no less important that the process by which they are appointed win public confidence.

12. In the light of these observations, we respectfully urge the Joint Committee to endorse the CALT recommendation and, in turn, to recommend to the federal and provincial governments:

    (1) the establishment of Judicial Nominating Councils for appointments to the Supreme Court and appointments to the pro-

vincial superior courts and the Federal Court of Canada;

(2) that these changes accompany the entrenchment of the Meech Lake Accord provisions in the Canadian constitution; and

(3) that the federal government should proceed without delay to consult with interested parties about the composition and terms of reference of the proposed Councils.

DAVID ELTON

THE ENIGMA OF MEECH LAKE
FOR SENATE REFORM *

Two very different views have emerged about the probability of meaningful reform of Canada's Senate given the Meech Lake Accord. For
many advocates of Senate reform Meech Lake has effectively killed any
chance for reform of the Canadian Senate.[1] These people feel Canada's
First Ministers have given them a Sisyphean task; Meech Lake condemns
them to an eternal task of rolling a huge stone up a hill which, once
reaching the top, will always roll back down. Two items in the Accord
are seen to perpetrate this purgatory: the requirement that all provinces
and federal government formally approve constitutional changes regarding Canada's national political institutions and the development of an
interim nomination and appointment procedure that requires premiers
to provide a list of nominees to the Senate from which the Prime Minister
will then appoint a senator.

For another group of Senate reform advocates, Meech Lake provides the first real step along the road to Senate reform taken since Confederation.[2] They point out that prior to the Accord, Senate reform
wasn't even on the national agenda, whereas as soon as Meech Lake
becomes a reality Senate reform obtains first priority on the constitutional agenda. In addition, proponents of Meech Lake point out that
from a practical point of view, Senate reform could not take place
without unanimous consent regardless of the formal amendment provisions. They also argue that the interim appointment procedure
provides provinces with a tool which can be used to ensure there is a
minimum of footdragging in realizing Senate reform.

This essay examines the assumptions underlying both points of
view. The implications of the Accord's requirement that all provinces

* In Roger Gibbins et al., eds., *Meech Lake and Canada. Perspectives from the West*
(Edmonton: Academic Printing and Publishing, 1988).

approve changes to the Senate are discussed, as are the possible ramifications of the newly established selection procedure for Senate appointments. Finally, two alternate approaches to dealing with Senate reform are discussed, alternatives which are outgrowths of the Meech Lake initiative. One approach requires a simple amendment to the Meech Lake Accord. The second approach outlines a plan of action available to committed Senate reformers regardless of the fate of the Meech Lake Accord initiative.

The Amending Process

From the outset of the debates on constitutional change it has been recognized that one of the primary obstacles to reform of the Senate lies in Canada's restrictive constitutional change process. Unlike other federations which provide for considerable public input into the initiation and ratification of constitutional changes, Canada's amending process severely restricts non-government participants. When it comes to changing the governing process, the very people with the greatest vested interest in maintaining the status quo, the eleven First Ministers, are the same people responsible for both initiating and ratifying changes in Canada's constitutional order. Canada's amending process is far more restrictive, far less open to public input than is the amending process in Australia, Switzerland or the United States. Substantiation of this observation was attained by developing a numeric index which rank ordered the degree of participation in the amending process in the four federations with regards to the initiation, amendment, and ratification of constitutional changes.[3] Australia and the United States turned out to be twice as open to influence by legislators and/or the public as did Canada, while Switzerland was three times as open.

Canada's existing government-controlled amending process (which requires the concurrence of the Parliament of Canada and seven provinces representing at least 50 percent of the population) creates a near insurmountable obstacle for those advocating changes to institutional structures. That Meech Lake moves the constitutional high jump bar from 2.4 metres (a height no Canadian has yet cleared) to 2.5 metres (a height that no one has ever cleared) seems quite academic. Because Senate reform seeks to modify the political powers of the very people charged with initiating and ratifying the necessary constitutional changes, First Ministers should not be expected to be overly anxious to see any significant reform initiative through to fruition. Indeed, it is to be expected that First Ministers and their advisors (who in a real sense have just as much to gain or lose as their ministers) will dwell on problems at the expense of an overall solution.

Not surprisingly, Senate reform serves up a number of very thorny problems. For example, finding agreement on the role and functions of the Senate will require First Ministers to voluntarily relinquish some of their existing powers. Second, to create a Senate capable of providing a balanced regional perspective on national policy making, there must be a significant shift in representation from both Ontario and Quebec to the eight smaller provinces. To complicate matters even more, there is every likelihood that the relative representation of two of the smaller provinces, New Brunswick and Nova Scotia, will also be diminished. Given these and other problems, it is questionable whether there would ever be a time when all eleven First Ministers would agree to a specific set of changes. To expect all eleven to rise simultaneously to the level of statesmanship required to ratify meaningful Senate reform as required under the Meech Lake Accord may be unrealistic, naive, or both.

It is instructive to recall that placing Senate reform on the national agenda required an implicit threat of blocking a constitutional change highly valued by both the federal and Quebec governments. If a simple acceptance for commitment to Senate reform was obtained under extraordinary circumstances where the self interests of the federal and Quebec governments were key factors, what set of circumstances must pertain for meaningful reform? Proponents of Meech Lake have not addressed this matter. Opponents to Meech Lake not only have asked this question, but have a disquieting answer, arguing that unless meaningful Senate reform takes place at the same time Quebec's demands are met, the only set of circumstances that would cause the central provinces and the federal government to agree to meaningful Senate reform is the existence of a viable and committed separatist threat from western Canada.[4]

Proponents of the Accord are equally adamant that the imposition of a unanimity requirement regarding Senate reform is not only reasonable but politically realistic for four reasons.[5] First, it is pointed out that the Meech Lake Accord itself attained unanimous agreement. Second, it is argued that the requirement gives Western and Atlantic provinces the ability to veto any attempts to reform the Senate in an unacceptable manner. Third, proponents point out that the probability of effecting fundamental change in Canada's national institutions without unanimous agreement is unrealistic. The problems created by the exclusion of Quebec from the 1982 constitutional changes are cited as a case in point. Finally, the interim appointment procedure is seen as a means by which Western and Atlantic provinces can ensure Senate reform will take place by recommending nominees who are themselves committed to seeing Senate reform take place and will therefore work within the Senate to this end.

Whether Meech Lake becomes a reality or not, the Accord has at least temporarily modified political practice in a way which, if used creatively by one or more provinces, could all but ensure that meaningful Senate reform will take place within the next decade or two. It is to this issue that we now turn.

Meech Lake and Senate Appointments

Undoubtedly, the most surprising and unexpected aspect of the Meech Lake Accord is the provision for an *immediate* change in the appointment procedure, a change which would become constitutionally binding if the Meech Lake Accord is implemented. The Accord provides that the selection of future appointees to the Senate be made by the Prime Minister from lists provided by the premier of the province in which the vacancy occurs. Whether these lists are to contain one or more names is not stated. Nor is there any indication regarding the manner premiers might use to determine whose name(s) to submit.

Unlike the argument for entrenching a commitment to discuss Senate reform, and the delineation of what should be discussed, all of which had been discussed prior to the Meech Lake meeting,[6] the temporary change in the appointment procedure was an outgrowth of the First Ministers' discussions. Whether it grew out of a Machiavellian ploy by the Prime Minister and some premiers to reduce the chances of further Senate reform by sharing a highly valued patronage appointment, or was operationalized to provide evidence of a real commitment to reform, is not clear. Yet regardless of the First Ministers' intent, it will be the actual practices which are followed by premiers and the Prime Minister in future appointments to the Senate which will determine whether this provision will enhance or hinder meaningful Senate reform. The decision to change Senate appointment procedures represents the first fundamental change in the makeup and, potentially, the powers of the Senate since Confederation. Ironically, at the same time that this provision could precipitate a significant breakup of the logjam facing Senate reform it could also create an Achilles' heel which will thwart further reform.

Models of Appointment

There are basically four models of appointment available to premiers in selecting nominees for the Senate, all of which have implications for further Senate reform. The first three models, which maintain previous Senate appointment practices, are discussed here while the fourth, which represents a fundamental change in Senate appointment procedures, is examined in the concluding section.

The first model available to premiers in making Senate nominees is the Triple P option: ''Premiers Perpetuating Patronage.'' The patronage model has proven to be the most appealing to prime ministers over the past 120 years, and undoubtedly provides the greatest benefits to a premier. Unless a premier is ideologically committed to Senate reform, an unlikely possibility given that Alberta's Premier Don Getty is the only premier in the past two decades who has given evidence of such a commitment, the Triple P model offers a premier the best of both worlds. Premiers are now in a position to give evidence of the extent to which they value the services of several faithful party workers at once by submitting a list of two or more names. This would leave the premier with the benefits of having indicated his desire to reward several of the party faithful while at the same time saddling the Prime Minister with the unsavory task of choosing only one of the nominees.

If the ''Triple P'' approach to Senate nominees is used by even one province it would effectively provide a near fatal blow to further reform. Not only would the individual premier using this approach be reticent to agree to meaningful reform in the future, but he or she would also have the absolute power to delay or stop Senate reform. In addition, the behavior of any individual premier would provide an appealing precedent for other premiers to follow. Because there is little or no precedent of political leaders foregoing patronage appointments, particularly of the magnitude of a Senate appointment, is it realistic to assume that ten premiers over an extended period of time will prove to be the exception to the rule in the name of meaningful Senate reform?

The second model of appointment is the ''qualified person'' option. The rationale underlying this model is that the province and its citizens plus the Senate and the country would be well served by appointing a highly qualified individual to the Senate. This option has been used from time to time by prime ministers. For example, Prime Minister Trudeau appointed Ernest Manning, a former Social Credit premier of Alberta, and Eugene Forsey, a constitutional law expert, neither of whom had Liberal party ties. If premiers adopt the "qualified person" model in making Senate nominations it is conceivable that over time the prestige of the Senate would be enhanced marginally. There is little likelihood, however, that even with several dozen nominations and appointments of qualified and respected persons, the Senate would obtain adequate legitimacy to effectively represent regional aspirations within the national government. The problem with the Senate is not that there are too few well qualified senators. The problem is that any appointment, however made, simply reinforces the anachronistic nature of the Senate. Appointment to a legislative body is incongruent with modern democratic practices.

Over the past 120 years many appointments to the Senate have been made using a mixture of patronage and merit, a mixture which accomplishes two things at once. First, premiers obtain the prestige and power that go with making appointments to individuals of their choice. Second, the public, the media, and even the opposition are satisfied the premier is working in the public interest. It is not surprising, therefore, that it is this mixed model of appointment that Newfoundland's premier operationalized in making the first nomination under the provisions of the Meech Lake Accord in early 1988. The premier's behavior fits well within the best traditions of Senate appointments and gives good evidence of Premier Peckford's desire to maintain the status quo regarding the Senate.

The third model of Senate appointment available to premiers can be called either the "do nothing" model or the "no nominee" model. It requires only that a province refrain from making nominations to the Senate. The rationale behind this model is that over time the existence of vacancies in the Senate will increase demands for reform of the institution. The success of this approach is dependent primarily upon provincial premiers being able to withstand the pressures within their own party to provide "jobs for the boys."

While it is conceivable that a particular premier could on principle refuse to provide nominees over a period of several years, it is unlikely that such constraint could be maintained over a long enough period of time to exert adequate pressure for reform. Given the slow rate of turnover in the Senate, real pressure for reform would not be exerted until the number of senators dropped below 70, something that will not occur for well over a decade. For example, at one point in the 1970s there were 20 vacancies in the Senate and the only sustained demand to rectify the situation came from those seeking patronage appointments.[7] It would probably be well into the 21st century before this approach would exert adequate pressure to precipitate the necessary reforms. Further, for the "no nominee" approach to take effect it would require that most if not all provinces take a similar approach, something which has not happened. While Ontario's Premier Peterson has already indicated that he is going to use this approach (Ontario has two vacancies in the Senate at present) there is no way for him to ensure that his own successor(s), much less any of the other premiers, will refrain from providing Senate nominees.

Alternate Approaches to Senate Reform

There are basically two alternate options open to proponents of Senate reform given the Meech Lake Accord: elect provincial nominees to the Senate, or place a political time bomb within the Accord. The first option requires that premiers use creatively the provinces' power to nominate senators, while the second option requires an amendment to the Accord.

Any one of Canada's ten premiers is currently in a position to provide for the election of a senatorial nominee. This option arises from the fact that the Meech Lake agreement is silent on the manner in which premiers obtain the names of their nominees. It is therefore open to any premier to pass provincial legislation providing for the election of senatorial nominees either at the time of a provincial election, or at some other convenient time. In addition, it is within the prerogative of a provincial government to informally limit the term of its nominees to whatever time it feels appropriate. This could be done by simply requiring a commitment from all candidates to resign after a specified period of time. In sum, no constitutional change of any kind is necessary to make the election of senators a reality.

There is no doubt but that the "election of a nominee" option would in and of itself go a long way towards creating a reformed Senate. The potential benefits of this option are considerable. Once one province elected a nominee there would be considerable pressure in other provinces to do likewise. In addition, the first two or three elected senators for a time would obtain a notoriety unparalleled by any other Canadian politician. This media exposure would dramatically increase awareness of the need for Senate reform and thus put pressure upon the First Ministers and their advisors to undertake the necessary constitutional changes to make meaningful Senate reform a reality. In addition, the election of a senatorial nominee would place within parliament a strong spokesman with a unique mandate for Senate reform.

While the Prime Minister retains the right to reject provincial nominees, for a prime minister to refuse to appoint an individual nominated by a majority of the electors of a province would have such serious political consequences that it reduces the likelihood of such an eventuality to nearly zero. In essence, the Prime Minister is placed in a Catch 22 situation. If he accepts the nominee the demand for Senate reform increases. If the Prime Minister chooses to reject an elected nominee his action would also dramatically increase the demand for Senate reform.

Although the election of nominees to the Senate holds out significant promise for creating an environment conducive to further Senate reform, there is also a potential dark side to this option. If all provinces were to adopt this approach over the next two decades, then it is possible to project the existence of a totally elected Senate which would further exacerbate the current maldistribution of seats in the Senate. The perpetuation of the existing distribution of seats would once again permit Ontario and Quebec to dominate national policy making and thwart the primary objective of enhancing regional input into the national policy making process. This possibility is highly unlikely, however, for it would be contrary to the self interests of all First Ministers to allow this state of affairs to pertain for any period of time. Such an elected Senate would also retain the existing senatorial powers and be able to challenge even the collective will of the First Ministers. Thus, given the First Ministers' power to reform the Senate without the Senate's concurrence, there is little doubt but that reform would take place well before the realization of an all elected Senate. A growing number of elected senators would provide an ever increasing incentive for First Ministers to undertake the necessary constitutional change.

The insertion of a legal timebomb with regards to Senate reform is a second approach. This could be done by simply constitutionalizing the "no nominee" model discussed earlier. Rather than leaving it up to the discretion of premiers to refrain or indulge in Senate appointments, the Accord could be changed to require that no further appointments be made until Senate reform was realized. While this provision would have little effect over the next five years, thereafter the decreasing numbers in the Senate would increase the relative powers of the remaining senators to the point where First Ministers would be obliged to act.

The key element in both alternatives is the creation of the necessary political incentive to induce First Ministers to reform the Senate. Experience indicates that the kind of constitutional changes necessary to realize Senate reform will take place only as a result of political necessity, not goodwill. After all, Senate reform was inserted into the Meech Lake Accord because it was the only way the federal and Quebec governments could obtain all province agreement to change the existing amending formula.

To expect that meaningful Senate reform will happen on the basis of goodwill among eleven heads of government all with differing constituencies and agendas is unrealistic in the extreme. Whereas the constitutional reforms of 1982 and the Meech Lake Accord dealt with more symbolic issues, Senate reform reaches to the very heart of the Canadian political system. It should therefore be expected that the practical political pressures upon First Ministers to undertake meaningful Senate reform will have to be considerably more intense than the pressures which brought about either the 1982 constitutional changes or the Meech Lake Accord of 1987.

Notes

1. One of the foremost advocates of Senate reform is the newly created Reform Party of Canada. Their presentation to the Special Joint Committee of the Senate and the House of Commons on the 1987 Constitutional Accord, August, 1987, exemplifies the extent of dismay among Senate reform advocates regarding the Meech Lake Accord.

2. Premier Don Getty's defence of the Meech Lake Accord in the Alberta legislature provides an excellent example of the rationale underlying the defence of Meech Lake's Senate reform provisions. *Alberta Hansard*, June 17, 1987, pp. 1969–1972.

3. This analysis was undertaken for a presentation to the Special Joint Committee of the Senate and the House of Commons on the 1987 Constitutional Accord. See "Western Perspective on the Meech Lake Accord," Presentation of the Constitutional Reform Committee of the Canada West Foundation, August 11, 1987.

4. David Elton and Roger Gibbins, "Western Alienation and Political Culture," in R. Schultz et al., editors, *Canadian Political Process*, 3rd ed. (Toronto: Holt, Rinehart and Winston 1979) 82–96.

5. James Horsman, "Sorry, Ted, but you're wrong about the Meech Lake Accord," *Alberta Report*, May 18, 1987, 15.

6. Peter McCormick and David Elton, "The Western Economy and Canadian Unity," *Western Perspectives* (Calgary: Canada West Foundation 1987) 18–19.

7. "Western Perspective on the Meech Lake Accord," op. cit., 15.

CHAPTER TEN

ABORIGINAL AND NORTHERN RIGHTS: Integrating the First Peoples into the Constitution

My question is, does this resolution accurately reflect Canada as it is and as it should be? I must answer for the aboriginal peoples I represent that it most certainly does not. It promotes a view of reality that ignores the first founding people of Canada—the aboriginal peoples. It provides a vision of the future in which aboriginal peoples cannot hope to share.

(Louis Bruyere, Native Council of Canada, submission to the Special Joint Committee of the Senate and the House of Commons on the 1987 Constitutional Accord, *Minutes of Proceedings and Evidence*, No. 12, August 25, 1987 [Ottawa: Queen's Printer, 1987]: 95–96)

The Meech Lake Accord discriminates against tens of thousands of Canadians solely because they have chosen to live north of the 60th parallel. It makes provincehood virtually impossible for the territories, it denies us the right to hold certain specific national offices and it was arrived at without either our knowledge or consent, and we are angry.

(Tony Penikett, this volume)

Reprinted with permission — Bob Krieger.

INTRODUCTION

Canada's four national aboriginal organizations were among the first to respond with consternation to the initial signing of the Meech Lake Accord. This was not surprising, considering that they had just completed, in March 1987, a series of four unsuccessful and frustrating constitutional conferences on aboriginal issues, in particular the thorny issue of self-government for their respective peoples. Indeed, a mood of betrayal and bewilderment prevailed among the organizations' leaders and supporters. So much effort had been expended over five years, with few, if any, results.

The four organizations—the Assembly of First Nations (AFN), the Métis National Council (MNC), the Inuit Committee on National Issues (ICNI) and the Native Council of Canada (NCC)—quickly convened a National Aboriginal Summit and fired off a long protest letter to the Prime Minister. The tone and the thrust of the manifesto set the pattern for their approach to the Meech Lake Accord. All four organizations expressed their support in principle for Quebec's five demands, while drawing attention to "some of the major adverse impacts of the Accord on aboriginal peoples." Their letter then outlined how the Accord could be altered to accommodate aboriginal concerns without derailing the process of the constitutional reconciliation of Quebec.

More importantly, perhaps, their letter revealed a deep sense of grievance associated with what the organizations' leaders considered a second betrayal by the Prime Minister and the premiers, particularly when it came so soon after the first. The aboriginal organizations had sensed something ominous was about to happen and, in April 1987, had formally requested participation in the constitutional talks pertaining to Quebec's demands. They now deplored the Prime Minister's decision to reject their request to participate, on the grounds that Quebec's demands had nothing to do with aboriginal or treaty rights. From their perspective, based on a decade of constitutional education and struggle, the Meech Lake Accord did affect, directly and indirectly, the rights and status of aboriginal peoples in far-reaching and prejudicial ways. Their letter concluded:

> We believe that the Constitution must stand as a symbol of hope and aspiration for aboriginal peoples, as well as for other peoples of Canada. It must not be converted by First Ministers, whether intentionally or not, into an instrument that limits or oppresses us. It must not be made so rigid as to perpetuate the status quo and deny aboriginal peoples equitable social and political development.[1]

The long road to the Meech Lake Accord was, for Canada's aboriginal organizations, strewn with hope and despair, reflecting both modest gains as well as a few major setbacks. Remarkably, through it all, the aboriginal peoples and their leaders demonstrated sheer dogged determination to be integrated, in a meaningful, non-threatening and constructive fashion, into the Canadian constitutional fabric and political culture. They referred to this aspiration as "closing the incomplete circle of Confederation."

This struggle by aboriginal peoples for integration into Confederation on their own terms has been, from a historical perspective, extremely slow.[2] It began in earnest only after World War II, with the emergence of the social welfare state, the dismantling of the church–state alliance in aboriginal education and the achievement of legal equality, including the right to vote. Initially, some of these developments threatened to undermine the system of treaties, reserves, exclusive federal jurisdiction—outlined in section 91(24) of the Constitution Act, 1867 and the Indian Act of 1876—and the Department of Indian Affairs, all of which provided the aboriginal peoples with a real, as well as symbolic, special status in Canadian society. There were also outright periodic demands that this special status be terminated so as to ensure socio-cultural and linguistic integration and eventual assimilation of Canada's aboriginal peoples into Canadian society. The most recent of these demands was contained in the Trudeau government's 1969 *White Paper on Indian Policy*, which proposed the repeal of the Indian Act and section 91(24) of the Constitution Act, 1867. Confronted by a vigorous outcry from the aboriginal communities, the Trudeau government quickly withdrew the *White Paper on Indian Policy* and pursued instead the reform and consolidation of special status for the aboriginal communities.[3]

This task was complicated by a legal clash that emerged in the 1970s over which of the two legislative measures—the Canadian Bill of Rights, 1960 and the Indian Act—would have priority over the other. It was a clash between individual rights advanced by the Canadian Bill of Rights and the collective special status rights of the aboriginal communities. In November 1969, the Supreme Court, in a six to three ruling on the *Drybones* case based on the Bill of Rights, struck down the liquor section of the Indian Act, which treated Indians more punitively than non-Indians. A precedent having been set, other individual rights cases soon emerged. The matter of sexual discrimination in the Indian Act was raised before the Royal Commission on the Status of Women, set up in 1967, by Mary Two Axe Earley and other women from the Caughnawaga Reserve near Montreal. The Commission's 1970 *Report* recommended that this discriminatory double standard be ended.

In 1970, the issue of sexual discrimination in Indian Band membership decisions found its way into the courts in the *Lavell* and *Bedard* cases. In the former case, an Indian woman, Jeanette Corbière, charged that there was sexual discrimination in the Indian Act. She had lost her Indian status when she married a non-Indian, David Lavell, whereas a non-Indian woman would acquire Indian status when she married a status Indian. In the latter case, Yvonne Bedard, who was separated from her non-Indian husband and thrown off the Six Nations Reserve where she was living in a house willed to her by her mother, charged the Band with sexual discrimination. When it became clear that both the Federal Court of Appeal and the Ontario High Court were giving precedence to the Canadian Bill of Rights over the Indian Act, various provincial and territorial aboriginal organizations, led by the National Indian Brotherhood (NIB) (the predecessor of the AFN) and funded by the federal government, intervened at the Supreme Court to defend the Indian Act and the special status it represented. The Supreme Court confirmed the Indian special status when it ruled in both cases that the Indian Act took precedence over the Canadian Bill of Rights by virtue of section 91(24) of the Constitution Act, 1867.

Although the Band Councils and the NIB were pleased with the verdict, the problem would not go away. Indeed, the sexual discrimination charge would continue to plague them through the next decade. Considerable pressure was brought to bear upon the organizations from

Indian and non-Indian women's organizations to reform the Indian Act rather than face the threat of having it superseded by the 1982 Charter of Rights and Freedoms. Reform of the Indian Act to end sexual discrimination took place under Bill C-31 in 1985. A modified special status had been preserved.[4]

By the late 1970s, mere survival was no longer the aspiration of Canada's aboriginal peoples. Growing poverty of Indians both on and off the reserves—revealed in the ever-increasing incarceration rates for Indians, Métis and Inuit—coupled with the increased threats to the ecosystems, economic resources and traditional way of life of the reserves forced Indian organizations to pursue land claims settlements with the federal and provincial governments. This process proved to be very expensive, time-consuming and not very successful—except for a few isolated cases, such as the James Bay Cree who stood in the way of the massive hydro project contemplated by the Liberal government of Robert Bourassa.

Aboriginal organizations concluded that they must adopt a more comprehensive political approach. The Indians in the Northwest Territories issued the Dene Declaration in 1975, which called for the creation of a Dene Nationhood within Canada. The Inuit called for a separate northern territory in their 1976 Nunuvut proposal. A year later, Saskatchewan's Indians envisioned the creation of autonomous "Indian governments," thereby doing away with the Department of Indian Affairs. The NIB sensed that the reopening of constitutional discussions in 1978 was an opportune moment to achieve two goals. The first and most important goal involved the right to participate in the constitutional reform process itself. "The aboriginal groups," explains Douglas Sanders, "were seeking recognition as political actors within Canadian federalism."[5] The second goal pertained to the practical entrenchment of aboriginal and treaty rights, as well as a more clearly defined special status for aboriginal peoples.

With these two goals clearly in mind, the NIB, supported by the non-status Indian, Métis and Inuit organizations, undertook a determined lobbying effort to obtain the right to participate in the constitutional reform process as full-fledged political actors—that is, as governments. Fully aware of this aspiration, the federal government tried to circumscribe aboriginal involvement in the process. Since there appeared to be a strong consensus regarding their involvement among all three national parties, some provincial parties and the Task Force on National Unity, the federal government granted the NIB, the NCC and the ICNI observer status at the October 1978 conference. At the second conference in February 1979, at which the aboriginal organizations were also present as observers, the first ministers agreed to add the aboriginal question to the constitutional agenda. At this point, aboriginal expectations had been raised to a very high level.[6] Consequently, the NIB was not satisfied with its highly limited role and decided to appeal the Canada Bill in Great Britain before the Queen. Anything less than a role on par with the first ministers was unacceptable to the NIB. Anything more than consultation at the ministerial level was unacceptable to the first ministers, who feared acknowledging the aboriginal peoples as autonomous governments. Nevertheless, the NIB pursued this objective throughout the entire debate on the Canada Bill, 1979–82.[7]

There was no single unified Indian lobby for aboriginal rights. Even after Trudeau returned to office and decided—after failing to get the approval of the premiers—on a constitutional reform package that protected treaty rights from the Charter but relegated aboriginal issues to a second round, the NIB refused to form a common front with the NCC and the ICNI. Militant and radical leaders within the NIB denounced the Charter as a direct threat to the special status of aboriginal peoples. In the fall of 1980, the NIB set in motion an elaborate and expensive lobbying process that included convening an AFN constitutional meeting, opening an office in London, England, and organizing a "constitutional express" to bring thousands of Indians to Ottawa and then on to the United Nations in New York.

In the interim, the NIB, unlike the NCC and the ICNI, submitted a brief to the Special Joint Committee of the Senate and the House of Commons on the constitutional proposal but boycotted the hearings. In January 1981, the Trudeau government, pursuing a strategy of consensus building, used the Special Joint Committee to work out a compromise among the three national parties and the three national aboriginal organizations. The patriated Constitution with a Charter would include three sections: one recognizing and affirming the aboriginal and treaty rights of the Indian, Inuit and Métis peoples of Canada; a second protecting the aboriginal peoples from the Charter; and a third requiring a constitutional conference on aboriginal issues with full aboriginal representation.

All three national aboriginal leaders claimed victory. Meanwhile, militant and radical western Canadian NIB affiliates felt betrayed by their leader, Del Riley, because the compromise failed to respond to their demands on the issues of self-government and a consent clause on all future amendments. The NIB was torn apart by this crisis, as the British Columbian, Albertan and Manitoban groups severed their ties with the national organization while its executive expressed serious objections to the compromise. A radicalized but divided NIB continued its strenuous lobbying efforts to derail the Canada Bill. Meanwhile, the NCC and the ICNI lobbied Ottawa to ensure that section 34, which recognized and affirmed aboriginal and treaty rights, would not be traded away during the make-it-or-break-it November 1981 Constitutional Conference. Their worst fears were borne out as section 34, at the request of the premiers, was dropped from the final resolution brought before the House.

This crisis catalysed all the aboriginal organizations, except the NIB, into frenetic action. They formed an Aboriginal Rights Coalition to obtain the reinstatement of section 34 by lobbying the premiers. As with the women's movement, the aboriginal coalition was only partially successful. Led by the NDP premiers—Alan Blakeney of Saskatchewan and Howard Pawley of Manitoba—the other seven premiers agreed within a matter of days to a modified section 34, referring to "existing" rights. Disappointed with the amended section 34, the Aboriginal Rights Coalition joined forces with the NIB in what ultimately would prove to be futile and expensive dual judicial/political strategy to derail the Canada Bill in Great Britain. After all was said and done, the Constitution Act, 1982 included the three sections—25, 35 (the amended version of 34) and 37, as outlined in the January 30, 1981, compromise—that had so divided the aboriginal organizations.[8]

Constitution building had proven to be a bittersweet experience. For the nationalist-imbued aboriginal leaders committed to full political participation in Confederation based upon aboriginal self-government, there remained plenty of unfinished constitutional business. Fortunately, they would be given another opportunity via the aboriginal constitutional conference called for by section 37(1) of the Constitution Act, 1982. The aboriginal perspective and continued sense of rising expectations are well described by Louis "Smokey" Bruyere, president of the Native Council of Canada during the four aboriginal conferences. The provision for the aboriginal constitutional conference, he explained:

> made plain the reality that aboriginal and treaty rights are not merely to be recognized and provided with general remedies in the courts for their breach, as is the case with the protection of individual and other minority rights. The difference is that aboriginal peoples have unique rights and relationships with Canada that can only be fully articulated by identifying and defining areas of executive and legislative capacity over which aboriginal peoples, as the third order of government in Canada, would have authority.[9]

Success in obtaining this ambitious goal via the aboriginal constitutional reform process, which involved four first ministers' conferences in 1983, 1984, 1985 and 1987, proved, in the end, to be as elusive as in the earlier rounds. It was relatively easy, despite Quebec's absence, to obtain agreement on urgent matters pertaining to sections 35, the aboriginal rights clause, and 37(1), the aboriginal constitutional conference clause, of the Constitution Act, 1982. The latter was amended to allow for additional conferences beyond the one called for in 1983. Two additions were made to section 35: subsection (3), stating that in "subsection (1) 'treaty rights' includes rights that now exist by way of land claims agreements or may be so acquired"; and subsection (4), addressing the thorny gender equality issue by guaranteeing aboriginal and treaty rights in section 35(1) "equally to male and female persons."[10]

During the 1984 and 1985 conferences, the aboriginal organizations sincerely believed that given the necessary political will they could make some progress in convincing the first ministers "that the essence of defining and identifying aboriginal and treaty rights lay in providing for the self-government of aboriginal peoples."[11] The process was complicated by a change of government in 1984, a development that events would later show to be a major turning point in the process. At the 1985 conference, the Mulroney government favoured a severely watered-down compromise amendment package and shied away from discussing the substantive but complex issues pertaining to the recognition and implementation of aboriginal self-government, particularly where agreement with the provinces was involved.

One thing became increasingly apparent after 1985—the Mulroney government had a very different constitutional agenda. During the 1984 election campaign, as leader of the Conservative party, Mulroney had promised the Quebec electorate that he would do whatever he could to accommodate the Bourassa Liberal government's constitutional demands so that the Quebec government might sign the 1982 Constitution Act. During 1986, prior to the fourth and last aboriginal conference scheduled for the spring of 1987, Mulroney managed to get the provinces to agree to set aside all other constitutional matters until the difficult matter of Quebec's demands for participation was resolved. Both the premiers and the Prime Minister argued that the aboriginal organizations' demand for self-government could not be decided effectively without the Quebec government at the table. Despite the valiant efforts of the NCC to salvage the March 1987 conference with the help of a rolling draft sponsored by Nova Scotia and a federal draft amendment, the outcome was a foregone conclusion. "Momentum was lost and the meeting failed, to paraphrase Zebedee Nungak, in a glorious non-success."[12]

Yet, within a month, these same first ministers had agreed to the Meech Lake Accord, which accommodated not only all of Robert Bourassa's five demands but also those of the other premiers on a wide range of issues. As mentioned earlier, the aboriginal organizations were quick to respond in a joint letter to Prime Minister Mulroney. They all submitted briefs to and appeared before the Special Joint Committee, substantiating their contention that the Accord affected, directly and indirectly, aboriginal rights and aspirations. The thrust of their critiques was that the Accord, in both the process as well as substantive amendments, completely ignored the existence of Canada's aboriginal peoples. While they had no objection to Quebec gaining recognition as a distinct society, they rejected the two-nation conception of Canada and called for the constitutional recognition of aboriginal peoples as distinct societies that constitute a fundamental characteristic of Canada. They wondered why the undefined concept of distinct society was so readily acceptable to the first ministers, who had rejected the concept of aboriginal self-government just the month before on the grounds that it was too vague. They expressed concern that the constraints placed upon the federal spending powers by section 106A would enable the provinces to prevent aboriginal communities from gaining access to or administering their own social service programs under some form of self-government.[13]

It was the process, pertaining to both the new amendment formula and future constitutional meetings, that drew the strongest objections from the aboriginal organizations. From their perspective, the expansion of the unanimity formula to national institutions and the creation of new provinces would make the achievement of aboriginal self-government virtually impossible. Furthermore, the provincial veto would block any reform concerning aboriginal representation in either the House of Commons or the Senate. Most damaging to their constitutional aspirations was the failure of the Accord to renew section 37(1) of the Constitutional Act, 1982, which lapsed in April 1987. Section 37(1) had provided a unique and dedicated process of aboriginal conferences coupled with a range of flexible amending formulas for first ministers to negotiate the constitutional future of aboriginal peoples. Instead, under section 50 of the Meech Lake Accord, the aboriginal peoples would have to plead annually with the first ministers to get their unfinished business on the constitutional agenda. Once there, aboriginal constitutional proposals would have to compete with various provincial agendas and be subject to provincial veto. Finally, the aboriginal organizations considered that section 16 of the Meech Lake Accord did not provide adequate protection for aboriginal constitutional rights. Section 35 of the Constitution Act, 1982 and section 91(24) of the Constitution Act, 1867 were immunized only from the distinct society/linguistic duality clause of the Meech Lake Accord. Aboriginal groups, through a number of provinces, had lobbied hard for a without-prejudice clause applicable to the entire Accord. The NCC's subsequent appeal for companion resolutions, one of which would restore the dedicated aboriginal amendment procedure and thereby assure aboriginal participation in second-round conferences, also fell on deaf ears. This lack of success demonstrated a marked decline of the aboriginal organizations' political and moral influence among the first ministers and intergovernmental bureaucrats.[14]

Professor Tony Hall, a historian of Indian treaties and aboriginal activist, contends that the lack of success of aboriginal peoples in the politics of constitutional reform is fundamentally structural.[15] The aboriginal communities, which lack any constitutional recognition of their right and practice of self-government, cannot participate as equals in the dual process of bureaucratic and executive federalism. Professor Hall sees a clear historical pattern of provincial rights versus aboriginal rights, reaffirmed with a vengeance in the 1980s. This pattern began with the provincial governments' initial rejection of the aboriginal and treaty rights clause in 1981, continued with their subsequent persistent rejection of some form of aboriginal self-government in the four aboriginal conferences and ended with the premiers' virtual exclusion of the aboriginal organizations from the constitutional process in the Meech Lake Accord.

Confronted by the rising tide of this provincial rights movement, successive national governments have proven incapable of fulfilling their constitutional role of "advocate or defender of Aboriginal claims against the competing claims of provincial jurisdiction." In this context, the aboriginal organizations' struggle to derail the Canada Bill in Great Britain was both valid and useful. It drew the Canadian public's attention to the constitutional, political and moral significance of the special relationship that existed between the Crown and Canada's aboriginal peoples. Unfortunately, this heightened awareness had only a moderate impact on the first ministers during the four constitutional conferences on aboriginal issues. "The Aboriginal spokespeople," contends Hall, "had held their places at the negotiating table across from the White first ministers, but the elected representatives of Native groups still sat technically apart from the institutions of Canadian self-government." Once again, the structural problem of outsiders trying to negotiate with insiders prevented a successful outcome.

Tony Hall describes well the shock and dismay experienced by the aboriginal organizations at the announcement of the Meech Lake Accord, which, in their view, froze them out of all future constitutional discussions. Hall, like them, questions the double standard at work among the first ministers and decries the total victory of the provinces opposed to aboriginal self-government. In nearly all of its provisions, the Accord was a disaster for the aboriginal communities. The Mulroney government had totally forsaken its constitutional responsibilities towards Canada's aboriginal peoples. This brutal crushing of aboriginal constitutional aspirations, Hall contends, will further alienate aboriginal peoples from the mainstream of Canadian society and break the trust that was developing in the resolution of their many problems via the political process of negotiations. He foresees the emergence of "more strident forms of Aboriginal activism," involving passive and not-so-passive forms of civil disobedience. Ironically, a constitutional process that was supposed to bring about national reconciliation instead resulted in a deepening sense of malaise and mistrust among the aboriginal organizations and the people they represent.

There is a very strong relationship between Canada's northern territories and the aboriginal peoples. The aboriginal peoples comprise nearly one-third of the population of the Yukon and a majority of the population of the Northwest Territories. These are the only two jurisdictions in which aboriginal and non-native organizations exercise control over semi-autonomous local governmental institutions. Citizens of both the Yukon and the Northwest Territories have been working very hard to achieve, at some appropriate time in the future, full provincial status in Confederation.[16] They were, to put it mildly, incensed and outraged at the altered amending provisions of the Meech Lake Accord, which gave each and every province a veto over the territories' political and constitutional development and denied their communities representation on the Supreme Court and the Senate.

Sensing that this oversight and blatant injustice of the first ministers towards Canada's northern citizens was the Achilles' heel of the Meech Lake Accord, the Liberal-dominated Senate took quick action. The Senate Committee of the Whole, chaired by Gil Molgat, established, in August 1987, a Task Force on the Meech Lake Constitutional Accord and on the Yukon and the Northwest Territories. Its members heard eloquent and revealing testimony from hundreds of citizens and groups at public hearings held in Whitehorse, Yukon, and in Yellowknife and Iqaluit, Northwest Territories. The Task Force *Report* made recommendations that would ensure northerners' participation in appointments to the Senate and the Supreme Court and all future constitutional and economic conferences; require consent of the territory concerned for all boundary changes; eliminate the provinces from the process whereby the Yukon and Northwest Territories would obtain provincial status; recognize the aboriginal peoples as distinct societies; and add aboriginal and treaty rights and the question of self-government to the constitutional agenda outlined in the Accord.[17] These Task Force recommendations were an accurate reflection of the concerns and aspirations of all northern citizens. It was also very clear that these recommendations had the full and unqualified support of virtually every provincial and national aboriginal organization. Through it all, the first ministers remained undaunted and unmoved.

No single source can adequately reflect the anger and frustration of Canada's northern citizens over the Meech Lake Accord. Yet Tony Penikett, government leader and president of the executive council of the Yukon, was able to articulate in a very clear and eloquent fashion the central grievances and aspirations of Canada's most northern citizens.[18] He argues that the Meech Lake Accord represents a denial of fundamental justice for northerners because they cannot designate representatives to the Supreme Court and the Senate. Furthermore, the Accord signifies a fundamental breach of trust between the first ministers and the aboriginal organizations and the territorial governments. Despite a vigorous and determined northern lobby, the amending formula of the Constitution Act, 1982—seven out of ten provinces with fifty per cent of the population—was stipulated to apply to the creation of new provinces and the extension of provincial boundaries.

Up to that time, all new provinces entering Confederation had been created on a bilateral negotiating basis between the national government and the people of the territory seeking provincial status. In the 1983 Constitutional Accord on Aboriginal Rights, signed by all the first ministers except the premier of Quebec, it was agreed that repeal of section 42(1)(e) and (f) pertaining to the creation of new provinces and extension of provincial boundaries would be item four on the agenda for reform.[19] In 1987, the first ministers, seven of whom had signed the political accord, reneged on this political accord. Adding insult to injury, the first ministers then barred the door shut forever by applying the unanimity formula to the creation of new provinces and provincial boundary extensions. This constitutionalization of the semi-colonial status of the northern territories was accomplished without ever consulting their representatives. Little wonder, Penikett concludes, that Canada's northern citizens felt so outraged and humiliated.

Notes

1. For a copy of this letter to the Prime Minister, dated May 27, 1987, see the Assembly of First Nations' brief to and testimony before the Special Joint Committee of the Senate and the House of Commons on the 1987 Constitutional Accord, *Minutes of Proceedings and Evidence*, No. 9, August 19, 1987 (Ottawa: Queen's Printer, 1987): 49–68.
2. See the lengthy and excellent articles entitled "Indian Treaties" and "Native People" in *The Canadian Encyclopedia* (Second edition, Edmonton: Hurtig Publishers, 1988).
3. Douglas Sanders, "The Renewal of Indian Special Status," in Anne F. Bayefsky and Mary Eberts, eds., *Equality Rights and the Canadian Charter of Rights and Freedoms* (Toronto: Carswell, 1985): 529–539.
4. *Ibid.*, 539–550.
5. Douglas Sanders, "The Indian Lobby," in Keith Banting and Richard Simeon, eds., *And No One Cheered: Federalism, Democracy and the Constitution Act* (Toronto: Methuen, 1983): 326.
6. Douglas Sanders, "Prior Claims: An Aboriginal People in the Constitution of Canada," in Stanley M. Beck and Ivan Bernier, eds., *Canada and the New Constitution: The Unfinished Agenda*, Vol. 1 (Montreal: Institute for Research on Public Policy, 1983): 225.
7. Sanders, "The Indian Lobby," 301–309.
8. *Ibid.*, 309–324.
9. Louis Bruyere, "Aboriginal Peoples and the Meech Lake Accord," in William Pentney and Daniel Proulx, eds., *Canadian Human Rights Yearbook/ Annuaire canadien des droits de la personne, 1988* (Ottawa: Les Presses de l'Université d'Ottawa, 1989): 54.
10. *Ibid.*, 55; Sanders, "The Renewal of Indian Special Status," 555–560. Sanders derides the restriction of the gender equality clause to section 35(1) and asks the rhetorical question: "What does the membership in the *Indian Act* have to do with aboriginal and treaty rights?" (quote 558). Sanders concluded that it had very little, indeed, to do with non-treaty Indians.
11. Bruyere, "Aboriginal Peoples and the Meech Lake Accord," 56; see Makivik Corporation, representing the interests of Inuit of Northern Quebec and affiliate of ICNI, brief to and testimony before the Special Joint Committee, *Minutes of Proceedings and Evidence*, No. 14, August 27, 1987, 25–40.
12. Bruyere, "Aboriginal Peoples and the Meech Lake Accord," 57–58. See also Douglas Sanders, "An Uncertain Path: The Aboriginal Constitutional Conferences," in Joseph M. Weiler and Robin M. Elliot, eds., *Litigating the Values of a Nation: The Canadian Charter of Rights and Freedoms* (Toronto: Carswell, 1986).
13. Inuit Committee on National Issues, Métis National Council and Native Council of Canada, testimony before the Special Joint Committee, *Minutes of Proceedings and Evidence*: ICNI, No. 3, August 5, 1987, 23–32; MNC, No. 9, August 19, 1987, 28–48; NCC, No. 12, August 25, 1987, 95–120; see also note 1.

14. For a detailed discussion of the impact of the Meech Lake Accord on the 1982 aboriginal package and amending process, consult the NCC's testimony, given by its president Louis Bruyere, to the Special Joint Committee, *Minutes of Proceedings and Evidence*, No. 12, August 25, 1987, 98–102; and Bruyere, "Aboriginal Peoples and the Meech Lake Accord," 66–72.

15. See Tony Hall's statement, entitled "Closing an Incomplete Circle of Confederation," to the Special Joint Committee, *Minutes of Proceedings and Evidence*, No. 14, August 27, 1987, 57–73, A1–A8; and his "Self-Government or Self-Delusion? Brian Mulroney and Aboriginal Rights," *Canadian Journal of Native Studies/Revue canadienne des études autochtones*, 6, No. 1 (1986): 77–90.

16. Cf. Kenneth Coates and Judith Powell, *The Modern North: People, Politics and the Struggle Against Colonialism* (Toronto: James Lorimer, 1988).

17. Senate Task Force on the Meech Lake Constitutional Accord and on the Yukon and the Northwest Territories, *Proceedings*, No. 1, September 3, October 24–25, 1987; No. 2, October 27–28, 1987; No. 3, November 2, 1987; No. 4, March 1, 1988. (This fourth issue was released separately as the Task Force *Report*, dated February 1988.)

18. Tony Penikett, testimony before the Special Joint Committee, *Minutes of Proceedings and Evidence*, No. 15, August 31, 1987, 91–108; and his "The Future of the Northern Territories," *Canadian Parliamentary Review*, 11, No. 1 (Spring 1988): 4–6.

19. For a copy of this 1983 Constitutional Accord on Aboriginal Rights and Schedule of Amendments, see the Senate Task Force *Report*, 43–46.

TONY HALL

WHAT ARE WE? CHOPPED LIVER? ABORIGINAL AFFAIRS IN THE CONSTITUTIONAL POLITICS OF CANADA IN THE 1980s*

A new verb has entered the spoken language of some Native communi-ties in Canada, and especially those in the Yukon and Northwest Terri-tories: to meech. If one has been cheated or betrayed, one has been meeched.

The new verb makes Aboriginal humour of a development in Cana-dian history that introduces yet further major causes for Aboriginal dis-trust in the fundamental institutions of Canadian democracy. Aboriginal leaders registered this heightened distrust within weeks after the first ministers reached their accord at Meech Lake in April of 1987. George Erasmus, National Chief of the Assembly of First Nations, asserted in a press conference that the accord "reeks of racism." At the same con-ference John Amagoalik, an Inuit spokesperson, compared bitterly the noncommittal treatment afforded his people by the first ministers with their ready willingness to recognize Quebec in the Canadian constitu-tion as a distinct society. He commented: "What are we? Chopped liver?"[1]

The Meech Lake accord offended many Aboriginal people for a variety of reasons. The agreement stipulates a definition of "the funda-mental characteristic of Canada," for instance, that remains absolutely mute on the existence of distinct Aboriginal societies and Aboriginal languages in this country. While an assessment along these lines accounts partially for the virtually uniform negative response of Aboriginal leaders to Meech Lake, however, a fuller explanation requires consideration of the process that led up to the agreement.

It can fairly be said that before April of 1987 Aboriginal people were more closely involved than any other major constituency in Canada

---

* Paper written specifically for inclusion in this volume.

in the process to patriate and then elaborate the Canadian constitution. There is a good deal of irony in this development for technically Aboriginal peoples are without any constitutional means of directly influencing the evolution of Canadian self-government beyond the small measure of power they can collectively exert as regular citizens at the ballot box. More precisely, the Canadian constitution denies Aboriginal communities any explicit recognition of their own powers of self-determination let alone any entrenched provision for the specific expression of Aboriginal political will within the larger political institutions of provincial and federal governments. It was largely because of these significant structural problems in Canadian federalism that Aboriginal politics became so thoroughly and, often, so awkwardly intertwined with constitutional politics in Canada during the 1980s.

1. Aboriginal and Treaty Rights in the New Constitution

Aboriginal involvement in the development of the Canadian constitution became most intense in the weeks and months following the first ministers' meeting of November 5, 1981. As part of their price for supporting the patriation of the Canadian constitution with a Charter of Rights and Freedoms, several of the provincial premiers exacted federal consent to delete from the agreement a phrase declaring that ''the aboriginal and treaty rights of the aboriginal peoples of Canada are hereby recognized and affirmed.'' The provision, originally titled section 34, had been included in the federal government's patriation package largely as a result of the persuasiveness of the Inuit Committee on National Issues who worked closely with several NDP MPs and with Liberal MP Warren Allmand.[2]

More generally, the inclusion of section 34 in the original patriation package put forth unilaterally by the federal government reflected the heightening profile of Aboriginal affairs in national politics during the 1970s. Episodes like the Native occupation of the headquarters of the Department of Indian Affairs in 1973, and the confrontation between police and the Ojibway Warriors' Society at Anishinabe Park in Kenora in 1974, had forced awareness of Aboriginal frustrations on the wider Canadian public.[3] These frustrations were given compelling articulation by a new generation of Aboriginal spokespeople such as Harold Cardinal from Alberta[4] and Billy Diamond from Quebec. Moreover, the judgement of the Supreme Court of Canada on the Nishga case in 1973,[5] the controversy over Cree and Inuit land claims in the development of massive hydro installations in the James Bay watershed,[6] and Thomas Berger's inquiry into the possibility of building a Mackenzie Valley pipeline[7] had all resulted in raising the visibility of Aboriginal issues as a significant if ill-understood feature of Canadian federalism.

The inclusion of section 34 in the proposed text of the new constitution marked a fitting culmination of Aboriginal activism during the 1970s. Similarly, the removal of section 34 on the insistence of several provincial premiers marked an ominous introduction to the mean-spirited politics of the 1980s that would eventually see Aboriginal people so badly betrayed at Meech Lake.

The provincial effort to eliminate a positive affirmation of Aboriginal and treaty rights from Canada's supreme law clarifies one of the basic tensions in the constitution since the entrenchment of the British North America Act of 1867. Officials of provincial governments, who claim exclusive jurisdiction over natural resources, have consistently felt compelled to oppose any suggestion that Aboriginal groups within provincial boundaries can retain any claim based on Aboriginal rights to the possession of legally enforceable interests in their ancestral domains.[8]

The result has been a constitutional dynamic that almost automatically sets the assertion of provincial rights at the opposite extreme from the assertion of Aboriginal and treaty rights. In this uneven match of opposing constitutional interests, the federal government has an obvious balancing role to play as an advocate or defender of Aboriginal claims against the competing claims of provincial jurisdiction. One of the principal constitutional foundations of this protectorship function is section 91(24) of the BNA Act which assigns "Indians and land reserved for the Indians" as the legislative responsibility of the federal Parliament.

On the night of November 5, 1981, however, the federal government abdicated its constitutional role as the protector of Aboriginal interests against the hostile encroachment of provincial jurisdiction. A Supreme Court of Canada ruling had forced upon Pierre Trudeau the necessity of obtaining "a substantial measure" of provincial government support for his patriation package[9] and the interests of Aboriginal groups were just simply traded away as one of the means to gain the signature of nine provincial first ministers on a constitutional accord.

This dark episode in the history of the Canadian federation reveals much about the difficulty of securing constitutional protection for numerically weak and politically marginalized groups within the framework of federal–provincial relations. What mechanisms are there to discourage federal politicians from trading away the interests of Aboriginal groups, linguistic minorities and residents of the federal territories in order to gain support from political constituencies represented by provincial first ministers? The events of November 5, 1981, demonstrate the enormous pressure that can tempt federal officials to sacrifice the rights of the vulnerable in order to widen a political base by gaining approval from elected representatives of regional majorities. The danger posed by this unfortunate and ill-considered feature of the new constitution could hardly have been more damagingly realized than in the bargain struck by the eleven first ministers at Meech Lake five and a half years later.

As well, the events of November 5, 1981, renewed a pattern that has repeatedly been characterized by an intertwining of Aboriginal affairs with the politics of Quebec. For rather obvious reasons no sanction was sought for the constitutional deal from Premier Lévesque or from Aboriginal leaders. It was the decision to press forward without such sanction that became a major factor in setting Canada's constitutional agenda for the remainder of the 1980s. As the tumult surrounding the life and death of Louis Riel had demonstrated in the latter half of the nineteenth century, the logic of history has closely linked the fate of *les canadiens* and of Aboriginal people within Confederation.[10]

Within a matter of days a torrent of public criticism developed over the removal of section 34. On November 16, the anniversary of the execution of Louis Riel and the eight Indians who were hanged along with him, angry Native demonstrators laid a wreath at the Ottawa conference hall where the deal had been struck. Three days later there were mass demonstrations in nine cities across Canada. Indians in Vancouver occupied the Museum of Anthropology. Five thousand Native protestors assembled in Edmonton in front of the Alberta Legislature.[11] In Ottawa medal-clad Native war veterans of World Wars I and II—men who reminded Canadians of the large Aboriginal contingents that have unfailingly defended the country since the War of 1812—led the procession to Parliament Hill.

The outrage went far beyond Aboriginal communities. Letters denouncing the removal of section 34 poured into the offices of newspapers and elected officials. Mr. Justice Thomas Berger publicly chastised the federal government for "repudiating" its trust responsibility to Aboriginal people, an intervention that later resulted in his being pushed to resign from the British Columbia Supreme Court.[12] A caustic Premier Lévesque pointed to the deletion as evidence that English Canada is "hypocritically, fundamentally racist."[13]

This wave of public protest forced a response from the politicians. Section 34 was re-introduced into the patriation package but with a modification. The new provision, now titled section 35, recognized and affirmed *existing* Aboriginal and treaty rights. While Jean Chrétien argued in Parliament that the new word was innocuous enough, Aboriginal leaders did not believe him.[14] It seems they were right in their distrust. As subsequent developments would demonstrate there is ample evidence that the addition of "existing" was understood by most legal advisers to the federal and provincial governments as a check that would substantially diminish the force and scope of section 35 in the eyes of its ultimate judicial interpreters.

While the authors of the revised patriation package may have looked upon the word "existing" as a kind of secret constitutional weapon to undermine Aboriginal interests, the indignant public response to the first ministers' original overt assault on Native people is perhaps the finest moment in the short history of Canada's new constitution. The widespread dissent expressed by fair-minded Canadians of many backgrounds modestly advanced the process of transforming the new constitution from a rather esoteric project of politicians and bureaucrats to a people's declaration of national purpose.[15] Activists in the women's movement shared in this moment of achievement for they too forced revisions in the patriation package. Hence, while the first ministers in private negotiations showed no hesitation in diminishing protection for fundamental human rights, the subsequent mobilization of broad public involvement in the process of constitution making resulted in the formulation of a modestly better document. The lessons of this experience have obvious implications vis à vis the Meech Lake accord and the subsequent course of constitutional deliberations it has set in motion.

2.   The British Parliamentary Debate on the Canada Bill

The scene of the next major episode in the patriation of the Canadian constitution was the floor of the British House of Commons. An Indian lobby group had been coalescing in London, England, since July of 1979 when 300 chiefs and elders visited the capital in order to draw attention to their fear that Aboriginal interests would be undermined if Canada was to sever its remaining constitutional links with Great Britain.

In the perception of many Native people, the greatest protection of their Aboriginal rights lies in Indian treaties, agreements that linked Indian groups directly with the British Sovereign. Patriation of the constitution, the Indians reasoned, would compromise the integrity of their old constitutional relationship directly with the supreme custodian of Crown authority in the British Empire. The chiefs and elders wanted assurances that there would be no transfer of constitutional authority without specific guarantees of a future continuity with historic commitments made on behalf of the Crown to recognize and accommodate their peoples' special Aboriginal status.[16]

In December of 1980 the elected chiefs of Indian bands throughout Canada responded to the growing imminence of patriation by generating the Assembly of First Nations from their national organization, the National Indian Brotherhood. The Assembly was founded upon a Declaration of the First Nations, a seminal articulation of the basic constitutional principles governing Aboriginal law.[17] While Indian politicians in Canada struggled to develop a better framework for Indian political solidarity in Canada, the initiative in developing Aboriginal political strategies in London was largely taken over by the older and more firmly constituted provincial Indian organizations. The Indian Association of Alberta, the Federation of Saskatchewan Indians and the Union of British Columbia Indian Chiefs lobbied especially forcefully, if not always in a co-ordinated fashion, to place their concerns before British parliamentarians, the media and the public.[18] Moreover, the IAA led a judicial challenge to the patriation process, arguing that the transfer of authority could not take place without Indian consent. Although the Indians formally lost this challenge, Lord Denning's judgement on the case included a proviso that ''[n]o Parliament should do anything to lessen the worth'' of the ''rights and freedoms that have been guaranteed to [the Indians] by the Crown.''[19]

The IAA's judicial challenge slowed the process sufficiently for the Indians' concerns to receive a rather thorough hearing in the British House of Commons. Of the thirty hours of debate on the Canada Bill, twenty-seven (or ninety per cent of the time) were devoted to Indian matters![20]

The centrality of Indian concerns in the final phase of the patriation process points to the relative importance of Aboriginal affairs in the constitutional politics of Canada. Historic, moral and international obligations compelled some British parliamentarians to look beyond the federal–provincial component of Canadian federalism. They looked beyond a relatively closed, two-tiered system of government that has tended to reduce Aboriginal peoples to the political status of small ethnic minorities, or of disadvantaged Canadians or of mere interest groups. Rather, the final phase of patriation necessitated some reference to the very genesis of Crown sovereignty in the northern portion of North America. And this reference naturally drew attention to the prominence of Crown–Indian dealings in the geopolitical and constitutional arrangements that established a territorial basis for the development of the Canadian state.[21] The clarification of these issues in the British Parliament became an historic episode in a worldwide phenomenon that increasingly is casting the problems of indigenous peoples into international forums for want of appropriate domestic forums to address the claims of Aboriginality.[22]

Bruce George, a Labour MP, was the British parliamentarian who worked most undauntingly to bring the Indians' case before the House of Commons. He saw the Indians' London campaign as

> but one stage in a broader campaign that will embrace the United Nations and many international organizations. Indians in Canada will take their case not only to a domestic public but to an international public. [Other] Indians and aboriginal peoples throughout the world will do likewise.[23]

Repeatedly throughout the debate George returned to the concept that the difficulties faced by Indians in Canada are part of a larger international problem. He argued that

> The trouble with academics and politicians is that they tend to confine their conceptions and analyses of human rights to Argentinians, South Africans, Poles and Russians. We tend to forget people on whom has been perpetrated one of the greatest international crimes of modern history— the destruction of the ways of life of indigenous populations, not just in the Americas but in Australia, Africa and China.[24]

Many of the MPs who spoke against the Canada Bill or who spoke for the various proposed amendments premised their arguments on the need to oppose human rights violations and the corresponding need to advance the development of international law. When criticized for interfering in the internal affairs of Canada, one MP answered that he was just as entitled to criticize Canadian Indian policy as he was to criticize human rights violations in South Africa or El Salvador.[25] The recourse to international law and convention was most forcefully developed by Sir Bernard Braine, a Conservative backbencher who had visited Canada on the invitation of the NIB. He based his intervention particularly on the International Covenant on Civil and Political Rights, ratified by both Canada and Great Britain in 1976. Article 1 of the document states simply: "All peoples have the right to self-determination." The Canada Bill, asserted Sir Bernard, prevented Indian groups in Canada from realizing their right to self-determination. It was therefore appropriate to amend the Canada Bill so that the British government would not place itself in contravention of an international covenant it had ratified.[26]

For Braine and for many other MPs a major target for criticism was the word "existing" in section 35. Braine wondered aloud why the word was added by those same Canadian politicians who had earlier attempted the outright removal of the provision on Aboriginal and treaty rights. He said:

> Is the answer perhaps that the addition of the word "existing" draws the line as regards native claims to land and self-government within Canada's sovereignty? In this way the little that has been achieved in the past by native interests, the little that remains to them after a century's erosion of their acknowledged rights, this tiny remaining portion of what they are entitled to, will be fixed immutably by the constitutional law of Canada. No unsatisfied claims arising out of the past will any longer be entertained by the Canadian courts. Past injustices will go without impartial remedy.[27]

Braine's relentless critique of this feature of the Canada Bill included reference to the cynical irony of affirming the *existing* rights of those peoples that can be shown by virtually all statistical indicators to be among the poorest and most disadvantaged of all groups in Canada.[28] He observed:

> What are these existing rights? Do they merely amount to the right of these people to continue to live in future in their existing state of deprivation? Is the right of the native peoples to suffer continuing erosion of their land, their land titles and their treaty rights under the Acts of the

Canadian Parliament? Is it their right to stand still and meekly accept the discriminatory provisions of the Indian Acts, the Territorial Land Act and other measures which have so gravely prejudiced them?

Is it the right of Indian peoples to continue to live with existing discriminations against native education, languages, cultures and customs? Is it the right to continue with an existing unemployment rate of 68 per cent? Is it their right to continue with their existing life expectancy, which is 20 years lower than that of the average Canadian? Is it their right to continue to suffer the existing suicide rate, which is the most cruel measure of any community's despair, which is out of all proportion to the national average?[29]

Forty-two members voted for an amendment to remove the word "existing" from section 35 of the Bill before them. The vote against was 154. While there was never any question that the ruling Conservatives would assure the passage of the unamended Canada Act through Parliament, the margin of support for the Indian position was politically respectable.[30]

Other dissenting parliamentarians justified their criticism of the Canada Act on the grounds that it infringed upon old British constitutional practice that respected the consensual basis of treaty relations between Indian groups and the Crown. One member explained that though he did not wish "to offend Canada," if he passed the Bill in its present form he would "disregard the rights of Indian nations given under 83 treaties between them and the British Sovereign."[31] Another member, Donald Stewart, went further. He explained:

> Throughout the period of colonisation, the Crown recognized the principle of bilateral negotiations with the Indians. The principle was formalized by the enactment of the Royal Proclamation of 1763. More than 80 treaties were concluded between the various Indian nations and the Crown. Although the terms of the treaties varied, all recognized the sovereignty of the Indian nations and the consensual nature of future negotiations. That relationship was intended to endure the passage of time and of Governments.[32]

Most of the bitter frustrations that Aboriginal people would experience in the new constitutional order during the remainder of the 1980s were accurately predicted in the British parliamentary debate on the

Canada Bill. As the making of the Meech Lake accord would demonstrate so starkly, there was nothing in the amending formula to require any Aboriginal involvement whatsoever in the process of constitutional change, even when that change might bear directly on the interests of Native people. The Indians "have no feeling that they are to be consulted realistically in the future," said Braine, adding:

> nothing in the Bill gives the native peoples any power to resist change in their status which may be to their disadvantage. The point is that their consent to a further curtailment of their rights is not required.[33]

While the Canada Bill afforded Aboriginal delegates no means of voting directly in the process of constitutional change, the Act did nevertheless include provision for one first ministers' meeting at which Aboriginal spokespeople would be invited "to participate" in "discussions" concerning "the identification and definition" of existing Aboriginal and treaty rights. As it happened this provision, section 37, created the opening for the later extension of the process of constitutional deliberations until March of 1987.

The existence of section 37 did nothing to erase the cynicism of the Bill's critics. Enoch Powell wondered if it was not possible to interpret section 37 "that there are no rights at all unless and until they have been identified by such a conference."[34] Bruce George was more blunt. He said: "I doubt whether such a conference will be anything but a disaster for the native peoples." The Labour MP explained further:

> The aboriginal peoples are invited merely to participate in discussions. Their treaty and other rights are at stake, yet the parties that agreed to remove section 34 and which control the amending formula will effectively adjudicate at the conference under section 37 (2). That is a biased jury, if ever I came across one.[35]

Here was the heart of the matter. Indians were being asked to accept that their Aboriginal and treaty rights were susceptible to constitutional definition by provincial officials. And, as Bruce George explained, "although Indians have no great trust in the Federal Government the trust they have in most provincial governments is infinitely and justifiably less."[36] Had not the provincial first ministers demonstrated only two and a half months earlier the extent of their hostility to Aboriginal and treaty rights? The actions of the first ministers on November 5, 1981, were explained as follows by Sir Bernard Braine:

> It is evident that the provinces which have major control over the resources in Canada's federal constitution were not prepared to concede that any aboriginal and treaty rights to land should be entrenched. The truth was that the treaty and aboriginal rights which had been solemnly conferred on native peoples of Canada by the Crown and which are part of the constitution of Canada had been overlaid in the past by the Federal Parliament for the benefit of the provinces.
>
> The provinces were determined to ensure that a continuation of this process of erosion of native rights would not, if they could help it, be stopped dead in its tracks by constitutional entrenchment . . . . Aboriginal interests and treaty rights became a token in the course of negotiation.[37]

There was nothing in the patriation package to prevent the continued treatment of Aboriginal interest as a token to be traded away—a token that was traded away at Meech Lake as surely as it was traded away in the federal–provincial negotiations of November 5, 1981.

The culmination of the debate took place on February 23, 1982. "Surely we are talking to Canada itself," Sir Bernard Braine hoped.[38] Surely the final arbiter of the discussion's significance would be "the bar of world opinion."[39]

Bruce George summed up his analysis as follows:

> There is now a renaissance and a resurgence. These [Aboriginal] peoples governed themselves in the past and they did so more competently than they have been governed subsequently under the paternalistic Indian Acts in the United States of America and Canada. They now seek to play a greater part in the running of their own affairs. If Canada does not recognize that and continues paternalistically to treat native people as their wards, governing them by Indian Acts while only allowing them some limited self-government, Canada will face considerable problems in the future.[40]

He added: "It would be terrible if Canada's career abroad were to be besmirched by its treatment of people at home."[41]

3.   From the Aboriginal Rounds to the Quebec Round, 1983–1987

Between March of 1983 and March of 1987, four first ministers' conferences on Aboriginal affairs took place in Ottawa. Generally it can be said that the results of these televised two-day events fulfilled the dire expectations of the Indian lobbyists and their parliamentary colleagues in Britain. In a sense, the critics of the Canada Bill were sadly vindicated by the inconclusive results of the extended process to enunciate with greater clarity the place of Aboriginal people within Canadian federalism. The disappointment felt by Native people at the end of March 1987 turned to outright anger one month later when they learned of the quick and sweeping agreement reached privately by the first ministers at Meech Lake.

Since first sitting down at the negotiating table in 1983, Aboriginal leaders had faced consistent resistance to the assertion that there must be constitutional reform to enable Aboriginal governments to preserve and promote the distinct identity of Aboriginal peoples. Within a few weeks of the termination of this process, Native people learned that the kind of recognition denied to them was to be extended to the provincial citizens of Quebec. A double standard of stunning proportions had been revealed. It seemed almost as if the first ministers had used Native spokespeople to gain deeper insight into the nature of cultural pluralism in Canada, but then taken the fruits of this understanding to reform the political relationship among their own predominantly Euro-Canadian constituents. Indians, Inuit and Métis looking at the process could legitimately ask if the real message of Meech Lake was not something like the following: Distinct Society Status—Only Whites Need Apply.

While the process of patriation had briefly required Canadian governments to relate to Native groups almost as distinct constituent parts of the Canadian federation, Canada's political leaders had now reverted back to their old practice of treating Aboriginal people as marginalized interest groups. What political incentive was there to do otherwise? The kind of fears that had first driven the Indian chiefs and elders to Great Britain in 1979 now seemed to be coming true.

The series of first ministers' conferences on Aboriginal affairs, the first and as yet only *public* exercise of constitutional negotiation conducted in post-patriation Canada, began on a far more positive note than it ended. The major agreement reached in March of 1983 was to hold three similar meetings over the subsequent four years. All delegations also consented to add several new provisions to section 35. An amendment was specified, stipulating that existing or future land claims agreements constitute ''treaty rights.'' Moreover, a section was inserted, 35.1, detailing that before any amendment of sections 25 and 35 of the Constitution Act, 1982, or of section 91(24) of the Constitution Act, 1867, a constitutional conference must take place that includes representatives of the Aboriginal people. These are the three provisions of the Canadian constitution that refer specifically to Aboriginal people, that is, to Indians, Inuit and Métis.

Finally, the accord reached in 1983, which was proclaimed as part of the Canadian constitution in June of 1984, included a statement that Aboriginal and treaty rights ''are guaranteed equally to male and female persons.'' This amendment marked an important stage in a concerted campaign to eliminate gender discrimination from the Indian Act and from all aspects of Canadian Aboriginal policy.[42] Discussions around the issue, a major focus of feminist politics in Canada during the 1970s and early 1980s, featured significantly in both the 1983 and 1984 constitutional conferences. The passage in 1985 of Bill C-31, a revision of the federal Indian Act which stipulated that Indian status can be neither gained nor lost through marriage, finally eliminated one of the most blatant instruments of sexual discrimination from Canadian law.[43]

No further accords were reached at the constitutional conferences in 1984, 1985 and 1987. At the last meeting only two provincial first ministers, Premier Pawley and Premier Hatfield, could agree with the Aboriginal position that Aboriginal self-government is an inherent right. Premiers Getty, Vander Zalm, Devine and Peckford would not accept even a weakly worded amendment that would have made the powers of Aboriginal governments entirely subject to the outcome of negotiations between Native groups and provincial authorities. The position taken by these premiers during the negotiations is evidence of their belief that the inclusion of the word ''existing'' in section 35 relieved the provinces from any legal necessity of changing the status quo in the relationship between Native people and provincial governments. Such recalcitrance on the part of the premiers was bolstered by a legal opinion shared by many law officers in Canada, including the federal Minister of Justice, that section 35 is an ''empty box''—a constitutional provision that in its present form would not be broadly interpreted by the Courts. Only fuller definition through constitutional amendment will ''fill the box.''[44]

While there was a failure to achieve any consensus on the status of Aboriginal self-government in Canadian federalism, it could be argued that the first ministers' conferences between 1983 and 1987, all broadcast live by the CBC, had the ameliorative effect of raising public awareness of Aboriginal issues. Almost certainly this was the case. Virtually all the news media in Canada devoted abundant coverage to these internationally unprecedented events. But the coverage, of course, could sometimes distort as well as clarify. Perhaps, for instance, there was a deceptively reassuring message conveyed in some of the images disseminated by the media. These images pictured first ministers and representatives of four Aboriginal organizations—the Assembly of First Nations, the Native Council of Canada, the Métis National Council and the Inuit Committee on National Issues—debating issues as if on a basis of equality. But, of course, there was no equality in the process of constitutional amendment. Aboriginal representatives had no vote.

Across the airwaves of the nation beamed the voices of Aboriginal leaders—voices that often spoke with great eloquence and conviction about visions of Canada at once ancient and startlingly new. But their voices spoke to an unhearing body of Canadian constitutional law lacking any current capacity for direct responsiveness to the political will of distinct Aboriginal constituencies. The Aboriginal spokespeople held their places at the negotiating table across from the White first ministers, but the elected representatives of Native groups still sat technically apart from the institutions of Canadian self-government. In that strange twist lies an anomaly of history resulting from a long-institutionalized conspiracy to transform insider to outsider and outsider to insider. In that uncorrected twist lies an historic opportunity tragically missed at the constitutional conferences on Aboriginal affairs.

While the images conveyed by the conferences may have given some observers a distorted sense of the extent of Aboriginal participation in the re-negotiation of Canadian federalism, the experience clarified much for those Native leaders most directly involved in the meetings. The latter could legitimately ask if the process had ultimately been more directed at confirming the encroachment of provincial jurisdiction over their communities than it was at the elaboration of how Aboriginal and treaty rights are to be exercised in Canada. If there was anything positive in the experience for them it probably had most to do with the political activity generated between Aboriginal people and between Aboriginal groups.

The four Aboriginal organizations represented at the negotiating table walked away from the last conference having tabled a Joint Aboriginal Proposal for Self-Government.[45] The degree of consensus represented by this document marks a significant political achievement by the Aboriginal leadership who had to overcome many obstacles in the way of unity. For instance, the organizations representing the Métis and non-status Indians, people whose Aboriginality had long gone largely unrecognized by governments in Canada,[46] stood to gain from almost any concession. Nevertheless they stood firm with the AFN. And the Indians and the Inuit too were able to hold common strategic ground. At a debriefing session after the 1987 conference, Zebedee Nungak, the young trilingual Inuit spokesperson who gave such compelling articulation to his people's frustrations and aspirations, described his part in the making of Aboriginal solidarity as the greatest single achievement of his political career.[47]

While the Aboriginal organizations that took part in the process were successful in working together, the conferences stimulated a good deal of sometimes divisive debate among registered Indians throughout Canada. After 1985 the provincial Indian organizations in Saskatchewan and Alberta withdrew from the process citing the inability of the AFN to represent their interests adequately. The westerners created a new organization, the Prairie Treaty Nations Alliance. The leadership of the PTNA sought their own separate seat at the first ministers' negotiating table. This split added a new crack in an already-fractured situation among the Indians.

Since 1983 the Coalition of First Nations had represented those Indians who wanted no part in the first ministers' conferences on Aboriginal matters as set in motion by section 37. The core group of the CFN had begun to coalesce among some of the Indians involved in the British parliamentary debates on the Canada Bill. As Bruce George told the British House of Commons in February of 1982:

> Many native groups say that if the legislation goes through they will play no part in the bogus conference, which will be stacked against them, and where their rights, far from being extended, are likely to be diminished.[48]

Given the position of the CFN,[49] then, the AFN's involvement in the conferences marked something of a vote of confidence in the willingness of Canada's political leadership to negotiate in good faith. In this sense, the AFN represented a more moderate school of Indian political strategy. Moreover, once seated at the negotiating table, the AFN's leadership had to contend with the problem of representing a variety of Indian groups divided by language, region, wealth, and the fact that some groups have treaties and others do not. The task was a formidable one, especially when facing first ministers who, with the exception of the Prime Minister, can devote their entire energies to representing the interests of their regionally defined constituencies. The lack of a suitable mechanism in this federal–provincial forum for the realistic expression of Indian diversity added yet a further distorting element to the proceedings.

The basic failure of the conferences on Aboriginal matters tends to strengthen the arguments of those Indians who saw the process from its inception as "bogus." The peak of their protest denouncing direct provincial involvement in Indians' historic relationship with the Crown occurred during the 1985 conference when several hundred Indian demonstrators assembled on Parliament Hill. Leading the march up towards the Parliament Buildings were several Indian war veterans carrying the Union Jack and the United Nations flag, symbols which evoke accurately the fundamental principles of the Coalition of First Nations.

By 1987 those Indian leaders taking part in the constitutional conferences were also orienting their political strategies increasingly back towards international forums. In the months before the conference the Crees covered by the James Bay and Northern Quebec Agreement succeeded in gaining non-governmental organization status at the United Nations. On the basis of this status the Crees invited Professor Erica-Irene Daes, Chairperson of the United Nations Working Group on Indigenous Populations, to attend the 1987 conference as an official observer. Attending the conference along with Professor Daes was Gudmundur Alfredsson, President of the Human Rights Centre in Geneva, Switzerland.[50]

There were further international ramifications surrounding the 1987 conference on Aboriginal affairs. These were set in motion by Prime Minister Brian Mulroney. He remarked to reporters after visiting the Pope at the Vatican: "there is no comparison at all between difficulties faced by our aboriginal peoples and the system of evil that exists in South Africa."[51] His comments led to a bizarre chain of events that saw a highly publicized visit to the Peguis Indian Reserve in Manitoba by the South African Ambassador to Canada.[52] The moves of the maverick Indian chief responsible for the visit were countered by the James Bay Cree and the AFN whose representatives held formal meetings with representatives of the African National Congress in the week before the first ministers' conference of March 1987. The process to clarify the constitutional relationship between Aboriginal groups and Canadian federalism was broken off,[53] therefore, in a manner that holds clear long-term implications for Canada's relationship with the wider international community. So too can the Meech Lake accord be viewed in the light of the same international considerations.

4. Aboriginal People and the Meech Lake Accord: Critical Perspectives

The scope of the first ministers' unanimous accords formulated at Meech Lake and the Langevin Block, and the short duration of the negotiations, shocked many Aboriginal people. The "blow" was especially "tremendous" for the Native leaders that were closest to the previous negotiations.[54] They felt they had been duped—that the March meeting had been an "orchestrated failure" to clear the way for the culmination of the bigger deal at Meech Lake. In the *Bulletin* of the Assembly of First Nations, George Erasmus was reported as having said that the Prime Minister and Premiers "cooked up" the basis of their accord the previous November, and that they "never intended to come to an agreement on Aboriginal rights." Chief Erasmus' comments appear in a story under the title "Constitutional Accord Makes for Disaster."[55]

After four years of being repeatedly lectured by White officials that nothing new could be put into the constitution until exhaustive negotiations clarified all the implications of the added language, Native people learned that the first ministers were unwilling to apply these same standards to themselves in their own private dealings. Hundreds of lines of dense constitutional language of the most significant kind were suddenly unveiled and presented as a seamless web of compromise that could not be changed.

The federal government immediately began advertising the accord as a constitutional fait accompli. A flyer was circulated throughout the country in the mailing of baby bonus cheques, for instance, informing Canadians that "[t]he Accord completes the process of constitutional renewal that began in 1981 . . . . The 1987 Constitutional Accord concludes our evolution to nationhood in a way that respects the traditions of our country and its people."[56] This kind of pronouncement was hardly calculated to instill confidence in Native people that the new constitution would ever become a vehicle through which they might realize their unfulfilled hopes of attaining a measure of justice and security for their posterity.

Hence, while the first ministers' abandonment without resolution of formal negotiations on Aboriginal matters seemed like a setback for Aboriginal aspirations, news of the Meech Lake accord left Native leaders feeling far more seriously isolated from the process of constitutional renewal. The accord, it seemed perfectly clear, would have the effect of closing off permanently so many possibilities for future movement towards constructive reform. "We could not believe that [the first ministers] were doing that to us," testified George Erasmus.[57]

But remarks made by Premier Don Getty in Ottawa on June 1st, the day before the first ministers reassembled at the Langevin Block to work their Meech Lake document into a legal text, could only confirm Native peoples' worst suspicions about what the accord held in store for them. Alberta's premier as much as proclaimed that with Meech Lake his provincial government was slamming the door on the possibility of making any future constitutional compromises in the area of Aboriginal rights. *The Edmonton Sun* reported his comments as follows:

> Getty said the recent First Ministers' meeting on aboriginal rights is a perfect example of the constitutional unfairness that could drive Alberta to consider separation.
>
> The premier said if Alberta had been forced to accept entrenchment of native rights in the Constitution, separatism would have been seriously considered.
>
> "We would have gone home and talked about maybe having to pull out of the bloody country. I have never thought you go about changing Canada by having 50 per cent of the people dominate the other 50 per cent," the Alberta Premier said here last night . . . .
>
> Getty said an example of why Alberta insists that change take place occurred at the March 26 meeting on whether to guarantee native rights in the Constitution.
>
> At the meeting, Mulroney and the premiers backing constitutionally guaranteed native rights tried to use the current [amending] formula to "bludgeon" Alberta, B.C. and Newfoundland into supporting them, Getty said.
>
> The bid failed, but Getty was adamant last night he fears a recurrence unless the changes proposed by the Meech Lake pact are signed, sealed and delivered at today's meeting.[58]

It is clear that from Premier Getty's perspective the rights and interests of Albertans generally are diametrically opposed to the rights and interests of Aboriginal people. He has no doubt about who must prevail. Similarly, he leaves little doubt that his interest in signing the Meech Lake documents had more to do with his desire to contain recognition of Aboriginal claims than to affirm the distinct character of Quebec society.

The provisions at the heart of the Meech Lake accord that define Quebec as a distinct society, and that would empower the government of Quebec to preserve and promote the distinct identity of that province, drew sharply negative response from a number of Native commentators.[59] It was galling for them to see such ready willingness among the first ministers to afford Quebecers the same kind of recognition that had been withheld from Native groups. "How can the distinctness of Quebec people be explicitly recognized following the continual denial of aboriginal rights?" asked Haida leader Miles Richardson.[60]

To make Quebec the one and only society in Canada that could be defined in the constitution as "distinct" seemed like a distortion of history and a misrepresentation of present realities. Aboriginal people, some of whom still speak Aboriginal languages that are often uniquely distinct to this country, felt themselves once again brushed aside by Euro-Canadian politicians whose respect for cultural pluralism seemed to begin and end with acknowledgment of their own major linguistic division. The fact that the accord would entrench the French and English languages as the exclusive expression of "the fundamental characteristic of Canada" added weight to Aboriginal peoples' contention that the Meech Lake accord symbolically confirmed their exclusion from the key theatres of Canadian public life. The exclusion was one that might eventually find strong reflection in the course of Canadian jurisprudence and in the institutional design of Canadian self-government.

The "distinct society" provision would seem even more inequitable if it proved that the language and the legal thinking behind the innovation were actually derived from previous unrealized efforts to define more precisely the relationship between Native people and the institutions of Canadian federalism. There is evidence, however, to suggest that this indeed may be the case. In the British parliamentary debates on the Canada Bill in 1982, for instance, Sir George Braine explained:

> The Native people of Canada are ethnically and culturally distinct peoples who deserve a separate status within Canada . . . . A greater degree of self-government will achieve for them the most important objective, which is the continuation in future generations of their distinct identity.[61]

In his questioning of George Erasmus in the Joint Committee of the Senate and House of Commons on the 1987 Constitutional Accord, Liberal MP Keith Penner expressed his belief that the idea for the "distinct society" provision originated in the key recommendation of the parliamentary report on Indian Self-Government tabled in 1983.[62] Penner, who was Chairperson of the Committee that produced the report, described the intensity of the debate leading to the decision to advocate that "Indian First Nation governments would form a distinct order of government in Canada."[63] The key phrase in the accord about the Quebec government's powers to "preserve and promote" the province's distinct identity could well have been borrowed directly from section 21(i) of the Cree–Naskapi (of Quebec) Act, legislation of the Parliament of Canada passed in 1984 to implement some features of the James Bay and Northern Quebec Agreement. The germane sections empower Cree and Naskapi Indian band governments "to promote and preserve the culture, values and traditions of the Crees or Naskapis." These powers were granted in recognition that "each band's people are distinct and the culture, values and traditions which make them distinct are of concern to them in their daily functions and activities."[64]

Regardless of whether or not the "distinct society" concept originates in the politics of Aboriginal affairs, the judges that would ultimately be called upon to interpret the new legal language would probably be compelled to study the constitutional use of the word "distinct" as it has historically been used by Crown officials in relationship to North American Indians. The case, Mohegan Indians v Connecticut colony (1749), for instance, might be consulted. The Privy Councillors who rendered judgement ruled that the Mohegans together constituted a distinct jurisdiction from the colony.

> The Indians, though living amongst the king's subjects in these countries, are a separate and distinct people from them, they are treated with as such, they have a polity of their own, they make peace or war with any nation of Indians when they think fit, without control from the English.
>
> It is apparent the Crown looks upon them not as subjects but as a distinct people, for they are mentioned as such throughout Queen Anne's and his present majesty's commission by which we now sit.[65]

As Native leaders were quick to point out, the problem of constitutionally designating a particular constituency as a distinct society, or of specifying a definition of the fundamental characteristic of Canada, is that those peoples not directly covered by the legal provisions are implicitly relegated to the periphery of Canadian statecraft.

At the Langevin Block meeting the first ministers added a provision titled section 16 to the Meech Lake accord. It stipulated that nothing in the "fundamental characteristic of Canada" section affected those parts of the constitution specifically mentioning Aboriginal people or multiculturalism. Rumour has it that Premier Howard Pawley of Manitoba demanded this protection for Aboriginal people while Premier David Peterson, pressured especially by the large Italian-Canadian community in Toronto, sought to defend multiculturalism. A more cynical view would be that section 16 was added as a means to avert any court challenge to the Meech Lake accord on the grounds that it transgressed the spirit and intent of section 35.1, an amendment to the Constitution Act, 1982.

The addition of section 16 aroused ire in several quarters. It worried women's groups whose leaders logically asked why the provisions on gender equality in the Charter of Rights and Freedoms had not also been exempted from the "distinct society" section of the accord. Some feminists saw in the first ministers' actions a constitutional change that would place women at the bottom of "a hierarchy of rights." And Aboriginal groups saw little in section 16 to ease their anxieties. The first ministers once again seemed to be acting on behalf of Native people without including them in the process. Moreover, by grouping the provisions on Aboriginal rights together with the provisions on multiculturalism, the first ministers seemed to be throwing Native people into the same constitutional pot as ethnic minorities. Native people justifiably reject most government efforts to deal with them through the ideological and administrative channels of multiculturalism, a vehicle most readily directed at the cultural requirements of newer Canadians whose first language is neither French nor English.[66]

Section 16 can be criticized further because of the deeper assumptions its inclusion seems to reflect.[67] By describing Native people as separate and apart from the effects of the "fundamental characteristic" section of the accord, there is the symbolic suggestion that Aboriginal groups are not to be included in the dynamic core of Canada. The provision, therefore, gives new articulation to old attitudes informed by a view that Aboriginal cultures are largely unadaptable; they are seen as static, even primitive clumps of humanity that are curious anachronisms in the modern world. Unfortunately, there is really nothing in the Meech Lake accord to give any assurance that its authors have rid themselves of such damaging assumptions long engendered, among other causes, by the way Canadian history has been taught.[68]

While section 16 speaks of isolating Aboriginal peoples from the effects of that part of the accord defining Canada's fundamental characteristic, there is nothing to exclude Native groups from the many other provisions of the Meech Lake documents. The accord's section on national shared-cost programmes, for instance, has important implications for Indians living within provincial boundaries. If a provincial government was to opt out of such a programme with compensation, as the accord would entitle it to do under certain conditions, what would be the impact on Indian bands in the province? Could these Native people continue to participate in the national programme or would they be tied to the decision of the provincial legislature? The Meech Lake accord is mute on the question, an issue that clearly would be of crucial significance for the future of Aboriginal governments.

Moreover, the spending formula outlined in the accord would entrench a structure without any room for developing Aboriginal governments to make their influence felt, however modestly, in this important field of national decision making. The same could be said of virtually all aspects of the accord. In the area of immigration, in the sections dealing with the appointment of Senators and Supreme Court judges and in the provisions for reform of the key federal institutions of national self-government, Meech Lake is constructed as if Aboriginal nationalities exist outside the democratic structures of Canada. Furthermore, in virtually every facet of its design, Meech Lake would set in motion a transfer of powers from the federal government to the provincial governments.[69]

If the unfolding of Aboriginal politics during the 1980s demonstrates any consistent lesson, it is the following: Aboriginal peoples who currently lack explicit recognition of their own inherent powers of collective self-government must continue to rely heavily on a strong and assertive federal authority to defend and assert Aboriginal claims against the counterclaims of provincial jurisdiction. The Meech Lake accord reflects a failure on the part of Prime Minister Mulroney to live up to this responsibility just as Prime Minister Trudeau yielded similarly in the negotiations of November 5, 1981. What must now be understood about Meech Lake, moreover, is that it would seriously incapacitate the federal government from ever again effectively fulfilling the Crown's old obligations to be vindicator and protector of the Aboriginal interest in Canada.

Meech Lake's yielding of federal prerogatives is nowhere so readily apparent as in the provision that would require unanimous consent of provincial legislatures to reform the rules governing democratic representation in the House of Commons and the Senate. The symbolism of this provision is that the federal government is created out of the deeper constitutional roots of provincial governments, each of which retains a veto power over how Canada's Parliament is structured. It is almost certain that this veto power would be employed by one or more provincial legislatures if ever there was a move towards modest reform of the House of Commons or the Senate to create a few entrenched places for the entry of elected officials primarily accountable to Aboriginal constituencies in various regions of the country. Without such an innovation, how is there ever to be a responsible integration of Aboriginal governments with the larger democratic institutions of Canadian self-government?

The fate that the Meech Lake accord would deal the residents of the Northwest Territories and the Yukon demonstrates a similar example of the results that flow from abandonment of the federal prerogative.[70] Control over the constitutional future of these federal territories was simply traded away to the premiers of B.C., Alberta and Saskatchewan largely so that their governments could gain a new political lever to regulate the northward development of provincial hinterlands into the arctic. This factor probably also figured in the bargaining strategy of Premier Bourassa of Quebec whose political career has largely been built on advancing the cause of northern development.[71]

The other side of the new provincial veto powers regulating if, when and how the federal territories become provinces is that territorial citizens are correspondingly blocked from having any formal vote in this same process. Of all the accord's transgressions, this feature is the most overt example of how the deal would place the greatest burden of ''Canadian unity'' on the most effectively disenfranchised elements of the citizenry. Native people, who still constitute a large percentage of the electorate in the federal territories, face double jeopardy from the accord, especially now that the government of Quebec seems to have joined the side of the assassins of Louis Riel.

5. After Meech Lake

The closing off of formal constitutional talks with Aboriginal delegates followed by the affrontive Meech Lake accord added weight to an already-heavy burden of frustration and alienation that too often comes by virtue of being a Native person in Canada. While the articulation of the new constitution had been seen as an ominous development in some Native circles, a significant portion of Aboriginal people had gotten behind their more optimistic spokespeople. They chose to hold to the hope that more equitable arrangements could be reached for their people through political efforts to elaborate Canada's fundamental laws; they had counted their vote on the side of confidence in the goodwill of Canadians as the nation embarked on its first exercise of full self-government, finally cut free from the old imperial structures of the Mother Country. But now that hope and that optimism too, however fragile, were undermined by the stark suggestion that for Aboriginal people Canada's new constitution had merged into the familiar old stream of broken promises. During the late 1980s tempers flared and tension mounted at a number of flashpoints of confrontation.

A catalyst for the re-emergence of more strident forms of Aboriginal activism, reminiscent of the rawer kinds of protests that took place in the early 1970s, was the Olympic torch run sponsored by Petro-Canada. During the autumn of 1987 and the winter of 1988 small groups of Native people and their supporters across Canada met the procession of runners carrying the Olympic torch to the 1988 Calgary Winter Games.[72] While the demonstrations were in the first instance to show solidarity with the Lubicon Crees' efforts to gain an Indian reserve for themselves in northern Alberta, the range of expressed grievances quickly widened. As the run proceeded the protesters replaced Petro-Canada's slogan of "Share the Flame" with "Share the Shame."

While the Lubicon struggle became something of a rallying point for the broader movement to affirm the human rights of Aboriginal people in Canada, the long, unnaturally hot summer of 1988 saw Aboriginal groups in many localities giving physical expression to their grievances. At Kahnawake, Quebec, RCMP officers and arms-bearing Mohawks only barely held back from violent confrontation over clashing interpretations of tax laws governing the sale of American cigarettes on the reserve.[73] At Goose Bay in Labrador, Innu Indians held protest demonstrations on the runway of the jet fighter base there, asserting their unceded Aboriginal interest in lands made less fruitful because of the destructive effects on wildlife of low-level jet training. In Northern Ontario, members of the Teme-Augama Anishinabai Band set up a blockade to stop the building of a logging road through the heart of their ancestral lands.[74] Their action marked a new phase of their fifteen-year-old court action to gain recognition as a distinct Indian band that has never signed a treaty covering its traditional hunting territories.[75]

Gary Potts, the erudite Chief of the Teme-Augama Anishinabai, announced the blockade from the steps of the Ontario Legislature during the last day of the Toronto Economic Summit. Among the speakers sharing the podium with Chief Potts were Aboriginal leaders engaged in most of the major hot spots of tension involving Aboriginal assertion of rights to land and jurisdiction. Haida leader Miles Richardson spoke of his people's struggle to protect with environmentalists the virgin forests of the South Moresby region in British Columbia. Also presented were Lubicon Chief Bernard Ominayak, Kahnawake Chief Joe Norton,

Inuit leader John Amagoalik and George Erasmus, National Chief of the AFN. The intent of bringing together these individuals was clearly to reveal the unifying patterns that make national issues of the various local struggles, to demonstrate Aboriginal willingness to stand together in more strident forms of activism, and to assert the various arguments in a context where the implications for Canada's international reputation became evident. As George Erasmus asserted from the steps of Queen's Park, Indians for a long time

> thought that reason was going to work. That kind of politics doesn't work in Canada. We must change our actions. We can't change theirs until we change ours . . . .[76] We are a people with tremendous patience but that patience is stretched so thin we must try other kinds of activities.[77]

These demonstrations of Aboriginal political will were made against a background of a truly appalling human tragedy that sets Native people at the extreme end of virtually every index of social and economic dislocation in Canada. While the last two decades have seen the entry of a small core of Native people into the middle class, the largest number of Indians, Inuit and Métis still lack any grasp of the levers that regulate the engines of economic productivity in Canada. In many northern communities in particular there has been little success, if not outright backward movement, in mitigating the ravages of alcohol abuse, drug abuse and family violence. Statistics on the suicides of Native youths and on the incarceration of Native people—four to seven times the national average—reveal absolutely unconscionable levels of inequity.

Against this background where police, courts, jails and social workers have become major regulators of the relationship between many Native people and the Canadian state, a series of episodes in the late 1980s suddenly placed a public spotlight on the tremendous suffering wrought by bias in the criminal justice system.[78] The inquiry into the wrongful conviction for murder of Nova Scotian Micmac Donald Marshall, the exposé on the woefully ill-managed investigation that shielded the murderer of Helen Betty Osborne for almost two decades, the killing by a policeman's bullet of J.J. Harper in the streets of Winnipeg,[79] and the alleged abuse and neglect by Hull police of accident victim Minnie Sutherland[80] each made haunting statements about the kind of mistreatment too often afforded Native people by officers of the law in Canada.

Given the proven propensity of some of Canada's first ministers to deal with Aboriginal groups as constitutional misfits ill adapted for either their own self-government or for direct participation in the broader exercise of Canadian self-government, it is fair to ask if the problems of law enforcement in the streets are connected to the difficulties in law making at the highest level. What signals are the law makers sending the law enforcers about the need to respect the individual and collective human rights of Native people in Canada? Smokey Bruyere, President of the Native Council of Canada, had little doubt about the answer in the autumn of 1988. He charged that the Meech Lake accord has "revived the worst prejudices of colonialism." He continued:

> Native people are furious and frustrated. And as the years go by, native people will decide there is no hope or worth to the constitutional reform process. They will decide on more direct action.[81]

Bruyere's remarks reflect the anxiety shared by many Native people that the best part of their precious political energies over the previous decade had been expended in rather fruitless dialogue with predominantly unhearing government officials. The experience had forced on Aboriginal observers recognition of the fundamental absence of will on the part of the country's political leadership to confront seriously the underlying structural problems in the federal system that so consistently seem to hold Native groups at the edges of the major forums of Canadian political, economic and social life. Perhaps the most macabre symbol of the renewed thrust to marginalize the Native agenda for change was Meech Lake's replacement of Aboriginal issues with the subject of fish as one of two priorities for future first ministers' conferences. The fact that the leaders of the federal Liberal and NDP parties would not make their support for Meech Lake conditional even on amendment of this particularly offensive element of the agreement revealed to Native people once again how easily their interests can be traded off by national politicians intent on courting the support of larger, more cohesive and more influential constituencies.

The most disturbing commentary on the possible consequences that might flow from the failures in negotiation was delivered by George Erasmus in Edmonton at the 1988 annual meeting of the AFN. As was widely reported in the press,[82] he addressed the assembled chiefs as follows:

Canada, we have something to say to you—we have a warning for you. We want to let you know that you're playing with fire. We may be the last generation of leaders that is prepared to sit down and peacefully negotiate our concerns with you. Canada, if you do not deal with this generation of leaders, then we cannot promise that you are going to like the kind of violent political action that we can just about guarantee the next generation is going to bring to you.

Were Chief Erasmus' words too strong? Did he not overstate the extent of the absence of progress in negotiations? After all, had not the 1980s seen the emergence of Aboriginal issues to unprecedented heights of visibility in national politics? Does not this fact alone vindicate the process even if there has been very little concretely to show for all the high-profile talks between Aboriginal leaders and the first ministers?

These questions, of course, defy the possibility of categoric response. A possible index of the relative status of Aboriginal issues in national politics, however, was the televised leaders' debates leading up to the federal election of November 1988. A reporter from Global TV drew the leaders into a discussion of Aboriginal affairs during the last three minutes of a six-hour event composed of three debating hours in French and three in English. Like the legal text of the Meech Lake accord itself, the televised debate reveals a political view of Aboriginal affairs as a kind of afterthought to be briefly considered once the more pressing concerns of the day are addressed. In spite of how integrally Aboriginal affairs impinged into the relatively new forum of constitutional politics during the 1980s, then, it is striking how marginal Aboriginal matters remained in the more familiar theatres of national decision making.

A related argument that could be advanced in defense of the process is the fact that the first ministers' meeting on Aboriginal affairs did succeed in introducing the concept of Aboriginal self-government, a novel idea to many at the beginning of the 1980s,[83] into the general currency of political exchange in Canada. Even if the concept was not explicitly introduced into the constitution, Canadians were made more familiar with the notion that Native peoples should have a larger say in determining their own collective futures within Canada. Of course a complicating factor is the vast range of political options that the term "Aboriginal self-government" can be employed to describe.

On the one hand the phrase can describe the transformation of Indian reserves into municipal-like structures whose citizens assume delegated responsibilities from the higher authority of the federal Parliament or provincial legislatures. The agreement concluded in 1988 covering the Sechelt band in British Columbia is of this type. At the other end of the spectrum is the idea of Aboriginal self-government as a distinct or third order of government in Canada. The Sechelt model sees Aboriginal self-government as a right created by Parliament—as a ''contingent right''—while the latter is founded on an understanding that treats Aboriginal self-determination as an inherent right rooted in the continuity of Aboriginal peoplehood from a time predating the existence of Canada.

Not surprisingly, government officials in Canada tend overwhelmingly to see the future of Aboriginal self-government more along the lines of the Sechelt model, while most Aboriginal leaders feel the responsibility to hold to the position that they represent peoples who retain the inherent right of self-determination—a right that must never be bargained away. Between 1983 and 1987 a process of first ministers' meetings developed that began to clarify the tensions between these different conceptions. The ground was being prepared for a political compromise that would establish a workable basis for Aboriginal self-determination within the framework of Canadian federalism. In March of 1987, however, Prime Minister Brian Mulroney unilaterally terminated that unfulfilled process with no provisions to continue the negotiations at some later date, or within an alternative political context.

While this termination held the possibility for continuing the process in uncertain abeyance, the terms of the Meech Lake accord seemed drastically to reduce the range of latitude within which future compromise could take place on the crucial issue of Aboriginal self-government. Basically, the accord advanced a vision of a Canadian state without the structural capacity to accommodate the inclusion of a distinct order of Aboriginal government. Instead, the accord was based on an idea of Canada as a pact between the two major linguistic groups and between ten regionally defined distinct societies. Within this rigid framework, with each province gaining veto power over the structural reform of federal institutions, what room would be available for the future expression of Aboriginal creativity in political, economic and cultural terms?

The Meech Lake accord allowed Native people little prospect that their Aboriginal governments would ever attain recognition as part of the fundamental characteristic of Canada. Instead a hidden agenda of Meech Lake seemed to be that Aboriginal governments must always be held to the status of a junior order of government with powers derived from the higher authority of federal–provincial structures. For Native people seeking to break free of the legacy of colonialism, what real progress was there to behold in such a prospect?

Of course all these arguments could be turned on their heads if the Meech Lake accord was significantly to advance contemplation among thoughtful Canadians of the parallel requirements that should fall on governments to promote the distinct identity of Aboriginal groups and of the French-speaking minority in the northern portion of North America. It should be no more acceptable to abandon the former to a kind of cultural laissez-faire than it would be to dismiss the historic responsibility to advance the vitality of the French fact in Canada. And yet by leaving Aboriginal governments as shadowy entities in Canadian constitutional law, and by disavowing any constitutional duty to preserve let alone to promote distinct Aboriginal societies, the authors of the Meech Lake accord leave Native groups stranded in inarticulated twilight zones of institutionalized marginalization. A particular difficulty imposed on Native people by these circumstances is the virtual impossibility of establishing a stable constitutional basis for the development of a distinct national system of Aboriginal education. Especially pressing is the need for a strong network of schools to reverse the tragically rapid process of Aboriginal language loss;[84] to promote instead a national plan for Aboriginal language renewal.[85]

The failure of Canadian politicians to find workable constitutional adaptations to deal with these problems, and the more general failure in the collective imagination to comprehend Aboriginal self-government as a strengthening feature of a renewed pluralistic federalism, only advance the diffusion of Aboriginal affairs into international forums. Rather than setting a high standard for the world in the treatment of indigenous societies, Canada is instead developing a reputation for human rights violations in this emerging field of international law. If the assessment of Meech Lake's flaws clarifies this current failure in Canada's federal system, then the formulation of the accord may have served a constructive purpose after all.

The importance of finding precisely correct constitutional language to illuminate the ideals that should inform relationships between individuals, groups and governments in Canada was given enlightened articulation in 1888 by Edward Blake before the Privy Council of the House of Lords in England. In the famous Indian Title Case that saw the governments of Ontario and Canada clash over conflicting interpretations of the rights of Aboriginal people,[86] Blake introduced his assessment of the constitutional meaning of the crucial section 91(24) of the British North America Act. Of the document's contents he explained:

One sentence, one phrase, even one word, deals with a whole code or system of law or politics, disposes of national or sovereign attributes, makes and unmakes political communities, touches the ancient liberties and the private and public rights of millions of free men, and sets new limits to them all.[87]

Blake's words serve as a sobering testimonial to the high responsibilities that fall on the shoulders of all parties with a role in transforming the fruits of constitutional deliberations in the 1980s into effective and fair constitutional language.

Notes

1. *Financial Post*, 1 June 1987, 1.
2. Simon McInnes, "The Inuit and the Constitutional Process: 1978–1981," in Ian A.L. Getty and Antoine S. Lussier, eds., *As Long as the Sun Shines and Water Flows: A Reader in Canadian Native Studies* (Vancouver: University of British Columbia Press, 1983), 329–31.
3. See articles by George W. Bauer in *The Canadian Forum*, May, 1973, 15–20; April 1974, 10–14; October 1974, 4–5.
4. See Harold Cardinal's seminal *The Unjust Society: The Tragedy of Canada's Indians* (Edmonton: Hurtig, 1969).
5. See Thomas R. Berger, *Fragile Freedoms: Human Rights and Dissent in Canada* (Toronto: Clarke, Irwin and Company, 1982), 219–54.
6. See Boyce Richardson, *Strangers Devour the Land: The Cree Hunters of the James Bay Area versus Premier Bourassa and the James Bay Development Corporation* (Toronto: Macmillan, 1975); Richard F. Salisbury, *A Homeland for the Cree: Regional Development in James Bay, 1971–1981* (Montreal: McGill-Queen's University Press, 1986).
7. See Thomas R. Berger, *Northern Frontier, Northern Homeland: The Report of the Mackenzie Valley Pipeline Inquiry*, 2 Vols. (Ottawa: Government of Canada, 1977).
8. See Tony Hall, "Self-Government or Self-Delusion: Brian Mulroney and Aboriginal Rights," *The Canadian Journal of Native Studies*, 6, 1 (1986), 81–82; Douglas Sanders, "The Constitution, the Provinces, and Aboriginal Peoples," in J. Anthony Long and Menno Boldt, eds., *Government in Conflict? Provinces and Indian Nations in Canada* (Toronto: University of Toronto Press, 1988), 151–74.
9. See Robert Sheppard and Michael Valpy, *The National Deal: The Fight for a National Constitution* (Toronto: Fleet Books, 1982), 224–44.
10. See Jean Morisset, "La Conquête du Nord-Ouest, 1885–1985: or The Imperial Quest of British North America," in Getty and Lussier, eds., *As Long as the Sun Shines*, 280–87; see also Morisset's fascinating introduction to

Morisset and Rose-Marie Pelletier, eds., *Ted Trindell, Métis Witness to the North* (Vancouver: Tillacum Library, 1986).

11. Douglas E. Sanders, "The Indian Lobby," in Keith Banting and Richard Simeon, eds., *And No One Cheered: Federalism, Democracy and the Constitution Act* (Toronto: Methuen, 1983), 319–21.

12. *The Globe and Mail,* 18 November 1981, A7; Carolyn Swayze, *Hard Choices: A Life of Tom Berger* (Vancouver: Douglas and McIntyre, 1987), 172–91.

13. *Vancouver Sun,* 20 November 1981, A14.

14. See the *Financial Post,* 5 December 1981, 8.

15. For a thorough discussion of the tension between the idea of a politicians' constitution and a people's constitution with special reference to the federal public hearings on the Meech Lake accord, see Alan C. Cairns, "Citizens (Outsiders) and Governments (Insiders) in Constitution-making: The Case of Meech Lake," *Canadian Public Policy/Analyse de Politiques,* 4, supplement/ numéro spécial (September 1988), S121–45.

16. Michael Woodward and Bruce George, "The Canadian Indian Lobby of Westminster, 1979–1982," *Journal of Native Studies,* 18, 3 (Autumn 1983), 119–26.

17. The Declaration is published in Getty and Lussier, eds., *As Long as the Sun Shines,* 337.

18. Woodward and George, "The Canadian Indian Lobby," 130–36.

19. Cited in Sanders, "The Indian Lobby," 323.

20. Ibid.

21. See Hall, "Indian Treaties," in *The Canadian Encyclopedia* (Second Edition) (Edmonton: Hurtig, 1988), Vol. 2, 1056–59.

22. See Ruth Thompson, ed., *The Rights of Indigenous Peoples in International Law: Selected Essays on Self-Determination* (Saskatoon: University of Saskatchewan Native Law Centre, 1987); Rudolph Ryser, "Fourth World Wars: Indigenous Nationalism and the Emerging New International Political Order," in Menno Boldt and J. Anthony Long, eds., *Quest for Justice: Aboriginal Peoples and Aboriginal Rights* (Toronto: University of Toronto Press, 1985), 304–15.

23. Great Britain, House of Commons, *Hansard,* 23 February 1982, 828.

24. Ibid., 803.

25. Ibid., 17 February 1982, 366.

26. Ibid., 313–19.

27. Ibid., 23 February 1982, 784.

28. See Canada, Indian and Northern Affairs, *Indian Conditions: A Survey* (1981); for a more recent study see James S. Frideres, *Native Peoples in Canada: Contemporary Conflicts* (Third Edition) (Scarborough: Prentice Hall, 1988), 138–206.

29. *Hansard,* 23 February 1982, 781.

30. Woodward and George, "The Canadian Indian Lobby," 137.

31. *Hansard,* 17 February 1982, 362.

32. Ibid., 342.

33. Ibid., 23 February 1982, 785–86.

34. Ibid., 811.
35. Ibid.
36. Ibid., 810.
37. Ibid., 783–84.
38. Ibid., 781–82.
39. Ibid., 782.
40. Ibid., 804.
41. Ibid., 817.
42. See Bryan Schwartz, *First Principles, Second Thoughts: Aboriginal Peoples, Constitutional Reform and Canadian Statecraft* (Montreal: Institute for Research on Public Policy, 1986), 329–52; Janet Silman, *Enough is Enough: Aboriginal Women Speak Out* (Toronto: The Women's Press, 1987).
43. Kathleen Jamieson, "Sex Discrimination and the Indian Act," in J. Rick Ponting, ed., *Arduous Journey: Canadian Indians and Decolonization* (Toronto: McClelland and Stewart, 1986), 112–36.
44. See Schwartz, *First Principles*, 353–64.
45. The proposal was tabled at the conference as Document 800–23/030.
46. See Sally M. Weaver, "Federal Policy-Making for Métis and Non-status Indians in the Context of Native Policy," *Canadian Ethnic Studies*, 27, 2 (1985), 80–102.
47. The author attended all the first ministers' conferences on Aboriginal affairs between 1983 and 1987. The account of the meetings and the surrounding events is based partly on this eye-witness testimony.
48. *Hansard*, 23 February 1982, 811.
49. See Hall, "Self-Government or Self-Delusion?," 82–85. See also Coalition of First Nations, *Sovereignty and Nationhood* (Second Edition) (Saddle Lake, Alberta, 1984); Eric Robinson and Henry Bird Quinney, *The Infested Blanket: Canada's Constitution—Genocide of Indian Nations* (Winnipeg: Queenston House, 1985).
50. *The Ottawa Citizen*, 21 March 1987, A3.
51. *The Globe and Mail*, 27 January 1987, A1–2.
52. *The Toronto Star*, 11 March 1987, A1, A25; The Chief of the Peguis Reserve explained his action in *Kainai News*, 11 March 1987, 5.
53. A reasoned assessment of the conferences with recommendations for the future is outlined by Peter Jull in "How Self-Government Must Come," *Policy Options*, 8, 6 (July/August 1987), 11–13.
54. The quoted words are from the testimony of George Erasmus. See the Senate of Canada, *Debates*, 18 November 1987.
55. *Assembly of First Nations Bulletin*, 4, 7 (May/June 1987), 1.
56. See *The Sudbury Star*, 27 July 1987, 1; 7 August 1984, 4.
57. Senate of Canada, *Debates*, 18 November 1987, 2200.
58. *The Edmonton Sun*, 2 June 1987.
59. See evidence of Zebedee Nungak, *Minutes of Proceedings and Evidence of the Special Joint Committee of the Senate and House of Commons on the 1987 Constitutional Accord*, No. 3, 5 August 1987, 28; evidence of George Erasmus

in ibid., No. 9, 19 August 1987; evidence of Ernie Daniels, Interim President of Prairie Treaty Nations Alliance, in Senate of Canada, *Debates*, 16 December 1987, 2458.

60. Richardson quoted in Ellie Kirzner, "Native Self-Rule Omens," *Now Magazine*, 13–26 August 1987, 9.

61. *Hansard*, 23 February 1982, 779–81.

62. Evidence of George Erasmus in *Special Joint Committee*, No. 3, 19 August 1987.

63. Canada, House of Commons, *Indian Self-Government in Canada: Report of the Special Committee*, 1983, 44.

64. Cree–Naskapi (of Quebec) Act, *Statutes of Canada*, Vol. 1, Chapter 18, 1984. See also Cree–Naskapi Commission, *1986 Report of the Cree–Naskapi Commission* (Ottawa, 1987), 7.

65. J.H. Smith, *Appeals to the Privy Council from the American Plantations* (New York: Columbia University Press, 1950), 426, cited in James Youngblood Henderson, "The Doctrine of Aboriginal Rights in Western Legal Tradition," in *Quest for Justice*, 199.

66. See Douglas Sanders, "Article 27 and the Aboriginal Peoples of Canada," in Canadian Human Rights Foundation, *Multiculturalism and the Charter: A Legal Perspective* (Toronto: Carswell, 1987), 155–66.

67. Much of the following is essentially the author's personal commentary on the Meech Lake accord. See Hall, *Special Joint Committee*, No. 14, 27 August 1987, 57–73, Appendix 1–17; Senate of Canada, *Proceedings of the Senate Submissions Group on the Meech Lake Constitutional Accord*, No. 5, 18 March 1988, 50–60; Legislative Assembly of Ontario, *Hansard Official Report of Debates, Select Committee on Constitutional Reform, 1987 Constitutional Accord*, No. C-24, 13 April 1988, C-1243–1251; *The Toronto Star*, 19 June 1987, A21; Hall, "Who Speaks for Canada? The Meech Lake–Free Trade Connection," *Humanist Canada*, 21, 1 (Summer 1988), 3–6.

68. See J.W. St. G. Walker, "The Indian in Canadian Historical Writing," *Canadian Historical Association, Historical Papers*, 1971, 21–47; Walker, "The Indian in Canadian Historical Writing, 1972–1982," in *As Long as the Sun Shines*, 340–57; Sylvie Vincent and Bernard Arcand, *L'image de l'Amérindien dans les manuels scolaires du Québec* (Quebec: Hurtubise, 1979).

69. Don Johnston, ed., *With a Bang, Not a Whimper. Pierre Trudeau Speaks Out* (Toronto: Stoddart, 1988).

70. See Senate of Canada, *Report of the Task Force on the Meech Lake Constitutional Accord and on the Yukon and the Northwest Territories* (Ottawa, 1988).

71. See Robert Bourassa, *Power from the North* (Scarborough: Prentice-Hall, 1985).

72. See, for instance, *The Toronto Star*, 20 December 1987, A14.

73. See *The Globe and Mail*, 2 August 1988, A7.

74. *The Globe and Mail*, 20 October 1988, A7.

75. See James Cullingham, "Home and Native Land," *Saturday Night*, 98, 4 (April 1983), 7–11.

76. *The Globe and Mail*, 22 June 1988, A1.
77. *The Toronto Star*, 22 June 1988.
78. See "Special Report: A Canadian Tragedy," *Maclean's*, 14 July 1986.
79. *The Globe and Mail*, 2 August 1988, A7.
80. *The Ottawa Sun*, 18 January 1989, 2.
81. *The Globe and Mail*, 26 September 1988, A5.
82. See *The Toronto Star*, 2 June 1988; *The Ottawa Citizen*, 4 June 1988, A3.
83. See Senator Lowell Murray's account of the failure of the first ministers' conferences on Aboriginal affairs compared to the "success" of Meech Lake in *Choices* (Montreal: Institute for Research on Public Policy, February 1988) (no pagination).
84. See Michael K. Foster, *Indigenous Languages in Canada* (Ottawa: Commissioner of Official Languages, 1982).
85. See Hall, *The N'ungosuk Project: A Study in Aboriginal Language Renewal* (West Bay: Two Bears Cultural Survival Group, 1987).
86. Joseph Schull, *Edward Blake*, Vol. 2, *Leader in Exile, 1881–1912* (Toronto: Macmillan, 1976), 103–111.
87. *The Ontario Lands Case: Arguments of Mr. Blake, Q.C., before the Privy Council* (Toronto: The Budget, 1888), 6.

TONY PENIKETT

CONSTITUTIONALIZING NORTHERN CANADA'S COLONIAL STATUS*

I am pleased to participate in this exercise in northern immersion.

Let me ask you to imagine that one morning Ontarians woke up and found that during the night, nine provinces and the federal government had, at a secret meeting by a lake, decided to suspend this province's membership in Confederation.

What if, perhaps in a fit of pique at Toronto, the other premiers and the Prime Minister of Canada had decided that Ontario could not re-enter Confederation until all 10 concurred? And what if there were no guidelines as to how the discretion of each premier and the Prime Minister was to be exercised on this question?

Surely Ontarians would be more than a little concerned if they found as well that the possibility of other provinces extending their boundaries into Ontario was suddenly a real possibility.

How would residents of Ontario feel when they discovered that they were no longer eligible to be appointed to the Senate or the Supreme Court of Canada? Would their bitterness at this treatment not be even greater when they considered how they had been denied access to or even input into the decision that had transformed their constitutional status?

Would people in this province accept such an arrangement if it were applied to them? I think not. "It couldn't happen to us," you might say. Perhaps not. But that, I submit, is what happened to the Yukon last year in April.

When most Ontarians hear the word "Yukon," they may perhaps think of the land described by Jack London, Robert Service or Pierre

---

* Brief to the Ontario Select Committee on Constitutional Reform, 1987 Constitutional Accord.

Berton. Perhaps members of the committee here picture a land peopled by Indians, prospectors, trappers, dance hall girls, gamblers and gold seekers. There is something of this still in the Yukon Territory, but Yukoners are more than quaint characters limited by the pages of Robert Service. We are citizens of Canada, and right now we are deeply concerned that our interests, our aspirations are being given short shrift by the rest of the country.

The Meech Lake accord discriminates against tens of thousands of Canadians solely because they have chosen to live north of the 60th parallel. It makes provincehood virtually impossible for the territories, it denies us the right to hold certain specific national offices and it was arrived at without either our knowledge or consent, and we are angry.

The proposal as it now stands states that the unanimous consent of all provinces as well as the federal government must be achieved before a territory can become a province. We know that unanimity has been rarely achieved by the first ministers. Our recent experience with the aboriginal self-government proposal gives us as northerners no reason to believe that this perfect apolitical harmony will be found in the future, especially when territorial as opposed to provincial interests are at stake.

But even if unanimity were possible, even if the north were over-reacting and all the first ministers decided to smile upon a proposal for provincehood at the same time, how can one justify allowing the representatives of every other region of Canada, except that region most affected, to decide the north's place in Confederation?

Surely this is the very opposite of self-determination. Surely this is a rule fit for a gentlemen's club in the 19th century rather than a democratic society in the 20th. And it is a rule, I suggest, that is ripe for abuse. Decades from now the territories could be a million strong but still be blackballed from the club for reasons of immediate political expediency if, for example, the south felt it needed guaranteed access to the north's oil and gas.

Some have insisted that this is not the intent of the unanimity rule. But then, what is? Why are the rules being changed for new provinces? What was wrong with the method whereby the present 10 joined Confederation? Prior to 1982, the door was open to us. In 1982, the door was closed. Now, in 1987, it has been barred.

We in the north feel strongly that the process by which the accord was reached was a violation of our right to self-determination. The first ministers failed to consult northern Canadians about matters fundamentally affecting their lives. It is bad enough that we have no vote, but to have been granted no voice in this process is simply outrageous.

In the north we feel strongly enough about our lack of input into this decision that we are challenging the constitutional accord in the courts. Our petition seeks a declaration by the court that the absence of consultation is inconsistent with conventional democratic principles, that we were, in short, denied natural justice. We also claim that there is a trust responsibility owed by the government and the Parliament of Canada to the people of the north, a trust responsibility writ larger by our absence from the table.

At present, our action and that of the government of the Northwest Territories are concentrating on preliminary questions of justiciability. Although both actions found some procedural favour at the trial level, both were reversed at the Court of Appeal. But this is not a publicity ploy for us. We intend to appeal those decisions to the Supreme Court of Canada. We are determined to explore fully every possible means for securing our rights as Canadians.

As well as jeopardizing our future constitutional status, the accord also wreaks a present-day injustice on some of our citizens. The territories, unlike the provinces, will not have the right to nominate senators or Supreme Court judges.

Yukoners are pleading today, pleading that you uphold their democratic rights in a way that is consistent with those enjoyed by Canadians from St. John's to Victoria. We urge you to extend to the Yukon nothing more or less than what the accord offers your own constituents.

Specifically, we urge you to amend the accord as presented to this body. We ask that (a) new sections 41(h) and (i) of the proposed amendment be deleted and (b) the word ''territories'' be added after the word ''provinces'' in sections 25(1), 25(2) and 101(c)(1) and 101(c)(2), so that Canadians living in the north might be nominated by their regional governments for appointments to the Senate and the Supreme Court respectively.

The deletion of the proposed sections 41(h) and (i) would leave the establishment of new provinces and the extension of existing boundaries to agreements between the federal government and the people directly affected.

I want to state quite clearly here that we are not opposed to the accord as a whole. It is vital to Canada to have Quebec endorse the Constitution as a full partner. Like other Canadians of every region and every political stripe, we are pleased to see national unity promoted through Quebec's signing of the Constitution. But we ask, is it necessary to freeze out the north in order to achieve this? We suggest that the Constitution can be amended to meet Quebec's legitimate needs and yet still allow for the creation of future provinces.

Keeping the door open for the creation of new provinces in the northern territories need not and does not threaten Quebec in any way. We do not work with a limited stock of federalism. To extend the full protection of the Constitution to one jurisdiction does not mean that corresponding rights must be taken from another.

It is understandable that Canadians greet with enthusiasm what appear to be solutions to long-standing constitutional conflicts, but that enthusiasm must not be allowed to blind us to the fact that solutions may be creating new conflicts. Canadian experience suggests that these new constitutional errors will not be remedied easily or quickly. Before we amend the Constitution, the practical implications ought to be clear. We ought to be positive that the proposed amendments will serve the future, as well as the present, interests of all Canadians.

Our national identity has been entwined in the north since the birth of our country. Our national image is built on the majesty of the north. In the eyes of the world and in the hearts of Canadians, the north is integral to the definition of Canada. We in the north wish to ensure that our treatment of northern Canada reflects the kind of country we are, the kind of country we want to be.

I will remind you that Canada at the time of Confederation had only four provinces: Nova Scotia, New Brunswick, Quebec, and, of course, Ontario. In contemplation of the creation of the Dominion, the London Resolution of 1865 stipulated that if Prince Edward Island, British Columbia and any other province which might be created from the Northwestern Territories wished to join in Confederation, they be admitted on "equitable terms."

When Manitoba was created, the Constitution Act of 1871 clearly set out Parliament's exclusive authority to admit new provinces:

> The Parliament of Canada may from time to time establish new provinces in any territories forming for the time being part of the Dominion of Canada, but not included in any province thereof, and may, at the time of such establishment, make provision for the constitution and administration of any such province, and for the passing of laws for the peace, order, and good government of such province, and for its representation in the said Parliament.

The subsequent admission of British Columbia, Prince Edward Island, Alberta and Saskatchewan was negotiated directly between each province and the federal government. In not one case was the assent of any other province required.

The existing conditions for entry faced by the Yukon and the Northwest Territories are already far more onerous than those met by any other province. As you know, the Constitution Act of 1982 amended the admission formula so that the seven-and-50 rule applies. The north was definitely being asked to leap higher hurdles than those who had gone before.

At the time of the amendment, northerners vigorously protested the imposition of these new requirements. Every single legislator from the Northwest Territories journeyed to Ottawa to press the northern case. Yukoners, too, voiced their concerns and their outrage.

One of the louder voices came from Erik Nielsen, then MP for the Yukon. In his statement in Hansard on November 26, 1981, he demonstrates that the constitutional status of the north is an issue about which every single northerner feels passionately. Let me quote him:

> For over half a century . . . the dream of provincial status has been the lodestone of northern hopes. It has been central to the vision of the north which sees the development of the Yukon and the Northwest Territories as the best and brightest hope for Canada's future. When the Prime Minister accepted the inclusion of two clauses in the April accord relating to 'the extension of existing provinces into the territories' and 'notwithstanding any other law or practice, the establishment of new provinces,' he dealt a crushing blow to the hopes and aspirations of thousands of Canadian citizens resident above 60. He gave away what was not his to give— the rights and privileges of Canadians of northern Canada above 60.

To use in the north the amending of the Constitution in a way which promised to make it impossible for northern territories ever to gain provincial status was a breaking of faith. We do not think we were alone in recognizing the fact that these entry provisions were unfair.

Attached to the 1983 constitutional accord on aboriginal rights, an accord mentioned by our colleagues from the Northwest Territories this morning, was appendix A, an agenda of outstanding items, items unresolved in the 1982 constitutional debate. Obviously, these were items that the federal government felt were of importance as the government wanted to deal with them at the next meeting.

Agenda item 4 specifically requested the repeal of sections 42(1)(e) and (f), which deal with the creation of new provinces and the extension of provincial boundaries. As well, in its discussion paper on the draft amendments, the federal government stated, "The intention would be that the Constitution of 1871 would operate rather than section 38(1) of the Constitution Act, 1982.'' In other words, it was the intention of the Trudeau government, at that time, to remove the impediments to the territories joining Confederation which had been placed in the Constitution at the last moment in 1982.

We in the territories, therefore, believed that the problems in the 1982 formula were apparent to all parties and that there was some consensus that they required change, because nine provinces and the federal government had signed the 1983 accord. The parties to the 1987 accord, unfortunately, did not improve the 1982 formula; they did not correct its unfairness and its inequities; incredibly to us, they made them worse. Seven people who signed the 1983 accord also signed the 1987 accord, completely contradictory positions. So far, we have been given no explanation whatsoever as to why the clear intention of 1983 was reversed in 1987, without, I might add, any consultation with the elected representatives of the people most directly affected.

I would ask you just to consider for a moment the Canada we would have today if the 1987 formula had been applied when the extension of boundaries and the creation of the post-Confederation provinces were being considered. A map of Canada would show only Nova Scotia, New Brunswick and a strip of land along the St. Lawrence River and the Great Lakes. Provinces seeking to maintain the status quo, to protect special interests and to exercise narrow jealousies could have refused the extension of boundaries and/or the admission of new provinces. Our map would show Canada as a small nation state with British territories or perhaps independent nations to the east, west and, dare I say, to the north of us.

Fortunately, earlier federal and provincial legislators had a larger vision of the federation that was to be Canada. They anticipated and encouraged the development of the territories and facilitated their admission into Confederation. We believe that this generosity of vision must be maintained.

Underlying the specific injustices that we in the north perceive is a fundamental wrong. Earlier, I spoke of natural justice and I cannot emphasize too strongly our anger, our frustration, at the denial of our right to be heard and to have reasons given for the decisions made which will affect us.

The leaders of the Yukon and the Northwest Territories were not invited to the original Meech Lake meeting, even though our constitutional fates were as much at stake as were those from any other jurisdiction.

In the weeks following the accord, I contacted each and every premier to explain our dilemma. We articulated many times our concerns to the Prime Minister's office. Our ministers contacted their federal and provincial counterparts, as did our officials. Even though Mr. Sibbeston, the then-leader of the government of the Northwest Territories, and I went to Ottawa on June 1, 1987, we were not invited to the premiers' all-night meeting at the Langevin Block.

On the evening before the meeting I finally received our first acknowledgement from the Prime Minister of Canada, a short note promising to represent the interests of the north. His complete failure to do so is what prompts me to continue to seek support for changes to the Meech Lake accord. I repeat, it is fundamentally unfair that our fate, the fate of the people of the north, should be decided by others, by every other region in Canada, by 11 men in a locked room, most of whom have never even seen the north, let alone lived there and known its people.

It is fundamentally undemocratic for our citizens to be denied representation in a process that affects their rights. You would not tolerate it here in your province. Why should you allow it to be imposed on others, your fellow Canadians?

The unfairness of this situation, as Mr. Richard mentioned this morning, was recognized in the recommendations of the special joint parliamentary committee on the accord. Although the majority report did not endorse amending the accord, it acknowledged, in paragraph 39 of chapter XV, "[t]he principle of the 'equality of the provinces' is important but in our opinion, it is carried too far if it imposes artificial and unnecessary constraints on the natural evolution and development of the northern third of the land mass of our country."

We in the north are perplexed and frustrated by the first ministers' apparent disregard for the rights of those of us who occupy the region of Canada so often linked to the country's future well-being. The normal evolutionary process of constitutional development would see the Yukon increasingly have the right to self-determination in matters of social, economic, cultural and, of course, political self-development, culminating someday in provincial status. Instead we see Canada turning its back on our progress, refusing to acknowledge our rights.

The Yukon and the Northwest Territories are not provinces now, nor do they seek provincial status at this time. Few people in the north would argue that we have reached the point where provincial status makes sense. We are keenly aware of the limitations imposed by our small dispersed population, our limited economic base and our under-developed infrastructure.

But this does not mean that additional, artificial limits should be imposed on us or that rights so fundamental to other Canadians that they take them for granted should be denied. Yukoners quite naturally wish to play a role in the country's major institutions. We want to continue to work for provincehood at some appropriate time in the future. To have that possibility extinguished at this time would erode our faith, not just in the future of the north, but in the vision of this country that Canadians have embraced since Confederation.

Ladies and gentlemen, what we are asking you, the leaders of Ontario, the members of this Legislature, is do you want the north to be part of Canada? Do you accept our right to determine our own future in Confederation or do you, in effect, believe that Confederation is now complete, that there is no more room? Do you admit the possibility of a Supreme Court judge or a senator from the north, or would you argue that Yukoners, who have sent a Speaker, a Deputy Prime Minister and Canada's second woman MP to Ottawa in this century, are not equal to national office?

I believe that your well-known commitment to democracy, fairness and equality should answer these questions for you.

CHAPTER ELEVEN

THE POLITICAL RUNOFF FROM MEECH LAKE: Will the Country Be Left High and Dry?

*The Meech Lake agreement shows that Brian Mulroney and the pro-
vincial premiers agree about the nation's future—a loose collection of
ten independent duchies.*

(Robert Fulford, "Surrendering Canada," *Saturday Night*, August 1987, 5)

*In view of the fact that it was only Quebec that was left out in
1982, there simply is no morally legitimate or pragmatic argument
for reopening the accord and putting it at risk, other than an
egregious error.*

(Senator Lowell Murray, brief to the Special Joint Committee of the
Senate and the House of Commons on the 1987 Constitutional Accord,
Minutes of Proceedings and Evidence, No. 16, September 1, 1987 [Ottawa:
Queen's Printer, 1987]: 9)

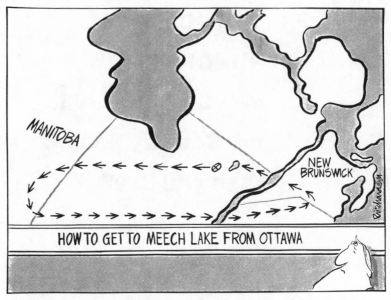

Reprinted with permission — Pritchard.

INTRODUCTION

From the moment it was announced on April 30, 1987, the Meech Lake Constitutional Accord has had a profound impact on Canadian politics and political parties, both nationally and provincially. Whether or not the Accord, or some amended version thereof, ever becomes an integral part of our Constitution, it will have left an indelible mark on contemporary Canadian history. Why is this so?—for the very straightforward reason that the Meech Lake Accord has contributed immensely to the process of political realignment set in motion by the September 4, 1984, national election. Ironically, this same process of political realignment can be interpreted as being partly responsible for the eventual demise of the Accord. It is this dialectic that I wish to explore in a very preliminary fashion in this somewhat unorthodox introduction to the concluding chapter of *The Meech Lake Primer*.

In the November 1984 election, the Progressive Conservative party of Brian Mulroney defeated the governing Liberal party of John Turner in a landslide victory that surpassed even that of J. G. Diefenbaker in 1958. Of the Tories' 211 seats, 58 came from the province of Quebec.[1] This was a most remarkable development, which, combined with the defeat of the Parti Québécois by Robert Bourassa's Liberal party in 1985, laid the groundwork for the Meech Lake Accord two years later.

The national Liberal party's stranglehold over Quebec had contributed to the downfall of the minority government of Prime Minister Joe Clark in 1979–80. Brian Mulroney, who replaced Joe Clark in a leadership race in June 1983, was determined that this was not going to happen a second time. Fortunately for him, he had the luck of the Irish. A rapid succession of coincidental and orchestrated events ensured him of that elusive breakthrough in Quebec. With Pierre Elliott Trudeau gone from the political scene and with the active support of the many Liberal party and Parti Québécois riding organizations, Mulroney's Conservative party was able to win over two-thirds of Quebec's seventy-five seats.

From the moment he entered politics in 1976, Brian Mulroney consistently portrayed himself as an ardent supporter of a bilingual and multicultural Canada. He was opposed to the theories of two nations and special status because, in his view, they threatened national unity. In fact, his vision of the country was very similar to that of Trudeau. In his maiden speech in the House in September 1983, Mulroney ardently supported a Trudeau government resolution calling for the full restoration of the constitutional rights of Manitoba's francophone minority as per the ruling of the Supreme Court. It was a superb performance that set him apart from his rival, John Turner, who appeared to waffle on the issue of minority rights. In the public imagination, Mulroney was beginning to take on the mantle of the defender of the linguistic minorities.[2]

Following a similar strategy, Mulroney made a valiant effort to appeal to the soft or federalist-oriented nationalists in Quebec. He made a vague but crucial promise during the 1984 election campaign to do whatever he had to in order to get the Quebec government's "signature on our constitution, with honour and enthusiasm." The strategy proved highly effective. Many nationalist-oriented Quebec voters, including a large number of Parti Québécois and Liberal supporters, threw their support behind relatively unknown Conservative candidates, believing that Mulroney and not Turner was the appropriate successor to former prime minister Trudeau. Like Trudeau, Mulroney came across as one of their own, a sympathetic and reliable defender of the francophone cause in the Canadian federal system.[3]

Firmly in office, it was not too long before Prime Minister Mulroney was called upon to live up to his promise to reconciliate Quebec. By 1986, negotiations with his friend, Robert Bourassa, re-elected premier of Quebec in 1985, were well under way. Both leaders were very eager to dispose of the constitutional question in a pragmatic and quick fashion. They wanted the political credit that would accompany such a coup. Most importantly, both leaders wanted to get on to what they considered to be an issue of greater importance—economic expansion via the deregulation of the Canadian and Quebec economies. It was an enormous gamble that would pay off in political spades, especially for Prime Minister Brian Mulroney.

Even before the ink on the Meech Lake Accord was dry, the once-powerful national Liberal party was thrown into complete disarray. Without any extensive consultation, the Liberal opposition leader, John Turner, committed his caucus to the Accord the very morning of its signature by the first ministers. This decision to chart new constitutional territory for his caucus and the party was encouraged by Raymond Garneau, former minister in the Bourassa government, who led the Quebec wing of the Liberal caucus. The decision would prove to be a fateful turn of events for Turner. Donald Johnston, a prominent Liberal MP for Saint Henri–Westmount and former leadership candidate, immediately denounced the Accord for creating "a dismembered confederation of fiefdoms." Johnston subsequently resigned from the shadow cabinet to carry out a personal campaign against the Accord within the rank and file of the Liberal party.[4] By the end of May 1987, John Turner also faced the scathing denunciation of the Accord by none other than his predecessor, Pierre Elliott Trudeau, who declared that the Accord rendered the Canadian state so totally impotent that it was destined, "given the dynamics of power, to be governed eventually by eunuchs."[5]

By June 1987, one-quarter of the Liberal caucus (eleven of forty) was openly in revolt against the leader over the Meech Lake Accord and would eventually vote against it in October. A significant number of Liberal senators, including Michael Pitfield and Michael Kirby, also opposed the Accord and moved quickly to create a separate Senate committee to study the Accord and make recommendations to the House. Over the next two years, these dissident Liberal MPs and senators remained adamant in their opposition to the Meech Lake Accord, despite repeated pleas by Turner to unite behind the caucus policy. As critics of the Accord proclaimed that it would fragment the country, it became readily apparent that the first victim of that fragmentation was the national Liberal party.[6]

Turner's strategy was to get his caucus to support the Accord while at the same time proposing a series of constitutional amendments—some of which would alter the Accord—that would be pursued once ratification was complete.[7] This dual strategy did not achieve the much-desired caucus unity, nor did it return the Liberal party to its longtime position of prominence in the province of Quebec in the national "free trade" election of 1988.[8] During April 1988, John Turner had to confront a concerted but unsuccessful attempt by twenty-two caucus members, encouraged by Liberal senators who had just voted to reject the Accord, to oust him from the leadership of his party.[9] Turner, while listening to the Quebec nationalist wing of his caucus on the constitutional question, did not appear to understand the economic aspirations of Quebeckers, especially those in the Montreal region. He tried desperately to gain the confidence of Robert Bourassa prior to the election, but to no avail. The Mulroney/Bourassa political partnership over the Meech Lake Accord and the Free Trade Agreement proved too powerful to be challenged by a Liberal party deeply divided over its constitutional vision of the country.[10]

With all three national parties formally adopting the Meech Lake Accord for a second time in June 1988, the issue was effectively eliminated from the national political agenda for the fall 1988 "free trade" election. When John Turner lost that election, his political future was once again in doubt. Although he managed to increase the number of Liberal seats from forty to eighty-three, with gains in Ontario and British Columbia, the party suffered a further decline in Quebec to an all-time low of twelve seats.[11] Bitter and humiliated over his treatment by Robert Bourassa and the Quebec Liberal party, Turner lashed out at Bourassa for resorting to the Charter's notwithstanding clause to ensure that Bill 178 on sign language was not contested in the Supreme Court. In the interim, it became clear that a majority of the larger Liberal caucus was hostile to the Meech Lake Accord. As a result, the long-stifled debate among the rank and file of the party began to take place, as Jean Chrétien and Paul Martin, to name only two, jockeyed for position in the leadership race. Unwilling to alter his stance on the Meech Lake Accord and seeing the writing on the wall, John Turner decided in early May 1989 to call upon the executive of the Liberal party to organize a leadership convention to choose his successor.[12]

Clearly, Turner's decision to step down did not terminate the Liberal party's bitter but necessary struggle over the Accord. Instead, it ensured for the first time that a genuine debate concerning both the process and substance of constitutional reform—and involving all the leadership aspirants—would take place at the grass-roots level of the party. Indeed, it appeared to many political commentators that the process of political realignment precipitated by the 1984 election and the Meech Lake Accord, and subsequently consolidated by the "free trade" election of 1988, was irreversible. The national Liberal party, encouraged by provincial party leaders opposed to the Meech Lake Accord—such as Sharon Carstairs and premiers Frank McKenna and Clyde Wells—and the rank and file from coast to coast, the commentators contended, was turning its back on a Quebec electorate that had swung massively to Brian Mulroney's Tory party.

This analysis seems to be confirmed by the inordinately influential role being exercised by Quebec's sixty-two Tories in the caucus and cabinet of Prime Minister Mulroney's second administration. In the minds of the Quebec electorate, the Conservative party has now replaced the Liberal party as their best vehicle for defending and promoting their national development within Confederation—a remarkable transformation; indeed, a development unthinkable only a decade ago when Joe Clark became prime minister and was soundly defeated within six months.[13]

The impact of the Accord on the political dynamics of the national New Democratic Party, although not as dramatic as with the Liberal party, was also quite significant. The outcome, in fact, was much the same. Indeed, the NDP leader, Ed Broadbent, ended up resigning several months after the 1988 election, in large measure because of his miscalculation over the constitutional policy of his party. Broadbent, like Turner, decided to support the Accord without widespread consultation within the party, because he was convinced by the party executive that such a policy would usher in an NDP breakthrough in the province of Quebec.

Broadbent was quite aware of the political realignment taking place in Canada, especially in Quebec, and he believed that the time was opportune for the NDP to benefit from this long-awaited development. The NDP was riding at a historic high in the polls in the province of Quebec, and this convinced Broadbent and most of his caucus that supporting the Québécois nationalist-inspired Accord would bring a significant political breakthrough in Quebec. Except for a couple of dissidents, Broadbent was able to maintain a unified caucus for both the October 1987 and June 1988 votes on the Accord. The NDP members of the Special Joint Committee of the Senate and the House of Commons on the 1987 Constitutional Accord signed its *Report*, and the NDP caucus proposed only three amendments to the Accord, none of which was considered essential for their support. Despite considerable vocal opposition from NDP militants in Manitoba and British Columbia, Broadbent skillfully managed to maintain support from all the provincial NDP leaders prior to and during the 1988 election. It was after the election that the strategy of the national executive on the constitutional question started to fall apart.[14]

Yet it was clear that this constitutional policy was very risky from the outset, especially when one considers that the Quebec NDP party, led by Jean-Paul Harney, was very critical of the Accord because the distinct society clause was too weak to bring the Québécois any tangible new powers. It was the NDP-Québec that provided most of the organizational structure at the level of individual ridings; if its militants were not on board, then the electoral gamble would certainly backfire.[15] During 1988, Broadbent stuck firmly to his strategy, despite every indication that the vaunted political payoff was not about to materialize.[16] The election came, and the NDP prospects of a political breakthrough in Quebec went up in smoke. All Broadbent received for his troubles was a stern lecture from Pierre Graveline, co-president of NDP-Québec, for not having endorsed the more nationalistic platform of the provincial party!

Graveline called for a formal break between the national and provincial parties, a development that occurred in May 1989.[17] In early March 1989, Broadbent indicated his desire to step down as leader of the national party. Indeed, a political realignment had taken place, but the NDP party proved incapable of capitalizing on that crucial development. Rather, as was the case with the Liberal leadership race, there was every indication that the new NDP leader, aware of the opposition to the Accord among the rank and file of the various provincial organizations, would be staunchly against the Meech Lake Accord as it now stands.[18]

It was as if the various provincial electorates sensed a political realignment in the making. The first political fallout at the provincial level that stemmed to some degree from the Meech Lake Accord occurred in New Brunswick. A young, brash and relatively inexperienced leader of the New Brunswick Liberal party, Frank McKenna, soundly defeated the seventeen-year administration of Premier Richard Hatfield on October 13, 1987. In a landslide victory, the Liberal party won all fifty-eight seats in the Legislative Assembly. Prior to and during the election campaign, McKenna had voiced his strong dissatisfaction with the Accord. Before the Special Joint Committee in late August 1987, McKenna had gone on record demanding that substantive amendments —pertaining to the Charter, linguistic minorities, spending powers, Senate reform, the Supreme Court and fisheries provisions of the Accord —be made before he would ask the New Brunswick Legislative Assembly to proceed with ratification.[19]

Since October 1987, grass-roots opposition to the Meech Lake Accord has become widespread throughout New Brunswick. Premier McKenna has skillfully used this strong and vocal opposition to ward off the incessant campaign by the Mulroney government—led by Senator Lowell Murray—and Premier Bourassa to have the agreement ratified without any amendments whatsoever. McKenna established a Committee of the Legislature to hear testimony on the Accord and to submit a *Report* with recommendations to the Assembly sometime in the fall of 1989. As expected, the vast majority of those intervening before this committee criticized various aspects of the Accord and demanded that it be amended or rejected. In the interim, many New Brunswickers continued to fear that Premier McKenna would cave in to the suggestion of a parallel accord that would not alter, in any shape or form, the Meech Lake Accord. Premier McKenna, trying to hold the middle ground, continually denied stories of either a provincial cabal against Ottawa or a sweetheart deal with Quebec.[20] Buoyed by growing opposition and the presence of another anti-Accord Liberal premier—Clyde Wells—on the political scene, Premier McKenna appeared to strengthen his resolve in 1989. In search for more time, he even questioned the Accord's ratification deadline of June 1990, hoping the entire matter could be put off indefinitely.[21]

In reality, the only effective political opposition to the Accord has surfaced in Manitoba. The defeat of the once-pre-eminent NDP provincial government in a surprise election on April 26, 1988, resulted in a minority Progressive Conservative government led by Premier Gary Filmon. The Manitoba Liberal party, led by the feisty and inveterate "anti-Meecher" Sharon Carstairs, had come out of obscurity to capture Her Majesty's loyal opposition in the legislature. Many observers, including Sharon Carstairs, pronounced the death of the Meech Lake Accord, while Premier Filmon promised, in his government's throne speech, to ratify the Accord at the first opportune moment.[22] Sensing the need to recuperate ground lost to the Liberal party, Gary Doer, the new Manitoba NDP leader, announced within days of the November 21, 1988, federal election that his party was committed to killing the Accord. The combination of free trade and the Meech Lake Accord, he argued, would prove to be a lethal blow to the political integrity of the country.[23]

In less than a month, Premier Filmon surprised the nation by withdrawing the Accord from the Manitoba legislature. His pretext was that Bourassa's new language law, Bill 178, which resorted to the Charter's notwithstanding clause to ban outdoor bilingual commercial signs, was a "national tragedy." It was also becoming quite apparent that at least half of the twenty-four-member Tory caucus were opposed to the Accord, particularly the distinct society clause. Early in 1989, Premier Filmon proposed that the federal government refer the distinct society clause to the Supreme Court for a ruling, but he could not muster support from the other premiers, even Frank McKenna, who publicly opposed the Accord.[24] The spring hearings of the Manitoba Legislature's Task

Force on the Meech Lake Accord demonstrated clearly that public opposition was very deep and widespread throughout the entire Manitoban society, including the small and beleaguered francophone community. When the western premiers met in their annual roundup in June 1989, both Premier Devine of Saskatchewan and Premier Vander Zalm of British Columbia indicated their growing sense of unease with the Accord.[25]

The full significance of the national political realignment hit home only on April 20, 1989, when the Liberal party of Clyde Wells was swept into office in Newfoundland. The provincial Liberal red tide had swept every Atlantic province except Nova Scotia. Sensing that the Mulroney Tory government was not addressing the social and economic needs and problems of Atlantic Canadians, Newfoundland voters roundly defeated the longstanding Conservative government of Brian Peckford, albeit under the new leadership of Tom Rideout. Former Premier Peckford, an unabashed supporter of the Mulroney government and the Accord, had pushed the Accord through the Legislative Assembly without public hearings.[26] Clyde Wells, the "intellectual, articulate and tough" new Liberal leader and premier, was opposed to many provisions of the Meech Lake Accord. His prime concern was with the interpretative nature of the distinct society clause, which would give Quebec "special powers to protect and promote that status." He vowed that his government would rescind the Assembly's ratification if changes were not made to the Accord before the deadline of June 1990.[27]

The two years since the signing of the Meech Lake Accord have demonstrated the degree to which the process of constitutional renewal has become intertwined with the political realignment that has been under way since the early 1980s. The Constitution Act, 1982 was achieved under very different political conditions and a very different procedural dynamic. First, the Constitution Act, 1982 was not subject to the unanimity formula and could well have passed muster with support of only six or seven provinces. As a result, the 1982 agreement did not face the prospect of falling apart after the first ministers—except for René Lévesque, who could not accept any constitutional agreement under any circumstance—had given their approval. Secondly, numerous amendments had been proposed and accepted at various stages in the lengthy process. Although all of the various interest groups were far from being fully satisfied, the Trudeau government continued to maintain widespread support for the final document among a broad cross-section of Canadian society throughout the entire ordeal. Both of these factors prevented a coalition of opposition forces from forming at the national and provincial levels, thereby seriously threatening final ratification of the Constitution Act, 1982.

The Meech Lake Accord epitomizes the more traditional style of elite accommodation politics between the eleven first ministers. Its drafting was predicated on the ability of all eleven first ministers to "make a deal" that had something in it for each of them. Its ratification was predicated on their ability to convince their respective cabinets, caucuses and legislatures to ratify the unamended "deal" while holding their noses to any of its perceived flaws, egregious or otherwise. What the Mulroney and Bourassa governments had not taken into account was the highly volatile nature of provincial politics during this era of political realignment. While both of these leaders pursued the Accord as a means of consolidating their respective regimes, they did not understand that the achievement of their respective political objectives would have the effect of a tidal wave moving through the Canadian political system. It is this reality, and not the combined opposition of a myriad of interest groups critical of the Meech Lake Accord, that will force either the alteration of the agreement or its relegation to the well-stocked graveyard of other constitutional proposals that suffered ignominious defeat.

Can the Accord be salvaged, or is it beyond reprieve? Some critics, such as George Radwanski and former senator Eugene Forsey, believe that the Accord is fundamentally and fatally flawed, and that it should be scrapped before it does irreparable damage to the constitutional and political fabric of the nation-state.[28] Other critics, such as Deborah Coyne, contend that Canada's politicians can put together a more circumscribed reform package that addresses the concerns of Quebec's political and social elites without dismantling the country and weakening the Charter. Coyne believes that the reconciliation of Quebec can be achieved under the terms originally put forward by Quebec, which called for the recognition of Quebec as a distinct society in an all-encompassing preamble rather than in the form of an interpretative clause.[29]

Peter Leslie, who headed up the Institute of Intergovernmental Relations at Queen's University before his recent move into the Federal–Provincial Relations Office in Ottawa, addresses, in a reasonable yet circumscribed fashion, several points made by the Accord's critics. He bases his support for the 1987 Constitutional Accord on a couple of assumptions generally shared by his political science colleagues. First, he believes that a majority of Canadians would have considered the process that culminated in the Constitution Act, 1982 as illegitimate had a federalist government rather than a separatist Quebec government represented its citizens at the bargaining table. While Quebec is legally bound by the 1982 Act, Leslie agrees with the leaders and members of Quebec's two major political parties that the 1982 Constitution Act and the process that created it are morally and politically illegitimate. Consequently, English-speaking Canada is morally bound to address and accommodate a reasonable set of constitutional demands from Quebec's federalist-oriented Liberal government. To refuse the Quebec government's reintegration into the process of executive federalism in general and constitutional reform in particular on its own terms, Leslie contends, will feed the cause of separatism and stifle the process of constitutional reform.

Working under this assumption, Peter Leslie readily disposes of the various and sundry criticisms advanced by the Accord's opponents, none of whom is ever identified. He rejects the argument that the undefined distinct society clause, coupled with the immigration and financial compensation provisions, will allow Quebec to acquire more powers than the other provinces. This clause is counterbalanced by both the linguistic duality clause and the principle of the equality of all the provinces. Yet this argument was qualified by the Special Joint Committee, which concluded in its *Report* that:

> the affirmation in section 2(3) of the role of the government and legislature of Quebec 'to protect and promote' Quebec's distinct society could be used by the courts to *interpret* the distribution of powers in a way not precisely the same as these powers would have been interpreted if the 'distinct society' clause were not part of the constitutional mix.[30]

Leslie does not address the shared critique of the linguistic and ethnocultural minorities and aboriginal peoples to the effect that the Accord totally ignores the issue of their respective collective rights. Nor does he have much sympathy for the women's organizations that want to immunize gender equality rights—section 28 of the Charter—from the distinct society clause.

The second assumption underlying Leslie's approach to the Accord is his adherence to the provincial compact theory of Confederation.[31] He equates federalism with decentralization, pluralism, diversity and asymmetry, whereas centralization and uniformity of policy making and program implementation are posited as characteristics of a unitary state. The Meech Lake Accord's various provisions, in Leslie's estimation, will constitutionalize a genuine form of federalism in Canada by intensifying "the processes of intergovernmental negotiation, mostly on a bilateral basis." The limitations on Ottawa's spending powers, the extension of the provincial veto over the amendment of national institutions and the creation of new provinces, provincial nomination of senators and Supreme Court justices and annual constitutional conferences of first ministers will more fully federalize operation of Canada's political system. The resulting depoliticization and bureaucratization of policy making envisioned and provided for in the Accord, Leslie argues, will help undermine the acrimonious and adversarial nature of federal–provincial relations by ushering in a new era of genuine co-operative federalism.

Howard McConnell, a professor of constitutional law at the University of Saskatchewan, analyses the Accord from the perspective of a western Canadian social democrat. He is concerned about the integrity of the Canadian nation-state and the ability of modern western Canada to integrate itself into the national decision-making process via a democratized Senate operating as a House of the Provinces:

> Quebec's willing acceptance of the 1982 Constitution is important, but not at any price. With the passage of the Free Trade agreement with the United States, a strong central government is needed to offset growing American political and economic influence and Meech Lake, with its marked centrifugal tendencies, could seriously undermine the powers of the federal government.[32]

McConnell views the constitutional agenda of the Mulroney government to have been dictated ''more by opportunistic politics than by a genuine desire to save the federation from some impending peril.'' He concurs with Pierre Elliott Trudeau's analysis of the distinct society clause, because it constitutionalizes the two-nations conception of Confederation. Furthermore, the Accord's linguistic duality clause will do little to reinforce bilingualism, because it is limited to simply preserving the very weak status quo of the linguistic minorities, especially francophones in western Canada.[33] Similarly, as a longtime resident of a province heavily dependent upon the national treasury, McConnell supports Donald Johnston's contention that the Accord's section 106A, which constrains Ottawa's spending powers, will fracture Canadian federalism.

McConnell is convinced that the Accord's deal on the ''Triple P'' Senate (Premiers Perpetuating Patronage) spells the end for the ''Triple E'' Senate (Elected, Equal, Efficient). The formula for appointments to the Supreme Court, according to McConnell, is also flawed, for two reasons. First, there is no guarantee of regional representation when

Ottawa selects a candidate from provincial lists. Secondly, there is no mechanism to ensure that Ottawa retains some influence over the Supreme Court when the chief justice is not appointed from among sitting judges. In a short period of time, the Supreme Court might well lose its national vision of Canada.

McConnell believes that Canada's northern citizens were denied their democratic right to accede to the status of provincehood because of Quebec's concern with being further outnumbered "in the councils of Canadian executive federalism." Provincial veto over the creation of new provinces, which could introduce non-meritorious political concerns, is a significant departure from the social and economic criteria used in other federal states. Finally, McConnell agrees with the women's organizations that argue that the distinct society clause jeopardizes section 28—gender equality rights—of the Charter by creating a hierarchy of rights. While this may not have been deliberate on the part of the first ministers, he concludes, the Accord "is mischievous" in its downgrading in section 28 of "the strongest affirmation of rights in the whole *Charter.*"

Notes

1. J. L. Findlay and D. N. Sprague, *The Structure of Canadian History* (Third Edition, Toronto: Prentice-Hall, 1989): 504, Table 14.

2. L. Ian MacDonald, *Mulroney. The Making of the Prime Minister* (Toronto: McClelland and Stewart, 1985): 263–267, 272–274, 300–301.

3. *Ibid.*, 288–290, quote 289. Mulroney won hands down in the French-language debate, which had a profound impact in Quebec.

4. Donald Johnston, "A Dismembered Confederation of Fiefdoms?," *The Ottawa Citizen*, May 16, 1987; his extensive brief to and testimony before the Senate Committee of the Whole on the Meech Lake Constitutional Accord, *Debates of the Senate*, March 23, 1988, 2912–2921; his testimony to the Legislative Assembly of Ontario, Select Committee on Constitutional Reform, 1987 Constitutional Accord, *Hansard Official Report of Debates*, March 7, 1988.

5. Pierre Elliott Trudeau, "Say Goodbye to the Dream of One Canada," *The Toronto Star*, May 27, 1987, reprinted in Donald Johnston, ed., *With a Bang, Not a Whimper. Pierre Trudeau Speaks Out* (Toronto: Stoddart, 1988): 8–22, quote 22.

6. Roy MacGregor, "Poll Pits Rebel Grits Against Turner," *The Ottawa Citizen*, June 5, 1987; Editorial: "The Liberal Knives," *The Globe and Mail*, August 27, 1987; Ross Howard, "Senate Liberals Plan Attack on Meech Lake Accord," *The Globe and Mail*, August 31, 1987.

7. Cf. Canada, Special Joint Committee of the Senate and the House of Commons on the 1987 Constitutional Accord, *Minutes of Proceedings and Evidence*, No. 17, September 9, 1987 (Ottawa: Queen's Printer, 1987): 151–154; and Bryan Schwartz, "Refashioning Meech Lake," *Manitoba Law Journal*, 18, No. 1 (1989): 59–63.

8. Marjorie Nichols, "Grits Playing Cynical Game with Meech Lake Strategy," *The Ottawa Citizen*, September 5, 1987; Gilbert Lavoie, "Turner n'a pas rassuré les libéraux," *La Presse*, 30 septembre 1987.

9. Carol Goar, "Why the Liberals Are Always in the Lurch," *The Toronto Star*, March 5, 1988; Michel Vastel, "Turner joue sa tête," *Le Devoir*, 28 avril 1988; his "Turner affronte les éminences grises du parti," *Le Devoir*, 30 avril 1988; Joan Cohen, "Meech Lake Symbolizes Liberal Woes," *Winnipeg Free Press*, May 11, 1988.

10. Lysianne Gagnon, "Turner et le Québec," *La Presse*, 11 juin 1988; Deborah McGregor, "Liberal Leaders' Meeting in Quebec Didn't Change Positions," *The Ottawa Citizen*, August 24, 1988.

11. Findlay and Sprague, *The Structure of Canadian History*, 504, Table 14.

12. Greg Weston, "Turner Attacks Bourassa for Quebec Language Policy," *The Ottawa Citizen*, April 6, 1989; Susan Delacourt, "Grits Bare Souls on Meech Lake," *The Globe and Mail*, April 17, 1989; her "Race is On as Turner Bows Out," *The Globe and Mail*, May 4, 1989; Paul-André Comeau, *Le Devoir*, 4 mai 1989.

13. Gretta Chambers, "Federal Liberals Turn Backs on Quebec," *The Gazette*, May 18, 1989; Michel Vastel, "Le leadership libéral se prépare sur le dos du Québec," *Le Devoir*, 19 juin 1989; Richard Cleroux, "Quebec MPs Emerge as Surprise Powerhouse," *The Globe and Mail*, May 24, 1989.

14. Ken MacQueen, "Broadbent Runs Caucus With an Iron Fist," *The Vancouver Sun*, November 19, 1987; Susan Delacourt, "NDP Weighs Liberal Revolt's Effect With Eye on Quebec, Tory Plans," *The Globe and Mail*, May 9, 1988.

15. Jean-Paul Harney, "À la dérive sur le Lac Meech," in Réal-A. Forest, ed., *L'adhésion du Québec à l'Accord du Lac Meech—Points de vue juridiques et politiques* (Montréal: Les Éditions Thémis, 1988): 206–217; Michel Vastel, "Le NDP et la société distincte," *Le Devoir*, 21 septembre 1987.

16. Pierre Cayouette, "La percée historique du NDP au Québec remise à plus tard," *Le Devoir*, 29 juillet 1988; his "Le NDP glisse partout sauf à Montréal," *Le Devoir*, 30 juillet 1988.

17. Pierre Graveline, "Ed Broadbent et le Québec, le rendez-vous manqué," *Le Devoir*, 1 décembre 1988; Peter Maser, "Quebec NDP Splits in Two," *The Ottawa Citizen*, May 1, 1989.

18. Hugh Winsor, "The NDP to Choose New Leader," *The Globe and Mail*, March 3, 1989; Daniel Drolet, "NDP MP Changes Tune on Meech," *The Ottawa Citizen*, May 31, 1989 (Drolet was referring to leadership hopeful, Steven Langdon); Geoffrey York, "Majority Now Opposed to Meech, NDP Leadership Hopefuls Claim," *The Globe and Mail*, May 31, 1989.

19. Frank McKenna, testimony before the Special Joint Committee of the Senate and the House of Commons on the 1987 Constitutional Accord, *Minutes of Proceedings and Evidence*, No. 12, August 25, 1987, 5–19.

20. Michel Vastel, "McKenna veut son petit lac Meech," *Le Devoir*, 27 novembre 1987; Don Richardson, "Delaying Ratification of Meech Lake," *The Telegraph-Journal*, February 17, 1988; his "Murray Confident N.B. Will Eventually Throw Its Support to Meech Lake Deal," *The Telegraph-Journal*, April 27, 1988; Bernard Descoteaux, "Lac Meech: McKenna envoie paître Bourassa," *Le Devoir*, 18 mars 1988; "Le Québec et le Nouveau-Brunswick ont fait la paix," *Le Devoir*, 23 août 1988.

21. "McKenna Steadfast on Meech Lake," *The Ottawa Citizen*, January 13, 1989; Susan Delacourt, "McKenna Questions Meech Lake Deadline," *The Globe and Mail*, January 13, 1989; Roy MacGregor, "McKenna Wants Answers from Mulroney, Bourassa," *The Ottawa Citizen*, May 24, 1989.

22. Don McGillivray, "Manitoba Catches Nation by Surprise," *The Ottawa Citizen*, April 25, 1989; William Johnson, "Liberal Votes in Manitoba Kill Meech Deal," *The Gazette*, April 27, 1989; "Filmon Gov't Makes Meech a Priority, Report Says," *The Ottawa Citizen*, July 21, 1989.

23. Geoffrey York, "Will Kill Meech Lake, Manitoba NDP Warns," *The Globe and Mail*, November 24, 1989; Michel Vastel, "Bourassa paiera cher son appui à Mulroney," *Le Devoir*, 18 décembre 1989.

24. Geoffrey York and Benoît Aubin, "Manitoba Premier Ends Meech Debate," *The Globe and Mail*, December 20, 1989; "Half Man. PCs Oppose Accord," *The Ottawa Citizen*, December 21, 1989; Geoffrey York, "Filmon Urges Judicial Clarification of Accord's Distinct Society Clause," *The Globe and Mail*, January 12, 1989.

25. Geoffrey York, "Meech Lake Accord Comes Under Attack at Manitoba Hearing," *The Globe and Mail*, April 7, 1989; his "Opposition to Meech Dominates Hearings," *The Globe and Mail*, April 12, 1989; Matthew Fisher and Christopher Donville, "Getty Holds Out, 3 Premiers Soft on Meech Pact," *The Globe and Mail*, June 29, 1989.

26. Kevin Cox, "Newfoundland Liberals Win Majority," *The Globe and Mail*, April 21, 1989; Hugh Winsor, "Newfoundland Liberals' Win Raises Alarms in Ottawa," *The Globe and Mail*, May 22, 1989; Don McGillivray, "Federal Tories Blew Nfld. Election," *The Ottawa Citizen*, April 21, 1989.

27. Michael Valpy, "Wells a New Star on Political Stage," *The Globe and Mail*, May 22, 1989; Hugh Winsor and Kevin Cox, "Wells Pledges to Oppose Meech Lake Agreement," *The Globe and Mail*, May 22, 1989.

28. George Radwanski, "Meech Lake Accord Seen as Threat to Canada as One Sovereign Nation," *The Toronto Star*, August 22, 24, 25, 1987; Eugene Forsey, "Meech Lake Does Weaken Federal Powers," *The Ottawa Citizen*, August 6, 1987; his "No! Submission to the New Brunswick Legislative Committee on the 1987 Constitutional Accord," *University of New Brunswick Law Journal* (forthcoming).

29. Deborah Coyne, "Beyond the Meech Lake Accord. Submission to the Manitoba Task Force on the Meech Lake Accord," April 4, 1989.

30. Special Joint Committee of the Senate and the House of Commons on the 1987 Constitutional Accord, *Report, Minutes of Proceedings and Evidence,* No. 17, September 9, 1987, 45.

31. Sharing Leslie's premises is political scientist Kenneth McRoberts in his "The Case for Meech Lake. Agreeing about the Obvious," *The Canadian Forum* (December 1987): 12-13.

32. Howard McConnell, "A Federalist on the Meech Lake Accord," *NeWest Review* (April/May 1989): 42.

33. Cf. Howard McConnell, "The French Language Controversy in Saskatchewan," *NeWest Review,* 13, No. 10 (Summer 1988): 8-9; his "The Meech Lake Accord and the West," *NeWest Review,* 13, No. 6 (February 1988): 12-13.

PETER M. LESLIE

IN DEFENCE OF THE "SPIRIT OF MEECH LAKE": EVALUATING THE CRITICISMS*

I Introduction

This submission expresses support for the 1987 Constitutional Accord, and urges Parliament and the provincial legislatures to endorse it. In what follows, I make the following arguments:

- it is urgent and important that changes be made in the Canadian constitution, so it becomes acceptable to Quebec
- the text of the Accord negotiated among First Ministers 2–3 June is almost certainly not amendable either in its principles or in its wording: thus Parliament and the provincial legislatures must make basically a "yes or no" decision
- while there should be a presumption in favour of endorsement of the Accord, Parliament and the legislatures of the nine provinces that signed the partial Accord of 1981 have an obligation to scrutinize the 1987 Constitutional Accord, to make sure it is acceptable to themselves as well as to Quebec (which the Quebec National Assembly has declared it to be)
- several of the arguments made by those who have urged rejection of the Accord, or else its fundamental amendment, do identify major issues that demand attention; but the concerns that

* First published in Queen's Quarterly and subsequently in Clive Thomson, ed., Navigating Meech Lake: The 1987 Constitutional Accord (Kingston: Institute of Intergovernmental Relations, 1988).

have been expressed are overblown, and can be alleviated by careful analysis of the Accord and its probable effects

- the Accord represents an attempt, and may offer an opportunity, to move into a new era of federal–provincial relations, in which governments can get away from the poisonous atmosphere of past battles; by virtue of the Accord, Canadian federalism may work a lot better in the future than it has in the past.

II An Agreement is Urgent and Important

"Government by consent" is generally acknowledged to be an essential characteristic of a free society. Violation of this principle offends against democracy and imperils the political stability of a country whose people are committed to democracy. It should therefore be of great concern to all Canadians that Quebec, alone among the provinces, has never assented to the present ground-rules of Confederation. Those rules were significantly changed by the Constitution Act, 1982, which implemented an agreement reached by the federal government and nine provinces, Quebec alone dissenting, in November 1981. The changes made at that time could not have been accomplished under the amending formula the 10 governments agreed upon at that time. In other words, the Constitution Act, 1982 could not meet the test of its own rules. The Act was denounced by unanimous vote of the Quebec National Assembly.

The extraordinary proceedings by which the constitution was fundamentally changed in 1982 would probably have been regarded throughout Canada as illegitimate, except for the fact that the Government of Quebec was in the hands of a political party committed to political independence. It could be argued, and was argued, that the Parti Québécois had a vested interest in denying its assent to any constitutional package, regardless how favourable to Quebec. For political reasons, the PQ could never be satisfied.

This argument is plausible, but, if invoked as justification for overriding Quebec's objections at the time, implies the following: as soon as a federalist party came to power in Quebec, giving evidence of wanting to cut a deal, the federal government and the nine provinces had a moral obligation to reopen the partial Accord of November 1981, and to bargain in good faith towards an amended Constitution Act acceptable to the government and people of Quebec. This process began a year ago. Now the First Ministers have fulfilled the promise implicit in the actions of an earlier group of First Ministers in November 1981. The Quebec National Assembly has endorsed the new agreement.

Some people have denied that there was good reason to reopen the substance of the partial Accord of November 1981, and they bristle when anyone speaks of "bringing Quebec into the constitution." Quebec is *in* the constitution, they say—and they are literally correct. The Government of Quebec has acknowledged that it is legally bound by the terms of the Constitution Act, 1982. The question, however, is one of *moral* exclusion, or the legitimacy of the Act and the propriety of the proceedings leading up to it. Evidently, for some people, it is enough that Quebec's representatives in the Parliament of Canada endorsed the Constitutional Resolution in 1982; they apparently consider the views of the Quebec National Assembly, then and subsequently, as irrelevant. Such people, it would seem, are unmoved by the fact that not a single Quebec provincial politician (to my knowledge) has ever endorsed the 1982 Act.

If, truly, the position consistently taken by all Quebec political parties is irrelevant or unimportant, nothing more remains to be said: there was no valid reason (at least none emanating from Quebec) to re-inscribe constitutional issues on the public agenda. But that, wisely, was not the view of the First Ministers. If the provinces have any place in the constitutional revision process, as by the Constitution Act, 1982 they do, Quebec has that right as much as others. In 1981, at the very moment the other provinces successfully asserted their claim to be involved, Quebec was excluded. Perhaps this was justifiable under the circumstances, but those circumstances no longer obtain. To refuse Quebec the moral right to participate fully (though after five years' delay) in framing the ground-rules of Confederation is not justifiable now. Implicitly recognizing this, the Premiers' Edmonton Declaration of August 1986 acknowledged the priority of Quebec's constitutional agenda, as set out by Mr. Gil Rémillard in May of that year; and they, together with the Government of Canada, have honoured their commitment to leave other constitutional issues for a later time. The moral validity of Quebec's position is the first and basic reason for negotiating, as the First Ministers have done, a new constitutional accord.

There are at least two additional reasons for wanting to bring Quebec into a constitutional framework it regards as legitimate. The first is that, at some unknown future time, there will probably be a new wave of Quebec nationalism. No one knows what form it will take, or what events may trigger it. However, the rest of Canada would be acting imprudently if it allowed a new independence movement to arise in a situation where the *indépendantistes* could evoke the events of 1981–82 as "a second Conquest," saying that the ground-rules for Confederation had been foisted upon Quebecers, and the province had never agreed to them. The 1987 Constitutional Accord removes a grievance, it blunts a weapon.

Finally, a constitutional accord is urgent and important for Canada because, reasonably enough, Quebec will not participate in any other constitutional changes until the agenda left over from 1981 has been settled. This makes the future development of the constitution, or its further adaptation to changing circumstances, extraordinarily difficult to achieve, and in some respects impossible. Some people regard Quebec's behaviour in this respect as blackmail: the word has been used. That attitude, however, can be justified only on the grounds that Quebec's exclusion in 1981 was its own fault, and the province must live with its mistakes. My own view, as I have explained, is different: the events of 1981 morally oblige the rest of Canada to reopen the partial Accord reached at that time. From this perspective it seems legitimate and reasonable that Quebec should refuse to join in making other changes in the constitution until its own agenda, if put forward in a constructive spirit, has been dealt with. I suspect any other province would behave likewise in similar circumstances.

As things now stand, the 1987 Constitutional Accord is a necessary first step towards any other changes desired by the Government of Canada or by provincial governments. One of the features of the Accord is the promise to return later to issues such as Senate reform and jurisdiction over the fisheries. (The prospects for doing so successfully will be discussed later in this submission.)

In conclusion: the First Ministers had strong moral reasons for tackling Quebec's constitutional agenda, which has shaped the 1987 Constitutional Accord. It was essential to do so because justice demanded it. However, a new constitutional accord is also important for at least two other reasons. First, in its absence Quebec *indépendantistes* carry a bludgeon. Second, without Quebec's full participation in the further development of the constitution it will be extremely difficult, and in some matters impossible, to bring about changes in other areas. *In short, the costs of failure at this stage would be incalculable.* They would be incalculable, even without taking into account the likelihood of a severe political backlash in Quebec, if the First Ministers' agreement should be rejected by Parliament or by any provincial legislature.

III Is the Accord Amendable?

To say that an accord is desirable does not imply that the particular Accord now before Parliament is worthy of its endorsement. Parliament is called upon to make a judgment on this, and, at least in a formal sense, may choose among three possible options: to endorse the 1987 Constitutional Accord without amendment, to endorse it, subject to certain amendments, or to reject it. In practice, however, the option of endorsing the Accord, subject to amendments, is almost certainly not available. If the Constitution Amendment, 1987, which forms part of the Accord, is amended in any particular by Parliament or by any *one* of the provincial legislatures, all the others too must accept the changes. While revisions at this stage are not absolutely inconceivable, the possibility of their being accepted by all the parties seems remote in the extreme. To take the improbable case, it may yet be shown that some clause or other appears to have implications not hitherto noticed. In other words, there may be a drafting error. In that situation all 11 governments and legislatures may agree to new wording that better represents the original intent. Except for changes to overcome a drafting error, however, it is hard to imagine changes at this stage. The "Langevin text" of 3 June, which adds precision to the "Meech Lake Accord" of 30 April and indeed somewhat alters it, represents a delicate balancing of divergent interests and preferences. This is the text that is now before Parliament. It reflects a consensus position that was arrived at only with the greatest difficulty. The fact that the First Ministers came within a hair's breadth of failure makes it hard to envision changes now, even changes that merely eliminate ambiguities.

It offends some Members of Parliament, and indeed many others, that there should be little if any opportunity for making changes at this stage. "Why hold hearings," it has been asked, "if the text is final?" The answer is clear: because Parliament and each of the provincial legislatures must have an opportunity to decide whether any part of the agreement is so thoroughly unacceptable that the whole must be rejected. If it seems undemocratic to present Parliament and the legislatures with a "yes or no" decision, one should remember that these are the first changes to the Canadian constitution, ever, where endorsement by all 11 legislatures has been required or sought. The process is far more rigorous than it has ever been before. Nor is it unusual or undemocratic that a legislature should be presented with a proposal on a take-it-or-leave-it basis. For example, the US Congress has voluntarily bound itself to accept or reject, without amendment, a bilateral trade agreement with Canada, if the President recommends it. That is the meaning of the so-called ''fast track'' procedure. Canada would not have entered into negotiations if the outcome were subject to re-negotiation on the floor of the Congress; and of course the restrictions that will apply to the Congress will apply also to Parliament. The radical nature of the decision, however, will not relieve either the Congress or Parliament of its responsibility to examine a draft agreement carefully and in detail. The same reasoning applies in the case of the Constitution Amendment, 1987.

The remainder of this submission assumes that the Meech Lake–Langevin Accord is not amendable in substance. The 1987 Constitutional Accord almost certainly represents the only possible chance of securing agreement on a set of changes that are acceptable both to Quebec and to its Confederation partners, the other 10 governments. If, therefore, it is acknowledged that an agreement of some kind is urgent and important, there must be a strong presumption in favour of endorsing the First Ministers' handiwork.

IV Evaluating the Criticisms

Regardless of the desirability of reaching a new constitutional settlement, it is important to review the main arguments made against the Accord, asking oneself the following questions:

- Does the Accord establish an overall political imbalance that would have long-term negative consequences for Canada? Two such arguments have been advanced: that Quebec has been given more powers than the rest of the provinces, an inherently unstable situation; and that Canada, already dangerously decentralized, has been set on a road to steadily increasing, debilitating, decentralization.
- Does the Accord diminish the rights of individuals and groups, weakening the guarantees established in the Canadian Charter of Rights and Freedoms? Arguments along these lines have been made in relation to official-language minorities and in relation to (in the words of s. 15 of the Charter) ''those that are disadvantaged because of race, national or ethnic origin, colour, religion, sex, age or mental or physical disability.''

- Will the Accord effectively block further progress, on a Canada-wide basis, in the field of social policy, as a result of limitations on the federal spending power?
- Will the modification of the amending formula block further desired constitutional change, for example as regards the status of the Yukon and Northwest Territories, and as regards the Senate of Canada?
- Does the Accord not create conditions for unending federal–provincial conflict, for example in its provisions for the appointment of Senators and Supreme Court judges?

I shall argue that the concerns implied by these questions, while understandable, either are unwarranted or have been blown out of reasonable proportion. Naturally I, like others, have reservations. The Accord is a compromise document. It is implausible that any of the First Ministers would, unconstrained by the political context, propose exactly the Langevin text. But no one has the luxury of asking, any more than the First Ministers had, "Can I imagine anything I would like better than this?" Each of us has to ask, instead, "Is the Accord, on balance, and given the situation inherited from the events of 1980–82, a positive achievement?" To make up one's mind on this, it is necessary to weigh the principal criticisms that have been made of it. In what follows, I do so under seven headings, reflecting the preceding set of questions.

Political Imbalance: Quebec and the Other Provinces

It has been vigorously argued in recent years that Quebecers must have the opportunity of participating in the national government of Canada equally with residents of other provinces. Former Prime Minister Trudeau committed much of his political career to working for this goal, and it led him to oppose giving the Quebec government wider powers or a larger policy role than the other provinces had. He reasoned that if this happened, some federal policies applying to most of Canada would not apply in Quebec, and it would be resented if Quebec MPs were constantly voting on issues that did not and could not affect their province—in effect, imposing on the rest of the country a set of policies that would not apply to themselves. Thus Trudeau opposed "special status" for Quebec and, even more, denounced the theory that Canada consists of "two nations" which may be equated roughly with Quebec on the one hand and the remaining nine provinces on the other. The question now at issue is whether or not the 1987 Constitutional Accord has moved

Canada towards a political structure based on the "two nations" theory. Arguments suggesting that it has done so are as follows:

- Article 1 of the Constitution Amendment, 1987—which is part of the Accord—inserts into the Constitution Act, 1867 a provision recognizing that "Quebec constitutes within Canada a distinct society"; the clause also affirms that the legislature and Government of Quebec have a responsibility "to preserve and promote the distinct identity of Quebec." Another part of the same clause reads: ". . . the existence of French-speaking Canadians, centred in Quebec but also present elsewhere in Canada, and English-speaking Canadians, concentrated outside Quebec but also present in Quebec, constitutes a fundamental characteristic of Canada." Parliament and the provincial legislatures are enjoined to "preserve"—but they are not enjoined also to "promote"—this fundamental characteristic of the country. In this respect the two declarations are treated differently. However, the courts are instructed to interpret the Constitution of Canada in a manner consistent with both declarations.
- The Accord promises that the Government of Canada will "as soon as possible" conclude an agreement with Quebec giving that province a degree of control over immigration that other provinces will, at least for a time, not exercise. The agreement will incorporate the principles of an administrative arrangement ("the Cullen–Couture agreement") made with Quebec in 1977. It will have the force of law and, under Article 3 of the Constitution Amendment, 1987, will limit Parliament's paramountcy in immigration matters, as established in s. 95 of the Constitution Act, 1867; furthermore, it will override in some respects Parliament's exclusive jurisdiction over "Naturalization and Aliens," as established by s. 91.25. It is provided that other provinces may negotiate agreements on immigration too, and thereby acquire similar powers; but of course they may choose not to do so.
- Article 7 of the Constitution Amendment, 1987 promises "reasonable compensation" to provinces not participating in future national shared-cost programmes (more details on this will be provided below). Were Quebec to avail itself of this opportunity while other provinces did not, it would acquire a larger policy role, or certainly the appearance of a larger policy role, than the other provinces.

In my opinion it is indeed correct to say that the immigration and cost-sharing provisions of the 1987 Accord would permit Quebec to play a larger policy role than other provinces. In the case of immigration, it has done so for 10 years, under the terms of an agreement negotiated while Mr. Trudeau was Prime Minister. In the case of shared-cost programmes, the principle of opting out was introduced in 1965, Quebec being the only province to avail itself of an offer made to all provinces under the Established Programs (Interim Arrangements) Act. I am not aware that this lack of symmetry, either as regards immigration or as regards the programmes covered by the opting-out scheme, has been damaging to Canada. It is certain that not many people know about it.

The "distinct society" clause, by contrast, has drawn a lot of attention. As noted, it is a guide to the interpretation of the Canadian constitution. It does not replace or invalidate any other part of the constitution. However, certain legal arguments based on other clauses may be strengthened by the description of Quebec as a distinct society, and by the affirmation that the Quebec government and legislature have responsibility for preserving and promoting its distinct identity. It would thus be incorrect to regard the clause as purely symbolic and without practical effect; but the extent to which it may ultimately affect the course of judicial interpretation is unknown. This makes some people nervous— Quebec nationalists, because they fear it may turn out to be an empty gesture, and also those hostile to any and every manifestation of Quebec nationalism, because they fear it may successfully be invoked to claim for Quebec a set of powers that other provinces have neither the incentive nor the constitutional basis to exercise. In short, people have given diametrically opposed interpretations of the clause and its long-run significance.

A response has been to say, in effect, "Let's be quite clear what it means before we assent to it." Or in other words, "Let's rewrite it to eliminate all ambiguity." But to demand this is tantamount to declaring that the search for a constitutional accord should have been abandoned well before the meeting at Meech Lake. In May 1986 Mr. Rémillard signalled that recognition of Quebec's character as a distinct society was an essential feature of a constitutional settlement. It must surely be clear to anyone who understands even a little about Quebec politics that no Quebec government could defend the wording of a "distinct society" clause which was utterly without practical effect, and shown to be so. Those opponents of Quebec nationalism who insist that the "distinct society" clause be rid of all imprecision or ambiguity are demanding exactly that.

Understandably, the desire to eliminate or reduce ambiguities is strong. However, ambiguity cannot be entirely avoided; nor is it desirable to try. Every constitution that lasts more than a brief span of years will eventually have meanings imputed to certain phrases that were not intended when they were drafted. If the drafters make the mistake of trying to cover every conceivable situation or problem they will inevitably fail. All they can reasonably hope to do is to formulate general principles which will later be applied to situations not imagined at an earlier time. In this sense, every constitution contains ambiguities; without them there would be no need for judicial interpretation. Moreover—and this is probably the more significant point—many of the ambiguities one sees in the 1987 Accord are evidently deliberate. They are there because the First Ministers had to find some form of words upon which they could all agree. At times they chose to be cryptic, relying upon future Supreme Courts to make their rulings in as fair a manner as they can, given the then-existing circumstances. Reliance upon decisional rules, frequently involving the exercise of broad judicial discretion, is an inevitable feature of constitution-making which it is not only futile to try to avoid, but a mistake to attempt.

While it is unreasonable to ask for 100-per-cent precision, it is important to note that the ''distinct society'' clause does not give the Quebec legislature a free hand to do whatever it thinks necessary to ''preserve and promote'' the distinctive character of Quebec. The division of powers is unchanged; only in cases of uncertainty, usually arising out of logical tension between two or more clauses of the constitution, can the ''distinct society'' clause be invoked as an aid to interpretation. Moreover, the clause is complex, affirming not only that Quebec constitutes *within Canada* a distinct society, but that the presence of English-speaking Canadians within Quebec (as of French-speaking Canadians in other provinces) is a fundamental characteristic of Canada. This is a declaration to which the courts must give effect. Further, the clause is counterbalanced by explicit recognition in the preamble to the Constitution Amendment, 1987 of ''the principle of the equality of all the provinces.''

These features of the Accord counterbalance the recognition of Quebec as ''a distinct society within Canada.'' It is unwarranted and alarmist to allege that these words may confer upon Quebec significant powers that are denied to other provinces. It is expected that there will be differences of role or of policy responsibilities, flowing from the facts that almost 90 per cent of Canadian francophones live in Quebec, and more than 80 per cent of Quebecers are francophone. The ''distinct society'' clause recognizes this, but the constitution as a whole provides that this role and these responsibilities be fulfilled within a constitutional status not greatly different from that of the other provinces. In short, the alleged political imbalance between Quebec and the other provinces is a bogey. Another form of political imbalance—the weakening of federal power *vis-à-vis* the provinces as a group—is also a matter of concern to many critics. This topic needs attention. However, it will be easier to consider it after other issues have been addressed.

The Accord and the Charter: Linguistic and Ethnic Minorities

Another concern that has been expressed about the "distinct society" clause is that it may diminish the scope of individual rights under the Canadian Charter of Rights and Freedoms. Critics have focussed especially upon the situation of official-language minorities, and other linguistic, cultural or ethnic minorities. The most charitable interpretation one can place upon these criticisms is that they reflect a misunderstanding of the intent of part of the Meech Lake agreement, before its clarification in the Langevin text. The Meech Lake statement referred to "French-speaking Canada" and "English-speaking Canada" and their concentration, respectively, in Quebec and in the other provinces. The explicit recognition of the facts that French-speaking Canada was "centred in *but not limited to* Quebec," and that English-speaking Canada was "concentrated outside Quebec *but also present in Quebec*," suggests that this was, both in conception and in its probable effects, a clause to reaffirm the rights of official-language minorities. The clause was evidently included in order to prevent misinterpretation of the words recognizing "that Quebec constitutes within Canada a distinct society." By itself, the latter statement might have been taken to mean that Quebec was to be equated with francophone Canada, the rest of the country being anglophone: thus it might have been taken to imply a backward step in relation to the rights of both anglophone and francophone minorities. To avoid this possibility, the recognition of Quebec as a distinct society within Canada was counterbalanced by the parts of the clause referring to the linguistically mixed character of Canada as a whole, although the two official-language groups are unevenly distributed across the territory. But this clause was interpreted by some critics as an attack on, rather than a reaffirmation of, the rights of linguistic minorities.

This reading of the clause struck me as perverse at the time, as it imputed, unconvincingly, great significance to the words "English-speaking Canada" and "French-speaking Canada," as if both were monoliths, each with its unique territory. Be that as it may, the Langevin text, as distinct from the Meech Lake agreement, rules out such interpretations. First, it refers to "English-speaking *Canadians*" and "French-speaking *Canadians*," clearly indicating that the reference is to individual rights. Second, the Langevin text contains the double disclaimer, that the clause is not to affect parts of the Charter referring to the multicultural heritage of Canada, or to aboriginal peoples. Finally, the Langevin text adds a non-derogation clause relating to legislative powers over language, both federally and at the provincial level.

These clarifications, together with the fact that the language clauses of the Charter are untouched in either version of the Accord, dispense with allegations that it weakens existing constitutional protections of the rights of linguistic, cultural or ethnic minorities.

The Accord and the Charter: "Section 15" Groups

After the Langevin meeting, new criticisms of the Accord were voiced. If the article referring to Quebec as a distinct society was to contain a non-derogation clause so no one can invoke it to weaken aboriginal rights or to override s. 27 of the Charter (which declares that the Charter "shall be interpreted in a manner consistent with the preservation and enhancement of the multicultural heritage of Canadians"), why could the principle of non-derogation not be made to apply also to all other groups? For example, s. 15 of the Charter prohibits discrimination based on "race, national or ethnic origin, colour, religion, sex, age, or mental or physical disability," and s. 28 states that "the rights and freedoms referred to in it are guaranteed equally to male and female persons." However, the "distinct society" clause (Langevin version) provides for non-derogation only in relation to sections of the Charter dealing with multicultural groups and aboriginal peoples. By implication, it has been claimed, others are not similarly protected. For this reason, the Langevin text has been said to put other groups at risk. By far the most strongly articulated and politically powerful objections along these lines have been those expressed by women's organizations.

What is needed here is a sense of proportion. It is hard to regard the risk as significant. The "distinct society" clause does not supplant any part of the Charter; as an interpretation clause, it can be called into play only when there is conflict between two or more other clauses in the constitution, for example between the non-discrimination rights in

s. 15, and s. 1, which reads: "The *Canadian Charter of Rights and Freedoms* guarantees the rights and freedoms set out in it subject only to such reasonable limits prescribed by law as can be demonstrably justified in a free and democratic society." The "distinct society" clause may have the effect of broadening the application of s. 1; women's and other groups are worried that this may occur, and that it may work to their detriment. Should one respond to this concern by providing that the "distinct society" clause will in no way diminish the force of s. 28? No, for this, truly, would place the "s. 15 groups" (other than women) in jeopardy. Such an amendment to the "distinct society" clause would single out gender equality rights for special protection. It would be indefensible to stop there. Then how about exempting the whole of s. 15? That could impact upon s. 1 in unpredictable ways, upsetting the carefully worked out balance between legislative powers and the powers of the courts in safeguarding individual rights, as achieved in 1981.

The underlying issue here poses the same questions of political philosophy as characterized many of the best contributions to the 1980–81 debate over the Charter itself. To what extent is it desirable to have judicial protection of individual rights? Conversely, to what extent ought political processes to regulate relations between the individual and the collectivity, and relations among social groups, for example as defined by categories referred to in s. 15? The debate over earlier drafts of the Charter resulted in amendments that strengthened and extended its basic principles. On the other hand s. 33, the *non obstante* or "notwithstanding" clause, conferred upon Parliament and the provincial legislatures additional powers to exempt laws and administrative measures from the purview of several key clauses, notably s. 15. The champions of individual rights, or rather of the judicial protection of individual rights, remained unreconciled to the powers vested in legislatures by s. 33.

Social Policy: The Spending Power

The issues remaining to be discussed have to do, in one way or another, with the federal government's capacity for leadership and policy control within the federation. On this topic, modifications to the spending power have been of prime concern to many critics. In Quebec, the main objection has been that the spending power has not only been constitutionally recognized for the first time, but dangerously strengthened. It has been asserted that the spending power clause narrows the provinces' role by explicitly acknowledging that Ottawa may impose upon them its own policy goals and budgetary priorities, while leaving to the provinces only a certain degree of administrative discretion at the level of implementation. Outside Quebec, critics have asserted that the conditions that Ottawa will retain authority to impose are so loose, or so easy for the provinces to circumvent, that there will be neither policy reasons nor political incentive to introduce any new social programmes. Both lines of attack strike me as somewhat off-target, though the Quebec ones get a lot closer to it.

The first point to notice is that the Accord touches only one aspect, though an important one, of the federal spending power. Broadly defined, the spending power is the capacity imputed to and frequently exercised by the federal government to spend in areas of exclusive provincial jurisdiction, thereby playing a policy role where it lacks regulatory authority. Payments may be made (i) to individuals, as in the area of family allowances, (ii) to organizations and institutions other than the provincial government, as in the case of research grants to universities, and (iii) to provincial governments. Typically, in the case of grants to provincial governments, the federal government pays a share of the costs of programmes or projects. Some are *ad hoc* arrangements negotiated bilaterally with each province, as in the case of regional development grants; others are continuing arrangements for sharing the costs, on a formula basis, of programmes which it is desired to see established across the country: hospital insurance and medicare are the outstanding examples. *The 1987 Constitutional Accord affects only new national shared-cost programmes; it does not touch existing ones, nor does it touch bilaterally negotiated, project-related, cost-sharing arrangements, and nor has it relevance to payments to individuals or non-government organizations and institutions. The most recent case of a shared-cost programme of the type that might, in the future, be affected by the Accord is medicare, introduced over 20 years ago in 1966.*

The dimension of the federal spending power that the Accord will affect became the subject of litigation two years ago, as a result of a challenge to the Canada Health Act (1984). The Supreme Court may eventually rule that parts of this Act constitute an attempt to exercise regulatory authority in an area of exclusive provincial jurisdiction, and are therefore *ultra vires*. The Accord will not apply in this case, because both medicare and the Canada Health Act pre-date it; but we may find it easier to understand the significance of the spending power clause if we imagine litigation on the Canada Health Act arising in a "post-Meech" context, as if the Constitution Amendment, 1987 had been in force from (say) 1965. Under its terms, in a new s. 106A inserted into the Constitution Act, 1867:

> The government of Canada shall provide reasonable compensation to the government of a province that chooses not to participate in a national shared-cost program that is established by the Government of Canada after the coming into force of this section in an area of exclusive provincial jurisdiction, if the province carries on a program or initiative that is compatible with the national objectives.
>
> Nothing in this section extends the legislative powers of the Parliament of Canada or of the legislatures of the provinces.

Under the terms of this article, the federal government would presumably have to satisfy the court, if the Canada Health Act were challenged under it, that the Act furthered a credibly "national" objective, such as making high-quality health care available to all Canadians—the principles of "comprehensiveness," "universality" and "accessibility"— and that the conditions it imposed (e.g., the ban on "extra billing") supported such objectives. Opponents would probably have difficulty arguing that the objective was not a national one, but they might have greater success in establishing that the ban on extra billing was not closely enough related to the objective to warrant a financial penalty such as the Canada Health Act authorizes the federal Minister of Health to impose on provinces that permit this practice. In other words, I think the new s. 106A, if it applied, might marginally assist opponents of the Canada Health Act.

There is no point trying to go further in guessing the outcome of litigation in hypothetical future cases, but the scenario I have sketched out may help us to imagine how the new s. 106A will work. First, Ottawa will have to be clear about the national objective or objectives it hopes to accomplish in introducing a new shared-cost programme, and it will have to be able to establish that any conditions imposed on transfers to provincial governments support the objective(s) in question. Second, if a province is to claim compensation for non-participation, it must have found its own way of meeting the objective(s) stated by Parliament. The obligations thus laid on (respectively) the federal and provincial governments will set up a bargaining dynamic in which, in future cases, Ottawa will be able to exercise leadership and policy initiative. But it will have an incentive to adapt any new programmes to the needs of individual provinces. The provinces, on the other hand, will have the latitude to find innovative solutions to problems that are felt across the country, or to devise new features of programme design that are more effective or efficient than Ottawa's. Further room for negotiation is provided by the fact that it may be unclear whether or not a programme is cost-shared (medicare and hospital insurance have not been cost-shared in the traditional sense since the introduction of Established Programs Financing, or EPF, in 1977). Another factor also giving both orders of government an incentive to bargain is that what constitutes "reasonable compensation" may be hard to establish when programme design varies considerably by province (as under the Canada Assistance Plan), when a formula results in widely varying shares of programme costs being met from the federal transfer (as in the early years of medicare), or a formula is not even based on programme costs (as, under EPF, it is not).

Will the federal government retain the incentive to launch new programmes when its control over programme design is less than absolute? Yes, I believe so, if the initiatives in question are supported by public opinion, as medicare was in 1966. If public opinion pressures Ottawa to "do something," it will also pressure the provinces to respond to the federal initiative. They may do so in different ways. However, if diversity dismays those critics of the Accord who are repelled by the thought of a patchwork of provincial programmes with differing standards, a useful corrective would be to examine the differences that now obtain among the provinces in the design of individual programmes that are cost-shared. The programs in question *are provincial programmes, in areas of exclusive provincial jurisdiction*; cost-sharing is a device to ensure that they have certain features in common, making them also, in a sense, national ones. I cannot see this dual character of the programmes in question being disturbed by the spending power clause in the Constitution Amendment, 1987, even if not all provinces participate in a given new programme. Some, conceivably all, may choose not to do so—but if they are to qualify for the federal fiscal transfer, they must design programmes of their own that are compatible with objectives written into federal law. To demand uniformity is to opt, not for federalism, but for a unitary state.

Amending Formula

In large measure, Quebec has been impelled to seek a constitutional settlement with its Confederation partners because of unfavourable demographic trends, the result of which is to diminish over time its political weight within the federation. It has sought constitutional protection against deterioration in its capacity to withstand encroachments on its powers, especially because other provinces, which do not have to defend a linguistic and cultural minority against assimilation, may not have the same determination to preserve certain of *their* powers. This explains the importance to Quebec not only of the "distinct society" clause, but of obtaining changes to the 1982 constitutional amending formula.

The amending formula in the Constitution Act, 1982 establishes a unanimity rule (favourable resolutions in Parliament and the provincial legislatures) for a narrowly defined class of amendments; otherwise, the approval of Parliament and two-thirds of the provincial legislatures is required, provided those provinces contain at least 50 per cent of the population of all provinces. It is also provided that where the general rule applies, a province may exempt itself from the effect of an amendment derogating from its legislative powers or proprietary rights (e.g., in natural resources), by resolution of the legislature. In the case of amendments transferring powers over education or cultural matters to the federal government, an opting-out province is entitled to "reasonable compensation." The intended effect of these provisions was apparently to place all provinces in a formally equal position, without requiring unanimity for everything and without setting up a situation where, at least in education or cultural matters, a province could be levered through financial inducements into giving up legislative powers.

The shortcomings of this amending formula for Quebec are twofold. First, the structure of certain central political institutions, such as the House of Commons, may be altered in ways that reduce Quebecers' influence within them, and Quebec may be powerless to stop such changes. The right of withdrawal may be effective in the case of legislative powers, but as Mr. Rémillard stated in May 1986, "One cannot withdraw from an institution." Second, withdrawal may be costly, except in the case of education or cultural matters, where the federal government is required to offer "reasonable compensation."

There were essentially three ways of accommodating the concerns expressed by Quebec.

- One, a non-starter, would be to give Quebec a veto where other provinces had none. This would have violated the principle of equality of status among the provinces, a key feature of the current amending formula.
- A second option would have been to tighten up the general amending formula, requiring the assent of two-thirds of the

provinces containing 75, 80 or even 85 per cent of the population. This would give Quebec an indirect veto, though if the required figure were 75 per cent its veto power would disappear if the clause were not "grandfathered." Grandfathering would also have violated the equal-status principle, and would probably have been unacceptable to some or all of the other provinces. Thus the formula would have had to stipulate 80 or 85 per cent.

- The third possible choice was the one preferred by the First Ministers: (i) to extend provinces' right to "reasonable compensation" in the case of subjects other than education and cultural matters, and (ii) to give all provinces a veto over major changes in the structure of the House of Commons, Senate and Supreme Court, and over the extension of existing provinces into the territories as well as the establishment of new provinces.

The criticism of the tightened-up formula is that it is too rigid. It has been said that the new formula will prevent further reforms in the structure or role of the Senate, and rule out the Yukon and the Northwest Territories ever acquiring provincial status. These criticisms, though perhaps over-categorical, are well taken, and I share them. But they are not the whole story. To round out the picture, one should acknowledge two facts. First, of the three options for a new amending formula, the one chosen is the least rigid. One could not have reached a settlement without responding to Quebec's deep and justifiable dissatisfaction with the existing formula. Second, specifically on the Senate and the status of the territories, the underlying issue is the relative political weight of the various provinces and regions. Reforms, especially as may relate to provincial representation in the Senate, are desired in some parts of the country because it is hoped they will reduce the political weight of central Canada, the provinces of Ontario and Quebec. These two provinces together can, under the present (1982) or any practically conceivable formula, stop any constitutional amendment. Thus it may be doubted that raising from seven to 10 the number of provinces whose endorsement is required for any amendment is a significant change, particularly when the smaller provinces are likely to endorse changes that will favour, precisely, small provinces. The matter is obvious in the case of Senate reform. However, it applies also to the creation of new provinces, because a change in the territories' status, involving the addition of two or three provinces to the existing 10, would strengthen any "small provinces' coalition."

I make no prediction about the likelihood of further Senate reform, or about the creation of new provinces, under the amending formula contained in the 1987 Accord. Obviously changes in these areas will be made marginally more difficult to accomplish than they are now. However, I would add, as a general observation, that one might envision such changes only as parts of a new "package deal." I do not know what would have to be included in the package to ensure its acceptance, but the contents might well be about the same under the proposed 1987 formula as under the 1982 one.

Appointments to Senate and Supreme Court

The federal government now appoints Senators and also Justices of the Supreme Court. The 1987 Constitutional Accord will alter this practice by binding the federal government to make such appointments only from lists submitted by the provincial governments; but the Accord provides also that the persons named must be "acceptable to the Queen's Privy Council for Canada." There is no provision for a deadlock-breaking mechanism in cases of disagreement. These provisions establish a mutual veto for both categories of appointment, but some critics have alleged that in practice the provinces will gain full control. They believe, in other words, that Ottawa has simply handed over the power of appointment to the provinces. In support of this interpretation it has been said that provinces will be able to go on indefinitely making nominations but that the federal government will not be able, for fear of appearing unreasonable, indefinitely to go on rejecting them: the provinces can simply wear Ottawa down, because the initiative rests exclusively with them.

This prognostication neglects some relevant considerations. It is necessary to recognize that a constitution establishes certain parts of the machinery of government, which, over time, are complemented by the creation of additional institutions and a set of practices or conventions that make the formally established parts of the machinery workable. Political parties and the principles of cabinet government are examples. In the case of appointments to the Supreme Court and the Senate it is conceivable that machinery will be devised to regularize the process (for example, consultative committees to screen potential nominees to the Supreme Court), and it is quite predictable that practices will arise that acquire the force of convention. For example, it has been suggested that when a Senate vacancy is to be filled, provinces submit a "list" of only one—that person having been elected in a form of primary election. In this case the federal government would find it impossible to reject the sole provincial "nominee" as unsuitable; but nor would the appointment have fallen to the provincial government. If such a convention became established, Canada would have acquired a Senate that was both elected and effective, though obviously not composed of an equal number of Senators from each province.

While one cannot safely predict what new machinery and processes may surround and envelop the appointments section of the 1987 Accord, more limited observations are possible. The federal government, faced with an unacceptable slate of provincial nominees to fill a Senate vacancy, could simply leave the position open. A standoff could be prolonged almost indefinitely. In filling vacancies in the Supreme Court, except in the case of the three justices from Quebec, the federal government can choose from among nominees put forward by two or more provinces. Provincial governments would have a strong incentive to nominate outstanding candidates.

The situation relating to Quebec nominees would be different, because here the federal government has not the latitude of accepting nominees from other provinces. Nonetheless, delay is an option if the Quebec nominee or nominees is (are) unacceptable. Should the provincial government start to play games with the nomination, "inadvertent" leaks could reveal this; and conversely, if Ottawa were being unreasonable, the same tactic could be employed on the provincial side. None of this I consider likely, and certainly not desirable; but it is necessary to imagine such scenarios in order to realize that both sides, under the provisions of the 1987 Accord, retain considerable bargaining power. The result is likely to be an informal process of negotiation, or a formal process of consultation involving third parties, such that appointments are truly *jointly made*. I believe both orders of government will have every incentive to act reasonably and responsibly in the appointments process. The Canadian public, particularly in the case of appointments to the Supreme Court, would not put up with anything else.

To those who say the absence of a deadlock-breaking mechanism sets up an unworkable situation, or a situation having the potential for endless and unresolvable conflict, I would point to the structure of government in the United States. In that country the "checks and balances" written into the constitution provide for multiple veto-points, but business does get conducted; the machinery is made to work, because the consequences of its not working would be intolerable. The mutual veto set up by the Constitution Amendment, 1987, as regards appointments to the Supreme Court and the Senate, can certainly be made to work, preserving a real voice for both the federal and the provincial governments. Finally, and this is the most important point, a mutual-veto procedure will result in high quality appointments, increasing the legitimacy of both institutions.

Political Imbalance: Excessive Decentralization

Where one line of criticism of the 1987 Constitutional Accord alleges that special powers have been given to Quebec, and deplores this, another line of criticism has been that, to satisfy the other provinces, everything Quebec wanted was given to all. The result has been, according to this second group of critics, the further decentralization of an already dangerously decentralized federation. This complaint is, to a large degree, a compendium of others that have already been discussed; they relate to immigration policy, the Charter of Rights and Freedoms, social policy and the spending power, the formula for new constitutional amendments, and the appointment process for Senators and for judges of the Supreme Court. I have argued that concerns raised under these heads are exaggerated, and in some cases without foundation.

Also mentioned as a change contributing to a dangerous—and debilitating—degree of decentralization are the provisions for annual First Ministers' meetings on the constitution as well as on the economy. Annual constitutional meetings are not, in my opinion, necessary: as much as possible, a constitution should be left alone. But I do not see that the mere fact of holding them will erode federal power. A federal government that is uninterested in protecting its jurisdiction will give parts of it away, or let policy control slip unobtrusively (if possible) into provincial hands; a stronger or more determined federal government will see that these things do not happen. Whether or not there are annual meetings on the constitution is irrelevant. What is vitally relevant, however, is the range of bargaining powers that the federal government retains, and whether these have been reduced by the 1987 Accord. On this subject, I think the pro-centralist critics have been shallow in their analysis.

The essence of the Meech Lake agreement is that almost all its clauses will intensify the processes of intergovernmental negotiation, mostly on a bilateral basis. This has been illustrated in my earlier comments, particularly those on the spending power and the appointment process (Senate and Supreme Court). In these sections I have argued that the federal government retains a great deal of leverage, though rather less capacity for unilateral action. Whether, as a result of future negotiations, power shifts to the provinces or to Ottawa will be determined by public opinion, by economic, fiscal, and social factors shaping the public agenda, and by the personalities and capacities of political leaders at both the federal and provincial levels. Decentralization is possible, but so is a reaffirmation of central power.

The most likely way that a centralizing trend may be brought on is by developments in the economic sphere, occurring to a large extent outside of Canada. I think some of the critics of the 1987 Accord have considered that economic factors will require a strengthening of central power, but that the Accord will lessen Ottawa's capacity to meet external economic challenges. *However, I can see nothing in the Accord that would have this effect.* None of its provisions touches federal powers over the economy. Perhaps the pro-centralist critics think the new rules affecting the spending power might do so, but most of the relevant initiatives would be, not "national shared-cost programmes," but bilaterally nego-tiated ones. The latter are not within the purview of the spending power clause. The only sort of national shared-cost programme I can think of as being relevant—and this is a real possibility—would be one for training technologically competent manpower, to facilitate the growth or implan-tation of "innovation-reliant" industries. My earlier analysis of the spending power provisions in the Accord suggests that such an initia-tive would be entirely feasible. Here, as in other respects, outcomes will be determined not by the institutions or rules put in place by the Accord, but by a whole complex of attitudinal, economic and social factors.

V The Future of Federal—Provincial Relations

The 1987 Constitutional Accord hardly touches the federal division of powers, but it will profoundly affect the manner in which they are exer-cised. It will alter the dynamic of federal–provincial relations, creating a modified framework for federal–provincial interaction in policy forma-tion. It will be an enormous achievement if such processes of interaction can be made less acrimonious, more productive. Intergovernmental co-operation will become all the more important if the external economic environment continues to deteriorate, and/or if budget deficits impose ever-tighter constraints on social policy. In the 1987 Constitutional Accord the First Ministers have taken a significant step toward improving the climate of federal–provincial relations. The spending power clause, in particular, provides a glimpse of how a better-mannered relationship may be brought about. There, the federal government retains significant policy initiative, but shows itself ready to relax unnecessary, unproductive, conflict-generating controls over policy design. In other areas—key appointments, First Ministers' conferences—a framework for cooperation has been established. In one area, immigration, a new division of policy responsibilities within a scarcely modified division of powers (the field has been a concurrent one since 1867) is foreshadowed, conceivably establishing a model for agreements in other areas, such as communications. In all these ways, the Accord encourages transition to a new era for federal–provincial relations, in which the poisonous atmosphere of past battles can dissipate. Governments and the public have become accustomed to viewing the operation of the federal system as a continuing contest, a rivalry in which one order of government loses whatever the other gains. The idea that there can be mutual gain has too often been overpowered by the participants' combative instincts.

The Accord cannot guarantee an end to such habits of mind, but it does establish a framework within which new, more co-operative habits can take hold. The hope that they will do so may prove too fond; in that case there remain plenty of opportunities for hard bargaining both by Ottawa and by the provincial governments. However, if "the spirit of Meech Lake" can be kept alive, more joint action to respond to domestic aspirations and foreign challenges may be forthcoming. The Accord will prove, in these circumstances, a facilitating instrument. That, as well as the desire to settle unfinished business from 1980–82, is a powerful reason to endorse the Accord.

W. H. McCONNELL

THE MEECH LAKE ACCORD: LAWS OR FLAWS?

The Constitution of Canada, like that of most federal states, has exhibited alternate phases of centralization and decentralization. *The Constitution Act, 1867*[1] was a highly centralist document. Macdonald and Tupper, particularly, were proponents of a powerful central authority, which they hoped to achieve by giving the residue of unallocated legislative powers to Ottawa,[2] and also by conferring on her a power of "disallowance" by which it could nullify any provincial statute by the unfettered executive action of the federal cabinet.[3] Although broad generalizations are hazardous, it may be suggested tentatively that from 1867 up to the Privy Council's decision in the *Local Prohibition Case*[4] in 1896, the centralist assumptions of the Fathers of Confederation prevailed. Thereafter, there was a powerful current of provincialist decisions until the Second World War with Lords Watson, Haldane and Atkin seeking explicitly to countervail what they regarded as excessive central power in the interest of a more viable federalism.[5] During and after the 1939–45 war, centralization again gathered force, and with the abolition of overseas appeals in 1949,[6] the Privy Council, which had come to be regarded by autonomist premiers as a guardian of provincial interests, was no longer a functioning part of the Canadian hierarchy of courts.

The collaborative effort to enshrine the April–June, 1987, Meech Lake Accord in the Canadian Constitution by Prime Minister Brian Mulroney and all ten provincial premiers creates a strong constitutional counter-current in the provincialist direction. The Accord would *inter alia* designate Quebec as a "distinct society,"[7] with the legislature and

* *Saskatchewan Law Review*, 52, No. 1 (1988): 115–141.

government of the province having a mandate to preserve and promote its "distinct identity."[8] It would vest the exclusive power to originate names for future Senate[9] and Supreme Court[10] appointments in provincial governments, allow much greater participation of the latter in decisions involving the federal spending power[11] and immigration procedures,[12] and generally broaden the ambit of the provinces' constitutional decision-making authority. If and when the Accord is entrenched, it is not fanciful to suggest that a whole new era of constitutional decentralization will be inaugurated. Moreover, because of the rigidity of the amending procedure introduced by the Accord,[13] which in some important respects adds new "unanimity" requirements for constitutional amendments, an element of inflexibility will be established which may make desirable change difficult in future.

Central to the calculations of the participants in the current constitutional process is, of course, the common aspiration to bring Quebec into a constitutional framework she rejected in 1980–82. In May, 1980, the provincial electorate, by a margin of 60 to 40 per cent, refused to give Premier René Lévesque's separatist government a mandate to negotiate the terms of "sovereignty-association" with the federal government in Ottawa.[14] Prime Minister Pierre E. Trudeau and his Justice Minister, Jean Chrétien, had intervened forcefully in the 1980 referendum, promising Quebec "constitutional renewal" in return for rejecting the separatist mandate sought by the Parti-Québécois government. Immediately after the referendum, the Continuing Committee of Ministers on the Constitution (CCMC), under the joint chairmanship of Chrétien and Saskatchewan Attorney-General Roy Romanow, attempted unsuccessfully to arrive at a federal–provincial consensus on constitutional reform.[15] With the collapse of the CCMC joint effort, Trudeau announced on October 2nd, 1980, that notwithstanding provincial opposition he was proceeding unilaterally to patriate the Constitution through the Joint Address procedure.[16] His only provincial allies were New Brunswick and Ontario. The Supreme Court of Canada decided in the following September that his initiative was unconstitutional in the conventional (but not in the legal) sense,[17] and the parties went back to the negotiating table. The separatist government of Quebec would not, however, join with the other nine provinces in accepting the ultimate constitutional compromise of November 5th, 1981, which brought about patriation of the Constitution with the Charter and a domestic amending formula.[18]

In the aftermath of patriation, tensions persisted between Quebec and Ottawa. The province was unsuccessful in an action brought before the Supreme Court to determine whether she possessed a historical veto power over constitutional change.[19] She inserted a "notwithstanding" clause in all of her laws, thereby symbolically rejecting a Charter she had no part in making, but the device was unanimously found unconstitutional by the Quebec Court of Appeal.[20] Moreover, she refused to participate in amending procedures, since to accept amendments would implicitly sanction a constitutional framework she continued to reject. It remained an unfinished task of Canadian statecraft to devise a mechanism which would induce Quebec to voluntarily accept that framework. From a strictly positivistic standpoint, there was no question that the Constitution applied to her, but she had not willingly embraced it.

In the forefront of Quebec's constitutional demands was some recognition that she was culturally unique in the Canadian federation.[21] And however contentious it might be to proponents of a single Canada to enshrine it in the Constitution, there was no doubt that Quebec was sociologically a "distinct society," as well as the historical nucleus from which contemporary Canada had developed. Legally, whether she assented to it or not, Quebec was bound by the constitutional accommodation of 1980–82. The question remained, however, concerning whether any Canadian constitutional framework from which she had abstained could have "political legitimacy"[22] without her consent.

The constitutional processes involving patriation in 1980–82 and Meech Lake in 1987 were exercises in executive federalism. However much we may pay lip service to "popular sovereignty" in the realm of constitution-making, it remains a republican virtue. Basic change in the Canadian Constitution appears to be, at this stage of history, the prerogative of ministers and legislatures, not of the people as a whole in referenda (the Quebec initiative in May, 1980, was an exception).

The final text of the Meech Lake Accord (known sometimes as the "Langevin" Agreement) was hammered out on Wednesday, June 3rd, at a marathon 19-hour negotiating session in which the First Ministers sent their expert constitutional advisers to the outer precincts in order not to be unduly distracted by technicalities.[23] The procedure resembled dispute resolution in the labour relations field, in which the Prime Minister was proficient in his legal practice before he entered politics. In such a context, it is not unusual to bring the parties together in a common forum and to keep them negotiating until they agree, perhaps strengthening the inducements gradually so that the reluctance of wavering participants is ultimately overcome. A deal was finally struck, but at what price?

On the day after the signing of the Accord by the eleven First Ministers, a senior federal official said: "It was essentially a search for language that everybody could live with. It was as much a problem-solving exercise as a negotiation.''[24] On the same day, in an address to the nation, Prime Minister Mulroney declared: "In recent days you have heard that we are rushing into this. It is normal and healthy that these questions should be asked . . . . Did we give up too much to get Quebec's signature on the Constitution? The answer is no. Fairness and equality have been the hallmarks of our actions.''[25]

As the ensuing debate was to reveal, critics of the Meech Lake Accord perceived that the Prime Minister had indeed given up too much to the provinces in return for Quebec's voluntary accession to the Constitution. Her accession was important, but it was in no way critical at this time. The agenda seemed to be dictated more by opportunistic politics than by a genuine desire to save the federation from some impending peril. In the September 4th, 1984, general election Quebec voters had uncharacteristically given Prime Minister Mulroney's Progressive Conservative party a massive vote along with four-fifths of the province's federal seats. The province later appeared to be inexorably slipping from his grasp. With the electorate in a volatile mood, and with Meech Lake highly popular in the province, however, federal politicians were wary and disinclined to challenge a constitutional arrangement that had found favour with provincial voters. The Prime Minister calculated that Meech Lake would assist him in restoring his party's ebbing fortunes in Quebec, whereas the Liberal and New Democratic Party oppositions also considered it politically expedient to support the Accord. No official voice was raised against Meech Lake in Parliament, although the Liberal caucus experienced severe strains because of the decentralist direction of the instrument, which conflicted with the policies of long-time Liberal Prime Minister (1968–79; 1980–84) Trudeau.

Women's organizations, aboriginal peoples and multicultural groups were among the more vigorous dissenters from the Accord. Many women were concerned that the loose language of the Accord, referring to certain Charter guarantees but not to others, would undermine sexual equality which was not expressly mentioned. Aboriginal peoples were dismayed that a constitutional agreement could be concluded with such secrecy and swiftness to meet Quebec's demands when no progress had been made towards their quest for self-determination at four successive constitutional conferences.[26] The final conference for this purpose had taken place earlier in 1987, moreover, and after its failure there had been no assurance of a resumption of negotiations in the near future. Aboriginal leaders considered that at least a renewed ''process'' should be incorporated in the Accord so that self-government could be brought about. There seemed to be no political will for this purpose, however, and multicultural groups were upset about the majoritarian thrust behind the strong affirmation of the English and French "communities" in section 2, fearing that their own distinctiveness, recognized in section 27 of the Charter, could be diminished or overlooked in the overall context of the Accord.

Reaction to the Meech Lake Accord: The "Distinct Society" Clause

As a political leader who habitually stood for a "single Canada," and deplored a narrow inward-looking nationalism, former Prime Minister Pierre Trudeau attacked particularly the provision in the Accord that would recognize Quebec as a "distinct society." "Those Canadians," he expostulated, "who fought for a single Canada, bilingual and multicultural, can say goodbye to their dream: we are henceforth to have two Canadas, each defined in terms of its language."[27] The provision was ominous indeed to Quebec Anglophones, because of the admonition addressed to the Quebec legislature and government in the same context "to preserve and promote (this) distinct identity." Trudeau, indeed, saw this injunction as superseding even conflicting Charter provisions, thus weakening the instrument he did so much to forge. The complementary pledge by Ottawa to withdraw from all services relating to cultural and linguistic integration of immigrants would further undermine single Canadian nationhood.

On the institutional level, the right extended to the provinces to designate future senators and Supreme Court judges could convert both national forums into bastions of adversarial provincial power. In a polemic marked by acid invective, Trudeau summarized the losses to the central power resulting from the Accord:

> What a dark day for Canada was this April 30, 1987. In addition to surrendering to the provinces important parts of its jurisdiction (the spending power, immigration), in addition to weakening the Charter of Rights, the Canadian state made subordinate to the provinces its legislative power (Senate) and its judicial power (Supreme Court), and it did this without ever hoping to get any of it back (a constitutional veto granted to each province). It even committed itself to a constitutional "second round" at which the demands of the provinces will dominate the agenda.[28]

While the result did not amount, precisely, to "sovereignty-association," it was "on the fast track to getting there." Trudeau sardonically castigated Mulroney for consummating the work of others whose policies would tend to sap national leadership and balkanize Canada. The Conservative Prime Minister was following in the path of Jean Lesage and Claude Ryan who called for Quebec's "special status," of Robert Stanfield who espoused the "two-nations" doctrine, and was endorsing the plea for a board of directors made up of eleven First Ministers championed by Allan Blakeney and Marcel Faribault, and lastly, was affirming the ideas of his vanquished opponent of February 1980, Joe Clark, who advocated Canada's restructuring into "a community of communities."

In a critique laced with anger and scorn, the centralist prime minister whose tenure of office was one of the longest in Canadian history showed that he was stung by what he regarded as Mulroney's betrayal of the one-Canada concept (a concept that, curiously, Trudeau shared with John Diefenbaker).

Trudeau's criticism raises the question of whether the Meech Lake Accord, while not amounting to outright separatism, could through time promote a kind of "incremental separatism." If Quebec and Ottawa legislators have an exclusive mission to "preserve and protect" the distinctiveness of Quebec society, what of the other distinct society that surrounds it and delimits it geographically? Can Quebec M.P.s who represent in Parliament their own "distinct society" legislate in areas which are distinctive in the territorially broader society which encompasses Quebec? If, in furtherance of a unilingual Francophone Quebec, Quebec M.N.A.s and M.P.s enhanced French language and culture in their home province, could they plausibly resist initiatives by Western Canadian M.P.s and M.L.A.s to promote Icelandic, Cree, Ukrainian and German at the expense of French? Would this contribute to national cohesion and unity? And if Quebec, and particularly Francophone M.P.s, have a particular mandate to promote and enhance the "distinct society" of Quebec, must they not acknowledge an implicit co-relative right of deputies from other parts of Canada to enhance the particular social and cultural attributes of their own regions? Trudeau's warning is that Meech Lake points to fragmentation of the federation rather than unity.

As an English-speaking Quebec M.P. Hon. Donald Johnston is naturally concerned about provisions in the Accord which could discriminate against the Anglophone minority in his province, but his concerns transcend those of the community of which he is an influential voice. In his Montreal *Gazette* article,[29] he emphasized the Accord's "further and irreversible strengthening of provincial powers at the

expense of the central government." The decentralization would be particularly felt in the areas of the federal spending power and on federal
institutions such as the Senate and the Supreme Court. Moreover,
Canada is already very decentralized: ". . . of all public money spent
in 1986, 60 per cent was spent by the provinces and municipalities, only
40 per cent by the federal government. Do they [supporters of the
Accord] know that in 1960 provincial and municipal spending was less
than 50 per cent?''

If the opting-out provision relating to the spending power were
extensively invoked by the provinces, "Canada could very well end up
with a patchwork quilt of provincial programs with little or no room
for co-ordination and transferability of benefits between them." Unlike
the situation prevailing in the past, the federal government would no
longer be able to ensure that spending programs conformed to "national
criteria or standards."

While Johnston favours the continuation of an appointed Senate,
he would reform it to represent occupational groups and the intellectual elite (e.g., scientists; educators; community, professional and labour
leaders; representatives of the fishery, agriculture and forestry sectors;
of the clergy and the press; and retiring provincial premiers).[30] Even
this modest reform proposal would be made difficult by the Accord's
individual vetoes for Parliament and the provinces on changes in the
Upper House. And in the case of appointments to the Supreme Court,
he ponders the eventual membership of the tribunal under the Accord:
"Imagine the composition of a Supreme Court with judges named over
20 years by Maurice Duplessis and for 10 years by separatists."

It was Johnston's qualms about the Accord's description of Quebec
as a distinct society that caused fellow Trudeau cabinet minister André
Ouellet to call him a "Westmount Rhodesian,"[31] a remark that was
later withdrawn. A "distinct society" promoted by the Quebec government and legislature not only could reinforce the linguistic rights of the
Francophone majority, it could foster distinctiveness in "communications, economic development, trade and even external affairs." In fact,
the well-known Quebec journalist Lise Bissonette has even suggested
it might provide constitutional support for a Quebec presidential system.

Dr. Eugene Forsey also criticizes the instrument for its "ambiguities
and obscurities" and generally sloppy draftsmanship.[32] Did the "distinct society" clause mean that any weakening of the *Official Languages
Act* was now constitutionally impermissible, or that the courts could
direct Parliament to make laws needed to live up to the new constitutional imperatives? Or, when it referred to the Francophone minority
outside Quebec, did it mean that the courts could order the Ontario

legislature to restore rights conferred on the minority which were later taken away? Or could it mean that if Franco-Ontarians considered legislative protection of their language and culture inadequate, the courts could order Queen's Park to add further rights for their protection? As others have queried, he wonders whether, in the clause on the spending power, "objectives" mean the same thing as "standards"? As well, who decides? As a former Liberal senator (1970–79), Forsey deplores the Accord's strengthening of requirements for altering the Senate, from a requirement for consent by Parliament and seven provinces having half the total population to a requirement for unanimity: "A single provincial legislature just keeping mum for three years would leave the change as dead as mutton."

The Accord, nevertheless, is not without its defenders. In a strongly supportive editorial, the *Globe and Mail* said: "Requiring courts to interpret the Constitution in a manner consistent with Quebec's distinctiveness within Canada is not isolationist, as Mr. Trudeau puts it. It gives a benefit of the doubt in hypothetical legal circumstances to the promotion of the French fact in North America—a Canadian achievement."[33] And one of the chief architects of the Accord, Senator Lowell Murray, the minister of state for federal–provincial relations, observes that the Accord's amendments "are not major" and allow the Constitution "to integrate the best of what a democratic people has learned about itself and the values it wishes its institutions to embody." "While the accord recognizes Quebec's distinct society," he adds, "it also recognizes that French-speaking Canadians do not reside exclusively in Quebec and that English-speaking Canadians do not live only outside it."[34] Professor Andrew J. Petter of the University of Victoria also notes that the criticism concerning the evisceration of the spending power may be misguided, since "many of the national social programs [the critics] rightly revere were born in the provinces, notably medicare."[35]

The Federal Spending Power

According to proposed section 106A of the Accord, the federal government is authorized to give "reasonable compensation" to a province choosing not to participate in a new national shared-cost program in an area of provincial jurisdiction, provided that the province's alternative "program or initiative" is "compatible with the national objectives."

The alteration in the legal guidelines for the use of the federal spending power could have profound implications for the Canadian federation. The spending power has been of great significance in Canadian history because of the disproportion between constitutional responsibilities for social welfare under the federal division of powers (largely provincial) and the capacity to raise adequate monies by taxes to meet such responsibilities, which the poorer provinces simply do not have.[36] The provinces, of course, are generally restricted to direct taxation,[37] while Parliament can impose any tax, direct or indirect, and it has powerful political and legal resources, in any competition for scarce fiscal resources with the provinces, to pre-empt some of the richer tax fields to itself.

Onerous provincial responsibilities in the social welfare, health and education sectors have long been funded jointly by the federal and provincial governments under the spending power. Federal grants to universities, especially after 1951, and for medicare and social programs have been made in this way. Provincial responsibilities in such areas could not be met by the poorer provinces, and could be met only with difficulty even by the richer ones, without such aid.[38]

As mentioned, Professor Petter has argued[39] that certain path-breaking social reforms were spawned by the provinces, and it should not be assumed that provincial social programs meeting "national objectives" will be defective. They may be superior. However, Professor Petter's point does not necessarily deflect the brunt of the criticism directed against the spending power proposal. While it is true that social experimentation by the provinces may engender worthy new programs, such as medicare, what critics fear is not essentially desirable innovation by provinces showing leadership in social policy, but defective compliance with "national objectives" by provinces sponsoring alternative programs of a less commendable character. It is not the vanguard provinces but the laggards that worry the critics. Under the pre-Meech Lake spending power procedure, uniform standards could be designed and enforced by the federal power for both progressive and refractory provinces, with non-receipt of transfer payments being the ultimate sanction against the latter. If Meech Lake is entrenched it will become more difficult for the federal government to ensure compliance with homogeneous coast-to-coast "standards" or "objectives."

The provinces rightly emphasize that when they embark on shared-cost social programs of this type with the federal government, the constitutional jurisdiction involved is ordinarily provincial. In the unemployment insurance and old age pension areas, the federal government acceded to new powers only by centralizing amendments.[40] In other areas, the bulk of social jurisdiction is provincial. In such a case is it not perfectly natural that the provinces should enjoy primary responsibility and control?

The answer to the above question cannot be divorced from historical factors. In 1867 when Confederation was achieved, what little social welfare there was emanated largely from private sources such as churches, cooperative societies and philanthropy. In the era of the "negative state," the role of government was smaller and was financed from indirect sources such as customs and excise duties, the sale of property, and so on. It was only with the devastating social depression of the 1930s that North American governments began to establish extensive social welfare programs requiring much greater financial outlays.

When such programs were planned, it was found that there was a large gap between fiscal resources and legal responsibilities. Cooperative federalism was the answer. Unless centralizing amendments could be agreed to, the parties would have to proceed on a shared-cost basis, jointly funding and administering such programs. While jurisdiction was provincial, a consensus emerged, however, that the programs should be uniform and national in scope. The federal government became, in effect, a "leveller" of the national economy, redistributing wealth by means of the tax system from the wealthier to the poorer areas. In essence, whenever it situated a military camp in a depressed area it had been doing the same thing. The principle began to emerge at this time that despite the vagaries of the climate and the regional inequities of nature, all Canadians were entitled to certain basic services as an attribute of citizenship. The leadership in defining social and economic benefits from coast to coast would be primarily federal.

There is some controversy as to precisely where the constitutional source of the federal spending power resides. Some writers find its source in section 91 1A of the *Constitution Act, 1867*, which confers jurisdiction over "The Public Debt and Property" on Parliament.[41] The late deputy minister of justice, Elmer Driedger, argued strongly against this view, however, on the basis that a grant of money by the federal government to the provinces is not a "law," such as those envisaged generally by section 91 of the *Constitution Act, 1867*, but the making of a conditional or unconditional gift to the provinces for some common purpose.[42] (There is also, it may be added, a provincial spending power, by which provinces can make expenditures for, but not legislate in relation to, federal objects.)

For a province like Saskatchewan, traditionally reliant for its prosperity on the sale of wheat,[43] the federal spending power has been vital as a shield against adversity. In 1986–87, in fact, Premier Grant Devine was promised a substantial segment of a $1 billion federal allocation for wheat farmers facing stiff competition from European and American competitors who were heavily subsidized, allowing them to sell their product on the international market at lower prices. A rough comparison can be made between Saskatchewan's traditional economic reliance on wheat and Cuba's reliance on sugar cane.[44] Both the Saskatchewan and Cuban economies have been prey to the vicissitudes of climate and uncontrollable external market forces, and have displayed frequent swings in economic prosperity. Arguably, both developed collectivist governments in an effort to reduce the impact of adverse economic forces on their primary producers.

In a national economy as diverse and fluctuating as Canada's, the vicissitudes of regional economic conditions over short periods of time necessitate a strong federal government which uses its spending power liberally as a buffer against local adversity. Arguably, this is more diffi-cult to achieve under Meech Lake. For one thing, nobody knows exactly what "national objectives" means. Within the context of a new national housing program for lower-income families under the "spending power," a left-wing provincial government might build public housing on an extensive scale, whereas a more "free-enterprise" provincial government might give applicants vouchers to rent or buy housing already on the market. In either case who would decide that the housing was of adequate quality and what the "reasonable compensation" would be? Would this post-Meech Lake situation be an improvement on a uni-form national housing program of a pre-Meech Lake character where the federal government set standards and exercised leadership? Such questions have no ready answer.

Another question that remains unanswered is what exactly consti-tutes a "new" program to which the Meech Lake spending power pro-visions are said alone to apply? Medicare, for example, is an enormously costly existing social program which consumes an increasing amount of provincial and federal tax revenues. Is it not possible that, to save some money, the whole program might have to be redesigned, conceiv-ably with some limitations on access, government user-fees to defray costs, and so forth? If a "new" shared-cost medicare program were designed under the spending power, would it not be open to Alberta and Ontario to opt out and devise their own variant medicare program with an extra-billing scheme? The *Canada Health Act, 1984*[45] would have to be repealed, of course, but that would be only a detail. The opting-out provinces could argue that they were maintaining the delivery of health care and that extra-billing was merely a subsidiary administrative feature of the overall scheme. Since it did not derogate from "national objectives" the provinces would be entitled to "reasonable compensation" from federal coffers.

One gets an uneasy feeling that social "standards" could become very elastic in opting-out provinces under the Meech Lake proposal. It is possible, also, that behind closed doors a number of provinces could virtually dictate the terms of a new "spending power" initiative to the federal government. They now have leverage to do so.

Appointments to the Senate

The Meech Lake Accord's provision envisaging provincial (instead of the present federal) nominations to the Senate will make Senate reform even more difficult than it formerly was. The thirteenth clause of the Accord[46] requires the Prime Minister to convene annual constitutional conferences, commencing in 1988, at which, *inter alia*, Senate reform will be an item on the agenda. However, once the Meech Lake system is in place, with its attractive new source of political patronage for provincial premiers, there will be a strong incentive to leave the present Senate otherwise intact for a lengthy period.[47]

Premier Donald Getty of Alberta has been the most forceful advocate of a "Triple E" (elected, equal and effective) Senate.[48] Since 1867, he would argue, the Canadian Parliament has unduly reflected the power and influence of Central Canada. With approximately two-thirds of the country's population concentrated in Ontario and Quebec, those provinces have a total of 170 M.P.s (out of 282) in the House of Commons, as compared with 109 for the Western and Atlantic provinces and three for the Territories. The unelected Senate is now relatively powerless, and even in the present Upper Chamber Ontario and Quebec each possess 24 members as compared with British Columbia's six and New Brunswick's ten. Although the Senate was designed to express regional interests and grievances in Parliament, it has not performed that role effectively. Instead, a federalized cabinet usually representing all provinces has articulated the interests of the provinces and regions. There have been frequent calls for Senate reform,[49] but serving as it does as a rich source of political patronage, no reform has ever materialized. In lieu of institutional reform, the Meech Lake proposals would merely substitute provincial for federal patronage. In other respects, the Red Chamber would remain the same.

Premier Getty could advance strong arguments for his proposed "Triple E" Senate. Over the past decade, for example, there has been a protracted series of bitter regional disputes—on the CF-18 contract, the Crow Rate, energy, patriation, fisheries, offshore resources, and other matters—leaving a lingering residue of hostility. Being substantially outnumbered by Central Canada in the House of Commons, there is no legislative forum like the American or Australian senates where equal representation of the local units would allow the extremities of Canada to reexamine disputes like the above on a more equitable footing.

Such a proposed reconstituted Upper House is sometimes objected to because of the great imbalances in population in the various provinces. How could Prince Edward Island have equal representation with Ontario, for example? In the American Senate, nevertheless, states with small populations, such as Alaska and Wyoming, each have two senators along with California, whose population is fifty times as great. And in Australia, Tasmania, which has only one-tenth of the population of New South Wales, has ten elected senators, the same number as the latter and the other Australian states.[50]

Prior to the adoption of the American Constitution of 1789, James Madison wrote in *Federalist Papers* that if the population principle was used in deciding the membership of both houses, the tendency would be to create an overcentralized *national* rather than a balanced *federal* governmental structure.[51] The Lower House (as in Canada at present) should represent population, but the Upper House should represent the local units (states or provinces) preferably on an equal basis. This is how the Americans and Australians have created well-balanced legislative systems. This is the direction that Premier Getty considered that parliamentary reform should take. With Meech Lake in place, however, the possibility of achieving any significant Senate reform becomes remote.

A reconstituted "Triple E" Senate would disturb important institutional elites. There would be an understandable apprehension by members of the Lower House, and by the federal executive, that their traditional legislative leadership would be subverted by such a reform. For an example of what could happen, one has only to look at the powerful U.S. Senate, which tends to dominate congressional government in the United States. A Canadian Senate of such a kind would be more compact than the House of Commons, and would have a political legitimacy that the present unelected chamber lacks. With such a reform, in any confrontation with the House of Commons, senators would not be subject to the taunt that they were an unelected anachronism in a democratic age. Such a Senate could become a strong institutional rival to the Lower House.

However, in any new Senate reform, adjustments could be made which would preserve the leadership of the Lower House while restructuring the Upper House to more effectively represent the provinces. For example: (1) By constitutional convention, a rule has now developed that the holders of major portfolios in the federal cabinet will sit in the Lower House. In the American system, members of the president's cabinet do not sit in either house, thereby contributing to the dominance of the U.S. Senate in a legislative framework that differs from the Canadian one; (2) by the convention of "responsible government," in Canada (unlike Australia) a rule also exists that only the Lower House can pass a want-of-confidence involving the defeat of the federal government;[52] and (3) only the Lower House can introduce financial bills, and the Senate cannot constitutionally (as in the Australian Upper House)[53] stop supply nor can it block constitutional amendments originating in the Lower House for more than 180 days.

Under the Meech Lake Accord, the greatest disincentive to reform could simply be the new requirement for provincial unanimity to change the system. Provincial premiers will enjoy a rich source of patronage they have never had before. A single resolute premier could block reform indefinitely, even if the other nine premiers and the prime minister desired it, simply by withholding his consent from any reform proposal. A single premier who did nothing for three years could terminate reform desired by everyone else in the federation. When, under existing arrangements, the premiers of Quebec and Ontario can forward names to Ottawa to fill up to 24 senatorial vacancies (compared to Saskatchewan's six), why would they opt for reform that would make them the mere equal of Prince Edward Island? The Meech Lake proposals are likely to freeze the Senate in its present mould indefinitely.

One of the unsettling things about the Meech Lake proposals is that they could give the Senate a superficial veneer of political legitimacy without effecting fundamental reform. Whenever a dispute arises between Parliament and the provinces in future, senators can accurately say that they owe their appointments to the provincial premiers and are consequently entitled to represent the provincial or regional point of view. They could argue, therefore, that they had a fresh mandate to obstruct measures emanating from the House of Commons that the pre-Meech Lake Senate, which owed its appointments not to the provinces but to the central government, did not. But aside from the provincial origins of the appointments, the Upper Chamber remains unchanged. Any substantive change in the Senate's powers, or any revision of the unequal number of senators from each province, or in the election of senators, would require the unanimous consent of Parliament and ten provincial legislatures. Except for increased provincial patronage, the institution remains as it was.

Appointments to the Supreme Court

In addition to unequivocally entrenching the Supreme Court,[54] the Meech Lake Accord decentralizes the appointing process for judges.[55] Quebec's present statutory entitlement to three out of nine judges is entrenched,[56] and when a vacancy occurs among the Quebec judges on the court, the replacement must be chosen by the Governor-General from a list of names submitted by the Government of Quebec.[57] In the case of vacancies from other provinces, the choice must be made from names submitted "by the government of a province other than Quebec."[58]

Because of Quebec's distinctive civil law system, it is essential to provide for a number of "civilians" on the court, and subsections 101B(2) and 101C(3)[59] accomplish this by requiring that only members of the Quebec bar chosen by Quebec and approved, in effect, by the federal cabinet will fill those vacancies.

While the unique position of Quebec is rightly recognized in the above proposals, there is disturbing ambiguity in the overall scheme. Prior appointments have been made on a regional basis, which recognizes the disparate character of the Canadian federation. All that the present proposals direct is that Ottawa should appoint new judges from outside Quebec from names originating with "the government of each province." If future vacancies arise in Ontario or on the Prairie provinces, there would seem to be no reason why nominees submitted by the several Atlantic provinces or British Columbia, from their own bars, could not fill the vacancies. It may be that there is an existing constitutional convention that appointments to the Supreme Court will represent all the main regions of the country, but in Meech Lake specific representation is assured only for Quebec, and a convention would certainly be superseded by an entrenched amendment to the extent that there was any inconsistency between them. There may be political factors that would deter governments from depriving any "region" of its representation on the court, but the Meech Lake text certainly does not reflect the federal reality.

There are other anomalies in the proposals. The Accord provides that when the Chief Justice is appointed by Ottawa from among sitting members of the Court, no provincial nominating power is involved.[60] If the Chief Justice is not appointed from among sitting judges, he or she will presumably be a provincial nominee, but will the federal government be involved here, and what consultative process (between Ottawa and the other provinces) will be employed? No consideration is given to this important problem. It is almost as if, in this respect, the Court had ceased to be a federal institution. And while section 101B(1) recognizes that judges may be selected from territorial bars, nowhere are the governments of the Northwest Territories and the Yukon permitted to forward names to the appointing power, since names can originate only with "provincial" governments.

The decentralized appointing power could lead to a Supreme Court of a much different character than the present one. As the Court decides more and more "policy" questions involving Charter issues, it is possible that it will become more politicized with discernible right and left wings, unlike the "pragmatic" Canadian courts of the past. A single centralized appointing power can oversee the development of the Court as an institution, as in the United States, where successive presidents can appoint left- or right-leaning members in order to create the balance on the tribunal that they desire.[61] In the polycentric appointing system emerging from the Meech Lake proposals, the effective balancing of the composition of the Court becomes more difficult. In future (except with appointments of Chief Justices from sitting members) no names will be generated by the federal power. There is a serious question here not only of whether the Court will have ideological balance, but of whether the members will have a national vision of Canada. With provincial premiers of not always progressive views making appointments, moreover, will women and minorities be represented adequately on future courts, and even if they are, what will their policy views reflect?

As with the Meech Lake reforms of the Senate, the Supreme Court changes ignore the important issue of patronage.[62] A more open appointing process, possibly with hearings concerning the fitness of nominees by a reconstituted Upper House, as in the American Senate, might allay public suspicions of undue political influence in the making of judicial appointments, but with Meech Lake suspicions are likely to be intensified if anything—there will be ten centres of patronage rather than one. And, as with the Senate, there is an individual provincial veto blocking any change in the appointing system or in other main features of the Supreme Court once the Accord is entrenched.[63]

The Accession of the Territories to Provincial Status

The conditions for admission of new provinces to the Canadian federation have through time become progressively more difficult. Provision was made for the admission of Newfoundland, Prince Edward Island, British Columbia, "Rupert's Land" and the "North-western Territory" in s. 146 of the *Constitution Act, 1867*, although Newfoundland did not finally join Canada until 1949, and the mentioned territorial units, which have undergone territorial changes since 1867, are not yet provinces. The various provinces which were admitted subsequent to the original four were admitted by different procedures—by imperial statute, imperial order-in-council, or ordinary domestic statute[64] until, with Newfoundland's admission,[65] the present complement of ten provinces was completed, leaving the Northwest Territories and the Yukon in what can only be described as a "semi-colonial" or dependent status.

In two referenda held in June and July 1948, Newfoundland ultimately voted by a small majority to federate with Canada, rather than to seek "responsible government," or sovereign self-governing status, which was the other alternative on the final ballot.[66] In the ensuing negotiations between Newfoundland and Ottawa on the "terms of union" the other provinces were simply not consulted. Fearing that Quebec's autonomist premier, Maurice Duplessis (who wanted, among other things, to negotiate the relocation of the Quebec–Labrador boundary), would oppose Newfoundland's admission, Prime Minister Louis St. Laurent bypassed the provinces entirely.[67] At that time, and for more than three decades thereafter, there was no formal constitutional requirement for the federal government to consult the provinces before Parliament enacted a statute admitting a new province.

Until 1982, the two northern territories could have achieved provincial status by a simple federal statute. Under a novel provision incorporated in section 42(1)(f) of the *Constitution Act, 1982*, the concurrence of Parliament and seven provinces (with half the total population) was required for the admission of new provinces. Even this provision made admission difficult, and the government of the Northwest Territories consulted Kenneth Lysyk, Q.C., in December, 1981, to ascertain if measures could be taken to delete the above provision from the impending British statute,[68] but this proved impossible. In section 9 of the Meech Lake proposals, a new section 41(i) of the foregoing Act makes the requirements for provincehood even more stringent. The consent of Parliament and *all* provinces is now required for admission. The prospects of either territory now being admitted under the revised procedure are so remote as to be virtually unattainable. If existing provinces feared that the admission of the territories would disturb the federal–provincial balance at annual meetings of First Ministers or that transfer payments from Ottawa to existing provinces could be reduced by such admissions, any province could individually veto admission out of the crassest motives of self-interest.

The practice in other federal states is instructive. Unlike Canada, which in 1867 consisted of only four of the present ten provinces, on federation in 1901 the six colonies now included in Australia became, and remain, the only states in the new Commonwealth. The Northern Territory was transferred to the Commonwealth by South Australia in 1911, and is governed by an Administrator and Legislative Council. It is also represented in the Commonwealth Parliament where it has had full voting rights since 1968. The procedure for admission of new states in Australia is much simpler than in Canada, since a simple federal statute, without the concurrence of any states, is all that is required.[69] As Professor Geoffrey Sawer says:

> The federal parliament can admit federal territories as new states without the consent of existing states; indeed, it could admit a completely non-Australian country that sought admission.[70]

Similarly, as Lord Bryce declares in the 1914 edition of his venerable work on American government,[71] the position in the United States was, and continues to be (as in Australia), that a simple federal statute, without the concurrence of any states, is all that is needed for the admission of new states to the Union:

> The . . . thirty-five States admitted to the Union, in addition to the original thirteen, have all entered it as organized self-governing communities, with their Constitutions already made by their respective peoples. Each Act of Congress which admits a new State admits it as a subsisting common-

wealth, sometimes empowering it to meet and enact a constitution for themselves . . . sometimes accepting and confirming a constitution already made by the people.[72]

Nothing could provide a starker contrast with the Meech Lake requirement than the American practice of admitting territories to statehood in the past. After a usually brief transitional territorial phase, which was expressly seen as a prelude to statehood, the territorial units acquired full membership in the American Union. The non-contiguous territories of Alaska and Hawaii, which were obtained by purchase or force, served a somewhat longer apprenticeship.[73] Is there, perhaps, in a republic, an underlying assumption that Canada does not share, that the residents of territories enjoy a democratic right to full membership in the federation as soon as it can be accomplished?

It is obvious that under the pre-existing system the federal government and Parliament could always control the admission of territories as provinces, since federal action in statutory form was required (at least in this century) for such admission. The reason for the increasing rigidity for admission must, accordingly, be sought elsewhere. Probably the desire to give Quebec a veto over such admissions figured prominently in the decision. Quebec, which is a guardian in the federation of what the Accord describes as a ''distinct society,'' is already outnumbered by nine provinces with English-speaking majorities in the councils of Canadian executive federalism, and the addition of two more non-Francophone northern provinces would create an even greater imbalance.

The new unanimity requirement imposed for the acquisition of provincial status raises an important policy issue. Should not the constitutional criteria for provincehood be social and economic progress as in other federal states? However, might they not become, under the Meech Lake formula, some extraneous political considerations not related to the merits at all?

Immigration and Alienage

Proposed section 95A of the *Constitution Act, 1867*[74] provides that any province can enter into an agreement with the federal government ''relating to immigration or the temporary admission of aliens into that province that is appropriate to the needs and circumstances of that province.'' Such an agreement is to have the force of law, moreover, notwithstanding section 91(25) of the *Constitution Act, 1867*, but any later and inconsistent Act of Parliament setting ''national standards and objectives'' is to have paramount force over such agreements, especially insofar as it establishes ''general classes of immigrants,'' or relates to ''levels of immigration,'' or prescribes categories of ''inadmissibility.'' The *Canadian Charter of Rights and Freedoms* is to apply, pursuant to section 95B(3),[75] in respect of any federal–provincial immigration agreement negotiated under subsection 95B(1).[76]

A chief purpose of the above provisions, although they are cast in general terms, is presumably to allow the province of Quebec to maintain the demographic balance, or existing proportion of Francophones to Anglophones, in its population, so that the relationship of French- to English-speaking residents can be preserved in the interests of the continuing vitality of the French language and culture. This could be facilitated, for example, by the province financially assisting immigration from countries such as France, Haiti or Vietnam, where French is spoken, in which cases the immigrants could adjust more readily to the majority French language and culture in the province. Arguably, the ''distinct society'' of Quebec would thereby be enhanced.

Any agreement to the above effect, however, is expressly made subject to the Charter,[77] and presumably could not legally impair the rights of ''permanent residents'' to move freely from place to place in Canada as permitted by subsection 6(2) of the Charter. The provincial inducement for immigrants to settle in the province could not require immigrants to remain indefinitely at their first destination, although it could offer attractive benefits to them such as the provision of relocation assistance, and aid with housing and employment. If an immigrant so assisted desired to move to another province, it could perhaps require repayment of the whole or part of the outlay provided, as long as such repayment was not construed by the courts to be an unreasonable fetter on mobility. Would such a system tend, however, to fractionalize citizenship within the country by fostering unduly strong local allegiance? Would such immigrants feel a greater obligation to the provincial government assisting them than to their adopted country as a whole, particularly if the immigrants moved to a province wherein, as constitutionally defined, there existed a ''distinct society''? Would Canadian citizenship thereby be depreciated? These are questions that should be addressed.

The Concerns of Women

Early in August, two women's groups expressed concern that the rapid drafting of the Meech Lake Accord had resulted in a text where courts, in interpreting the document, could overlook the Charter's guarantees of equality.[78] The National Association of Women and the Law as well as the Legal Education and Action Fund (LEAF) contended that the "distinct society" clause could be interpreted as overriding the *Canadian Charter of Rights and Freedoms*. Section 16 of the Accord made the "distinct society" clause subject only to sections 25 and 27 of the Charter, section 35 of the *Constitution Act, 1982*, and section 91(24) of the *Constitution Act, 1867*, dealing, respectively, with aboriginal and treaty rights, the multicultural heritage, and federal jurisdiction over Indians.[79]

The argument can be put simply. The "distinct society" clause is made subject to certain Charter provisions expressly mentioned in the text, but not to others which are not mentioned (such as sexual equality). Why could the drafters of the document not have declared that the instrument was subject to *all* of the Charter, removing any doubts on the matter? If one invokes the interpretive maxim *expressio unius est exclusio alterius*,[80] a systematic interpretation of the document would lead to only those guarantees being applied to the "distinct society" clause as were expressly mentioned in the text; why should other unmentioned guarantees also be applied when they are not said to apply? A court has only to look, for comparative purposes, to subsection 95B(3) which applies the whole of the Charter to federal–provincial immigration agreements concluded under subsection 95B(1). If equality rights were to apply to the "distinct society" clause, why could sections 15 and 28 of the Charter not have been referred to in Accord section 16, or better still, the Accord made subject to the entire Charter? Women and civil libertarians generally may, consequently, be reasonably apprehensive that express reference to some Charter guarantees but the omission of others (e.g. "equality") would lead the courts to infer that the latter were not to apply.[81]

The legal advisers of LEAF raised some pertinent questions about the possible erosion of equality rights under the Accord.

A recent Supreme Court of Canada decision, *Ref re an Act to Amend the Education Act*,[82] in face of a challenge predicated partly on the Charter's equality provisions, upheld as constitutionally valid the extension of public funding to the final two years of Catholic high schools in Ontario. In this decision Wilson J., for the larger four-member faction of the Court, construed the denominational school guarantee in section 93 of the *Constitution Act, 1867* as ''a fundamental part of the Confederation compromise,''[83] which might override, and did here override, entrenched Charter rights to equality which were inconsistent with it. Such an accommodation could not be attacked on Charter grounds. Independent Christian schools, and other non-publicly funded private schools, had argued that such grants, without similar grants to them, infringed their equality rights. There is a disturbing parallelism here. If the 1867 Confederation compromise were immune from attack on Charter grounds, would not the 1987 Accord's Confederation compromise, establishing the ''distinct society'' clause to secure Quebec's consent to the Constitution, similarly be immune from legal attack? It could be seen as equally basic. In either case, an intention would be inferable that such central and fundamental constitutional compromises of a presumably inviolable character overrode inconsistent Charter guarantees, *inter alia*, to equality.

Professor Catherine A. MacKinnon makes an additional strong objection to the manner in which the Accord potentially undermines gender rights.[84] By explicitly recognizing aboriginal and multicultural rights, but declining to recognize others, the Accord creates, in effect, a hierarchy of rights in which unmentioned equality or gender rights are made subordinate to others. Lawyers often use analogical arguments. They compare what has been decided in one area of law to what has not yet been decided in another area having similar features. Thus, a positive future decision in the area of ''cultural'' rights in the 1987 Accord could ordinarily be cited as an analogy, perhaps to reinforce an argument against sexual inequality, in a pending case. The obvious answer to such an argument, however, is that the analogy is imperfect because the rights expressly singled out in the Accord have been placed on a higher level:

> . . . by choosing to affirm some interests and not to include gender, the Accord makes some rights structural to Canadian federalism in a way that excludes gender from a comparable structural place. The record for women in the U.S. Constitution makes all too clear that neglecting to mention women's rights at constitutive moments is predictably not gender neutral in its effects. Facial gender neutrality in a non-gender neutral world does not guarantee gender neutrality, far less sexual equality.[85]

Some Charter rights, consequently, are, by the very terms of the Accord, placed on a higher plane than others. Accordingly, it cannot persuasively be argued that legal advances in areas relating to these specifically mentioned rights should form good analogies for advances in the realm of sexual equality. The whole social process of constitution-building is defective, since the Accord undermines ''the Charter's political culture and its actual delivery of promised rights.''[86]

The Accord is mischievous in that it tends to downgrade in section 28 what by its text would appear to be the strongest affirmation of rights in the whole Charter: "Notwithstanding anything in this Charter, the rights and freedoms referred to in it are guaranteed equally to male and female persons." In construing rights to sexual equality in the United States, courts have not customarily placed discrimination on the basis of sex on the same high level as they have placed discrimination on the basis of ''race'' or ''national origin.''[87] Statutory provisions possibly violating racial equality were subjected by courts to ''strict scrutiny,'' whereas those violating sexual equality received only ''intermediate scrutiny.'' In Canada, such provisions as section 28 suggested that, unlike the situation prevailing under the U.S. *Bill of Rights*, the highest level of scrutiny would be reserved for possible legislative subversion of gender rights. As Professor MacKinnon argues, the very words of the Accord—its selective reference to some rights and silence on others—count against this.

Conclusion

Some of the constitutional infirmities discussed above were recognized by the Liberal and New Democratic parliamentary oppositions during the Joint Committee Hearings on the 1987 Constitutional Accord,[88] and proposed amendments were prepared by both parties to cure some of the more palpable defects.[89] The amendments were bound to prove abortive, however, since Prime Minister Mulroney's continuing position was that the Meech Lake text would not be altered.[90] Since any change in the text would require the concurrence of all eleven participating governments, to entertain *any* changes, however defective the text, could lead to endless complications. The committee took refuge in the prospect that whatever defects might exist in the Accord could be left for rectification at future constitutional conferences.[91] One problem with this proposal, of course, will be that with the new ''unanimity'' requirements for amendment, it will be much more difficult to rectify defects at future conferences. In general, the opposition parties on the Joint Committee did not play a constructive role. They adopted the attitude that the acquiescence of Quebec in the 1982 constitutional arrangements was so greatly desirable that this was paramount to everything else and that any blunders in the Accord were minor and could be left for future correction. Were it not for the perceived need to bring Quebec into the new arrangements, it may be safely affirmed that the proposed Accord would never have been put forward. It has simply too many serious flaws. As Dean John D. Whyte of the Queen's University law faculty told the Joint Committee on August 20, 1987:

> If the Accord's extensive and far-reaching changes are wrong for Canada we do not owe it to Quebec to accept it. The isolation of a province from the processes of statecraft has weakened, and will weaken, Canada. But the restoration of that province to the status of full participant is not in itself justification for fundamental changes that will alter Canada for the worse and will erode Canada's presence as a nation.[92]

The reintegration of Quebec in the Canadian constitutional framework is, of course, a valuable objective which Dean Whyte shares with most Canadians. A question that must be asked, however, is at what cost? The uncritical attitude of both government and opposition members on the Joint Committee deprived the Accord of the searching examination it needed and made the resultant report into a bland and self-serving document.

Concluded swiftly at a 19-hour marathon drafting session, the Meech Lake Accord seeks to bring Quebec, which rejected the constitutional changes of 1982, into a more harmonious relationship with the rest of Canada. Admirable as this aim may be, there is no national crisis requiring that it be done immediately, without a meticulous examination of a badly flawed document. Once it is accepted, the rigidity of the amending procedure it brings with it, which requires unanimity for basic change, may make desirable change virtually impossible. Its bad features may be with us for a very long time. Flaws notwithstanding, all three national parties and all ten provincial legislative assemblies appear to be resolved to support it. Humans rarely act from unmixed motives, and both idealism and expediency figured in its supporters' calculations. To a large extent, by supporting it, all the federal parties hope to improve their future political fortunes in Quebec, where the Accord is popular. Although Meech Lake has badly divided the federal Liberal caucus, the party officially supports the Accord. Prime Minister Mulroney's governing Progressive Conservatives are redeeming a 1984 election pledge through sponsorship of the Accord, and the New Democrats see electoral gains in Quebec on the horizon which rejection of Meech Lake could imperil. Long regarded as the party of conscience, they appear to be governed here more by opportunism. Arguably, the provisions of Meech Lake will make Senate reform, the elimination of judicial patronage and strong central leadership more difficult for any federal government to achieve.

The only small hope that critics of the Accord had that desired changes might be made to it before it was entrenched (possibly in the summer of 1988) resided in the election of Premier Frank McKenna in New Brunswick on October 13, 1987.[93] Premier McKenna had opposed parts of the Accord, notably insofar as Quebec's "distinct society" clause could relegate French-speaking Acadians in the north of the province to second-class constitutional status. Opponents of Meech Lake hoped that McKenna would either veto or renegotiate the Accord.

Notes

1. 30 & 31 Vic., c. 3, (U.K.).
2. W.H. McConnell, *Commentary on the British North America Act* (Toronto: MacMillan, 1977) at 138–40.
3. G.V. LaForest, *Disallowance and Reservation of Provincial Legislation* (Ottawa: Department of Justice, 1955).
4. *A.G. Ont. v A.G. Can.* (1896), [1896] A.C. 348 (P.C.).
5. See Haldane's post-mortem eulogy of Watson ([1899] 11 Juridical Rev. 278 at 280), where he says of Lord Watson's work in interpreting the Canadian Constitution: "He completely altered the tendency of the decisions of the Supreme Court, and established in the first place the Sovereignty . . . of the legislatures of Ontario, Quebec and the other provinces." See Haldane's address, to the same effect, to the Cambridge Law Society in (1923) 1 *Cambridge Law Journal* 143 at 150.
6. Cf. s. 54(2) of the *Supreme Court Act*, R.S.C. 1952, c. 259, enacted by S.C. 1949 (2d sess.), c. 37, s. 3.
7. See s. 1 of the proposed *Constitution Amendment, 1987*, which recognizes Quebec as a "distinct society" by adding s. 2(1)(b) to the *Constitution Act, 1867*.
8. S. 1 of the *Constitution Amendment, 1987*, adding s. 2(3) to the *Constitution Act, 1867*.
9. *Ibid.*, s. 2, adding s. 25(1) to the *Constitution Act, 1867*.

10. *Ibid.*, s. 6, adding s. 101C to the *Constitution Act, 1867.*

11. *Ibid.*, s. 7, adding s. 106A to the *Constitution Act, 1867.*

12. *Ibid.*, s. 3, adding ss. 95A to 95D to the *Constitution Act, 1867.*

13. *Ibid.*, s. 9, adding amended s. 41 to the *Constitution Act, 1982.*

14. Richard S. Kay, ''The Creation of Constitutions in Canada and the United States,'' (1984) 7 *Canada-United States L.J.* 111 at 113.

15. See Ray Romanow, John Whyte and Howard Leeson, *Canada . . . Notwithstanding* (Toronto: Carswell, 1984) at 66–94.

16. W.H. McConnell, ''Cutting the Gordian Knot: The Amending Process in Canada,'' (1981) 44 *Law and Contemporary Problems* 195 at 197–99.

17. *Reference re Amendment of the Constitution of Canada* (Nos. 1, 2 and 3) [1981] 1 S.C.R. 753 (*Patriation Case*).

18. McConnell, *supra*, note 16 at 223.

19. *Re A.G. Quebec and A.G. Canada* (1982), 140 D.L.R. (3d) 385 (S.C.C.).

20. *Alliance des Professeurs de Montreal* v *A.G. Quebec* (1985), [1985] C.A. 376; 21 D.L.R. (4th) 354.

21. See P. Jessell, ''A Secret Proposal'' *Maclean's* (28 July 1986) 12. Quebec's five conditions for accepting the 1982 constitutional provisions were: 1. explicit recognition of Quebec as a distinct society; 2. guarantee of increased powers in matters of immigration; 3. limitation of the federal spending power; 4. recognition of a right of veto; and 5. Quebec's participation in appointing judges to the Supreme Court of Canada.

22. B.L. Strayer, ''The Patriation and Legitimacy of the Canadian Constitution'' (*Cronkite Memorial Lectures*, 3rd series, October 1982, College of Law, University of Saskatchewan) at 3–26.

23. Stanley Oziewicz, ''19 Hours of Negotiations, A Gruelling Search for Words'' *The [Toronto] Globe and Mail* (4 June 1987) A3.

24. *Ibid.*

25. Rt. Hon. Brian Mulroney, ''Notes for an Address to the Nation by Prime Minister Brian Mulroney on the Constitution'' (Ottawa: Office of the Prime Minister, 4 June 1987) at 2.

26. See s. 37 *Constitution Act, 1982,* enacted as Schedule B to the *Canada Act, 1982,* (U.K.) 1982, c. 11, now repealed by *Proclamation Amending the Constitution of Canada,* 118 *Canada Gazette,* Pt. 1 (1984), 5238.

27. See the text of Mr. Trudeau's statement ''The Meech Lake Accord: Nothing Left but Tears for Trudeau'' *The [Toronto] Globe and Mail* (28 May 1987) A8. Unless otherwise indicated, subsequent quotations from Mr. Trudeau are taken from this text.

28. *Ibid.*

29. See the text of Mr. Johnston's statement ''Meech Lake: Marry in Haste: Repent at Leisure'' *[Montreal] Gazette* (15 May 1987). Unless otherwise indicated, subsequent quotations from Mr. Johnston are taken from this text.

30. Donald Johnston, *Up the Hill* (Toronto: 1985) at 245–46.

31. Michael Rose, ''A Liberal Family Feud'' *Maclean's* (25 May 1987) 12.

32. Eugene Forsey, "Vague Aspects of the Meech Deal Pose a Big Threat" *The* [*Toronto*] *Globe and Mail* (1 June 1987) A7. Unless otherwise indicated, subsequent quotations from Dr. Forsey are taken from this text. The distinguished constitutional counsel John Robinette expresses a similar concern to Forsey's on the ambiguities of the Accord: "What is the legal meaning of distinct society? What is the legal meaning of distinct identity? Why a shift from the phrase distinct society to distinct identity?

"We all have good will towards the province of Quebec. And we respect our fellow Canadians. But this is a legal document, and to use words so indefinite as distinct society or distinct identity will cause a great deal of difficulty in the future." See: "Robinette Feels Constitutional Wording Will Cause Problems" *The* [*Regina*] *Leader Post* (5 June 1987) C–14.

33. "A Strong Accord" *The* [*Toronto*] *Globe and Mail* (29 August 1987) D6.

34. "The Meech Lake Accord Strengthens Bonds that Link Canada" *The* [*Toronto*] *Globe and Mail* (15 June 1987) A7.

35. A.J. Petter, "Meech Won't Stall Social Reform in the Provinces" *The* [*Toronto*] *Globe and Mail* (30 June 1987) A7.

36. See, e.g., W.H. McConnell, "The Judicial Review of Prime Minister Bennett's 'New Deal' " (1968) *Osgoode Hall L.J.* 39.

37. Except that, by a 1982 constitutional amendment, the provinces were given certain powers over the indirect taxation of national resources; see s. 92A added to the *Constitution Act, 1867* by the *Constitution Act, 1982*, and Moull, "Section 92A of the *Constitution Act, 1867*" (1983) 61 *Can. Bar Rev.* 715.

38. See, e.g., Peter W. Hogg, *Constitutional Law of Canada*, 2nd ed. (Toronto: Carswell, 1985) at 123–26, and G.E. Carter, *Canadian Conditional Grants since World War II* (Toronto: Canadian Tax Foundation, 1971).

39. Petter, *supra*, note 35.

40. See McConnell, *supra*, note 2, at 181–84 and 296–300.

41. See, e.g., Joseph E. Magnet, "The Constitutional Distribution of Taxation Powers in Canada" (1978) 10 *Ottawa L. Rev.* 473 at 480–84.

42. Elmer Driedger, "The Spending Power" (1981) 7 *Queen's Law J.* 124 at 133–34.

43. John H. Archer, *Saskatchewan: A History* (Saskatoon, 1980) at 269.

44. Cf. J.-P. Sartre, *Sartre on Cuba* (New York, 1961) at 26.

45. S.C. 32–33 Eliz. 11, c. 6; ss. 18 and 20 of the Act provide for a corresponding reduction of transfer payments from Ottawa to those provinces which permitted extra-billing. These provisions effectively ended the acquiescence in extra-billing in Canada by provincial governments.

46. See clause 13, in Part VI, "Constitutional Conferences," in the proposed *Constitution Amendment, 1987*.

47. See Geoffrey Simpson, "Premiers with Lists" *The* [*Toronto*] *Globe and Mail* (5 May 1987) A7, and the remark of former Manitoba Liberal leader Izzy Asper that in the Meech Lake Accord: "Instead of a 'Triple E Senate' [the premiers] got a promise of a 'Triple P Senate'—provincial premier patronage"; Deanna Herman, "West Got Nothing from Accord" [*Saskatoon*] *Star-*

Phoenix (25 September 1987) A9.

48. Robert Lee, "Canadians Question Relevance: Senate Reform Difficult Course to Navigate" [*Saskatoon*] *Star-Phoenix* (2 May 1987) E13.

49. See, e.g., F.A. Kunz, *The Modern Senate of Canada, 1925-63* (Toronto, 1965); R.A. Mckay, *The Unreformed Senate of Canada*, r.p. (Toronto, 1963); and W.H. McConnell, "The Canadian Debate on Senate Reform," in V. Venkataramaniah, ed., *Essays on Constitutional Law* (New Delhi, India, 1986) at 3–12.

50. The *Representation Act 1948-49*, s. 4 (Australia) increased the number of senators for each of the six Australian states from six to ten; and see c. 7, "The Upper Houses," in Geoffrey Sawer, *Australian Government Today*, 11th ed. (Melbourne, 1973).

51. James Madison, Alexander Hamilton and John Jay, *The Federalist Papers* (New York, 1961) at 244.

52. Five Canadian governments have fallen through adverse votes in the House of Commons: Macdonald (1873); Meighen (1926); Diefenbaker (1963); Trudeau (1974); and Clark (1979).

53. See the letter to the editor by Senator Eugene Forsey in the *Ottawa Journal* (21 November 1975) 7, where he discusses the dismissal of Australian Prime Minister Gough Whitlam by Governor General Sir John Kerr because Whitlam was not granted supply by the Australian Senate, and refused to resign.

54. See proposed revised s. 41(g) of the *Constitution Act, 1982*, in s. 9 of the *Constitution Amendment, 1987*.

55. See proposed ss. 101A–101E of the *Constitution Act, 1867*, in s. 6 of the *Constitution Amendment, 1987*.

56. The *Supreme Court Act*, R.S.C. 1970, S-19, s. 6, as entrenched by proposed s. 101C(3) of the *Constitution Act, 1867*, in s. 6 of the *Constitution Amendment, 1987*.

57. *Ibid.*

58. See proposed s. 101C(4) of the *Constitution Act, 1867*, in s. 6 of the *Constitution Amendment, 1987*.

59. S. 6, *Constitution Amendment, 1987*.

60. Proposed s. 101C(2) of the *Constitution Act, 1867*, in s. 6 of the *Constitution Amendment, 1987*.

61. President Reagan's nominations of William Rehnquist to be Chief Justice and Anthony Scalia, Robert H. Bork and Anthony Kennedy to be Associate Justices in 1986–87 are examples of conservative jurists nominated by a conservative president; see *Time* (30 June 1986) 10.

62. Kirk Makin, "Showdown at the Bench, Critics Fear Meech Lake Accord Will Mire Appointment of Judges in the Pork Barrel" *The* [*Toronto*] *Globe and Mail* (15 August 1987) D1, and see also The Canadian Bar Association Committee Report, *The Appointment of Judges in Canada* (Ottawa: The Canadian Bar Foundation, 1985), which deals extensively with political patronage in Canada.

63. Proposed s. 41(g) of the *Constitution Act, 1987*, in s. 9 of the *Constitution Amendment, 1987*.

64. McConnell, *supra*, note 2 at 26–28.

65. The *Constitution Act, 1949*, S.C., 12–13 Geo. V1, c. 22.

66. McConnell, *supra*, note 2 at 421.

67. P. Gerin-Lajoie, *Constitutional Amendment in Canada* (Toronto, 1950) at 125; Joseph Smallwood, *I Chose Canada* (Toronto, 1973) at 316.

68. "NWT Studies Court Action on BNA Pact" *The [Toronto] Globe and Mail* (4 December 1981) 8.

69. S. 121 of the Australian *Constitution Act, 1900* (U.K.), 63 & 64 Vic., c. 12 stipulates: "The Parliament may admit to the Commonwealth or establish new States, and may upon such admission or establishment make or impose such terms and conditions, including the extent of representation in either House of the Parliament, as it thinks fit."

70. Geoffrey Sawer, *supra*, note 50 at 127–28.

71. *The American Commonwealth* (New Edition), 2 vols. (New York, 1914).

72. *Ibid.*, vol. 1, at 430–31.

73. Both were admitted as states in 1959.

74. S. 3, *Constitution Amendment, 1987*.

75. *Ibid.*

76. *Ibid.*

77. Proposed s. 95B(3), in s. 3 of the *Constitution Amendment, 1987*.

78. "Women May Have Found Flaw to Force Accord Revisions" [*Saskatoon*] *Star-Phoenix* (11 August 1987). The guarantees of equality are contained in ss. 15 and 28 of the Charter.

79. *Ibid.*

80. See, e.g., P.J. Fitzgerald, ed., *Salmond on Jurisprudence*, 12th ed. (London, 1966) at 134.

81. But see Donna Greschner, "A Constitution with 'Instructions Included': Some Questions About Interpretation After Meech Lake," in *The Meech Lake Accord* (proceedings of a symposium held at the University of Toronto, 30 October 1987) (Toronto, 1987) where, on Dworkinian premises, it is argued that if s. 28 is interpreted as a rule rather than a principle (because of the strength and clarity of its language) any conflict between s. 28 and a "principle" such as clause 1 of the Accord, containing the "distinct society" clause, should be resolved judicially in favour of the rule, thus giving priority to the Charter's guarantee of male and female equality.

82. (Unreported, 25 June 1987); see also the letter from Professor Robin Elliott, Faculty of Law, University of British Columbia, to Beth Symes, dated 28 August 1987, in LEAF's "Brief to the Joint Committee of the Senate and the House of Commons on the 1987 Constitutional Accord, September 1987" (hereinafter referred to as LEAF's Brief).

83. Unreported judgment, *supra*, note 81 at 48.

84. Catherine A. MacKinnon to Women's Legal Education and Action Fund, dated 6 September 1987, in LEAF's Brief.

85. *Ibid.* at 3; an example of the rejection of "women's rights" at such a constitutive moment was the failure of the Equal Rights Amendment (ERA) to secure ratification by the necessary 38 states within ten years of its passage (1972) by Congress.

86. *Ibid.*

87. See, e.g., *Brown* v. *Board of Educ.*, 347 U.S. 483 (1954), which deals with racial discrimination, and *Craig* v. *Boren*, 429 U.S. 190 (1976), which deals with sexual discrimination. See also *U.S.* v. *Carolene Prod. Co.*, 304 U.S. 144 (1938) where Stone J. (as he then was) first propounded his "rational basis" test for economic classifications.

88. Special Joint Committee of the Senate and the House of Commons, *The 1987 Constitutional Accord* (Ottawa: Queen's Printer, 1987) (Joint Chairs: A. Tremblay and C. Speyer).

89. *Ibid.* at 151–57.

90. Pierre April, "Mulroney Refuses to Alter Meech Lake Agreement" *The [Toronto] Globe and Mail* (23 June 1987) 1.

91. *The 1987 Constitutional Accord, supra,* note 88 at 142.

92. Dean John D. Whyte, "Submission to the Special Joint Committee of the Senate and the House of Commons on the 1987 Constitutional Accord," 20 August 1987, at 1.

93. Ross Howard, "Meech Lake Accord Could Come Into Effect by Early Next Summer" *The [Toronto] Globe and Mail* (10 October 1987) A2; see also "Grits Sought Mandate to 'Negotiate' Accord" *[Saskatoon] Star-Phoenix* (14 October 1987) C11.

APPENDIX

MEETING OF FIRST MINISTERS ON THE CONSTITUTION.

1987 CONSTITUTIONAL ACCORD

June 3, 1987

1987

Constitutional

Accord

WHEREAS first ministers, assembled in Ottawa, have arrived at a unanimous accord on constitutional amendments that would bring about the full and active participation of Quebec in Canada's constitutional evolution, *would recognize the principle of equality of all the provinces*, would provide new arrangements to foster greater harmony and cooperation between the Government of Canada and the governments of the provinces and would require that annual first ministers' conferences on the state of the Canadian economy and such other matters as may be appropriate be convened and that annual constitutional conferences composed of first ministers be convened commencing not later than December 31, 1988;

AND WHEREAS first ministers have also reached unanimous agreement on certain additional commitments in relation to some of those amendments;

NOW THEREFORE the Prime Minister of Canada and the first ministers of the provinces commit themselves and the governments they represent to the following:

1. The Prime Minister of Canada will lay or cause to be laid before the Senate and House of Commons, and the first ministers of the provinces will lay or cause to be laid before their legislative assemblies, as soon as possible, a resolution, in the form appended hereto, to authorize a proclamation to be issued by the Governor General under the Great Seal of Canada to amend the Constitution of Canada.

2. The Government of Canada will, as soon as possible, conclude an agreement with the Government of Quebec that would

(a) incorporate the principles of the Cullen-Couture agreement on the selection abroad and in Canada of independent immigrants, visitors for medical treatment, students and temporary workers, and on the selection of refugees abroad and economic criteria for family reunification and assisted relatives,

(b) guarantee that Quebec will receive a number of immigrants, including refugees, within the annual total established by the federal government for all of Canada proportionate to its share of the population of Canada, with the right to exceed that figure by five per cent for demographic reasons, and

(c) provide an undertaking by Canada to withdraw services (except citizenship services) for the reception and integration (including linguistic and cultural) of all foreign nationals wishing to settle in Quebec where services are to be provided by Quebec, with such withdrawal to be accompanied by reasonable compensation,

and the Government of Canada and the Government of Quebec will take the necessary steps to give the agreement the force of law under the proposed amendment relating to such agreements.

3. Nothing in this Accord should be construed as preventing the negotiation of similar agreements with other provinces relating to immigration and the temporary admission of aliens.

4. Until the proposed amendment relating to appointments to the Senate comes into force, any person summoned to fill a vacancy in the Senate shall be chosen from among persons whose names have been submitted by the government of the province to which the vacancy relates and must be acceptable to the Queen's Privy Council for Canada.

Motion for a Resolution to authorize an amendment to the Constitution of Canada

WHEREAS the *Constitution Act, 1982* came into force on April 17, 1982, following an agreement between Canada and all the provinces except Quebec;

AND WHEREAS the Government of Quebec has established a set of five proposals for constitutional change and has stated that amendments to give effect to those proposals would enable Quebec to resume a full role in the constitutional councils of Canada;

AND WHEREAS the amendment proposed in the schedule hereto sets out the basis on which Quebec's five constitutional proposals may be met;

AND WHEREAS the amendment proposed in the schedule hereto also recognizes the principle of the equality of all the provinces, provides new arrangements to foster greater harmony and cooperation between the Government of Canada and the governments of the provinces and requires that conferences be convened to consider important constitutional, economic and other issues;

AND WHEREAS certain portions of the amendment proposed in the schedule hereto relate to matters referred to in section 41 of the *Constitution Act, 1982*;

AND WHEREAS section 41 of the *Constitution Act, 1982* provides that an amendment to the Constitution of Canada may be made by proclamation issued by the Governor General under the Great Seal of Canada where so authorized by resolutions of the Senate and the House of Commons and of the legislative assembly of each province;

NOW THEREFORE the (Senate) (House of Commons) (legislative assembly) resolves that an amendment to the Constitution of Canada be authorized to be made by proclamation issued by Her Excellency the Governor General under the Great Seal of Canada in accordance with the schedule hereto.

Schedule
Constitution Amendment, 1987

Constitution Act, 1867

1. The *Constitution Act, 1867* is amended by adding thereto, immediately after section 1 thereof, the following section:

Interpretation

"2. (1) The Constitution of Canada shall be interpreted in a manner consistent with

(a) the recognition that the existence of French-speaking Canadians, centred in Quebec but also present elsewhere in Canada, and English-speaking Canadians, concentrated outside Quebec but also present in Quebec, constitutes a fundamental characteristic of Canada; and

(b) the recognition that Quebec constitutes within Canada a distinct society.

Role of Parliament and legislature

(2) The role of the Parliament of Canada and the provincial legislatures to preserve the fundamental characteristic of Canada referred to in paragraph (1)(a) is affirmed.

Role of legislature and Government of Quebec

(3) The role of the legislature and Government of Quebec to preserve and promote the distinct identity of Quebec referred to in paragraph (1)(b) is affirmed.

Rights of legislatures and governments preserved

(4) Nothing in this section derogates from the powers, rights or privileges of Parliament or the Government of Canada, or of the legislatures or governments of the provinces, including any powers, rights or privileges relating to language."

2. The said Act is further amended by adding thereto, immediately after section 24 thereof, the following section:

"25.(1) Where a vacancy occurs in the Senate, the government of the province to which the vacancy relates may, in relation to that vacancy, submit to the Queen's Privy Council for Canada the names of persons who may be summoned to the Senate.

(2) Until an amendment to the Constitution of Canada is made in relation to the Senate pursuant to section 41 of the *Constitution Act, 1982*, the person summoned to fill a vacancy in the Senate shall be chosen from among persons whose names have been submitted under subsection (1) by the government of the province to which the vacancy relates and must be acceptable to the Queen's Privy Council for Canada."

3. The said Act is further amended by adding thereto, immediately after section 95 thereof, the following heading and sections:

"Agreements on Immigration and Aliens

95A. The Government of Canada shall, at the request of the government of any province, negotiate with the government of that province for the purpose of concluding an agreement relating to immigration or the temporary admission of aliens into that province that is appropriate to the needs and circumstances of that province.

95B. (1) Any agreement concluded between Canada and a province in relation to immigration or the temporary admission of aliens into that province has the force of law from the time it is declared to do so in accordance with subsection 95C(1) and shall from that time have effect notwithstanding class 25 of section 91 or section 95.

(2) An agreement that has the force of law under subsection (1) shall have effect only so long and so far as it is not repugnant to any provision of an Act of the Parliament of Canada that sets national standards and objectives relating to immigration or aliens, including any provision that establishes general classes of immigrants or relates to levels of immigration for Canada or that prescribes classes of individuals who are inadmissible into Canada.

(3) The *Canadian Charter of Rights and Freedoms* applies in respect of any agreement that has the force of law under subsection (1) and in respect of anything done by the Parliament or Government of Canada, or the legislature or government of a province, pursuant to any such agreement.

95C.(1) A declaration that an agreement referred to in subsection 95B(1) has the force of law may be made by proclamation issued by the Governor General under the Great Seal of Canada only where so authorized by resolutions of the Senate and House of Commons and of the legislative assembly of the province that is a party to the agreement.

Amendment of
agreements

(2) An amendment to an agreement referred to in subsection 95B(1) may be made by proclamation issued by the Governor General under the Great Seal of Canada only where so authorized

(a) by resolutions of the Senate and House of Commons and of the legislative assembly of the province that is a party to the agreement; or

(b) in such other manner as is set out in the agreement.

Application
of sections
46 to 48 of
*Constitution
Act, 1982*

95D. Sections 46 to 48 of the *Constitution Act, 1982* apply, with such modifications as the circumstances require, in respect of any declaration made pursuant to subsection 95C(1), any amendment to an agreement made pursuant to subsection 95C(2) or any amendment made pursuant to section 95E.

Amendments
to sections
95A to 95D
or this
section

95E. An amendment to sections 95A to 95D or this section may be made in accordance with the procedure set out in subsection 38(1) of the *Constitution Act, 1982*, but only if the amendment is authorized by resolutions of the legislative assemblies of all the provinces that are, at the time of the amendment, parties to an agreement that has the force of law under subsection 95B(1).''

4. The said Act is further amended by adding thereto, immediately preceding section 96 thereof, the following heading:

''*General*''

5. The said Act is further amended by adding thereto, immediately preceding section 101 thereof, the following heading:

''*Courts Established by the Parliament of Canada*''

6. The said Act is further amended by adding thereto, immediately after section 101 thereof, the following heading and sections:

''*Supreme Court of Canada*

Supreme
Court
continued

101A.(1) The court existing under the name of the Supreme Court of Canada is hereby continued as the general court of appeal for Canada, and as an additional court for the better administration of the laws of Canada, and shall continue to be a superior court of record.

Constitution
of court

(2) The Supreme Court of Canada shall consist of a chief justice to be called the Chief Justice of Canada and eight other judges, who shall be appointed by the Governor General in Council by letters patent under the Great Seal.

Who may be
appointed
judges

101B.(1) Any person may be appointed a judge of the Supreme Court of Canada who, after having been admitted to the bar of any province or territory, has, for a total of at least ten years, been a judge of any court in Canada or a member of the bar of any province or territory.

Three judges
from Quebec

(2) At least three judges of the Supreme Court of Canada shall be appointed from among persons who, after having been admitted to the bar of Quebec, have, for a total of at least ten years, been judges of any court of Quebec or of any court established by the Parliament of Canada, or members of the bar of Quebec.

Names may
be submitted

101C.(1) Where a vacancy occurs in the Supreme Court of Canada, the government of each province may, in relation to that vacancy, submit to the Minister of Justice of Canada the names of any of the persons who have been admitted to the bar of that province and are qualified under section 101B for appointment to that court.

Appointment
from names
submitted

(2) Where an appointment is made to the Supreme Court of Canada, the Governor General in Council shall, except where the Chief Justice is appointed from among members of the Court, appoint a person whose name has been submitted under subsection (1) and who is acceptable to the Queen's Privy Council for Canada.

Appointment
from Quebec

(3) Where an appointment is made in accordance with subsection (2) of any of the three judges necessary to meet the requirement set out in subsection 101B(2), the Governor General in Council shall appoint a person whose name has been submitted by the Government of Quebec.

Appointment
from other
provinces

(4) Where an appointment is made in accordance with subsection (2) otherwise than as required under subsection (3), the Governor General in Council shall appoint a person whose name has been submitted by the government of a province other than Quebec.

Tenure, salaries,
etc. of judges

101D. Sections 99 and 100 apply in respect of the judges of the Supreme Court of Canada.

Relationship
to section 101

101E.(1) Sections 101A to 101D shall not be construed as abrogating or derogating from the powers of the Parliament of Canada to make laws under section 101 except to the extent that such laws are inconsistent with those sections.

References
to the
Supreme Court
of Canada

(2) For greater certainty, section 101A shall not be construed as abrogating or derogating from the powers of the Parliament of Canada to make laws relating to the reference of questions of law or fact, or any other matters, to the Supreme Court of Canada.''

7. The said Act is further amended by adding thereto, immediately after section 106 thereof, the following section:

Shared-cost
program

''106A.(1) The Government of Canada shall provide reasonable compensation to the government of a province that chooses not to participate in a national shared-cost program that is established by the Government of Canada after the coming into force of this section in an area of exclusive provincial jurisdiction, if the province carries on a program or initiative that is compatible with the national objectives.

Legislative power
not extended

(2) Nothing in this section extends the legislative powers of the Parliament of Canada or of the legislatures of the provinces.''

8. The said Act is further amended by adding thereto the following heading and sections:

''XII — CONFERENCES ON THE ECONOMY AND OTHER MATTERS

Conferences on the economy and other matters

148. A conference composed of the Prime Minister of Canada and the first ministers of the provinces shall be convened by the Prime Minister of Canada at least once each year to discuss the state of the Canadian economy and such other matters as may be appropriate.

XIII — REFERENCES

Reference includes amendments

149. A reference to this Act shall be deemed to include a reference to any amendments thereto.''

Constitution Act, 1982

9. Sections 40 to 42 of the *Constitution Act, 1982* are repealed and the following substituted therefor:

Compensation

''40. Where an amendment is made under subsection 38(1) that transfers legislative powers from provincial legislatures to Parliament, Canada shall provide reasonable compensation to any province to which the amendment does not apply.

Amendment by unanimous consent

41. An amendment to the Constitution of Canada in relation to the following matters may be made by proclamation issued by the Governor General under the Great Seal of Canada only where authorized by resolutions of the Senate and House of Commons and of the legislative assembly of each province:

(a) the office of the Queen, the Governor General and the Lieutenant Governor of a province;

(b) the powers of the Senate and the method of selecting Senators;

(c) the number of members by which a province is entitled to be represented in the Senate and the residence qualifications of Senators;

(d) the right of a province to a number of members in the House of Commons not less than the number of Senators by which the province was entitled to be represented on *April 17, 1982*;

(e) the principle of proportionate representation of the provinces in the House of Commons prescribed by the Constitution of Canada;

(f) subject to section 43, the use of the English or the French language;

(g) the Supreme Court of Canada;

(h) the extension of existing provinces into the territories;

(i) notwithstanding any other law or practice, the establishment of new provinces; and

(j) an amendment to this Part.''

10. Section 44 of the said Act is repealed and the following substituted therefor:

Amendments by Parliament

''44. Subject to section 41, Parliament may exclusively make laws amending the Constitution of Canada in relation to the executive government of Canada or the Senate and House of Commons.''

11. Subsection 46(1) of the said Act is repealed and the following substituted therefor:

Initiation
of amendment
procedures

"46.(1) The procedures for amendment under sections 38, 41 and 43 may be initiated either by the Senate or the House of Commons or by the legislative assembly of a province."

12. Subsection 47(1) of the said Act is repealed and the following substituted therefor:

Amendments
without
Senate
resolution

"47.(1) An amendment to the Constitution of Canada made by proclamation under section 38, 41 or 43 may be made without a resolution of the Senate authorizing the issue of the proclamation if, within one hundred and eighty days after the adoption by the House of Commons of a resolution authorizing its issue, the Senate has not adopted such a resolution and if, at any time after the expiration of that period, the House of Commons again adopts the resolution."

13. Part VI of the said Act is repealed and the following substituted therefor:

"PART VI

CONSTITUTIONAL CONFERENCES

Constitutional
conference

50.(1) A constitutional conference composed of the Prime Minister of Canada and the first ministers of the provinces shall be convened by the Prime Minister of Canada at least once each year, commencing in 1988.

(2) The conferences convened under subsection (1) shall have included on their agenda the following matters:

(a) Senate reform, including the role and functions of the Senate, its powers, the method of selecting Senators and representation in the Senate;

(b) roles and responsibilities in relation to fisheries; and

(c) such other matters as are agreed upon."

14. Subsection 52(2) of the said Act is amended by striking out the word "and" at the end of paragraph (b) thereof, by adding the word "and" at the end of paragraph (c) thereof and by adding thereto the following paragraph:

"(d) any other amendment to the Constitution of Canada."

15. Section 61 of the said Act is repealed and the following substituted therefor:

References

"61. *A reference to the Constitution Act 1982, or a reference to the Constitution Acts 1867 to 1982, shall be deemed to include a reference to any amendments thereto.*"

General

Multicultural
heritage and
aboriginal
peoples

16. Nothing in section 2 of the *Constitution Act, 1867* affects section 25 or 27 of the *Canadian Charter of Rights and Freedoms*, section 35 of the *Constitution Act, 1982* or class 24 of section 91 of the *Constitution Act, 1867.*

CITATION

Citation

17. This amendment may be cited as the *Constitution Amendment, 1987.*

SELECTED
BIBLIOGRAPHY

GENERAL

Banting, Keith, and Richard Simeon, eds. *And No One Cheered: Federalism, Democracy and the Constitution Act* (Toronto: Methuen, 1983).

Bastarache, Michel. *Les droits linguistiques au Canada* (Cowansville: Les Éditions Y. Blais, 1986).

Bayefsky, Anne F., and Mary Eberts, eds. *Equality Rights and the Canadian Charter of Rights and Freedoms* (Toronto: Carswell, 1985).

Beck, Stanley M., and Ivan Bernier, eds. *Canada and the New Constitution: The Unfinished Agenda*, Vol. 1 (Montreal: Institute for Research on Public Policy, 1983).

Belobaba, Edward P., and Eric Gertner, eds. *The New Constitution and the Charter of Rights* (Toronto: Butterworths, 1983).

Boldt, Menno, and J. Anthony Long, eds. *Quest for Justice: Aboriginal Peoples and Aboriginal Rights* (Toronto: University of Toronto Press, 1985).

Cairns, Alan, and Cynthia Williams, eds. *Constitutionalism, Citizenship, and Society in Canada*. Macdonald Commission Studies 33 (Toronto: University of Toronto Press, 1985).

Canada. Special Joint Committee of the Senate and the House of Commons on the 1987 Constitutional Accord. *Minutes of Proceedings and Evidence*, Nos. 1–16, June 30, 1987, to September 1, 1987 (Ottawa: Queen's Printer, 1987).

———. Special Joint Committee of the Senate and the House of Commons on the 1987 Constitutional Accord. *Report* (Ottawa: Queen's Printer, 1987).

———. *Strengthening the Canadian Federation: The Constitution Amendment* (Ottawa: Queen's Printer, 1987).

Canadian Human Rights Foundation, ed. *Multiculturalism and the Charter: A Legal Perspective* (Toronto: Carswell, 1987).

Doerr, Audrey, and Micheline Carrier, eds. *Women and the Constitution in Canada* (Ottawa: Canadian Advisory Council on the Status of Women, 1981).

Gibbins, Roger, et al., eds. *Meech Lake and Canada. Perspectives from the West* (Edmonton: Academic Printing and Publishing, 1988).

Hogg, P. *Canada Act 1982 Annotated* (Toronto: Carswell, 1982).

——— . *Meech Lake Constitutional Accord Annotated* (Toronto: Carswell, 1988).

Lesage, Gilles, ed. *Le Québec et le Lac Meech. Un Dossier du Devoir* (Montréal: Guérin littérature, 1987).

Long, J. Anthony, and Menno Boldt, eds. *Government in Conflict? Provinces and Indian Nations in Canada* (Toronto: University of Toronto Press, 1988).

Mandel, Michael. *The Charter of Rights and the Legalization of Politics in Canada* (Toronto: Wall & Thompson, 1989).

McWhinney, Edward. *Constitution-making: Principles, Processes, Practice* (Toronto: University of Toronto Press, 1981).

Nevitte, Neil, and Allan Kornberg, eds. *Minorities and the Canadian State* (Oakville: Mosaic Press, 1985).

Ontario. Select Committee on Constitutional Reform, 1987 Constitutional Accord. *Report on the Constitution Amendment 1987* (Toronto: Queen's Park, 1988).

Romanow, Roy, John Whyte and Howard Leeson. *Canada . . . Notwithstanding: The Making of the Constitution 1976–1982* (Toronto: Carswell/Methuen, 1984).

Schwartz, Bryan. *First Principles, Second Thoughts: Aboriginal Peoples, Constitutional Reform and Canadian Statecraft* (Montreal: Institute for Research on Public Policy, 1986).

——— . *Fathoming Meech Lake* (Winnipeg: Legal Research Institute, University of Manitoba, 1987).

Sheppard, R., and M. Valpy. *The National Deal: The Fight for a Canadian Constitution* (Toronto: Fleet Books, 1982).

Swinton, K. E., and C. J. Rogerson, eds. *Competing Constitutional Visions— The Meech Lake Accord* (Toronto: Carswell, 1988).

The Meech Lake Accord—L'Accord du Lac Meech. Special Issue. *Canadian Public Policy/Analyse de Politiques*, XIV (September/septembre 1988).

Thomson, Clive, ed. *Navigating Meech Lake: The 1987 Constitutional Accord* (Kingston: Institute of Intergovernmental Relations and Queen's Quarterly, 1988).

Weiler, Joseph M., and Robin M. Elliot, eds. *Litigating the Values of a Nation: The Canadian Charter of Rights and Freedoms* (Toronto: Carswell, 1986).

CHAPTER ONE
THE GENESIS AND NATURE OF THE ACCORD:
The Proponents Present Their Case

Banting, Keith, and Richard Simeon, eds. *And No One Cheered: Federalism, Democracy and the Constitution Act* (Toronto: Methuen, 1983).

Beck, Stanley M., and Ivan Bernier, eds. *Canada and the New Constitution: The Unfinished Agenda*, Vol. 1 (Montreal: Institute for Research on Public Policy, 1983).

Chrétien, Jean. *Straight from the Heart* (Toronto: Key Porter Books, 1985).

Lesage, Gilles, ed. *Le Québec et le Lac Meech. Un Dossier du Devoir* (Montréal: Guérin littérature, 1987).

Leslie, Peter M. "Submission to the Special Joint Committee of the Senate and the House of Commons on the 1987 Constitutional Accord." In Clive Thomson, ed., *Navigating Meech Lake: The 1987 Constitutional Accord* (Kingston: Institute of Intergovernmental Relations and *Queen's Quarterly*, 1988) and in Chapter Eleven of this book.

Milne, David. *Tug of War: Ottawa and the Provinces Under Trudeau and Mulroney* (Toronto: Lorimer, 1986).

Morin, Claude. *Lendemains piégés. Du Référendum à la nuit des longs couteaux* (Montréal: Boréal Express, 1988).

Rémillard, Gil. "Under What Conditions Could Quebec Sign the Constitution Act of 1982?" In Michael D. Behiels, ed., *Quebec Since 1945* (Toronto: Copp Clark Pitman, 1987).

——— . "Speech to the Conference on Rebuilding the Relationship: Quebec and its Confederation Partners." In Peter Leslie, ed., *The State of the Federation 1986* (Kingston: Institute of Intergovernmental Relations, Queen's University, 1987).

Romanow, Roy, John Whyte and Howard Leeson. *Canada . . . Notwithstanding: The Making of the Constitution 1976–1982* (Toronto: Carswell/Methuen, 1984).

Schwartz, Bryan. *Fathoming Meech Lake* (Winnipeg: Legal Research Institute, University of Manitoba, 1987).

Stevenson, Garth. *Unfulfilled Union. Canadian Federalism and National Unity* (Third Edition, Toronto: Gage, 1989).

CHAPTER TWO
CONSTITUTIONALIZING CONFLICTING VISIONS OF CANADA

Adam, Marcel. "Laisser le Canada anglais faire de l'accord Meech son problème." *La Presse,* 4 mars 1989.

Leslie, Peter M. "Submission to the Special Joint Committee of the Senate and the House of Commons on the 1987 Constitutional Accord." In Clive Thomson, ed., *Navigating Meech Lake: The 1987 Constitutional Accord* (Kingston: Institute of Intergovernmental Relations and *Queen's Quarterly,* 1988) and in Chapter Eleven of this book.

Morin, Claude. "Trudeau nous a légué un héritage empoisonné." *La Presse,* 13 mars 1989.

Murray, Lowell. "Référendum et Constitution. Lowell Murray répond à Pierre Trudeau." *La Presse,* 5 avril 1989.

Ontario. Select Committee on Constitutional Reform, 1987 Constitutional Accord. *Report on the Constitution Amendment 1987* (Toronto: Queen's Park, 1988).

Simeon, Richard. "Meech Lake and Shifting Conceptions of Canadian Federalism." *Canadian Public Policy/Analyse de Politiques,* Supplement to XIV (1988).

———. "Meech Lake and Visions of Canada." In K. E. Swinton and C. J. Rogerson, eds., *Competing Constitutional Visions—The Meech Lake Accord* (Toronto: Carswell, 1988).

Trudeau, Pierre. "Say Goodbye to the Dream of One Canada." *The Toronto Star,* May 27, 1987. Reprinted in Donald Johnston, ed., *With a Bang, Not a Whimper. Pierre Trudeau Speaks Out* (Toronto: Stoddart, 1988).

———. "L'accord constitutionnel de 1982 n'a pas été un marché de dupes pour le Québec." *La Presse,* 10 mars 1988.

———. "Ce n'est pas comme cela qu'il faut écrire l'Histoire." *La Presse,* 22 mars 1989.

CHAPTER THREE
DIVINING A DEMOCRATIC PROCESS:
The Citizens' versus the Politicians' Constitution

Behiels, Michael D. "Brief on the Meech Lake Accord." Brief to the Ontario Select Committee on Constitutional Reform, 1987 Constitutional Accord, *Hansard Official Report of Debates,* March 21, 1988.

Boli, John. "Human Rights or State Expansion? Cross-National Definitions of Constitutional Rights, 1870-1970." In George M. Thomas et al., eds., *Insti-*

tutional Structure: Constituting State, Society, and the Individual (Beverly Hills: Sage Publications, 1987).

Cairns, Alan C. "The Changing Nature of Citizen Rights." In Alan Cairns and Cynthia Williams, eds., *Constitutionalism, Citizenship, and Society in Canada.* Macdonald Commission Studies 33 (Toronto: University of Toronto Press, 1985).

———. "Citizens (Outsiders) and Governments (Insiders) in Constitution-making: The Case of Meech Lake." *Canadian Public Policy/Analyse de Politiques,* Supplement to XIV (1988).

Canada. Special Joint Committee of the Senate and the House of Commons on the 1987 Constitutional Accord. *Minutes of Proceedings and Evidence,* No. 5, August 11, 1987 (Ottawa: Queen's Printer, 1987).

Gibbins, Roger. "A Sense of Unease: The Meech Lake Accord and Constitution-making in Canada." In Roger Gibbins et al., eds., *Meech Lake and Canada. Perspectives from the West* (Edmonton: Academic Printing and Publishing, 1988).

Murray, Lowell. "The Process of Constitutional Change in Canada: The Lessons of Meech Lake." *Choices* (Montreal: Institute for Research on Public Policy, February 1988).

Smiley, D. V. "An Outsider's Observations on Federal–Provincial Relations Among Consenting Adults." In Richard Simeon, ed., *Confrontation or Collaboration: Intergovernmental Relations in Canada Today* (Toronto: Institute of Public Administration, 1979).

Whyte, John D. "More Than Small Change: The Meaning of Meech Lake for the Canadian Polity." Submission to the Select Committee on the 1987 Constitutional Accord of the Legislative Assembly of New Brunswick, Fredericton, October 20, 1988.

CHAPTER FOUR
DECIPHERING THE DISTINCT SOCIETY CLAUSE

Anand, Raj. "Ethnic Equality." In Anne F. Bayefsky and Mary Eberts, eds., *Equality Rights and the Canadian Charter of Rights and Freedoms* (Toronto: Carswell, 1985).

Bastarache, Michel. "La clause relative à la dualité linguistique et la reconnais-sance du Québec comme société distincte." In Réal-A. Forest, ed., *L'adhé-sion du Québec à l'Accord du Lac Meech—Points de vue juridiques et politiques* (Montréal: Les Éditions Thémis, 1988).

———. "Le principe d'égalité des langues officielles." In Michel Bastarache, *Les droits linguistiques au Canada* (Cowansville: Les Éditions Y. Blais, 1986).

Behiels, Michael D. *Prelude to Quebec's Quiet Revolution* (Montreal/Kingston: McGill–Queen's University Press, 1985).

——— . "Francophone/Anglophone Relations, 1760–1987." In *The Canadian Encyclopedia* (Second Edition, Edmonton: Hurtig Publishers, 1988).

Bouchard, Gérard. "Une ambiguité québécoise: les bonnes élites et le méchant peuple." In *Présentations* (Société royale du Canada, 1985–86).

Brun, H. "The Canadian Charter of Rights and Freedoms as an Instrument of Social Development." In C. Beckton and W. MacKay, eds., *The Courts and the Charter* (Ottawa: Canadian Government Publishing Centre, 1986).

Canada. Royal Commission on Bilingualism and Biculturalism. *A Preliminary Report* (Ottawa: Queen's Printer, 1965).

——— . Royal Commission on Bilingualism and Biculturalism. *Report*, Book 1. *General Introduction: The Official Languages* (Ottawa: Queen's Printer, 1967).

Clift, Dominique. *Le déclin du nationalisme au Québec* (Montréal: Libre expression, 1981).

Conseil de la langue française. *Les compétences linguistiques du Québec après l'Accord du lac Meech.* Avis au Ministre responsable de l'application de la Charte de la langue française (Québec, 1988).

Cook, Ramsay. *Canada and the French-Canadian Question* (Toronto: Macmillan, 1966).

——— . *Canada, Quebec and the Uses of Nationalism* (Toronto: McClelland and Stewart, 1986).

——— . *The Maple Leaf Forever* (Toronto: Macmillan, 1971).

Courchene, T. J. "Meech Lake and Federalism: Accord or Discord?" In K. E. Swinton and C. J. Rogerson, eds., *Competing Constitutional Visions— The Meech Lake Accord* (Toronto: Carswell, 1988).

de Jong, K. J. "Sexual Equality: Interpreting Section 28." In Anne F. Bayefsky and Mary Eberts, eds., *Equality Rights and the Canadian Charter of Rights and Freedoms* (Toronto: Carswell, 1985).

Duplé, Nicole. "L'Accord du Lac Meech: les inquiétudes féministes sont-elles fondées?" In Réal-A. Forest, ed., *L'adhésion du Québec à l'Accord du Lac Meech—Points de vue juridiques et politiques* (Montréal: Les Éditions Thémis, 1988).

Hogg, P. *Meech Lake Constitutional Accord Annotated* (Toronto: Carswell, 1988).

Kallen, E. "The Meech Lake Accord: Entrenching A Pecking Order of Minority Rights. *Canadian Public Policy/Analyse de Politiques*, Supplement to XIV (September/septembre 1988) and in Chapter Eight of this book.

Laforest, Guy. "The Meaning and Centrality of Recognition." In Roger Gibbins et al., eds., *Meech Lake and Canada. Perspectives from the West* (Edmonton: Academic Printing and Publishing, 1988).

Lamarche, L. "Perspective féministe d'une certaine société distincte: les Québécoises et l'Accord du Lac Meech." In K. E. Swinton and C. J. Rogerson, eds., *Competing Constitutional Visions—The Meech Lake Accord* (Toronto: Carswell, 1988).

Lesage, Gilles, ed. *Le Québec et le Lac Meech. Un Dossier du Devoir* (Montréal: Guérin littérature, 1987).

Magnet, J. E. "The Charter's Official Languages Provisions: The Implications of Entrenched Bilingualism." *Supreme Court Law Review*, 4 (1982).

Mahoney, K. "Women's Rights." In Roger Gibbins et al., eds., *Meech Lake and Canada. Perspectives from the West* (Edmonton: Academic Printing and Publishing, 1988).

McRoberts, Kenneth. *Quebec. Social Change and Political Crisis* (Third Edition, Toronto: McClelland and Stewart, 1988).

Morel, André. "La reconnaissance du Québec comme société distincte dans le respect de la Charte." In Réal-A. Forest, ed., *L'adhésion du Québec à l'Accord du Lac Meech—Points de vue juridiques et politiques* (Montréal: Les Éditions Thémis, 1988).

Morissonneau, C. "Mobilité et identité québécoise." *Cahiers de Géographie du Québec*, 23 (1979).

Murray, Lowell. "Le Canada doit répondre 'oui' au Québec." *Le Devoir*, 28 août 1987.

Québec. *Projet d'accord constitutionnel. Propositions du Gouvernement du Québec* (Québec, 1985).

Smith, L. "The Distinct Society Clause in the Meech Lake Accord: Could It Affect Equality Rights for Women?" In K. E. Swinton and C. J. Rogerson, eds., *Competing Constitutional Visions—The Meech Lake Accord* (Toronto: Carswell, 1988).

Swinton, K. "Competing Visions of Constitutionalism: Of Federalism and Rights." In K. E. Swinton and C. J. Rogerson, eds., *Competing Constitutional Visions—The Meech Lake Accord* (Toronto: Carswell, 1988).

Task Force on National Unity. *A Future Together* (Ottawa: Supply and Services Canada, 1979).

Trofimenkoff, Susan Mann. *The Dream of Nation: A Social and Intellectual History of Quebec* (Toronto: Gage, 1983).

Woehrling, J. "Minority Cultural and Linguistic Rights and Equality Rights in the *Canadian Charter of Rights and Freedoms.*" *McGill Law Journal*, 31 (1985).

——— . "La réglementation linguistique de l'affichage public et la liberté d'expression: *P.G. Québec c. Chaussure Brown's Inc.*" *McGill Law Journal*, 32 (1987).

——— . "La modification constitutionnelle de 1987, la reconnaissance du Québec comme société distincte et la dualité linguistique du Canada." *Cahiers de Droit*, 29 (1988).

—— . "La reconnaissance du Québec comme société distincte et la dualité linguistique du Canada: conséquences juridiques et constitutionnelles." *Canadian Public Policy/Analyse de Politiques*, Supplement to XIV (September/septembre 1988).

CHAPTER FIVE
THE DILEMMA OF THE LINGUISTIC MINORITIES

Apps, E. "Minority Language Education Rights." *University of Toronto Faculty of Law Review*, 43 (1985).

Bastarache, Michel. *Les droits linguistiques au Canada* (Cowansville: Les Éditions Y. Blais, 1986).

Commission of Official Languages. *Annual Report 1987* (Ottawa: Supply and Services Canada, 1988).

—— . "Special Report. English and French in Canada." (On the 25th Anniversary of the B and B Commission and the 20th Anniversary of the Official Languages Act.) *Language and Society* (Summer 1989).

Foucher, Pierre. "*L'Accord du lac Meech* et les francophones hors Québec." In William Pentney and Daniel Proulx, eds., *Canadian Human Rights Yearbook/Annuaire des droits de la personne, 1988* (Ottawa: Les Presses de l'Université d'Ottawa, 1989).

Johnson, William. "The Other Minority." *The Gazette*, June 30, July 2–10, 1989.

Proulx, D. "La précarité des droits linguistiques scolaires ou les singulières difficultés de mise en oeuvre de l'article 23 de la Charte canadienne des droits et libertés." *Revue Générale de Droit*, 14 (1983).

Schwartz, Bryan. *Fathoming Meech Lake* (Winnipeg: Legal Research Institute, University of Manitoba, 1987).

Silver, Arthur. *The French Canadian Idea of Confederation, 1864–1900* (Toronto: University of Toronto Press, 1982).

Taylor-Browne, Karen. "The Francophone Minority." In Roger Gibbins et al., eds., *Meech Lake and Canada. Perspectives from the West* (Edmonton: Academic Printing and Publishing, 1988).

CHAPTER SIX
SPENDING POWERS: Provincializing National Programs?

Banting, Keith G. *Universality and the Development of the Welfare State* (Kingston: John Deutsch Institute, Queen's University, 1985).

————— . "Federalism, Social Reform and the Spending Power." *Canadian Public Policy/Analyse de Politiques*, Supplement to XIV (1988).

————— . "Political Meaning and Social Reform." In K. E. Swinton and C. J. Rogerson, eds., *Competing Constitutional Visions—The Meech Lake Accord* (Toronto: Carswell, 1988).

Banting, Keith, and Richard Simeon, eds. *And No One Cheered: Federalism, Democracy and the Constitution Act* (Toronto: Methuen, 1983).

Behiels, Michael D. *Prelude to Quebec's Quiet Revolution. Liberalism versus Neonationalism 1945-1960* (Montreal/Kingston: McGill–Queen's University Press, 1985).

Brown, Malcolm. "An Economic Perspective." In Roger Gibbins et al., eds., *Meech Lake and Canada. Perspectives from the West* (Edmonton: Academic Printing and Publishing, 1988).

Cairns, A. "The Embedded State: State–Society Relations in Canada." In Keith Banting, ed., *State and Society: Canada in Comparative Perspective*. Macdonald Commission Studies 31 (Toronto: University of Toronto Press, 1986).

Cameron, D. M., and J. S. Dupré. "The Financial Framework of Income Distribution and Social Services." In Stanley M. Beck and Ivan Bernier, eds., *Canada and the New Constitution: The Unfinished Agenda*, Vol. 1 (Montreal: Institute for Research on Public Policy, 1983).

Courchene, Thomas J. "Meech Lake and Socio-economic Policy." *Canadian Public Policy/Analyse de Politiques*, Supplement to XIV (1988).

Dupré, J. S. "Reflections on the Workability of Executive Federalism." In Richard Simeon, ed., *Intergovernmental Relations*. Macdonald Commission Studies 63 (Toronto: University of Toronto Press, 1985).

Hogg, Peter. "Analysis of the New Spending Provision (Section 106A)." In K. E. Swinton and C. J. Rogerson, eds., *Competing Constitutional Visions— The Meech Lake Accord* (Toronto: Carswell, 1988).

Johnson, A. W. *Giving Point and Purpose to the Federal Financing of Post-secondary Education and Research in Canada* (Ottawa: Queen's Printer, 1985).

————— . "The Meech Lake Accord and the Bonds of Nationhood." In K. E. Swinton and C. J. Rogerson, eds., *Competing Constitutional Visions—The Meech Lake Accord* (Toronto: Carswell, 1988).

LaForest, Gerald. *The Allocation of Taxing Power Under the Canadian Constitution* (Canadian Tax Foundation, 1967).

Lajoie, Andrée. "The Federal Spending Power and Meech Lake." In K. E. Swinton and C. J. Rogerson, eds., *Competing Constitutional Visions— The Meech Lake Accord* (Toronto: Carswell, 1988).

Marier, Roger. "Les objectifs sociaux du Québec." *Canadian Public Administration*, 12, No. 2 (1969).

Maslove, A., and B. Rubashewsky. "Cooperation and Confrontation: The Challenges of Fiscal Federalism." In *How Ottawa Spends 1986* (Ottawa: Carleton University, 1986).

Petter, Andrew. "Meech Ado About Nothing? Federalism, Democracy and the Spending Power." In K. E. Swinton and C. J. Rogerson, eds., *Competing Constitutional Visions—The Meech Lake Accord* (Toronto: Carswell, 1988).

Stevenson, Garth. *Unfulfilled Union. Canadian Federalism and National Unity* (Third Edition, Toronto: Gage, 1989).

CHAPTER SEVEN
WOMEN'S RIGHTS:
Does Meech Lake Undermine the Gains of 1982?

Anderson, Doris. "Preface." In Audrey Doerr and Micheline Carrier, eds., *Women and the Constitution in Canada* (Ottawa: Canadian Advisory Council on the Status of Women, 1981).

Baines, Beverley. "Gender and the Meech Lake Committee." In Clive Thomson, ed., *Navigating Meech Lake: The 1987 Constitutional Accord* (Kingston: Institute of Intergovernmental Relations and *Queen's Quarterly*, 1988).

de Jong, Katherine J. "Sexual Equality: Interpreting Section 28." In Anne F. Bayefsky and Mary Eberts, eds., *Equality Rights and the Canadian Charter of Rights and Freedoms* (Toronto: Carswell, 1985).

Eberts, Mary. "Women and Constitutional Renewal." In Audrey Doerr and Micheline Carrier, eds., *Women and the Constitution in Canada* (Ottawa: Canadian Advisory Council on the Status of Women, 1981).

———. "Sex-based Discrimination and the Charter." In Anne F. Bayefsky and Mary Eberts, eds., *Equality Rights and the Canadian Charter of Rights and Freedoms* (Toronto: Carswell, 1985).

Hosêk, Chaviva. "Women and the Constitutional Process." In Keith Banting and Richard Simeon, eds., *And No One Cheered: Federalism, Democracy and the Constitution Act* (Toronto: Methuen, 1983).

Kome, Penny. *The Taking of Twenty-Eight: Women Challenge the Constitution* (Toronto: The Women's Press, 1983).

Murray, Lowell. "Could the Meech Lake Accord Override Sexual Equality Rights?" *CAUT Bulletin* (February 1988).

Roberts, Barbara. *Smooth Sailing or Storm Warning? Canadian and Quebec Women's Groups on the Meech Lake Accord* (Ottawa: Canadian Research Institute for the Advancement of Women, n.d.).

Smith, Lynn. "The Distinct Society Clause in the Meech Lake Accord: Could It Affect Equality Rights for Women?" In K. E. Swinton and C. J. Rogerson, eds., *Competing Constitutional Visions—The Meech Lake Accord* (Toronto: Carswell, 1988).

CHAPTER EIGHT
ETHNOCULTURAL MINORITIES:
The Struggle for Constitutional Equality

Anand, Raj. "Ethnic Equality." In Anne F. Bayefsky and Mary Eberts, eds., *Equality Rights and the Canadian Charter of Rights and Freedoms* (Toronto: Carswell, 1985).

Beckton, Clare F. "Section 27 and Section 15 of the Charter." In Canadian Human Rights Foundation, ed., *Multiculturalism and the Charter: A Legal Perspective* (Toronto: Carswell, 1987).

Behiels, Michael D. "Francophone/Anglophone Relations, 1760–1987." In *The Canadian Encyclopedia*, Vol. II (Second Edition, Edmonton: Hurtig Publishers, 1988).

——— . "Neo-Canadians and Schools in Montreal, 1900–1970." *Journal of Cultural Geography*, 8, No. 2 (1988).

Berger, Thomas R. *Fragile Freedoms: Human Rights and Dissent in Canada* (Toronto: Clarke, Irwin and Co., 1981).

Burnet, Jean. "The Social and Historical Context of Ethnic Relations." In R. C. Gardner and R. Kalin, eds., *A Canadian Social Psychology of Ethnic Relations* (Agincourt: Methuen, 1981).

——— . "Multiculturalism in Canada." In Leo Driedger, ed., *Ethnic Canada. Identities and Inequalities* (Toronto: Copp Clark Pitman, 1987).

Canada. Royal Commission on Bilingualism and Biculturalism. *The Cultural Contribution of Other Ethnic Groups*, Book IV (Ottawa: Supply and Services Canada, 1969).

Christopher, T. C. "The 1982 Canadian Charter of Rights and Freedoms and Multiculturalism." *Canadian Review of Studies in Nationalism*, XIV, No. 2 (1987).

Cook, Ramsay. *Canada and the French-Canadian Question* (Toronto: Macmillan, 1966).

Eberts, Mary. "The Use of Litigation Under the Canadian Charter of Rights and Freedoms as a Strategy for Achieving Change." In Neil Nevitte and Allan Kornberg, eds., *Minorities and the Canadian State* (Oakville: Mosaic Press, 1985).

Gall, G. L. "Multiculturalism and the Fundamental Freedoms: Section 27 and Section 2." In Canadian Human Rights Foundation, ed., *Multiculturalism and the Charter: A Legal Perspective* (Toronto: Carswell, 1987).

Gibson, Dale. "Protection of Minority Rights Under the Canadian Charter of Rights and Freedoms: Can Politicians and Judges Sing Harmony?" In Neil Nevitte and Allan Kornberg, eds., *Minorities and the Canadian State* (Oakville: Mosaic Press, 1985).

Hudson, Michael R. "Multiculturalism, Government Policy and Constitutional Enshrinement—A Comparative Study." In Canadian Human Rights Foundation, ed., *Multiculturalism and the Charter: A Legal Perspective* (Toronto: Carswell, 1987).

Kalbach, Warren E. "Growth and Distribution of Canada's Ethnic Populations, 1871–1981." In Leo Driedger, ed., *Ethnic Canada. Identities and Inequalities* (Toronto: Copp Clark Pitman, 1987).

Kallen, Evelyn. *Ethnicity and Human Rights in Canada* (Toronto: Gage, 1982).

——— . "Multiculturalism: Ideology, Policy and Reality." *Journal of Canadian Studies*, 17, No. 1 (Spring 1982).

——— . "Multiculturalism, Minorities, and Motherhood: A Social Scientific Critique of Section 27." In Canadian Human Rights Foundation, ed., *Multiculturalism and the Charter: A Legal Perspective* (Toronto: Carswell, 1987).

Krulak, Orest M. "Constitutional Reform and Immigration." In Roger Gibbins et al., eds., *Meech Lake and Canada. Perspectives from the West* (Edmonton: Academic Printing and Publishing, 1988).

Palmer, Howard. "Reluctant Hosts: Anglo-Canadian Views of Multiculturalism in the Twentieth Century." In R. Douglas Francis and Donald B. Smith, eds., *Readings in Canadian History. Post-Confederation* (Second Edition, Toronto: Holt, Rinehart and Winston, 1986).

CHAPTER NINE
PROVINCIALIZING NATIONAL INSTITUTIONS:
The Amending Formula, the Senate and the Supreme Court

Aucoin, Peter. "Regionalism, Party and National Government." In Peter Aucoin, ed., *Party Government and Regional Representation in Canada* (Toronto: University of Toronto Press, 1985).

Canada. Library of Parliament. *Bibliographies. The Senate/Le Sénat*, No. 58 (Ottawa: Information and Technical Services Branch, June 1988).

——— . Special Joint Committee on Senate Reform (Joint Chairmen: Senator Gildas Malgat and Paul Cosgrove, M.P.). *Report* (Ottawa: Queen's Printer, 1989).

Cheffinns, Ronald. "The Constitution Act, 1982 and the Amending Formula: Political and Legal Implications." In Edward P. Belobaba and Eric Gertner, eds., *The New Constitution and the Charter of Rights* (Toronto: Butterworths, 1983).

Décary, Robert. "L'Accord du Lac Meech et la Cour suprême du Canada." In Réal-A. Forest, ed., *L'adhésion du Québec à l'Accord du Lac Meech—Points de vue juridiques et politiques* (Montréal: Les Éditions Thémis, 1988).

Elton, David, and Roger Gibbins. "Western Alienation and Political Culture." In R. Schultz et al., eds., *Canadian Political Process* (Third Edition, Toronto: Holt, Rinehart and Winston, 1979).

Engelman, Frederick C. "Prologue to Structural Reform of the Government of Canada." *Canadian Journal of Political Science*, 19 (December 1986).

Hogg, Peter W. *Canada Act 1982 Annotated* (Toronto: Carswell, 1982).

Lederman, W. R. "Current Proposals for Reform of the Supreme Court of Canada." *Canadian Bar Review*, 57 (1979). Reprinted in W. R. Lederman, ed., *Continuing Canadian Constitutional Dilemmas* (Toronto: Butterworths, 1981).

Macpherson, James C. "The Potential Implications of Constitutional Reform for the Supreme Court of Canada." In Stanley M. Beck and Ivan Bernier, eds., *Canada and the New Constitution: The Unfinished Agenda*, Vol. 1 (Montreal: Institute for Research on Public Policy, 1983).

Mandel, Michael. *The Charter of Rights and the Legalization of Politics in Canada* (Toronto: Wall & Thompson, 1989).

McCormick, Peter. "Toward a Provincial Role in Judicial Appointments." In Roger Gibbins et al., eds., *Meech Lake and Canada. Perspectives from the West* (Edmonton: Academic Printing and Publishing, 1988).

——— , and David Elton. "The Western Economy and Canadian Unity." In *Western Perspectives* (Calgary: Canada West Foundation, 1987).

Morin, Jacques-Yvan. "Les blocages concertés de l'Accord constitutionnel de 1987." In Réal-A. Forest, ed., *L'adhésion du Québec à l'Accord du Lac Meech—Points de vue juridiques et politiques* (Montréal: Les Éditions Thémis, 1988).

Russell, Peter H. "The Jurisdiction of the Supreme Court of Canada: Present Policies and a Programme for Reform." *Osgoode Hall Law Journal*, 6, No. 1 (October 1968).

——— . "Constitutional Reform of the Judicial Branch: Symbolic vs. Operational Considerations." *Canadian Journal of Political Science/Revue canadienne de science politique*, XVII, No. 2 (June/juin 1984).

Scott, Stephen A. "The Supreme Court of Canada and the 1987 Constitutional Accord." In Réal-A. Forest, ed., *L'adhésion du Québec à l'Accord du Lac Meech—Points de vue juridiques et politiques* (Montréal: Les Éditions Thémis, 1988).

Smiley, Donald. "Central Institutions." In Stanley M. Beck and Ivan Bernier, eds., *Canada and the New Constitution: The Unfinished Agenda*, Vol. 1 (Montreal: Institute for Research on Public Policy, 1983).

Tremblay, Guy. "La réforme des institutions et de la formule d'amendement dans l'Accord du Lac Meech." In Réal-A. Forest, ed., *L'adhésion du Québec à l'Accord du Lac Meech—Points de vue juridiques et politiques* (Montréal: Les Éditions Thémis, 1988).

Ziegel, Jacob S. "Federal Judicial Appointments in Canada: The Time is Ripe for Change." *University of Toronto Law Journal*, 37, No. 1 (1987).

CHAPTER TEN
NATIVE RIGHTS:
Integrating the First Peoples into the Constitution

Berger, Thomas R. *Northern Frontier, Northern Homeland: The Report of the Mackenzie Valley Pipeline Inquiry*, 2 vols. (Ottawa: Government of Canada, 1977).

———. *Fragile Freedoms: Human Rights and Dissent in Canada* (Toronto: Clarke, Irwin and Co., 1981).

Bruyere, Louis. "Aboriginal Peoples and the Meech Lake Accord." In William Pentney and Daniel Proulx, eds., *Canadian Human Rights Yearbook/Annuaire canadien des droits de la personne, 1988* (Ottawa: Les Presses de l'Université d'Ottawa, 1989).

Cardinal, Harold. *The Unjust Society: The Tragedy of Canada's Indians* (Edmonton: Hurtig Publishers, 1969).

Coates, Kenneth, and Judith Powell. *The Modern North: People, Politics and the Struggle Against Colonialism* (Toronto: James Lorimer, 1988).

Foster, Michael K. *Indigenous Languages in Canada* (Ottawa: Commissioner of Official Languages, 1982).

Hall, Tony. "Self-Government or Self-Delusion? Brian Mulroney and Aboriginal Rights." *Canadian Journal of Native Studies/Revue canadienne des études autochtones*, 6, No. 1 (1986).

———. *The N'ungosuk Project: A Study in Aboriginal Language Renewal* (West Bay: Two Bears Cultural Survival Group, 1987).

———. "Indian Treaties." In *The Canadian Encyclopedia* (Second Edition, Edmonton: Hurtig Publishers, 1988).

———. "Who Speaks for Canada? The Meech Lake–Free Trade Connection." *Humanist Canada*, 21, No. 1 (1988).

Jamieson, Kathleen. "Sex Discrimination and the Indian Act." In J. Rick Ponting, ed., *Arduous Journey: Canadian Indians and Decolonization* (Toronto: McClelland and Stewart, 1986).

McInnes, Simon. "The Inuit and the Constitutional Process: 1978–1981." In Ian A. L. Getty and Antoine S. Lussier, eds., *As Long as the Sun Shines and Water Flows: A Reader in Canadian Native Studies* (Vancouver: University of British Columbia Press, 1983).

Morisset, Jean. "La Conquête du Nord-Ouest, 1885–1985; or The Imperial Quest of British North America." In Ian A. L. Getty and Antoine S. Lussier, eds., *As Long as the Sun Shines and Water Flows: A Reader in Canadian Native Studies* (Vancouver: University of British Columbia Press, 1983).

———. "Introduction." In Jean Morisset and Rose-Marie Pelletier, eds., *Ted Trindell, Métis Witness to the North* (Vancouver: Tillacum Library, 1986).

Robinson, Eric, and Henry Bird Quinney. *The Infested Blanket: Canada's Constitution—Genocide of Indian Nations* (Winnipeg: Queenston House, 1985).

Ryser, Rudolph. "Fourth World Wars: Indigenous Nationalism and the Emerging New International Political Order." In Menno Boldt and J. Anthony Long, eds., *Quest for Justice: Aboriginal Peoples and Aboriginal Rights* (Toronto: University of Toronto Press, 1985).

Sanders, Douglas. "Prior Claims: An Aboriginal People in the Constitution of Canada." In Stanley M. Beck and Ivan Bernier, eds., *Canada and the New Constitution: The Unfinished Agenda*, Vol. 1 (Montreal: Institute for Research on Public Policy, 1983).

——— . "The Indian Lobby." In Keith Banting and Richard Simeon, eds., *And No One Cheered: Federalism, Democracy and the Constitution Act* (Toronto: Methuen, 1983).

——— . "The Renewal of Indian Special Status." In Anne F. Bayefsky and Mary Eberts, eds., *Equality Rights and the Canadian Charter of Rights and Freedoms* (Toronto: Carswell, 1985).

——— . "An Uncertain Path: The Aboriginal Constitutional Conferences." In Joseph M. Weiler and Robin M. Elliot, eds., *Litigating the Values of a Nation: The Canadian Charter of Rights and Freedoms* (Toronto: Carswell, 1986).

——— . "Article 27 and the Aboriginal Peoples of Canada." In Canadian Human Rights Foundation, ed., *Multiculturalism and the Charter: A Legal Perspective* (Toronto: Carswell, 1987).

——— . "The Constitution, the Provinces, and Aboriginal Peoples." In J. Anthony Long and Menno Boldt, eds., *Government in Conflict? Provinces and Indian Nations in Canada* (Toronto: University of Toronto Press, 1988).

Schwartz, Bryan. *First Principles, Second Thoughts: Aboriginal Peoples, Constitutional Reform and Canadian Statecraft* (Montreal: Institute for Research on Public Policy, 1986).

Silman, Janet. *Enough is Enough: Aboriginal Women Speak Out* (Toronto: The Women's Press, 1987).

Thompson, Ruth, ed. *The Rights of Indigenous Peoples in International Law: Selected Essays on Self-Determination* (Saskatoon: University of Saskatchewan Native Law Centre, 1987).

Weaver, Sally M. "Federal Policy-Making for Métis and Non-Status Indians in the Context of Native Policy." *Canadian Ethnic Studies*, 27, No. 2 (1985).

Woodward, Michael, and Bruce George. "The Canadian Indian Lobby of Westminster, 1979–1982." *Journal of Native Studies*, 18, No. 3 (1983).

CHAPTER ELEVEN
THE POLITICAL RUNOFF FROM MEECH LAKE:
Will the Country Be Left High and Dry?

Coyne, Deborah. "Beyond the Meech Lake Accord. Submission to the Manitoba Task Force on the Meech Lake Accord." April 4, 1989.

Forsey, Eugene. "No! Submission to the New Brunswick Legislative Committee on the 1987 Constitutional Accord." *University of New Brunswick Law Journal* (forthcoming).

Harney, Jean-Paul. "À la dérive sur le Lac Meech." In Réal-A. Forest, ed., *L'adhésion du Québec à l'Accord du Lac Meech—Points de vue juridiques et politiques* (Montréal: Les Éditions Thémis, 1988).

LaForest, G. V. *Disallowance and Reservation of Provincial Legislation* (Ottawa: Department of Justice, 1955).

MacDonald, L. Ian. *Mulroney. The Making of the Prime Minister* (Toronto: McClelland and Stewart, 1985).

McConnell, W. H. *Commentary on the British North America Act* (Toronto: Macmillan, 1977).

——— . "Cutting the Gordian Knot: The Amending Process in Canada." *Law and Contemporary Problems*, 44 (1981).

Schwartz, Bryan. "Refashioning Meech Lake." *Manitoba Law Journal*, 18, No. 1 (1989).

Smiley, Donald. "A Dangerous Deed: The Constitution Act, 1982." In Keith Banting and Richard Simeon, eds., *And No One Cheered: Federalism, Democracy and the Constitution Act* (Toronto: Methuen, 1983).

Strayer, B. L. "The Patriation and Legitimacy of the Canadian Constitution." In *Cronkite Memorial Lectures*, 3rd ser. (Saskatoon: College of Law, University of Saskatchewan, 1982).

CONTRIBUTORS

INDIVIDUALS

Georges Arès   President, l'Association canadienne-française de l'Alberta (ACFA), Edmonton, Alberta.

Gérald-A. Beaudoin   Senator, and Professor of Civil Law, Faculty of Law, University of Ottawa, Ottawa, Ontario.

Alan C. Cairns   Professor, Department of Political Science, University of British Columbia, Vancouver, British Columbia.

Ramsay Cook   Professor, Department of History, York University, North York, Ontario, and Co-editor of the *Dictionary of Canadian Biography*.

Deborah Coyne   Program Officer, The Walter and Duncan Gordon Charitable Foundation, Toronto, Ontario.

Stefan Dupré   Professor, Department of Political Science, University of Toronto, Toronto, Ontario.

Mary Eberts   Lawyer with Tory, Tory, Deslauriers & Binnington, Toronto, Ontario.

David Elton   President of the Canada West Foundation, and Professor, Department of Political Science, University of Lethbridge, Lethbridge, Alberta.

Tony Hall   Assistant Professor, Department of Native Studies, University of Sudbury in federation with Laurentian University, Sudbury, Ontario.

Evelyn Kallen   Professor, Department of Social Science and Anthropology, York University, North York, Ontario.

Peter Leslie   Assistant Secretary for the Cabinet, Policy Development, Federal–Provincial Relations Office, Ottawa, Ontario.

W. Howard McConnell   Professor, College of Law, University of Saskatchewan, Saskatoon, Saskatchewan.

Lowell Murray   Leader of the Government in the Senate and Minister of State (Federal–Provincial Relations).

Tony Penikett   Government Leader and MLA for Whitehorse West.

Gil Rémillard   Gouvernement du Québec, Cabinet du ministre de la Justice, Procureur général et ministre délégué aux Affaires intergouvernementales canadiennes.

Ian Scott   Attorney General for Ontario, Queen's Park, Toronto, Ontario.

Stephen A. Scott   Professor, Faculty of Law, McGill University, Montreal, Quebec.

Richard Simeon   Director, School of Public Administration, Queen's University, Kingston, Ontario.

Pierre E. Trudeau   Former prime minister of Canada (1968–79, 1980–84), currently a lawyer with Heenan Blaikie, Montreal, Quebec.

José Woehrling   Professeur de droit public, Faculté de droit, Université de Montréal, Montreal, Quebec.

ORGANIZATIONS

Alliance Quebec   Quebec.

Canadian Association of Law Teachers   Ottawa, Ontario.

Canadian Ethnocultural Council   Ottawa, Ontario.

Fédération des Femmes du Québec   Quebec.

DATE DUE